Chicago

timeout.com/chicago

Published by Time Out Guides Ltd, a wholly owned subsidiary of Time Out Group Ltd.
Time Out and the Time Out logo are trademarks of Time Out Group Ltd.

© Time Out Group Ltd 2007
Previous editions 2000, 2002, 2004.

10 9 8 7 6 5 4 3 2 1

This edition first published in Great Britain in 2007 by Ebury Publishing
Ebury Publishing is a division of The Random House Group Ltd,
20 Vauxhall Bridge Road, London SW1V 2SA

Random House Australia Pty Limited 20 Alfred Street, Milsons Point, Sydney, New South Wales 2061, Australia
Random House New Zealand Limited 18 Poland Road, Glenfield, Auckland 10, New Zealand
Random House South Africa (Pty) Limited Isle of Houghton, Corner Boundary
Road & Carse O'Gowrie, Houghton 2198, South Africa

Random House UK Limited Reg. No. 954009

Distributed in USA by Publishers Group West
1700 Fourth Street, Berkeley, California 94710

Distributed in Canada by Publishers Group Canada
250A Carlton Street, Toronto, Ontario M5A 2L1

For further distribution details, see www.timeout.com

ISBN 10: 1-904978-57-6
ISBN 13: 9781904978572

A CIP catalogue record for this book is available from the British Library

Colour reprographics by Wyndeham Icon, 3 & 4 Maverton Road, London E3 2JE

Printed and bound by Firmengruppe APPL, aprinta druck, Wemding, Germany

Papers used by Ebury Publishing are natural, recyclable products made from wood grown in sustainable forests

Time Out Guides Limited
Universal House
251 Tottenham Court Road
London W1T 7AB
Tel + 44 (0)20 7813 3000
Fax + 44 (0)20 7813 6001
Email guides@timeout.com
www.timeout.com

Editorial

Editor Will Fulford-Jones
Consultant Editor Amy Carr
Copy Editors Edoardo Albert, Ismay Atkins, Dominic
Earle, Hugh Graham, Phil Harriss
Listings Editors Steve Heisler, Jessica Linn
Proofreader Simon Cropper
Indexer Sam Le Quesne

Managing Director Peter Fiennes
Financial Director Gareth Garner
Editorial Director Ruth Jarvis
Deputy Series Editor Dominic Earle
Editorial Manager Holly Pick

Design

Art Director Scott Moore
Art Editor Pinelope Kourmouzoglou
Senior Designer Josephine Spencer
Graphic Designer Henry Elphick
Digital Imaging Simon Foster
Ad Make-up Jenni Prichard

Picture Desk

Picture Editor Jael Marschner
Deputy Picture Editor Tracey Kerrigan
Picture Researcher Helen McFarland

Advertising

Sales Director Mark Phillips
International Sales Manager Fred Durman
International Sales Consultant Ross Canadé
International Sales Executive Simon Davies
Advertising Sales (Chicago) Time Out Chicago

Marketing

Group Marketing Director John Luck
Marketing Manager Yvonne Poon
Marketing & Publicity Manager, US Rosella Albanese

Production

Group Production Director Mark Lamond
Production Manager Brendan McKeown
Production Coordinator Caroline Bradford

Time Out Group

Chairman Tony Elliott
Financial Director Richard Waterlow
Time Out Magazine Ltd MD David Pepper
Group General Manager/Director Nichola Coulthard
Time Out Communications Ltd MD David Pepper
Time Out International MD Cathy Runciman
Group Art Director John Oakey
Group IT Director Simon Chappell

Contributors

Introduction Will Fulford-Jones. **History** Victoria Cunha, Will Fulford-Jones (*Strike one* Will Fulford-Jones; *Unsteady as she goes* Web Behrens; *What's in a name?* Judy Sutton Taylor). **Chicago Today** Web Behrens. **Architecture** Madeline Nusser (*A history of height* Web Behrens). **The Machine** John Dugan. **Mojo Working** Will Fulford-Jones. **The Great Divide** Dan Epstein. **Where to Stay** Lori Rackl (*Seen it all before?* Will Fulford-Jones). **Sightseeing Introduction** Will Fulford-Jones. **Museum reviews throughout Sightseeing** Martina Sheehan. **The Loop** Madeline Nusser (*We'll always have Paris* Valerie Nahmad; *Walk* Will Fulford-Jones). **The South Loop & Chinatown** Madeline Nusser; *additional material* John Dugan (*Walk* Madeline Nusser). **The Near North Side** John Dugan; *additional material* Will Fulford-Jones (*Beachy keen* Madeline Nusser, Rose Spinelli). **Old Town & Lincoln Park** John Dugan (*Easy riders* Will Fulford-Jones). **Lakeview & Around** John Dugan; *additional material* Web Behrens (*Talkin' all that jazz* Judy Sutton Taylor). **Wicker Park & Around** John Dugan. **Oak Park** Web Behrens (*Wright on* Will Fulford-Jones). **The South Side** John Dugan, Marc Geelhoed (*Walk* Will Fulford-Jones). **Restaurants** Heather Shouse, *Time Out Chicago* staff (*Loop lunchin'* Heather Shouse, David Tamarkin; *Made in Chicago* Tim Lowery, Margaret Lyons; *Sweet things* David Tamarkin; *Up all night* Heather Shouse; *The brunch bunch* Laura Baginski, Will Fulford-Jones, Heather Shouse, David Tamarkin; *Going native* Nicholas Day). **Bars** Heather Shouse, *Time Out Chicago* staff (*The golden gander* Will Fulford-Jones; *Smoke alarm* Heather Shouse). **Shops & Services** Annie Tomlin (*Farmers' markets* Judy Sutton Taylor; *Golden oldies* Judy Sutton Taylor). **Festivals & Events** Madeline Nusser (*Hug a hoodie* Judy Sutton Taylor). **Art Galleries** Madeline Nusser. **Children** Judy Sutton Taylor. **Comedy** Jonathan Messinger (*Bronze mettle* Steve Heisler). **Dance** Asimina Chremos. **Film** Cliff Doerksen. **Gay & Lesbian** Jason Heidemann. **Music** Antonia Simigis (*Artists in residence* Matthew Lurie, James Porter, Antonia Simigis). **Nightclubs** John Dugan. **Sports & Fitness** Isaac Davis (*Spare change* Mark Sinclair; *Life cycle* Will Fulford-Jones). **Theatre** Christopher Piatt. **Day Trips** Lauren Viera (*Kidding around* Judy Sutton Taylor). **Directory** Will Fulford-Jones.

Maps john@jsgraphics.co.uk, except page 335 © Chicago Transit Authority.

Photography Martha Williams, except page 12 Getty Images; pages 15, 18 Corbis; pages 20, 21, 23, 41, 42 Bettmann/Corbis; page 45 Rob Greig; pages 130, 131 Yvonne Dostatni; pages 145, 151, 154, 158, 171, 173, 205 Donna Rickles; page 178 David Tamarkin; page 258 Nolan Wells/Bloodshot Records. The following images were provided by the featured establishments/artists: pages 233, 235, 251, 279, 284.

The Editor would like to thank the staff of *Time Out Chicago*, especially Chad Schlegel, Amy Carr, Nicole Radja, Kim R Russell, David Gibson and all those who contributed to this guide; Nyx Bradley; Tony Coppoletta; Elizabeth Walasin Lulla at the Chicago Office of Tourism; Susan Ross at the Chicago Architecture Foundation; Greg Stepanek at the CTA; and all contributors to previous editions of *Time Out Chicago*, whose work forms the basis for parts of this book.

Contents

Introduction 6

In Context 11

History 12
Chicago Today 27
Architecture 31
  Map: Loop Architecture 33
The Machine 41
Mojo Working 45
The Great Divide 49

Where to Stay 53

Where to Stay 54

Sightseeing 71

Introduction 72
The Loop 75
The South Loop & Chinatown 87
The Near North Side 95
Old Town & Lincoln Park 106
Lakeview & Around 112
The North Shore 116
The Near West Side 119
Wicker Park & Around 126
Oak Park 131
The South Side 135

Eat, Drink, Shop 143

Restaurants 144
Bars 176
Shops & Services 190

Arts & Entertainment 215

Festivals & Events 216
Art Galleries 221
Children 225
Comedy 230
Dance 233
Film 236
Gay & Lesbian 240
Music 250
Nightclubs 263
Sports & Fitness 271
Theatre 278

Water Tower. *See p98.*

Trips Out of Town 285

Day Trips 286
  Map: Day Trips 287
  Map: Milwaukee 293

Directory 299

Getting Around 300
Resources A-Z 303
Further Reference 311
Index 313
Advertisers' Index 320

Maps 321

Chicago Overview 322
Street Maps 324
Street Index 333
CTA Rail System 335
Chicago Neighbourhoods 336

Introduction

While New York wears its arrogance as a badge of honour and Los Angeles rarely pays attention to anything or anyone outside its ever-broadening boundaries, Chicago has always been desperate to impress. Since the World's Columbian Exposition of 1893 put the town on the global map, city fathers and business moguls have been hatching increasingly grandiose plans in the hope of wowing outsiders. It's why the clouds are punctured by innumerable skyscrapers, why the city spent seven years and almost $500 million building Millennium Park, and why a team of optimists in the mayor's office are attempting to lure the Olympics to town.

Indeed, no survey of Chicago is complete without mention of the man who presides over it. For almost two decades, this has been Mayor Richard M Daley's town, just as it was his father's town from 1955 to 1976. Beloved and loathed, respected and feared, Daley dominates Chicago, never far from the spotlight or the headlines. His public image has come to reflect that of the city itself: vibrant, vigorous and somewhat controversial.

Still, not even his detractors deny that Daley gets things done like few other American mayors, constantly effecting cultural and structural change to his city. And the mayor's boundless energy finds echoes all over Chicago. From the stages of its music venues to the stages of its theatres (Sinatra's observation that here 'they do things they don't do on Broadway' still holds true), few cities carry such cultural sparkle. Despite Daley's best efforts, the bars and the nightclubs remain abuzz. The city's dining is second to none, in terms of both its quality and its variety. And even the weather is restless, capable in winter of lurching from balmy autumnal afternoon to blizzard-riddled night to sun-soaked morning.

The locals here respect and perhaps even cherish the city's storied past. When, in 2006, Macy's rebranded the grand old Marshall Field's department store, mere months after the equally venerable Berghoff bar closed its doors, the outcry was loud and fierce. And yet, mere weeks later, everyone had moved on: to other shops, other bars, other lives. Chicago's past may be bright, but its future is surely brighter.

ABOUT TIME OUT CITY GUIDES

This is the fourth edition of *Time Out Chicago*, one of an expanding series of more than 50 Time Out guides produced by the people behind the successful listings magazines in Chicago, New York, London and a variety of other cities around the globe. Our guides are all written by resident experts: this particular book has been compiled by the staff of the weekly *Time Out Chicago* magazine, the definitive guide to what's on in the city. Whether you're a long-time local or a first-time visitor, the guidebook contains all the most up-to-date information you'll need to explore the city or read up on its background.

THE LOWDOWN ON THE LISTINGS

Above all, we've tried to make this book as useful as possible. Addresses, phone numbers, websites, public transport information, opening times, admission prices and credit card details are all included in the listings, as are details of selected other services and facilities. However, businesses can change their arrangements at any time. Before you go out of your way, we

strongly advise you to phone ahead to check opening times and other particulars. While every effort and care has been made to ensure the accuracy of the information contained in this guide, the publishers cannot accept responsibility for any errors it may contain.

PRICES AND PAYMENT

Our listings detail which of the five major credit cards – American Express (AmEx), Diners Club (DC), Discover (Disc), MasterCard (MC) and Visa (V) – are accepted by each venue in the guide. Some venues will also accept travellers' cheques issued by a major financial institution, such as American Express.

The prices we've listed in this guide should be treated as guidelines, not gospel. Fluctuating exchange rates and inflation can cause prices to change rapidly, especially in shops and restaurants. If prices vary wildly from those we've quoted, ask whether there's a good reason, and please email to let us know. We aim to give the best and most up-to-date advice, so we always want to know if you've been badly treated or overcharged.

Navy Pier. *See p101*.

THE LIE OF THE LAND

Chicago is laid out on a grid system, and is relatively easy to negotiate. Ground zero is at the corner of State and Madison Streets in the Loop; addresses on north–south streets are numbered according to how many blocks north or south of Madison they sit, with the same principle at work for east–west roads and State Street.

To make both book and city easier to navigate, we've divided the city into neighbourhoods. The same area names and designations are used in all addresses throughout the guide. Although these designations are a slight simplification of the city's geography, we hope they'll help you to understand its layout. An overview map on page 336 illustrates these areas. For more on finding your way around the city, *see p72*.

The back of this book includes street maps of the most commonly visited parts of Chicago, along with a full street index. The street maps start on page 321; on them are pinpointed the locations of hotels (❶), restaurants (❶) and bars (❶) featured elsewhere in the guide. For all addresses throughout the book,

we've given both a cross-street and a map reference, along with details of the closest public transport options, so finding your way around town should be straightforward.

TELEPHONE NUMBERS

Chicagoland boasts five telephone area codes. The majority of numbers in this guide fall into the 312 and 773 area codes, with codes 847, 708 and 630 covering the suburbs. All numbers in this guide are prefaced by a 1 and an area code: for example, 1-312 123 4567.

If you're dialling from within a given area, you can drop the 1 and the area code, and dial only the remaining seven digits. If you're calling from outside the area code, dial the 11-digit number as listed in this guide. To reach numbers listed in this book from outside the US, dial your country's international access code (from the UK, it's 00 or, on mobile phones, the '+' symbol) and then dial the number as listed. For more on phones, including details of local cellphone coverage, *see pp308-309*.

ESSENTIAL INFORMATION

For all the practical information you might need for visiting Chicago, including visa, customs and immigration information, details of the local transport network, a listing of emergency numbers and a selection of useful websites, please turn to the Directory at the back of the book (*see pp300-312*).

There is an online version of this book, along with guides to over 100 international cities, at **www.timeout.com**.

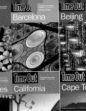

In Context

History	**12**
Chicago Today	**27**
Architecture	**31**
The Machine	**41**
Mojo Working	**45**
The Great Divide	**49**

Features

Strike one	17
Unsteady as she goes	21
What's in a name?	24
Key events	26
Five gold rings	28
A history of height	35
A whole lot of nothing	38
Gun crazy	42
Baseball timeline	50

Maps

Loop Architecture	33

Marina City. *See p39*.

Flower power at the 1968 **Democratic Convention**.

History

Rivers, railroads and resilience.

The location, a boggy swampland on the edge of Lake Michigan, was not especially ideal. But the efforts of those that chose to settle here turned it from a potential curse into an undoubted blessing. Ever since a Haitian traveller made his home here in the 1770s, successive residents have fought tooth and nail to turn their city into a major player. Indeed, 21st-century Chicago can only be explained by a look at the 250 years that preceded it.

IN THE BEGINNING

Missionary Father Jacques Marquette and cartographer Louis Jolliet were the first Europeans to explore the lower Lake Michigan region. In 1673, chartered and funded by the governor of New France (now Quebec), the pair attempted to follow the Mississippi and its tributaries as far as possible to the north-east. After travelling to the native village of Kaskaskia (near what is now Utica, Illinois) on the Illinois River, the intrepid duo proceeded north-east on the Des Plaines River.

When they reached what the local Native Americans called 'Checagou' (believed to translate as 'wild onion', which grew in the area), Marquette and Jolliet's party floated on down the Chicago River to Lake Michigan before heading north to Green Bay in the autumn of 1673. The trip was deemed a success, so much so that Marquette returned to the area in 1674 and spent the winter as a temporary resident of what would later become known as Chicago before heading back to Kaskaskia in the spring. Jolliet never again visited the area.

The first permanent non-native resident of Chicago, Haitian pioneer Jean-Baptiste Point du Sable, came to the area almost exactly a century later. The son of French parents, the black Du Sable is believed to have established a fur trading post at the mouth of the Chicago River as early as 1772, marrying a Potawatomie native named Catherine around the same time. During the War of Independence, Du Sable was suspected of being an enemy sympathiser and was held captive at a military outpost, but he returned to the Chicago River area in 1779. Two decades later, he sold his property on to a fur trapper, who in turn flogged it almost immediately to a trader named John Kinzie. The area's first permanent white settler, Kinzie eventually came to be known as 'the Father of Chicago'. However, it's the more unassuming Du Sable who really deserves the nickname.

THEY FORT THE LAW

Fearful of further trouble after the War of Independence, the government decided a military presence was necessary in the area, and so Fort Dearborn was built in 1803 at what is now the south end of the Michigan Avenue Bridge. Then the major western US Army garrison in the country, it occupied a strategic point near the southern end of Lake Michigan on the south side of the Chicago River, just across from the cabin built by Du Sable. Sure enough, the US was soon once more battling the British; by the summer of 1812, tensions between soldiers and natives, who were bought off by the British, were at an all-time high.

Despite efforts to appease the Potawatomie leaders, it was clear to Captain Nathaniel Heald that safety concerns were so great that Fort Dearborn should be evacuated. Accompanied by an escort of friendly Miami natives from Indiana led by Captain William Wells, the garrison began its journey along the lake, but was ambushed by natives. Heald and his wife were taken prisoner, but almost all the others who were attempting to leave the fort were executed; in all, 53 settlers and natives died. The Potawatomies returned three days later and burnt the fort.

After the war was over, though, things returned to normal, and trading once more began to take place in the area. Having fled during the massacre, Kinzie came back in 1816 and resumed his business activities. His descendants continued to make themselves known through their various civic and industrial ventures in the remaining years of the 19th century; his son, John H Kinzie, even stood for mayor in 1834. Today's Kinzie Street, which lies just north of the Chicago River, is testimony to his influence.

Gurdon Hubbard, another early settler, arrived from Montreal in 1818, the same year Illinois joined the union as a state, and quickly established a fur trade route from Danville, Illinois, to Chicago. A decade later, he bought the Illinois branch of the massively profitable American Fur Company franchise; in so doing, he cemented his own position on the trading ladder and set the stage for the city's future expansion. By the time Chicago was incorporated as a town in 1833, Hubbard had

begun to diversify into meatpacking, shipping, insurance and real estate, while also campaigning tirelessly for the construction of the Illinois–Michigan Canal. For the next three decades, his own prosperity mirrored that of his adopted home town, which expanded apace.

PIONEER CHECKPOINT

When the Erie Canal opened in 1825, it linked the Hudson River – and, thus, the East Coast – with Buffalo, New York (on Lake Erie). The canal opened up Illinois to travel and commerce, a great boon to the pioneers who were arriving from more populous areas in the east. A prime example was William Ogden, a transplanted Yankee who came west in 1835 to sell a parcel of land for a family member, but who stayed and, two years later, became mayor of Chicago.

Famed meatpacking mogul Philip Armour also moved to Chicago (from Milwaukee) after the Civil War ended, and earned millions selling barrels of pork. Armour employed refrigerated train cars for shipping fresh meat, expanded the use of animal by-products, and diversified into other businesses. Meanwhile, Cyrus McCormick found Chicago to be just as hospitable to his Virginia-bred sensibilities, even borrowing money from Ogden to build the factory that would produce the mechanical reapers he had invented. During his time in Chicago, the belligerent McCormick became active in Democratic politics, and ran unsuccessfully for Congress in 1864. Today, he's commemorated in the name of the city's convention centre.

But few outsiders went on to have as much influence over the growth of Chicago as 'Long' John Wentworth, whose appetites for food, drink and good living matched his stature (he stood six feet six inches tall and weighed more than 300 pounds). After arriving in 1836 at the age of 21, Wentworth became the managing editor and, later, the owner-publisher of the *Chicago Democrat*, the city's first newspaper. He closed the newspaper in 1861, effectively merging it with the *Tribune*, but at the time, he had rather bigger fish to fry: having served five terms in the House of Representatives as a Democrat, Wentworth had been elected as the city's Republican mayor in 1857.

Along with Scottish-born detective Allan Pinkerton, Wentworth attempted to quell the town's growing lawlessness. Police raids commissioned by Wentworth on the city's red-light districts were unsuccessful, and he retreated to spend the rest of his post-political life on a farm in suburban Summit. Pinkerton, though, continued to enjoy a rich and colourful career: having founded what is now recognised to be the world's first detective agency and purportedly saved President Lincoln from assassination during the Civil War, he worked in every facet of his field until his death in 1884.

TRAINS AND BOATS AND PLAINS

An economic depression that swept the country in 1837, known as the Panic, threatened to put a lid on Chicago's growth. However, the Panic also coincided with Chicago achieving official city status; the city duly revitalised, things weren't slow to pick up after the worst had passed. In 1848, two projects were completed that between them signalled the beginnings of Chicago's immense growth: the first telegraph line reached the city, radically improving communications, and the Illinois–Michigan Canal was finally completed, almost two decades after work on it had begun.

While the establishment of the Erie Canal had boosted the city's business, the new canal created an even more crucial connection: with vessels sailing to and from the Atlantic Ocean via the Great Lakes. A year earlier, the River and Harbor Convention in Chicago had promoted waterway trade to thousands of attendees, many from the east. The event began Chicago's long tenure as a host city for major conferences and meetings. Furthermore, the same savvy investors soon became aware of the city's potential as a railway hub.

Because of its central location and existing trade connections, Chicago became a crucial checkpoint for railway commerce in the US. Soon, livestock, timber, grain and other goods were transported speedily through Chicago in previously unheard-of quantities. More and more industries established their headquarters on the south-western shores of Lake Michigan rather than at rival St Louis, roughly 300 miles away in Missouri. By 1856, Chicago had become the largest railroad centre in the country.

Chicago's steel industry was also boosted by the unmatched transportation links. Situated along the banks of Lake Michigan at the mouth of the Calumet River, South Chicago became home to a number of blast furnaces, which set the stage for further growth. By the turn of the century, steel production in the area accounted for 50 per cent of the entire domestic output.

Coming at the juncture of such technological development, the Civil War also spurred the city's growth. St Louis's port on the Mississippi was blockaded by Navy vessels for the duration of the war, constricting trade movement. Chicago, further north and thus away from the worst of the conflict, benefited hugely. The employment of unskilled immigrant labour in the city's steel mills was a major factor in the growth and development of Chicago's extreme south-east neighbourhoods.

By 1870, more than half of Chicago's 300,000-strong population was foreign-born, with Germans, Irish, Bohemians and Scandinavians representing the majority of the city's new arrivals. The rapid population growth led, by necessity, to the construction of cheap, wooden buildings – at the time, timber was both cheap and easy to obtain. Fires sprang up around Chicago from time to time, but few imagined the horror that lay just around the corner.

FIRE AND RAIN

On 8 October 1871, a fire broke out adjacent to an immigrant neighbourhood that bordered the central business district. Spreading to the north-east, the blaze gained momentum, and didn't slow even upon reaching the south branch of the Chicago River. A dry summer, a concentration of wooden constructions (including roadways), and the presence of convection whirls (nicknamed 'fire devils, they enabled the blazes to leap over rivers) all stoked the appalling inferno.

> ## 'Two aldermen lined their pockets with illicit lucre from businesses grateful for their support.'

Over the next 36 hours, Chicago's citizens fled with only their most essential possessions. By the time the blaze finally burned itself out in Lincoln Park, several miles north of where it had started, it had left an unprecedented trail of destruction. Over an area stretching from Taylor Street north to Fullerton and from the Chicago River east to Lake Michigan, 17,000 buildings were destroyed, 98,000 people were left homeless, and more than 300 lives were lost.

But if the fire was dramatic, the city's efforts to regenerate itself in the wake of the disaster were nothing short of spectacular. Relief efforts soon gave way to rebuilding ventures; bloodied but unbowed, the downtown business district merchants wasted no time in obtaining loans and hiring crews to construct new, fireproof buildings. A mere 12 months on, 300 new structures had been erected; a few years down the line, taller, fireproof buildings stood proudly in place of the shambolic wooden structures that once made up downtown Chicago. Attracted by a blank canvas, and motivated by the enthusiasms of the city fathers, architects began to develop the extant elevator buildings into what were later termed 'skyscrapers'. The ultimate result of the fire was what remains, to this day, the finest collection of urban architecture in the US.

City in ruins: locals survey the remains of their town after the **Chicago Fire**. *See p14.*

Another elemental problem, that of water, also needed to be addressed by city planners. Despite the seemingly unlimited supply of freshwater provided by Lake Michigan, the vast quantities of polluting matter dumped into the Chicago River were in danger of permanently befouling the city's water supplies. By 1879, the heavy rains that swept the filth further into the lake prompted such severe outbreaks of cholera and dysentery that state leaders formed the Chicago Board of Sewerage Commissioners.

The eventual solution to the problem affected not only city residents but also those from downstate, since the plan involved forcing the river to run not towards but away from the lake. The sewage that had previously flowed unchecked into the clear waters of Lake Michigan would be redirected to the Mississippi River by means of a channel built to extend as far as a tributary in Lockport, Illinois. This channel, later known as the Sanitary and Ship Canal, was commissioned in 1889 and opened in 1900 against legal protests on behalf of the city of St Louis. The suit was dropped when the water was deemed to be safe by the time it reached its new destination in the south.

RIOT AND REFORM

But for all the successful regenerative efforts, not everything went smoothly. A nationwide railroad strike in the 1870s affected Chicago more than most, pitting out-of-work rioters against state militia units. During the strike, crowds assembled in their thousands to hear speeches espousing workers' rights. The mayor issued warnings to those not affected by the walkout to stay at home, away from the out-of-control mobs, but not everyone heeded them. A number of protesters and civilians died in the violence. Events in Chicago mirrored the national climate, as workers everywhere struggled to gain rights and power.

The Haymarket Square riot of 1886 was a watershed in the struggle between self-described 'anarchist' workers and their bosses. On the night of 4 May, a public gathering to protest against the treatment of workers at Cyrus McCormick's factory turned violent when a bomb was thrown at the police. Eight officers and three protestors died in the riots, yet only eight men stood trial. Four were executed for their part in the demonstrations, but three were pardoned, largely thanks to attorney John Peter Altgeld. The 'Haymarket martyrs', as they came to be known, inspired the socialist celebrations of ordinary workers that continue around the world each May Day.

Throughout this period, immigrants continued to descend on Chicago, the majority from Poland, Germany, Italy and Ireland. Not all of them immediately found work, and many of those who did were nonetheless forced to live in abject poverty. Jane Addams and Ellen Gates Starr decided to do something about it. The

Your connection
to Chicago.

DEPARTURES

destination	flight #	time
AMSTERDAM	3847	4:43P
BANGKOK	5623	4:55P
BOSTON	1459	5:07P
CHICAGO LOOP	BLUE/ ORANGE LINES	EVERY 6-20 MINS
HOUSTON	2473	5:12P
LONDON	9126	5:31P
NEW YORK	4962	5:39P

The Chicago Transit Authority provides frequent, convenient trains from O'Hare and Midway Airports to downtown Chicago. Take our buses and famous elevated trains to Chicago's top attractions, from the Art Institute to Millennium Park, Navy Pier and beyond!

Unlimited ride 1, 2, 3 and 5-Day Visitor Passes are available for $5 a day – or less. Passes can be purchased in advance by visiting transitchicago.com.

twentysomething duo, who'd met as teenagers at Rockford Female Seminary (now Rockford College), returned in 1888 from a tour of Europe inspired by what they'd seen at Toynbee Hall in London. The following year, in a mansion on Halsted Street donated by Charles Hull, they founded Hull-House to provide social services to a deprived local community on the West Side of the city.

Unafraid of controversy, Addams constantly wrestled with the city's political bodies, whose responses to the needs of the neighbourhoods she found inadequate. More often than not, she won the arguments. One of the first such settlement houses in the US, Hull-House proved immensely influential in the late 19th- and early 20th-century push for social reform in America. In 1931, Addams' humanitarian, feminist and internationalist work led to her being awarded the Nobel Peace Prize.

The year after Addams and Starr opened Hull House, the wheels were set in motion for the creation of a different but equally important Chicago institution. Founded (and, for the most part, funded) by John D Rockefeller, and with Ohio-born academic William Rainey Harper as its first president, the University of Chicago eventually held its first classes in 1892 on a

Strike one

By the 1870s, George Pullman was well on his way to becoming one of Chicago's wealthiest men. The confident businessman's designs for railroad cars in which passengers could dine and sleep had quickly become industry standards, a lucrative proposition during an era in which train travel was becoming ever more popular. Successful entrepreneurs are often said to have had one big idea. Pullman's downfall was that he had a second.

While searching for a way to reduce unrest among his workers, a major problem in post-Civil War America, Pullman hit upon the idea of housing them all in a planned community. The idea had already been tried in industrial England, and Pullman saw little reason why it couldn't succeed in the US. Hiring New York architect Solon Beman as his designer, Pullman set about realising his vision for a self-contained industrial city over 3,000 acres, which he purchased in Lake Calumet to the south of Chicago. Immodestly, but not altogether surprisingly, he named the new town after himself.

His big mistake was to try and run Pullman the town like he ran Pullman the business: carefully, fiercely, and with profit the ultimate and overriding motive. Decent amenities were provided for its 9,000-strong population of workers and their families: the site contained a park, a church, a theatre, shops and even a hotel. Although a few things niggled, not least Pullman's insistence that the town remain dry, most residents were content in their new accommodation.

When, in the early 1890s, demand for the sleeper cars fell, Pullman laid off a number of workers, and decided to cut the wages of others by around 30 per cent. However, he kept the rents for their properties at the same level, taking the cash directly from their pay packets and leaving many of them with virtually nothing in the way of disposable income. The hunger for profit that had built his business into a behemoth was soon to prove the downfall of his would-be capitalist idyll.

On 11 May 1894, 50,000 Pullman workers walked out on strike over the conditions in which their boss had left them. Ever-averse to pragmatism, Pullman not only refused to negotiate, but proceeded to lock them out. Eugene V Debs, president of the American Railway Union, soon intervened on behalf of the workers, instigating a boycott of Pullman cars across the nation. Rioting ensued, before President Grover Cleveland sent in the Army.

Eventually, in July, the strike was broken, and the Pullman plant reopened the following month with a substantial percentage of new workers. However, the damage was done. Pullman was harshly criticised by the media and, damningly, by a subsequent federal investigation into the disturbances. His reputation remained in tatters at the time of his death in 1897 at the age of 66, so much so that his family were forced to bury him in a lead-lined coffin to prevent his still-angry workers from desecrating his corpse.

The following year, the state supreme court decreed that the town should be annexed by Chicago, and ordered the Pullman company to sell all non-industrial property within it. Over the next few years, Pullman was gently absorbed into the suburbs of the South Side. And in 1971, it was designated a National Landmark District (for information on visiting the site, *see p142*), ensuring that Pullman's folly is remembered more than a century after its ignominious demise.

World's Columbian Exposition of 1893

parcel of land at 57th Street and Ellis Avenue. Something of a progressive for his time, Harper envisioned his university offering an equal education for both male and female students, operating a press in order to disseminate its teachings throughout the country, and using a then-novel 'quarter' system to allow for greater flexibility in the schedules of faculty and staff.

Although Harper's premature death in 1906, at the age of 49, came prior to the establishment of a medical school at the campus, it is partly thanks to his quest for excellence that today's University of Chicago Hospitals, as well as its other schools, are among the best in their field. That said, the university is best known for the key role it played in the development of nuclear energy when, in 1942, a team led by Enrico Fermi built the first ever nuclear reactor. The event led to the Manhattan Project and the creation of the world's first atomic bomb.

FAIR'S FARE

Held just 22 years after the Chicago Fire, the World's Columbian Exposition of 1893 was a perfect opportunity for Chicago to showcase its growth. A team of planners and designers led by Daniel Burnham and Frederick Law Olmsted created a series of grand attractions in a specially created 'White City', with 46 nations providing 250,000 displays in its various halls. The first ever Ferris wheel, standing 250 feet (76 metres) tall and kitted out with 36 cars that each held up to 60 people, was built for the fair.

However, the Streets in Cairo section was the fair's most profitable attraction, due in no small part to the suggestive cavortings of an exotic dancer named Little Egypt.

Leaving aside its rather anticlimactic ending (a planned parade was cancelled when, three days prior to it, Chicago mayor Carter Henry Harrison, Sr was shot and killed in his own home), the event was an almost unparalleled success. More than 25 million visitors came to the city during the six months the fair was in place, putting Chicago back on the map in the eyes of outsiders who'd written it off after the fire. However, it also kicked off a more general renaissance of popular entertainment in the city that lasted long after the fair had ended. Dance halls, movie palaces, nightclubs, amusement parks and vaudeville shows all sprang up around the time of the event and in the years immediately after it, greatly expanding the array of cultural options available to locals.

SODOM AND TOMORROW

Around the time of the Columbian Exposition, the Levee district in Chicago's First Ward took corruption and decadence to levels previously unmatched in the city's already fairly rich history. Centred around State and 22nd Streets on the Near South Side, close to modern-day Chinatown, the area was flooded with gamblers, drunks, penny-ante criminals and prostitutes. The latter plied their trade in an astonishing 200 brothels, revelling in such colourful names as the Everleigh Club (run by sisters Minna and Ada), Freiberg's Dance Hall, the Library, the House of All Nations and the Opium Den. For such activity to flourish, favours had to be granted and eyes had to look the other way.

The politicos in charge of the area were only to happy to oblige. Machine politics had yet to take hold on a grand scale, but corruption still flourished, with the First Ward a particularly iffy locale. Colourfully nicknamed Chicago aldermen Michael 'Hinky Dink' Kenna and 'Bathhouse' John Coughlin got into the habit of lining their own pockets with illicit lucre from businesses grateful for their support; the duo then used some of this cash to buy votes in First Ward elections. The pair were even said to have run an unofficial office out of Freiberg's Dance Hall, perfect for entertaining influential figures whose favours they needed to court.

Eventually, the moral adversaries of the goings-on in the Levee were prompted to put an end to the lawlessness. A Vice Commission appointed by the mayor enabled enforcers to shut down brothels based on the lost taxable income to the city. Once the Everleigh closed its doors in 1911, ground down by moral crusaders (and, in truth, something of a victim of its own success), the rest of the Levee's bordellos, saloons and gambling houses were systematically raided until both patrons and proprietors wearied of the law's interference. A few later reopened under a cloak of darkness, but the area never again flourished.

One of the beneficiaries of Kenna's and Coughlin's largesse was Charles Tyson Yerkes. A Philadelphian by birth and a broker by trade, he settled in Chicago in the 1880s and began to buy favours from the aldermen in a bid to gain ownership of the city's streetcar lines. Using stockholders' money to pay himself (investors went without), the brash Yerkes systematically expanded his activities into ownership of trolley cars and elevated train car lines.

But finally, the 'traction king', as Yerkes was by then known, stepped too far over the line, when he inspired his political cohorts to introduce a bill that would extend his transit franchise for another 50 years without any compensation to the city. Although the bill was passed in 1895, it was repealed after two years of public protest. Yerkes soon tired of the fray and moved to London; some 42 years after his death in 1905, the Chicago Transit Authority was created as a municipal agency to oversee the city's various mass transportation entities.

INSULLATION

Another man who left an impression on the city at the end of the 19th century, this time through his business dealings and philanthropy, was

Samuel Insull. After emigrating from Britain to the US in 1881 to work as Thomas Edison's assistant, Insull proved his worth by increasing Edison's domestic business fourfold, before becoming president of the Chicago Edison Company in 1892. Insull was also one of the forces behind the creation of the railroad system that connects Chicago to its suburbs, now known as Metra.

However, for all his entreprenurial spirit, the stubborn, starchy Insull's true passion was for opera. So much so, in fact, that he proposed building a new opera house for the town that would be financially supported by offices within its building (much like Adler and Sullivan's Auditorium Building, completed in 1889). Insull soon had the support of the major arts patrons, but insisted on looking after the entire project himself, hiring the firm of Graham, Anderson, Probst and White to design the structure.

> **'Capone ended up at Alcatraz, his empire disintegrating as he collapsed into insanity.'**

Upon its completion, the Civic Opera House was revealed to be a magnificent building, fêted by the city fathers who'd help fund its construction. Unfortunately, its completion came in 1929, shortly after the stock market crashed; as Insull's pride and joy opened to huge public acclaim, his empire was already beginning to crumble. After losing all of his companies, he travelled to Europe for a brief respite, before returning to the States to face court proceedings relating to fraud and embezzlement. He was acquitted, but his reputation never recovered. Nor, just as crucially, did his finances: when he died in 1938, suffering a heart attack in the Paris métro, he was found to have less than a dollar's worth of change in his pocket.

PAYING THE BILL

The father-and-son mayoral legacies of Carter Harrison senior and junior, which dated back to the 1870s, left large shoes to fill. The 24th mayor of Chicago (he went on to win five terms in office), Harrison, Sr took charge for the first time in 1879 and presided over much of the rebuilding that followed the Chicago Fire; he later served as mayor during the World's Columbian Exposition, until he was murdered three days before it ended. Later, Harrison, Jr, the 30th mayor of Chicago but the first born in the city, proved to be even more reform-minded than his father. Also winning five terms in office, he was known for his fair dealings with

The South Side's **Union Stock Yards**, an industrial behemoth in 19th-century Chicago.

immigrant and minority groups, and was one of the driving forces behind the moral clean-up in the Levee during the early 1910s.

By the end of his fifth term, Harrison Jr's popularity was waning, and he was defeated in the Democratic primary by Robert Sweitzer. It scarcely mattered. The pragmatic Democrat was roundly thrashed at the mayoral elections by William Hale Thompson, scion of a real estate business family and a powerful friend to the likes of Al Capone. 'Big Bill', as he was almost universally known, was not a clever man, but his belligerence suited the mood of the city, desperate to escape a financial recession that had begun to envelop the country as a whole.

Thompson was re-elected mayor of Chicago in 1919. However, while he was an enthusiastic recipient of many minority votes, his passivity during the Chicago Race Riots that same year hurt his chances of re-election. In the summer of 1919, an isolated incident on one of Chicago's beaches set off five days of rioting between whites and blacks, leaving more than 35 people dead and hundreds more injured. Things escalated further with the death of black teenager Eugene Williams, who drowned at the segregated 29th Street beach on 27 July 1919 after a confrontation between blacks and whites reputedly prevented him from coming ashore.

Williams' death was the spark that set alight a series of violent racial battles. When word got out about it, the story soon changed: rumours spread that Williams had been stoned to death, prompting fury among the black community. After several attempts to quell the violence

without force, Mayor Thompson asked the governor of Illinois for the assistance of state troops. Too late, 5,000 men were summoned to keep the peace. Coupled with his pro-German stance during World War I, the reasons for Thompson's fall from grace become obvious. He failed to win re-election in 1923, and was replaced in office by Democratic candidate William Dever.

PROHIBITION AND DEPRESSION

The Prohibition era in the US began when, on 16 January 1920, Congress ratified the 18th Amendment banning the manufacture and sale of alcohol. Chicago's involvement in the days prior to the amendment came chiefly through Evanston's Frances Willard, president of the Women's Christian Temperance Union for four decades and a tireless anti-alcohol campaigner.

Spurred on by the WCTU, the temperance movement gained momentum in the years after World War I, its followers obtaining signed pledge cards from untold numbers of US citizens. The pledge of temperance was a factor in the political climate that fuelled the need for alcohol restrictions, first at the community and state levels and then across the entire county. However, the ideals of the 18th Amendment created incredible hypocrisy within American society, corruption at all levels of government, and a massive increase in organised crime. Chicago was in the thick of the action.

Mayor Dever was in favour of Prohibition, and made every effort to enforce it. But then, as now, Chicago was a drinking city: while the temperance campaigners were undoubtedly influential, Dever's attitudes were less than popular with the electorate at large, and opened the door to competition in the mayoral election in 1927. Opposing him was the indefatigable Thompson; raucous in his condemnation of Prohibition, he promised to reopen bars that had been closed by Dever and his cronies.

There was more to Thompson's pro-alcohol stance than social liberalism. Under Prohibition, the Mob essentially controlled the city's alcohol supply. During his first two terms in office, it was often muttered that Thompson was in the

pockets of the town's gangsters: first Johnny Torrio and then, after Torrio retired following an attempt on his life in 1925, Al Capone. While Dever was incorruptible, Torrio and Capone were both careful to keep Thompson on their side even after he lost office in 1923, reputedly with regular financial backhanders. Thompson, for his part, enjoyed the Mob support, not least because it helped get him re-elected in 1927.

During Thompson's third term in office, Mob influence spiralled. Capone ruled over his empire safe in the knowledge that Thompson would never prosecute, keeping the mayor and

Unsteady as she goes

In the wake of the *Titanic* catastrophe in 1912, a flurry of new regulations led to a vast number of lifeboats being fitted to cruise ships. The laws were designed to increase passengers' chance of survival in the event of another major mishap. However, with tragic irony, the well-intentioned safety mandate combined almost immediately with human error to cause one of the worst disasters in the US. No icebergs were present when the *Eastland*, a passenger ship docked in peaceful waters in the Chicago River and still moored to a downtown wharf, rolled on to its side on a calm summer morning. Some 845 people died in the event.

Already a top-heavy ship with an insufficient ballast system, the *Eastland* acquired additional lifeboats and rafts on its top deck in early July 1915 to comply with a new *Titanic*-inspired federal law. The 265-foot vessel was a disaster waiting to happen, a disaster that fell with tragic timing only two weeks later. On Saturday 24 July, thousands of employees of Western Electric arrived at the river to board the boat. The company had intended to ferry its workers and their families across Lake Michigan for its annual picnic. However, shortly after the lurching ship reached its 2,500-person capacity, it pitched over.

Just a few feet from land, hundreds of men, women and children were

tossed into the river. Others were stuck inside cabins that quickly filled with water; still others were crushed by the sudden avalanche of furniture and other passengers. With the ship's port side now resting on the river bottom, a few lucky passengers who clung to the starboard side were able to hop to safety when a second cruise ship pulled alongside it to bring about their rescue. Though penned inside the fallen ship, others managed to survive for hours until rescuers were finally able to cut them loose.

Though the tragedy claimed three times as many lives as the Great Chicago Fire of 1871, it's been more or less forgotten today. A memorial plaque marks the site on Wacker Drive just east of LaSalle Street, while a private historian's collection of *Eastland* artefacts is part of the Center for History in the far western suburb of Wheaton.

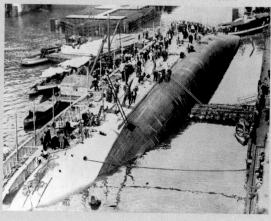

his local police chiefs sweet with regular payoffs. He even escaped prosecution for the St Valentine's Day Massacre in 1929, in which seven members of a rival North Side gang were summarily executed behind a garage in Lincoln Park by his associates.

It took a group of outsiders to challenge Mob hegemony: US marshal and special Prohibition task force agent Eliot Ness, charged with gathering evidence against booze-running gangsters such as Capone and Dion O'Banion from a tiny office on Wabash Street. Ness and his team, later nicknamed the Untouchables due to their resistance to Mob bribery, worked hard, but couldn't pin the St Valentine's Day Massacre on Capone. However, federal investigators did tag him with 22 charges of tax evasion, charges that stuck. Convicted in 1931, Capone ended up at Alcatraz, his empire disintegrating as he collapsed into insanity. In the same year, Thompson was forced out of office by a city weary of his inveterate corruption, never to return. He was the last Republican to serve as Chicago mayor in the 20th century.

During the later 1920s and early 1930s, according to some historians, the Depression itself acted as a force for the repeal of the 18th Amendment, due to the changes it had produced within American society and the accompanying political and economic shifts that it had simultaneously brought about. In 1933, with the 21st Amendment that repealed Prohibition, it was clear that individual states would again take control of the regulation and taxation of alcohol, and that the public sale of 'demon rum' would be legal across the nation once more.

'Daley stuck with his tough approach, but few stood alongside him.'

During the Depression, the city's immigrant population base altered once more, a shift that was subsequently, and dramatically, reflected in Chicago politics. The changes began to take hold in 1931, when the disgraced Thompson was soundly defeated in 1931 by Anton 'Tony' Cermak, a coal-miner's son and street vendor who had emigrated to the US from Bohemia as a child in the 1870s. It was Cermak who really set in motion the type of machine politics that typified Chicago government for much of the remainder of the 20th century (for more on this, see pp41-44), but he didn't get long to act out his plans. On 15 February 1933 in Miami, Cermak was struck by an assassin's bullet apparently intended for President Franklin D Roosevelt. Although he lingered for over two weeks, the wound proved fatal (see p42 **Gun crazy**).

Cermak didn't live long enough to see Chicago's second World's Fair. Entitled the 'Century of Progress', it was held 40 years after the Columbian Exposition – in a neat nod to the earlier wing-ding, Daniel Burnham's two sons Hubert and Daniel were appointed, as architect and secretary, to the board of trustees – and stayed open for two summers, 1933 and 1934. While not as influential as its predecessor, it proved both popular and profitable. The money raised aided the arts organisations involved in preserving the fair's exhibits, including the Museum of Science and Industry (built for the earlier Columbian Exposition), the Adler Planetarium and the South Park Corporation (later taken over by the Chicago Park District).

After World War II, Chicago benefited from a huge boom. In 1950, its population topped 3.6 million; affluence was everywhere, as people began to move from the city to the suburbs. Five years later, the city was to reach a turning point with the election of one of the most famous American city mayors of the century.

DEUS EX MACHINE

In 1955, Richard J Daley won the first of six straight terms as mayor. Skilled in the machine politics tradition through his chairmanship of the Cook County Democratic Organization, Daley was an Irish American Democrat who gained the trust of minority and working-class voters with straight talk and a get-the-job-done attitude. But while he reigned more or less unchallenged for his first decade in office, aided in no small part by the patronage system (see pp41-44), his mettle was tested by spiralling crime and racial tensions, epitomised in the civil unrest triggered by the assassination of Dr Martin Luther King, Jr.

King had come to Chicago several times during the 1960s. With each visit, he flagged up more of the problems faced by minority communities. Poor housing, job discrimination, poverty and illiteracy were just a few of the issues that King hoped to bring to the fore. However, he was greeted with scorn by white Chicagoans, even after several meetings with Daley in a bid to set up a Citizens Advisory Committee that could address racial tensions.

When King announced his intention to take up residence in a slum building in the Lawndale neighbourhood, the owners of the structure took him to court. Various rallies and marches led by King in white neighbourhoods led to police intervention, which in turn set the stage for the widespread burning and looting of white-owned businesses that occurred mainly in black neighbourhoods on the West Side immediately following King's death in April 1968. To stem the chaos, Daley called in the

National Guard, but it was only the beginning of a turbulent year, which culminated in a national PR disaster for the mayor and his administration.

RIOT POLICE

The Democratic National Convention of 1968 was meant to be a glorious celebration of Chicago, as the party descended on the city to choose its candidate for the upcoming presidential election. However, with both party and country split over the Vietnam War, it proved far tougher than Daley had anticipated.

As they arrived in late August, the Democrats were joined in the city by anti-war protesters. Encouraged by a group of counter-cultural mischief-makers known as the Yippies, they had descended on Chicago in their hundreds to celebrate what they provocatively called the Festival of Life. Daley immediately settled on a hard line approach to their presence, denying them permission to gather in a number of apparently sensitive locations.

To begin with, the Yippies' protests passed relatively quietly. But at the first sign of inevitable trouble, the 12,000-strong Chicago police force – supplemented by 15,000 troops from the National Guard and the US Army, called in by Daley – waded in with nightsticks and tear gas, meeting mild dissent with fearsome violence. In the disarray, a number of journalists were gassed, beaten and arrested as they attempted to cover the melées between the 'pigs' and the 'flower children'. They filed their stories, but the damage to the city's reputation had already been done: many disturbances were broadcast live on national TV. Daley stuck with his tougher-than-tough approach throughout the troubles, but few Democrats stood alongside him. He, and his city, were humiliated.

The subsequent scapegoating of several protesters, in what became known as the 'Chicago Eight' trial, only prolonged the embarrassment. Indicted for conspiracy to cause riots, the recalcitrant defendants – among them Abbie Hoffman and Jerry Rubin – found themselves at the centre of the controversy, and made the most of it by hiring brash New Yorker William M Kunstler as their attorney. Judge Julius Hoffman presided over the chaotic but entertaining 100-day trial, highlighted by a parade of well-known witnesses. A handful of the charges stuck, but not for long: all convictions were quashed on appeal in 1972. It was established three years later that the FBI, with the complicity of Judge Hoffman, had bugged the offices of the defendants' attorneys.

A further confrontation between police and radicals occurred in 1969, when the Weathermen's 'Days of Rage' were fashioned after ambushes by the Black Panther party. The Weathermen were an offshoot radical subgroup of the Students for a Democratic Society (SDS) who advocated armed overthrow of US governmental entities to atone for the country's exploitation of foreign nations and

Snow practically closed the entire city during the fearful winter of 1978-79.

What's in a name?

Some say it's the **City of Neighborhoods**. Writer Donald Miller called it the **City of the Century**. But given all its sundry aliases, Chicago might as well be dubbed the City of Nicknames.

Chicago is most famously referred to as the **Windy City**, but the tag has nothing to do with the weather. Though the precise origins are still widely debated, it's generally agreed that the term was coined in the middle of the 19th century as a nod to the long-windedness of its politicians and the verbosity of its local boosters.

The **Second City** nickname is, if anything, even more confusing. While many believe it emerged simply because of Chicago's status as the largest town in the US outside New York City (though it's since been surpassed in the population stakes by LA), others claim it was pejoratively bestowed on the city by *New Yorker* writer AJ Liebling in the belief that Chicago was a notch down from New York in more than just its size. Still others argue that the pseudonym has less to do with census figures than the ugly stepsister complex Chicagoans seem to have when they compare their hometown with the grandeur of the Big Apple. And yet another school of thought suggests the term was first coined to describe the shiny new sections of town built after the Great Fire of 1871.

'Chicago', a poem by local historian and author Carl Sandburg, is the source of two of the city's other well-known nicknames. The **City of the Big Shoulders** nods to the tough, workhorse mentality and pivotal role Chicago played in the growth of the US in the 19th century, while the **Hog Butcher for the World** is a reference to the stockyards that drove the city's economy around the same time. Some years later, the city even adopted the nickname **Porkopolis** in tribute to its meatpackers. Thankfully, it never caught on.

A couple of nicknames have official city approval. **City in a Garden** is a straightforward translation of *Urbs in Horto*, the city's Latin motto, while **The City that Works** was coined by Mayor Richard J Daley. Less common are the **Big Onion** and the **Wild Onion**; both are homages to (and quasi-translations of) 'Checagou', the name given to the area by the Native American tribe who settled in it.

But perhaps the strangest nickname is one bestowed on it in 1922 by Fred Fisher in his song 'Chicago' (popularised in 1964 by Frank Sinatra, who had earlier granted the city another *nom de plume* with his recording of the Sammy Cahn/Jimmy Van Heusen track **My Kind of Town**). In it, Fisher referred to Chicago as **That Toddlin' Town**. The nickname quickly caught on, without anyone knowing quite what it actually means.

its military action in Vietnam. Members of the group vandalised property and attacked police in the Loop and the Gold Coast, and there were further skirmishes between civilians and uniformed cops on the North Side and in the Civic Center.

> **'For all his populism, Daley has often let finance muscle get in the way of sentiment.'**

By the time the violence had ceased, dozens of police and demonstrators had been injured. Neither side came out of it especially well; indeed, it may have been symbolic that Fred Hampton, the leader of the Chicago chapter of the Black Panther party, died in a police raid that same December. What's more, racial problems in the city continued well into the following decade. For better or worse, many white residents chose to leave for the suburbs in a phenomenon termed 'white flight'.

ONWARDS AND UPWARDS

During the 1970s, the Loop was transformed into a financial centre as never before, priapic skyscrapers such as the Sears Tower springing up as testament to its economic virility. But on the whole, it was a difficult decade for Chicago, much as it was for most of the Midwest. Daley retained office, but struggled to galvanise his electorate as he had in previous decades; still in office, he died of a massive heart attack in 1976. In the face of economic instability, the city battled gamely on until the winter of 1978-79, when it was essentially closed by an amazing 82 inches of snow. Otherwise popular mayor Michael Bilandic was blamed by the electorate for the city's slow reaction to the blizzard, and was replaced in office the same year by Daley protégée Jane Byrne.

As they had with Bilandic, Chicago voters quickly tired of the strident Byrne, who excelled at headline-grabbing gestures but proved less skilled at negotiating the machine politicians who still dominated the council. Chicago's first female mayor was then replaced by its first black mayor, as Harold Washington snuck through to win in a three-way heat for the Democratic nomination in 1983. But after winning office the same year, Washington was left a lame duck when the council split into two camps: the reformers, led by Washington, and the old-school machine politicians, led by Edward Vrdolyak (*see pp43-44*).

After Washington won re-election in 1987, things improved. The 29, as they had become known, no longer wielded the power they once did, and Washington was able to make progress at last. After his sudden death (like Daley, he suffered a heart attack while in office), former alderman Eugene Sawyer continued with many of his reforms. But he was defeated in the 1989 mayoral primary by Richard M Daley, who has proved to be very much his father's son.

BACK TO THE FUTURE

Over the last decade and a half, the machine politics tradition that Byrne and Washington tried to eradicate seems to have returned in earnest. But there's little doubt that the city has dramatically improved under Daley's watch, thanks in no small part to his tireless efforts to publicise and promote it to a national and international audience.

The Loop continued to grow ever more powerful and influential during the 1990s, while the city's convention industry expanded to unprecedented levels. Daley has thrown money at city beautification schemes, in turn encouraging huge private investment in new commercial buildings and residential space. The numbers of tourists travelling to the city has also risen, attracted by Daley-sponsored measures such as the redevelopment of Navy Pier and, more recently, the late, expensive but already widely cherished Millennium Park. Chicago's status as an industrial city may be gone, but it has regained much of the prosperity that illuminated its early years.

But just as Daley inherited his father's can-do attitude towards bettering the city, so he's been dogged by controversy about alleged corruption within his administration (*see pp41-44*). For all his populism, he's often let financial muscle get in the way of sentiment: witness the shameful demolition in 1994 of the Maxwell Street Market, breeding ground for several generations of blues musicians. The city remains one of the most racially divided in the US, a legacy of the separationist housing policies enacted by Daley Sr in the 1950s and '60s and not remedied by his successors. And then there's the curious incident of the airport in the night-time. Daley had long argued that Meigs Field airport, which occupied a prime piece of real estate just south of the Adler Planetarium, should be turned into a public park. Even so, the city was astonished when, around midnight on 30 March 2003, Daley sent bulldozers into the airfield to destroy its runways.

Yet for all the mayor's faults (perceived and otherwise), and for all the deep-cut societal problems that still exist in a city largely split along racial lines, Chicagoans in all corners of the city go about their business much as they ever have. The staunch resilience that characterised Chicago in the days of Kinzie and Wentworth is still present today; indeed, given the difficulties the city has had to overcome (and, for that matter, has yet to address), it's arguably the town's dominant characteristic. For all its faults, the Windy City remains a town on the rise.

Millennium Park.

Key events

1673 Father Jacques Marquette and Louis Jolliet discover what later becomes Chicago.
1779 Jean Baptiste Point du Sable becomes the first permanent resident of the area.
1812 53 settlers are killed by natives in the Fort Dearborn Massacre.
1837 Chicago incorporates as a city.
1847 The Chicago River and Harbor Convention promotes waterway commerce.
1848 The Illinois–Michigan Canal is built; the Chicago Board of Trade is established.
1850 Northwestern University opens.
1860 Abraham Lincoln is nominated as Republican presidential candidate in Chicago.
1871 The Chicago Fire destroys $200 million worth of property and claims 300 lives.
1879 The Chicago Academy of Fine Arts (later the Art Institute of Chicago) is incorporated.
1886 The Haymarket Square labour riot takes place; 11 people are killed.
1889 Social reformer Jane Addams opens Hull-House; architect Frank Lloyd Wright builds his own residence in Oak Park.
1891 The Chicago Orchestra, later the Chicago Symphony Orchestra, is established.
1892 The first elevated train service is offered to commuters in the central district.
1893 The World's Columbian Exposition opens on the South Side.
1894 Pullman train employees strike for improved working conditions.
1900 Chicago River is diverted towards the Mississippi for sanitary purposes.
1903 A fire at the Iroquois Theatre kills 600, prompting national laws for public buildings.
1909 Daniel Burnham, city visionary, unveils his park-filled Plan of Chicago.
1915 The Eastland pleasure vessel capsizes in the Chicago River, killing 812.
1919 Race riots rage in July; 38 die.
1920 Eight Chicago White Sox players, among them 'Shoeless' Joe Jackson, are banned from baseball after fixing the 1919 World Series.
1921 The Field Museum opens.
1924 Leopold and Loeb are sentenced to life in prison for murder.
1929 Seven bootleggers are executed in the St Valentine's Day Massacre.
1933 The Century of Progress World's Fair opens, as does the Museum of Science and Industry; Mayor Anton Cermak is killed in Miami by a gunman apparently intending to shoot President-elect Franklin D Roosevelt.

1934 John Dillinger is shot and killed at the Biograph movie theatre in Lincoln Park.
1942 Physicist Enrico Fermi conducts successful nuclear chain reaction experiments at the University of Chicago.
1953 Hugh Hefner publishes the inaugural monthly issue of *Playboy* in December.
1955 Richard J Daley is elected mayor; O'Hare International Airport opens.
1958 A fire at Our Lady of the Angels school kills three nuns and 87 children.
1959 The first ever Second City cabaret show takes place; Chicago becomes an ocean port with the opening of the St Lawrence Seaway.
1967 A blizzard in January closes down the city with 22 inches of snow.
1968 Riots take place after the murder of Martin Luther King, Jr; the Democratic National Convention is marred by violence.
1969 The Chicago Seven trial takes place; two radicals die in a Black Panther raid.
1971 The Union Stockyards close after 105 years of continuous livestock trading.
1973 The Sears Tower opens.
1976 Mayor Richard J Daley dies in office.
1979 *The Blues Brothers* is filmed in the city; an American Airlines DC-10 crashes near O'Hare Airport, claiming 273 lives.
1986 The Chicago Bears rout the New England Patriots 46-10 to win their first Super Bowl.
1987 Mayor Harold Washington dies in office.
1988 Floodlights are at long last installed at Wrigley Field.
1989 Richard M Daley, son of Richard J Daley, is elected mayor of Chicago.
1992 The Chicago River floods underground tunnels, causing $1 billion of damage.
1994 The United Center opens.
1995 Temperatures top 100 degrees for five straight days in July, killing 550 people.
1996 Michael Jordan and the Chicago Bulls win their sixth NBA championship.
1999 Over 200 statues are displayed as part of the 'Cows on Parade' outdoor exhibition; Richard M Daley is re-elected for a third term.
2003 21 people are trampled to death in the E2 nightclub as they try to escape a fire.
2004 Four years late, Millennium Park opens to the public.
2005 The Chicago White Sox win the World Series for the first time since 1917.
2006 Federal investigators launch a probe into corruption at City Hall.

Construction continues at **Trump** Tower.

Chicago Today

A city on the make.

Any discussion about 21st-century Chicago begins – and, to some degree, ends – with its mayor. Richard J Daley, who reigned over the city from 1955 until his death in 1976, is often referred to as the 'last of the big-city bosses' by historians. However, they underestimated the town's talent for keeping it in the family. Barring an electoral earthquake in early 2007, or the kind of fatal tragedy that curtailed Daley Sr's term in office, Mayor Richard M Daley will exceed his dad's 21-plus years in office at the end of 2010. He is very much his father's son.

Few mayors wield such influence over their cities as does Daley over Chicago. Cannily reaching out to a wide variety of constituencies, guaranteeing him repeated re-election, Daley presides with unflappable confidence over his town. Trouble has circled him constantly, but he's withstood the criticism while propelling the city forwards. Indeed, his track record could scarcely be showier: in the course of beautifying Chicago, he's added flower gardens to Lake Shore Drive, regenerated Navy Pier and built the already-beloved Millennium Park. Daley can look voters in the face when he declares that Chicago remains 'the city that works'.

Exactly how it works, and for whom, is another matter entirely. But despite ongoing investigations into municipal graft that have snagged Daley allies (*see pp41-44*), corruption charges have yet to penetrate the upper echelons of City Hall. And when the Democrats triumphed in the national elections of 2006, Daley's two main obstacles to re-election were removed. Luis Gutiérrez and Jesse Jackson, Jr, two prominent members of the US House of Representatives, were rumoured to be planning to stand against Daley, but were assuaged by their party's return to power in Washington. The mayor looks set to remain in charge for some time yet.

GROWING PAINS

Chicagoans generally agree about a few key current concerns. Yes, the education system needs to improve; no, it's not OK for the police to practice racial profiling. However, while it's not a headline-grabber, perhaps the major issue facing the city is gentrification. Encouraged by Daley in some neighbourhoods, arriving in others almost despite his best efforts, and eluding still others entirely, it's complex, difficult and fascinating.

Five gold rings

In the last decade, Mayor Daley has made it a priority to spruce up Chicago, partly in an attempt to position it once more on the world stage. Some of his aesthetic choices have been iffy; the majority have proven surprisingly successful. However, he's not done yet: his biggest project may still be a decade away.

In April 2007, the US Olympic Committee will decide whether to submit a city to the International Olympic Committee in the hope of being awarded the 2016 games. Chicago is one of two cities under consideration; the other is Los Angeles, which hosted the games in 1984. If the USOC selects Chicago, the city fathers will then have two years in which to prepare and campaign before the IOC chooses a host city in October 2009.

The Olympics would be Chicago's most ambitious gambit since the World's Columbian Exposition in 1893. But the question on many minds' is not whether the city could host the Olympics (it successfully hosted the Gay Games in 2006, admittedly on a far smaller scale), but whether it should. The main worry is financial: the Athens games of 2004 came

in at twice the original $6 billion plan, and the budget to prepare London for the 2012 games has tripled from its initial $5 billion guesstimate. Chicago, of course, has past form here: Millennium Park ran way behind schedule and wildly over-budget, eventually requiring a big bailout from private investors.

The Olympics might seem like a vanity project, but the mayor hopes that the city will continue to benefit from the games long after they've ended. The proposed Olympic Village, along the lakefront just south of McCormick Place, would become private housing after 2016, some of it priced below market value in an attempt to facilitate a mixed-income neighbourhood. The stadium would be situated at Washington Park on the South Side, an area in need of regeneration. And a number of the city's harbours would be overhauled to accommodate sailing and rowing events. If Daley and his team, headed by Patrick Ryan, can lure the necessary private investors and stay true to their vision, Chicago could end up a more unified city a decade from now. Watch this space.

The benefits of gentrification are undeniable. Property values increase as crime rates decline, and a range of previously unavailable shops and services (galleries, theatres, cafés, even schools) spring up. However, the measurable financial benefits are not evenly distributed, and what's generally good news for existing homeowners is bad for those who rent their properties. Rental units are disappearing across the city, subsumed by condo developers who, adding aesthetic insult to housing injury, have been erecting cinder-block behemoths at the expense of green space.

One north side district provides an excellent study in the tightrope perils of gentrification. Rogers Park is one of the city's most racially mixed neighbourhoods, with large Latino, African American and European American populations living side by side. But the area's diversity is being threatened by the condo-conversion wave. Whites make up less than a third of Rogers Park residents but almost two-thirds of homeowners. And according to a 2006 study by the non-profit Lakeside Community Development Corporation, whites are securing mortgages at six and seven times the rate of black and Hispanic borrowers, while rental units evaporate. Gentrification in Rogers Park, as elsewhere, has thus far come at the expense of racial, economic and cultural diversity.

In poorer areas, Daley's strategy to reform public housing has accelerated gentrification, most visibly with the gradual dismantling of the notorious Cabrini-Green public housing project. By 2008, only the original 1942 row houses should remain in what, for decades, was a no-go ghetto. Cabrini-Green's ugliest units, built in the late 1950s and early '60s, are being replaced, but they're coming down at a faster rate than new mixed-income housing is going up. Current residents are concerned that they're being squeezed out, and with good reason. It's surely no coincidence that the gentrifying area bumps right up against the Gold Coast, one Chicago's swankest, richest locales.

The question of where low-income residents can turn for better-paying jobs roiled the city council in 2006, when a majority of aldermen went against Daley's wishes and approved a so-called 'big box' ordinance requiring übersized retailers such as Target and Home Depot to pay their workers at least $10 an hour (almost twice the federal minimum wage). There was no unified voice among demographic groups: some African American aldermen representing West and South Side districts lobbied for the bill, but others insisted that the economic revival of their wards was tied to the arrival of mega-chains such as Wal-Mart. Although Daley lost in the first round of voting, the decision of three council members to switch their votes meant that when Daley then vetoed the bill, his first veto in 17 years as mayor, the scheme's supporters were unable to overrule him.

Gentrification needn't always mean the arrival of huge chains. In fast-rising areas such as Lincoln Square and Wicker Park, economic revival has been linked directly to the small and proudly independent businesses in residence. But other areas of the city are already clogged with megastores, and concomitantly clogged with the traffic they attract. Around North and Clybourn Avenues, the streets are almost as congested as the huge parking lots.

ON THE ROAD

Of course, fewer people would drive if the city's mass transit system was more reliable. But frustration has been mounting at the Chicago Transit Authority, with fares rising as the quality of service declines. Some recent delays were unavoidable: parts of the network have needed refurbishment for years. But the programmes to repair and/or rebuild the infrastructure on the Brown and Red lines have been extended by the need to keep running trains along them. Patience is the only answer.

Long-term (if temporary) station closures are one thing; major snafus and travel calamities are another. In summer 2006, a Blue line train derailed, stranding hundreds of passengers in a smoke-filled tunnel. In a separate incident later in the year, Orange line trains ran in the 'wrong' direction around the Loop circuit, thanks to an aging track switch that took an entire day to repair. Just two weeks later, two train cars on the same line fell off their elevated tracks.

Worse, passengers are often left in the dark about what's going on during crises. In a cost-cutting move, the CTA eliminated conductors from its trains, but some aldermen have called for them to be reinstated, using federal funds allocated for homeland security. The presence of another employee to roam the cars, it's hoped, would provide greater security while curtailing anti-social behaviour and vandalism.

LOOKING UP

Chicago's local schools system was once regarded as among the worst in the nation. The system still has major shortcomings, and the number of high school graduates who go on to earn a bachelor's degree is half the national average. However, things are changing: several new college-prep magnet schools (such as Walter Payton College Prep on the edge of the Gold Coast) are benefitting from increased funding, and other schools are also on the up.

When Daley took on jurisdiction over the city's schools in 1995, he created a CEO position in the hope of streamlining school reform. After the influential Paul Vallas resigned in 2001, new CEO Arne Duncan set in motion a plan to create 100 new schools in the city over six years. By restructuring underperforming schools or building replacements, the Renaissance 2010 programme has led to improvements to neighbourhood schools in struggling areas such as Austin and Englewood.

There's also progress being made on an environmental front. The city regularly announces eco-friendly initiatives, and recycled materials are inventively employed in several areas of infrastructure, including CTA railroad ties made of recycled plastic milk jugs and rubber sidewalks fashioned from recycled tires. One new pilot programme will test the efficacy of solar-powered lighting in 100 bus shelters, with the hope of eventually saving $200 a year in electricity for every shelter in the city.

The most anticipated change is an overhaul of the city's much-debated 'Blue Bag' recycling program. For years, residents have been asked to dump most of their recyclables in one blue bag, for collection by garbage trucks. In theory, someone picked out the blue bags later in the collection cycle, and sorted the recyclables. In reality, many of the bags have been following the rest of the rubbish into Indiana landfills. However, Daley has at long last yielded to protestors: the system is set for a major revamp in 2007, with the introduction of a curbside recycling programme. Cynics have already started to wonder which of City Hall's favorite contractors will diversify into the presumably lucrative curbside pick-up business. But at least tons of recyclable material will find a new life.

Meanwhile, the city has become ever more bike-friendly. Existing bike trails have been enhanced (most obviously, the lakefront lanes; see p111 **Easy riders**) and new routes added to the network; bike parking has proliferated; and CTA buses have been equipped with bike racks, making it easy to pedal one way and take the bus back. Further improvements should come through the Bike 2015 Plan, developed by city officials in partnership with the Chicagoland Bicycling Federation.

Indeed, these days, Chicago's got a plan for just about everything. And there are more being mapped out all the time, not least Daley's ambitious plan to stage the Olympics in 2016 (see p28 **Five gold rings**). The goal is to prove to newcomers and outsiders what most of the city's residents already know: unless you're trying to raise a family on minimum wage, or fretting about how to balance a fixed income against escalating property taxes, Chicago is the most friendly and liveable big city in the United States.

Marina City. *See p39.*

Architecture

High and mighty.

Could it have been the Midwest's unequivocal flatness that gave rise to a skyline of such soaring heights? Perhaps, but the city that invented the skyscraper in the 19th century, and now boasts a dynamic and ever-expanding line-up of towering structures, has also moved beyond it. Outside of flamboyant downtown, Chicago is home to a host of interesting smaller buildings, some of which have rivalled their lofty counterparts in importance by themselves giving rise to new architectural movements and modern methods of construction.

For unimpeded views of the city's skyline, take one of many boat tours (*see p73*) that launch on to the Chicago River every day. The city's waterways helped Chicago become one of the country's largest transportation hubs; in turn, buildings of every sort – commercial, industrial, residential and even cultural – have sprouted on the banks of the river. It's a spectacular sight.

BURNING AMBITIONS

The story of Chicago's ascent from ramshackle Midwestern burg to world-class architectural showcase began in 1871, although it must have seemed like the end for those who lived in the city at the time. On the night of 8 October, a fire broke out in the barn behind the home of Patrick and Catherine O'Leary on the city's Near West Side and raced north and east. When it finally burned itself out two days later, much of the city was reduced to smouldering ruins.

While many theories exist about what caused the fire, from Mrs O'Leary's much-maligned cow to a fiery meteorite, most will agree that poor urban planning was ultimately to blame for the way it spread. At the time, Chicago

❶ Orange numbers given in this chapter correspond to the location of each building on the architecture map. See p33.

was a veritable tinderbox: two-thirds of its 60,000 buildings were made of wood, and most of the city's 60-odd miles of paved streets were covered with wooden planks. Add the crowded conditions and the lack of fire codes, and disaster seems inevitable. Yet although its immediate impact was catastrophic, the blaze proved to be the spur for the city to rebuild itself with dramatic immediacy.

THE CHICAGO SCHOOL

Refusing to be defeated by the tragedy, the city was determined to rebuild with a daring, original vision. Once the charred buildings were cleared away, scores of architects converged on the city, drawn by the idea of working with a clean slate and without a confining architectural heritage.

Among them was Louis Sullivan. Born and educated in Boston, Sullivan arrived in Chicago in 1873 and went to work for Dankmar Adler, a German émigré with a firmly established architectural practice. Despite – or, more likely, because of – their differences in personality, the two worked well together, Sullivan's erratic moods and artistic hauteur tempered by Adler's sober professionalism. Along with a handful of noteworthy contemporaries, among them William LeBaron Jenney and Daniel Burnham, Sullivan would help define what came to be known as the Chicago School.

The Chicago School's biggest innovation was the use of an interior steel structure to distribute the weight of a building. Previously, constructing taller buildings meant thickening the load-bearing exterior masonry walls to support the weight of the upper floors. Particularly notable among such structures is Adler and Sullivan's **Auditorium Building** (50 E Congress Parkway, at S Wabash Avenue; map ❶), which combined a 4,200-seat theatre with offices and a hotel when it was completed in 1889. Owned by Roosevelt University since 1946, it remains one of the city's premier theatre and music venues. Catch a performance by the Joffrey Ballet in order to see the spectacular interior, with its dramatic arches, gilded reliefs and rows of sparkling electric lights.

'The American fashion for art deco never really developed in Chicago.'

The **Fine Arts Building** (410 S Michigan Avenue, at E Van Buren Street; map ❷), constructed by Solon Spencer Beman in 1885 as a showroom for Studebaker carriages, is another classic example of load-bearing masonry construction. As, too, is the **Monadnock Building** (53 W Jackson Street, at S Dearborn Street; map ❸). Designed by

Charles Beersman's grand, gum-coloured **Wrigley Building**. *See p34.*

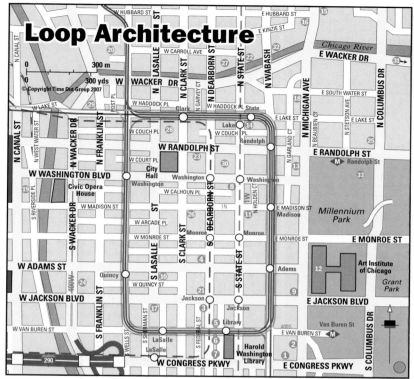

Loop Architecture

Burnham and John Wellborn Root in 1891, the hulking Monadnock was the last skyscraper to be built from solid masonry construction, and remains an impressive sight more than a century after its completion.

Most experts agree that the first official 'skyscraper' to use a steel skeletal frame was the **Home Insurance Building**, constructed in 1885 by Jenney at LaSalle and Adams Streets (and, unfortunately, demolished in 1931). Perhaps the most attractive of the pioneering steel-framed constructions still standing in the Loop is the **Marquette Building** (140 S Dearborn Street, at W Adams Street; map ❹), built by William Holabird and Martin Roche in 1895. Continuing along S Dearborn as far as Congress Parkway will lead you past three other excellent examples of the form: Burnham's 1896 **Fisher Building** (No.343; map ❺), Holabird and Roche's 1894 **Old Colony Building** (No.407; map ❻) and William LeBaron Jenney's 1891 **Manhattan Building** (No.431; map ❼).

Chicago School buildings are tall and rectangular with flat roofs, and often made up of three distinct elements: base, rise and capital. Their grid-like steel structure is often recognisable on the structure's outer surfaces. With the steel frame taking care of the heavy lifting, the exterior walls are opened up for windows and other non-load-bearing materials, most often light-coloured terracotta. The buildings generally avoid ornamentation in favour of utilitarian simplicity; after all, it was Chicago School heavy-hitter Sullivan who declared that 'form follows function'.

The Reliance Building, at the intersection of State Street and Washington Boulevard, is a classic example of Chicago School innovations. Completed in 1895 by Charles Atwood and Burnham using foundations laid four years earlier by Root, the elegant Reliance makes use of a Chicago School mainstay: the oriel window, a protruding bay window that runs the length of the building and underscores its soaring verticality. With its abundance of large plate glass windows, the Reliance presaged the future of the modern-day skyscraper. In recent years, it's undergone effective renovations and is now the **Hotel Burnham** (*see p58*; map ❽).

Other Loop buildings are just as typical of the style. Take the **Santa Fe Center** (née the Railway Exchange Building; 224 S Michigan Avenue, at E Jackson Boulevard; map ❾): when it was completed in 1904, Burnham was so proud of it that he moved his own offices there. Appropriately, it's now home to the Chicago Architecture Foundation (*see p80*). And don't miss Burnham and Root's majestic 1888 **Rookery** (209 S Lasalle Street, at W Adams Street; map ❿), named for the birds that once inhabited it, or Sullivan's turn-of-the-century **Carson Pirie Scott Building** (1 S State Street, at Madison Street; map ⓫), which makes use of another common design element: the Chicago Window, a large pane of glass flanked by two smaller opening windows.

THE WHITE CITY

When the World's Columbian Exposition (aka the World's Fair) came to Chicago in 1893, Burnham oversaw the construction of the buildings in which the exhibits were to be housed. But the popularity of his gleaming white Beaux Arts classical constructions changed the course of architecture in the early 20th century, effectively – and ironically – outmoding the reigning Chicago School in the process.

Burnham's White City was levelled when the Columbian Exposition ended in order to make way for Meigs Field airstrip. Yet its influence remains in three classic Chicago landmarks: Shepley, Rutan and Coolidge's **Art Institute of Chicago**, completed in 1893 (111 S Michigan Avenue, at W Adams Street; map ⓬); the ostentatious Chicago Public Library, built by the same firm in 1897 and now the **Chicago Cultural Center** (78 E Washington Boulevard, at N Michigan Avenue; map ⓭); and Rapp and Rapp's restored **Chicago Theater** (175 N State Street, at E Lake Street; map ⓮). Of a similar period, too, is Cyrus Eidlitz's beautiful Romanesque Revival **Dearborn Station** (47 W Polk Street, at Dearborn Street), completed in 1885 as one of the city's first train stations.

Burnham is now best remembered for a contribution that lasted a little longer: the 1909 Chicago Plan, which mapped out the city's development. In addition to the introduction of traffic-relieving bi-level thoroughfares around the downtown area (such as Wacker Drive), Burnham's plan minimised lakefront development, a shrewd move that resulted in the expansive lakefront parks that stretch from the South Side to the northern suburbs.

Despite Burnham's prominence and influence, some designers remained unimpressed by the Beaux Arts aesthetic, with one Wisconsin-born architect making a particular impact. Frank Lloyd Wright began his professional career at the office of Adler and Sullivan, but set up his own practice in Oak Park after being fired for moonlighting. It was here that he formulated what would become known as the Prairie Style of architecture; a walk around the neighbourhood in which he built 25 homes remains an enlightening experience. For more on Frank Lloyd Wright, *see pp132-133* **Wright on**; for his **Robie House** in Hyde Park, *see p142*.

TOWARDS MODERNISM

The Chicago School had become old hat by the 1920s, and architects began looking elsewhere for inspiration. The result was a 20-year period when architects didn't concentrate on one style but instead toyed with many. Indeed, designs in a panoply of different styles were submitted to a competition staged by the *Tribune* newspaper in 1922, as they searched for an architect to design their new offices. The winner was John Mead Howells and Raymond Hood's limestone-clad 456-foot (139-metre) **Tribune Tower** (435 N Michigan Avenue, at E Hubbard Street; map ⓯), a Gothic tower that arrived complete with flying buttresses at its ornate crown. Embedded in the walls around the building's entrance are artefacts from significant structures around the world, among them the Great Pyramids at Cheops to Notre-Dame Cathedral. Their presence was designed to draw attention to the newspaper's global reach, but they also inadvertently nod towards the growing eclecticism of local architectural fashions.

Just across the street is Charles Beersman's **Wrigley Building** (400 N Michigan Avenue, at E Kinzie Street; map ⓰), a massive wall of a building completed in 1924 that rises majestically over the Chicago River. The white terracotta that covers the building is cream-coloured at street level, but gets lighter towards the top. At night, when the façade is illuminated by giant floodlights, the trompe l'oeil gives the building a glorious, glowing aspect.

The American fashion for art deco never really developed in Chicago, but a few buildings in the style were constructed here. Chief among them is Holabird and Root's **Chicago Board of Trade Building** (141 W Jackson Boulevard, at S Lasalle Street; map ⓱), completed in 1930 (and dramatically addended a half-century later). Approach it along Lasalle for the full, dramatic effect, and look up to see the crowning statue of Ceres 45 storeys above street level. Other admirable art deco buildings

A history of height

Chicago's skyline is probably the best example – or, at least, the most prominent, priapic example – of so-called 'Second City syndrome'. During the first decades of its existence, Chicago was always runner-up to Miss New York in measures of greatness. As a result, the locals decided on an architectural strategy to prove their worth. 'Higher! Taller! Longer!' went the mantra. 'Big? Bigger than yours! So there!'

As in Europe, Chicago's tallest buildings started out as sacred sites for the reverent. **Holy Name Cathedral** (733 N State Street), built in 1854, **St Michael's Church** (1633 N Cleveland Avenue; **1**), constructed 15 years later, were two early sky-piercers, reaching 245 feet (75 metres) and 290 feet (88 metres) respectively. Pointing high towards the heavens, the spires seemed to declare a greater connection to the divine. This way of thinking has vanished from religious architecture in the urban US, but it lingers in Red State America, where women's hairdos rival their megachurches: the higher the hair, the closer to God.)

The next building to assume the mantle of Chicago's tallest was the first structure constructed specifically to house the **Chicago Board of Trade** (141 W Jackson Street; **2**). But when the owners removed its clock tower due to structural instability, the title passed to Burnham & Root's long since demolished **Masonic Temple** (at State & Randolph Streets). Its 302 feet (92 metres) made it officially the world's tallest building, but its 22 floors didn't hold the record for long: New York seized back the title in 1894 when the Manhattan Life Insurance Building was completed. And so it followed that American architecture came down to its dominant religion, as various temples to capitalism asserted the gospel of commerce by reaching for the sky.

The 394-foot (120-metre) **Montgomery Ward Building** (6 N Michigan Avenue; **3**), built in 1899, was topped in 1922 by the **Wrigley Building** (400 N Michigan Avenue; **4**), which still looms 438 feet (134 metres) over the Chicago River. Two years later, it was beaten by the **Chicago Temple** (77 W Washington Street; **5**), but even this grand old gem didn't last long at the top of the skyscraping charts. In 1930, the **Chicago Board of Trade** (141 W Jackson Street; **6**) opened its 605-foot (184-metre) monument to Art Deco beauty, with the goddess Ceres standing proudly atop its pinnacle.

A futher building boom in the 1960s and '70s raised the bar once more. The Chicago Civic Center (now the **Daley Center**; 50 W Washington Street; **7**) reached 648 feet (198 metres) in 1965, but was made to look feeble with the 1969 arrival of the now-iconic **John Hancock Center** (875 N Michigan Avenue; **8**), towering 1,127 feet (344 metres) over the Magnificent Mile. It was the city's tallest until 1973, when the Standard Oil Building (now the **Aon Center**, 200 E Randolph Street; **9**) squeaked nine feet above it. But then the very next year, Chicago reclaimed the World's Tallest title from New York, beaming with pride for almost three decades over the 1,451 feet (442 metres) of the **Sears Tower** (233 S Wacker Drive; **10**).

The fun ended when the dubious Council on Tall Buildings sided with some Kuala Lumpur yahoos. The Petronas Towers didn't have as many inhabitable floors as the Sears Tower; however, its spires counted while the Sears' antenna didn't. Whatever. The height to the top of the Sears antenna is still taller than any other structure. If (when?) the Calatrava-designed Chicago Spire comes to pass – it's due to break ground in 2007 along Lake Shore Drive – it'll be taller still. So no matter what goes on in East Asia, Chicago will still be kicking New York's ass.

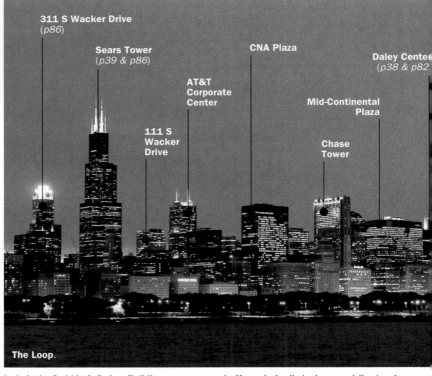

311 S Wacker Drive
(p86)

Sears Tower
(p39 & p86)

CNA Plaza

Daley Center
(p38 & p82)

AT&T
Corporate
Center

Mid-Continental
Plaza

111 S
Wacker
Drive

Chase
Tower

The Loop.

include the Carbide & Carbon Building, now
the **Hard Rock Hotel** (230 N Michigan
Avenue, at E Lake Street; *see p57*; map ⑲),
and two further Holabird and Root productions:
the former **Palmolive Building**, later the
offices of *Playboy* (919 N Michigan Avenue,
at E Walton Street), and **2 Riverside Plaza**,
formerly home to the *Chicago Daily News* (400
W Madison Street, at N Canal Street; map ⑲).

And then there's the huge, art deco-styled
Merchandise Mart, the largest building in the
world when it was completed on the north bank
of the Chicago River (by N Wells Street; map ⑳)
in 1930. Designed by the firm of Graham,
Anderson, Probst & White, the building's
dramatic waterfall-style limestone façade rises
25 storeys above the river; busts of some of
America's leading merchants, among them
Marshall Field, A Montgomery Ward and Frank
W Woolworth, line the esplanade. Commissioned
by Marshall Field to house wholesale operation
of his department store, along with those of other
furniture and interior design shops, it was sold

to the Kennedy family in the years following the
Depression. A 1991 renovation created a public
mall on the first two floors.

GLASS AND STEEL

Despite all the local innovation, it took an
outsider to kick off arguably the most striking
period in Chicago's architectural history.
Ludwig Mies van der Rohe arrived in the city in
1938, bringing with him the International Style.
The aesthetic had its roots in the architect's
native Germany but borrowed heavily from
the strident simplicity of the Chicago School,
ultimately carrying it to new extremes.

Buildings in the International Style feature
cubic shapes, long horizontal bands of glass
called 'ribbon windows', low, flat roofs, and
open floorplans divided by movable screen
walls. Usually constructed from glass, steel
and concrete, the structures are devoid of
ornamentation and regional characteristics.
The emphasis is on the horizontal plane, even –
perhaps perversely – in skyscrapers.

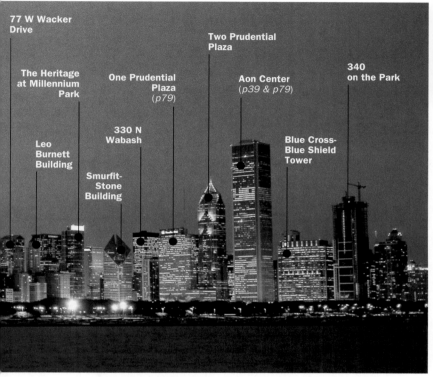

77 W Wacker Drive

Two Prudential Plaza

The Heritage at Millennium Park

One Prudential Plaza (p79)

Aon Center (p39 & p79)

340 on the Park

Leo Burnett Building

330 N Wabash

Blue Cross-Blue Shield Tower

Smurfit-Stone Building

After serving as director of the Bauhaus in the early 1930s, Mies came to the US in 1937 at the relatively advanced age of 51, settling first in Wyoming before, a year later, moving to Chicago in order to take up a professorship at the Armour Institute (later renamed the Illinois Institute of Technology). In 1939, he set about redesigning the South Side campus, creating a handful of striking buildings that demonstrated his affection for steel-framed glass and cubic abstraction. These are functional buildings, their lack of frills wholly deliberate. 'I don't want to be interesting,' Mies once commented. 'I want to be good.'

Upon their completion in 1951, the stunning, state-of-the-art **Lake Shore Drive Apartments** (860-880 N Lake Shore Drive, at E Chestnut Street) were light years ahead of their time. An indelibly classic example of the International Style, the 26-storey twin towers were an instant commercial and critical success. A few years later, Mies turned his talents to the **Federal Center**, the unofficial name of a

grouping of buildings constructed between 1959 and 1974 in the Loop (200 S Dearborn Street, at W Adams Street; map ㉑). You'll immediately recognise his signature curtain wall of glass, supported by steel black I-beams that support individual panes, emphasising the building's internal skeletal structure (and, in the process, almost turning it inside out). The grey granite that was used to pave the plaza continues uninterrupted into the lobby, creating a feeling of openness.

'As full as the skyline may appear, there's plenty of construction work ongoing.'

Famously telling students that 'God is in the detail', Mies lavished careful attention on every aspect of his creations, even going so far as to design their furniture. Take the 52-storey **330 N Wabash** (formerly IBM Plaza; 330 N Wabash Avenue, at E Wacker Drive; map ㉒),

A whole lot of nothing

Chicago is arguably most famous to outsiders for two local characteristics: forward-thinking architecture and deep-seated political corruption. Block 37 is what happens when the two collide. After three decades, four developers, more than $100 million dollars and innumerable false starts, this sizeable plot of dirt in the heart of the Loop stands pathetically empty. Some have pinned the blame for the lack of progess on the politicians who started the reconstruction ball rolling in 1979; others have grumbled about the developers who have singularly failed to develop the land. The truth presumably lies somewhere in between, but it hardly matters: all that concerns Chicagoans these days is when – if? – the vacant lot will finally be filled.

The story begins in the 1820s, when civil engineer James Thompson mapped out the burgeoning city in time for the 1830 election. On his survey, Thompson broke up the city into 58 numbered blocks; the area of land hemmed in by State, Washington, Dearborn and Randoph Streets was designated Block 37 on his schematic. After the city was destroyed by the Great Fire, skyscrapers rose from the ashes and 16 buildings were erected on the block, housing movie palaces, billiard halls and other multifarious, crowd-pulling enterprises. These were the glory days of the Loop, then Chicago's entertainment district.

By the 1970s, though downtown Chicago was crumbling. Two decades of post-war suburban flight had drained the city of its affluent residents, leaving the Loop to rot. Against this backdrop, the buildings that occupied Block 37 were deemed unsound by city planners, subjected to compulsory purchase orders and slated for demolition. Appalled by the city's heavy-handed behaviour, local architecture activists managed to stave off the wrecking ball until 1989, when Daley bulldozed the entire block.

While the condemned buildings sat in limbo during the early 1980s, the rights to their redevelopment were sold to the Chicago-based JMB Realty Corporation. By the time the lot was cleared, Daley had a multi-use skyscraper ready for construction, designed by Helmut Jahn to accommodate retail units, office space, a hotel and apartments. But while other simultaneously demolished blocks in the city boomed with new construction projects, JMB made little progress in the wake of the countrywide real estate crash of 1990. The lot lay empty throughout the 1990s, a symbol of local government folly and national economic trauma.

Eventually, the city doled out $35 million in 2002 to retake the project back from JMB, selling the land to the Maryland-based Mills Corporation. The price was a relatively measly $12.4 million, but there was a catch: Mills was required to lease the land to 'unique retailers' that had little or no presence in Illinois. In 2006, plagued by accounting problems apparently unrelated to the development, Mills passed on its interest to yet more developers: the retail, parking and CTA parts of the development were sold to to local developer Joseph Freed & Associates, with Golub & Co purchasing the office portion.

As of early 2007, the developers were making all the right noises. The retail units are, they assured the city, on track to open in early 2008, at around the same time that construction is due to begin on two residential high-rises above them. Discussion continues about the construction of a CTA station under the development that would provide travellers with a much-needed express service to both the city's airports. But after 28 years, no one in Chicago is holding their breath.

begun in 1969 and, after Mies's death the same year, completed in 1971 by one of the architect's associates. The building's voluminous glass-walled lobby, a Mies staple, is decorated with his chrome and leather Barcelona chairs, designed for an exposition in 1929.

But perhaps the most spectacular local building designed by Mies sits roughly two hours south-west of downtown Chicago in the small town of Plano, Illinois. The **Farnsworth House** (14520 River Road, Plano, 1-630 552 0052, www.farnsworthhouse.org) completed in 1951 for Dr Edith Farnsworth, the architect's alleged love interest. This one-room, box-like house on stilts was designed by Mies to be decorated only with travertine marble floors, wooden cabinets and a rustic fireplace, and walled from the outside by mere sheets of glass. Situated on the wooded banks of the Fox River, the structure sits in stunning contrast with its natural surroundings. Tours are available six days a week from April to November.

MOVING ON UP

Mies's influence over his contemporaries and successors is visible in a number of buildings downtown. The most notable is perhaps the **Richard J Daley Center** (55 W Randolph Street, at N Dearborn Street; map ㉓), completed as the Chicago Civic Center in 1965 to designs by Jacques Brownson of CF Murphy Associates. However, it's been metaphorically overshadowed by what is, given the prominence of its location, arguably Chicago's most dominant structure.

Designed by Bruce Graham of Skidmore, Owings & Merrill and towering 1,127 feet (344 metres) above the Magnificent Mile, the **John Hancock Center** (875 N Michigan Avenue, at E Chestnut Street) became the city's tallest building when it was completed in 1969. Vaguely pyramid-shaped, the structure gradually tapers from street level to its top floor, its visible X-shaped structural supports evenly distributing the building's weight and helping it resist the tremendous forces of wind at its higher elevations. The Hancock's lower floors are occupied by retail outlets and restaurants, with office space and apartments further up. It's topped by an exclusive bar/restaurant and a slightly less exclusive observatory.

Five years after the Hancock was completed, a second Mies-influenced, Graham-designed monster opened its doors. In doing so, the **Sears Tower** (233 S Wacker Drive, at W Adams Street; map ㉓) became the world's tallest building (a title it relinquished two decades later). Standing a ludicrous 1,454 feet (443 metres) tall, the aluminium and amber glass tower clearly owes a debt to the International Style with its chunky, cubist proportions. Although it's not an especially dynamic structure, it's easier on the eye than other Chicago cloudbusters from the same era, such as the 1,136-foot (346-metre) **Aon Center**, completed in 1973 as the Standard Oil Building (200 E Randolph Street, at N Columbus Drive; map ㉓), and the 859-foot (262-metre) **Water Tower Place** (845 N Michigan Avenue, at E Pearson Street). However, it lacks the easy elegance of the nearby **Chase Tower** (built in 1969 as the First National Bank of Chicago Building; 21 N Clark Street, at W Madison Street; map ㉓).

Not everyone took to Mies's aesthetic, something immediately apparent from the two 61-storey 'corncob' towers of Bertrand Goldberg's **Marina City** apartment complex, situated west of the Wrigley Building on the north bank of the river (map ㉓). Constructed of reinforced concrete, the towers were completed in 1967 and could hardly be more distinctive: the individual floors are cantilevered out from the main core, which houses lift shafts and rubbish chutes. A theatre venue built between the two towers in 1966 is now occupied by the **House of Blues** (see p60).

While Mies's Federal Center pushed the boundaries of what a government building should look like, Helmut Jahn's dome-shaped **James R Thompson Center** (formerly the State of Illinois Centre; 100 W Randolph Street, at N Clark Street; map ㉓) blew away critics when it was completed in 1985. Despite its stridently modern appearance, the building pays subtle homage to traditional government buildings, with its abstract suggestion of the classic cupola. The main attraction, though, is the 230-foot (70-metre) atrium created by the rotunda: ample lighting, exposed lift shafts and mechanics, and reflective surfaces give the space a vibrant sense of movement.

Lakeshore East. *See p40.*

The **Sears Tower**, between
225 and **333 W Wacker Drive**.

development, on a site just east of the
Michigan Avenue Bridge that most recently
housed a ridiculously bijou golf course (map ③).
The first few condo towers completed as part
of the development aren't architecturally
memorable, but they're nonetheless notable
in the way they illustrate a 21st-century
Chicago trend: the way in which young
professionals are once more keen to make
their homes in the centre of the city.

A rather more high-profile tower is currently
been constructed just along the river, on the
north bank close to the junction with Wabash
Avenue. Donald Trump originally planned to
build the world's tallest building on the Chicago
riverfront, plans that fell by the wayside in
the wake of 9/11. However, after a brief delay,
Trump eventually settled on the slightly shorter
Trump International Tower & Hotel (map
③); designed, perhaps inevitably, by Skidmore,
Owings & Merrill, it should become the city's
second tallest building when it's ready in 2008.

There's more to come. If all goes according
to plan, 2010 should also see the opening of
the Santiago Calatrava-designed **400 N Lake
Shore Drive**, a $550-million, 124-storey hotel
and condominium tower near the entrance to
Navy Pier. When complete, the building will be
the tallest in the US, topping out at a scarcely
credible 2,000 feet (610 metres). Although plans
for the tower (modelled in the shape of a twisted
branch or, according to harsher critics, a screw)
were approved in 2006, developer Christopher
Carley struggled to raise the necessary funds.
However, with Irish developer Garrett Kelleher
stepping into the breach, construction on the
massive skyscraper and its circular plaza,
six-storey parking garage and riverwalk
promenade is scheduled to begin in 2007.

But for all the towering skyscrapers
springing up downtown, the most impressive
recent development keeps its extremities rather
closer to ground level. Located east of Michigan
Avenue between Randolph and Monroe Streets
and unveiled in 2004, the 24-acre **Millennium
Park** (*see p75*) was four years late in arriving,
and, at nearly $500 million, cost considerably
more than originally budgeted. However,
Chicagoans have taken with great enthusiasm
to the completed park, and especially to Frank
Gehry's **Jay Pritzker Pavilion** (map ③).
Whether building up or staying ground-bound,
Chicago remains a thoroughly modern city.

Another attention-grabbingly curvaceous
modern building sits a few blocks west on
the banks of the Chicago River. William E
Pedersen's **333 W Wacker Drive** (map ㉙)
was built between 1979 and 1983 on the bend
of the river, and its curved frontage echoes the
shape of the waterway in spectacular fashion.
Look at it from the opposite bank or – better
still – from a moving boat, from where the
subtly stunning ways the light plays on the
rounded frontage are best appreciated.

NEW HEIGHTS

As full as the Chicago skyline may appear,
there's still plenty of construction work
ongoing, filling patches of land previously
neglected by or unavailable to developers.
Aside from the long-running, muddled **Block
37** development (*see p38* **A whole lot of
nothing**; map ㉚), the most high-profile project
is the 28-acre **Lakeshore East** riverfront

▶ For **books about architecture**, see *p311*.
▶ For the **Chicago Architecture
Foundation**, which stages exhibits and
runs regular tours, see *p73* and *p80*.

Mayor Richard J Daley. See p43.

The Machine

The well-oiled cogs of machine politics once dominated
Chicago. Though rusty, are some still spinning today?

'I didn't come over on the Mayflower,
but I came over as soon as I could.'
– Anton (Tony) Joseph Cermak,
Mayor of Chicago, 1931-1933

The history of the political machine in urban
America is, in many ways, a chapter in the
story of immigration. Virtually every major city
in the US was run by a machine during the late
19th and early 20th centuries, when immigration
to the country was at its peak. At their best,
machines provided a means for immigrant
groups to secure, expand and redistribute
the spoils of power. Previously excluded from
political participation, they found the chance
to grab a piece of the pie impossible to resist.

But while all politics, to some extent, is about
distributing resources to loyal constituents, the
political machines took the idea to extremes.
Under them, public office went hand in hand
with the pursuit of profit, in a power structure
built on patronage and reliant on corruption,
nepotism and malfeasance. The chief aim of
political machines was the retention of their
own power, and few of their protagonists cared
too much how crookedly they went about it.

The 1930s saw fatal blows dealt to many of
the major political machines: by reformers such
as the Progressives, but also by the massive
expansion of federal New Deal programmes.
New York's famous Tammany Hall was one
of many machines to see its influence all but
eradicated after Franklin D Roosevelt was
elected president in 1932. But in Chicago, long
renowned as fertile ground for corruption (even
the baseball team was crooked; *see p49*), the
machine was just beginning to thrive.

IMMIGRANT SONG
Machine politics in Chicago really begins with
Anton Cermak, an immigrant from Bohemia
who became mayor in 1931. Assisted by his
background as the secretary of the United
Societies for Local Self-Government, a coalition
of Germans, Czechs and other immigrant
communities, 'Pushcart Tony' is credited with
uniting new Chicagoans into a voting block
that became the backbone of an ascendant
Democratic party machine. Those who swore
allegiance to Cermak were rewarded with jobs,
which meant feeding the family during the
Depression. The machine provided.

Many of Cermak's supporters were fellow Bohemians, but just as crucial to his success was the loyalty of Irish Americans from the South Side neighbourhoods of Bridgeport and Back of the Yards. Indeed, following Cermak's death in 1933 (*see below* **Gun crazy**), Bridgeport sent three successive Irish American residents to City Hall, who between them went on to rule the city for 43 years. The Irish had a head start in American politics: they immigrated earlier, they spoke the language, and they understood the English-modelled political system. The unique outsider-insider status they came to assume meant they could count on votes from other European immigrant groups.

The Irish came to dominate politics in Bridgeport, and particularly in Hamburg parish. The ward headquarters was the machine's home base, and local social organisations such as the Hamburg Athletic Club served as a training ground for politicians (while also sheltering thugs who enforced the area's racial divide with violence). In 1924, at the age of 22, Richard J Daley was elected president of the club, a position he held for 15 years.

Replacing Cermak in 1933, Edward J Kelly became the first of Bridgeport's Irish American mayors. Kelly's machine was distinguished by its ties to organised crime, which kept it flush with money, and for its efforts to reach out to

Gun crazy

On 15 February 1933, a 33-year-old unemployed bricklayer by the name of Giuseppe Zangara fired five shots from an eight-dollar .32-calibre revolver at Franklin D Roosevelt as the president-elect rode through Miami in an open-top Buick. Zangara missed FDR but struck five other men; among them was Chicago mayor Anton Cermak, who died of his wounds three weeks later. Just a month after the shooting, Zangara was sent to the electric chair.

It was a little ironic that Cermak, a great uniter who had brought disenfranchised immigrants into democratic politics, died at the hands of a European-born worker. Indeed, Cermak, a barely educated man from Bohemia (now the Czech Republic), perhaps had more in common with Zangara than with his more famous co-passenger. But did Cermak's death simply come down to a stray bullet, or was he the intended target all along?

Some Chicagoans, crime buffs and conspiracy theorists have another explanation. Zangara, they contend, was financially comfortable, making a good hourly rate as a union bricklayer and mason. However, so the story goes, he also had mob ties, and even served time for racketeering. This shady background adds up to Zangara being a perfect trigger-man for a mob hit on Cermak, who had been active against the Chicago-area Cosa Nostra gangs of Al Capone.

It is tantalising stuff, to be sure, and very Hollywood-friendly. We know that Zangara, a self-styled but largely apolitical anarchist, blamed the upper classes for his Depression-era woes and, more bafflingly, for his crippling stomach pain. However, he pretty much hated everyone, and Cermak is still generally held to

have been an unintended victim of his fury. Being barely five feet tall, Zangara fired his shots while standing on an unstable folding chair, which explains why the US got the New Deal and Cermak got a punctured lung.

The Cermak/Zangara affair is discussed surprisingly infrequently these days. However, it has occasionally been retold in movies, literature and even music. The 1933 film *The Man Who Dared* ends with the shooting, which was also dramatised in 1960 on two episodes of the TV show *The Untouchables*. Latterly, Stephen Sondheim included Zangara in his musical *Assassins*, while local punk writer Al Burian penned a short story about the event as seen from Cermak's point of view.

the growing population of African Americans, which kept it thick with votes. Public concerns about mob violence, as well as Kelly's support for desegregation, eventually resulted in the machine replacing him with fellow Bridgeport-based Irish American Martin Kennelly in 1947. But when, after two terms, the machine wearied of Kennelly's independent stance on a variety of issues, he too was cast aside.

OUR DALEY BREAD

The machine reached full throttle under a highly organised Democratic party led by Richard J Daley, elected as the city's mayor in 1955. As was the case with his predecessors, Daley's machine was headed by Irish Catholics, but he was also careful to call on other immigrant groups, from African Americans to Eastern Europeans. With such a broad spread of support, he was able to remain in power, virtually uncontested, for more than two decades.

'After the '68 protests, Daley complained that the police were too tentative.'

Daley's machine was built on the loyalty of often corrupt ward bosses and their many precinct captains. Jobs were given out not on the basis of the candidate's suitability for the position, but as reward for their political work and campaigning. Daley's 40,000 patronage employees had to kick back part of their salaries to their ward organisations; staff were fired if they did not fulfill their obligations to the party, work that was often done on city time.

The Cook County Democratic Organization, as the Chicago machine was formally known, was rigidly hierarchical, but also came to be connected to almost every businessman and family at street level. Its ward committeemen might have operated law firms or insurance companies on the side, making the posts extra lucrative. But in exchange for this sweetheart position, a committeeman had to make vote totals for bosses or they would be 'vised' and replaced. The machine required results.

Daley exacted loyalty from most of the cities' aldermen, but there's never been any evidence that he gained financially from it, or wanted to. His pursuit of power for power's sake meant that his hands stayed clean. His desire for influence extended to a national level: without Daley's help, John F Kennedy almost certainly would have lost the crucial state of Illinois in 1960, and with it the Presidential election. That said, there's been little evidence to support long-standing allegations of vote-rigging, either locally or nationally.

For all its corrupt internal practices, the Daley administration gained a reputation for getting things done. Under Daley's watch, construction boomed: O'Hare Airport, the Sears Tower, McCormick Place and the UIC campus were all built during his reign. But the mayor was by no means loved by all. Daley presided over – indeed, encouraged – a profoundly segregated city, and resisted Martin Luther King's attempts to integrate Chicago's schools. After rioting broke out in the wake of King's assassination (*see p22*), Daley further fanned the flames of discontent when he alleged that the police reaction to the protests was too tentative.

Greater embarrassment was to follow several months later. When US TV broadcast images of women and children being beaten and tear-gassed in the wake of anti-war demonstrations outside the Democratic Convention in August 1968, an incident that came to be known as the Battle of Chicago, Daley was left exposed on the national stage (*see p23*). The reputation of the Chicago police was permanently stained even before the Chicago Police and agents of the Cook County State's Attorney's office shot and killed Black Panther organiser Fred Hampton in 1969 under dubious circumstances.

Boss, Mike Royko's 1971 biography of Daley, portrayed the mayor as being ruthless, corrupt and thoroughly unenlightened on the subject of race. But today, historians generally agree that by revitalising downtown and keeping some vestige of a middle class in the city, the mayor prevented the kind of dramatic decline seen in other rust-belt cities. And though some have argued that they amount to one and the same thing, it's generally accepted that Daley tolerated corruption more than he practised it.

RAGE AGAINST THE MACHINE

In the 1970s, racial tension and the flight of the machine's ethnic base to the suburbs weakened its structure. Some of Daley's efforts in the field of public works, such as his high-rise housing projects, came to be considered failures, while his defence of residential segregation and his opposition to affirmative action in government made him increasingly unpopular with African Americans. Daley's sudden death in 1976, after 21 years in power, left a power vacuum, but his cohorts had already begun to leave the roost.

By the time Harold Washington became Chicago's first black mayor in 1983, riding in on the split loyalties of white voters and a balloon in black voter registration, the machine seemed mostly washed up. But Washington, himself a Democrat, was left to battle the Democratic machine when his council split along racial lines. Led by Edward Vrdolyak, 29 old-school white Democratic aldermen teamed up and refused to approve Washington's reform policies, but their majority wasn't sufficient to push through their own measures: they needed 30 of the council's 50 votes in order to override Washington's mayoral veto, which he was not shy about wielding. Stalemate ensued in what became known as the Council Wars. It was a poisonous time.

After he was re-elected in 1987, the 29 (as they were known) dispersed, and Washington eventually managed to institute policies that promoted more open government and minority contracting. But Washington died in office of a heart attack later that same year, and Chicagoans were soon reminded of their past with the emergence of a new yet somewhat familiar candidate for the city's top job.

THE DALEY DOUBLE
Upon defeating Eugene Sawyer, Washington's replacement, in the 1989 mayoral primary, Richard J Daley's eldest son Richard M Daley won election to City Hall. His 'pin-striped machine', named for its use of lawyers and bright young advisors, quickly developed a powerful hold over Chicago, courting the city's most respected minority leaders and political independents with city services and contracts in order to ensure a new era of loyalty.

For many mainstream liberals, Daley represents smart, sophisticated city government, supporting gun control, gay rights and various 'green' programmes. But his programme to reform public housing, a ten-year, $5 billion plan to tear down high-rises and replace them with mixed-income row houses and condos, has proved controversial. Even affluent Chicagoans seem sceptical that programmes such as the city's Blue Bag recycling scheme are anything other than evidence of Daley's deft PR talents.

Daley has presided over an economic and cultural boom, and has been praised for revitalising the city's schools, rejuvenating downtown and spending more than $2 billion restoring smaller neighbourhoods. But his rock-solid hold on the city has developed more than a few cracks. Recently, some last vestiges of Chicago's patronage system have surfaced and come under attack in three major scandals. The resemblance between father and son appears to go beyond a physical likeness and a shared propensity for malapropisms.

In 2004, the *Chicago Sun-Times* broke the story of corruption in the city's Hired Truck Program, which it termed 'clout on wheels'. In a nutshell, the city was found to be hiring trucks from local firms at inflated rates, often paying them to sit idle for days or weeks at a time. The city gave around $40 million annually to these private truck companies, many based

in Daley's ward; some firms were found to have kicked back donations to politicians. More than 30 people have been convicted in connection with the scheme.

'Allegations of police brutality have dogged the administration for years.'

Out of the scandal, another came to light. High-level Daley staffers from his secretive Intergovernmental Affairs office were found to have been practising systematic hiring, based on political connections rather than merit, for possibly thousands of City jobs. By the middle of 2006, US Attorney Patrick Fitzgerald had charged and convicted Daley's former patronage chief and three other one-time officials on charges of mail fraud.

Further controversy arose when James Duff, an associate of Daley and a major donor to the Democrats, was found to have fraudulently won more than $100 million in work from the city through a programme set up to provide contracts to minority- and female-owned businesses. Duff was jailed in 2005 for ten years, and asked to repay $22 million to the city (in restitution) and the US government (in fines).

Various scandal investigations conducted over the last few years have led closer and closer to the mayor's office. Allegations of police brutality in the city have dogged the administration for years, with a 2006 report confirming that a police torture ring acted with virtual impunity between the 1970s and the '90s. Tack on to these controversies a series of massive cost overruns on major construction projects, such as the renovation of a terminal at O'Hare International Airport and the development of Millennium Park, and Daley's empire started to look fragile. The mayoral election due to be held in early 2007 initially looked like it could turn into a close-run thing.

Representative Jesse Jackson, Jr, son of the former presidential candidate, had been making noises about running against Daley at the mayoral elections in early 2007, pointing out that the economic success of lakefront Chicago hasn't had much effect on the South Side. But after the Democrats won the national elections in 2006, Jackson and fellow US Representative Luis Gutiérrez opted to stay in Washington, leaving Daley to retain the power he's held for almost two decades. The machine, it seems, is now just part of the Chicago furniture.

▶ For **reading recommendations**, see p311.

Mojo Working

How Chicago got, and kept, the blues.

Many styles of music are closely associated with one city. New Orleans and jazz, Memphis and rock 'n' roll, and Nashville and country, to name but three. Yet few cities are so wedded to a style that a subgenre takes its name from the town. It may have found its origins elsewhere in the US, but modern-day blues music is inextricably linked to Chicago.

IN THE BEGINNING

Blues has its musical origins in the Deep South at the turn of the 20th century, finding direct musical antecedents in the call-and-response songs and improvised, often mournful, field hollers sung by black slaves as they worked in the fields and on the plantations. As the music began to develop as a performing art, echoes of ragtime, minstrelsy and even church music began to be heard in it. Not that anyone knew at the time, mind: a century ago, musicologists cared not a jot for black music, and the white public, whose money fuelled the fledgling music industry, cared even less.

In the early 20th century, there was no real repertoire of popular song. The pop and jazz compositions that grew to define the period from 1920 until the emergence of rock 'n' roll were yet to be written; the only pre-World War I popular songwriter whose songs are still played with anything approaching regularity and respect is Stephen Foster, the composer of (among others) 'Gentle Annie', 'Camptown Races' and 'My Old Kentucky Home'. However, although no songs had grown to become standards, the forms taken by the songs were beginning to become standardised. The most resonant took as its lyrical skeleton two repeated lines followed by a different but rhyming third line that acts as a pay-off: an AAB structure. It's this format that has held firm for a century as the hook on which a 12-bar blues is hung.

Still, more fundamental to the genesis of the blues was the use of microtonally flattened notes that fell outside the realms of the normal 12-note chromatic scale, and that hadn't yet been heard in American or European music. Specifically, the irregular flattening of the third meant that the music was essentially in neither a major nor minor key. That's the science bit. In layman's terms? It sounds *sad*. These notes, the flattened thirds and (less genre-defining) flattened fifths, are known as 'blue notes'.

It wasn't until Memphis composer WC Handy published *Memphis Blues* in 1912 that the word and the style became widely known. Handy was nicknamed the Father of the Blues, although he was nothing of the sort: he merely popularised the style, and his music has little in common with latter-day blues. But Handy's success brought the music if not into the mainstream, then certainly some way towards it. His music these days sounds polite, comfortable, even edge-less. But 90 years ago, to his largely white audience, it was out-and-out exotica.

From here, the blues took a number of turnings. On one hand were the garrulous, almost vaudevillian female blues belters of the 1920s, such as Bessie Smith and Ma Rainey. On the other were the likes of Robert Johnson and Charlie Patton, downbeat Delta bluesmen who accompanied themselves on acoustic guitars. The songs were still mostly built around the AAB structure, yet they were being interpreted in wildly different ways, from Texas to Georgia and various points en route. But not, yet, in Chicago, then still a largely white town.

MELROSE PLACE

The story of blues in Chicago starts some two decades after Handy, with an ambitious local music publisher. Lester Melrose was strictly a small-time industry figure when, in the early 1930s, he approached two national record labels, Victor and Columbia, with a pitch to supply them with what were then called 'race records' (jazz and blues made mostly by African Americans) with which to stock the town's newly popular jukeboxes. Everything went to plan. The labels bought the proposal; all Melrose needed now were the musicians. He was in the right place. Hundreds of thousands of black Americans had moved to Chicago in the two decades leading up to World War I in search of prosperity during what was known as the Great Migration, and the town had a deep and varied pool of black musical talent.

Melrose's production business flourished; without him, it's likely that many Chicagoan musicians of the 1930s would have gone unrecorded. Among those he captured on tape and sold to Victor, which then released them on its Bluebird imprint, were Big Bill Broonzy, raised in Arkansas but resident in Chicago since 1920; pianist Memphis Slim, who arrived 17 years later; and Sonny Boy Williamson, known to his mother in Jackson, Tennessee as John Lee Williamson. These three, though, were just the tip of a very large iceberg. Post-Depression, optimism was high and business was good. Melrose supplied the cuts, and Victor paid him. So he supplied it with more.

The fun ended with World War II, when shellac rationing meant fewer records could be cut. Then, in 1942, after a dispute over royalties owed from jukebox broadcasts, musicians' union head JC Petrillo ordered a ban on recording. However, the impact had been made. Melrose's work had established Chicago as a thriving blues capital of sorts, even if many of his musicians were not native to the city, and the blues they played – often with a full band, yet mostly acoustic and strangely easygoing in comparison to what came only a decade later – could hardly be pinned as uniquely Chicagoan.

Melrose is best remembered for two things. The first is that he was one of the first record producers to employ a house band to back up his artists, an idea later adopted by countless labels from Motown to PWL. Broonzy, 'Blind' John Davis and Washboard Sam were among the regulars Melrose used as sidemen. Yet Melrose also found fame for his tight-fistedness, a characteristic most apparent from the story of Arthur 'Big Boy' Crudup, who moved from Mississippi to Chicago in the late 1930s.

'Chess was no labour of love for the brothers: it was purely business.'

When Crudup arrived in town, he was so poor that his home was a cardboard box under the now-demolished 39th Street Station. After being spotted by Melrose at a party, he signed to Bluebird and had several minor hits. But the relationship turned sour when, in 1947, Crudup became aware that Melrose had not paid him royalties he was owed. When Elvis Presley's 1954 recording of Crudup's 'That's All Right, Mama' hit the jackpot, Crudup was again denied his due; by the time of his death 30 years later, he still hadn't seen a penny. It wouldn't be the first time a white executive was accused of exploiting black musicians in Chicago.

CHECKMATES

The irony of the black, urban, working-class Chicago blues that emerged in the 1940s is that it took two urbane, middle-class Polish Jews to bring it to an audience. Leonard and Phil Chess had arrived in Chicago from Poland as children in 1928, Leonard aged 11 and Phil four years his junior. By the early 1940s, the pair were running bars in black neighbourhoods on the South Side.

Live music was essential to the Chess brothers' business, with the Macomba Lounge at 3905 S Cottage Grove Avenue doing a particularly brisk trade. Coupled with the brothers' realisation that many of the musicians they were hiring had no means to record or release their music, the success of the Macomba led the pair to buy into a jazz-dominated local label called Aristocrat.

By the late 1940s, the blues had morphed wildly from its southern roots, as much out of necessity as anything. The old all-acoustic set-up just wouldn't do here: the bars in which the musicians played were too noisy, and the music got drowned out by boozy chatter. In order to make themselves heard, musicians began to turn to electric guitars and other amplification. The blues, once plaintive and rustic, was now urban, aggressive and lascivious.

One of the first records the Chess brothers cut for the label was 'Johnson Machine Gun', recorded by local pianist Sunnyland Slim. It was a notable disc in that it didn't fit tidily into Aristocrat's jazz-leaning catalogue. But it was also important in that it brought to the brothers' attention Slim's guitarist, a 33-year-old named McKinley Morganfield. The guitarist was soon cutting his own discs for Chess under the name Muddy Waters; by 1950, when the brothers bought Aristocrat outright, changed its name to Chess Records and began to concentrate solely on blues, he had become the label's anchor.

The following decade made Chess and, with it, what became known as the Chicago blues. Waters enjoyed success with tunes such as

'Mannish Boy', 'Rollin' Stone' (from which a certain British band took their name) and 'I Just Want to Make Love to You'. But soon, the American public was becoming acquainted with other local musicians. Harmonica wizard Little Walter, bottleneck guitarist Elmore James and feisty singer Sonny Boy Williamson (no relation to the Melrose protégé, who was murdered by muggers in 1948) all had hits.

Others had less commercial success but a considerable cultural impact. Howlin' Wolf's furious take on the electric blues, for example, was only really appreciated in later years. And multi-tasking producer/bassist/fixer Willie Dixon stayed largely in the background during this golden age, though his name appears on the writing credits for such staples as 'Hoochie Coochie Man', 'Wang Dang Doodle' and 'Little Red Rooster'.

It's hard to overestimate the impact the newly electrified Chicago blues had on popular culture. The music and its makers were still, of course, largely ghettoised. But change was slowly on its way. Jackie Robinson's debut on a Major League Baseball field in 1947, the first African American to play in the majors, was a signal event in the history of black America, but it found parallels in the quietly growing acceptance of black culture among whites. It would be many more years before significant progress was made, but this was a start.

History preserved at the **Chicago Blues Museum**. *See p137.*

SHOW ME THE MONEY

Having found success with Chicago blues, the Chess brothers branched out beyond the city, and beyond the blues, to greater rewards. Doo-wop acts such as the Moonglows and the Flamingos signed with Chess, but the real success came in 1955, when the brothers signed St Louis, Missouri's Chuck Berry and hit pay dirt with 'Maybelline'. Bo Didley, too, was attracting attention with his chugging rock 'n' roll on Checker Records, a Chess subsidiary.

The success of Chess spawned several local imitators. Vee-Jay issued early records by John Lee Hooker and Jimmie Reed in the years after its founding in 1953, while Cobra's most notable artist was Otis Rush. But by the time the 1960s rolled around, the popularity of Chicago blues was on the wane, a fact illustrated by the decision of Phil and Leonard Chess to let go of many of their blues artists. Junior Wells, Koko Taylor and Buddy Guy, Chicagoans all, emerged during the 1960s, but pickings were generally slim. And while the blues had a positive influence on the music of Jimi Hendrix and Led Zeppelin, the tributes paid to it in the work of the Rolling Stones and local guitarist Paul Butterfield were ultimately unconvincing.

> **'The blues still carries on, with a respectability that it took 40 years to earn.'**

Like Melrose, the Chess brothers have often been accused of exploiting black musicians on their books. In 1964, the Stones visited Chess to find Muddy Waters employed not as a musician but as a painter in the studio where they were about to record. And Bo Diddley was not alone in griping about his lack of royalty payments. Certainly, neither brother was a particular fan of the blues. The running of Chess Records was no labour of love: it was purely business. Like all good entrepreneurs, the Chess brothers saw a gap in the market and worked flat out to fill it; the proof of this is apparent in the haste with which they cut back on their blues releases when rock 'n' roll hit big.

Yet the musicians wanted and needed an outlet for their music, and Chess was more beneficial to them than competitors might have been. There was a respect between the two camps that there never was between Melrose and his musicians. As Nadine Cohodas puts it in *Spinning Blues into Gold*, her history of the label, the brothers earned their spurs with the musicians because they made their living within the black community, not merely from it. It helped, too, that their Jewishness led some blacks to see them as outsiders.

21ST CENTURY BLUES

The late 20th century saw the blues settle into an easy predictability, not just in Chicago but across the world. While popular, its most famous protagonists fell short of the mark. The music of Stevie Ray Vaughan was all bluff and bluster; for all his passionate live shows, the similarly heralded Robert Cray failed to catch fire on record; and Eric Clapton's attempts at the music have been far too reverent to convince. Those acts with a little fire in their bellies, such as the Jon Spencer Blues Explosion, stayed resolutely underground.

But in the past few years, the music has come full circle, its newest practitioners playing with the kind of raw intensity that defined the early Chicago blues a decade ago. Acts such as Detroit, Michigan's White Stripes and Akron, Ohio's Black Keys deliver the blues, or at least a version of it, with a fearsome power that sits in stunning contrast to the likes of Cray and Clapton. Oxford, Mississippi record label Fat Possum has also tried to reclaim the grittiness of the blues, building a catalogue of newly recorded but old-school blues.

The blues still carries on in Chicago, now with a respectability that it took 40 years to earn. The **Harold Washington Library** (*see p306*) holds a sizeable archive of blues-related documents, interviews and recordings, while the newly opened **Chicago Blues Museum** (*see p137*) highlights the music's history. The music has also become quite a draw for wide-eyed, lily-white tourists and conventioneers, who stay at the extravagant **House of Blues** hotel before crawling several blocks up the road to one of two branches of **Blue Chicago** (*see p260*) for innumerable choruses of 'Sweet Home Chicago'.

That said, authenticity is notoriously elusive. The consensus pick among aficionados, musicians and purists as the town's best blues club is probably **Rosa's Lounge** (*see p261*), which opened barely two decades ago and sits about as far from the South Side as it's possible to get. Although you'll find both at gritty neighbourhood hangouts on the South Side such as **Lee's Unleaded Blues** (*see p260*), authenticity doesn't guarantee quality.

But then what constitutes authenticity anyway? Even the decision made by a handful of local musicians to go electric, *the* characteristic of Chicago blues, was born less from artistic and creative urges than from pure commercial pragmatism. The musicians simply needed to find a way to be heard, and plugging their guitars into amplifiers happened to be it. And as long as they're still singing about loves decayed and chances lost, they'll always be an audience of empathisers ready to soak it up.

The Great Divide

Cubs or White Sox? Baseball in the Windy City.

In October 2005, the Chicago White Sox won the World Series, humiliating the Houston Astros four games to none. It was a momentous achievement for the South Side ball club, which hadn't been to the Fall Classic since 1959 and hadn't won it since 1917. So momentous, in fact, that rival Chicago Cubs fans on the North Side joined in the celebrations. Surely, they reasoned, the back-to-back triumphs of the White Sox and the long-suffering Boston Red Sox (who won it all in 2004, having not done so since 1918) meant one thing above all others: the Cubs, who hadn't won the Series since 1908, were going to go all the way in 2006.

And lo, the Cubs did indeed go all the way in 2006: all the way to the bottom of the National League's Central division, with a wretched win-loss record of 66-96. But despite the team's horrendous play, the Cubs still managed to draw over 3.1 million fans to Wrigley Field during the season, the fifth-highest attendance figure in the NL and the second best turnstile tally in the 130-year history of the franchise. They even out-drew the White Sox, who set their own record by drawing nearly three million punters of their own.

While the teams' combined attendance tally of more than six million speaks well of the city's affection for the national pastime, the Sox have only recently begun to enjoy the same levels of fan support and media attention as their uptown cousins, and they had to win a World Series in order to do it. The Cubs, on the other hand, could field a team of winos straight off Skid Row and probably still draw 35,000 fans a game. The White Sox are a baseball team. The Cubs, though, are one of Chicago's biggest summertime tourist attractions.

EARLY DAYS
It hasn't always been this way. Back in 1906, the only season thus far that's ended with the two Chicago teams facing each other in the World Series, the clubs were equally popular. Both teams were competitive during the pre-1920 'dead-ball era': the Cubs won five NL pennants while the White Sox won four American League titles, and the franchises achieved two World Series apiece. But after the 1919 World Series and the ensuing 'Black Sox' scandal, in which Eddie Cicotte, 'Shoeless' Joe Jackson and six other players were accused of intentionally throwing the Series to the Cincinnati Reds at

the behest of a well-heeled gambling consortium, the Sox gradually assumed the mantle of the Second City's second team.

The Cubs generally fielded better teams than the White Sox between the wars, but the North Siders also had the advantage of playing in a far more pleasant environment. Built in 1914 at the corner of Clark and Addison Streets for the short-lived Chicago Whales (of the equally short-lived Federal League), Weeghman Field became the Cubs' new home in 1916. A decade later, it was rechristened Wrigley Field, after the team's new owner (and famed chewing gum magnate) William Wrigley, Jr. From 1920 until shortly before World War II, Wrigley and his son Philip, who took over the team in 1932, poured much of the family fortune into making Wrigley Field the most attractive ballpark in the country. Cubs treasurer Bill Veeck planted the famous ivy on the outfield walls in 1937, the same year that work began on the manual scoreboard that still stands in centre field.

The Wrigleys also took time to promote the ballpark as a family-friendly environment, a novel notion at a time when baseball was still considered a disreputable pastime. 'Ladies' Day', a regular promotion in which the first 20,000 women to arrive at the ballpark would get in free, was a great success. Add in the great Cubs teams of the 1930s, which won the National League four times in ten years thanks to future Hall of Famers such as Hack Wilson and Kiki Cuyler, and it's small wonder that both team and ballpark became deeply embedded in the hearts and minds of local sports fans.

The original Comiskey Park also had its share of magic moments. However, the grey and grimy home of the White Sox lacked Wrigley Field's intimacy and charm, and the rough working-class neighbourhood in which it sits was far less hospitable to strangers. The White Sox didn't clear the one million single-season attendance mark until 1951, 24 years after the Cubs had first posted a similar figure.

GOATS AND GROOVES

The White Sox struggled mightily in the decades following the Black Sox scandal, failing to finish higher than third in the American League between 1921 and 1956. But after their loss to the Detroit Tigers in the 1945 World Series, the Cubs began to have serious troubles of their own. The 20 seasons that followed a respectable third-place finish in 1946 saw them finish above the .500 mark just once, and that with an 82-80 showing that was good enough only for a seventh-place finish out of ten teams in 1963.

According to Cubs lore, this precipitous slide, and virtually every calamity that's befallen the team in subsequent years, comes down to one event. Like the Curse of the Bambino, which supposedly plagued Boston for 85 years, one misstep by the owner consigned the team to perpetual failure. Harry Frazee doomed the Red Sox by selling Babe Ruth to the Yankees, but it was Philip Wrigley's inhospitable attitude towards a farm animal that sent the Cubs on the road to a pennant-less existence.

The story goes that Billy Sianis, the owner of a local tavern, purchased two box seats for Game 4 of the 1945 World Series: one for him and one for his pet goat. Though Sianis and his cloven-hoofed friend were allowed in to Wrigley Field, and were somehow even permitted to stroll around the playing field before the first pitch, Wrigley took umbrage at the goat's odour and ordered that the pair be ejected from the park. Incensed at the disrespect shown to him and his pet, Sianis allegedly placed a curse on the Cubs, promising that they would never win another pennant. The Cubs lost both the game and the Series, and haven't won the NL since. Naturally, the **Billy Goat Tavern** (*see p178*), Sianis's watering hole, continues to thrive.

While it's fun to blame the Cubs' six subsequent decades of futility on Sianis, the club's endlessly inept management also has

1876 Chicago White Stockings founded; win inaugural NL title

1902 Renamed the Cubs

1906 Win 116 games, but lose to White Sox in World Series

1907/08 Win two straight World Series

1916 Move to Weeghman (now Wrigley) Field

1800s — **1900** — **1910** — **1920**

1900 Chicago White Stockings founded; win inaugural AL title

1910 Comiskey Park opens

1919 'Black Sox' throws World Series

1904 Renamed the White Sox

1906 Beat Cubs to win World Series

something to do with it. There have been awful trades, such as the 1964 deal that sent future stolen-base king Lou Brock to St Louis for weak-armed pitcher Ernie Broglio. There have been the hilariously misguided tactical moves, chiefly Philip Wrigley's ill-fated 1961 decision to do away with the manager's position in favour of a rotating 'college of coaches'. The Cubs lost 103 games that year.

Nor has there been any shortage of crucial coaching blunders, whether it's Leo Durocher running his would-be championship squad into the ground in 1969 by putting the same eight players in the line-up day after day, or Dusty Baker failing to walk to the mound to calm down pitcher Mark Prior after Cubs fan Steve Bartman leaned over the fence and took a catch away from left fielder Moises Alou in Game 6 of the 2003 NL Championship Series. At the time, the team were five outs away from reaching the World Series, but lost their concentration after Bartman's intervention. The Marlins went on to score eight runs in the inning; the Cubs lost the game and, the next day, the pennant.

Still, leaving aside their 2005 world title, the Sox haven't exactly distinguished themselves in the long haul. The Cubs may have made it to the postseason only four times in the last 60 years, but the Sox have only been there five times during the same period. Even their successes have been tainted: the team's AL-winning run of 1959 is best remembered not for the electrifying play of 'Go-Go' Sox greats such as Luis Aparicio and Nellie Fox, but for the air-raid sirens that the city fathers inadvisedly set off when the team clinched the pennant, triggering panic across the region. And while legendary Cubs such as Ernie Banks and Ron Santo never got a chance to play in the World Series, at least they were spared the indignity of taking the field in short pants, as the White Sox did for one game in 1976, or in unwieldy, 19th-century throwback tunics, which the Sox sported from 1977 through 1981.

Both these fashion faux pas were the brainchild of Bill Veeck, who'd emerged from the Cubs organisation to become one of the most entertaining and enterprising owners in sporting history. While in charge of the St Louis Brown, Veeck sent a midget up to bat (wearing the uniform number ⅛); as the owner of the Cleveland Indians, he employed rubber-faced clown Max Patkin as one of the team's coaches. And after taking charge of the Sox for the second time in 1975, Veeck showed he'd lost none of his showman's instinct. With help from popular local rock DJ Steve Dahl, Veeck and his son Mike concocted a promotion wherein any fan who brought a disco record to Comiskey would be admitted to a double-header between the Sox and the Detroit Tigers for a mere 98 cents. The records would then be piled on the field and blown up between the two games in an event billed as Disco Demolition Night.

'On game days, Wrigleyville erupts into a giant fraternity bacchanal.'

Dahl's explosive destruction of the vinyl was even more impressive than planned. But so, too, was the ensuing on-field riot between an estimated 7,000 fans and the various mounted police, firemen and SWAT team members who were called in to restore order. Noting the scorched outfield grass, the ripped-up infield and the cloud of tear gas still hovering overhead in the aftermath, the umpiring crew pronounced the field unfit for play, forcing the Sox to forfeit the second game of the twin-bill.

A LITTLE RESPECT
The Disco Demolition demons, and the ghosts of the Black Sox, seem to have been exorcised when the original Comiskey Park was razed in 1990. After White Sox owner Jerry Reinsdorf threatened to move the team to Tampa Bay, the

1931 Hack Wilson clubs 191 RBI

1932 Beaten by NY in World Series

1929/30 Lose two straight World Series

1945 Lose to Detroit in World Series as Curse of the Billy Goat is laid

1953 Ernie Banks makes his debut

1960 Cubs forgo manager in favour of 'College of Coaches'

— **1930** ——— **1940** ——— **1950** ——— **1960** —

1931 Team owner Charles Comiskey dies

1944 Begin run of seven straight losing seasons

1930 Shortstop Luke Appling makes his debut

1958 Bill Veeck takes over the team

1969 Astroturf installed at Comiskey Park

1959 Sox win AL for first time in 40 years ▶

state legislature voted to grant the team public funding for the construction of a new ballpark. The result was New Comiskey Park (now US Cellular Field), the last in a long line of dismal 'ashtray' baseball stadia dating back to the mid 1960s. The sightlines are agreeably obstruction-free, but the Cell is not the sort of place that draws fans by itself. Still, the Sox have mostly played winning baseball while ensconced in it, never finishing lower than third in their division since moving into the stadium in 1991. Fans have finally begun showing up to watch.

Wrigley Field, on the other hand, is a bigger draw these days than the Cubs themselves. Indeed, many have argued that its success has been impeding the team. After all, if more than three million masochistic fans are willing to pay an average of almost $35 a ticket (only the Red Sox charge more) to watch lousy baseball, why should the Tribune Company, which bought the club from the Wrigley family in 1981, spend money on a better team? The eight-year, $136-million contract awarded to outfielder Alfonso Soriano in November 2006 dug a hole in that logic. But then with rumours circulating that the Tribune is on the verge of selling the team, it adds up: they made the deal safe in the knowledge that they won't be on the hook for it.

Though William Wrigley would surely turn in his grave, Wrigley Field is now really just the epicentre of a full-on party zone known as Wrigleyville. On game days (and, following the installation of lights at the stadium in 1988, game nights), the neighbourhood erupts into a giant fraternity bacchanal, complete with inebriated Cubs fans urinating on the steps of the multi-million-dollar townhouses that dot the surrounding blocks.

Many serious fans make the pilgrimage to the country's second oldest major league park in hopes of communing with baseball history (and maybe even seeing a good game). But for others, going to the game is merely something to do between hitting the late-morning bratwurst cookout on the porch and putting the finishing touches to your beer buzz at one of Wrigleyville's innumerable sports bars. In a gloriously foul-mouthed 1983 tirade against 'the fuckin' nickel-dime people who turn up' at Wrigley, beleagured Cubs manager Lee Elia expressed what many Sox fans had argued for years. 'Eighty-five per cent of the fuckin' world's working. The other 15 come out here. [It's] a fuckin' playground for the cocksuckers.' Elia himself was forced to look for a new job four months later.

Of course, one could easily postulate that such egregious displays of public drunkenness are actually unconscious cries for help. Perhaps the fans have been so damaged by their lifelong loyalty to the Cubs that they've been driven to drink themselves into oblivion. Still, while those who bleed Cubbie blue all dream of some day watching the World Series at Wrigley, most would also admit that it's far easier on the psyche to root for a team of loveable losers (the Cubs have lost more games than they've won in 45 of the last 60 seasons) than to pull for a good one that breaks your heart, like the Cubs squads that so spectacularly sprawled just short of greatness in 1969, 1984 and 2003.

And yet, hope springs eternal in Wrigleyville. While the White Sox have the strongest major-league squad and the most promising minor-league system, all the optimistic chirping seems to be emanating from the North Side. 'Our goal is to win the World Series next year and the year after that,' announced interim Cubs president John McDonough at a press conference following the 2006 season finale. It was rumoured that McDonough was also intent on travelling back in time for a torrid three-way with Marilyn Monroe and Clara Bow in the back lounge of the *Hindenburg*. At press time, Vegas bookmakers were giving equal odds on either goal actually being accomplished.

1979 Cubs score 22 against Philadelphia... and still lose the game

1992 Star pitcher Greg Maddux leaves the team

2003 Five outs from World Series, Cubs collapse

1971 Pitcher Ferguson Jenkins wins the Cy Young Award

1988 First night game at Wrigley Field

1998 Sammy Sosa belts 66 home runs

1970 — 1980 — 1990 — 2000

1975 Bill Veeck takes over for a second time

1991 New Comiskey Park opens

2005 Sox win World Series for first time since 1917

1981 Jerry Reinsdorf buys the team

1978 Disco Demolition Night

1990 Frank Thomas makes his debut

Where to Stay

Where to Stay   **54**

Features

The best Hotels   54
Seen it all before?   57
The chain gang   61
Bed & backrub   66
Hostels   69

Wheeler Mansion. *See p59.*

Where to Stay

From blockbuster chain hotels to low-key B&Bs, Chicago is packed with accommodation options – but you'll have to pay for the privilege.

If a city's popularity with the world at large can be measured by the quality and variety of its hotels, then Chicago is growing more well-liked by the day. The city's assortment of quaint inns, funky boutiques, business-friendly blocks and lavish palaces combine to hold 30,000-plus guestrooms, more than half within a mile of Navy Pier. And the deep holes in the ground and soaring cranes in the sky are clues that the city's hotel scene is continuing to develop at an impressive clip. Some 3,000 new rooms are slated for completion by 2009, among them the first **Shangri-la Hotel** in the US and the high-profile 90-storey **Trump Tower**.

Business travellers on expense accounts take comfort in the knowledge that they'll never have to slum it here. The **Peninsula**, the **Four Seasons** and the **Ritz-Carlton** are among the best in their respective chains, awash with luxurious amenities. At the other end of the scale, the likes of **Comfort Inn** and **Red Roof Inn** provide budget travellers with a place to stay. And somewhere in between sit a slew of independent operations, from the glamorous **James Chicago** to the more casual **Rick's Bucktown B&B**.

In this chapter, we've listed only those hotels within a reasonable distance of downtown. Other chain hotels can be found further out, especially around O'Hare International Airport. For a list of 1-800 numbers and websites for the main hotel chains, *see p61* **The chain gang**.

INFORMATION AND PRICES

With such an impressive inventory of hotels, finding a room in Chicago shouldn't pose too many problems. Finding one at a price you want to pay is another matter. The average Chicago hotel room in 2006 came in at a not insubstantial $197 per night; given the high levels of business traffic passing through town, it's a price the market can easily support. When major conventions hit town, which they do with alarming regularity, prices head in the direction of the skyscrapers. That room you're eyeing up just off the Magnificent Mile with a rack rate of $225 could possibly be yours for less than $100 during a lean weekend in February. A week later, 10,000 conventioneers could show up and the price might triple on the spot.

Deals can be had at virtually all of the hotels if you put in a little work and build in a little flexibility with your dates. When searching for a hotel room, start by contacting the hotel directly, either by phone or (better still) online: many hotels offer internet-only specials that can shave as much as $50 from the room rate. It's also worth checking online systems such as **www.hotels.com**, **www.priceline.com**, **www.lastminute.com** and **www.expedia. com**, all of which may have bargains (especially at short notice away from peak season). In addition, Chicago-based **Hot Rooms** (1-800 468 3500, 1-773 468 7666, www.hotrooms.com) offers regular deals.

Bed and breakfast is an increasingly popular option in Chicago, especially among travellers keen to avoid the big downtown properties and their big downtown prices. The **Chicago Bed & Breakfast Association** (www.chicago-bed-breakfast.com) has an online calendar of availability at a dozen licensed B&Bs in the city, while stays can also be arranged through **Bed & Breakfast Chicago** (1-800 375 7084, 1-312 640 1050, www.athomeinnchicago.com).

However you book your hotel room, always ask about cancellation policies when booking. Most hotels require at least 24 hours' notice, but

The best Hotels

For the lap of luxury
Peninsula Chicago. *See p62*.

For a room with a view
Swissôtel. *See p56*.

For staying in with the in-crowd
James Chicago. *See p63*.

For hospitality plus history
Hotel Burnham. *See p58*.

For bed, breakfast and books
Windy City Urban Inn. *See p69*.

❶ Green numbers given in this chapter correspond to the location of each hotel on the street maps. *See pp322-332*.

Life is suite: the stunning **W Chicago City Center**. *See p56.*

some smaller hotels and B&Bs may require as much as two weeks. Try and ensure you don't get caught out. The rates listed below are meant as a guide, with the highest figure in each category being the amount you can expect to pay in peak season. All rates exclude the city's crippling hotel tax, which runs at 15.4 per cent.

We've listed a selection of services for each hotel at the bottom of all reviews, detailing everything from in-room entertainment options to the cost of parking. The majority of hotels feature dataports for dial-up users; however, most also offer high-speed internet access for laptop-toters, whether via a cable connection or with wireless technology. Prices for internet access are for any given 24-hour period unless otherwise stated. Where two parking rates are listed, the first is for self-parking and the second is for valet parking.

The Loop

Deluxe

Crowne Plaza Silversmith

10 S Wabash Drive, at E Madison Street, IL 60603 (1-877 227 6963/1-312 372 7696/fax 1-312 372 7320/www.crowneplaza.com/silversmith). El: Blue or Red to Monroe; Brown, Green, Orange, Pink or Purple to Madison. **Rates** $289-$329 double; $389-$450 suite. **Credit** AmEx, DC, Disc, MC, V. **Map** p305 H12 ❶

This 144-room boutique hotel on Jewelers Row is an architectural gem. The late 19th-century Arts and Crafts style is evident outside and in, with wrought-iron pieces adding accents to the comfortable (if slightly dated) decorations in each guestroom. The building is handsomely clad in dark green, highly glazed terracotta, and was built to house silversmiths (hence the name) and jewellers. Guests can get their sweet fix during the complimentary dessert hour. *Bar. Business centre. CD. Concierge. Disabled-adapted rooms. Gym. High-speed internet (free wireless). Parking ($30-$37). Restaurant. Room service. Spa.*

Fairmont Chicago

200 N Columbus Drive, at E Lake Street, IL 60601 (1-866 540 4409/1-312 565 8000/fax 1-312 856 1032/www.fairmont.com). El: Brown, Green, Orange, Pink or Purple to State; Red to Lake. **Rates** $169-$439 double; $319-$619 suite. **Credit** AmEx, DC, Disc, MC, V. **Map** p325 J11 ❷

A feeling of refined romance pervades in these cushy digs: oversized bathrooms, separate dressing rooms, fluffy robes, and in-room spa services complete with chocolate-covered strawberries and champagne. The generously sized rooms, with views of the city or lake, are easy to reach: none of the Fairmont's 692 rooms and suites is more than four doors away from a lift. Tea and frothy coffees are served in the art-filled sunken lobby, while the classy, revamped Aria bar (*see p176*) serves sushi with glasses of Evolution, its signature champagne and sake cocktail. *Bar. Business centre. Concierge. Disabled-adapted rooms. DVD. Gym. High-speed internet (free wireless in public spaces; $14.95 via cable in rooms). Parking ($45). Pool. Restaurant. Room service. Spa.*

Hotel Monaco. *See p58.*

Renaissance Chicago Hotel

*1 W Wacker Drive, at N State Street, IL 60601
(1-800 468 3571/1-312 372 7200/fax 1-312 372
0093/www.renaissancehotel.com). El: Brown,
Green, Orange, Pink or Purple to State; Red to
Lake.* **Rates** *$289-$369 double; $429-$639 suite.*
Credit AmEx, Disc, MC, V. **Map** p326 H11 ❸
This 27-storey hotel features 553 rooms, including
40 sprawling suites that are bigger than many condos. Neutral colours and standard furnishings give
guestrooms a tasteful yet somewhat generic feel; the
bay windows provide impressive views of the skyline, river and Lake Michigan. A funky fountain and
wall murals add some interest to the public areas.
The location is perfect for the Loop, the Magnificent
Mile and the restaurants of River North, but those
who prefer to eat in are well served by the contemporary American fare in the Great Street eaterie.
*Bar. Business centre. Concierge. Disabled-adapted
rooms. Gym. High-speed internet (free wireless in
public spaces; $9.95 via cable in rooms). Parking
($39). Pool. Restaurants (2). Room service. Spa.*

Swissôtel

*323 E Wacker Drive, at N Columbus Drive, IL
60601 (1-800 654 7263/1-312 565 0565/fax
1-312 565 0540/www.chicago.swissotel.com). El:
Brown, Green, Orange, Pink or Purple to State; Red
to Lake.* **Rates** *$229-$429 double; $569-$899 suite.*
Credit AmEx, DC, Disc, MC, V. **Map** p326 J11 ❹
Though not as Swiss as it once was (it's now owned
by the Raffles group of Singapore), this outpost
of the global chain still offers up European-style

breakfasts in Geneva, its breakfast-only eaterie.
Otherwise, the hotel is a thoroughly high-tech operation, from the ergonomically designed furniture to
the 42nd-floor state-of-the-art fitness spa offering
jaw-dropping views of Lake Michigan. Indeed, even
the building is modern: the hotel occupies a triangular glass high-rise, with each of the 632 rooms
designed to provide a lake or river view. Carnivores
will find prime beef at Chicago's version of the Palm.
*Bar. Business centre. Concierge. Disabled-adapted
rooms. Gym ($10.80). High-speed internet ($9.95 via
cable in rooms). Parking ($45). Pool. Restaurants (2).
Room service.*

W Chicago City Center

*172 W Adams Street, at N LaSalle Street, IL 60603
(1-877 946 8357/1-312 332 1200/fax 1-312 917
5771/www.starwoodhotels.com). El: Blue or Red to
Jackson; Brown, Orange, Pink or Purple to Quincy.*
Rates *$249-$500 double; $549-$2,000 suite.*
Credit AmEx, DC, Disc, MC, V. **Map** p325 H12 ❺
This stunning Beaux Arts building, which started
out as a private men's club in 1929, has been transformed into one of Starwood's sleek W Hotels. Set
over two storeys, the ornate, candlelit lobby is an
ideal spot for people-watching while nursing a fancy
Martini. The 369 rooms (including 12 spacious suites)
come with pillow-top mattresses, CD libraries and
the option of an in-room shiatsu massage. You can
request just about anything (legal) you desire from
W's signature Whatever/Whenever service, which
once reportedly hired a helicopter to fetch a guest's
wedding cake. **Photo** *p55.*

Bars (2). Business centre. CD. Concierge. Disabled-adapted rooms. DVD. Gym. High-speed internet ($14.95 via cable in rooms). Parking ($39). Restaurant. Room service. Spa.

Expensive

Hard Rock Hotel

230 N Michigan Avenue, at E South Water Street, IL 60601 (1-866 966 5166/1-312 345 1000/fax 1-312 345 1012/www.hardrock.com). El: Brown, Green, Orange, Pink or Purple to State; Red to Lake. **Rates** $149-$409 double; $469-$1,500 suite. **Credit** AmEx, DC, Disc, MC, V. **Map** p325 J11 ❻

With Beatles in the bathrooms and Madonna in the corridors, there's little doubt about this hotel's theme. But although the public spaces feature showcases devoted to musical legends, the rock 'n' roll aspect is toned down in the guestrooms, where amenities include flat-screen TVs and a selection of Aveda toiletries. Boasting 381 rooms and 13 suites, the hotel occupies the 40-storey Carbide & Carbon Building, an art deco superstar built in 1929 as a high-rise office tower by the sons of famed architect Daniel Burnham. Its exterior colours, so the story goes, are intended to mimic a dark green champagne bottle with gold foil. For a review of the bar, see p176.

Bar. Business centre. CD. Concierge. Disabled-adapted rooms. DVD. Gym. High-speed internet (free wireless in public spaces & via cable in rooms). Parking ($35/$38). Restaurants (2). Room service.

Hotel Allegro

171 W Randolph Street, at N LaSalle Street, IL 60601 (1-866 672 6143/1-312 236 0123/fax 1-312 236 0917/www.allegrochicago.com). El: Blue, Brown, Green, Orange, Pink or Purple to Clark; Red to Lake. **Rates** $199-$349 double; $179-$399 suite. **Credit** AmEx, DC, Disc, MC, V. **Map** p355 H12 ❼

From the Tootsie Roll candies at the front desk to the zebra-print robes in the suites, the Allegro boasts a whimsical sense of style. There's a showbiz theme to the Kimpton Group's late-'90s transformation: rooms are decorated in vibrant colours, and the theatrically themed suites include one decorated like the set of The Lion King. Original brass and woodwork details make a sharp backdrop for the overstuffed red and blue couches in the dramatic lobby. As at the other Kimpton hotels, guests enjoy a daily wine hour in the lobby (5-6pm) and an in-room yoga channel. The 312 Chicago restaurant serves creative Italian-American specialities in a handsome setting. Bar. Business centre. CD. Concierge. Disabled-adapted rooms. DVD. Gym. High-speed internet (free wireless). Parking ($34/$40). Restaurant (2). Room service.

Seen it all before?

If this lobby or that ballroom looks familiar when you check into your hotel, don't worry. You haven't stayed here in a past life. You're probably just having a cinematic flashback. Many of Chicago's iconic hotels developed and/or exploited their iconography on the silver screen, taking starring roles or bit parts in the movies that have helped define the city to the public outside it.

The **Drake** (see p65) has long attracted a cosmopolitan crowd in real life. Down the years, it's been little different in the movies. Cary Grant, James Mason and Eva Marie Saint graced its lobby in Hitchcock's North by Northwest, Julia Roberts plotted against precious Cameron Diaz here in My Best Friend's Wedding, and Tom Cruise awaited Risky Business girl-for-hire Rebecca de Mornay in the hotel's Palm Court.

Another hotel, the **Hilton Chicago** (see p58), dates to 1927, and was featured in The Package, My Best Friend's Wedding and Home Alone II: Lost in New York (well, why not?). However, it's best known for its role in The Fugitive, in which its Grand Ballroom, its three-storeyed laundry room and its towering rooftop provide the backdrop

for Harrison Ford's athletic escapades. The same film set its charity fundraising dinner in the ballroom at the **Four Seasons** (see p65), on the other side of the Chicago River.

Built in 1910, the formerly luxurious **Blackstone Hotel** on the corner of Michigan Avenue and Balbo Drive in the South Loop has been closed since 1999, but is scheduled to reopen in late 2007 after an expensive programme of renovations. With any luck, the refurbishment will preserve the hotel's longstanding grandeur, a favourite of film-makers down the years. The Coen Brothers used its ballroom in The Hudsucker Proxy, and Tom Cruise stayed here in The Color of Money. The violent banquet scene in The Untouchables was filmed here in the ballroom at the Blackstone, but it didn't stand in for the **Lexington**, the hotel in which Al Capone actually kept a suite: that task fell to the foyers of the **Chicago Theatre** (175 N State Street, at E Lake Street) and **Roosevelt University** (430 S Michigan Avenue, at E Van Buren Street). Formerly on the corner of Michigan Avenue and 22nd Street, the Lexington itself was demolished in the 1990s.

Hotel Blake

500 S Dearborn Street, at E Congress Parkway,
IL 60605 (1-312 986 1234/fax 1-312 939 2468/
www.hotelblake.com). El: Blue or Red to Jackson;
Brown, Green, Orange, Pink or Purple to Library.
Rates $199-$499 double. **Credit** AmEx, DC, Disc,
MC, V. **Map** p325 H13 ❽

Housed in the recently renovated former 19th-
century headquarters of the Morton Salt Company
in the heart of Printers Row, the Blake has a historic
exterior that belies the chic, contemporary digs that
lie within its walls. The 162 spacious rooms have
retained their crown moulding but have otherwise
been brought gently up to date with casually handsome furnishings and hi-tech fittings. A 24-hour
complimentary business centre and fitness room are
other attractions; the upmarket, carnivore-focused
Custom House, the latest brainchild of Chicago über-
chef Shawn McClain, provides sustenance.
Business centre. CD. Concierge. Disabled-adapted
rooms. DVD. Gym. High-speed internet (free
wireless). Parking ($36). Restaurant. Room service.

Hotel Burnham

1 W Washington Street, at N State Street, IL
60602 (1-877 294 9712/1-312 782 1111/fax 1-312
782 0899/www.burnhamhotel.com). El: Blue to
Washington; Brown, Green, Orange, Pink or Purple
to Randolph; Red to Lake. **Rates** $229-$299 double;
$300-$409 suite. **Credit** AmEx, DC, Disc, MC, V.
Map p325 H12 ❾

This historic but forgotten architectural treasure
morphed from the Reliance Building into the Hotel
Burnham, named for the architect whose firm created
it. The restoration job was beautiful (appropriately,
for a building designated as a National Historic
Landmark), but it didn't leave the building stuck in
the 19th century: the Kimpton Group has brought
its trademark exuberance to the design of the 103
guestrooms and 19 suites, doing them out with rich
indigo blue and gold fabrics mixed with mischievous
cherubs and musical figures. Grab a sidewalk table
for some tasty nosh at Café Atwood, and don't miss
the free wine hour (5-6pm) each night in the lobby.
Bar. Business centre. CD. Concierge. Disabled-
adapted rooms. Gym. High-speed internet (free
wireless). Parking ($35). Restaurant. Room service.

Hotel Monaco

225 N Wabash Avenue, at E Wacker Drive, IL
60601 (1-866 610 0081/1-312 960 8500/fax 1-312
960 1883/www.monaco-chicago.com). El: Brown,
Green, Orange, Pink or Purple to State; Red to Lake.
Rates $289-$389 double; $250-$499 suite. **Credit**
AmEx, Disc, MC, V. **Map** p325 H11 ❿

Its facilities and location have made it popular with
business travellers, but this funky Kimpton hotel
rewards those who are simply here to relax. Guests
let go of their stress with the help of free chair massages and wine, served nightly around a limestone
fireplace in the French deco lobby. Serenity also
beckons in the 192 stylishly decorated rooms, where
windowsills filled with plush pillows are referred to
as 'meditation stations'. Another nice gimmick:

guests are offered a 'pet' goldfish for the duration of
their stay. Off the lobby, the South Water Kitchen
dishes up comfort food such as meatloaf. **Photo** *p56.*
Bar. Business centre. CD. Concierge. Disabled-
adapted rooms. Gym. High-speed internet (free
wireless). Parking ($36). Restaurant. Room service.

Hyatt Regency

151 E Wacker Drive, at N Michigan Avenue, IL
60601 (1-888 591 1234/1-312 565 1234/fax 1-312
239 4414/http://chicagoregency.hyatt.com). El:
Brown, Green, Orange, Pink or Purple to State; Red
to Lake. **Rates** $109-$469 double; $450-$5,400 suite.
Credit AmEx, DC, Disc, MC, V. **Map** p325 J11 ⓫

The Hyatt's 2,019-room Loop operation is a popular
choice for business travellers, and with good reason:
this is a slick operation, if dauntingly large. The lofty
lobby bar backs up to a wall of glass, making for a
dramatic backdrop; at weekends, the area morphs
into the Hard Drive nightclub (*see p264*). The rooms
are comfortably and comparatively modern; many
offer terrific views across the Chicago River.
Bar. Business centre. Concierge. Disabled-adapted
rooms. Gym. High-speed internet ($11.95 wireless in
public spaces & via cable in rooms). Parking ($41).
Restaurant. Room service. Spa.

Palmer House Hilton

17 E Monroe Street, at S State Street, IL 60603
(1-800 445 8667/1-312 726 7500/fax 1-312 917
1707/www.hilton.com). El: Blue or Red to Monroe;
Brown, Green, Orange, Pink or Purple to Madison.
Rates $150-$400 double; $250-$500 suite. **Credit**
AmEx, Disc, MC, V. **Map** p325 H12 ⓬

On 26 September 1871, the Palmer House opened to
the public. Less than two weeks later, it burned to
the ground in the Chicago Fire. Undaunted, Potter
Palmer rebuilt it and was back in business just two
years later, which makes this the longest continuously operating hotel in America. The opulent Beaux
Arts lobby is a showpiece, with museum-worthy
frescoes and a ceiling by 19th-century muralist Louis
Pierre Rigal. Guests can get a taste of history by
ordering a decadent brownie, baked using the recipe
the hotel chef invented back in 1893. **Photo** *p59.*
Bar. Business centre. Concierge. Disabled-adapted
rooms. Gym. High-speed internet ($6/hr wireless in
public spaces; $10 via cable in rooms). Parking
($30/$38). Pool. Restaurant. Room service.

The South Loop & Chinatown

The South Loop

Expensive

Hilton Chicago

720 S Michigan Avenue, at E Balbo Drive, IL
60605 (1-800 445 8667/1-312 922 4400/fax
1-312 922 5240/www.chicagohilton.com).

Palmer House Hilton. *See p58.*

El: Red to Harrison. **Rates** $179-$429 double; $279-$699 suite. **Credit** AmEx, DC, Disc, MC, V. **Map** p325 J13 ⑬

Back in 1927, the Stevens was the largest hotel in the world: there were roughly 3,000 rooms here at the time. Although it's gone through countless changes since then, not least in its name, it remains something of a beast: with 1,634 guestrooms, it's virtually a city within a city. The vast public spaces are decorated with fine art, flower arrangements and plush carpets; an 'executive' level in the tower has its own check-in and levels of pampering consistent with the prices. Thanks to a staff exchange programme with Ireland, its pub, Kitty O'Shea's, has at least a hint of authenticity. A free shuttle runs to the Magnificent Mile. *Bars (4). Business centre. Concierge. Disabled-adapted rooms. Gym. High-speed internet ($5.95 wireless in public spaces; $12.95 wireless in rooms). Parking ($38-$41). Pool. Restaurants (4). Room service. Spa.*

Budget

Essex Inn

800 S Michigan Avenue, at E 8th Street, IL 60605 (1-800 621 6909/1-312 939 2800/fax 1-312 939 0526/www.essexinn.com). El: Red to Harrison. **Rates** $99-$329 double; $299-499 suite. **Credit** AmEx, DC, Disc, MC, V. **Map** p324 J14 ⑭

The 1999 makeover of this '70s-style hotel, located in the shadow of the hulking Hilton, has placed it squarely in the 'best buy' category. The 254 rooms aren't dazzling, but they are clean, comfortable and decorated in good taste. The Savoy Bar & Grill offers a full menu, and the hotel shuttles guests free of charge to the Magnificent Mile. But the key attraction is the indoor pool with a retractable glass roof, offering million-dollar views of Lake Michigan, Museum Campus and Soldier Field. *Bar. Business centre. Concierge. Disabled-adapted rooms. Gym. High-speed internet ($3.95 wireless). Parking ($21-$30). Pool. Restaurant. Room service.*

Chinatown & around

Expensive

Wheeler Mansion

2020 S Calumet Avenue, at E Cullerton Street, IL 60616 (1-312 945 2020/fax 1-312 945 2021/www. wheelermansion.com). El: Red to Cermak-Chinatown. **Rates** $230-$285 double; $285-$365 suite. **Credit** AmEx, DC, Disc, MC, V. **Map** p324 J16 ⑮

One of the few mansions to survive the Chicago Fire, the Wheeler is typical of the elegant domiciles that once housed the city's elite. Built in 1870 for Chicago Board of Trade President Calvin T Wheeler, this opulent mansion had fallen on hard times and was slated to become a parking lot until preservationists snapped it up in 1999 and turned it into a classy B&B. A five-minute walk from McCormick Place, the 11-room inn is an intimate alternative to convention centre lodging. Daily gourmet breakfasts and turn-down service are included, along with Egyptian cotton linens and robes. **Photo** *p60.* *Concierge. High-speed internet ($9.95 wireless). Parking (free).*

Bed and gourmet breakfast at the venerated **Wheeler Mansion**. *See p59.*

Moderate

Hyatt Regency McCormick Place

2233 S Martin Luther King Drive, at E Cermak Road, IL 60616 (1-800 633 7313/1-312 567 1234/ fax 1-312 528 4000/http://mccormickplace.hyatt. com). El: Red to Cermak-Chinatown. **Rates** $150-$400 double; $650-$850 suite. **Credit** AmEx, DC, Disc, MC, V.

The only hotel adjoining McCormick Place, this Hyatt offers 800 rooms to convention-going patrons. The convenience to conventioneers is obvious; while the hotel is a bit removed from the city, the prices are pretty fair. Chinatown is a short taxi ride away, and an hourly complimentary shuttle is available for downtown access. Although the Cermak El train stop looks close, it's not a fun walk, especially at night. *Bar. Business centre. Concierge. Disabled-adapted rooms. Gym. High-speed internet ($9.95 wireless in public spaces & via cable in rooms). Parking ($24/$29). Pool. Restaurant. Room service.*

The Near North Side

Expensive

Amalfi Hotel

20 W Kinzie Street, at N State Street, IL 60610 (1-877 262 5341/1-312 395 9000/fax 1-312 395 9001/www.amalfihotelchicago.com). El: Red to

Grand. **Rates** $189-$489 double; $209-$549 suite. **Credit** AmEx, DC, Disc, MC, V. **Map** p325 H11 ⑯

The 215-room Amalfi welcomes guests by sitting them down at an individual check-in desk with what it grandly calls an 'experience designer', who might suggest a complimentary Amalfitini cocktail in the Ravello lounge. Pretensions aside, staff do load your visit with plenty of value-added amenities, such as free high-speed internet access, no annoying extras for local and toll-free phone calls, and a nightly reception with complimentary drinks and hors d'oeuvres. The Amalfi also delivers on comfort, serving up fine Egyptian cotton sheets, pillow-top mattresses, terry robes and slippers, plus a free continental breakfast.

Business centre. CD. Concierge. Disabled-adapted rooms. DVD. Gym. High-speed internet (free wireless). Parking ($37). Room service.

House of Blues

333 N Dearborn Street, at the Chicago River, IL 60610 (1-877 569 3742/1-312 245 0333/ fax 1-312 923 2458/www.houseofblueshotel.com). El: Red to Grand. **Rates** $199-$309 double; $259-$995 suite. **Credit** AmEx, DC, Disc, MC, V. **Map** p325 H11 ⑰

Guests get plenty of exposure to music at this spunky hotel nestled in the towering Marina City complex. There's often a worthwhile act playing at the adjoining music venue (*see p257*); what's more, hotel guests get free entry into the popular Foundation Room club. The hotel's outlandish design, in its 366 guestrooms and throughout its public spaces, is a wildly entertaining mix of Morocco and the Deep South. The facilities have been overtaken in recent years by

Where to Stay

some of the hotel's higher-tech neighbours, but this is still a good and agreeably individualistic option in the middle of town. **Photo** *p62.*
Bar. CD. Concierge. Disabled-adapted rooms. DVD. Gym. High-speed internet ($9.95 via cable in rooms). Parking ($39). Room service.

Moderate

Hampton Inn & Suites

33 W Illinois Street, at N Dearborn Street, IL 60610 (1-800 426 7866/1-312 832 0330/fax 1-312 832 0333/www.hamptoninnchicago.com). El: Red to Grand. **Rates** $169-$350 double; $210-$370 suite. **Credit** AmEx, DC, Disc, MC, V. **Map** p326 H11 ⑱
Yet another chain-affiliated hotel striving for individuality. Built in 1998, this 230-room property is mindful of Chicago's architectural heritage; the Prairie-style touches are deliberately reminiscent of Frank Lloyd Wright. Guests are treated to displays of artefacts from historic buildings, such as a stair stringer from Adler and Sullivan's Chicago Stock Exchange building. Accommodation is in 130 standard guestrooms, 40 studio suites and 60 two-room full-kitchen suites. Rates include hot breakfasts, free local calls and a daily newspaper.
Business centre. Concierge. Disabled-adapted rooms. Gym. High-speed internet (free via cable in rooms). Parking ($38). Pool. Room service.

Hilton Garden Inn

10 E Grand Avenue, at N State Street, IL 60611 (1-800 445 8667/1-312 595 0000/fax 1-312 595 0955/www.chicagodowntownnorth.gardeninn.com). El: Red to Grand. **Rates** $109-$449 double; $159-$499 suite. **Credit** AmEx, DC, Disc, MC, V. **Map** p326 H10 ⑲
This spin-off may be small compared to Hilton's Chicago flagship (*see p58*), but it is North America's largest Hilton Garden Inn, offering spacious (if colourless) guestrooms at prices that are pretty low for the area. All the rooms have refrigerators and microwaves, and a 24-hour pantry in the lobby

stocks microwaveable cuisine if you can't be bothered even to wander across to the adjacent and highly popular Weber Grill. The hotel offers complimentary access to the nearby Crunch Fitness club, a free business centre and high-speed internet access, and none of those extras that you won't use but will end up paying for.
Bar. Business centre. CD. Concierge. Disabled-adapted rooms. Gym. High-speed internet (free wireless & via cable in rooms). Parking ($22/$36). Pool. Restaurant. Room service.

Budget

Comfort Inn & Suites Downtown

15 E Ohio Street, between N State & N Wabash Streets, IL 60611 (1-888 775 9223/1-312 894 0900/fax 1-312 894 0999/www.chicagocomfort inn.com). El: Red to Grand. **Rates** $89-$209 double; $159-$309 suite. **Credit** AmEx, DC, Disc, MC, V. **Map** p326 H10 ⑳
Forget what you know about this mid-price chain: this is no formulaic property. Fashioned from a gutted transients' hotel, it retains many original 1920s art deco elements. A shabby-chic lobby features a cheerful gas fireplace and a mahogany Tudor-style beamed ceiling, with hot orange accents to brighten up the woodwork. You'll find good value here, with high-speed internet access, a fitness room, a jacuzzi and a sauna, and continental breakfast all included.
CD. Concierge. Disabled-adapted rooms. Gym. High-speed internet (free via cable in rooms). Parking ($21).

Howard Johnson Inn

720 N LaSalle Street, at W Superior Street, IL 60610 (1-800 446 4656/1-312 664 8100/fax 1-312 664 2365/www.hojo.com). El: Brown, Purple or Red to Chicago. **Rates** $149-$169 double; $199 suite. **Credit** AmEx, DC, Disc, MC, V. **Map** p326 H10 ㉑
Don't expect a mint on your pillow at this decidedly modest – indeed, slightly scruffy – two-storey motor court, an anachronism in the heart of River North. You're here, if you're here at all, purely to

---

The chain gang

The following hotel chains all have branches in and around Chicago.

Expensive/Moderate

Hilton 1-800 445 8667/www.hilton.com.
Hyatt 1-888 591 1234/www.hyatt.com.
Marriott 1-888 236 2427/ www.marriott.com.
Radisson 1-800 333 3333/ www.radisson.com.
Ramada 1-800 272 6232/ www.ramada.com.
Sheraton 1-888 625 5144/ www.starwoodhotels.com.

Budget

Best Western 1-800 780 7234/ www.bestwestern.com.
Comfort Inn 1-877 424 6423/ www.comfortinn.com.
Holiday Inn 1-800 465 4329/ www.holiday-inn.com.
Motel 6 1-800 466 8356/ www.motel6.com.
Travelodge 1-800 578 7878/ www.travelodge.com.

save a little cash. Its central courtyard provides free parking, though it's strictly first come, first served: there are only about 30 parking spots to divvy up among 71 rooms. Attached to the hotel is a cheerful diner where food prices fall squarely in the bargain category.

High-speed internet (free wireless in public spaces). Parking (free). Restaurant.

Ohio House

600 N LaSalle Street, at W Ontario Street, IL 60610 (1-866 601 6446/1-312 943 6000/fax 1-312 943 6063/www.ohiohousemotel.com). El: Red to Grand. **Rates** $95-$110 double; $140-$180 suite. **Credit** AmEx, DC, Disc, MC, V. **Map** p326 H10 ㉒

This timeworn motel seems straight from a 1960s movie set, offering clean, no-frills rooms at budget rates in a desirable location. Penny pinchers will appreciate the coffee shop, which offers mammoth breakfasts (two each of eggs, pancakes, bacon and sausages) for a few bucks. A large room above the office – the management calls it a 'suite' – includes a refrigerator, microwave and sleeper sofa, and could conceivably hold a family of five or six.

High-speed internet ($9.99 wireless). Parking (free).

The Magnificent Mile & Streeterville

Deluxe

Omni Chicago

676 N Michigan Avenue, at E Erie Street, IL 60611 (1-800 843 6664/1-312 944 6664/fax 1-312 266 3015/www.omnihotels.com). El: Red to Chicago. **Rates** $329-$899 suite. **Credit** AmEx, DC, Disc, MC, V. **Map** p326 J10 ㉓

This 347-suite property is apparently favoured by Oprah when she needs somewhere to house her talk-show guests. Guests can choose from a variety of spacious suites, some of which come with stow-away treadmills, a 'get fit kit' and a refreshment centre stocked with healthy snacks; all come with plush robes, plasma TVs, wet bars and a true rarity: windows that open. Sun worshippers can take advantage of the two rooftop sundecks. On the fourth floor, the 676 restaurant and bar serves Northern Italian and American cuisine.

Bar. Business centre. CD. Concierge. Disabled-adapted rooms. Gym. High-speed internet (free wireless). Parking ($40). Pool. Restaurant. Room service. Spa.

Park Hyatt Chicago

800 N Michigan Avenue, at W Chicago Avenue, IL 60611 (1-800 778 7477/1-312 335 1234/fax 1-312 239 4000/http://parkchicago.hyatt.com). El: Red to Chicago. **Rates** $250-$525 double; $695-$3,000 suite. **Credit** AmEx, DC, Disc, MC, V. **Map** p326 J10 ㉔

Little expense has been spared at this 198-room Magnificent Mile property, housed in the lower third of a slender, 67-storey residential tower. The walls and halls are home to an estimated $23 million's worth of artwork; a scent expert recently created

House of Blues. *See p60.*

signature smells to waft through the modern lobby and NoMI, the much-lauded restaurant. High-tech to the core, guestrooms have DVD players, flat-screen LCD televisions and iPod connectivity, along with black leather Eames chairs and 300-thread-count linens. NoMI's garden terrace is a happening place on summer nights; at other times, the sleek lounge is an ideal spot to rub Rolexes with the out-crowd.

Bar. Business centre. CD. Concierge. Disabled-adapted rooms. DVD. Gym. High-speed internet (free wireless). Parking ($39). Pool. Restaurant. Room service. Spa.

Peninsula Chicago

108 E Superior Street, at N Michigan Avenue, IL 60611 (1-866 288 8889/1-312 337 2888/ fax 1-312 751 2888/www.chicago.peninsula.com). El: Red to Chicago. **Rates** $490-$575 double; $695-$6,500 suite. **Credit** AmEx, Disc, DC, MC, V. **Map** p326 J10 ㉕

This swanky icon spells luxury all the way, from its distinguished art collection to the award-winning top-floor spa and fitness centre (*see p66* **Bed & backrub**). As you soak in a marble tub looking out over Michigan Avenue, you may feel equally laudatory. High-tech bedside control panels mean guests don't need to get up to draw the curtains or adjust the temperature. Afternoon tea in the sun-drenched lobby is a refined treat; the G&T brigade gathers nightly around the grand fireplaces in the bar. Grab dim sum at Shanghai Terrace, a modern version of a 1930s Shanghai supper club.

Bar. Business centre. CD. Concierge. Disabled-adapted rooms. DVD. Gym. High-speed internet (free wireless). Parking ($42). Pool. Restaurants (4). Room service. Spa.

Expensive

Allerton Crowne Plaza

701 N Michigan Avenue, at E Huron Street, IL 60611 (1-800 972 2494/1-312 440 1500/ fax 1-312 440 1819/www.crowneplaza.com). El: Red to Chicago. **Rates** $189-$359 double; $300-$500 suite. **Credit** AmEx, DC, Disc, MC, V. **Map** p326 J10 ㉖

Travellers visiting Chicago after a long absence may be in for a serious bout of déjà vu upon catching sight of this historic 443-room hotel, built in 1924 as Michigan Avenue's first high-rise. As part of a $50 million restoration, vintage photographs and blue-prints were used to restore the brickwork and carved stone details of the northern Italian Renaissance exterior. The property was widely known around town for the popular Tip Top Tap lounge; it's long gone, but its sign still glows from atop the building. Further tribute is paid in the name of Taps on Two, which serves breakfast, lunch, dinner and, during the evening happy hour, free appetisers.

Bar. Business centre. CD. Concierge. Disabled-adapted rooms. DVD. Gym. High-speed internet ($9.95 wireless). Parking ($40). Pool. Restaurant. Room service. Spa.

Chicago Marriott

540 N Michigan Avenue, at E Ohio Street, IL 60611 (1-800 228 9290/1-312 836 0100/fax 1-312 836 6139/www.marriott.com). El: Red to Grand. **Rates** $199-$509 double; $700-$3,000 suite. **Credit** AmEx, DC, Disc, MC, V. **Map** p326 J10 ㉗

With 46 storeys, 1,192 rooms and loads of meeting space, this Magnificent Mile monster is the antithesis of the boutique hotel. Indeed, its massive lobby is more reminiscent of a railway station, albeit a plush one with bright lights, comfortable seats and a bar to tempt thirsty travellers who use the space as a short cut between Michigan Avenue and Rush Street. A recent $15 million renovation injected some much-needed flair into the formerly boring rooms.

Bar. Business centre. CD. Concierge. Disabled-adapted rooms. Gym. High-speed internet ($14.95 via cable in rooms). Parking ($26/$35). Pool. Restaurant. Room service. Spa.

Conrad Chicago

521 N Rush Street, at E Ohio Street, IL 60611 (1-312 645 1500/fax 1-312 645 1550/www.conrad hotels.com). El: Red to Grand. **Rates** $275-$375 double; $575-$1,200 suite. **Credit** AmEx, DC, Disc, MC, V. **Map** p326 J10 ㉘

Shopaholics will appreciate the location of this 311-room, Hilton-operated player, perched above the high-end shops at North Bridge mall. Each guest-room is decked out with a 42-inch flat-screen TV, a state-of-the-art sound system and 500-thread-count Pratesi linens; guests get to choose their pillows from an extensive menu. In warm weather, kick back on the smart outdoor couches on the hotel's terrace, while sipping a cocktail or tucking into some tapas. Classic Hollywood flicks play in the background on Sunday and Monday nights. **Photo** *p65.*

Bars (2). Business centre. CD. Concierge. Disabled-adapted rooms. DVD. Gym. High-speed internet (free wireless). Parking ($29/$40). Restaurants (3). Room service.

InterContinental Chicago

505 N Michigan Avenue, at E Grand Avenue, IL 60611 (1-800 972 2492/1-312 944 4100/fax 1-312 944 1320/www.chicago.intercontinental.com). El: Red to Grand. **Rates** $189-$449 double; $369-$2,500 suite. **Credit** AmEx, DC, Disc, MC, V. **Map** p326 J10 ㉙

A dramatic four-storey rotunda greets guests entering this architectural showpiece, which started out in 1929 as the Medinah Athletic Club. The stock market crash put an end to its first incarnation (the opulent pool, where Johnny Weissmuller trained, has survived), before the property reopened in 1944 as a hotel. The concierge hands out audio tours that give listeners the lowdown on the hotel's many architectural styles. But although it hangs on to its history, the hotel is constantly upgrading itself: witness the emergence of contemporary bistro Zest. The 792 guestrooms are luxurious.

Bars (2). Business centre. Concierge. Disabled-adapted rooms. Gym. High-speed internet ($9.95 wireless). Parking ($41). Pool. Restaurant. Room service.

James Chicago

55 E Ontario Street, at N Rush Street, IL 60611 (1-877 526 3755/1-312 337 1000/fax 1-312 337 7217/www.jameshotels.com). El: Red to Grand. **Rates** $229-$489 double; $269-$629 suite. **Credit** AmEx, DC, Disc, MC, V. **Map** p326 H10 ㉚

The most fashionable lodging in the city continues to draw the crowds: to Primehouse David Burke, its all-conquering steakhouse (*see p154*), and to the oft-buzzing J Bar (*see p179*), but also to the surprisingly capacious hotel side of the operation. The 300 sleek, fashionable rooms all come with large-screen TVs, a stereo system and good-sized bathrooms; the roll call of amenities is led by an impressive gym and spa (*see p66* **Bed & backrub**). The location is plum: a block from the shops of Michigan Avenue.

Bar. Business centre. CD. Concierge. Disabled-adapted rooms. DVD. Gym. High-speed internet (free wireless). Parking ($32/$40). Restaurant. Room service. Spa.

Sheraton Chicago Hotel & Towers

301 E North Water Street, at N Columbus Drive, IL 60611 (1-877 242 2558/1-312 464 1000/fax 1-312 464 9140/www.sheratonchicago.com). El: Red to Grand. **Rates** $199-$419 double; $599-$899 suite. **Credit** AmEx, DC, Disc, MC, V. **Map** p326 J11 ㉛

This darling of the convention circuit is an absolute behemoth, boasting 1,209 rooms and the largest hotel ballroom in the Midwest. An equally spacious lobby with imported marble and rich wood accents has huge picture windows overlooking the river, making it a sedate spot in which to sip a cup of coffee from the Java Bar. For something stronger, head to stylish Chibar, which has views of the Centennial Fountain that throws arcs of water across the river in summer. The aquatic theme continues with the lobby's quiet, perpetual waterfalls in black granite.
Bar. Business centre. Concierge. Disabled-adapted rooms. Gym. High-speed internet ($10 wireless). Parking ($23/$36). Pool. Restaurants (3). Room service.

W Chicago Lakeshore

644 N Lake Shore Drive, at E Ohio Street, IL 60611 (1-877 946 8357/1-312 943 9200/fax 1-312 255 4411/www.starwoodhotels.com). El: Red to Grand. **Rates** $229-$429 double; $499-$700 suite. **Credit** AmEx, DC, Disc, MC, V. **Map** p326 K10 **32**
The city's second W hotel has come a long way from its previous incarnation as a Days Inn. At these prices, so it should have. If you've stayed at a W before, the cool vibe and the sleek, casually expensive decor will be familiar. Some of the 520 guestrooms, featuring teak furniture and dark red accents, look out on to Lake Michigan. An indoor pool adjoins the outdoor sundeck, and the new Bliss Spa (*see p66* **Bed & backrub**) provides pampering from head to toe. The Asian-influenced look has the young urban professional crowd swarming to both its lobby bar and lofty lounge, Whiskey Sky.
Bars (2). Business centre. CD. Concierge. Disabled-adapted rooms. DVD. Gym. High-speed internet ($14.95 via cable in rooms). Parking ($41). Pool. Restaurant. Room service. Spa.

Moderate

Courtyard by Marriott

165 E Ontario Street, at N St Clair Street (1-800 321-2211/1-312 573 0800/fax 1-312 573 0573/ www.marriott.com). El: Red to Grand. **Rates** $199-$309 double; $229-$439 suite. **Credit** AmEx, DC, Disc, MC, V. **Map** p326 J10 **33**
While other Streeterville hotels have been painstakingly renovated of late, this surprisingly sleek 24-storey property was recently built from scratch to recall the art deco style of 1930s Michigan Avenue. The lobby features warm crimsons and cherry wood accented with granite and brushed chrome, as well as a chandelier of fluted blown-glass tubes. Free high-speed internet access is standard in all 306 rooms; guests can also request a microwave or tiny fridge if their room doesn't already have them. Just off the lobby, Viand is a contemporary American brasserie with a friendly bar.
Bar. Business centre. Concierge. Disabled-adapted rooms. Gym. High-speed internet (free via cable in rooms). Parking ($26/$36). Pool. Restaurant. Room service.

Embassy Suites Chicago Downtown Lakefront

511 N Columbus Drive, at E Ohio Street, IL 60611 (1-888 903 8884/1-312 836 5900/fax 1-312 423 6300/www.chicagoembassy.com). El: Red to Grand. **Rates** $129-$459 suite. **Credit** AmEx, DC, Disc, MC, V. **Map** p326 J10 **34**
A signature atrium, soaring 15 storeys high, lends a wide-open feel to this all-suites hotel, which ups the drama with the lobby's waterfall and reflective pool. Room rates include cooked-to-order breakfasts and complimentary early evening cocktails. Stretch your budget further by taking advantage of the suite's tiny 'kitchen' that consists of a mini-fridge and a microwave. On weekdays, the hotel is popular with business travellers and those who oversee their expense accounts; on weekends, economy-minded families take over.
Sister property the Embassy Suites Chicago Downtown (600 N State Street, at E Ohio Street, 1-800 362 1779, 1-312 943 3800) recently underwent a major remodelling programme. While still not quite as swish as the lakefront operation, it offers serviceable accommodation at similar prices, and also boasts a pool and fitness centre.
Bar. Business centre. Concierge. Disabled-adapted rooms. Gym. High-speed internet ($9.95 wireless). Parking ($34/$39). Pool. Restaurant. Room service.

Fairfield Inn & Suites

216 E Ontario Street, at N St Clair Street, IL 60611 (1-800 228 2800/1-312 787 3777/fax 1-312 787 8714/www.fairfieldsuiteschicago.com). El: Red to Grand. **Rates** $99-$329 double; $139-$539 suite. **Credit** AmEx, DC, Disc, MC, V. **Map** p326 J10 **35**
The minimalist lobby at this flagship Fairfield hotel on Ontario Street proves that wallet-friendly hotels don't need to skimp on style. A cheerfully bright common room with a flat-screen TV hosts the complimentary breakfast, which features hot waffles and oatmeal. In addition to the 159 respectable (if not exactly character-packed) rooms, the hotel offers 26 suites containing microwaves, 32-inch TVs and CD systems. Suites are an especially good buy if you snag one at the low end.
Business centre. CD. Disabled-adapted rooms. Gym. High-speed internet (free via cable in rooms). Parking ($26/$38). Room service.

Budget

Red Roof Inn

162 E Ontario Street, at N St Clair Street, IL 60611 (1-800 733 7663/1-312 787 3580/fax 1-312 787 1299/www.redroof-chicago-downtown. com). El: Red to Grand. **Rates** $109-$129 double; $129-$149 suite. **Credit** AmEx, DC, Disc, MC, V. **Map** p326 J10 **36**
You'll usually find this economy lodging chain along the nation's highways or in the far-flung suburbs. But here's one in the heart of the city: just a block east of fashionable Boul Mich, in the shell of a what was once a French-owned boutique hotel. As a nod

Conrad Chicago. See p63.

to style – and perhaps to its antecedents – it may well be the only Red Roof Inn with chandeliers in the lobby. Renovated in 2001, the rooms are clean, comfortable, cheap and devoid of any individuality. Adjoining the hotel is the Coco Pazzo Café, a branch of the fine Coco Pazzo mini-chain.
Bar. Disabled-adapted rooms. High-speed internet ($9.99 wireless). Parking ($33). Restaurant.

The Gold Coast

Deluxe

Drake

140 E Walton Place, at N Michigan Avenue, IL 60611 (1-800 553 7253/1-312 787 2200/fax 1-312 787 1431/www.thedrakehotel.com). El: Red to Chicago. **Rates** $209-$389 double; $329-$449 suite. **Credit** AmEx, DC, Disc, MC, V. **Map** p326 J9 ③⑦
A traditional 'old money' stomping ground favoured by Chicago socialites, this stately icon exudes old-school style, with velvet seats in elevators, bowls of fresh fruit lining the check-in desk, enormous chandeliers and a spectacular flower arrangement in the picturesque lobby. Staying in one of the 535 graceful guestrooms, which have been accommodating celebrities and heads of state since 1920, feels a bit like crashing a rich aunt's downtown condo. The decor is upmarket but slightly passé; some parts of the hotel are a bit tired, despite a $45-million renovation in 2003. Still, the classic Palm Court remains a wonderful setting for high tea.

Bars (4). Business centre. CD. Concierge. Disabled-adapted rooms. Gym. High-speed internet ($12.99 wireless in public spaces; $11.40 via cable in rooms). Parking ($25/$41). Restaurants (4). Room service.

Four Seasons

120 E Delaware Place, at N Michigan Avenue, IL 60611 (1-800 332 3442/1-312 280 8800/fax 1-312 280 1748/www.fourseasons.com). El: Red to Chicago. **Rates** $480-$680 double; $680-$3,500 suite. **Credit** AmEx, DC, Disc, MC, V. **Map** p326 J9 ③⑧
You can practically smell the money at this opulent hotel. The public spaces are decked out with Italian marble, glittering crystal and exquisite woodwork; rooms and suites come with classy furnishings, high-end toiletries and twice-daily maid service. Those in search of edibles and potables will find ample refreshment at Seasons, a clubby cigar bar and lounge with a companionable fireplace, a waterfall and views of the Magnificent Mile. The swimming pool is covered by a skylight and surrounded by Romanesque columns.
Bar. Business centre. CD. Concierge. Disabled-adapted rooms. DVD. Gym. High-speed internet (free wireless in public spaces & via cable in rooms). Parking ($25/$40). Pool. Restaurants (3). Room service. Spa.

Ritz-Carlton Chicago

160 E Pearson Street, at N Michigan Avenue, IL 60611 (1-800 621 6906/1-312 266 1000/fax 1-312 266 1194/www.fourseasons.com/chicagorc). El: Red to Chicago. **Rates** $480-$615 double; $645-$2,500 suite. **Credit** AmEx, DC, Disc, MC, V. **Map** p326 J9 ③⑨

The Ritz-Carlton has a team of seasoned staff who will deliver anything from shoelaces to saline solution 24 hours a day. The lavish lobby is a soothing place, with a massive skylight and fountain. The 435 richly appointed rooms take up the top 15 floors of Water Tower Place and come with high ceilings, marble bathrooms and picture windows. The Spa at the Carlton Club (*see below* **Bed & backrub**) offers more than 25 treatments; the four-star Dining Room (*see p155*) is one of the best restaurants in town.

Bar. Business centre. CD. Concierge. Disabled-adapted rooms. DVD. Gym. High-speed internet (free wireless). Parking ($19-$40). Pool. Restaurants (3). Room service. Spa.

Sofitel Chicago Water Tower

20 E Chestnut Street, at N Wabash Avenue, IL 60611 (1-877 813 7700/1-312 324 4000/fax 1-312 324 4026/www.sofitel.com). El: Red to Chicago. **Rates** $225-$440 double; $355-$675 suite. **Credit** AmEx, DC, Disc, MC, V. **Map** p326 H9 ⑩

Bed & backrub

There are masses of museums, an enviable shopping scene and seemingly limitless cultural opportunities in Chicago. But the ever more luxurious array of amenities laid on by the city's hotels are making it increasingly difficult for visitors to get out and explore them.

According to *Condé Nast Traveler*'s most recent survey, three of the country's top five urban spas are clustered within a few blocks of each other close by Michigan Avenue. And they have plenty of competition: every hotel worth its salt seems to be adding a spa to its range of amenities. Here are five of the best hotel spas in the city.

The Peninsula (*see p62*) recently spent $1 million renovating its award-winning facility, which is perched on the hotel's top two floors. The 15,000-square foot (1,400-square metre) **Peninsula Spa** now features a pair of private treatment suites that can accommodate couples, as well as a new relaxation area (christened the Quiet Zone) that overlooks the indoor swimming pool (*pictured*). Asian-inspired treatments, such as the Japanese mint aromatherapy wrap, dominate the spa's extensive and expensive menu of treatments.

The **Spa at the Ritz-Carlton Chicago** (*see p65*), open only to hotel guests and private members, is hardly any less impressive than its near-neighbour. Prepare to be doted on at this tranquil spot, where the treats on offer include herbal and mineral wraps, facials and nail care, as well as in-room massages and indulgent baths.

Also on the Gold Coast, the **Spa at the Four Seasons** (*see p65*) exudes an old-money, sophisticated vibe, right down to the menu of treatments that includes a rose petal wrap for tired tootsies and a Perle de Caviar facial. After your skin has been revitalised, you can top off the experience with a split of champagne and a caviar canapé.

Don't expect any carrot sticks and cheesy new-age music at the W Chicago Lakeshore's **Bliss Spa** (*see p64*), the first Midwest outpost of this New York enterprise. This ultra-modern relaxation oasis is all about having fun: you can even watch *Sex and the City* re-runs on your personal flat-screen TV at one of the four movie-while-you-manicure stations. Check in early so you have plenty of time to load up at the sinful brownie buffet, served in the comfortable eighth-floor lounge.

Most recently, the relatively small **Spa at the James Chicago** (*see p63*) has proved a big hit with locals looking for a little pick-me-up over their lunch breaks. The popular mini-menu at the hipster haven features massages, nail treatments and facials that take 30 minutes or less.

The radical prism-shaped design of this 32-storey building by French architect Jean-Paul Viguier is a striking addition to the Chicago skyline. The hotel opened in a plum Gold Coast location in 2002, with 415 sleekly designed rooms featuring spacious marble bathrooms. As French as the croissants baked daily on the premises, the Sofitel offers haute cuisine in a cool, modern setting at the stylish Café des Architectes. Meanwhile, staff at Le Bar (*see p179*) pour killer Martinis and serve them with complimentary dishes of olives and snacks.
Bars (2). Business centre. CD. Concierge. Disabled-adapted rooms. Gym. High-speed internet ($9.99 wireless). Parking ($39). Restaurant. Room service. Spa.

Expensive

Hilton Suites
198 E Delaware Place, at N Mies van der Rohe Way, IL 60611 (1 800 445 8667/1-312 664 1100/fax 1-312 664 9881/www.hilton.com). El: Red to Chicago. **Rates** $289-$1,000 suite. **Credit** AmEx, DC, Disc, MC, V. **Map** p326 J9 ⁣④
Freshly baked cookies at check-in make for a warm welcome at this all-suites hotel in the shadow of the Hancock Center. The modern, comfortable suites feature a separate 'parlour' and a convertible sofa. As you climb out of the indoor pool on the 30th floor, huge windows reveal a larger body of water, Lake Michigan, stretching toward the horizon. The higher rooms on the lakeside have similarly enviable views.
Bars (2). Business centre. Concierge. Disabled-adapted rooms. Gym. High-speed internet ($9.95 wireless). Parking ($40). Pool. Restaurant. Room service.

Hotel Indigo
1244 N Dearborn Parkway, at W Goethe Street, IL 60610 (1-800 972 2494/1-312 787 4980/fax 1-312 787 4069/www.ichotelsgroup.com). El: Red to Clark/Division. **Rates** $159-$379 double; $499-$699 suite. **Credit** AmEx, DC, Disc, MC, V. **Map** p327 H8 ④
Original artwork from Chicago neo-Impressionist Bill Olendorf is the only remnant held over from the recent renovation of this 1929 property, formerly known as the Claridge. Whimsical wall murals, hardwood floors and a bold colour palette make for a refreshing change from standard hotel decor. The colourful, cheery tone is set by the inviting lobby, filled with well-stuffed chairs. The well-equipped fitness centre and window-front bar (serving sangria and tapas) are further bonuses. **Photo** *p68*.
Bar. Business centre. CD. Concierge. Disabled-adapted rooms. DVD. Gym. High-speed internet (free wireless). Parking ($35). Restaurant. Room service. Spa.

Millennium Knickerbocker
163 E Walton Place, at N Michigan Avenue, IL 60611 (1-866 866 8086/1-312 751 8100/fax 1-312 751 9205/www.millenniumhotels.com). El: Red to Chicago. **Rates** $139-$369 double; $369-$1,000 suite. **Credit** AmEx, DC, Disc, MC, V. **Map** p326 J9 ④

Formerly Hugh Hefner's swinging Playboy Towers, this regal property now caters to a more refined crowd. Guests and locals populate the renovated two-storey lobby bar, which has a jazz piano soundtrack and a choice of more than 50 Martinis. As of early 2007, bathrooms were being upgraded in a bid to keep the historic property up to speed: the small tubs are to be replaced with walk-in showers, and flat-screen TVs were also being added to the rooms.
Bar. Business centre. CD. Concierge. Disabled-adapted rooms. Gym. High-speed internet ($2.99/hr wireless in public spaces; $9.95 via cable in rooms). Parking ($40). Restaurant. Room service.

Raffaello
201 E Delaware Place, at N Seneca Street, IL 60611 (1-800 983 7870/1-312 943 5000/fax 1-312 601 8260/www.chicagoraffaello.com). El: Red to Chicago. **Rates** $229-$399 double; $279-$479 suite. **Credit** AmEx, DC, Disc, MC, V. **Map** p326 J9 ④
A $20-million renovation of this landmark building in Streeterville has improved things enormously. The old Raphael Hotel was looking a bit tired by the time it closed in 2005; its replacement is rather more eye-catching. The opulent lobby has Mediterranean touches, and there's a hydroponic garden on the green roof. In between, the spacious guestrooms come with 500-thread-count bedding. An organic spa and restaurant are among the appealing extras.
Business centre. CD. Disabled-adapted rooms. DVD. Gym. High-speed internet ($9.95 wireless). Parking ($40). Restaurant. Room service. Spa.

Sutton Place
21 E Bellevue Place, at N Rush Street, IL 60611 (1-866 378 8866/1-312 266 2100/fax 1-312 266 2141/www.suttonplace.com). El: Red to Clark/Division. **Rates** $179-$499 double; $329-$649 suite. **Credit** AmEx, DC, MC, V. **Map** p326 H9 ④
This 246-room hotel is unabashedly modern, with its original Robert Mapplethorpe photos, soft lighting and modish furniture. The classy detailing extends to each of the 246 guestrooms, appointed with DVD players, CD collections, deep-soaking tubs and fluffy robes. Six penthouse suites have floor-to-ceiling windows and private balconies, offering a great vantage point from which to spy on Gold Coasters as they shop away the day and party by night. Guests won't need to go far to party themselves: downstairs sits the Whiskey Bar & Grill.
Business centre. CD. Concierge. Disabled-adapted rooms. DVD. Gym. High-speed internet ($9.95 wireless). Parking ($39). Restaurant. Room service.

Talbott Hotel
20 E Delaware Place, at N Rush Street, IL 60611 (1-800 825 2688/1-312 944 4970/fax 1-312 944 7241/www.talbotthotel.com). El: Red to Chicago. **Rates** $179-$499 double; $329-$649 suite. **Credit** AmEx, DC, Disc, MC, V. **Map** p326 J9 ④
Quite possibly the only hotel in the world with a life-sized cow mounted on its frontage (a remnant of the city's bovine-themed public art display a few years back), this boutique hotel is reminiscent of a small,

All things bright and beautiful: the artsy **Hotel Indigo**. *See p67.*

upmarket European inn. The classically furnished guestrooms (with canopied beds) and the granite and marble lobby were treated to a massive renovation in 2006. Guests get complimentary passes to a nearby health club. The showpiece at Basil's, a 45-seat lounge, is a 19th-century walnut bar.
Bar. Business centre. CD. Concierge. Disabled-adapted rooms. High-speed internet (free wireless). Parking ($36). Restaurant. Room service.

Westin

909 N Michigan Avenue, at E Delaware Place, IL 60611 (1-800 228 3000/1-312 943 7200/fax 1-312 397 5580/www.westin.com). El: Red to Chicago. **Rates** $229-$489 double; $499-$2,500 suite. **Credit** AmEx, DC, Disc, MC, V. **Map** p326 J9 ⑰
Hotels are basically in the business of selling sleep. Acknowledging this, the nationwide Westin group equips its hotel rooms with what it calls the Heavenly Bed, designed to encourage zzzzs. By and large, it lives up to its name. The 751 guestrooms include 23 suites. Steaks and seafood are served up in the 300-seat Grill on the Alley. The other Westin in Chicago, the Westin River North (320 N Dearborn Street, 1-800 937 8461, 1-312 744 1900), offers fine business services.
Bar. Business centre. Concierge. Disabled-adapted rooms. Gym. High-speed internet (free wireless in public spaces; $12.95 first day/$6 additional days via cable in rooms). Parking ($41). Room service. Spa.

Moderate

Gold Coast Guest House

113 W Elm Street, at N Clark Street, IL60610 (1-312 337 0361/fax 1-312 337 0362/www.bb chicago.com). El: Red to Clark/Division. **Rates** $129-$229 double. **Credit** AmEx, Disc, MC, V. **Map** p326 H9 ⑱
Housed in a 19th-century Victorian townhouse (built just after the Great Fire had ravaged the town), this B&B is a welcome oasis of good-value accommodation in a swanky neighbourhood. Sally, the friendly owner, is happy to chat with guests over a glass of wine in the lush garden. Be sure to book ahead, as there are only four guestrooms. Guests looking for more privacy and longer stays should ask about Sally's nearby studios and one-bedroom apartments.
Business centre. CD. DVD. High-speed internet (free wireless). Parking ($25).

Seneca

200 E Chestnut Street, at N Mies van der Rohe Way, IL 60611 (1-312 988 4438/www.senecahotel.com). El: Red to Chicago. **Rates** $99-$249 double; $109-$289 suite. **Credit** AmEx, DC, Disc, MC, V. **Map** p326 J9 ⑱
Don't let the doorman and classical music in the tastefully elegant lobby fool you: the Seneca's prices are refreshingly low for this part of town. The hotel's deluxe one-bedroom suites arguably represent the

best value of the hotel's 270 rooms, which once made up a residential hotel in this 1924 building. The adjacent Saloon steakhouse is popular.
Bars (2). Disabled-adapted rooms. Gym. High-speed internet (free wireless). Parking ($40). Restaurants (3). Spa.

Whitehall Hotel

105 E Delaware Place, at N Michigan Avenue, IL 60611 (1-800 948 4255/1-312 944 6300/fax 1-312 944 8552/www.thewhitehallhotel.com). El: Red to Chicago. **Credit** AmEx, DC, Disc, MC, V. **Map** p326 J9 ⑤⓪
The 222-room Whitehall occupies a landmark building, developed in 1928 to house luxury apartments. The panelled lobby retains its clubby English look, while a stylish Italian eaterie, Fornetto Mei, has supplanted the private dining club that used to be here. Its sidewalk atrium is a great place for people-watching in this moneyed neighbourhood. The rooms feature mahogany furniture and Chippendale desks. Guests in the Pinnacle level rooms get complimentary car service within a two-mile radius.
Bar. Business centre. Concierge. Disabled-adapted rooms. Gym. High-speed internet ($9.95 wireless in public spaces & via cable in rooms). Parking ($39). Restaurant. Room service.

Old Town & Lincoln Park

Lincoln Park

Budget

Days Inn Lincoln Park

644 W Diversey Parkway, at N Clark Street, IL 60614 (1-888 576 3297/1-773 525 7010/fax 1-773 525 6998/www.lpndaysinn.com). El: Brown or Purple to Diversey. **Rates** $110-$156 double; $145-$260 suite. **Credit** AmEx, DC, Disc, MC, V. **Map** p328 F4 ⑤①
This notch in the ever-expanding Days Inn belt is no more (or less) characterful than their other gazillion hotels around the world. However, it has one great advantage: a plum location at the busy intersection of Broadway, Clark and Diversey, on the cusp of Lincoln Park and Lakeview. The rooms aren't anything special, but they are clean and, given the competition, good value for money. Continental breakfast is served in a comfortable sitting area; the hotel also offers complimentary admission to the Bally's health club next door.
Disabled-adapted rooms. Gym. High-speed internet (free wireless). Parking ($20).

Windy City Urban Inn

607 W Deming Place, at N Clark Street, IL 60614 (1-877 897 7091/1-773 248 7091/fax 1-773 529 4183/www.windycityinn.com). Bus 22, 36. **Rates** $125-$185 double; $195-$325 suite. **Credit** AmEx, DC, Disc, MC, V. **Map** p328 F4 ⑤②

Visitors will find a home away from home at this Victorian mansion owned by local TV newsman Andy Shaw and his wife Mary. Tucked away on a quiet, leafy street in Lincoln Park, the five cosy guestrooms and three apartments (in the neighbouring coach house; there may be a minimum-stay requirement at busy times) are themed on and named after local writers, from the tough-talking Nelson Algren to the more demure Gwendolyn Brooks. Continuing the literary theme, the B&B boasts an extensive selection of Chicago literature: guests are invited to grab a book and a glass of sherry and lounge in the ivy-covered garden or snuggle up by the fireplace.
Business centre. Concierge. DVD. High-speed internet (free wireless). Parking ($12).

Hostels

Travelling on a budget? No problem. Chicago has a number of hostels that offer a welcome alternative to the city's often expensive hotels. Amenities vary at the quartet listed below, but all offer a mix of dorm accommodation and private rooms. Book ahead, especially at the HI-Chicago hostel in the Loop.

Arlington International House

616 W Arlington Place, at N Geneva Terrace, Lincoln Park, IL 60614 (1-800 467 8355/1-773 929 5380/ fax 1-773 665 5485/www.arlingtonhouse. com). El: Brown, Purple or Red to Fullerton. **Rates** $29-$74. **Credit** MC, V. **Map** p328 F5.

Chicago International Hostel

6318 N Winthrop Avenue, at W Rosemont Avenue, North Side, IL 60660 (1-773 262 1011/fax 1-773 262 3632/www.hostel inchicago.com). El: Red to Loyola. **Rates** $35-$81. **Credit** AmEx, Disc, MC, V.

HI-Chicago

24 E Congress Parkway, at S State Street, the Loop, IL 60605 (1-312 360 0300/ fax 1-312 360 0313/www.hichicago.org). El: Blue or Red to Jackson; Brown, Green, Orange, Pink or Purple to Library. **Rates** $31. **Credit** MC, V. **Map** p325 H13.

International House of Chicago

1414 E 59th Street, at S Dorchester Avenue, Hyde Park, IL 60637 (1-773 753 2270/fax 1-773 753 1227/ http://ihouse.uchicago.edu). Metra: 55th-56th-57th Street. **Rates** $52-$120. **Credit** MC, V. **Map** p332 Y18.

Lakeview & Around

Budget

City Suites

933 W Belmont Avenue, at N Sheffield Avenue,
IL 60657 (1-800 248 9108/1-773 404 3400/fax
1-773 404 3405/www.cityinns.com). El: Brown,
Purple or Red to Belmont. **Rates** $139-$239 double;
$159-$349 suite. **Credit** AmEx, DC, Disc, MC, V.
Map p329 E3 ⏺

This 45-room boutique hotel in a part-gentrified,
part-bohemian neighbourhood is right next to the
Belmont El station, from where it's a mere 15-minute
train ride to downtown. Walk four blocks north,
meanwhile, and you'll be at Wrigley Field. The hotel
itself has an appealing art deco feel, and its spotless
suites include a sleeper sofa, an armchair and a
spacious workstation. A continental breakfast is
included, but Ann Sather and its peerless Swedish
pancakes and cinnamon rolls are temptingly close.
Concierge. High-speed internet ($9.95 wireless).
Parking ($18).

Majestic

528 W Brompton Avenue, at N Lake Shore Drive,
IL 60657 (1-800 727 5108/1-773 404 3499/
fax 1-773 404 3495/www.cityinns.com). Bus
145, 146, 151. **Rates** $89-$399 double; $120-
$499 suite. **Credit** AmEx, DC, Disc, MC, V.
Map p329 G1 ⏺

Set on a quiet, tree-lined residential street within
walking distance of the delightful Lincoln Park Zoo,
the Majestic is housed in a building dating from the
1920s, and offers 29 rooms and 23 suites fitted out
with microwaves and wet bars. It's not especially
handy for the El, but buses along nearby Lake Shore
Drive get you to the Magnificent Mile in about 15
minutes. As with its sister properties City Suites and
the Willows, guests are greeted each morning with
a complimentary breakfast.
Business centre. Concierge. High-speed internet
($9.95 wireless). Parking ($22).

Willows

555 W Surf Street, at N Broadway, IL 60657 (1-800
787 3108/1-773 528 8400/fax 1-773 528 8483/
www.cityinns.com). El: Brown or Purple to Diversey.
Rates $119-$199 double; $139-$289 suite. **Credit**
AmEx, DC, Disc, MC, V. **Map** p328 F4 ⏺

This quaint, 55-room hotel near the busy intersection of Clark and Diversey has an old-fashioned
French country feel. Fans of minor hotel curiosities
(and, for that matter, of vintage private-eye movies)
will enjoy riding in the original 1920s Otis elevator,
creaks and all. Room rates include a continental
breakfast and complimentary cookies every afternoon at 4pm. Good value.
Concierge. High-speed internet ($9.95 wireless).
Parking ($22).

Wicker Park & Around

Budget

House of Two Urns B&B

1239 N Greenview Avenue, at W Division Street, IL
60622 (1-877 896 8767/1-773 235 1408/fax 1-773
235 1410/www.twourns.com). El: Blue to Division.
Rates $109-$159 double; $139-$179 suite. **Credit**
Disc, MC, V. **Map** p331 D8 ⏺

Wicker Park's reputation as a quirky, artistic enclave
fits perfectly with this friendly, off-beat B&B. Named
after the urn motif found in the stained-glass window and façade of this 1912 brownstone, the Two
Urns has four rooms with eccentric themes such as
European antique plates or the tale of the princess
and the pea. Some rooms have shared baths. Sweet
smells still fill this former Polish bakery in the morning, when the owner whips up a full breakfast for
guests. Those looking for more privacy can book one
of three apartments across the street.
Business centre. CD. Concierge. DVD. High-speed
internet (free wireless). Parking (free).

Ray's Bucktown B&B

2144 N Leavitt Street, at W Webster Avenue, IL
60622 (1-800 355 2324/1-773 384 3245/www.rays
bucktownbandb.com). El: Blue to Western. **Rates**
$139-$169 double. **Credit** AmEx, Disc, MC, V.
Map p331 B5 ⏺

Sitting several worlds away from B&B's traditionally chintzy image, Ray Reiss's Bucktown operation
is a bed-and-breakfast for the 21st century. The
rooms are crisp, fresh and modern, and the facilities
are awesome: aside from Wi-Fi throughout the building, rooms have TiVo-equipped televisions, and
there's even a photographic studio available to rent.
A two-night minimum is usually in effect, though
single-night stays can sometimes be accommodated.
High-speed internet (free wireless & via cable in rooms).

Wicker Park Inn

1329 N Wicker Park Avenue, at W Wolcott Avenue
IL 60622 (1-773 486 2743/fax 1-773 278 3802/
www.wickerparkinn.com). El: Blue to Damen.
Rates $115-$185 double. **Credit** AmEx, DC, MC, V.
Map p331 C8 ⏺

You won't find the usual frilly curtains and old-fashioned furniture at this modern B&B, located on a
tree-lined street of turn-of-the-century row houses in
the city's hippest 'hood. The popular property
recently doubled its number of guestrooms to seven,
each with private baths, televisions and free wireless internet access. Wake up to a shot of espresso
and a continental breakfast buffet brought in fresh
from a nearby bakery.
High-speed internet (free wireless). Parking (free).

Sightseeing

Introduction	**72**
The Loop	**75**
The South Loop & Chinatown	**87**
The Near North Side	**95**
Old Town & Lincoln Park	**106**
Lakeview & Around	**112**
The North Shore	**116**
The Near West Side	**119**
Wicker Park & Around	**126**
Oak Park	**131**
The South Side	**135**

Features

Top ten Things to do	72
The city in brief	73
We'll always have Paris	79
Out of print	80
Walk Art for art's sake	84
Walk Chinese whispers	92
Beachy keen	102
Easy riders	111
Talkin' all that jazz	114
Walk Painting on Pilsen	124
Ablution solution	127
Wright on	132
Walk Back to school	140

Crown Fountain. *See p77.*

Introduction

Our kind of town.

Its buildings range from historic landmarks to modern masterpieces. Its world-class museums explore everything from history to holography, African-American culture to the natural world. The restaurants and shops cover every budget and taste. In short, you won't come up short of things to do in this most visitor-friendly of cities.

If you plan to visit several sights, consider the **Citypass**. For $49.50 ($39 3-11s), bearers gain entry to the Adler Planetarium, the Field Museum, the Shedd Aquarium, the Museum of Science & Industry (including the Omnimax) and the Hancock Center. (Note: some of these museums are free on Mondays and/or Tuesdays in winter.) You can buy a Citypass at any of these sights. For more, see www.citypass.com.

Top ten Things to do

Build up the city
... with one of the **Chicago Architecture Foundation**'s numerous tours. *See right.*

Catch a home run ball
... at **Wrigley Field**. *See p272.*

Get out of town
... and beyond the tourist trail on a **Chicago Greeter** neighbourhood tour. *See right.*

Go back in time
... at the **Chicago History Museum**. *See p108.*

Learn a little
... at **Museum Campus**. *See pp87-90.*

Look down on the locals
... from the **John Hancock Center**. *See p98.*

Loop the Loop
... with an amble or an El ride around downtown's buzzing hub. *See pp75-86.*

Picture this
... at the **Art Institute of Chicago**. *See p78.*

Take to the lake
... along the **Lakefront Trail**. *See p111.*

Talk to the animals
... at the bijou **Lincoln Park Zoo**. *See p109.*

ORIENTATION
Ground zero is at the corner of Madison and State Streets. Addresses on north–south streets are numbered according to how many blocks north or south of Madison they sit; the same is true of east–west roads and State Street. Addresses increase by 100 for each block with the exception of Downtown, where block size varies. Generally, a street number range of 800 corresponds to a mile; for example, it's two miles between 1 N Clark Street and 1601 N Clark Street. For public transit, *see pp300-302.* For a map of local neighbourhoods, *see p336.*

Tours

Bobby's Bike Hike
1-312 915 0995/www.bobbysbikehike.com. **Tours** *Late May-early Sept* 10am, 1.30pm, 7pm daily. *Apr-late May, early Sept-Nov* 10am, 1.30pm Mon-Fri, Sun; 10am, 1.30pm, 7pm Sat. **Tickets** $25-$35; $15-$28 discounts. **Credit** AmEx, MC, V.
Bobby's runs a nice selection of bike tours, centred on downtown but also exploring the quiet streets of Old Town, the inviting Lincoln Park and the gorgeous lakefront. None of the tours is strenuous; on a nice day, there's no better way to explore the city than by bike. Tours leave from a central location (call or check online for details and directions); rates include bike hire. Bobby's also offers keenly priced bike rentals ($15-$20/half-day, $20-$25/day).

Chicago Architecture Foundation
Information 1-312 922 3432/tickets 1-312 902 1500/ www.architecture.org. **Tours** times vary. **Tickets** prices vary. **Credit** AmEx, DC, Disc, MC, V.
Chicago's architecture gets the boosters it deserves with the excellent CAF. The most popular tour is the Architecture River Cruise ($27), the best of the city's water tours, but other itineraries take in everything from modern skyscrapers to quiet 'hoods, and are conducted on foot, by coach and by bike. Advance booking isn't available for all tours, but it is recommended for the River Cruise; snag tickets by phone, online, from the CAF's ArchiCenter (*see p80*), or from Hot Tix in the Water Works (*see p278*).

Chicago Greeter
1-312 744 8000/www.chicagogreeter.com. **Tours** 10am, 1pm daily. *InstaGreeter* 10am-4pm Fri, Sat; 11am-4pm Sun. **Tickets** free.
See the city through the eyes of volunteer locals, who guide guests through their neighbourhood with personal anecdotes. Some tours focus on downtown, but it's a great way to experience off-the-beaten-track but

The city in brief

THE LOOP
The financial centre of Chicago stretches south and east of the river as far Congress Parkway. *See pp75-86.*

THE SOUTH LOOP AND CHINATOWN
South of the Loop but north of I-55, this stretch of town includes the attraction-packed **Museum Campus**. *See pp87-94.*

THE NEAR NORTH SIDE
The tourist-packed Near North Side takes in the fast-rising **River North** area; the world-famous shopping of the **Magnificent Mile**; **Streeterville**, where you'll find Navy Pier; and the swanky **Gold Coast**. *See pp95-105.*

OLD TOWN AND LINCOLN PARK
Old Town is a historic residential area. To its east is the southern edge of lengthy **Lincoln Park**, which lends its name to the handsome 'hood that adjoins it. *See pp106-111.*

LAKEVIEW AND AROUND
This lively locale encompasses **Boystown**, Chicago's main gay drag, and **Wrigleyville**, named after Wrigley Field. Slightly further north are residential neighbourhoods such as **Uptown**, **Andersonville** and historic, Teutonic **Lincoln Square**. *See pp112-115.*

THE NORTH SHORE
Beyond the city limits lies a string of smart suburbs, the most interesting of which is **Evanston**. *See pp116-118.*

THE NEAR WEST SIDE
The streets directly west of the Loop, known as the **West Loop** or **River West**, have come up a lot in recent years. Also here are **Greektown**, **Little Italy** and **Pilsen**. *See pp119-125.*

WICKER PARK AND AROUND
Just north of the West Loop sits **Ukrainian Village**, now home to as many hipsters and Mexicans as Eastern Europeans. Directly above it, **Wicker Park** and **Bucktown** hold many of the city's most interesting bars, restaurants and shops. *See pp126-130.*

OAK PARK
This cultured little town is best approached for its preponderance of Frank Lloyd Wright-designed houses. *See pp131-134.*

THE SOUTH SIDE
Several neighbourhoods stand out on Chicago's sprawling South Side, among them collegiate **Hyde Park** and the historic African American area of **Bronzeville**. *See pp135-142.*

fascinating areas such as Ukrainian Village. You need to register seven business days in advance; if not, try the walk-up InstaGreeter tours of the Loop. Tours leave from the Chicago Cultural Center (*see p80*).

Chicago Neighbourhood Tours
1-312 742 1190/www.chicagoneighborhoodtours.com. **Tours** *June-Aug* 10am Thur, Sat. *Sept-May* 10am Sat. **Tickets** $25-$50; $20-$45 discounts. **Credit** AmEx, MC, V.

Leaving from the Chicago Cultural Center (*see p80*), these city-run tours focus on a different neighbourhood each week, with visits to historic sites, museums and even restaurants. The Special Interest tours focus on subjects as diverse as Greek immigration and the city's cemeteries; Thursday's Summertime Sampler takes visitors around three 'hoods in one go.

Chicago Trolley Company
1-773 648 5000/www.chicagotrolley.com. **Tours** *Apr-Oct* 9am-6.30pm (last pick-up 5pm) daily. *Nov-Mar* 9am-5pm (last pick-up 4pm) daily. **Tickets** *1-day* $25; $10-$20 discounts. *2-day* $35; $10-$20 discounts. **Credit** AmEx, DC, Disc, MC, V.

This hop-on/hop-off trawls sights and landmarks in the Loop and on the Near North Side. A route map is available online, where prices are reduced by 10%.

Lake cruises
Countless operators offer cruises on Lake Michigan from Navy Pier, including **Mystic Blue** (1-877 299 7783, www.mysticbluecruises.com) and **Seadog** (1-888 636 7737, www.seadogcruises.com). An alternative is provided by the 150-foot schooner **Windy** (1-312 595 5555, www.tallshipwindy.com).

Loop Tour Train
1-312 744 2400/www.cityofchicago.org. **Tours** *May-Sept* 11.35am, 12.15pm, 12.55pm, 1.35pm Sat. **Tickets** free.

Another city-sponsored programme, the Loop Tour Train uses the elevated train tracks to offer insight into Chicago's business district. Tickets are available on a first-come, first-served basis from 10am on the day from the Chicago Cultural Center (*see p80*).

Untouchables Tour
1-773 881 1195/www.gangstertour.com. **Tours** 10am Mon-Wed; 10am, 1pm Thur, Sun; 10am, 1pm, 7.30pm Fri; 10am, 1pm, 5pm Sat. **Tickets** $25; $19 discounts. **Credit** MC, V.

Kicking off at the Rock 'n' Roll McDonald's (Clark & Ohio Streets), this camp-as-Christmas tour takes wide-eyed tourists to the sites of some of the city's biggest gangster incidents.

LOOK IN THE LOOP
LOOPTOPIA
Chicago's Own All-Night Cultural Celebration
LOOP THE LOOP
Free Downloadable Audio Tours
Featuring the best of the Loop, new and old
THEATER
Most vibrant theater district in the Midwest
Shop / Wine / Dine
Sample retailers from boutique to flagship; international markets, culinary delights and refreshing spirits
www.chicagoloopalliance.com
CHICAGO LOOP ALLIANCE

The Loop

Big business and even bigger buildings in Chicago's central business district.

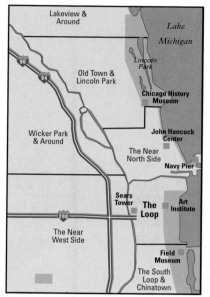

Map p325

El: numerous stations on all lines.

Taking its name from the cable cars that encircled it during its first heyday in the late 19th century, the Loop is the hub around which Chicago revolves. While it's positively soaked in history, it's also undeniably modern, constantly refreshing and regenerating itself in order to keep pace with competing business districts around the US and the globe. During the day, at least, the energy that emanates from it is positively infectious.

The Loop suffered a set-back after World War II, when suburban development accelerated and the area became less essential to everyday Chicago life. But big business kept the area afloat, and the 1980s saw the neighbourhood gradually come back to life as the local economy enjoyed a boom. While it has had its ups and downs in the intervening years, with businesses moving in and out of the area, it has generally held steady ever since, and remains vital to big business in the US.

Less than a decade ago, recreation in the Loop after 5pm was reserved for tourists, confined to the many hotels here, and play-goers, drawn to the handful of grand old picture palaces adapted for modern theatrical use. These days, it's a different story. A cluster of new condominium developments has gone up of late, attracting affluent residents back from the suburbs to the heart of the city. At the same time, high-rise college dormitories have been built, accommodating thousands of students. And that's without mentioning **Millennium Park**, one of the city's most popular attractions almost from the day it opened in 2004. During the warmer months, there are free concerts here more or less nightly, drawing thousands of visitors to a once forlorn part of town.

Commercial enterprises have sprung up to serve these new residents and visitors. Some are simple operations hawking everyday goods: groceries, coffees, office supplies. Others, though, are more interesting: a posh restaurant here, a glamorous hotel bar there. And as more locals move back downtown and real estate grows ever more precious, the Loop's boundaries have been extending. For the chiefly residential South Loop, *see pp87-93*; for the nightlife-heavy West Loop, *see pp119-125*. That said, the Loop's primary purpose remains not residential but commercial, and it's at its most interesting and lively during the day.

For the casual sightseer, many of the Loop's highlights are architectural. While we touch on many in this section, the **Architecture** chapter contains more detail, along with a map of the Loop on which more than 40 of these buildings are marked. For the chapter, *see pp31-40*; for the map, *see p33*.

Millennium Park & Grant Park

Millennium Park

Its name doesn't quite tell the whole story. Conceived and constructed to celebrate the turning of the 21st century, **Millennium Park** eventually opened in 2004, four years behind schedule and more than $300 million over its original budget of $150 million. The 24.5-acre park was dogged by controversy during the run-up to its completion, not least when details

Millennium Park (top) and the Art Institute of Chicago. *See pp75-79.*

of the spectacular budgetary excesses emerged in the local press. How quickly people forget. Almost immediately after opening, Millennium Park became one of the city's most beloved attractions, as much among locals as visitors.

At the north end of the park, which takes as its boundaries Randolph Street, Columbus Drive, Monroe Street and Michigan Avenue, sits **Wrigley Square**, named for the virtually legendary Wrigley family who once all but ruled the city. The square is anchored by a replica of the Greek columns that graced the north-west corner of Grant Park between 1917 and 1953. On it is detailed a lengthy list of 'Millennium Park founders', the city's rather grand way of letting people know who paid for it. ('Millennium Park funders' would have done the job just as well, and saved a few bucks on stonemasonry into the bargain.)

Directly east of Wrigley Square sits the park's **Welcome Center** (201 E Randolph Street, 1-312 742 1168), from where maps and audio guides to the park can be collected. Both are also available for free download at www.millenniumpark.org, which offers a host of resources. Just by the Welcome Center sits the sturdy **Harris Theater for Music & Dance** (see p234); designed by Tom Beeby, it welcomes troupes both conservative and challenging.

Millennium Park's most striking structure sits immediately adjacent to the Harris Theater, and dominates the immediate landscape. Designed by the inimitable Frank Gehry, the **Jay Pritzker Pavilion** (see p252) is a dazzling piece of work, striking steel ribbons curling 35 to 40 feet (ten to 12 metres) into the air above the 60-foot (18-metre) bandstand. That said, it's even more astonishing when it's in use. At the free concerts staged regularly here during the summer, the music is pumped through a state-of-the-art sound system contained within the trellis that lopes over the lawn. There's room for 11,000 people here, 4,000 on fixed seats near the stage and the remainder on the grass.

Gehry also designed the **BP Bridge**, which connects the south-eastern corner of the Pritzker's lawn to **Daley Bicentennial Plaza** across Columbus Drive to the east. It's the only Gehry bridge in existence. Just south of the bridge sit the **Lurie Gardens**, a beautiful 2.5-acre oasis divided into two 'plates' in an attempt to echo the city's history. The dark plate re-creates the lakefront's natural topography of rolling prairie, shade trees and lush, muted vegetation; to the west, the light plate represents the city that emerged after the Chicago Fire, its orderly beds of perennials carefully orchestrated to pay attention to plant progressions and bloom times.

The western and south-western portions of the park are dominated by two pieces of public art. In the south-west corner sits Jaume Plensa's **Crown Fountain**, two 50-foot (15-metre) towers that face each other across a black granite plaza. On to each tower, which between them use 122,000 glass bricks, is projected the face of one of 1,000 Chicagoans. Sporadically, the lips on each face purse tightly, and out shoots a torrent of water. (The water supply is shut down during winter, but the images remain.) It's an agreeably cheeky twist on traditional park fountains.

North of here, and perhaps the park's most popular attraction, is Anish Kapoor's sculpture **Cloud Gate**, popularly known as 'the Bean'. Some 66 feet long and 33 feet high (20 metres by ten metres), the corpuscular structure is constructed of quarter-inch polished stainless steel plates on a steel support skeleton. From a distance, it's sleek, ultramodern and even chilly, but up close, it takes on a kinetic intensity, swimming with reflections of the skyline, shifting clouds, trees and you, the viewer. If you stand beneath the structure and gaze up at its concave underside, the polished surfaces create endless reflections: mirrors of mirrors. Looming over the **McCormick Tribune Ice Rink** (see p277), it's a genuinely thrilling piece of work.

Grant Park

The land on which Millennium Park was constructed was formerly part of **Grant Park**, which stretches south to Roosevelt Road and Museum Campus (see p87). Built on landfill in the 1920s, the park has been overshadowed in the last couple of years by its flashier and more heavily landscaped neighbour to the north, but it remains a handsome place, and a busy one in summer. The Pritzker Pavilion may now be home to the **Grant Park Music Festival**, but other prominent summer events, among them the **Taste of Chicago** (see p217) and the **Chicago Blues Festival** (see p254) remain firmly rooted in Grant Park.

Aside from the **Art Institute of Chicago** (see p78), one of the city's most magnificent buildings, Grant Park's other main point of interest is the **Buckingham Fountain**, which sits directly east of Congress Parkway. A gift to the city in 1927 from the family of Clarence Buckingham, a trustee and benefactor of the Art Institute, it's modelled on the fountain at Versailles but stands twice the size and contains more than a million gallons of water. It's at it most impressive (and popular) on summer evenings, when its pink marble is illuminated and the Loop skyline is burnished by the sunset behind it.

Auditorium Building. *See p80.*

Art Institute of Chicago

*111 S Michigan Avenue, at W Adams Street
(1-312 443 3600/www.artic.edu).* El: Brown, Green,
Orange, Pink or Purple to Adams. **Open** *Sept-May*
10.30am-5pm Mon-Fri; 10am-5pm Sat, Sun. *June-Aug*
10.30am-5pm Mon-Wed; 10.30am-9pm Thur, Fri;
10am-5pm Sat, Sun. **Admission** $12; $7 discounts;
free under-12s; free to all 5-8pm Thur & (June-Aug)
5-9pm Thur, Fri. **Credit** AmEx, DC, Disc, MC, V.
Map p325 J12.

The intrigue of Chicago's most noteworthy museum
begins even before you cross the threshold, when
you meet two of the city's most beloved characters
just outside its Michigan Avenue entrance. Donated
by Mrs Henry Field, sister-in-law to department
store mogul Marshall, sculptor Edward Kemeys'
two bronze lions have guarded the Art Institute of
Chicago since 1894. But few locals realise that the
pair aren't identical twins: the south lion is said to
stand in an attitude of defiance, while the north lion
is reportedly 'on the prowl'.

Past these leonine doormen lies a world-class institution, and one that looks the part from the moment
you reach the atrium lobby. The Art Institute has
the building its impressive collections deserve: built
by Shepley, Rutan and Coolidge in 1892 for the
World's Columbian Exposition the following year,
it's as grand as it's large. The signage around the
museum is generally good, and the free museum
map is comprehensive enough for most visitors.
However, the museum's sheer size can still make it
a daunting place. The aforementioned map, which
is distributed at the ticket office, is a useful guide,
but you might also want to invest in the excellent
audio guide ($6), which provides an overview of the
museum's highlights. **Photo** *p76.*

Collections

The museum's three buildings each feature two to
three storeys of exhibition space, so stealing more
than a glance at each work will make it nearly
impossible to cover the entire museum in a single
day. (The task will become even more difficult in
2009, assuming the new Modern Wing is completed
on schedule). However, by prioritising the Modern
and Contemporary collections on the second floor of
the Allerton Building, and the American 1900-1950
collection on the second floor of the newer Rice
Building, you'll still get to see many of the Art
Institute's most notable and famous works.

That said, one enjoyable way to start a tour of the
museum is by taking a quick look at some of the sal-
vaged architectural gems on display in the **Crown
Gallery**. One of the Institute's quirkier spaces, at
the top of the stairs by the Michigan Avenue
entrance, it contains elevator grilles rescued from
the Chicago Stock Exchange (donated by architect
Louis Sullivan), various spandrels and lunettes, and
even some stained-glass windows that formerly
belonged to some of the city's forgotten buildings.

After this whimsical beginning, move on to the
Pritzker Galleries, where you'll find many of
the Institute's most prized canvases. The museum

has managed to accumulate amazing collections
of Impressionist and post-Impressionist paintings
since opening in the late 19th century, and it's here
that you'll find them. Look out in particular for
Caillebotte's famous *Paris Street; Rainy Day* (room
201) and Seurat's *A Sunday on La Grande Jatte –
1884* (205), at which Ferris Bueller gawped on his
day off, along with other notable works such as
Renoir's *Acrobats at the Cirque Fernando* and
Cézanne's *The Basket of Apples.*

The nearby **Modern Collection** delivers a succession of textbook classics. Numerous works by
Salvador Dali (236, 243) sit alongside Magritte's
Time Transfixed (236), Picasso's *The Old Guitarist*
(234B) and countless other instantly recognisable
pieces. The **American 1900-1950 Collection** in
the nearby Rice Building is scarcely any less impressive, containing such gems as Edward Hopper's
Nighthawks (262), Grant Wood's *American Gothic*
(263), and works by Georgia O'Keeffe (265), Winslow
Homer (170) and Mary Cassatt (273). Sadly, Marc
Chagall's exquisite *American Window,* three panels
of intricate stained glass donated by the artist to the
city of Chicago, has been temporarily removed from
its perch next to the Rice Building entrance while
construction continues on the new Modern Wing.
Designed by Renzo Piano, the wing will be dedicated
solely to modern and contemporary art, and will feature 65,000 square feet (6,000 square metres) of exhibition space spread over three floors. There will also
be educational facilities, an outdoor sculpture terrace
and a bridge across to Millennium Park. The new
wing is due to open in 2009.

Less celebrated but equally worthy are the **Asian,
Medieval** and **Renaissance Art Collections,** all
of which are of interest to more than just aficionados. And we're still not done: other diversions

include a faithfully rebuilt model of the old Chicago Stock Exchange, a sculpture garden, a paperweight collection and the **Kraft Education Center**, which has dozens of games to keep children interested. Nearby are the **Thorne Miniature Rooms**, a fascinating collection of scale models of American, European and oriental houses spanning four centuries. And after all that, it's little surprise that many visitors completely overlook the museum's **Photography Collection** on the lower level. These four galleries of images are well worth a gander, most notably for rotating selections from the 15,000-piece Alfred Stieglitz collection.

Despite the strength of its permanent collection, the Institute nonetheless stages regular temporary exhibitions, some of which are more high-profile than others. Check the website (and *Time Out Chicago*) for details of what's on while you're in town.

Michigan Avenue

The mile-long stretch of Michigan Avenue that runs south of the Chicago River isn't officially Magnificent, like its counterpart to the north, but it's nonetheless packed with buildings of artistic and architectural interest. What's more, this wide, handsome thoroughfare offers walkers a glimpse of both aspects of the Loop. To the west stands an array of tall, imposing and often historic buildings, housing hotels, businesses and cultural institutions. And to the east are the wide-open spaces of Grant Park and, beyond them, Lake Michigan. It's a quietly impressive street.

Start at the **Michigan Avenue Bridge**, which affords spectacular views of the Loop from its northern tip (by the Tribune Tower and the Wrigley Building, for which *see p98*). The bridge's south-west tower now houses the **McCormick Tribune Bridgehouse & Chicago River Museum** (*see p80*), which celebrates the role of the river in the history of Chicago while also providing some fantastic views of the waterway itself. East of the bridge, along Wacker Drive towards the lake, sits

the **Lakeshore East** development, a new collection of condo towers that have quickly become popular with local celebs.

Strolling south of the bridge along N Michigan Avenue, the ground-level businesses aren't always interesting (a souvenir shop here, a middle-American chain restaurant there), but the buildings housing them often are. Close to the river sits the **Carbide & Carbon Building** (No.230, at E South Water Street), an art deco skyscraper built in 1929 that reopened in January 2004 as the **Hard Rock Hotel** (*see p57*). It's a handsome building both inside and out: the exterior of the green terracotta tower is trimmed in gold leaf, while the awe-inspiring lobby features plenty of marble with glass ornamentation. Just down the road sits the **Smurfit-Stone Building** (No.150, at E Randolph Street), built in 1983 and highlighted by Yaacov Agam's aluminium sculpture *Communication X9*.

Just off Michigan Avenue itself, immediately north of Millennium Park, sit a pair of towering skyscrapers. **One Prudential Plaza** (130 E Randolph Street, at N Stetson Avenue) is notable for its sculptural relief of the Rock of Gibraltar, the company's trademark, while the **Aon Center** (*née* the Amoco Building; 200 E Randolph Street, at N Columbus Drive) is distinguished only for its unreasonably immense height. Just behind them, fronting on to Wacker Drive and the river, stands the equally unprepossessing (and similarly drab) towers of the **Hyatt Regency** hotel (*see p58*).

Things get more interesting further down Michigan Avenue, with a trio of buildings used not for business but for pleasure. Chief among them is the **Chicago Cultural Center** (*see p80*): Michigan Avenue's *pièce de résistance* (though its official street address is Washington Boulevard), it was built as a library but is now an architectural gem, a tourist resource, a gallery, a concert venue and an office block rolled into one. Every visitor should at least pop in for a look on their travels around the Loop.

We'll always have Paris

No, your eyes aren't deceiving you: that really is a traditional Paris Métro sign guarding the entrance to the Metra station at E Van Buren Street and S Michigan Avenue. In 1900, the city of Paris hired Hector Guimard, France's first and foremost Art Nouveau architect, to create the design, now a Paris icon. More than 100 years later, Chicago was presented with its own version by the Régie Autonome

des Transports Parisiens (RATP), responsible for the Paris transit system. The entryway was dedicated on 14 July 2005 (Bastille Day), and sits in good historic company: the Roman Revival-esque Chicago Club (the Art Institute's original home) and the Fine Arts Building and Auditorium, both of which were built around the time Guimard designed his sign, are just blocks away.

Out of print

Centred on the stretch of Dearborn Street running south from Congress Parkway to Polk Street, **Printers' Row** was once a bustling hub of travel and industry. From the late 19th century, its focal point was the Dearborn Station, at the time the city's busiest rail terminus; also here were the 100 or so printing companies that lent the area its nickname.

By the 1970s, the area was spiralling into decline, abandoned and nearly forgotten. The printers had vanished and trains had ceased to serve the station, which was demolished. But the following decade and a half brought a new spirit of opportunism. Developers gutted the print shops and built residential lofts, and the station was converted into office space. And in 1985, the **Printers' Row Book Fair** (*see p217*) was established in an attempt to welcome Chicagoans back to an area that many had spent the last few decades carefully avoiding.

Today, a stroll along Dearborn Street, with diversions into its surrounding roads, is a lesson in urban regeneration. Housed in two renovated 19th-century buildings, the Hyatt on Printers' Row, now the **Hotel Blake** (*see p58*), opened here in the late 1980s. Down the block, on the western side of Dearborn on opposite sides of Harrison Street, the **Pontiac Building** (No.542) and the imposing, 22-floor **Transportation Building** (No.600) have both been upgraded for the newly affluent age. Close at hand, **Kasey's Tavern** (No.700, 1-312 427 7992, www.kaseystavern.com) has been serving neighbourhood locals since 1899.

Further south, at the junction with Jackson Boulevard, sits **Symphony Center** (*see p253*), home to the Chicago Symphony Orchestra. Made up of three wings connected by a central rotunda, the facility encompasses the 1904 Orchestra Hall, a park, a store and an education and administration wing. And just down the block from the Symphony Center is the **Santa Fe Building** (224 S Michigan Avenue, at E Jackson Boulevard), designed in 1904 by Daniel Burnham (who liked it so much that he moved his own offices here). Firmly ensconced inside is the marvellous **Chicago Architecture Foundation** (www.architecture.org; *see p73*), which supplements its huge programme of tours with lectures and small-scale exhibits in what it calls its 'ArchiCenter'. There's an excellent shop on site selling books and gifts.

Continuing south, the **Fine Arts Building** (410 S Michigan Avenue, between E Van Buren Street & E Congress Parkway) once housed the showrooms of the Studebaker Company, which in 1895 was showing carriages rather than cars. Soon after, it was converted into a theatre on the first floor and artists' studios above, and the words 'All Passes – Art Alone Endures' were carved inside the entrance. Frank Lloyd Wright had a studio here at one time, as did L Frank Baum, author of *The Wizard of Oz*.

The **Auditorium Building** (S Michigan Avenue, at E Congress Parkway; **photo** *p78*) is sometimes billed as the edifice that put Chicago on the cultural map. When it was conceived by Dankmar Adler and Louis Sullivan, the building was the tallest in the world, housing a theatre, a hotel and offices. It was dedicated in 1889 by President Benjamin Harrison as the first home of the Chicago Opera. During World War II, it was converted into a servicemen's centre, and the stage was used as a bowling alley. The building was left to wither away, until the Auditorium Theatre Council was formed and raised $3 million for some much-needed restoration work. The building reopened in 1967 and is now on the National Register of Historic Places; for the theatre programme, visit www.auditoriumtheatre.org. A couple of blocks south is the new **Spertus Museum** (*see p81*).

Chicago Cultural Center
78 E Washington Boulevard, at N Michigan Avenue (1-312 744 6630/www.chicagoculturalcenter.org). El: Blue to Washington; Brown, Green, Orange, Pink or Purple to Randolph; Red to Lake. **Open** *Apr-Oct* 8am-7pm Mon-Thur; 8am-6pm Fri; 9am-6pm Sat; 10am-6pm Sun. *Nov-Mar* 10am-7pm Mon-Thur; 10am-6pm Fri; 10am-5pm Sat; 11am-5pm Sun. **Admission** free. **Map** p325 J12.
This block-long building was built in 1897, and is something of a honeypot for the architectural and design connoisseur, with two Tiffany domes (one of which is said to be worth $35 million), a marble staircase and several glass mosaics. It's an invaluable resource for information about what's on in the city, and an excellent cultural venue in its own right: free concerts are staged here every lunchtime, many of a very high standard. **Photo** *p81*.

McCormick Tribune Bridgehouse & Chicago River Museum
Southwest tower, Michigan Avenue Bridge, 376 N Michigan Avenue, at E Wacker Drive (1-312 939 0490 x1/www.bridgehousemuseum.org). El: Brown, Green, Orange, Pink or Purple to State; Red to Lake. **Open** 10am-5.30pm daily. **Admission** *Suggested donation* $3; free under-5s. **Credit** AmEx, Disc, MC, V. **Map** p326 J11.

In the last few years, the Friends of the Chicago River converted the famous 1920 Michigan Avenue Bridgehouse into a museum that celebrates the river's role in building Chicago into a major metropolitan city. The five-storey space might prove difficult to traverse if you're travelling with children or grandma; however, if you make it to the top, you'll be rewarded with a unique viewpoint of the Chicago River, the bridge itself and the gradually growing Trump Tower on the northern bank. The archival photographs, maps, newspaper articles and historical titbits are a feast for history buffs, riverphiles or anyone with a keen interest in urban planning, though the insider views of the massive gears, mechanisms and counterweights used to lift the bridge lend the museum a broader appeal. **Photo** *p82.*

Spertus Museum

Spertus Institute of Jewish Studies, 610 S Michigan Avenue, at E Harrison Street (1-312 322 1747/www. spertus.edu). El: Orange, Green or Red to Harrison. **Open** from late 2007; call for details. **Admission** call for details. **Credit** MC, V. **Map** p325 J13.
The Spertus Museum's new ten-storey, Kruek & Sexton-designed digs, fronted by an illuminated glass façade, is one of the first new construction projects in decades on Michigan Avenue's landmark-protected 'street wall'. Once completed in late 2007, the museum's expanded displays will continue where those in the old building left off: detailing the rich diversity of Jewish culture, with a 10,000-strong collection of artefacts from all over the world. The Asher Library holds some 100,000 books, alongside periodicals, sound recordings and videos.

State Street & around

Or 'State Street, that great street', the stuff of which songs are made. Closed to traffic in 1979 to form a pedestrian mall, the stretch about which Sinatra sang was reopened to vehicles in 1996. A $25-million facelift widened the streets, added landscaping and helped restore life to the long-beleaguered road.

At the top of State Street's list of landmarks is **Macy's** (No.111, at E Randolph Street; *see p192*), a block-long retail extravaganza still defiantly known to some by its original name. First opened on this site in 1868 (and twice destroyed by fire, once in the Chicago Fire of 1871 and again six years later), Marshall Field's department store served seven generations of Chicagoans and became the flagship shop in a pioneering nationwide chain. When Macy's bought the store in 2005 and changed its name the following year (exactly a century after Field's death), Chicagoans were outraged, fearing that the traditions, from Field's philosophy of 'Give the lady what she wants' to annual dinners at the Walnut Room, would be lost.

So far, at least, their worries have proven relatively unfounded. The Tiffany mosaic dome (c.1907) still stands high above one atrium, and the clock at State and Randolph, the inspiration for a Norman Rockwell painting that graced the cover of the *Saturday Evening*

Sightseeing

Masterpiece in marble: the stairs at the beaux arts **Chicago Cultural Center**. *See p80.*

McCormick Tribune Bridgehouse & Chicago River Museum. See p80.

Post on 3 November 1945, still keeps perfect time. (The original Rockwell work hangs near the seventh-floor visitors' centre.) During holidays, crowds line up to take in the store's window displays.

The long-awaited **Block 37** development, occupying the block bounded by State, Washington, Randolph and Dearborn Streets (directly opposite Macy's) is at last showing signs of life. In the pipeline since 1989, the multi-use structure broke ground in 2005, and is slated to open in 2008. For more, *see p38* **A whole lot of nothing**. North on State sits the **Chicago Theater** (175 N State Street, at W Randolph Street; *see p254*). You can't miss the red vertical marquee of this former movie house, which opened in 1928 and today plays host to a variety of shows. Opposite is the **Gene Siskel Film Center** (164 N State Street, at W Randolph Street; *see p237*), which has monthly thematic film series.

Look south on State, meanwhile, and you'll be face to face with one of Chicago's greatest restoration projects. Built in 1895, the **Reliance Building** (1 W Washington Street, at N State Street) was once one of the more elegant early Chicago skyscrapers, but years of neglect left it in disrepair. The city bought the building in 1996, before the Kimpton Group moved in and converted it into a hotel three years later. The **Hotel Burnham** (*see p58*) is named after famed architect Daniel Burnham, whose firm designed the building.

Immediately to the south of Macy's sits the **Carson Pirie Scott** building (1 S State Street, at E Madison Street; *see p34*), built between 1899 and 1903 by Louis Sullivan for Schlesinger & Mayer retail company, but sold to Carson Pirie Scott in 1903. After just over a century on State Street, the company announced that it was to close the shop by Easter 2007; with downtown retail slowly making a comeback, it'll be interesting to see what fills the building once it has been vacated.

Two notable buildings sit just off State Street on Monroe. To the west is the **LaSalle Bank Theatre** (22 W Monroe Street, at S State Street; *see p283*); formerly known as the Shubert Theatre, it was built in 1905 and is now home to some of the biggest Broadway shows to visit Chicago. And just east of State is the block-long **Palmer House Hilton** (17 E Monroe Street, at S State Street; *see p58*), which was built in 1927 by Holabird & Roche. Even if you're not staying here, the elegant lobby is worth a peek.

A couple of blocks south and east of here is yet another architectural landmark. When the 16-storey **Monadnock Building** (53 W Jackson Boulevard, at S Dearborn Street) was erected in 1891, it was the highest and heaviest load-bearing structure in the world. It remains the world's tallest all-masonry building; in order to support the building's weight, its walls are six feet thick at the base and thin out as the building rises.

A further block south and east sits perhaps the Loop's most extraordinary building. Rising from the ground like a gigantic cheese, Harry Weese's **Metropolitan Correctional Center** (71 W Van Buren Street, at S Federal Street) is an astonishing piece of design. Distinguished by their skinny windows, the top 16 floors of this triangular structure house federal prisoners and suspects awaiting trial. Peer down on the building from above, and you may see some of these inmates stretching their legs in the rooftop exercise yard. Offices occupy the bottom 11 floors.

Heading back to State Street, the **Harold Washington Library Center** (400 S State Street, at W Van Buren Street, 1-312 747 4300, www.chipublib.org) makes a little more effort to settle in with its long-standing neighbours. Designed by Thomas Beeby and named after the city's first African American mayor, it was constructed in 1991 from granite and brick but with a terracotta exterior, borrowing details from some of Chicago's most famous structures. Talks, discussions and concerts are held regularly at the library; check online for details.

Randolph Street & around

Chicago's politics – and that of much of Cook County – play out in the buildings along Randolph Street between LaSalle and Dearborn. Indeed, the huge building on Randolph between LaSalle and Clark bears the name of a former governor of Illinois, and houses hundreds of city workers. The **James R Thompson Center** (1-312 814 6684; *see also p39*) is named after the former governor who commissioned it, and does little to blend in with its surroundings. Thompson himself called it 'a building for the 21st century' when it was dedicated in 1985, which seems to be pushing the point a little. Still, there's no doubt that it catches the eye. Offices circle an indoor atrium, skylights flood the granite floor and glass elevators shoot visitors up and down the 17 storeys. Shops and a food court occupy the lower levels, while state offices line the other floors.

City Hall and the adjoining **County Building** (Cook County, that is) sit opposite the Thompson Center, on the block bounded by Randolph, Washington, Clark and LaSalle. The fifth floor is home to the city's mayor and city council; on good days, a meeting of the council can be the best show in town. Meetings are held every two weeks and are open to the public: call 1-312 744 6870 for details.

Across the street from City Hall, located on Randolph between Clark and Dearborn, stands the **Daley Center**, named after mayor Richard

J Daley. Cook County's court system also has its headquarters in this rust-coloured high-rise, but it's best known for the sculpture by Picasso that graces **Daley Plaza** (*see p84* **Walk**). The building was erected in 1965 with the sculpture following two years later; much to the dismay, it's said, of Mayor Daley, who apparently wasn't much of a Picasso fan. A Christmas tree is put up each year in Daley Plaza, which also plays host to concerts, farmers' markets and the occasional protest every weekday. An eternal flame burns in memory of war dead.

Rising 400 feet (120 metres) above ground from its base a block south of City Hall on Washington, the **Chicago Temple** (77 W Washington Street, at N Clark Street, 1-312 236 4548, www.chicagotemple.org) is known as the 'Chapel in the Sky'. The headquarters of the First United Methodist Church of Chicago has an eight-storey spire (visible only from a distance), a sanctuary and office space. On an exterior first-level wall, a series of stained-glass windows depict the church's history in Chicago. Services generally take place at 8.30am and 11am on Sunday, though tours are also offered of the Sky Chapel.

LaSalle Street

LaSalle Street is the beating heart of the Midwest's financial industry. Running south from City Hall, the street is lined with financial institutions, housed in a series of ever-grander buildings. But the origins of LaSalle's influence are rooted as far back as 1848, when a group of merchants founded the **Chicago Board of Trade** (141 W Jackson Boulevard, at S LaSalle Street, 1-312 435 3590, www.cbot.com) to regulate the grain futures market.

Both buildings constructed specifically to house the Board of Trade were, on completion, the largest in the city. Completed in 1930 by Holabird & Roche as the replacement for William Boyington's 1885 structure, the current Art Deco model is one of the Loop's most gracious buildings. Sculptures of men holding wheat and corn loom over the entrance; atop the roof sits a 30-foot statue of Ceres, the Roman goddess of grain and harvest. A 1980 addition to the Board of Trade connected the building via a pedestrian bridge to the **Chicago Board Options Exchange** (400 S LaSalle Street, at W Van Buren Street, 1-312 786 5600, www.cboe.com), creating the largest contiguous trading floor space in the US. Due to security worries, the Board of Trade's visitors' centre is currently open only to pre-booked groups, but it may reopen in the future; check online for details.

Walk Art for art's sake

The prevalence of skyscrapers in the Loop means it's easy to walk around with your eyes to the sky. But if you snap your head back to eye level, you'll notice some striking sculptures. Many are huge: given the imposing surroundings, the artists had to think big in order to be noticed.

There are countless examples of public art around the Loop. Chicagoans can thank City Hall, which passed a groundbreaking ordinance 30 years ago that forced those in charge of building projects to set aside a small fraction of construction costs for art. Private companies followed suit, and the result has been an array of sculptures that complement the excellence of the architecture. Here's a baker's dozen of the finest pieces, strung together into a walk that ought to take a leisurely 90 minutes or so.

Start at Madison Plaza, on the north-west corner of Madison and Wells.

Recently moved indoors under a glass-walled atrium (200 W Madison, open 8am-7pm daily), **Louise Nevelson**'s *Dawn Shadows* (1983) is purported to have been influenced by the design of the El. Don't worry, though: Chicago's rail system is more reliable than this monstrous black form might suggest.

Head east along Madison, then take a left and walk along LaSalle.

Freeform, which sits on the façade of the Illinois State Office Building at 160 N LaSalle Street, is one of several Loop works by local artists. **Richard Hunt** has many works on display in the city, though this eye-catching abstract piece is perhaps his most prominent.

Walk back down LaSalle and take a left along Randolph to the front of the James R Thompson Center.

Located on Thompson Center's plaza, **Jean Dubuffet**'s fibreglass *Monument With Standing Beast* demands attention. Dubuffet always had affection for Chicago after a 1951 lecture he gave at the Arts Club of Chicago was rapturously received.

Carry on east to the corner with Dearborn, and head south to the plaza outside the Daley Center.

This striking piece of work is known locally only as 'the Picasso'; its creator, **Pablo Picasso**, didn't give it a title when he donated it to the city in 1967. Its lack of title helped to stoke the confusion – and, in some quarters, the contempt – that greeted its installation. It's believed to be based on the head of a woman. Or perhaps a baboon.

Continue down Dearborn, then turn right into Washington.

Outside the Brunswick Building at 69 W Washington sits Miró's *Chicago*. Created by **Joan Miró** in collaboration with ceramics expert Joan Artigas, it was completed in 1981.

Double back up Washington; take a right at the junction with Dearborn and go south.

Back in the 19th century, birds nested in the run-down temporary City Hall at 209 S LaSalle Street, at W Adams Street. When the current structure was built in 1888, the birds were remembered in the new name of the building, the **Rookery**. Two (sculpted) rooks at the LaSalle Street entrance serve as further reminders, though a 1991 renovation ensured there is nothing dilapidated about the Rookery today. A spiral staircase climbs up to the top floor of the building; the lobby walls, redesigned by Frank Lloyd Wright in 1905, are lined with marble.

The **One Financial Place** building (440 S LaSalle Street, at W Congress Parkway) stands above the Eisenhower Expressway. If you're in a car, you can't miss it: traffic heading in or out of the Loop drives under the building, through arches that serve as stilts. Built in 1985 by the same architects who drew the Sears Tower, it's

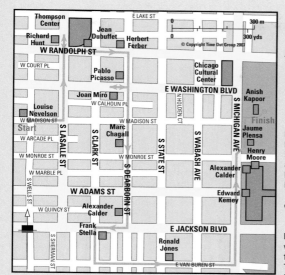

influenced by *Moby Dick*. Few are more striking than *The Town-Ho's Story* (pictured), a jarring collection of mangled metal that dominates the lobby of the Ralph H Metcalfe Federal Building.

Continue east to Clark, then take a left; then take the next left along Van Buren to State Street.
Pritzker Park, designed by **Ronald Jones** and completed in 1991, is less sculpture and more landscape garden. However, its highlight, an interpretation of Magritte's *The Banquet*, is reason enough to make a detour.

Continue down Van Buren to Michigan; turn left.
Edward Kemey's *Lions* is without doubt the most famous sculpture in Chicago. These two striking local landmarks have guarded the entrance of the Art Institute of Chicago for almost a century. Just north of the main entrance, in the Institute's McCormick Memorial Court, sit two more works by notable sculptors: *Flying Dragon*, another vast piece by **Alexander Calder**; and *Large Interior Form*, whose three holes distinguish it as a work by British sculptor **Henry Moore**.

Continue north up Michigan Avenue to Millennium Park.
The two most popular pieces of public art in Chicago are two of the newest. The vast faces beamed on to **Jaume Plensa**'s *Crown Fountain* (see p77) unnerve adults but tickle kids. Almost everyone, though, loves **Anish Kapoor**'s *Cloud Gate*, aka 'the Bean' (see p77).

He may be best known for his paintings, but Chicagoans know **Marc Chagall** more as a sculptor, thanks to his vibrant, 70-foot (21-metre) mosaic *The Four Seasons*, now under a glass cover at Bank One Plaza.

Continue south down Dearborn for two blocks to Federal Center Plaza.
Alexander Calder was once asked why he had called his vast, hooped sculpture *Flamingo*. The questioner doubtless expected an answer swamped in rhetoric. Calder replied, 'It was sort of pink and has a long neck.' He got that right.

Carry on south. At the next junction, cross the road and turn right into Jackson.
Between 1986 and 1997, **Frank Stella** created 266 works of art based on or

home to the top-rated **Everest** restaurant (*see p144*) and the Midwest Stock Exchange, the second largest in the US.

W Wacker Drive & the Chicago River

Edging up through a crowded Loop skyline that it tries its hardest to dominate, the **Sears Tower** (*see p86*) is probably Chicago's most recognisable landmark. When it was completed in 1974, topping out at 1,454 feet (443 metres) excluding its protuding antennnae, it was the world's tallest building. Nine steel tubes of varying heights form the frame of the black aluminium- and glass-covered edifice, designed by Bruce Graham of Chicago firm Skidmore, Owings & Merrill. Tickets for the observatory can be bought in the atrium off Wacker Drive, where visitors are welcomed by an Alexander

Calder sculpture – *Universe* – representing the sun, a pendulum and three flowers.

Other landmark structures line Wacker Drive to the north and south of the Sears Tower. Just below it, **311 S Wacker Drive** (at W Jackson Boulevard) is the tallest reinforced concrete building in the world. Its exterior of glass and pink granite is surrounded by a neatly landscaped concourse; at night, the crown of the 65-storey structure is lit up like a Christmas tree. To the north, meanwhile, Henry Cobb's 2005 **Hyatt Center** (71 S Wacker Drive, at W Monroe Street) is a curvaceous, almost sexy construction, one of the Loop's more feline and glamorous skyscrapers.

Unfortunately, the fourth-floor gallery that allowed the public to watch the frantic trading at the **Chicago Mercantile Exchange** (30 S Wacker Drive, at W Madison Street, 1-312 930 8249, www.cme.com) is currently shut due to security concerns. However, curious visitors can find out a little more about what goes on behind the now-closed doors at the lobby-level visitors' centre, open from 8am until 4.30pm during the week.

Home to the Lyric Opera since 1950, the **Civic Opera House** (20 N Wacker Drive, at E Madison Street; *see p250*) is centred on a lavish art deco auditorium adorned in red and orange with gold leaf accents. With a capacity of over 3,500, it's the second-largest opera house in the country. Renovated in 1996, the 1929 building still boasts the terracotta and bronze forms of a trumpet, a lyre and the masks of tragedy and comedy on its interior and exterior walls.

The Loop extends west over the Chicago River to encompass the **Citicorp Center**, home to the Ogilvie Transportation Center (aka Northwestern Station; 500 W Madison Street, at N Canal Street) and the former Northwestern Atrium Center. It's busy with commuters daily, but it's nothing like as handsome as nearby **Union Station** (210 S Canal Street, at W Adams Street, 1-312 655 2385). Sunlight streams through skylights ten storeys high and on to the statues inside the station, completed in 1925 and beautifully restored in 1992.

Heading west from Union Station, you'll soon enter the **West Loop** and **Greektown** (*see pp119-125*). But before you get there, you'll run into arguably the most eye-catching of all Chicago's sculptures: Claes Oldenburg's *Batcolumn*, a 100-foot (31-metre) baseball bat, which stands ominously outside the Social Security Administration Building (600 W Madison Street, at N Jefferson Street).

Sears Tower

233 S Wacker Drive, at W Jackson Boulevard (1-312 875 9696/www.the-skydeck.com). El: Brown, Orange, Pink or Purple to Quincy. **Open** *May-Sept* 10am-10pm daily. *Oct-Apr* 10am-8pm daily. **Admission** $11.95; $8.50-$9.95 discounts; free under-3s. **Credit** AmEx, Disc, MC, V. **Map** p325 G12.

Designed by Bruce Graham as the world's tallest building (it's since been overtaken by the Petronas Towers in Kuala Lumpur and Taipei 101 in Taiwan, and will soon be topped by two other Chicago skyscrapers), the Sears Tower hasn't had an untroubled history. The building received mixed reviews from architecture critics when it opened in 1973, after which Sears had trouble renting out all the office space in its 110-floor behemoth; they eventually left the complex in 1995. However, a quarter of a century after its completion, it has earned its status as arguably the city's most iconic building.

A relatively recent renovation spruced up the overall visitor experience with a (too-long) introductory movie and additional exhibits on the building and the city. But of course, everyone's really here for the views from the 103rd-floor Skydeck. They're great, of course: on a clear day, you can see 60 miles. However, the views from the John Hancock Center are rather more impressive, chiefly because they afford perspective on the Loop's skyline that the Sears Tower can never hope to offer.

Let's get the El out of here.

The South Loop & Chinatown

From Victorian high society to 21st-century high rises.

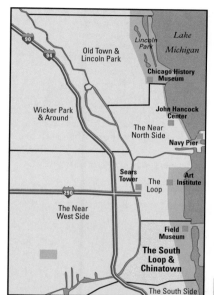

with dozens of high-rise condominium complexes sprouting in the past few years.

Loosely defined as stretching from Roosevelt Road in the north down to McCormick Place and I-55 (by 25th Street), the South Loop is still a ragged area. The neighbourhood's character can change significantly in a block or two: a glossy convention centre stands alongside a scruffy Chinese community, while swankily converted warehouse apartments sit uneasily close to deprived public housing complexes. (The housing projects surrounding Cermak Road, which fall halfway between the Prairie Avenue Historic District and Chinatown, are best avoided for safety reasons.)

If you're here for a convention, you're likely to find yourself at **McCormick Place** (E 23rd Street, at S Lake Shore Drive) for much of your stay. Best accessed via the Metra service from the Randolph Street station (by Millennium Park), it's a gargantuan site, with over two million square feet (186,000 square metres) of meeting space and excellent facilities. For more information, see www.mccormickplace.com, or call 1-312 791 7000.

The South Loop

Map p324

El: Green or Orange to Roosevelt; Red to Cermak-Chinatown, Harrison or Roosevelt.

As is the way in so many major US cities, population overspill and entrepreneurial savvy have meant that previously run-down areas in Chicago are rapidly being converted into bijou locales for urbanites who have the ability to drop several hundred thousand dollars on an apartment. Fulton Market (*see p119*) and Bucktown (*see p126*), both formerly dilapidated neighbourhoods, are the most obvious examples of such gentrification, but parts of the South Loop are also being upgraded in a similar fashion. The difference is that while the other neighbourhoods have been rehabbed and outfitted, the South Loop has grown upwards,

Museum Campus

Map p324

El: Green, Orange or Red to Roosevelt.

Three of the country's finest museums share the grassy plot of land known as **Museum Campus**, jutting out into Lake Michigan at the southern edge of Grant Park (just south of Roosevelt Road). Although they've changed considerably in the intervening years, the **Shedd Aquarium** (*see p90*), the **Adler Planetarium** (*see p89*) and the **Field Museum** (*see p89*) were erected here in time for the Century of Progress World's Fair of 1933-34; each is named after the Chicago business mogul who commissioned it.

Lake Shore Drive once ran right through Museum Campus, making itself a significant obstacle for pedestrians. Thankfully, it was shunted west in the 1990s; you can get off the Red Line at Harrison, take the sidewalk that heads east from 9th Street and Michigan

Avenue, and stroll easily between museums. However, be warned that the trio aren't as close together as they might look from a distance.

In 2005, **Northerly Island Park** (1400 S Lynn White Drive, 1-312 745 2910) was added to the area's recreational attractions. The island was previously occupied by Meigs Field, an airport used by the prosperous to jet in and out of downtown. On 30 March 2003, citing post-9/11 concerns over terrorism, Mayor Daley shocked the city by bulldozing the runways in the middle of the night, instantly closing the airport (and stranding a number of aircraft at it). These days, the redeveloped, city-owned stretch of parkland offers fishing and walking opportunities, and is home to the **Charter One Pavilion** (*see p253*), an open-air music venue.

A football's throw or two from here is **Soldier Field**, home to the Chicago Bears football team (*see p272*). Built in the early 1920s as a memorial to America's war dead, the stadium was substantially renovated in the early 21st century, a programme that wasn't without controversy. The austere old façades remain, but the modern grandstands that peek over the top make little effort to blend with them. As a direct result of the work, the stadium was removed from the National Register of Historic Places in 2004.

Adler Planetarium

1300 S Lake Shore Drive, at E Solidarity Drive (1-312 322 0590/www.adlerplanetarium.org). El: Green, Orange or Red to Roosevelt. **Open** 9.30am-4.30pm daily (until 10pm 1st Fri of mth). **Admission** $7; $5-$6 discounts; free to all Mon & Tue in Sept-Dec. *Museum, audio tour & 1 show* $16; $14-$15 discounts. *Additional show* $5. **Credit** AmEx, Disc, MC, V. **Map** p324 L14.

The name of this facility on the banks of Lake Michigan is only semi-appropriate: this excellent enterprise is a lot more than just a planetarium. For a start, there are actually two planetariums here: the high-tech StarRider Theater, which was added as part of a $40-million facelift in the late 1990s, and the Sky Theater, a much more old-school affair. Between them, they offer six shows that run in rotation throughout the day.

Be sure to spend some time in the Astronomy Museum, underplayed in the promotional literature (and, for that matter, in other guidebooks) but actually every bit as appealing as the planetariums themselves. Former astronaut James Lovell, who lives in the area, has recently donated artefacts and souvenirs from his adventures and helped bring NASA relics to the museum. Particularly notable was a recent exhibition on Lovell's own Apollo 13 mission, the ill-fated return to earth of which prompted the Tom Hanks film of the same name. Shoot for the Moon, a new permanent exhibition gallery, features a fully-restored Gemini 12 spacecraft and more than 30 related items.

The rest of the permanent collection is reached via a disorienting walkway, and the opening exhibit offers assorted titbits (if the earth is a baseball, the moon is a ping-pong ball eight feet away) that set the tone for what follows: it's interactive, interesting and kid-friendly without being dumbed-down. Look out, in particular, for the vast Dearborn telescope, part of the museum's enviable collection of historically significant scientific instruments; the Great Scott Rock, a piece of the moon named after astronaut David Scott; and the fun 3-D Milky Way Theater.

Built in 1930, the building that holds the planetarium is a 12-sided architectural marvel, each side representing a sign of the zodiac. Even if you don't plan on going inside, it's worth strolling around it: the grass verge outside offers one of the best landlocked, ground-level views of Chicago's skyline.

Field Museum

1400 S Lake Shore Drive, at E Roosevelt Road (1-312 922 9410/www.fieldmuseum.org). El: Green, Orange or Red to Roosevelt. **Open** *Jan-Sept* 9am-5pm daily. *Oct-Dec* 9am-5pm Mon-Fri; 8am-5pm Sat, Sun. **Admission** $12; $7 discounts; free under-4s; free to all Mon & Tue in Jan-Mar, Sept & Oct. **Credit** AmEx, Disc, MC, V. **Map** p324 J14.

Field Museum.

Sightseeing

The Field Museum opened as part of the World's Columbian Exposition in 1893 as the Columbia Museum of Chicago, but was renamed after philanthropist and department store magnate Marshall Field in the early 20th century and moved to this impressive location soon after. A Chicago must-see, the museum is one of the most impressive natural science centres in the world, with a wealth of biological and anthropological exhibits alongside world-class on-site research facilities.

The big draw here is Sue, the world's largest Tyrannosaurus rex. Since she made her debut here in the late 1990s, Sue has become a mini-industry all by herself. Suitably awed children are normally to be found in her vicinity (near the north entrance of the museum), while parents rue the amount and variety of Sue merchandise available at the well-stocked museum shops. Sue even gets a store all to herself on the Upper Level, though all this is little wonder when you learn that the dinosaur cost the museum a cool $8.36 million at auction. Despite the name, its sex is unknown: it's named after Susan Hendrickson, who unearthed the skeleton in North Dakota in 1990.

Popular though Sue is, she's by no means the whole story. The Field is too big to get around comfortably in a day, but pick up a map and plan your visit carefully, and you'll be rewarded. Among the standout exhibits are the display on North American Indians, the World of Birds corner ('Hear the kookaburra laugh!'), the taxidermic Mammals of Asia, the large section on Africa (which includes an instructive section on slavery), the educational What is an Animal? section, and the famed (and stuffed) lions of Tsavo. Egyptology remains one of the major thrusts of the museum: in one of the most popular attractions, Inside Ancient Egypt, visitors explore a burial chamber rife with mummies, coffins and ushabti figurines; and visit a re-created village by a stream.

All these exhibits are on the Ground Level. The displays on the Upper Level are slightly more adult-oriented (with the exception of the McDonald's Fossil Preparation Laboratory), while the Lower Level is largely set aside for temporary exhibits on topics from the eruption of Pompeii to King Tut. Otherwise, displays well worth a look include Evolving Planet, a revamped dinosaur exhibit that pleases young ones with dozens of towering remains; and Pacific Spirits, which shows off masks, carvings and spears from Polynesia, Micronesia and other Pacific archipelagos. If you still can't decide what to see, time your visit to coincide with one of the free tours of the museum's highlights, held at 11am and 2pm (Mon-Fri only).

Shedd Aquarium

1200 S Lake Shore Drive, at E McFetridge Drive (1-312 939 2438/www.sheddaquarium.org). El: Green, Orange or Red to Roosevelt. **Open** *June-Aug* 9am-6pm Mon-Wed, Fri-Sun; 9am-10pm Thur. *Sept-May* 9am-5pm Mon-Fri; 9am-6pm Sat, Sun. **Admission** *Aquarium* $8; $6 discounts; free under-2s; free to all Mon & Tue in Oct, Nov, Jan & Feb. *Aquarium & oceanarium* $18; $14 discounts; free under-2s. $7 ($5 discounts; free under-2s) Mon & Tue in Oct, Nov, Jan

& Feb. *All-access pass* $23; $16 discounts; free under-2s. *Oceanarium* $7; $5 discounts; free under-2s. **Credit** AmEx, Disc, MC, V. **Map** p324 K14.

Housed in a beautiful, circular 1920s building on the lake, the Shedd Aquarium holds every conceivable kind of fish and water mammal. Enter through the main lobby and you'll be greeted by a large Caribbean coral reef exhibit, spectacularly plonked in the middle of a domed hall. From this central root protrude a number of branches – corridor-like exhibition spaces devoted to themes from the exotic (African tropical fish) to the everyday (invasive species found in the Great Lakes). The displays are clearly labelled, and the layout of the exhibits (you can approach them in any order) means that even when the museum's busy, there are always displays that are less crammed than others. Be sure to get a look at Granddad, the lungfish in the Waters of the World gallery. He was plucked from the waters of Australia in 1933 for the Century of Progress World's Fair; at an estimated age of 100 years of age, he's thought to be the oldest aquatic animal living in captivity anywhere in the world.

The aquarium doubled in size in 1991 with the addition of a spectacular $45-million Oceanarium. It's an extraordinary place, dominated by a vast tank (flooded with natural light and with great views of the lake) in which whales and dolphins swim and perform shows several times daily for enthusiastic crowds. After showtime, it looks strangely empty, until you discover the downstairs viewing galleries that offer a window on to underwater life. Elsewhere, there are exhibits on sea lions and penguins (more graceful in water than out of it). However, though the Oceanarium's raison d'être is to recreate the conditions of the Pacific Northwest, one of its most successful exhibits was the long-running Project Seahorse, which raised a great deal of awareness about the potential extinction of the species.

After eight years of construction, the Wild Reef wing was completed in 2003. Now one of the Shedd's top attractions, it's a faithful recreation of a coral reef habitat in the Philippines, with various sections devoted to the many facets of reef life, from the creatures that inhabit the shoreline surf to those that patrol the drop-off. Superb interactive displays provide more information than you could possibly absorb in one visit. However, among the highlights are shark tanks that span the tunnel in an overhead arch, giving visitors an all-consuming diver's-eye view of the fierce predators. Amid all the fun, a few little lessons on the importance of maintaining reef habitats have also been included.

The aquarium also offers a rotating series of exhibitions, which in the past has included an assortment of crabs and a show titled *Lizards & the Komodo King*. And don't miss *Man with Fish*, a painted bronze fountain (created by German artist Stephan Balkenhol) that sits just outside the aquarium. It's a humorous comment on stewardship, with an inexpressive everyman hugging a huge speckled fish.

The Prairie Avenue Historic District

Map p324

El: Red to Cermak-Chinatown.

During the late 19th century, before the city's rich and powerful moved to the North Side, the roads around 18th Street and Prairie Avenue were the grandest part of town, the centre of Chicago's high society and home to well over a hundred mansions. Only five properties from this era remain, but they still provide a sense of what life must have been like among the city's privileged Victorian elite.

On the south-west corner of 18th Street and Prairie Avenue sits the **Glessner House Museum** (*see below*), one of the key stops on a historical tour of Chicago. The property was built for John Jacob Glessner, who made his fortune in farm machinery. His neighbours were just as wealthy and even more esteemed: among them were the train car-designing Pullmans (*see p17* **Strike one**), whose mansion has long since vanished, and the piano-making Kimballs, whose pad at 1801 S Prairie Avenue is now

Prairie Avenue Historic District.

home to the US Soccer Federation (which also occupies the Coleman House next door). To the south lived both Marshall Field, Sr and Marshall Field, Jr. However, the area's oldest house is an intruder: the **Clarke House Museum** (*see below*) originally sat on 20 acres of land at 16th Street and Michigan Avenue, and was moved to the area three decades ago.

Roughly a century after the area began to fade from prominence, it's undergoing a resurgence and revitalisation. Old warehouses have been converted into lofts, and entirely new apartment complexes have sprung up from nothing: the rowhouses going up along Prairie Avenue are valued at well over $1 million. Plans are in place for several high-rises on the edge of the officially designated Historic District, but not even the properties within it are safe: Marshall Field, Jr's old home is being converted into six swanky townhouses. It all stands in stark contrast to the streets that run roughly four blocks west, drenched in impoverished public housing.

Clarke House Museum

1827 S Indiana Avenue, at E 18th Street (1-312 745 0040/www.glessnerhouse.org). El: Red to Cermak-Chinatown. **Open** *Tours* noon, 1pm, 2pm Wed-Sun. **Admission** $10; $8-$9 discounts. *Clarke & Glessner Houses* $15; $8-$12 discounts. *Prairie Avenue walking tour* $9; $5-$8 discounts. **Credit** MC, V. **Map** p324 J16.

Built in 1837 for hardware dealer Henry Clarke, this impressive property is the oldest house in Chicago. It's also the hardest place for the post office to keep track of: it's been moved twice in its long history, most recently in 1977 when the city lifted the building over a set of El tracks and on to its present (and hopefully permanent) home. Unlike the fortress-like Glessner House (*see below*), this Greek revival property was built before electricity, indoor plumbing and the Chicago Plan (*see p34*) changed the nature of architectural design in the city. Even so, the timber frame and mortise-and-tenon joints have travelled well, with ongoing restoration work enabling visitors to get a window into early upper-class life in Chicago. Tours begin at the Glessner House Museum; combined tours are available.

Glessner House Museum

1800 S Prairie Avenue, at E 18th Street (1-312 326 1480/www.glessnerhouse.org). El: Red to Cermak-Chinatown. **Open** *Tours* 1pm, 2pm, 3pm Wed-Sun. **Admission** $10; $8-$9 discounts; *Clarke & Glessner Houses* $15; $8-$12 discounts. *Prairie Avenue walking tour* $9; $5-$8 discounts. **Credit** MC, V. **Map** p324 J16.

A stroll through the Prairie Avenue Historic District is enjoyable in its own right, but it's incomplete without a tour of this museum. The imposing stone mansion was designed by Henry Hobson Richardson (who died in 1886, the year before it was completed).

Sightseeing

Walk Chinese whispers

Although it's been well established for years, Chicago's Chinese community hasn't always called the city's modern-day Chinatown home. Chinese immigrants originally settled around Clark and Van Buren Streets in the Loop and only headed south after 1910, when rents in the business district began to soar.

Before the Chinese arrived, the area around Wentworth Avenue was home to working-class Italians. Though few locals will recall their presence here, which lasted until the 1960s, a few vestiges of Italian culture remain. However, for the most part, Chinese businesses dominate along Wentworth Avenue and Cermak Road: restaurants and bakeries feed the hungry, while small shops hawk everything from healing herbs and acupuncture services to samurai swords and parade-ready papier mâché dragon heads.

Even today, almost a century after the Chinese first arrived in the neighbourhood, Chinatown remains modest. Intersected by every imaginable thoroughfare – Amtrak rail lines and the Chicago River to the west, I-55 to the south, the El network to the north and east – the neighbourhood hasn't had much room to grow, which helps explain its bustling, often overcrowded streets.

Start at the El's Red Line Cermak-Chinatown stop (W Cermak Avenue, east of S Wentworth Avenue).

The Chinatown gate arching over this intersection welcomes visitors to Wentworth Avenue, the main drag of Chinese shops and restaurants. On the west side of the street is the attractive **On Leong Merchants Association Building** (2216 S Wentworth Avenue), also known as the Pui Tak Center. The impressively frescoed three-storey building blends architectural styles typical of 1926, the year it was built, with traditional Chinese design elements, such as a duo of lion sculptures guarding the entrance, pagoda-topped towers, green-tiled roofs and red-painted trim. It never betrays the fact that it was designed by a pair of Norwegian-American architects, Christian Michaelsen and Sigurd Rognstad.

Walk south on Wentworth Avenue, turning west on 23rd Street.

The **Chinese-American Museum**, which opened in 2005, mixes temporary exhibitions from around the US with personal collections of Chicago's own Chinese-American community. For more details, *see p94*.

Head back to Wentworth Avenue. Turn left to walk north, then turn west on to Alexander Street.

Completed in 1904, the **Saint Therese Chinese Catholic Mission** (218 W Alexander Street) paints a poignant historical and cultural portrait of the neighbourhood. It was originally an Italian parish, but it now offers masses in Cantonese, Mandarin and Indonesian alongside its monthly Italian services. Between masses on Sundays, visitors are often allowed to take a look at the vestibule's intricately carved statues of

---

It's dark, drafty and Victorian, yet still manages to maintain a certain cosiness, thanks to oak-panelled walls and gold-leaf ceilings. The house was furnished in part by local furniture maker Isaac Scott, and covered in William Morris carpets and wallpaper.

A number of Glessner's artefacts are on display in the house, among them a solid silver candlestick on the concert grand and bronze casts of President-Elect Abraham Lincoln's face and hands. The casts mysteriously disappeared in 1992, only to reappear on the doorstep a few days later, after a great deal of publicity. An afternoon spent in the conservatory on the top floor, or browsing the bookshelves in the study, would make a visit here sublime. Unfortunately, you only get an hour in the house, tailed the entire time by a security guard armed with three words: 'Do not touch'. Tours begin inside the main doors on Prairie Avenue; combination tickets are available if you've also got time to see the nearby Clarke House.

National Vietnam Veterans' Art Museum

1801 S Indiana Avenue, at E 18th Street (1-312 326 0270/www.nvvam.org). El: Green, Orange or Red to Roosevelt. **Open** 11am-6pm Tue-Fri; 10am-5pm Sat. **Admission** $10; $7 discounts. **Credit** MC, V. **Map** p324 J16.

The only institution in the US devoted entirely to art produced by veterans of the Vietnam conflict is a moving memorial. That said, it's a troublesome task deciding what constitutes art when the living memory is still so raw. Some pieces offer vivid representations of violence and death, with visual examples of the difficult emotional journey many soldiers faced then and continue to face today. That said, the less literal the art, the more powerful the message. The 58,235 dog tags that hang in the foyer, gently rattling against each other, together make a far more gripping expression of death than hackneyed paintings of the Grim Reaper.

Mary, Jesus and St Rocco; the latter, honoured with a parade in early August, is the patron saint of Simbario, a small village in Italy from which the majority of the church's earliest parishioners emigrated. Next to the altar hangs a wooden cross, apparently a gift from Al Capone's mother (a former parishioner) in a last-ditch effort to save her son's soul. Below it are traditional Chinese candles and alter pillows, reflecting the parish's current dominant demographic.

Head back to Wentworth Avenue and turn left to walk north along it, before heading west on Cermak Avenue to Archer Avenue.

Chinatown Square (2130 S Archer Avenue, 1-312 808 1745), a two-storey outdoor shopping complex erected in 1993, speaks of the enclave's growing prosperity. During summer, the open plaza in front of the mall hosts a market at which vendors sell more or less the same trinkets, turtles and household wares found in Wentworth stores, albeit for about 30 to 40 per cent less. **Joy Yee's Noodles** (2159 S China Place, 1-312 328 0001) is a favourite spot for bubble tea, the sweet, milky, chilled drink loaded down with tapioca balls.

Walk back to Wentworth Avenue, head north and turn west on 19th Street.

Another early 1990s addition to the area, **Ping Tom Memorial Park** (300 W 19th Street, 1-312 746 5962) isn't too easy to find; it's tucked away behind a new housing development. However, it's worth the effort to witness the miraculous transformation of what was once 12 acres of abandoned railway yard into a welcome green space.

The Chicago River runs along the west border of the park. Locals come here to meditate, relax on the grass or picnic. Visible just to the north is a still-functioning relic of Chicago's industrial age. The imposing steel Amtrak lift bridge, built circa 1917, is one of the few remaining vertical lift bridges of its kind. If you're lucky enough to be in the park at the right time, you'll be able to watch its massive concrete counterweights lift the suspension tracks 130 feet (40 metres) above the water as boats pass through.

Regardless of your definition, the voices that echo in this museum – those of the soldiers, curators, visiting schoolchildren, tourists – make a stronger statement than any single piece of art. Be sure to read the museum's publications: leaf through the guestbook before then spending time with Mike Helbing's *Wall Drawing/Work in Progress*, a participatory drawing created by the layered graffiti of visitors. There's meaning bound up in this museum, between a handful of mature works of art and the many very painful memories.

Chinatown & around

El: Red to Cermak-Chinatown.

Just below the South Loop is **Chinatown** (**photo** *p94*), a slew of Chinese eateries, stores and cultural attractions clustered around Wentworth and Archer Avenues. For a tour of the area, *see above* **Walk**; if you've not got time, the **Chinese-American Museum of Chicago** (*see p94*) makes for an interesting diversion. To see the area at its most vibrant, visit for the **New Year Parade** (late January or early February; *see p220*), the **Chinatown Summer Fair** (mid July) or the **Dragon Boat Races** (late July), when locals race elaborately painted wooden boats down the river in an effort to raise funds for local charities.

Nearby, at State Street and Cermak Road, sits the dicey but intriguing **Hilliard Homes** public housing complex. Designed by Chicago's Bauhaus-trained Bertrand Goldberg in 1966 (and added to the National Register of Historic Places 33 years later), the estate together comprises the most notable buildings under the care of the Chicago Housing Authority. Reminiscent of Goldberg's earlier Marina City corncobs (*see p39*), the honeycomb-windowed residences have been rehabbed to serve as mixed income housing for families and seniors (not, as was proposed at one point, luxury residences). They're perhaps best admired from the safety of the El station that they overlook.

There are more notable buildings nearby on Michigan Avenue (2200-2500 blocks) and parallel Indiana Avenue (2200-3500 blocks), in an area informally known as **Motor Row**. Back in the early 20th century, this was the city's main area for car sales and repair. In the area's prime, 116 makes of automobile were sold and repaired along its streets. Many of the showrooms, some of which featured rotating display areas and elevators for the cars, occupied architecturally significant buildings; several of them have retained their terra cotta facades. Originally an auto club, the third home of the *Chicago Defender* newspaper at 2400 S Michigan Avenue is a notable example of Prairie School style architecture.

Blues Heaven

2120 S Michigan Avenue, between E 21st & E 22nd Streets (1-312 808 1286/www.bluesheaven.com). El: Red to Cermak-Chinatown. **Open** noon-3pm Mon-Fri; noon-2pm Sat. **Admission** $10. **No credit cards.**
From 1957 to '67, this building was the home of the legendary Chess label and Chess/Ter-Mar studios, recording and releasing records from legendary

bluesmen such as Muddy Waters, Howlin' Wolf and Buddy Guy. It's said that when the building was sold in the '70s, the new owners destroyed 250,000 records that had been abandoned here. Decades later, Willie Dixon's widow purchased the site and opened a museum and educational foundation in 1997. Today, you can tour the recording, rehearsal and office spaces, which feature guitars, memorabilia and a bit of the original soundproofing.

Chinese-American Museum of Chicago

238 W 23rd Street, at S Wentworth Avenue (1-312 949 1000/www.ccamuseum.org). El: Red to Cermak-Chinatown. **Open** 9.30am-1.30pm Fri; 10am-5pm Sat, Sun. **Admission** $2; $1 discounts. **No credit cards.**
Chinatown has more to offer than dim sum and cheap gifts, as this museum of Chinese-American history and culture proves. That said, it won't take long to get through the two floors of exhibition space. The rotating displays, some better curated than others, include travelling exhibitions from around the country, but the most fascinating shows are those culled from the personal collections of Chicago's own Chinese-American community. Past topics have included a survey of traditional Chinese furniture and clothing, an examination of Chinese Chicagoans' role in the 1893 and 1933 World's Fair, and a look at the versatility of tofu.

Head to **Chinatown** for everything from healing herbs to bubble tea. *See p93.*

The Near North Side

Shop 'til you drop, gallery-hop or just get high.

Lakeview &
Around

Lake
Michigan

Lincoln Park

Old Town &
Lincoln Park

Chicago History
Museum

Wicker Park
& Around

John Hancock
Center

**The Near
North Side**

Navy Pier

Sears
Tower

The
Loop

Art
Institute

The Near
West Side

Field
Museum

The South
Loop &
Chinatown

The downtown area of Chicago just north of
the river mixes business and pleasure to lively
effect. The central attraction is N Michigan
Avenue, aka the **Magnificent Mile**, one of
the country's most famous shopping streets, but
it's far from the only worthwhile diversion. To
the west of it sprawls the **River North** district,
a fast-rising muddle of galleries, nightclubs,
restaurants and apartments. Directly east sits
Streeterville, a tidy little district dotted with
hotels, residential towers, and attractions both
cultured (the **Museum of Contemporary
Art**) and commercial (**Navy Pier**). And just
to the north rolls the **Gold Coast**, one of the
city's most chichi neighbourhoods.

Getting around the Near North Side is safe
and simple. For a start, it's relatively compact
and thus very walkable: the Magnificent Mile is
actually a Magnificent Three-Quarters-of-a-Mile.
The shopping, dining, nightlife and big-ticket
entertainment around here mean that for
millions of tourists, the experience of visiting
Chicago never extends beyond these streets. In
other words, don't expect much peace and quiet.

River North

Map p326

*El: Brown or Purple to Chicago or Merchandise
Mart; Red to Chicago or Grand.*

The north banks of the Chicago River were
staked out by French-Canadian and Potawatomi
Indian traders in the 1830s, making the area
that would eventually become known as River
North one of Chicago's earliest settlements.
European immigrants settled into the area as
it experienced an industrial boom. Eventually,
though, the neighbourhood established itself
as a warehouse district.

It remained as such until the 1970s, when,
with post-industrial rust setting in, it morphed
into a low-rent enclave for starving artists and
creative types. Today, a little ironically, the
area around the intersection of Clark and Ohio
Streets traps many tourists into eating at
expensive themed restaurants. If you're being
ogled by the big frog atop the **Rainforest Café**
(605 N Clark Street, at W Ohio Street, 1-312 787
1501), you know you're in the danger zone.

In recent years, the western portion of River
North has been reborn as a desirable business
district. Interior designers, dotcom start-ups,
designer furniture stores and art dealers have
all been quick to take up leases on converted
loft spaces, offset by a rash of new luxurious
high-rises. The blocks bound by Chicago Street
(north), Wells (east), Erie (south) and Orleans
(west) comprise the **River North Gallery
District**, an area that more than 100 galleries
(and numerous antique stores) call home;
for details, *see pp221-223*. The area has also
become a hotbed for nightlife, attracting both
chic city dwellers and suburban weekenders;
for details of clubs in the area, *see pp264-267*.

Back towards Michigan Avenue sits a handful
of notable churches providing solace from the
hectic streetlife (and just about making their
presence felt amid the towering skyscrapers,
malls and hotels). Two cathedrals stand only
a few blocks apart: the Catholic **Holy Name
Cathedral** (735 N State Street, at E Chicago
Avenue, 1-312 787 8040, www.holyname
cathedral.org), a Victorian Gothic edifice built
in 1875, and the Episcopalian **St James
Cathedral** (65 E Huron Street, at N Wabash
Avenue, 1-312 787 7360, www.saintjames
cathedral.org), the unusual interior walls of

Magnificent Mile.

which are decorated with stencil patterns in more than 20 colours. However, Chicagoans tend to associate the area with another former church, often known as 'the Castle' (632 N Dearborn Street, at W Ontario Street). Designed by Henry Ives Cobb, architect of the Fisheries Building at the 1893 World's Fair, this red granite Romanesque revival building was for years the home of the Chicago Historical Society building, but now houses the **Vision/ Excalibur** nightclub (*see p266*).

Close by, the **Tree Studios** (4 E Ohio Street, at N State Street) are proof that the area's association with artists is nothing new. Built by lawyer and philanthropist Lambert Tree in 1894 and later expanded, the studios were used as work or lodging by some of the city's best-known artists for decades, until they were threatened by developers. For once, the story has a happy ending: in 2001, the city fathers saved Queen Anne and Arts & Crafts buildings from the wrecking ball, and the complex continues to thrive. The ground floor of the sensitively restored main building now houses the **Design Within Reach** (1-312 280 4677, www.dwr.com) furniture showroom and the upmarket **Hildt Galleries** (1-312 255 0005, www.hildtgalleries.com), among others, and is also the new home of jazz bar **Pops for Champagne** (*see p262*).

For a time, artists at Tree Studios shared their space with the Medinah Temple Association (600 N Wabash Avenue, at Ohio Street). Built for the national Shrine fraternal organisation in 1912, the temple was considered one of the nation's finest examples of a Middle Eastern-style Shrine temple. In 2003, **Bloomingdale's Home & Furniture Store** (*see p212*) took over the space; the multi-million-dollar renovation that ensued preserved much of the exterior architecture and restored the interior's former glory.

Several blocks south-west of Tree Studios stands the former nemesis of Chicago's criminal contingent: **Courthouse Place** (54 W Hubbard Street, at N Dearborn Street). The former Cook County Court building was built in 1892 as the second county court facility. Over the years, it was the site of some momentous legal wrangles, including attorney Clarence Darrow's successful bid to save convicted murderers Leopold and Loeb from the death sentence in 1924. Even more chillingly, it was also once used for hangings, and is purported to be haunted. These days, it's an office building.

South of here, overlooking the river, stands Bertrand Goldberg's distinctive **Marina City** (300 N State Street). Its two iconic structures, nicknamed the Corncob Towers for obvious reasons, have made cameos in everything from

Steve McQueen's final movie to a Wilco album cover. The top 40 storeys house trapezoid apartments, with the lower 20 storeys used for parking. The complex is also home to the **House of Blues** (*see p60 and p257*). The new **Museum of Broadcast Communications** (*see below*) sits in the towers' shadow (literally, depending on the time of day and the position of the sun). And east of the Corncobs along the river, 'the Donald' is currently constructing his modestly named **Trump International Hotel & Towers**, scheduled for completion in 2009.

Just as Trump's new skyscraper stands (or will eventually stand) as testament to a 21st-century economic optimism in Chicago, so the hulking riverfront building to its west pays tribute to earlier wealth and enthusiasm. Built in 1930 as showrooms and a wholesale office for Marshall Field, the **Merchandise Mart** (between Wells and Orleans, on the Chicago River, www.merchandisemart.com) is the second-largest building in the world (second only to the Pentagon), boasting an astonishing 4.2 million square feet (390,000 square metres) of floor space.

When the Merchandise Mart hit hard times in the 1940s, Fields sold the building to Joseph P Kennedy; it was Kennedy who installed the outdoor Merchandise Mart Hall of Fame in 1953, honouring captains of industry with Romanesque bronze busts placed along the river. These days, visitors head here for the Design Center, which boasts more than 130 showrooms of design products, and for the retail shopping area on the first two floors. In 2006, the owners took over the annual **Art Chicago** event, and immediately announced plans to expand it into a citywide **Artropolis** from 2007 onwards (*see p222* **Festivals**).

Museum of Broadcast Communications

360 N State Street, at W Kinzie Street (1-312 245 8200/www.museum.tv). El: Red to Grand. **Open** from 2007; call for hours. **Admission** call for details. **Credit** call for details. **Map** p326 H11.
Radioheads, TV lovers and history buffs have been staying tuned for the much-anticipated reopening of the Museum of Broadcast Communications, one of the city's most entertaining cultural institutions. Formerly housed in the Chicago Cultural Center, the museum will reopen in sleek new River North digs in spring 2007 following a three-year intermission. Old interactive favourites – such as the Play by Play Press Box, where you can record yourself calling a half-inning of baseball, and the television studio, where you can film yourself reading the news, are likely to remain popular. So, too, is the Radio Hall of Fame, with exhibits devoted to innovative broad-casters such as Jack Benny and Don O'Neill. But fans are also preparing for a few surprises in the lineup.

To go along with its glass-fronted, environmentally-friendly home, the museum will boast several new high-tech bells and whistles. Among them will be the Media Café, in which visitors can sit back on cushy recliners, munch away on snacks, and view selected clips from radio and TV shows from the gigantic house archives (which include more than 13,000 TV shows, 4,000 radio shows, 11,000 com-mercials and 5,000 newscasts).

The Magnificent Mile & Streeterville

Map p326

El: Red to Chicago or Grand.

The stretch of Michigan Avenue running north from the river was dubbed the 'Magnificent Mile' long before there was much magnificence about it. Perhaps inevitably, the man responsible was a real estate developer: Arthur Rubloff, who christened the street in the years after World War II as he went about renovating old buildings and erecting new ones.

In due course, the road grew into its moniker. Big shops flocked to the road, which is now a who's who of American retail. It's at its best in the run up to Christmas, when the buildings and trees are garlanded with lights, but it's pleasant (if congested) all year round, the broad expanse of the road dotted with small flower gardens and handsome greenery.

Michigan Avenue is best approached by walking up it from south to north, especially if you first take in the views from the southern side of the **Michigan Avenue Bridge**. After it opened in 1920, the bridge quickly became an asset to the area north of the river, making access to the Loop much easier for residents and businessmen. A plaque at the south-eastern end commemorates Fort Dearborn, the military outpost from which the city developed, and four sculptures on pylons along the bridge nod to major events in the city's history: the arrival of Joliet and Marquette, trader Jean Baptiste Point du Sable's settlement, the Fort Dearborn Massacre and the rebuilding following the Chicago Fire of 1871.

Once visible from here, the former offices of the *Chicago Sun-Times* were demolished in 2004 to make way for Donald Trump's **Trump International Hotel & Tower** skyscraper (401 N Wabash Street), expected to open in 2009 (*see p40*). While the *Sun-Times* has relocated, the city's other daily paper, located north-west of the Trump Tower, has stayed in the building it's occupied for more than eight decades.

John Howells' and Raymond Hood's Gothic design for **Tribune Tower** (435 N Michigan Avenue) was selected in 1922 by then-publisher

Sightseeing

Colonel Robert McCormick from a field of international entries, and was completed to great acclaim three years later. The Gothic block houses the offices of the daily newspaper, the *Tribune*-owned WGN radio station (the letters stand for World's Greatest Newspaper) and CLTV, Chicago's 24-hour local news station. As you walk around the first level, look for the stones purportedly swiped by *Tribune* correspondents from the Alamo, the Berlin Wall, the Parthenon and St Peter's Basilica, along with a rock from the moon. Head inside to visit the **McCormick Tribune Freedom Museum** (*see p100*), an exploration into the First Amendment rights of the US Constitution.

Time your arrival right, and you might catch a live radio broadcast from the Tribune Tower's streetfront studio. Close by it, NBC has gone one better: the **NBC 5 Streetside TV Studio** (401 N Michigan Avenue, www.nbc5.com) stages regular live television broadcasts. The schedule usually includes a daily 5am newcast (6am on weekends), and then further news round-ups at 11am, 4.30pm and 5pm. The public is encouraged to watch from the street.

Just across the street is the stunning **Wrigley Building** (400 N Michigan Avenue). A white terracotta-clad structure designed by Charles Beersman for Graham, Anderson, Probst & White, the firm later responsible for Merchandise Mart, it has stood at the base of Michigan Avenue since 1924, and remains home to the Wrigley gum company. The handsome clock tower was based on a cathedral tower in the Spanish city of Seville.

Further north, Michigan Avenue has its share of breathtaking architecture, not least the formerly exclusive (and men-only) Medinah Athletic Club building that's now home to the **Hotel Intercontinental** (*see p63*). However, the main reason people flock here is for the shops. From Gap to Gucci, Apple to Armani, the Magnificent Mile is one long paean to consumerism. Some shops have their own individual premises, but many others lie within malls. For details, *see pp190-214*.

Just across Chicago Avenue stand the **Water Tower** and the **Chicago Water Works** (163 E Pearson Street, at N Michigan Avenue, 1-312 744 2400), two of only a handful of structures to survive the Chicago Fire of 1871. The plaza around the Water Tower is a favourite spot for amateur musicians and artists to pass the hat, and for tourists to snag a ride on a horse-drawn carriage. Inside the Water Tower is the compact City Gallery, which favours Chicago-oriented exhibits; the Water Works across the street houses a visitors' centre, a gift shop and the **Lookingglass Theatre Company** (*see p281*). Also right here is the **Loyola University**

Museum of Art (820 N Michigan Avenue, at E Pearson Street, 1-312 915 7600, www.luc.edu/luma), which stages temporary shows.

The Water Tower is a handsome building, but these days it's very much in the shadow of the **John Hancock Center** (*see below*) just to the north. Towering 1,107 feet (337 metres) above the Magnificent Mile and the Gold Coast, it's smaller than the Sears Tower but affords more impressive views, chiefly because it has little competition from nearby skyscrapers. The criss-cross braces that form the building's outer frame were designed to keep the structure from swaying in the wind. Much of the building is residential, but the lower levels and the sunken plaza are home to assorted shops and eateries.

Across the street from the Hancock is the impressive **Fourth Presbyterian Church** (126 E Chestnut Street, at N Michigan Avenue, 1-312 787 4570, www.fourthchurch.org), built in 1914. A block north is the **Drake Hotel** (140 E Walton Street, at N Michigan Avenue; *see p65*), which has long been a stopover for the rich and famous. The hotel was designed to resemble a Renaissance palace: a gorgeous second-floor lobby ushers guests to over 500 plush rooms, while the first floor is lined with small retail shops. This is where the **Gold Coast** (*see p101*) really begins.

John Hancock Center

875 N Michigan Avenue, at E Delaware Place (1-888 875 8439/www.hancock-observatory.com). El: Red to Chicago. **Open** 9am-11pm daily. **Admission** $9.95; $6-$7.50 discounts; free under-4s. **Credit** Disc, MC, V. **Map** p326 J9.

Though it stands a few storeys shorter than the Sears Tower, Big John arguably offers even more stunning views. For one thing, it's far enough north to take in the Loop's skyline, and close enough to the water to allow glimpses of boats miles out on Lake Michigan. For another, the 94th-floor Hancock Observatory has an outdoor walkway: it's not for the faint of heart, granted, but it's guaranteed to blow the cobwebs away. Buy your ticket on the ground floor and take the ear-popping, 40-second elevator ride to the observatory, where you'll find floor-to-ceiling windows and plenty of maps to show you what you're looking at. As well as the aforementioned Skywalk outdoor walkway, there are historical displays and a few daft set-piece photo opportunities.

Another point in the Hancock's favour is its 96th-floor Signature Lounge. Though the restaurant below is (predictably) pricey, locals like to bring out-of-town guests to the bar here: even taking into account the cost of a cocktail, you're likely to break even on the deal, as there's no admission charge and you won't have to endure the tourist kitsch of the observation deck. The secret's out, so even people arriving when the bar opens at 5pm may be met with queues for the elevator, followed by queues for a

Looking south, west and north from the top of the **John Hancock Center**.

Explore your constitutional rights at the **McCormick Tribune Freedom Museum**.

table. But if you're willing to pay more than you usually would for a drink, the views are worth the wait, particularly as the sun goes down.

McCormick Tribune Freedom Museum

445 N Michigan Avenue, at E Illinois Street (1-312 222 4860/www.freedommuseum.us). **El:** *Red to Grand.* **Open** 10am-6pm Mon, Wed-Sun. **Admission** $5; free under-5s. **Credit** AmEx, Disc, MC, V. **Map** p326 J11.

It would be easy to write off this relatively new museum for no other reason than its name. The word 'freedom' may in recent years have become associated with rampant nationalism, and even with a dash of imperialism. But don't let this deter you: the freedoms addressed here are of a more traditional variety. The First Amendment rights of the American Constitution are the focus here, with exhibits covering everything from the Declaration of Independence to recent debates over war protests. One display lets you make decisions on Supreme Court cases, while another lets you check out symbols and music that were once banned. However, the museum's central exhibit is *12151791*, a two-storey sculpture named after the date on which the First Amendment was ratified. Thought-provoking stuff.

Streeterville

Loosely defined as the area south of the Hancock Center and east of Michigan Avenue, Streeterville takes its name from the scoundrel who ran his steamboat aground on a sandbar near the lakeshore in 1886 and immediately claimed the area as independent territory. As rubble was dumped in the lake, Captain George Wellington Streeter began taking waste (and money) from building contractors, and

eventually managed to expand his sandbar, which he called the 'District of Lake Michigan', by 186 acres with the landfill. His fight was valiant and lengthy, but his mansion was finally torched by the Chicago Title & Trust Company in 1918. Two decades later, his relatives gave up the fight.

The area is these days considerably calmer than in Streeter's day, when thieves, prostitutes and marauders roamed the locale. Much of the neighbourhood is given over to expensive residential property and grand hotels, though it's also home to Northwestern University's downtown campus and, at N Columbus Drive and W Illinois Street, **NBC Tower**. Built in 1989 but designed to blend in with the 1920s and '30s art deco skyscrapers that surround it, the block is home to the studio in which Jerry Springer records his notorious talk show. The show is filmed from Monday to Wednesday between September and April; for tickets, call 1-312 321 5365 or see www.jerryspringertv.com.

Located along the stretch of the Chicago River that flows into Lake Michigan, **North Pier** (435 E Illinois Street, at N Lake Shore Drive, 1-312 836 4300) doesn't compare to neighbouring **Navy Pier** (*see p101*) in terms of size and the number of attractions. But it does have peace and quiet in its favour. There are plenty of places to sit outside and watch boaters heading out to the lake. At the far eastern end you'll find the Centennial Fountain and Arc, commemorating the city's Water Reclamation District. An arc of water shoots out of the fountain and into the river – and sometimes on to passing boaters – every hour, on the hour (10am-2pm, 5pm-midnight, Map-Sept).

This pocket has been the site of much activity in recent years, with the establishment of new residential buildings and a handful of new, big-ticket shops and restaurants. E Illinois Street alone is home to the new **AMC River East 21** cineplex (No.322; *see p237*); the flashy **Lucky Strike Lanes** (in the same building; *see p275*); the sprawling **Fox & Obel** (No.401; *see p206*), Chicago's finest gourmet food market; and **DeLaCosta** (No.465; *see p153*), a new, rather glamorous Mexican-slanted restaurant. The latter duo sit in the **River East Art Center** (www.rivereastartcenter.com), a new development housing retail space and a handful of galleries. However, if it's art you're after, you're better served by the temporary shows at the low-key **Arts Club of Chicago** (201 E Ontario Street, at N St Clair Street, 1-312 787 3997) or the rather more high-profile **Museum of Contemporary Art** (*see below*).

Museum of Contemporary Art

220 E Chicago Avenue, at N Mies van der Rohe Way (1-312 280 2660/www.mcachicago.org).
El: Red to Chicago. **Open** 10am-8pm Tue; 10am-5pm Wed-Sun. **Admission** $10; $6 discounts; free under-12s; free to all Tue. **Credit** AmEx, DC, Disc, MC, V. **Map** p326 J9.

While the Art Institute has a pair of lions to guard it, the MCA needs no such deterrents: the $46-million building, designed by Berlin architect Josef Paul Kleihues and opened to coincide with the MCA's 30th birthday in 1997, is imposing enough. However, while its exterior is daunting (and not universally admired), it's a different story inside: since it opened, its vast spaces have proved supremely adaptable.

The emphasis here is on temporary shows. The MCA's scattershot approach to programming is admirable and pays plenty of dividends, both with its exhibitions and the performances that take place within its walls (theatre, dance, performance art and chamber music); there's also a library, a lecture hall, a sculpture garden, a Wolfgang Puck restaurant and an excellent shop. The 2007-08 calendar gives some idea of the variety on offer: Escultura Social: A New Generation of Art from Mexico City (June-Sept 2007), which features the work of young Mexico City artists working in non-traditional sculptural materials, is followed by Sympathy for the Devil: Art and Rock 'n' Roll Since 1967 (Sept 2007-Jan 2008), which explores the relationship between rock and visual art, which in turn will be followed by a retrospective of American painter Jim Nutt (Feb-June 2008).

Navy Pier

Navy Pier hasn't always been the glittering tourist façade it is today. Built as the rather plain-sounding Municipal Pier No.2 by Charles Frost as a commercial shipping pier in 1916, one of five piers proposed six years earlier by architect Daniel Burnham (who didn't live to see it built), it became more or less deserted when most commercial ships were re-routed to a pier on the South Side. During World Wars I and II, the 50-acre site was occupied by the US Navy, before serving as the first campus for the University of Illinois at Chicago until 1965.

Following a period of relative dereliction, the city renovated the pier as a leisure destination in the late 1980s. The multi-million-dollar project was completed in 1995, since when it's been one of the city's leading family attractions. A 15-storey Ferris wheel, a crazy golf course and a hand-painted musical carousel provide old-fashioned entertainment, as does the **Smith Museum of Stained Glass Windows** (1-312 595 5024; admission free). An IMAX cinema (*see p237*) and the Skyline Stage (1-312 595 7437), at which concerts are held in summer, bring things into the 21st century; shops, food stands, restaurants, the **Chicago Children's Museum** (*see p226*) and the **Chicago Shakespeare Theater** (*see p279*) complete the list of permanent attractions.

Time your visit carefully and you'll be seduced by the crisp breeze whipping in off the lake. Ambitious visitors take a ride on one of the boats that dock along the south side of the pier; most offer trips throughout the day and evening. Navy Pier also receives yearly visits from the tall ships and acts as a showcase for public art. Recently unveiled plans for the pier from Metropolitan Pier and Exposition Authority include the addition of a monorail, a rollercoaster, a floating hotel and a water park.

Just outside Navy Pier to the north, off Lake Shore Drive, is **Olive Park**, a quiet green space with room for picnicking. The small **Ohio Street Beach**, just to the west, contains a sculpture garden honouring Jane Addams (*see p122*) and offers superb views of the skyline.

Navy Pier

600 E Grand Avenue, at Lake Michigan (1-312 595 7437/www.navypier.com). El: Red to Grand. **Open** *late May-early Sept* 10am-10pm Mon-Thur, Sun; 10am-midnight Fri, Sat. *Early Sept-Oct* 10am-9pm Mon-Thur; 10am-11pm Fri, Sat; 10am-7pm Sun. *Nov-late May* 10am-8pm Mon-Thur; 10am-10pm Fri, Sat; 10am-7pm Sun. **Admission** free. **Credit** varies. **Map** p326 K10.

The Gold Coast

Map p327

El: Red to Chicago or Clark/Division.

You can tell a lot about a neighbourhood by the company it keeps. When, in 1882, entrepreneur Potter Palmer built a $250,000 'mansion to end all mansions' on what now equates to 1350 N Lake Shore Drive, he became as much a pioneer in real estate as he had previously been in retail

(Palmer was one of the leading lights in the establishment of a commercial district in downtown Chicago). This area had been marshland up until Palmer's arrival, but when a string of rich and influential Chicagoans followed in his wake, the locale soon came to replace Prairie Avenue (*see p90*) as the preferred address of Chicago's elite.

As the Gold Coast's reputation grew, it became a destination to which many Chicagoans aspired. The area attracted the Roman Catholic Church, whose archbishop of the city resides at an expansive red-brick building on State Street (*see p105*). Just blocks away, Hugh Hefner chose the building at 1340 N State Street for his Playboy Mansion, though he eventually moved his headquarters and his bunnies to California. Palmer's mansion was torn down in 1950 to make room for one of the area's multiple high-rises, some of which are of architectural merit. However, many of the Gold Coast's early stately homes have been left standing, in styles ranging from Tudor to art deco.

Technically, the Gold Coast is bounded by Chicago and North Avenues, Clark Street and Lake Michigan. While the northern half of this area is chiefly residential, the southern block is mostly commercial. Oak Street is home to many of the city's ritziest boutiques, while the area around Rush and Division Street has had more bars and restaurants per square foot than any other corner of Chicago since the 1920s. The 1986 film *About Last Night* was set here, but the area's now been dubbed the 'Viagra Triangle' on account of its popularity with greying men on the prowl for younger women. On weekends, the bars on Division Street are

Beachy keen

Chicago loves its beaches, but when they're covered by snow six months of the year, it's hard to tell which ones are worth a visit during the relatively fleeting summer. Picking one gets trickier when you consider the vast stretches of sandy shoreline. So we've boiled down your lakefront options to three beaches with distinctive, lovable personalities.

Beaches are open from 9am to 9.30pm in summer. The Park District tests the waters for bacteria on a frequent basis, so check www.chicagoparkdistrict.com (and click on 'Swim Report') for daily updates on weather and water conditions. And put on that sunscreen: the red lobster look is *so* out.

12th Street Beach, South Loop
Snuggled between the Adler Planetarium and Northerly Island Park (formerly Meigs Field), this cute little sandy cove is empty in the early afternoon aside from a few beach bums and a family or two. For privacy and a scenic view of the lakefront, head to the far north side and cast your towel on the sand under the shade of a tree. The strip of beach is small, but there's plenty of room for the kids to play, judging by the numerous sandcastles and the smiling faces peeping out from buried bodies, and it's perfect for a BYOG (that's 'bring your own grill') barbecue on the lawn.
Amenities: New landscaping has provided gardens and walkways that add to the beach's simple charm. Facilities include no-frills bathrooms, showers, drinking fountains and a beach café.

Where to eat: To save a buck on that hot dog and Gatorade, bypass the beach café and head over to the south-west side of the beach to the pretzel stand. For more variety on the menu, duck into Galileo's Café at the Adler Planetarium for lunch (*see p89*): you won't have to pay admission if you stick to the dining area.
1200 S Lake Shore Drive, at Solidarity Drive, South Loop (1-312 747 2524).

North Avenue Beach, Old Town
Seething with sexy singles playing beach sports and muscle-bound men cycling down the lakefront path, North Avenue Beach is the West Coast minus the surf. If you're not into scoping and getting scoped, you might find this strip of sand a bit run-down. Still, it's worth it for the beautiful skyline views of the city.
Amenities: That big boat-shaped building on the beach houses bathrooms, showers and a host of services. Get a beach towel or an umbrella for $10 a day, or rent a bike for a beachfront ride. You'll also find a newspaper stand, a counter-service café, and Castaways Bar & Grill (1-773 281 1200), which affords rooftop views of the bikini- and shorts-packed beach and stages sets by cover bands happy to butcher classic rock tunes for your inebriated pleasure. However, by far the biggest attraction is volleyball. The Chicago Sport & Social Club provides more than 50 volleyball nets for registered league play and a few for walk-ons.

a rowdy, booze-soaked whirlpool in which tourists, conventioneers, suburbanites and college grads happily drown their dignity.

Oak Street & around

The Gold Coast's greatest jewel sits just on the shoulder of the city, along Lake Michigan off Oak Street. During summer, the **Oak Street Beach** is the Riviera of Chicago's shoreline, where the city's buff and beautiful people go to sun, swim and show off. In summer, there's a flurry of activity around the volleyball nets and the lakeside paths. As in-line skaters, runners and cyclists fly by, vendors sell food and drink; for a beach, the pace is relentless. Pedestrian access to the beach is via underpasses located across from the Drake Hotel at Michigan Avenue and Oak Street. However, it's far from

the only beach along Lake Michigan; for details of the others, *see p102* **Beachy keen**.

The Gold Coast's other attractions are considerably less frenetic. **Oak Street** itself is the city's high-end fashion strip (*see p195*); walking west along it will lead you to within a stone's throw of **Washington Square**, a green space bound by Delaware, Walton, Dearborn and Clark Streets. Throughout its history, the square saw spirited demonstrations from all kinds of lively orators and protestors, until Mayor Richard J Daley cracked down on it in the 1960s. These days, it's an extremely calm place for 364 days a year. The exception is the last Sunday of July, when the square hosts the lively, politicised Bughouse Debates in tribute to the park's past life.

The debates are organised by the **Newberry Library** (60 W Walton Street, at N Clark Street,

Where to eat: Castaways is open until 11pm, but if you want to nosh on the beach, be sure to pack a picnic: all the cafés and hot-dog stands close at 5pm.
1600 N Lake Shore Drive, at N LaSalle Drive, Old Town (1-312 742 7725).

Montrose Beach, Uptown

The first thing to realise about Montrose Beach is that the name is a misnomer. The lakefront activities stretch from Montrose Avenue all the way to Wilson Avenue. Get over it and roam around: you'll stumble upon loads of fun activities. This swathe of lakefront attracts more doers than spectators: most prominent are the Latino families cooking out, and the Eastern Europeans who've brought their tradition of promenading to the Midwest. The water is surprisingly clean; unfortunately, other than the breakwater rocks, it's not enclosed.
Amenities: Bike Chicago (1-312 595 9600) rents hybrids and cruisers for $8-$9 an hour, and surrey bikes (canopied quadracycles) for $20-$25 an hour. Montrose Harbor is home to the venerable Corinthian Yacht Club, which regularly hosts races. Closer to Wilson Avenue, there's a six-lane

launch for boats and personal watercraft; kayaks, sailboats and paddle boats are available through www.h2ofun.com. Fishermen can be seen wetting a line at the Montrose Pier thanks to its proximity to the Park Bait Company (600 W Montrose Avenue, 1-773 271 2838). Landlubbers love charging around Cricket Hill, a popular runner's course.
Where to eat: On the beach side is LA Concessions (1-312 782 9855), serving snacks such as ice-cream, chips and hot dogs. Siam Cafe (4712 N Sheridan Road, 1-773 769 6602) serves good, cheap Thai food, and wine and beer.
4400 N Lake Shore Drive, at W Montrose Avenue, Uptown (1-312 742 7526).

Sightseeing

1-312 943 9090, www.newberry.org), Chicago's research library for the humanities. Founded in 1887 by banker Walter L Newberry, it's not a lending library but a research centre, housing a vast variety of history, literature, genealogy and cartography texts, along with a collection of Thomas Jefferson's letters. The building itself, overlooking Washington Square, was designed by Henry Ives Cobb and completed in 1893. Non-academics can see inside by visiting one of the seminars, lectures and concerts staged at the library, or visiting its annual fund-raising Christmas bazaar.

Astor Street

Running north from Division Street, close by the impressively colourful and exuberant **Lake Shore Drive Synagogue** (70 E Elm Street, 1-312 337 6811, tours by request), sits handsome, historic **Astor Street**. A stroll along these quiet pavements offers a window into an era when Chicago's wealthiest citizens jostled for bragging rights by building more luxurious mansions than their neighbours, mansions that have been immaculately preserved by their current residents. Astor Street went up in the world after the Chicago Fire of 1871, when the city was forced to rebuild its downtown with a vengeance. However, the quarter-mile stretch of road didn't really come into its own until the turn of the 20th century.

Unlike the barn-like palaces that languished on Prairie Avenue (*see p90*), previously the city's most desirable address, the mansions built on Astor Street by the likes of Cyrus McCormick and the Goodmans were more akin to overgrown townhouses. Most of the properties were built in the Queen Anne, Romanesque or Georgian Revival architectural styles, though their gaudy coats of arms, turrets and balconies were later dubbed 'Stockyard Renaissance' by one wag.

From the late 19th century until World War II, the street was home to many of the richest men and women in the city. But after the war, the lure of the North Shore put the area on the skids: many of the buildings were knocked down in the 1960s to make room for the faceless high-rise condo buildings that stud the Gold Coast. However, community protest got the area declared a Landmark District in 1975, the first such area in Chicago, and the homes are now largely in excellent shape.

Even the apartment towers along Astor Street carry with them a little class. Take the pair **Nos.1260 and 1301**, for example: built in the early 1930s by Philip B Maher, they're almost identical examples of art deco luxury, the artful minimalism of their design providing a bridge between the new and old Gold Coasts. And at the same intersection (with Goethe Street) stands **No.1300**, the most eye-catchingly modern building on the road. Designed by one-time Astor Street resident Bertrand Goldberg (who also built the corncob towers of Marina City; *see p96*) and completed in 1963, the 28-storey tower sits perched on a small glass box and some precariously slender columns.

Before continuing up Astor Street, take a quick stroll east to the **Three Arts Club** (1300 N Dearborn Street, at W Goethe Street, 1-312 944 6250, www.threearts.org). This long-established enterprise harks back to an era when society women felt the need to protect young ladies from the 'wicked city' by giving them a refuge in which study painting, drama or music. Built by Holabird & Root in 1914 to resemble a Tuscan villa, it's the only club of its kind still in operation (similar clubs operated in Paris, New York and London). Sadly, the club announced in 2006 – with a heavy heart – that the building will be put up for sale, after anticipated public funding for renovation did not materialise.

Head back to Astor Street and continue north to No.1355, also known as **Astor Court**. This Georgian mansion was designed by Howard Van Doren Shaw in 1914 for William O Goodman, who funded the construction of the Goodman Theatre in the Loop (*see p279*) in tribute to their late playwright son. The marble archway and spiked fence give it a hint of Versailles, as does the tantalising glimpse through a gate of a lost-in-time courtyard.

Next door is one of the real landmarks on the street, the **Charnley House** (No.1365). A simple but compact building, it was built in 1892 and designed by the great Frank Lloyd Wright while he was still working under the auspices of Louis Sullivan's firm (he was later fired for moonlighting). It's a mix of the duo's styles, combining Lloyd Wright's sweeping horizontal lines and Sullivan's ornamentation. It's now the headquarters of the Society of Architectural Historians, which conducts tours of the house every Wednesday at noon and every Saturday at 10am (and also at 1pm from April to November). For details, call 1-312 915 0105 or see www.charnleyhouse.org.

Across the junction with Schiller Street sits the **Ryerson House** (No.1406), designed by David Adler in 1922 for steel magnate Joseph T Ryerson. Its look was patterned, mostly successfully, after Paris hotels. Just beyond it stands a tall, skinny slice of Art Deco simplicity: completed in 1929 by the firm of Holabird & Root, the **Russell House** (No.1444) faces the world with a sleek stone façade imported from France and carved decorative panels. Opposite, the **Fortune House** (No.1451) was built in the Jacobethan style in 1910 by Howard Van Doren Shaw. It has a clean country house look to it that is more akin to the houses in Wilmette.

At the junction with Burton Place stands the imposing edifice of the palazzo that former mayor Joseph Medill built for his daughter, Mrs Robert Patterson, in 1893. The orange brick walls, terracotta trim and inviting courtyard of **No.1500** have all aged well, though the property has now been divided into frighteningly exclusive condominiums. Just west off Astor Street, the thick, immovable **Madlener House** (4 W Burton Place) was built in 1902 by Richard Schmidt and is now home to an arts organisation. Its interior can be seen as part of the Saturday tours of Charnley House (*see p104*).

Its postal address is 1555 N State Parkway, but the **Archbishop's Residence** stretches an entire block along Astor Street. This 1885 Queen Anne mansion is built of red brick with sandstone trim and has 19 chimneys poking up to the sky. At the top of Astor Street, either turn right in the direction of the **International Museum of Surgical Science** (*see below*), or wander left along W North Avenue. At No.59 is one of the city's oldest and most expensive private schools, the **Latin School of Chicago**. Founded in 1888, it counts guitarist Roger McGuinn and sculptor Claes Oldenburg among its alumni. Just across the road is the **Chicago History Museum** (*see p108*) and the **Old Town** neighbourhood (*see p106*).

International Museum of Surgical Science

1524 N Lake Shore Drive, at E North Avenue (1-312 642 6502/www.imss.org). El: Red to Clark/Division. Bus: 72, 73, 151. **Open** 10am-4pm Tue-Sat. **Admission** $6; $3 discounts; free to all Tue. **Credit** AmEx, MC, V. **Map** p327 H7.

Not everyone will appreciate the assortment of surgery-related artefacts at this unusual museum. Indeed, many will probably shudder at the sight of a 3,000-year-old Peruvian skull drill or the Civil War-era amputation kit. Still, as with a gruesome car accident, it's difficult to look away. Operated by the neighbouring International College of Surgeons since 1954, the rather creepy International Museum of Surgical Science also houses a rare (working) iron lung; a re-created x-ray lab that includes Emil Grubbe's turn-of-the-century equipment; oddly captivating surgery-related murals by Gregorio Calvi di Bergolo; anatomy- and surgery-related art exhibitions; and, for the kids, a walk-in re-creation of a 19th-century apothecary. A small gallery space features revolving anatomy- and surgery-related art exhibitions. If your stomach starts to turn, make a dash for outside: the façade of the lakefront mansion, which was designed by renowned architect Howard Van Doren in 1917, is also worth a look.

Historic **Astor Street**, where the other half liked to live. *See p104*.

Old Town & Lincoln Park

A former cabbage patch and an old cemetery make up two desirable 'hoods.

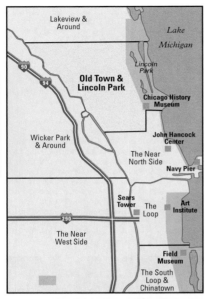

El: Brown or Purple to Sedgwick; Red to North/Clybourn.

Sightseeing

Old Town

Map p327

El: Brown or Purple to Sedgwick; Red to North/Clybourn.

Once a trading spot for Indian tribes, the neighbourhood now known as Old Town was properly settled by German immigrants, who were pushed north following the Chicago Fire of 1871. At the time, the stretch of land between North Avenue, Clark Street, Armitage Avenue and Larrabee Street was little more than a patchwork of gardens and cow pastures, but it was redeveloped after the blaze; the influx of German shops and restaurants along North Avenue earned it the moniker 'German Broadway'. After World War II, the neighbourhood was finally considered venerable enough to assume its current name.

The development of the Cabrini-Green public housing project along Division Street and the collapse of industry in the area in the 1950s changed the face of Old Town's south-west corner. Home to 20,000 people, the project became a symbol of the city's neglect of its urban poor, the extremes of gang violence and the local drug trade. Ever conscious of its public image (and ever aware of the escalating price of real estate), the city has recently begun to tear down the development's main towers and relocate its residents, a programme of enforced gentrification that's not been without its critics. Nearby, upmarket apartment blocks, grocery stores and coffee shops have sprouted.

The downturn of Old Town made it financially viable territory for movers and shakers in the 1950s counterculture, who began to lend the neighbourhood a new character. During the following decade, the area became a kind of Midwestern equivalent to New York's Greenwich Village and San Francisco's Haight. The likes of Miles Davis and John Coltrane played (and recorded) at the Plugged Nickel (1321 N Wells Street); just down the road sat Mother Blues (No.1305), a no less important music venue at the time. Folk singers also descended on the district, to the **Old Town School of Folk Music** on Armitage Avenue (*see p259*) and the Earl of Old Town pub at 1615 N Wells Street. Just opposite the latter, Mike Nichols' and Elaine May's **Second City** crew (*see p232*) went about defining modern sketch comedy after emerging from the ashes of the Compass Players troupe.

It couldn't last, and didn't. As has been the case with many such fashionable and forward-thinking neighbourhoods across the world, Old Town proved too attractive for its own good. As its reputation rose, so did the rents, and the hippies, beatniks and folkies were gradually forced to look elsewhere. The cutting edge is conspicuous by its absence in what is now a relatively affluent and cultured part of town. Along Wells Street and Armitage Avenue sits a slew of smart restaurants and one of the city's longest string of boutiques. Still, some of the old raffishness remains in the **Old Town Ale House** (*see p181*), a glorious imbiberie that continues to draw a democratic mix of working stiffs, theatrical luvvies, rabblerousing twentysomethings and hopeless old soaks.

Bona fide sights and attractions are largely absent from Old Town, but a wander around its confines is nonetheless an agreeable way to lose track of an afternoon. It remains a handsome place, nowhere more so than in the historic **Old Town Triangle**. Hemmed in by Wells Street to the east, North Avenue to the south and a vaguely diagonal line connecting the Lincoln Avenue/Wisconsin Street junction with the corner of North and Larrabee, this cosy district has retained many of its 19th-century cottages, built in the three decades after the Chicago Fire. It's easy to see why the locals are so proud of their neighbourhood.

One such street is **Crilly Court**, constructed by developer Daniel F Crilly in the middle of an entire block he purchased in the early 1880s. Between 1885 and 1893, Crilly built row houses on the west side of the block and four-storey apartment buildings on the east, carving the names of his four children above the doors. Some five decades later, son Edgar renovated the buildings, closing off the alleys to form a series of courtyards. The renovation was one of the first in the Old Town Triangle, and the younger Crilly is credited with leading the way in the historical preservation of the locale.

Several homes near Crilly Court have their own historic significance. The residence at 216 W Menomonee Street is believed to have been a 'fire relief cottage', built by the city following the Chicago Fire (at a cost of $75) to provide shelter for homeless residents. The 1872 frame house at 1802 N Lincoln Park West, meanwhile, is one of only a handful of wooden farmhouses left in the area; the restrictions on building materials after the fire made such structures scarce.

Just north are two other frame houses built in the 1870s for the Swiss-born Wacker brewing family. Frederick's son Charles, then a member of Chicago's planning commission and the man after whom Wacker Drive is named, lived in the carriage house at 1836 N Lincoln Park West, while his father resided in the Swiss chalet-style residence at 1838. Down the street, the row houses at 1828-1834 N Lincoln Park West were designed by Dankmar Adler and Louis Sullivan in 1884 and 1885. Displaying Sullivan's love of geometric ornamentation, they're rare examples of his early residential work.

One of the oldest buildings in Old Town is also one of its tallest. Built in 1869 on land donated by beer baron Michael Diversey, the Romanesque **St Michael's Church** (1633 N Cleveland Avenue, at W North Avenue, 1-312 642 2498, www.st-mikes.org) was partially gutted by the Chicago Fire, but rebuilt in next to no time by the Germans who worshipped in it. Local tradition dictates that if you can hear the ringing of the bells (the largest of which weighs an amazing 6,000 pounds (2,800 kilos), you're in Old Town. The interior, open to the public, contains a carved wooden altar and stained-glass windows; outside are stone columns and several roofs with intricate brickwork.

A few streets away sits the **Midwest Buddhist Temple** (435 W Menomonee Street, at N Hudson Avenue, 1-312 943 7801, www. midwestbuddhisttemple.org), a modernist structure built in the early 1970s by Japanese

Crilly Court.

immigrants who began to settle in the area. The one-storey concrete base is topped by a pagoda-like roof; inside sits a sizeable gold Buddha. The congregation, still about 80 per cent Japanese, hosts an annual Ginza Holiday in the middle of August, celebrating Japanese culture, dance, music and food.

Heading east, it's hard to miss the enormous **Moody Church** (1609 N LaSalle Street, 1-312 943 0466, www.moodychurch.org), named after the 19th-century evangelist Dwight L Moody and completed in 1925. Directly beyond it is the south-western corner of **Lincoln Park** (*see below*), and the excellent **Chicago History Museum** (*see below*).

Chicago History Museum

1601 N Clark Street, at W North Avenue (1-312 642 4600/www.chicagohistory.org). El: Brown, Purple to Sedgwick. **Open** 9.30am-4.30pm Mon-Wed, Fri, Sat; 9.30am-8pm Thur; noon-5pm Sun. **Admission** $12; $1-$10 discounts; free under-12s. Free to all Mon. **Credit** AmEx, DC, Disc, MC, V. **Map** p327 H7.

The museum formerly known as the Chicago Historical Society has given its facility, and its image, a major makeover. Founded in 1852, it's the city's oldest cultural institution. After a massive refurbishment, it returned in 2006 with a younger, more populist identity.

That said, it hasn't changed beyond recognition. Permanent exhibitions, which are now presented thematically rather than chronologically, include old favourites such as Chicago's first locomotive, the table upon which Lincoln signed the Emancipation Proclamation, and George Washington's inaugural

suit. Of the new displays, City in Crisis remembers some of the city's disasters, such as the Chicago Fire of 1871, the Eastland boat disaster (*see p21* **Unsteady as she goes**) and the race riots of 1919. Conversely, City on the Make and My Kind of Town recall some of the city's more positive moments, such as its rapid growth and early industry, as well as great moments in sports and recreation. The temporary exhibitions are just as interesting and varied, taking in everything from Chicago sports memorabilia to local photography. The spruced-up building still houses a tastefully stocked gift shop; the selection of books, in particular, is impeccable. A programme of lectures, discussions and tours rounds things out nicely.

Lincoln Park

Map p327 & p328

El: Brown or Purple to Armitage, Diversey or Fullerton; Red to Fullerton.

In the middle of the 19th century, the area around **Lincoln Park** contained little more than a smallpox hospital and a conveniently located cemetery. Today, it's one of Chicago's most desirable neighbourhoods, its popularity due in no small part to the picturesque, 1,200-acre lakefront space from which it takes its name. The park runs along Lake Michigan from North Avenue (1600 N) up to Hollywood Avenue (5700 N) on the edge of Andersonville. The neighbourhood, however, extends only as far as Diversey Avenue (2800 N), running westwards all the way to the Chicago River.

Lincoln Park.

The park

The same urban utopian spirit that inspired the design for New York's Central Park made Lincoln Park a reality. Named after Abraham Lincoln in the wake of his 1865 assassination, the park was created on drained swampland (and the city's cemetery) over several decades. Not even the Chicago Fire put a stop to its construction, which continued into the 20th century with the addition of several of its most beloved institutions and the extension of the park far into northern Chicago. It's grown into one of the city's most cherished sites.

Lincoln Park is laced with paths that invite aimless strolling or unimpeded cycling (*see p111* **Easy riders**), but also has facilities for other activities. There are playing fields and golf courses, tennis courts and chess tables; you can even rent a paddleboat on the South Pond, from a kiosk right by the historic **Café Brauer** (2021 N Stockton Drive, 1-312 742 2400). The park is undoubtedly at its best on weekdays during summer, when it's a relatively peaceful place. Even at weekends, though, it's not too hectic: its immense size and reach mean the crowds tend to spread out along its length.

When the city began work on the park in the 1860s, it decided to move all the bodies from the cemetery to other locations in the north of the city. Most went quietly, as one might expect dead people to go. However, the family of hotelier Ira Crouch went to court to prevent the city from shifting their beloved's corpse. Much to their surprise, and to the city's irritation, they won; as a result, the **Couch Mausoleum** stands near the junction of LaSalle and Clark Streets, not far from the world's oldest statue of the president who lends his name to the park.

The park's main attraction, and the one area that can get a little too busy in summer, is the **Lincoln Park Zoo** (*see below*), a small and much beloved operation located at around 2200 N (near Webster Avenue). Just north of the elephant house sits the **Alfred Caldwell Lily Pool**, built in 1889 and redesigned four decades later by the Prairie School architect whose name it bears. Restored in 2005, it's now a National Historic Landmark, and well worth a look.

Just north of the zoo's main entrance is the **Shakespeare Garden**, which contains a variety of flowers and plants mentioned in the Bard's plays. The garden also contains the Bates Fountain, a popular cooling destination in summer, and a bronze bust of the playwright that dates back to 1894; it's one of more than 20 sculptural monuments dating from the late 19th century, maintained with funds raised by an advocacy group.

The broad lawn leads to the **Lincoln Park Conservatory** (1-312 742 7736), a Victorian greenhouse erected in 1892. The four halls of the conservatory retain a variety of climates and allow plants from all over the world to flourish. The conservatory is open 9am-5pm daily, and admission is free. Just across from it is the **Notebaert Nature Museum** (*see p110*).

Lincoln Park Zoo

2200 N Cannon Drive, at W Webster Avenue (1-312 742 2000/www.lpzoo.org). El: Brown, Purple or Red to Fullerton. **Open** *Zoo buildings: Apr, May, Sept, Oct* 10am-5pm daily. *June-Aug* 10am-5pm Mon-Fri; 10am-6.30pm Sat, Sun. *Nov-Mar* 10am-4.30pm daily. *Zoo grounds: Apr, May, Sept, Oct* 9am-6pm daily. *June-Aug* 9am-6pm Mon-Fri; 9am-7pm Sat, Sun. *Nov-Mar* 9am-5pm daily. **Admission** free. **No credit cards**. **Map** p328 H5.

Compared to its direct competitors, it's small. Next to other local attractions, it lacks modern, whizz-bang technology. That said, there are few quintessentially Chicagoan activities more enjoyable than strolling through Lincoln Park Zoo on a sunny weekday afternoon. It opened in 1868 after the park was presented with two swans by New York's Central Park; 140 years later, it's one of the oldest zoos in the country, its 35-acre site home to 1,000 species.

The zoo was the subject of some controversy in the last few years, when a trio of elephants died in relatively quick succession. Even without them, there's still plenty to enjoy. The Kovler Lion House remains popular; so, too, does the Regenstein African Journey, which re-creates an African landscape and houses a variety of species native to the continent. Another top draw is the Regenstein Center for African Apes. The zoo is a world leader in gorilla breeding, with nearly 50 born here since 1970. Added in 2005, the Pritzker Family Children's Zoo features a re-created wooded environment complete with beavers, wolves and bears. All told, it's an attractive place, and it's a wonder it's still free: since 1995, it's been run not by the city but by the Lincoln Park Zoological Society, with two-thirds of its income coming from private sources.

Notebaert Nature Museum

2430 N Cannon Drive, at W Fullerton Avenue (1-773 755 5100/www.naturemuseum.org). El: Brown, Purple or Red to Fullerton. **Open** 9am-4.30pm Mon-Fri; 10am-5pm Sat, Sun. **Admission** $7; $4-$5 discounts; free under-3s. Free to all Thur. **Credit** AmEx, Disc, MC, V. **Map** p328 H5.
Its location, along Lincoln Park's North Pond, is ideal. Its $31-million, 73,000sq ft (6,600sq m) building is grand. And the fanfare that greeted its opening in 1999 was enormous. Still, the Notebaert Nature Museum is a bit of a disappointment, due chiefly to the fact that few of its exhibits are as exciting as they should be. Highlights include the Extreme Green House, a mock bungalow that aims to teach kids domestic science; and the Hands-On Habitat, which aims to teach kids about how animals live. The temporary exhibitions also occasionally hit the mark. But the museum's main selling point is the Judy Istock Butterfly Haven, a glass-topped space populated by over 50 species of butterfly. The most attractive parts of the museum are the outdoor pond and walkway; these can be enjoyed for free, leaving the admission fee to be invested in a good lunch instead. For a few dollars more, it's well worth heading to North Pond (*see p159*), one of Chicago's premier eateries.

The neighbourhood

Lincoln Park began to take off as a residential neighbourhood in the late 1970s, after the Puerto Rican Young Lords turf gang that once rumbled around its streets began to disperse. These days, it's a sought-after address among the North Side's burgeoning population of youngish urban professionals and career-focused post-collegiates with money to burn. (This image of Lincoln Park locals has become something of a cliché, but is still grounded in truth.) As with Old Town, its neighbour to the south, Lincoln Park doesn't contain many sights per se, but it's no less appealing for all that. Wide, tree-lined streets lead – if you're lucky – to attractive corner bars and appealing shops, frequented by a mostly laid-back bunch.

The neighbourhood is anchored by **DePaul University**, the campus of which ebbs quietly out from around the intersection of Fullerton and Sheffield Avenues. The college connection is most obvious along the nearby stretches of Lincoln Avenue and Clark Street, dotted with sports bars and low-key party palaces that get flooded with people, and alcohol, on weekends. Pockets of the area are essentially a collegiate equivalent to the similarly crass Rush/Division axis down in the Gold Coast, but it's easily avoided. Armitage Avenue and Halsted Street are more easygoing alternatives.

Over half of the buildings in Lincoln Park were built between 1880 and 1904. These days, there's a battle raging between preservationists, who want to hang on to the area's heritage, and developers, who'd prefer to tear parts of it down and start again. Quaint Victorian houses are increasingly having to fight for attention with giant new mansions, but they're winning the battle so far. One of the architectural highlights is the **Francis J Dewes Mansion** (www.dewesmansion.com), built at 503 W Wrightwood Avenue (at N Hampden Court) for a local beer baron in 1896.

Just west of the zoo (*see p109*) is the site of the infamous **St Valentine's Day Massacre**, where, on 14 February 1929, seven members of Bugs Moran's gang were executed against a garage wall by Al Capone's henchmen. Though Moran escaped (he'd overslept), the killings broke his resistance and cemented Capone's position at the forefront of Chicago's lucrative organised crime world. Film fans will have seen a fictional and comical version of the massacre at the beginning of *Some Like it Hot*. The garage, at 2122 N Clark Street, has since been replaced by a lawn. But the incident still resonates: the nearby **Chicago Pizza & Oven Grinder Company** (*see p157*) tells the tale on its menus.

Several blocks north-west is the site of yet another fabled gangland killing: that of John Dillinger, a professional criminal who had escaped from police custody in Crown Point, Indiana, where he was awaiting trial for the murder of a cop. He'd been pinned as Public Enemy Number One by the FBI, who tracked him down to the **Biograph Theatre** (2433 N Lincoln Avenue, at W Fullerton Avenue) on 22 July 1934. As he left a screening of *Manhattan Melodrama*, police shot him dead; bystanders dipped their skirts and handkerchiefs in his blood as souvenirs. The Biograph closed as a cinema several years ago, but was recently taken over by the **Victory Gardens Theater** (*see p282*). Dillinger, meanwhile, is remembered on the anniversary of his death each year with a parade from the **Red Lion Pub** (*see p182*) to the site of his grisly demise.

For more green pleasantness, pop by **Oz Park** (2021 N Burling Street, at W Dickens Avenue). Guarded by a statue of the Tin Man, it takes its name from the seminal book and Judy Garland-starring movie, whose author L Frank Baum lived in Chicago.

Easy riders

Linking the Osterman Beach on the North Side with 71st Street on the South Side, Chicago's **Lakefront Trail** is one of the city's great glories. Clocking in at a little under 20 miles of gloriously car-free traffic, it's packed on summer weekends with joggers, inline skaters and cyclists; it's far quieter (and, thus, nicer) during the week.

Keen riders and fit runners should consider tackling the trail in its entirety. However, it's just as accessible for novices who fancy taking in some great views from the comfort of a saddle (several shops en route offer bikes for hire). If your time or energy is limited, the trail is at its most scenic and enjoyable between Museum Campus (1500 S) and Belmont Avenue (3200 N), a manageable five-mile stretch. Here are some highlights.

HOLLYWOOD AVENUE (5700 N)
The **Kathy Osterman Beach** is at the northern end of Lincoln Park and of the Lakefront Trail. You might have the place to yourself.

WILSON AVENUE (4600 N)
Who says Americans don't care for soccer? There's usually a lively game going on at the pitch here, near a handful of tennis courts.

IRVING PARK ROAD TO BELMONT AVENUE (4000 N TO 3200 N)
The lakefront location of the **Sydney R Marovitz Golf Course** (see p276) is almost picturesque enough to make diehard golf-haters take up the game. The clubhouse is at roughly Addison Street (3600 N), close to Edwin Clark's handsome, clock tower-topped **Waveland Field House**.

A little inland sits **Kwanusila**, a replica of an Indian totem pole presented to the city in 1929 by businessman James Kraft. It's a stone's throw from **Belmont Marina**, one of the mellowest docks along the lake.

DIVERSEY PARKWAY TO FULLERTON AVENUE (2400 N TO 2800 N)
Look out at Diversey for Cyrus Dallin's striking statue of a Native American warrior on horseback, completed in 1890. Past the North Pond care is needed to safely negotiate the bottleneck of walkers, joggers and riders around what is a surprisingly tight little corner.

NORTH AVENUE (1600 N)
The views of the city skyline from the **North Avenue Beach** are stunning, especially from the promontory. The daring can also chance their arm by challenging the locals to a game of chess or beach volleyball. Rental bikes are available from **Bike Chicago** (see p275).

OAK STREET TO NAVY PIER (1100 N TO 500 N)
Sweep past the **Oak Street Beach** and the **Drake Hotel**, and **Navy Pier** will come into view. Just before it is the **Ohio Street Beach**, barely a beach at all. South of Navy Pier, take the eastern sidewalk of Lake Shore Drive's lower level to get across the Chicago River. A block or so off the trail, you can rent a bike at **Bobby's Bikes** (see p72).

RANDOLPH STREET TO MUSEUM CAMPUS (150 N TO 1400 S)
Founded in 1892, the **Columbia Yacht Club** is one of the city's most renowned boating organisations; just inland, in **Millennium Park**, is another branch of **Bike Chicago** (see p275). Directly south, you'll roll alongside the boat-packed **Monroe Harbor** before cruising down the edge of Grant Park in the shadow of **Lake Shore Drive**. Follow the path as it rounds the **Shedd Aquarium** (see p90), then stop to take in the Loop skyline.

MCCORMICK PLACE TO 31ST STREET (2300 S TO 3100 S)
In the shadow of the huge convention centre, the **McCormick Place Bird Sanctuary** might be the most unexpected sight on the trail. Just south stands the **Fallen Firefighter & Paramedic Memorial Park**; just south is the sweet little **31st Street Beach**.

Sightseeing

Lakeview & Around

Uptown girls, Boystown bears and beer-soaked Cubs.

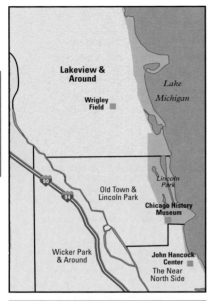

Lakeview

Map p329 & p330

El: Brown to Belmont, Southport or Wellington; Purple to Belmont or Wellington; Red to Addison or Belmont.

Lakeview is said to take its name from a hotel built in 1853 by James Rees and EE Hundley. Having completed the construction, the pair struggled to decide on a name until their friend Walter Newberry turned up to see the place. Impressed by the waterside vistas, Newberry suggested that they call it the Hotel Lake View. The name eventually carried over to the neighbourhood, and has since expanded to take in huge swathes of the surrounding area.

At the time Rees and Hundley were building their property, the area was countryside, farmed by a handful of European immigrants. Things changed dramatically in 1854, when a devastating cholera swept Chicago and many locals fled north to escape it. As there were no roads to the area from Chicago, Rees and Hundley laid down a plank thoroughfare. Lake View Plank Road, as it was rather plainly christened (it has since morphed into modern-day Broadway), spurred on immediate and dramatic expansion of the area.

During the following three decades, the now-incorporated Lakeview Township stretched as far north as Devon Avenue and all the way to Western Avenue in the west. In 1887, it lost its independence and was annexed by the city. The event led to the area shrinking – in a manner of speaking: only the southernmost portion of the old township retains the name Lakeview, the northern reaches having been absorbed into Roscoe Village, Andersonville, Edgewater, Buena Park, North Center, St Ben's, Lincoln Square and Uptown.

Lakeview developed as a residential and entertainment district during the 20th century, with relatively high rents keeping factory industries away. For a time, Lakeview had a hip cachet; the punky shops around Belmont and Clark are testament to an edgier past, as was the presence at 3448 N Greenview Avenue of Smashing Pumpkins singer Billy Corgan (he has since sold up and moved out). However, the district has since grown more affluent and less cutting-edge, and is nowadays visited mainly for its reliable restaurants, its baseball team and its lakefront and marina, located at the northern end of Lincoln Park. In summer, the park offers a multitude of activities (jogging, tennis) and inactivities (snoozing on the grass).

The hubs of Lakeview's culture, nightlife and commerce are the stretches of Clark and Broadway Streets to the immediate north and south of Belmont Avenue, home to an array of kitschy shops, bars and restaurants. Among the best are the **Unabridged Bookstore** (*see p193*) and **Uncle Fun** (*see p214*), which offers a selection of bizarre knick-knacks, kitsch and gag gifts. Close at hand are two very different cinemas. The 1912 **Vic Theatre** (*see p237*) is a former vaudeville house that stages touring rock acts alongside the rowdy Brew & View movie nights. The rather more demure **Music Box** (*see p237*), meanwhile, is an over-the-top, Italian Renaissance-inspired spot. The main theatre, seating 750, uses trompe l'oeil paintings of garden walls to create the illusion of sitting in an outdoor courtyard, with a ceiling covered with stars and moving cloud formations.

In the south-east corner of Lakeview sits a small pocket of town known as **Boystown**, Chicago's main gay neighbourhood. Bordered by Addison, Broadway and Halsted Streets and Belmont Avenue, it's awash with nightlife and shopping options; for details, *see pp240-249*.

Wrigleyville

Central Lakeview was changed forever in 1914 with the construction of **Wrigley Field** (*see p272*), a genuine American landmark. The park was originally built for the Whales of the Federal League, set up by Charles Weeghman to challenge the American and National Leagues. When the league folded just a year later, Weeghman bought the NL's Cubs and moved them across town. In 1920, Weeghman sold both team and ballpark to Philip Wrigley. Six years later, the stadium changed its name to Wrigley Field, a name that has since been extended to the streets surrounding it.

On game days (the Cubs play here 81 times a year, and more on the rare occasions they reach the play-offs), Lakeview morphs from a sedate, cultured enclave to a wild, beer-soaked bacchanal. Cubs culture rules near the junction of Clark and Addison: sports bars and pubs such as **Hi Tops** (3551 N Sheffield Avenue, at W Cornelia Avenue, 1-773 348 0009) and the **Cubby Bear** (*see p182*) dominate the area. Even Boystown gets in on the act: the **North End** (3733 N Halsted Street, at W Bradley Place, 1-773 477 7999) is a gay sports bar.

However, not every hangout around here focuses on baseball. Chief among the avoiders is the **Metro** (*see p257*), one of the country's favourite music venues. Originally a Swedish community centre, John Shanahan's club has hosted the Chicago debuts of bands including REM and Nirvana. The adjoining **Smartbar** (*see p269*) was a key centre in the emergence of both the industrial and house scenes. A few doors down sits the **Gingerman** (*see p183*), where the ambience is miles away from the likes of **Murphy's Bleachers** (*see p183*).

Roscoe Village

West of Lakeview, around the junction of Roscoe and Damen, is **Roscoe Village**, a formerly down-at-heel neighbourhood that has seen property prices climb as it becomes an affordable alternative to Lincoln Park. The quietly reserved neighbourhood has generally stood slightly apart from the nightlife loop, but an influx of new restaurants, bars and shops has brought new vigour to the area.

Heading north

El: various Red line stations north of Addison.

Chicago's Swedish Americans have historically called **Andersonville** home. Many remain in the area; for more on the history of their community, visit the **Swedish American Museum Center** (*see p115*). However, the neighbourhood, centred on N Clark Street

Swedish American Museum Center.

Sightseeing

Talkin' all that jazz

Though you wouldn't know it these days, the Uptown neighbourhood was once one of Chicago's glitziest and liveliest districts. Back before the Depression, partygoers from all corners of the town flooded to the streets around the intersection of Clark and Lawrence to party the night away in ballrooms and lounges both upscale and downmarket. This unlikely corner was the heart of Chicago's Jazz Age, a buzzing and vibrant entertainment district to rival any in the city's history. Some of these grand old venues have since been demolished, most notably the Arcadia Ballroom (formerly at 4432 N Broadway Street, at W Montrose Avenue) and the Rainbo Gardens (4812 N Clark Street, at W Lawrence Avenue). However, a surprising number remain, in various states of repair.

The grandest of them all is the **Aragon Ballroom** (1106 W Lawrence Avenue, at N Winthrop Avenue; *see p255*; *pictured*), built in 1926 for the then astronomical sum of $2 million. Despite the price, owner Andrew Karzas got his money's worth: the ballroom's Moorish design, by Ralph Huszagh and Boyd Hill, was spectacular. Mosaic tiling lined the walls and crystal chandeliers hung from the ceilings; the dome was fitted with twinkling lights designed to mimic a starry sky.

The Aragon had room for more than 7,000 revellers, but it always busy. The decor was one attraction; another was the calibre of the dance bands, led by such notables as Tommy Dorsey and Lawrence Welk. But Karzas's masterstroke was locating the Aragon next to the newly extended El service. The theatre was a mere stone's throw from Lawrence station, which had opened three years earlier.

The Aragon's popularity lasted roughly three decades, before an explosion at an adjacent bar forced its closure. When it reopened, with both ballroom and neighbourhood deteriorating, it drew far smaller crowds than in its heyday. But after a spell in the doldrums, it seems to have settled nicely into its current role as a rock and pop venue.

Across Broadway sits the **Riviera Theatre** (4746 N Racine Avenue, at W Lawrence Avenue; *see p259*), built during World War I to designs by the famous firm of Rapp & Rapp. The 2,600-capacity theatre was one of the first erected specifically to screen films rather than to stage vaudeville shows; it was also a pioneer in that it supplemented the screenings with live music. Thanks in no small part to the management's insistence on targeting an affluent, stylish crowd, the Riv remained popular for decades. These days, like the Aragon, it's a music venue.

A few doors down is the **Uptown Theatre** (4816 N Broadway, at W Lawrence Avenue), a movie palace built in 1925. At first glance, it would seem to have been built as a direct competitor to the nearby Riv; in fact, it was conceived by the same developers (Balaban & Katz, who also ran the Chicago Theatre in the Loop) and designed by the same architects. The Spanish Revival-style movie theatre had room for 4,500, making it the second largest in the US. Indeed, it proved too big for its boots: having struggled for decades to sustain a profit, it closed its doors in 1981. The last quarter of a century has taken its toll on the still striking structure, but preservationists are hopeful that it has a future. Visit www.uptown theatre.com for details of their campaign.

The clearest view of 1920s Uptown can be glimpsed at the **Green Mill** (4802 N Broadway, at W Lawrence Avenue; *see p262*), an Art Deco-style jazz club once owned by one of Al Capone's henchmen. It hasn't changed much since the days when jazz was king: it's still crowded, slightly cramped and loaded with atmosphere. The jazz remains, but the Green Mill is also now known as the birthplace of America's poetry slam movement.

and W Foster Avenue, is changing fast, its resurgence driven in no small part by a large gay community put off by the excesses of Boystown. And why not: after all, who wouldn't want to live close to **Hopleaf** (*see p161*), with its mussels and Belgian ales?

North-east of Andersonville sits **Uptown**, a neighbourhood that's still finding its gritty way along the comeback trail. In the past, the neighbourhood was a centre for entertainment and a playground for gangsters such as Al Capone, who appreciated the anonymity afforded by hanging out away from his native South Side. Indeed, Uptown is more notable for its past than for its present. Alongside the slew of grand Jazz Age theatres (*see p114* **Talkin' all that jazz**) sit some of the city's most handsome old building façades, such as Louis Sullivan's **Krause Music Store** (4611 N Lincoln Avenue, at W Wilson Avenue).

North of here but south of **Evanston** (*see p116*) lie some primarily residential neighbourhoods. Among them are **Rogers Park**, home to Loyola University and the unrelated but nonetheless curiously educational **Leather Archives & Museum** (*see below*).

Leather Archives & Museum

6418 N Greenview Avenue, at W Devon Avenue, Rogers Park (1-773 761 9200/www.leatherarchives. org). El: Red to Loyola. **Open** noon-8pm Thur, Fri; noon-5pm Sat, Sun. **Admission** *Membership* $5.
Housed in a former synagogue, this museum is purportedly the only one in the US devoted to the leather lifestyle. Paintings of men with perfect 'packages' adorn the walls of the former worship hall; downstairs, visitors can thumb through 10,000 sex magazines and peruse leather whips, 19th-century male chastity belts and common kitchen tools used for sex play. The museum takes a serious approach to preserving the history of leather as an object of fetish; not an easy undertaking, as the S&M community has traditionally operated underground.

Swedish American Museum Center

5211 N Clark Street, at W Foster Street, Andersonville (1-773 728 8111/www.samac.org). El: Purple or Red to Berwyn. **Open** 10am-4pm Tue-Fri; 11am-4pm Sat, Sun. *Children's Museum* 1-4pm Tue-Fri; 11am-4pm Sat, Sun. **Admission** (suggested donation) $4; $3 discounts; free under-1s; free to all 2nd Tue of mth. **No credit cards**.
The Center enjoys healthy support in Andersonville, a neighbourhood that's long been populated by Swedish immigrants. Recent years have seen the opening of an interactive Children's Museum of Immigration, although the museum has also gained a reputation for its modern art exhibitions, which often feature Swedish or Swedish-American artists working with textiles. Classes in everything from cooking to the Swedish language, plus screenings, round off this excellent enterprise.

Ravenswood & Lincoln Square

El: Brown to Damen or Western.

Occupying a fascinating cultural space between Old World traditions and New World trendiness, **Ravenswood** manages the neat trick of being simultaneously quaint and hip. Gentrification has arrived in this nook of the city north-west of Roscoe Village, bringing music and art schools, clothing and antique shops, and a wide range of restaurants. Still, many of the characteristics that people cherish about the area, such as the park and the large library, were here decades ago, back when Ravenswood was the Germanic part of town. You can still hear German spoken in some of the shops, though these days it competes with Croatian and Spanish.

Newcomers to the area will tell you that they live in **Lincoln Square**, although longtime residents – like the two women who co-own the marvellous **Café Selmarie** (4729 N Lincoln Avenue, 1-773 989 5595) – prefer the old title. Historically, the 'Lincoln Square' label was reserved for a one-block prime business stretch of Lincoln Avenue (between W Leland and W Lawrence Avenues) in which Café Selmarie sits dead centre, flanked by a pedestrian square.

A handful of old establishments still remain on this stretch of Lincoln Avenue, each within walking distance of the Western station on the Brown line. The grandmother is **Delicatessen Meyer** (No.4750, 1-773 561 3377), which has sold imported groceries for more than half a century. Another old-timer is the **Chicago Brauhaus** restaurant (No.4732, 1-773 784 4444), dishing up classic German fare such as *sauerbraten* and *spätzle*; it's open late (midnight during the week, 1am on weekends) with music and dancing. However, while it was established in 1875, the famous **Merz Apothecary** (*see p210*) didn't move to the area until 1982.

Cultural venues dot the streets around Lincoln Square. Housed in a former library building, the **Old Town School of Folk Music** (*see p259*) retains two whimsical WPA-era murals, one of them above the stage in the intimate, acoustically stellar concert hall. The space is used for concerts and also for more casual jam sessions, open to all. The nearby **Lillstreet Art Center** (4401 N Ravenswood Avenue, at W Montrose Avenue, 1-773 769 4426, www.lillstreet.com) contains a gallery, a café (First Slice) and studio space. And though it doesn't sport a fancy lit-up marquee, the **Davis Theater** (*see p237*) remains a treasure. How many other movie houses are decorated with a framed poster of Bette Davis's axe-wielding romp *The Anniversary*?

Sightseeing

The North Shore

First-class honours and middle-class manners in the shadow of the city.

Evanston

El: Purple to Davis.

The good-sized suburb of Evanston marks the southern end of the affluent region known as the North Shore. Bounded on the east by the lake, on the west by Skokie and on the south by Howard Street, the last stop on the Red line and the dividing line between Chicago and the North Shore, Evanston is perhaps best known as the home of **Northwestern University** (*see below*). But thanks to a dedicated El line (the Purple one, which runs north from Howard) and an increasing array of decent civic amenities, it's surpassed its initial status as a mere dormitory community (the town wasn't incorporated until 1863, more than a decade after NWU was founded).

Although it will probably seem a little bland after the architectural assault that is downtown Chicago, Evanston has freshened up its appearance in a big way of late. The condominium construction that was rampant during the last decade has attracted a more upmarket, youthful demographic of singles and couples to join the existing mix of students, families and elderly residents.

The immense mansions on Sheridan Road, along the lakefront, are among the North Shore's most impressive sights. But even inland, Evanston's streets are very attractive, lined with old maples, oaks and elms thriving in the rich prairie soil, amid wonderful public parks. Year-round festivals, generally safe neighbourhoods, a handsome little downtown (centred on Church and Davis Street just east of the lake) and scores of shops and eateries have all enhanced the town's desirability among those looking for a quieter life in the shadow of the noisy big city.

A handful of museums dot the town, all low-key affairs. The **Mitchell Museum of the American Indian** (*see below*) offers a scholarly survey of ancient American life, while the **Frances Willard House** (1730 Chicago Avenue, at Church Street, 1-847 328 7500, www.franceswillardhouse.org) pays tribute to one of the leading lights in the Temperance movement of the 19th century. It's open for tours ($5, $3 discounts) from 1pm to 4pm on the first and third Sundays of the month. Also worth a look, though it's only open for tours

on weekends from June to September, is the **Grosse Point Lighthouse**, constructed in 1873 at the corner of Central Street and Sheridan Road (1-847 328 6961, www.grosse pointlighthouse.net). The **Noyes Cultural Arts Center** (927 Noyes Street, at Maple Avenue, 1-847 448 8260, www.cityofevanston. org) offers an array of additional cultural entertainments in the shape of theatrical performances and gallery exhibits.

Mitchell Museum of the American Indian

2600 Central Park Avenue, Evanston (1-847 475 1030/www.mitchellmuseum.org). El: Purple to Central. **Open** 10am-5pm Tue, Wed, Fri, Sat; 10am-8pm Thur; noon-4pm Sun. **Admission** (suggested donation) $5; $2.50 discounts; $10 family. **No credit cards**.
An avid collector of Native American artefacts, John Mitchell founded this museum with his personal collection in 1977. Now housing more than 10,000 artefacts, it features ceremonial dolls, beadwork, masks, carvings and Paleolithic-era tools from native peoples throughout the US and Canada.

Northwestern University

Since 1851, this highly selective, intellectually rigorous institution has earned a reputation for academic and sporting excellence. Northwestern's medical, law and business graduate schools rank as some of the most innovative in the world, and its performing and fine arts departments are deservedly respected. Its combined library holdings are also held in high regard.

The university's 240-acre campus lacks the gravitas of the University of Chicago in Hyde Park (*see p139*), but it's still a picturesque place that benefits from its lakeside location. Unusually for a university, the campus was once considerably bigger than it is now, but the authorities were forced to sell off more than half its original 380-acre site due to financial difficulties. When the university grew in the middle of the 20th century, it needed some of this land back, but it had by then been developed into housing. The university's novel response was to expand eastwards by filling in a large chunk of Lake Michigan.

The campus, officially located at 2001 Sheridan Road (1-847 491 3741, www.north western.edu), is a pleasant place for a wander,

The outdoor sculpture garden at the **Mary & Leigh Block Museum of Art**.

its site dotted with a mix of buildings old and new. In the former category is **University Hall** (1897 Sheridan Road), a grand structure that was constructed in 1869 and is now the oldest remaining building on campus. In the latter is the 1975 **Pick-Staiger Concert Hall** (1977 S Campus Drive, on the Arts Circle, 1-847 467 4000), a combined classroom and performance facility that stages everything from solo recitals to orchestra concerts. If it's a nice day, grab some lunch and head away to munch it in the handsome, becalmed **Shakespeare Garden**, perhaps via the **Mary & Leigh Block Museum of Art** (*see below*). A self-guided tour of the campus is downloadable (in PDF format) from the university's website by following the link marked 'Visiting Campus'.

Big Ten football fans enthusiastically support the Northwestern Wildcats each fall, if only to see the opposing teams run roughshod over the home field. Still, a festive air pervades the masses near the stadium, located on Central Avenue just west of the Purple line El stop.

Mary & Leigh Block Museum of Art
Northwestern University, 1967 S Campus Drive (on the Arts Circle), Evanston (1-847 491 4000/www. blockmuseum.northwestern.edu). El: Purple to Davis. **Open** 10am-5pm Tue; 10am-8pm Wed-Fri; noon-5pm Sat, Sun. **Admission** free. **No credit cards.**

The visual arts are celebrated at this multi-faceted university space, which encompasses four galleries and additional venues for film screenings (*see p237*), concerts and symposia. The museum's extensive collection of works on paper includes prints, photographs and drawings spanning the 16th to the 20th centuries; exhibitions drawn from it are supplemented by interesting (if niche) temporary shows. The outdoor sculpture garden includes works by Miró, Hepworth and Arp.

Further north
Various transportation stations.

Chicagoans generally head up beyond Evanston for either of two reasons. The main one, usually at the behest of their kids, is to visit **Six Flags Great America & Hurricane Harbor** (I-94/I-294 from Chicago, exit at Route 132, 1-847 249 4636, www.sixflags.com; hours vary by season), a vast, loud and thoroughly exhausting amusement park in the far northern suburb of **Gurnee**. After a day at this thrillfest, most parents (and a fair few kids) come away sunburned, foot-weary and broke. For revenge, drag the young 'uns across the road to the **Gurnee Mills** outlet mall (*see p191*).

Other attractions are dotted around the North Shore between Evanston and Gurnee, and are generally a little quieter than Six Flags. Immediately to the north of Evanston, **Wilmette** is best visited for the vast and amazing **Bahá'í Temple House of Worship** (*see below*) or, on a more down-to-earth level, for a scrumptious apple pancake at the **Walker Bros Original Pancake House** (153 Green Bay Road, Wilmette, 1-847 251 6000, http://walkerbrosoph.com). **Glencoe** is home to the **Chicago Botanic Garden** (*see below*); inland, the **Long Grove Historic Village** (*see below*) has been charming visitors for decades.

Two other North Shore spots come into their own in summer. During the warmer months, the century-old **Ravinia Festival** in Highland Park (*see p252*) provides an outdoor home for the Chicago Symphony Orchestra and the Hubbard Street Dance Company, but also mixes in a variety of pop acts. The venue has been slightly overshadowed by the belated opening of Millennium Park (*see p75*), but it's still an immensely popular place. Unlike at many music festivals, the cheap seats are a big draw here, offering concertgoers a chance to spread out and picnic on the lawn. But if you want to see the musicians while you hear them, you'll need to pony up for the pavilion seats.

And then further north, not too far from the Wisconsin border at the town of **Zion**, sits **Illinois Beach State Park** (1-847 662 4811, www.dnr.state.il.us). Whether you choose

overnight accommodation at a fully equipped inn, beachside camping or just a day trip, it's not hard to take it easy at this clean and uncomplicated lakeside beach park that stretches six miles and covers 4,000 acres. Nearby **Tempel Farms** (17000 Wadsworth Road, Wadsworth, 1-847 623 7272, www.tempel farms.com) breeds Lipizzan horses, which give full dressage performances in July and August.

Bahá'í Temple House of Worship

100 Linden Avenue, Wilmette (1-847 853 2300/ www.bahaitemple.org). El: Red, then Purple to Linden. **Open** *Auditorium* 7am-10pm daily. *Visitor Centre May-Sept* 10am-10pm daily. *Oct-Apr* 10am-5pm daily. **Admission** free. **No credit cards**.
No visit to the North Shore is complete without taking in the enormous, whitewashed Bahá'í Temple House of Worship, which resembles nothing so much as the world's largest lemon squeezer. Inspiring prayer, devotion and countless photo ops – and visible for miles – this 164ft (50m) spiritual dome is magnificent when illuminated at night; its surrounding manicured garden add to its beauty by day. It was completed in 1953 as a place of prayer and meditation for the Bahá'í faith, which advocates the 'oneness of God, the oneness of mankind and the oneness of religion'.

Chicago Botanic Garden

1000 Lake Cook Road, Glencoe (1-847 835 5440/ www.chicagobotanic.org). Metra: Glencoe. **Open** *Sept-May* 8am-sunset daily. *June-Aug* 7am-9pm. **Admission** free. **No credit cards**.
A variety of planting styles has delighted visitors to the Botanic Garden since 1972. The sprawling yet calm oasis is beautifully maintained, with trails that encourage walkers and cyclists to linger. Highlights include a walled English garden, the series of islands that make up the Japanese gardens, a 15-acre prairie and carillon concerts. There's also a pleasant restaurant, plus galleries that host rotating exhibitions of botanic-themed art. Note that although admission is free, parking costs $12 (reduced to $7 on Tuesdays); take the Metra to avoid the charges.

Long Grove Historic Village

307 Old McHenry Road (Route 53 & Route 83 intersection), Long Grove (1-847 634 0888/www. longgroveonline.com). Metra: Deerfield, then taxi. **Open** *Village Information Centre* 10am-5pm Mon-Sat; noon-5pm Sun. *Shops* times vary per shop; all closed Mon. **Credit** varies.
This charming if slightly touristy, open-air historic attraction contains over 80 free-standing stores and restaurants, and is at its best in summer and autumn, when it hosts a variety of festivals celebrating the merits of everything from strawberries (June) and apples (October) to Greeks (August) and the Irish (early September). At the Long Grove Confectionery Company (220 Robert Parker Coffin Road, 1-847 634 0080), the chocolate-dipped pretzels, fresh strawberries and sandwich cookies are to die for.

Bahá'í Temple House of Worship.

The Near West Side

Change doesn't stop in this patchwork of immigrant villages and industry.

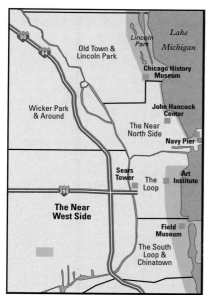

city's hip and gainfully employed, its mix of dining and nightlife taking after New York's meatpacking district. The development continues, albeit rather more slowly, north of here (and south of Ukrainian Village, *see p128*).

Beyond the West Loop, much of the West Side was stigmatised by the riots that followed the assassination of Martin Luther King, Jr. A long period of neglect followed, with neighbourhoods such as **Garfield Park** and **Lawndale** left to rot by the city fathers. Chicago's expansion westwards has resulted in improvements in these once-beleaguered neighbourhoods, but numerous empty lots stand testament to the fact that there's still a long way to go.

Back closer to the Loop, it's possible to explore Little Italy, Greektown and Pilsen by foot along their main streets. The commercial areas of each neighbourhood are increasingly busy with activity, but it's wise to keep your wits about you when venturing into the long stretches of no man's land that separate them. Start by taking the Blue line to UIC-Halsted, and walking north on Halsted to the corner with four pseudo-Greek columns, which Mayor Richard M Daley had installed in 1996 for the Democratic Convention.

From the late 1880s until the 1920s, German, Irish, Russian, Greek and Eastern European immigrants streamed (with a shove) into the industrial and residential areas around Chicago's city centre. **Greektown, Little Italy** and **Pilsen** are the remnants of these once-vital enclaves. With assimilation, the next generation of immigrants dispersed: neither Greektown or Little Italy contain sizeable Greek or Italian communities these days, while the Europeans who once lived in Pilsen made way years ago for the Latino immigrants that now lend the neighbourhood its prevailing character.

The streets immediately west of the Kennedy Expressway and Greektown, masquerading as the **West Loop, West Loop Gate** or **River West** (the name depends on the real estate agent), have been reworked in recent years by savvy property developers, and are now home to a number of restaurants, nightclubs and expensive apartments. In particular, Fulton Market has proved highly desirable among the

The West Loop & River West

Map p330

El: Green or Pink to Ashland or Clinton.

Once an uninviting maze of warehouses and garment factories, the West Loop now hosts some of the hottest real estate in this post-industrial town. The blocks immediately to the west of the Kennedy Expressway are the centre of a development craze that encompasses both residential conversions and new businesses. Along Randolph Street (between Halsted and Racine Streets), a slew of highly regarded restaurants compete for attention with bars and nightclubs; as they do so, old-line wholesalers such as the Puckered Pickle Company look on with bemusement and occasional irritation. Randolph hosts a monthly Chicago Antique Market between May and October and a street fest in Summer.

The **Fulton Market** area is in flux, to say the least. During the day, the streets are full of trucks and men in white jackets working in the meatpacking industry and lunching at greasy diners. Come sundown, it's a nightlife hot spot. There's no greater example of the tension between the two neighbourhoods than the chic **Victor Hotel** nightclub (see p269), housed in what was once a cold storage facility. Reportedly, the area will soon welcome an outpost of Robert Redford's Sundance Cinemas.

It's a similar story along Lake Street between Halsted and Morgan Streets, where meat and veg cash-and-carry outposts share the street with restaurants such as the **Reserve Ultra Lounge** (see p269) and the seemingly obligatory loft apartments. But, from the looks of it, the meat business is still in pretty good shape. For a vision of the area's bone-hacking present, check out the **Peoria Packing Butcher Shop** (1300 W Lake Street, at N Elizabeth Street, 1-312 738 1800), where piles of raw meat and pigs' feet are heaped up for the benefit of eager budget buyers.

Before real estate prices spiralled, a colony of artists had discovered the West Loop. A number of relatively edgy galleries remain in place here, clustered at Peoria and Washington and in the Fulton Market area between Peoria and Racine (see pp223-224). They have an impact on local culture, but it's dwarfed by that of **Harpo Studios** (1058 W Washington Boulevard, 1-312 591 9222, www.oprah.com), from where the most powerful woman in American media shoots her shows and oversees her empire. In theory, visitors can book free tickets to recordings of *The Oprah Winfrey Show* by phone, but it's notoriously impossible: you'll need to work months ahead and prepare for an almost constant busy signal (or get lucky with last-minute reservations). Perhaps unsurprisingly, very few of Oprah's audience kill time before the show with a trip to the nearby **Museum of Holography** (see below).

About a mile west on Madison Street is the massive **United Center** (see pp272). The home to the famed Chicago Bulls basketball team and the Chicago Blackhawks hockey team, it also welcomes big-time music acts and circuses. The once-bleak blocks around the arena are sprouting with new development, but it's still not currently an area in which to linger.

Museum of Holography

1134 W Washington Boulevard, at N Racine Avenue (1-312 226 1007/holographiccenter.com). El: Blue to Racine; Green to Ashland. **Open** 12.30-4.30pm Wed-Sun. **Admission** $4; $3 discounts; free under-6s. **No credit cards. Map** p330 E12.

In the unlikely event that you're fascinated by holography, this is a dream come true. The holograms themselves are varied, and a room full of voxgrams (medical holograms made from a series of CT scans) will intrigue anyone who's been wondering what

the inside of a larynx looks like. For the rest of us, it takes only a minimal interest in holography and a good sense of humour to see this place as one of the campest museums in the city. While it's proven useful to science and Princess Leia, holography as an art form is stuck in a 1980s suburban mall; the best that can be said about most of the art on display here is that it's technically interesting.

Greektown

Map p330
El: Blue to UIC-Halsted.

In the late 1970s, there were more than 125,000 Greeks in Chicago. It's a different story today, though you might not know it from a walk along Halsted Street from Monroe Street south to Van Buren Street in the West Loop. Although there are far fewer Greeks living in Greektown than there once were, this stretch remains the Midwest's biggest Hellenic commercial area. Scattered between welcoming Greek restaurants is an eclectic array of shops selling everything from baklava and Greek pop music to candles and evil eye stones (at the fabulously odd **Athenian Candle Company** (300 S Halsted Street, at W Jackson Street, 1-312 332 6988). The **Hellenic Museum & Cultural Center** provides what remains of the community with an anchor.

On Adams Street, one block east of Halsted and across the freeway, sits the decidedly un-Greek **Old St Patrick's Church** (700 W Adams Street, at S Desplaines Street, 1-312 648 1021). Built in 1856, it was one of the first churches in America built to serve Irish immigrants; having survived the Chicago Fire in 1871, it's also the oldest church building in the city. The interior is decorated with muted stained-glass windows and a mix of pagan and Christian symbols. Each July, the church hosts the World's Largest Block Party.

Hellenic Museum & Cultural Center

801 W Adams Street, at S Halsted Street (1-312 655 1234/www.hellenicmuseum.org). El: Blue to UIC-Halsted. **Open** 10am-4pm Tue-Fri; 11am-4pm Sat; noon-5pm Sun. **Admission** *Suggested donation* $5. **Credit** MC, V. **Map** p330 F12.

While work progresses on the Hellenic Museum & Cultural Center's intended home, on the site of the former N Turek & Sons hardware store at 333 S Halsted Street, operations have moved to this temporary space. Until the new premises are ready (hopefully in 2008), it's business as usual at this shrine to immigrant Greek culture. The museum derives many of its pieces from the collections of local Greek families, but it's by no means only of interest to those with Greek ancestry. The 2006 Road to Rembetika display, which chronicled the music of the Greek underground, is one example of the

Sightseeing

Old St Patrick's Church.

museum's rotating historical exhibitions, which change frequently and are consistently noteworthy. The museum's modern and conceptual art exhibitions, on the other hand, aren't quite as dazzling.

Heading south

Map p330

El: Blue to UIC-Halsted.

Stroll down Halsted south from Greektown, and you'll soon find yourself surrounded by the brutalist architecture of the **University of Illinois at Chicago** (UIC) campus, built in the 1960s and still a sprawling and ever-expanding interruption to the historic neighbourhoods that surround it. The casual observer may have difficulty discerning the university's attempts to soften its concrete landscape with trees and grassy medians. Still, this uninviting landscape is well worth negotiating simply for the purposes of visiting the **Jane Addams Hull-House Museum** (*see below*).

A couple of blocks south lies the area that gave birth to the Chicago blues. The old **Maxwell Street** attracted communities of immigrants for years, from Europe, from the South and then from Mexico, who met here and tried to make their way in the brave new world by setting up shops and businesses. However, its fame comes largely from the fact that, from the 1920s onwards, it was the hub of the then-nascent Chicago blues community. Musicians gathered on sidewalks, plugged in their instruments and cranked up the volume.

No longer. In the early 1990s, UIC got permission from Mayor Daley to raze the entire site, demolishing landmarks such as Nate's Deli (where Aretha Franklin bursts into song in *The Blues Brothers*) as the campus expanded. These days, you can get a Jamba juice here, but you sure ain't gonna hear any decent blues.

The multi-ethnic market that once stood here was forced sideways to Canal Street, but is being forced to move again in 2007 to the stretch of Desplaines Street between Roosevelt and Harrison Roads. On Sundays (7am-3pm), expect to find stalls selling everything from power tools to bootleg DVDs, plus a parade of Mexican food stands hawking tacos, churros, carne asada, candies and fresh fruit.

Jane Addams Hull-House Museum

University of Illinois at Chicago, 800 S Halsted Street, at W Polk Street (1-312 413 5353/www.uic. edu/jaddams/hull). El: Blue to UIC-Halsted. **Open** 10am-4pm Tue-Fri; noon-4pm Sun. **Admission** free. **No credit cards. Map** p330 F14.

After an 1888 visit to London's Toynbee Hall, a pioneering settlement house that provided social services for a working-class neighbourhood, a pair of young women named Jane Addams and Ellen Gates Starr returned to Chicago vowing to start something similar. A year later, Hull-House opened its doors. It began as a relatively small operation, but eventually expanded to include educational facilities, social assistance offices, and the city's first swimming pool, public kitchen and gymnasium. One beneficiary of the music programme was a young Benny Goodman, who learned to play clarinet there.

The fame of Addams and Hull-House grew, inspiring other socially conscious people in the US just as Addams herself had been inspired by Toynbee Hall. She died in 1935, aged 74, but her work is commemorated in the two structures that remain of her 13-building complex. In the original 1856 mansion (donated to Addams by Charles Hull, hence the name) sit displays of paintings that once hung at the settlement, pottery and tableware created through Addams' community art programme, and her desk. Next door is the dining hall, which now houses photographs, exhibits and a 15-minute slide-show introduction to the American labour movement and the social problems faced by the West Side's immigrants. Enlightening and inspiring.

National Italian American Sports Hall of Fame. *See p123.*

Little Italy

Map p330

El: Blue to Polk or Racine; Pink to Polk.

Sauntering west from Halsted on Taylor Street along the south side of the UIC campus leads into **Little Italy**. It's said that pizza first made its way from Naples to the US in this once-thriving neighbourhood. Like Greektown, it's a shadow of its former self, with the Italians who once lived here long since forced out by the construction of the Eisenhower Expressway or driven away by the the creation of the UIC's Circle Campus. What remains is a nostalgia trip, but it's not an unenjoyable one.

Aside from the **National Italian American Sports Hall of Fame** (*see below*), the main attractions today are culinary, with most of the action along Taylor Street between S Morgan Street and S Ashland Avenue. At the **Scafuri Bakery** (No.1337, 1-312 733 8881), the eightysomething proprietress serves up bread rolls, freshly baked cookies and pastries; down the street, there are prime people-watching opportunities and stomach-stretchingly large pasta portions at the **Rosebud Café** (No.1500, 1-312 942 1117). Italian sandwiches and gourmet goods can be procured at the perennial **Conte di Savoia** deli (No.1438, 1-312 666 3471, www.contedi savoia.com). In summer, folk from miles around queue for flavoured ices at **Mario's Italian Lemonade** (1068 W Taylor Street, at S Carpenter Street, no phone, closed Oct-Apr). During term, students gravitate towards the vegetarian-friendly, Latin-slanted **Che Café** (No.1058, 1-312 850 4665).

To the west, Little Italy has a maze of fascinating residential sidestreets that reward exploration. From Taylor, head north on Loomis to view the classic Chicago three-flats

Artifact Info

and stoops that line the street, then turn east on Lexington to enjoy the beautiful old homes that overlook Arrigo Park, a peaceful green that stands out amid the brick, stone and stucco landscape. The area is the home to a portion of the city's less handsome ABLA public housing, and is being considered as a site for the city's putative Public Housing Museum.

South of Little Italy, one modern structure stands out amid a stretch of empty lots. The former **Illinois Regional Library for the Blind & Physically Handicapped** (1055 W Roosevelt Road) has been converted into a bank, but retains its 165-foot (50-metre) window and unique curving shape.

National Italian American Sports Hall of Fame

1431 W Taylor Street, at S Bishop Street (1-312 226 5566/www.niashf.org). El: Blue to Racine. **Open** 9am-5pm Mon-Fri; 11am-4pm Sat, Sun. **Admission** free. **No credit cards**. **Map** p330 D14.

This recent addition to Little Italy honours more than 200 sports heroes with a collection that includes Mario Andretti's racing car and Rocky Marciano's championship belt. Piazza DiMaggio, a small plaza dedicated to every Italian American's favourite son, lies directly across the street and makes a convenient picnic spot for an espresso and a mozzarella sandwich from Conte di Savoia. **Photo** *p122*.

Pilsen

El: Blue or Pink to 18th.

Historically a bit isolated, Pilsen has seen its profile rise in recent years. It's an easy walk from the north (albeit a slightly grim one), but the neighbourhood's southern edge is blocked off by the Chicago River and an array of shipping, storage and trucking facilities. Having provided a home for numerous different communities over the last 150-plus years, it's now home to the largest Mexican and Mexican American community in the Midwest. The **National Museum of Mexican Art** (*see p125*) provides it with a cultural focus.

Pilsen was originally settled in the 1800s by German, Czech, Polish and Yugoslavian immigrants drawn to work on the railroads; in 1857, under orders from Mayor Wentworth, police forced Bohemians out of the Near North Side to join them. By the late 19th century, industrialisation and its concomitant social pressures had transformed the locale into a hub of labour activism. But as immigrant quotas began to restrict the influx of Southern and Eastern Europeans in the '20s, Pilsen's Mexican heritage took root. The murals on and around 18th Street (*see p124* **Walk**) echo the area's continuing activism.

Pilsen's main commercial activity takes place on W 18th Street between S Racine Avenue and S Paulina Street, where street vendors abound and salsa music pours out of passing vehicles. At the **Tortilleria Sabinas** factory (No.1509), watch through giant glass windows as the staff make tortillas. For a cup o' joe, hit the left-leaning **Café Jumping Bean** (No.1439, 1-312 455 0019); and if you're hungry, hit cash-only **Restaurante Nuevo León** (*see p167*), flagged by its huge mural.

A sizeable artistic community inhabits the blocks around the intersection of 18th and Halsted Streets. Many artists rent from the Podmajersky family, which has supported creative entrepreneurs and historic preservation in the community for several generations. Art scenesters tend to congregate at the **Skylark** (2149 S Halsted Street, at W 21st Street, 1-312 948 5275), a boho bar with a fine beer selection.

Other notable buildings include the old **Schoenhofen Brewery** (W 18th Street & S Canalport Avenue), built in 1902 and a well preserved example of American architecture's movement away from revivalist styles. It sits on an artesian spring-fed well, some 1,600 feet deep, and could conceivably brew beer again in the future. Nearby, **Rustico's Rancho Viejo** (1812 S Ashland Street, at W 18th Street, 1-312 733 9251) inhabits a building that encapsulates

Walk Painting on Pilsen

When Mexicans and Mexican Americans settled in the formerly Czech Pilsen neighbourhood in the 1960s, wall murals emerged as a powerful form of community expression. Influenced both by the Mexican muralists of the 1910 Revolution, among them Diego Rivera and Jose Orozco, and the African American muralists on the city's South Side, Pilsen's street painters advocated civil rights and a united neighbourhood. The murals and mosaics were created by the community and its artists, who received no government grants and no private funding. Most murals in Pilsen are part of what a loose group of artists has forthrightly dubbed the community mural movement.

These days, things have changed. Tourists and locals regularly visit Pilsen's artistic community, which encompasses studios, galleries and the much-loved Mexican Fine Arts Center Museum. What's more, several local muralists these days do receive money from the Public Art Fund. However, the local landscape has also altered dramatically since the 1960s. Never officially protected, most of the murals from the 1960s and '70s have vanished, among them the more politically charged works that aggressively bemoaned the Vietnam War and Latino struggles. Fortunately, though, several artists from that generation are alive and well and still making murals, alongside a younger generation who've picked up the torch. This walk links some of the area's highlights.

Start by taking the Pink line to Damen.
To the north of Damen station, **Juan Chavez**'s glass mosaic collage *Vida Simple* (Damen Avenue & Cullerton Street) depicts residents of the Pilsen neighbourhood atop a collage of buildings, plants and gesturing hands. Co-commissioned by the CTA and the city's Public Art Program, it's one of two mosaics that Chavez has made for the transport system.

Head east along Cullerton Street.
Take a left on Paulina Street, then take the second right on to 18th Street.
Francisco Mendoza's Orozco Community Academy mosaics (1645 W 18th Place) include portraits of Mexican and Chicano

the 'hood's ethnic history. Once a *sokol* (school) for Czech and Polish immigrants, then a dancehall, it's now an artisans' store that sells a variety of Mexican crafts. Wooden furniture, Oaxacan figurines and vibrant paintings adorn the former stage, balcony and dancefloor.

National Museum of Mexican Art

1852 W 19th Street, at S Damen Avenue (1-312 738 1503/www.nationalmuseumofmexicanart.org). El: Blue or Pink to 18th Street. **Open** 10am-5pm Tue-Sun. **Admission** free. **No credit cards**.
Having expanded in recent years (and, in December 2006, renamed itself from the Mexican Fine Arts Center Museum), this is Chicago's most enjoyable community museum. The permanent displays are

intriguing; in particular, Mexicanidad: Our Past is Present, which offers a whistle-stop chronological tour of Mexican arts and culture with the aid of music, art, religious artefacts and other ephemera. Several of the galleries are given over to temporary exhibits, such as a recent display of Cheech Marin's noteworthy Chicano art collection and a show of paintings by Frida Kahlo and Diego Rivera, which brought a new audience through the museum's doors. All the exhibits come with informative and engaging captions in English and Spanish. Call ahead for details of music, dance and other performances, especially if you're here during the annual Day of the Dead festival (*see p220*). The crafts-packed Tienda Tzintzuntzan gift shop is one of the best museum shops in town.

people made from coloured bits of tile. Among them are Frida Kahlo stoically posing, and neighbourhood folk hitting the books at the library.
Keep walking down 18th Street, then head right at Ashland Avenue.
St Pius V Parish & School (1919 S Ashland Avenue) is covered by murals. In *Dejen Que Los Niños Se Acerquen a Mí*, one of the largest and most emotive, a priest christens a crying baby. Artist **Jeff Zimmerman** is a young, hip voice in the mural movement, with several other works dotting the South Side.
Carry on south along Ashland Avenue, then head left on Cullerton Street, and head east for three blocks. Take a left on Throop Street, a right on 19th Street, a right on Racine Avenue, a left on 19th Place and then a left on Carpenter Street.
In **Bill Campillo**'s *Untitled, 1985* (1900 S Carpenter Street), the workmen look as though they're building the wall on which they're portrayed, hanging out of painted windows and laying painted bricks.
Continue down Carpenter Street, then go left on 19th Street and right up Racine Avenue.

In 1972, on the walls of the still-thriving Casa Aztlan community centre (1831 S Racine Avenue), **Raymond Patlán** and a group of neighbourhood kids painted an array of Mexican historical and cultural themes, including portraits of revolutionaries and Aztec symbols. After a fire in 1974 burnt parts of the building, other artists restored and revised the mural.
Go left and head west on 18th Street until you hit Bishop Street.
Longtime mural painter **Hector Duarte** headed the group that painted a small mural entitled *Alto al desplazamiento* (18th & Bishop Streets). In it, a claw reaches out from behind two Latino workers. The name of the 1994 mural loosely translates as 'Stop the gentrification'.
Continue west on 18th Street to Paulina Street.
On the 18th Street CTA station (1710 W 18th Street and Paulina Street), **Francisco Mendoza**, **Joy Anderson** and others have made a pre-Columbian themed mural with traditional symbols. To finish your tour, follow the symbols up the stairs to the El platform and jump on a train heading back to the Loop.

Wicker Park & Around

The run-down area where bohemia blossomed… and then got bought up.

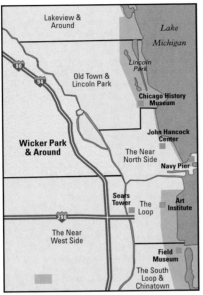

In the 1960s, Wicker Park was one of Chicago's most notorious, crime-ridden and unapproachable neighbourhoods, a deindustrialised void in a metropolis that was crumbling around it. Drawn by the low rents that such circumstances dictate, artists and musicians began to move to the district during the 1980s. The seeds they planted for a Greenwich Village-style bohemian enclave blossomed into a vibrant music and arts scene in the '90s.

Fast-forward to the 21st century, and the neighbourhood has changed almost beyond recognition. New luxury condos house affluent young professionals, who eat at swanky restaurants and drink at chic cocktail bars. By day, women in stilettos push strollers around the area's high-end boutiques. The creative classes are feeling the squeeze. But although the character of the neighbourhood has shifted dramatically over the last decade or so (the tipping point came when MTV filmed *The Real World* here in 2001), Wicker Park still contains traces of its famed bohemian flavour.

In centuries gone by, the area's main artery was the road now known as Milwaukee Avenue. It was worn into a pathway by several tribes of Native Americans, who used it to access the game-rich outer prairies. Following the 1871 Chicago Fire, however, the character of the area changed dramatically. The pattern of immigration that ensued in and around the locale is a microcosm of Chicago's ethnic settlement.

The Wicker Park neighbourhood was first settled after the fire by German immigrants, who built stately houses in the area around the plot of recreational land that is the actual Wicker Park. Poles moved into **Bucktown**, directly north of Wicker Park, while Ukrainians and Russians began arriving in the area to the south, a neighbourhood now known as **Ukrainian Village**. Paved after the fire, Milwaukee Avenue connected these new European settlements with downtown.

Many fourth- or fifth-generation East European immigrants continue to make their homes here; especially in Ukrainian Village, which remains one of the city's largest East Slavic population bubbles. However, the Spanish-language billboards that dot the streets speak of a more recent Puerto Rican and Mexican influence. As Eastern Europeans began to resettle in the suburbs during the 1950s and '60s, Latin Americans came to Wicker Park seeking solid blue-collar work in the apparel industry. Many arrived too late: the jobs had begun to move overseas, and the area became something of a vacuum. The gentrification of the area doesn't extend much further than Western Avenue; the streets west of here, in the **Humboldt Park** area, remain gang territory and are best avoided at night.

The borders of Wicker Park, Bucktown and Ukrainian Village are far from rigid. Beginning where Milwaukee Avenue meets the Kennedy Expressway, the Milwaukee Avenue corridor trails Chicago Avenue west to Western Avenue, and then follows Milwaukee north until around Armitage. The lower portion of this area, south of Division, is known as West Town, contained within which is Ukrainian Village. Above it, bordered roughly by Division Street and Western, Ashland and Bloomingdale Avenues, is Wicker Park. And north of Wicker Park, stretching to Fullerton Avenue, is Bucktown.

Ablution solution

During the late 19th and early 20th centuries, millions of Russians emigrated to the US. Many ended up in Chicago; a few of the more fortunate Russian Jews opened bathhouses to make themselves feel more at home.

At the time, Chicago's population of industrial workers lived in run-down tenements with few or no bathing facilities. A group of women physicians known as the Free Bath & Sanitary League convinced the city government to build its first public baths, basic utilitarian facilities for slum dwellers.

Most such bathhouses closed after World War II, though the Luxor Baths at 2039 W North Avenue hung on a little longer. Formerly favoured by Nelson Algren and assorted members of the Chicago underworld, it closed its doors relatively recently and is now home to a restaurant called Spring (*see p173*); the new owners have left the old façade intact. However, one facility has survived into the 21st century: the **Division Street Russian & Turkish Bathhouse** (1914 Division Street, at N Winchester Avenue, 1-773 384 9671), extant since 1906, is one of only a handful of public bathhouses still operating in the US.

Described by Saul Bellow in *Humboldt's Gift* as 'hotter than the tropics and rotting sweetly', the baths have survived a century, clinging on in a world that's moved forward without them. In the process, they've reputedly become a favoured haunt of everyone from Jesse Jackson to John Belushi, Mike Ditka to Russell Crowe. The baths are open daily, with admission costing $25.

A renovation of the western half of the bathhouse was completed in late 2006, adding new facilities such as two whirlpools and a steam room for both men and women. There's also a small bar, serving soups and sandwiches for post-bath nourishment. But the bathing takes place in the basement: there's a wet area locker room, massage rooms with tables, hot and cold pools, divided showers, a steam room and a hot room.

The hot room is a Russian 'banya', and is rather more humid than a sauna. Granite boulders are heated by gas jets in a brick oven; splash the boulders to produce steam and heat up the eucalyptus-scented room. Bathers sit on wooden benches; when the heat gets too much, they soak themselves with cold water or head to a cold pool.

For $10 extra, attendants are on hand in the steam room to give *plaitza* (or *platka*) rubdowns: traditionally, a scrubbing with a hand-held birch broom or a bundle of leafy oak twigs, but these days, it's given with a seaweed sponge. Vigorous old-school massages are also available for an extra fee.

Beer Baron Row. *See p130.*

Ukrainian Village & West Town

Map p331

El: Blue to Chicago or Division.

Any tour of West Town and, more particularly, Ukrainian Village should begin at the south-west corner of Milwaukee Avenue and Augusta Boulevard, where you'll find the **Polish Roman Catholic Union of America**. The building is the home of the oldest Polish fraternal organisation in the US, established in 1873; Vincent Barzynski, one of its founders, was a vital figure in the development of Chicago's Polish community. It's now home to the **Polish Museum of America** (*see p129*): established in 1935 and opened two years later, it's the country's oldest ethnic museum.

A block to the west and north stands the **Northwestern University Settlement House** (1400 W Augusta Boulevard, at N Noble Street), home base of the organisation founded by sociologist Charles Zeublin. A lesser-known cousin of **Hull-House** (*see p122*), it played a major role in the development of American social service. The building was designed by architect Irving K Pond, who earned a name as a developer of settlement houses; it still houses several social service organisations.

To the north-west, the three-way intersection of Milwaukee, Division and Ashland marks the **Polonia Triangle**, known throughout the city's history as Polish Downtown and the one-time heart of Polish Chicago. The large white terracotta building, now a bank and clothing store, was once the home of *Dziennik Zwiazkowy*, Chicago's largest Polish-language daily newspaper, as well as the Jan Smulski Bank Polski. Just to the east, at 1520 W Division Street, is a large grey building that once housed the Polish National Alliance, the largest fraternal Polish organisation in the country. Meanwhile, further west is the **Division Street Russian & Turkish Bathhouse** (*see p127* **Ablution solution**), which opened in 1906 and remains one of the country's few traditional bathhouses still in operation.

On the corner of Evergreen and Noble stands the gigantic **St Stanislaus Kostka** (1351 W Evergreen Avenue, at N Noble Street, 1-773 278 2470, www.ststansk.com), completed in 1881 and home to Chicago's first Polish-Catholic congregation. Modelled after a church in Krakow, St Stanislaus boasted one of the largest congregations in the US – close to 5,000 families – at the turn of the 19th century. The church was dedicated and served by Barzynski until his death in 1899. Outside service hours, it's open only by appointment.

One block north of the church is Blackhawk Street, which will take you back to Ashland. Though redevelopment has reared its ugly head here, a few pre-20th-century homes remain, built at the height of the area's economic prosperity. The oldest homes are easily distinguished by the fact that they are built below sidewalk level, an oddity resulting from an 1850 decision by the city to raise sidewalks to facilitate better drainage.

The heart of Ukrainian Village, though, is further west. At the south-west corner of Haddon and Leavitt stands the **Holy Trinity Orthodox Cathedral** (1121 N Leavitt Street, at W Haddon Street, 1-773 486 6064), the first Orthodox/Greek Rites church to drop anchor in the community. Founded in 1892 by Carpatho-Ukrainian immigrants as St Vladimir's Russian Orthodox Church, it was redesigned by Louis Sullivan to resemble a Slavic church, with Tsar Nicholas II donating $4,000 towards the construction. The new church was consecrated in 1903 and was designated as a cathedral by the Russian Orthodox Church two decades later. Added to the National Register of Historic Places over 30 years ago, it's open to visitors by appointment only.

A couple of blocks away, on the north-eastern corner of Oakley and Cortez, is **St Volodymyr Ukrainian Orthodox Cathedral** (2238 W Cortez Street, at N Oakley Avenue, 1-773 278 2827). Built in 1911, it marks the proper entrance to Ukrainian Village, and was the first religious institution formed by local Ukrainians in the area. Call ahead if you want to look around.

From here, head south on Oakley until Rice. You can't miss the huge, Byzantine-styled **St Nicholas Ukrainian Catholic Cathedral** (2238 W Rice Street, at N Oakley Avenue, 1-773 276 4537, www.stnicholascathedralukrcath. org), modelled after the Basilica of St Sophia in Kiev, Ukraine. Completed in 1915, it was founded by Uniate Catholics, who hailed from Galicia and Carpatho-Ukraine. The interior is among Chicago's most elaborate, with ornate paintings, an enormous Greek chandelier and carpentry dominating the interior cupolas and imparting a distinctive Byzantine flavour. Call ahead to look around, or show up for a service.

St Nicholas was the community centre for Ukrainians until 1968, when a split in the parish over the use of the Gregorian and Julian calendars divided the congregation and sent many to the **Sts Volodymyr & Olha Church** (2245 W Superior Street, at N Oakley Avenue, 1-312 829 5209, www.stsvo.org). The church is modern Byzantine edifice with golden cupolas and a gigantic mosaic depicting the conversion of the Ukraine to Christianity in AD 988 by St

Volodymyr. It's also a piece of living history: the Eastern Rites are still conducted here in Ukrainian. Pop your head in between 9am and 4pm on weekdays. The **Ukrainian Institute of Modern Art** (*see below*) is a block north.

From here, wander east along Chicago Avenue, past an array of authentic Ukrainian and Russian businesses, towards the south-east corner of the neighbourhood. At Chicago and Ashland stands the **Goldblatt Bros** building (1609 W Chicago Avenue, at N Ashland Avenue), established as a discount department store in 1914 by two sons of Polish immigrants. From this store, Maurice and Nathan set about creating an impressive empire that eventually stretched to more than 40 locations by the 1970s. After years of neglect and requests from locals to spare it from demolition, the restored building now houses city workers and, unexpectedly, occasional art exhibits.

Polish Museum of America

984 N Milwaukee Avenue, at W Augusta Boulevard (1-773 384 3352/http://pma.prcua.org). El: Blue to Chicago. **Open** 11am-4pm Mon-Wed, Fri-Sun. **Admission** $5; $3-$4 discounts. **No credit cards.**
While it does a fine job of explaining the history of the city's Polish settlers, the Polish Museum of America, opened in 1937, has a colourful history of its own. Its collection expanded dramatically when exhibits sent by the Polish government to New York for the 1939 World's Fair became stuck in the US after Poland was invaded. The museum purchased many of the artefacts for its archives, which grew further when Ignacy Paderewski, noted Polish pianist and the first prime minister of a free Poland, left many personal effects to the museum in 1941. Paderewski was exiled to the US when war broke out; a plaque recognising his contribution to the city stands at the entrance of Wicker Park.

These days, the museum complements its permanent collection with temporary shows, classes and talks. Staff are only too happy to explain the history of Chicago's Polish community, or to recommend one of the many Polish restaurants in Little Warsaw, further up Milwaukee Avenue.

Ukrainian Institute of Modern Art

2320 W Chicago Avenue, at N Oakley Avenue (1-773 227 5522/www.uima-art.org). Bus 66. **Open** noon-4pm Wed-Sun. **Admission** free. **No credit cards.**
As its name suggests, this operation is devoted to modern art by Ukrainian artists. One of the city's better-kept secrets, the not-for-profit organisation has a small permanent collection, which usually takes second billing to notable temporary shows on topics such as graphics and war art.

Ukrainian National Museum

2249 W Superior Street, at N Oakley Avenue (1-312 421 8020/www.ukrainiannationalmuseum. org). Bus 49, X49, 66. **Open** 11am-4pm Thur-Sun. **Admission** $5; free under-12s. **No credit cards.**

Located in the heart of Ukrainian Village, this sweet little museum houses traditional clothing, musical instruments, agricultural tools and folk art from the Eastern European nation. A library houses some 16,000 books and periodicals and cultural archives.

Wicker Park & Bucktown

Map p331

El: Blue to Damen, Division or Western.

From the Goldblatt Bros building, wander north up Ashland and then north-west up Milwaukee towards the bewildering 'Six Corners' intersection of Milwaukee, North and Damen. This is the beating heart of the Wicker Park neighbourhood, but also the junction at which its gentrification is most pronounced. A liver-boggling number of nightclubs, bars and restaurants sit within a stone's throw of here.

And yet for all the moneyed development that's swept the area in the last half-decade or so, many iconic old buildings remain, relics from previous periods of prosperity but also, at the same time, veterans of intermittent depressions and recessions. Perhaps chief among these landmarks is the **Northwest Tower** (1600 N Milwaukee Avenue, at W North Avenue), a triangular, 12-storey art deco building completed just before the

Wicker Park.

Depression in 1929 by the architectural firm Holabird & Root. The one-time centre of Wicker Park's business activity, it was virtually empty by 1970, but a restoration plan in 1984 again filled the building with offices and businesses.

Across the street from the Northwest Tower stands the two-block-long, three-storey **Flat Iron Building** (1579 Milwaukee Avenue, at W North Avenue), a less venerable structure than its neighbour but one that has also found a new lease of life. Much of the building is occupied by young artists, with cult retail outlets such as the **Occult Bookstore** (1-773 292 0995) also on site. A large proportion of the neighbourhood's galleries are found nearby.

South of the Milwaukee–Damen–North intersection, things get a little quieter. For a glimpse into Wicker Park's history, wander along W Pierce Avenue, lined with large homes built by earlier German and Polish residents. The **Gingerbread House** (No.2137) was constructed in 1888 by Herman Weinhardt; across the street stands the **Paderewski House** (No.2138), built two years earlier and since renamed after the Polish pianist who once entertained a crowd from the verandah of the property. And at No. 2141 stands a house adorned with an Orthodox cross on top. Built in the late 19th century, it was once the home of the archbishop of the Russian Orthodox Holy Virgin Protection Church. There are more handsome old mansions on nearby Hoyne Avenue between Pierce and Schiller: known as Beer Baron Row, it was formerly a retreat for Chicago's prosperous brewers (**photo** *p128*).

Further south along Damen Avenue, you'll find the plot of land that gives the area its name. Although it's named after German Protestants Charles and Joel Wicker, **Wicker Park** was actually donated by Mary L Stewart in 1870. Once a dangerous corner of the city, the park has become much safer in recent years: the crack dealers have been replaced by farmers' markets, with annual events such as the Renegade Craft Fair (www.renegadecraft.com) adding colour to the calendar.

The literary-minded should walk one block south of the park to Evergreen Avenue, aka Nelson Algren Honorary Boulevard. Algren, author of *The Man with the Golden Arm* and one of Chicago's most accomplished writers, lived at No.1958 from 1959 to 1975. The city erected a Historical Wicker Park monument to help the curious locate the house; a plaque commemorates his residency. Further south on Damen (at Division Street) is the **Rainbo Club** (*see p187*), formerly favoured by Algren but now a popular haunt for local hipsters, artists and musicians.

Oak Park

Head out west for Hemingway and Lloyd Wright, the stars of the suburbs.

Ernest Hemingway Museum. *See p134.*

El: Green to Harlem, Oak Park or Ridgeland.

Heading west on the Green line from the Loop, you'll see some of the city's most deprived areas once you've crossed the Chicago River. The views from the window of the El train are less than inspiring: abandoned public housing, empty warehouses, boarded-up storefronts and trash-littered vacant lots. But towards the end of the line, it's another story entirely.

The first town over the border as you head west from downtown, **Oak Park** is one of Chicago's oldest suburbs, and easily one of its most beautiful. The village grew up in the years following the Great Fire of Chicago, and still retains a historic ambience. Yet despite appearances, it's long been a progressive place. Interracial couples historically found Oak Park more relaxed than Chicago, and the town elected an openly lesbian trustee (who later became Village Board President) long before Chicagoans voted into office a gay alderman.

Three Green-line El stops serve the suburb: Ridgeland station lies at its eastern extremity, while Harlem/Lake station in downtown Oak Park is at the end of the line. (The latter station is also served by the less frequent Metra service from the Ogilvie Transportation Center in the Loop.) Exit at Ridgeland and stroll west along Lake Street, browsing the shops – perhaps with a diversion to the kid-oriented **Wonder Works** (*see p226*) – until you reach the Green line's alpha/omega point for your return to the city.

Halfway along this Lake Street corridor, you'll hit Oak Park Avenue and many of the area's shopping highlights. The eclectic **Fly Bird** (719 Lake Street, 1-708 383 3330, www.fly-bird.net) is stocked with what the shop calls 'curious items', from the practical (housewares) to the amusing (ugly dolls). Women looking to splurge should investigate the **Ananas** fashion boutique (109 N Oak Park Avenue, 1-708 524 8585, www.shopananas.com), while kids of all ages will enjoy the **Magic Tree Bookstore** (141 N Oak Park Avenue, 1-708 848 0770, www.magictreebookstore.com).

A little further along Oak Park Avenue are the **Ernest Hemingway Birthplace & Museum** (*see p134*), a pair of buildings dedicated to one of the two famous residents to whom Oak Park owes much of its tourist appeal. A little further north-west, up around the junction of Chicago and Forest Avenues, sit the world's largest concentration of Frank Lloyd Wright-designed residences. The architect built 25 structures in the area; his early life is celebrated at the **Frank Lloyd Wright Home & Studio**. For more, *see pp132-133* **Wright on**.

Closer to Harlem Avenue, you'll find more commercial evidence of Oak Park's independent mindset, with a number of small local shops thriving despite the presence nearby of mega-chains. The quirky-fun staff and regular author appearances at **Barbara's Bookstore** (1100 Lake Street, 1-708 848 9140, www.barbarasbookstore.com) assure it a loyal customer base despite competition from Borders a half-block away, while the fresh-baked goods and fine coffee at the **Prairie Bread Kitchen** in the pedestrian mall by the train station (103 N Marion Street, 1-708 445 1234) keep locals coming back, even with branches of Starbucks and Caribou close at hand. The family-owned **Lake Theatre** (1022 Lake Street, 1-708 848 9088, www.classiccinemas.com) books art films as well as Hollywood blockbusters; follow a screening with a classic old sundae at **Petersen's Ice Cream Parlor** (1100 Chicago Avenue, 1-708 386 6131, http://petersens.biz).

Sightseeing

Wright on

The majority of eye-catching and headline-grabbing buildings in Chicago are priapic, sky-piercing affairs. Spend a mere five minutes walking around the Loop and it'll become apparent why the city is known as the home of the skyscraper. It's perhaps ironic, then, that Chicagoland's most celebrated architect made his name not by designing grandiose public buildings or flashy towers, but by constructing isolated residences for rich suburbanites, shuttered from the prying eyes of the common man. Nowadays, Frank Lloyd Wright's style is taken for granted. A century ago, it was virtually revolutionary.

Raised in Wisconsin, Wright arrived in Chicago in the years following the Great Fire and went to work in the offices of Adler and Sullivan, where he was assigned to the firm's residential design department. Eschewing the beaux-arts style so popular at the time, Wright's residential designs had much in common stylistically with the International Style of architecture, which was taking hold in Europe around the end of the 19th century.

In 1893, though, Wright was fired from Adler and Sullivan for moonlighting and set up his own practice at his home in suburban Oak Park, which he shared with his wife Catherine Tobin and their six children. At his home studio, Wright spent the next decade defining

what would come to be known as the Prairie Style, building more than 20 homes for his Oak Park neighbours. Miraculously, all of them survive today.

Mostly constructed of light-coloured brick and stucco, Wright's early Prairie Style homes are low, ground-hugging, rectangular structures featuring broad gabled roofs, sweeping horizontal lines and open, flowing floor plans. Wright was careful that they should blend in with their surroundings, imitating the wide open and flat topography of the Midwest plains. Common features include enclosed porches, stout chimneys and overhanging eaves.

Among the more notable Wright-designed properties in Oak Park are, chronologically, the relatively early **Parker** and **Gale Houses** (1019 and 1027 W Chicago Avenue); the **Thomas House** (210 N Forest Avenue), considered Wright's first true Prairie Style home; the **Moore House** (333 N Forest Avenue; *pictured right*), which Wright himself reworked almost three decades after its 1895 completion; the **Hills House** (313 Forest Avenue; *pictured above*), reconstructed after a fire in 1977; and the **Gale House** (6 Elizabeth Court), one of the last homes he built in the area. None of them is open to the public (they're all occupied), but you can see the exteriors simply by strolling around the neighbourhood. For more insight, get an audio tour from the Frank Lloyd Wright Home & Studio (*see p134*), or join one of the weekend guided tours (booking may be required).

Wright also designed Oak Park's **Unity Temple** (875 Lake Street, www.unity temple.org), a liberal Protestant church currently undergoing a massive restoration timed to commemorate its centenary in 1908. Both of Wright's parents belonged to the Unitarian Church, which encourages followers to approach religion through nature, science and art. Followers believe such disciplines reveal the underlying principles of God's universe. Indeed, Wright's respect for natural elements and precise geometry is apparent in the designs of his homes and the temple.

Wright left his home studio in 1909 and sold the property in 1925. Five decades later, the building had been so abused and altered by subsequent owners that it barely resembled the architect's original design. In 1974, the Frank Lloyd Wright Home & Studio Foundation was formed to acquire the property, oversee a $3-million restoration that returned the property to its 1909 appearance, and eventually open it to the public as a museum and education centre. Tours of the **Frank Lloyd Wright Home & Studio** (for details, *see p134*) offer fascinating insights into Wright's early life and creative influences. If you're lucky, you'll get one of the more entertaining tour guides, who won't gloss over the soapy details of Wright's philandering ways. Joint tickets are available with the aforementioned guided tours of Oak Park; see www.wrightplus.org for full details of the many tours available.

One of the last designs to come out of Wright's Oak Park studio was the **Robie House** (*see p142*), located near the University of Chicago on the city's South Side. Wright began work on the home of Chicago industrialist Frederick C Robie in 1909, a project the architect would later proclaim 'the cornerstone of modern architecture'.

When asked what his best building was, the self-aggrandising Wright answered, 'My next one'. He may have had a point: New York City's Guggenheim Museum was the last structure he designed before his death in 1959. Yet although Wright went on to design notable buildings all over the country, the small town where he got his start remains the best place to investigate his work.

Sightseeing

Along the southern edge of Oak Park, a few blocks west of the Austin stop on the Blue line lies the Harrison Street shopping district, also dominated by local shops. Many of the clothes sold at **Willow** (147 Harrison Street, 1-708 763 8770) are designed by the mother-daughter owners; nearby sits the new location of Oak Park legend **Val's Halla** (239 Harrison Street, 1-708 524 1004, www.valshalla.com),which has been recommending vinyl and CDs to eager customers for 30 years.

A mostly dry town, Oak Park doesn't have any straight-up bars; those lie on the other side of Harlem Avenue in neighbouring Forest Park. If you're looking for alcohol within the town, you'll have to find one of the restaurants with liquor licences. Among them is **Philander's**, where the terrific seafood is often served to the accompaniment of a jazz group. It's located within the **Carleton Hotel** (1120 Pleasant Street, at S Maple Avenue, 1-708 848 4250, www.carletonhotel.com), built in 1928 and expanded in 2000 to incorporate an adjacent building erected for the World's Columbian Exposition of 1893.

Ernest Hemingway Birthplace & Museum

Birthplace: 339 N Oak Park Avenue, at Erie Street. Museum: 200 N Oak Park Avenue, at Ontario Street (1-708 848 2222/www.ehfop.org). El: Green to Oak Park. **Open** *1-5pm Thur, Fri, Sun; 10am-5pm Sat.* **Admission** $7; $5.50 discounts; free under-5s. **No credit cards.**

Looked after by the Hemingway Foundation, the Oak Park house where Ernie emerged has been open to the public for years. The displays include photographs, furnishings and the like, all connected with Hemingway's childhood years. A museum two blocks away continues the theme with videos, books, posters and other Ernestabilia. All very well and good, of course, but the fact that Hemingway himself despised Oak Park, leaving as soon as he could (aged 18, for Kansas City, Missouri, and a job on a newspaper) and memorably referring to it as a place of 'wide lawns and narrow minds', is skimmed over. Hemingway may have been in Oak Park, but Oak Park certainly wasn't in Hemingway. **Photo** *p131.*

Frank Lloyd Wright Home & Studio

951 Chicago Avenue, at N Forest Avenue, Oak Park (1-708 848 1976/www.wrightplus.org). El: Green to Oak Park. **Open** *11am-4pm daily. Tours (45mins) 11am, 1pm & 3pm Mon-Fri; every 20mins, 11am-3.30pm Sat, Sun.* **Admission** $12; $5-$10 discounts. *See p132* **Wright on**.

Oak Park Conservatory

615 Garfield Street, between S Clarence & S East Avenues (1-708 386 4700/www.oakparkparks.com). El: Green to Oak Park. **Open** *2-4pm Mon; 10am-4pm Tue-Sun.* **Admission** *(suggested donation) $1; 50¢ discounts. Audio tour free.* **No credit cards.**

Much more than a greenhouse, this 73-year-old windowed structure contains three large themed rooms (tropical, fern and desert). A 5,000sq ft (450sq m) building, opened in 2000, provides space for social and educational events. Next door, Rehn Park has a play area for children, tennis courts and a pool.

Pleasant Home/Historical Society of Oak Park & River Forest

217 S Home Avenue, at Pleasant Street (1-708 848 6755/www.oprf.com/oprfhist). El: Green to Oak Park. **Tours** *Mar-Nov* 12.30pm, 1.30pm & 2.30pm Thur-Sun. *Dec-Feb* 12.30pm & 1.30pm Thur-Sun. **Admission** $5; $3-$4 discounts. Free to all Fri. **No credit cards.**

Designed in 1897 by Prairie School architect George W Maher, Pleasant Home is used primarily for meetings and wedding receptions. However, there's also a photograph and document archive here, plus a charming little local museum with exhibits relating to long-time local resident Edgar Rice Burroughs and the ubiquitous Mr Hemingway. You can only visit the museum and home as part of a tour.

Unity Temple

875 Lake Street, at N Kenilworth Avenue (1-708 383 8873/www.unitytemple-utrf.org). El: Green to Oak Park. **Open** *10.30am-4.30pm Mon-Fri; 1-4pm Sat, Sun. Tours* 1pm, 2pm & 3pm Sat, Sun. **Admission** $8; $5-$6 discounts. **Credit** AmEx, MC, V.

This Unitarian Universalist church, designed by Lloyd Wright in 1905 and eventually completed in 1908, is notable for its striking first-floor sanctuary and community room. Also of interest are the physical expressions of Wright's notions of divinity and sacred space found throughout (such as light fixtures, leaded glass windows and furniture); his love of music is reflected in the regular concerts that are held here. During the week, you can take a self-guided tour; at weekends, it's guided tours only.

Also in the area

Brookfield Zoo

3300 Golf Road, at 31st Street & 1st Avenue, Brookfield (1-708 485 0263/www.brookfieldzoo.org). Metra: Hollywood (Zoo Stop). **Open** *Memorial Day (last Mon in May)-Labor Day (1st Mon in Sept)* 9.30am-6pm daily. *Labor Day-Memorial Day* 10am-5pm daily. **Admission** $10; $6 discounts; free under-2s; Free to all Tue-Thur, Sat, Sun Oct-Feb & Tue-Thur Mar-Sept. **Credit** AmEx, DC, Disc, MC, V.

Brookfield Zoo, about five miles from Oak Park, is worlds apart from its compatriot in Lincoln Park (*see p109*) in terms of geography, tone and size. Over 200 acres of land are dedicated to keeping more than 400 species of wildlife. Cages are largely eschewed in favour of letting the animals roam free, to the delight of the kid-heavy crowds. The dolphin shows in the Seven Seas Panorama are predictably popular. And, of course, everyone loves the inquisitive meerkats. Parents should come prepared for an expensive time in the well-stocked gift shop afterwards.

The South Side

Home to Hyde Park liberals and modern-day blues.

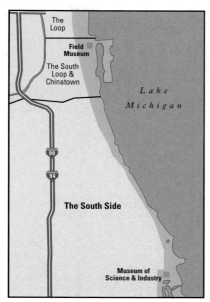

The cultural and political influence of the South Side, a fairly all-encompassing term for the towns and districts that sprawl south from I-55, extends far beyond the city limits. The area has immeasurable musical clout: the blues were cultivated here in the 1940s and '50s (*see pp45-48*), while Gospel music was born and baptised in the Pilgrim Baptist Church (which tragically burned down in January 2006). **Bronzeville** spawned the Chicago Renaissance, a blossoming of African American scholarship, arts and activism. But the South Side's greatest influence over Chicago has been political, with the Democratic machine that emanated from the tough neighbourhood of **Bridgeport**.

Even the most fleeting of visits will reveal that the South Side has borne the brunt of the city's depressions, and seen less of the fruits of the recent good times. This is still a poor part of town, and somewhat dangerous in places. However, pockets of it – most notably leafy, collegiate **Hyde Park** – are well worth a visit. The Red and Green lines travel through parts

of the area, with the Metra service from Downtown reaching other neighbourhoods not served by the El.

The Near South Side

El: Red to Cermak-Chinatown.

The streets immediately beyond the **South Loop** and **Chinatown** (*see pp87-93*), which end around I-55, are either uninspiring or downright shady. However, there are a few notable landmarks here, chief among them the **Wood-Maxey-Boyd House** at 2801 S Prairie Avenue (near E 28th Street). This Queen Anne-style building was saved from demolition during the 1950s, and again in 2003, when owner Alva Maxey-Boyd faced down the city and won. Her neighbours weren't as tough or as lucky: after a programme of systematic demolition, it's the only house on the block.

Given the amount of ink and paper expended on describing the Ludwig Mies van der Rohe buildings in the Loop and on the Near North Side, it's surprising that his designs for the main campus of the **Illinois Institute of Technology** (IIT) are generally overlooked in guidebooks. After all, this is one of the more important modernist sites in the country. Guided tours of the site ($5) are run at 10am and 1pm every day except Sunday, with self-guided audio tours ($5) also available (10am-3pm Mon-Sat). All tours depart from the ultra-postmodern **McCormick Tribune Campus Center** (3201 S State Street, at S 32nd Street), itself designed by noted Dutch architect Rem Koolhaas. The giant graphic of a head pays tribute to Mies with a wink and a nudge, while the stainless steel tube around the El trains helps to reduce the noise emanating from them. For more on the tours, call 1-312 567 5014 or see http://mies.iit.edu. The site is easily accessible by catching the 29 bus that runs down State Street.

Bronzeville

El: Green to 35th-Bronzeville-IIT.

Taking as its approximate borders Wentworth and Cottage Grove Avenues, and 26th and 51st Streets, Bronzeville emerged as a product of racial segregation and de facto residential restrictions. The neighbourhood came to be symbolic of the Chicago Renaissance, a period of African American cultural flowering in the city, before fading under the weight of underinvestment and neglect. In recent years, it's begun to make a comeback, but this long-beleaguered district still has a little way to go.

African Americans began to settle in the area during the late 19th century, joining the Irish Americans who already called it home. By the 1920s, the area had become what many referred to as a 'Black Metropolis': two major waves of migration brought some 200,000 southerners to the South Side, and the area prospered accordingly. Around this time, the area was christened Bronzeville by the *Chicago Bee*, an African American newspaper that elected a 'mayor' for the district every year.

It didn't last. The Depression and ongoing, city-approved segregation contributed to a downturn in the area's fortunes (as chronicled by local resident Richard Wright in his 1940 novel *Native Son*). The city's response was to drop more than 30 blocks of public housing on the neighbourhood and starve it of investment and attention, two acts that essentially rubber-stamped its earlier segregationist policies and invited economic decline. As factories shuttered and businesses fled, Bronzeville degenerated throughout the 1970s and '80s, riddled with abandoned buildings, cheque-cashing dens and seedy liquor stores.

Bronzeville still hasn't quite recovered from years of neglect and blight. Not all the promised new investment has yet materialised; indeed,

many abandoned properties have been boarded up for so long that even the wood covering their windows is rotting away. However, slowly but surely, an array of new local businesses is helping the neighbourhood rebound. At E 47th Street and S King Drive, a new complex houses contemporary American eaterie **Blu 47** (*see p174*) and the **Spoken Word Café** (4655 S King Drive, at E 47th Street, 1-773 373 2233), a cosy coffee shop with open-mic readings. A few blocks away sits the baseball-themed **Negro League Café** (301 E 43rd Street, at S Prairie Avenue, 1-773 536 7000, www.thenegroleague cafe.info). The area even boasts a B&B: **Bronzeville's First Bed & Breakfast Club** (3911 S King Drive, at 39th Street, 1-773 373 8081, www.bronzevillesbnb.com).

But perhaps the most revealing clue to the city's renaissance sits by the Blu 47 complex. Opened in 1928 at the corner of 47th Street and what is now King Drive (at the time, it was called South Park Avenue), the Regal Theater hosted virtually every African American superstar musician during its four decades in operation, among them Duke Ellington, Billie Holiday and Sam Cooke. After years in the doldrums, the site was taken over in 2004 by the **Harold Washington Cultural Center** (1-773 373 1900, 4701 S King Drive, at E 47th Street, www.haroldwashingtoncultural center.com), a multi-million-dollar arts facility featuring a gallery, a museum and a 1,000-seat theatre. Call for details of tours of the centre.

Other relics from Bronzeville's glory days have survived intact into the 21st century. The **Chicago Defender Building** (3435 S Indiana Avenue, at E 35th Street) was built as a synagogue, but went on to house the newspaper that agitated for civil rights and encouraged the Great Migration. Not far away sit the elaborate offices of its competitor, the *Chicago Bee* (3647-3655 S State Street, at E 36th Street). Opposite each other at the corner of 35th Street and King Drive are the old **Supreme Life Offices**, once the home of the country's first African American insurance agency, and the **Victory Monument**, erected in 1926 to honour black soldiers who fought in World War I.

But perhaps the most unlikely point of interest in Bronzeville dates back to the 19th century. Ironically, given his somewhat racist tendencies, 19th-century politician Stephen A Douglas once owned the land now occupied by the neighbourhood. Douglas died in 1861, the year after he was defeated by Abraham Lincoln in the presidential elections; two decades later, he was commemorated at 35th Street and Cottage Grove Avenues with an ostentatious tomb, a 46-foot (12-metre) column topped by a statue of the man himself.

Victory Monument.

Although Bronzeville is definitely on the up, parts of it still remain sketchy, especially at night. Take care when visiting the area. **Chicago Neighborhood Tours** (*see p73*) offers tours of Bronzeville three times a year.

Bridgeport

El: Orange to Halsted; Red to Sox-35th.

Originally and fatefully dubbed Hardscrabble, Bridgeport (south from 26th Street to Pershing Road, between Wentworth and Ashland Avenues) grew up around the Illinois–Michigan Canal as a settlement of Irish Americans willing to work for land. During the early and mid 20th century, it was known for its hostility to outsiders and for the violent gangs that enforced its boundaries. However, such behaviour didn't prevent it from exerting a massive influence over the development of the city; indeed, it might even have helped. For it was from here that the fabled Democratic political machine really cranked into action. For more on this era, *see pp12-26*.

For years, Bridgeport's economy was driven by meat. Opened in 1865, the Union Stock Yards was the centre of the country's meatpacking industry, a sprawling site that eventually grew to cover an area constrained by Pershing Road in the north, Halsted Street to the east, 47th Street to the south and Ashland Avenue to the west. Upton Sinclair's book *The Jungle* passed damning judgment on conditions within the collection of slaughterhouses, but it continued to thrive and closed as recently as 1971. Its presence is commemorated by the limestone Stockyards Gate over Exchange Avenue (at Peoria Street), next to a memorial for firefighters who died in a fire here in 1910.

Centred around Halsted Street, Bridgeport has maintained a working-class Irish character, but is now home to communities of Mexican Americans and Lithuanian Americans; the latter hang out at **Healthy Food Lithuanian**, 3236 S Halsted Street, at W 32nd Street, 1-312 326 2724), a neighbourhood survivor known for its juices and home-made *kugelis*. And while Bridgeport remains tight-knit, an influx of condo conversions and an assortment of 'space available' signs on nearby warehouses tell their own story. The **Polo Café** (3322 S Morgan Street, at W 33rd Place, 1-773 927 7656, www. polocafe.com), a former candy shop, has become a focal point for the new and fast-rising district, which also saw the recent opening of the **Chicago Blues Museum** (*see below*).

However, most Chicagoans visit Bridgeport to take in a Chicago White Sox baseball game at **US Cellular Field** (S Wentworth Avenue & E 35th Street; *see p272*), a hulking concrete bowl

Note-worthy: the **Chicago Blues Museum**.

built in the early 1990s. Aesthetically, it's not a patch on Wrigley Field, but the fans don't mind. After all, since it opened, the Cubs haven't been a patch on the White Sox, who won the World Series in 2005. For more on the city's baseball rivalry, *see pp49-52*.

Chicago Blues Museum

3636 S Iron Street, at W 37th Street (1-773 828 8118/www.chicagobluesmuseum.com). Bus 9, 35. **Open** by appointment only. **Admission** $10; $5 discounts; free under-10s. **No credit cards**.

This highly anticipated South Side museum lost some of its sizzle when its appointments-only policy left countless visitors frustrated and out in the cold. If you're smart enough to plan ahead, you may be lucky enough to get in and peruse the history of Chicago blues and jazz music. On tap are related films and artefacts, as well as images culled from the museum's 350,000-piece photographic archive. Among relics left over from the golden age are seats from the famed Regal Theater (*see p136*), Vee-Jay Records star Jimmy Reed's guitar and the basement door from Muddy Waters' South Side home.

Hyde Park

Map p332

Metra: 55th-56th-57th Street.

With the University of Chicago as its anchor, Hyde Park enjoys a reputation as an oasis of intellectualism and community activism. Indeed, 'Hyde Park liberal' is a familiar term of both abuse and affection among Chicagoans. The neighbourhood is much more low-key than the equivalent, college-dominated districts on

the North Side counterparts; largely geared towards the middle-class families that settle there, it has far fewer bars, restaurants and nightclubs than (for example) Lincoln Park. But its true campus culture also makes it feel much more self-enclosed, like a village of its own.

The aforementioned campus of the **University of Chicago** is at the heart of Hyde Park, both figuratively and literally. Many of the buildings are neo-Gothic, but several newer structures are worthy of attention. Chief among them is Cesar Pelli's flowing and airy Ratner Athletic Center, which houses a pool visible from the sidewalk between 55th and 56th Streets on Ellis Avenue. In addition to the **Oriental Institute** (*see p141*), the campus is home to a pair of galleries. The **Renaissance Society** (5811 S Ellis Avenue, at E 58th Street, 1-773 702 8670, http://renaissancesociety.org) offers a roster of temporary modern-art shows, while the **Smart Museum of Art** (*see p142*) boasts an enviable permanent collection. For a detailed tour of the campus, *see p140* **Walk**.

As you might expect, the leafy streets around the college are dotted with bookstores, such as **Powell's** (*see p194*) and the **Seminary Co-Operative** (*see p193*), and music shops (including **Hyde Park Records**, *see p213*). Close by sits **Robie House** (*see p142*), a Frank Lloyd Wright masterpiece. Other attractions sit slightly further away. To the east, in pretty, lakefront Jackson Park, sits the **Museum of Science and Industry** (*see below*), one of the city's premier family-friendly museums. And to the west, in Washington Park, is the **DuSable Museum of African American History**

(*see below*). Both parks are ideal for finding pensive pauses unavailable in other parts of the city, rather like the neighbourhood as a whole.

DuSable Museum of African American History

740 E 56th Place, at E 57th Street (1-773 947 0600/ www.dusablemuseum.org). Metra: 55th-56th-57th Street. **Open** 10am-5pm Mon-Sat; noon-5pm Sun. (closed Mon July-Dec). **Admission** $3; $2; $1-$2 discounts; free under-6s; free to all Sun. **No credit cards. Map** p332 X17.

When the DuSable Museum opened in the early '60s, African American history was suffering serious neglect at the hands of the nation's cultural institutions. The seeds of change were planted when, in 1961, printmaker and schoolteacher Margaret Burroughs cleared the furniture out of her South Side home's living room, replaced it with an enviable collection of African American art and artefacts, and hung a shingle outside reading 'African American Museum'. And so the DuSable Museum was born.

One of the country's first museums dedicated to black history, the DuSable Museum is now housed in a stately former Park District building in Washington Park. Revolving exhibitions spotlight everything from African American entrepreneurship and the civil rights movement to traditional quilt-making techniques. The museum also focuses on Chicago's own African American community, with an ongoing exhibit on the life of Bronzeville beauty product pioneer Annie Malone. Organisation and interpretive materials don't seem to be of utmost importance, but the helpful staff compensate.

Museum of Science & Industry

5700 S Lake Shore Drive, at 57th Street (1-773 684 1414/www.msichicago.org). Metra: 55th-56th-57th Street. **Open** 9.30am-4pm Mon-Sat; 11am-4pm Sun.

DuSable Museum of African American History.

Hammurabi Robb

Ralph Turner

Walk Back to school

Hyde Park is dominated by the University of Chicago, and strollers can't help but pass by its landmarks. Here are a few of the more interesting structures on campus.

Begin at the corner of 58th and Woodlawn.
Just south of the **Robie House** (*see p142*) sits the relatively new **Graduate School of Business** building (1101 E 58th Street). Designed by Rafael Vinoly, it's in part a modern re-interpretation of its Frank Lloyd Wright-designed neighbour. Approach from the south to see how the two buildings interact, and also to gauge Vinoly's sensitivity to his predecessor.

Head south down Woodlawn until you get to the junction of Woodlawn and 59th.
It looks pretty big out front, but **Ida Noyes Hall** (1212 E 59th Street) is even bigger inside. It was built in 1916 as a women's hall of residence; these days, there's a cinema and a swimming pool tucked away inside it. Across the way, the **Rockefeller Memorial Chapel** (5850 S Woodlawn Avenue, 1-773 702 2100, http://rockefeller.uchicago.edu) is named after the man whose cash funded the building of the university. Constructed to the dauntingly Gothic designs of Bertram Goodhue in 1928, the chapel is notable for some wonderful stained glass and a surfeit of exterior statues.

Walk a block west down Woodlawn, then take the next right up University.
Steps away from the university's **Oriental Institute Museum** (*see below*) sits the **Chicago Theological Seminary** (1164 E 58th Street, www.ctschicago.edu). Visit the quietly lovely Thorndike Hilton Memorial Chapel and the **Seminary Co-operative Bookstore** (5757 S University Avenue, 1-773 752 4381) downstairs.

Continue north up University Avenue to the south-west corner with E 57th Street.
If you're lucky, your visit to Hyde Park will coincide with a concert at **Mandel Hall** (*see p251*). Some top-notch classical ensembles perform in its beautifully maintained auditorium.

Walk north up University Avenue for a block.
George and William Keck designed the three-flat, International-style **Keck-Gottschalk-Keck Apartments** (5551 S University Avenue) for themselves and Professor Louis Gottschalk in 1937. It's now a designated Chicago landmark known for the external blinds attached to its street-facing windows.

Turn left on to E 56th Street.
The **Smart Museum of Art** (*see p142*) is the second university museum en route. Stop to see which items from its extensive collection are on display in its intimate space.

Admission $11; $7-$9.50 discounts; free under-2s; free to all Mon-Tue Jan-Feb. **Credit** AmEx, Disc, MC, V. **Map** p332 Z17.

If you're into exhibits loaded with interactive features, this expansive Hyde Park operation should be just the ticket. Built in 1893 as the Palace of Fine Arts for the World's Columbian Exposition, the building was converted to its present incarnation in the 1920s. Although it's a fair way from downtown, it's one of the city's top attractions.

The challenge for every science museum is not only to track the history of technological progress, but also to keep pace with it. While some of the whizbang exhibits are good – notably the Toymaker 3000 robotic production line and the predictably oversubscribed IMAX Theater, which features science-related films on a massive screen – there are some real clunkers here, too. The simulated take-off and landing of an actual 727 (Balcony West), for example, is so underwhelming that the model trains on the floor below come alive with wonder.

Overall, the museum's focus is broad, as witnessed by low-tech displays such as Colleen Moore's Fairy Castle (Ground Floor, by the Yellow Stairs), a gaudy but fabulous multi-room miniature that's just a bit too big to be called a doll's house. Nearby, the huge John Deere combine harvester in the Farm (Ground Floor, by the Red Stairs) is equally amazing, mostly due to its overwhelming mechanical presence. The long queues that form outside the Coal Mine (Main Floor, by the Rotunda) hide an exhibit that kids enjoy immensely, at least if they don't go mad during the boring wait on the staircase. If you're interested, go during the earlier portion of your visit, as seats on 'Old Ben #17' often fill to capacity and the exhibit closes earlier than the rest of the museum.

Of all the vehicles in the museum, the 1934 Pioneer Zephyr train (Great Hall) is one of the highlights, as is the not-to-be-missed U-505 German submarine (Ground Floor). One of only five surviving World War II subs in the world, it recently underwent a $35-million overhaul that afforded it its very own vast underground chamber. It's now surrounded by lots of interpretative materials, short films and artefacts found on board when, in June of 1944, it was captured by American seamen off the coast of West Africa. The vast exhibition is included with admission but the on-board tour requires additional tickets ($5).

Continue west down E 56th Street for a block, then turn left down Ellis Avenue.

A Henry Moore sculpture, *Nuclear Energy*, stands on the site of Stagg Field, the long since demolished football field. It was here, on 2 December 1942, that Enrico Fermi conducted the first successful nuclear experiment. Moore's statue was unveiled exactly 25 years later.

Stroll down Ellis Avenue and then turn left into E 57th Street.

The Gothic **Cobb Gate** makes for a grand entrance to the college, and made for an equally grand exit for Billy Crystal and Meg Ryan when they set off for New York City from here in Nora Ephron's likeable 1989 cinematic comedy *When Harry Met Sally*. Ask a savvy student to explain the frivolous collegiate myth that has grown up around the figures on the gate, from the admissions secretary at ground level to the final-year students up top.

Walk through the Cobb Gate and continue south to the roundabout.

The portentous **Swift Hall**, located right in the heart of the campus, is home to the university's Divinity School. It figures, then, that right next to it should be the **Bond Chapel**, all dark woods and studied calm behind its imposing double doors. Close by, **Cobb Hall** is the oldest building on campus, dating back to 1892. It takes its name from Henry Ives Cobb, the architect who designed 18 of the college

buildings. Inside, the university mounts exhibitions of unapologetically modern art in the **Renaissance Society** (*see p139*).

Cut through the passageway between Cobb Hall and the Administration building and head north up Ellis Avenue.

It's the least interesting of all the literary outlets in bookstore-dominated Hyde Park, but the Barnes & Noble-run **University of Chicago Bookstore** (970 E 58th Street, 1-773 702 8729) still succeeds in drawing a mix of students needing textbooks and tourists needing souvenirs.

Elsewhere in the museum, young visitors especially will wonder agog at the interactive science displays, whether whispering to a friend across the hall at the Whispering Gallery (Main Floor), marvelling at Foucault's endlessly swinging pendulum or watching a chick hatch before their eyes in the hatchery (Main Floor). It'll take at least a day to see everything and it's easy to get disoriented, even without temporary exhibits such as the groundbreaking but controversial blockbuster Body Worlds show and a Da Vinci exhibition that featured models of never-before-executed plans from the Renaissance Man's renderings. Still, it's well worth a visit. **Photo** *p142*.

Oriental Institute Museum

University of Chicago, 1155 E 58th Street, at S University Avenue (1-773 702 9520/oi.uchicago. edu). Metra: 55th-56th-57th Street. **Open** 10am-6pm Tue, Thur-Sat; 10am-8.30pm Wed; noon-6pm Sun. **Admission** (suggested donation) $5; $2 under-12s. **No credit cards. Map** p332 X17.

This University of Chicago-run archaeological treasure trove forgoes the current museum trend of providing hokey interactive displays that pander to the Nintendo generation's short attention spans. Instead, it allows some stunning architectural finds to speak for themselves in old-fashioned glass display cases. John D Rockefeller bankrolled the institute so archaeologist-Egyptologist James Breasted and his colleagues could lead expeditions to excavate lost civilisations. The vast collection that resulted, which includes cuneiform tablets, mummies and larger-than-life stone statues from Egypt and the Near East, evokes all the mystery and intrigue any whip-cracking, fedora-wearing action hero could handle.

The space is divided into galleries themed around Mesopotamia, Egypt and Persia, along with newer East Wing Galleries that take in the Assyrian, Syro-Anatolian and Megiddo collections. Among the highlights are the hard-to-miss, 16-foot (five-metre), solid-stone, human-headed winged bull that guarded King Sargon II's palace court more than 2,700 years ago, and the equally imposing 3,000-year-old King Tut statue uncovered in Thebes. The institute's newest gallery focuses on ancient Nubia (now southern Egypt and northern Sudan), with artefacts that include what's believed to be the world's oldest rug.

Which came first? Find out at the **Museum of Science & Industry**. See p139.

Robie House

5757 S Woodlawn Avenue, at E 58th Street (1-708 848 1976/www.wrightplus.org). Metra 55th-56th-57th Street. **Tours** 11am, 1pm & 3pm Mon-Fri; every 30 mins 11am-3.30pm Sat, Sun. **Admission** $12; $10 discounts. **Credit** AmEx, Disc, MC, V. **Map** p332 Y17.
If you have even a basic knowledge of architecture, you'll know who's behind this place. Commissioned by Chicago industrialist Frederick C Robie and completed in 1910, this is Frank Lloyd Wright at his finest. A masterpiece of the Prairie Style, the house features dramatic horizontal lines, cantilevered roofs, expansive stretches of glass and Wright's signature open floor plan. It's free to admire from the street, but the 45-minute guided tour, operated by the Frank Lloyd Wright Preservation Trust, is the best way to experience it. Tickets for selected tours are available in advance; otherwise, it's first come, first served.

Smart Museum of Art

University of Chicago, 5550 S Greenwood Avenue, at E 55th Street (1-773 702 0200/http://smartmuseum. uchicago.edu). Metra: 55th-56th-57th Street. **Open** 10am-4pm Tue, Wed, Fri; 10am-8pm Thur; 11am-5pm Sat, Sun. **Admission** free. **Map** p332 X17.
Named after the two publishers of *Esquire* magazine, whose family foundation provided the funds to open the facility, the Smart Museum of Art houses a dizzyingly eclectic collection of more than 10,000 objects, spanning 5,000 years from ancient Shang Dynasty bronzes to high-concept contemporary works of art. The mind reels, stepping from Shinto prints in one room to Anselm Kiefer in the next. The under-appreciated work of HC Westermann is also well represented.

The Pullman District

Metra: 111th Street.

Originally outside the city limits, the Pullman District (roughly bounded by 104th, 115th, Cottage Grove and Langley Streets) is the preserved remains of the first model planned industrial community in the US. Tycoon George Pullman conceived a workers' utopia to be built alongside his new vertically integrated railcar factory, and set about creating it on a 3,000-acre site. Erected from 1880, the 1,300 structures included houses, shops, churches, parks and a library for his employees. Sadly, Pullman's dream turned into a nightmare when workers' dissatisfaction resulted in a violent and destructive strike. As a result, the town was annexed by Chicago in 1898, though Pullman wasn't around to see it happen; he'd died a year earlier. For more, *see p17* **Strike one**.

Unfortunately, much of the original town is gone, destroyed by overzealous construction workers and, in the case of the old clock tower, arsonists (it burned down in 1998). Still, the buildings that remain give a decent impression of what this community was like during its first decade. The Hotel Florence, the Greenstone Church and some rowhouse-lined sidestreets are all either intact or have been restored in what is now a National Landmark District. Start your visit at the **Historic Pullman Foundation Visitor Center** (*see below*).

Historic Pullman Foundation Visitors Center

11141 S Cottage Grove Avenue, at S 112th Street (1-773 785 8901/www.pullmanil.org). Metra: 111th Street. **Open** 11am-3pm Tue-Sun. *Tours* May-Oct 1.30pm 1st Sun of mth. **Admission** (suggested donation) $5; $3-$4 discounts; free under-6s. **Credit** AmEx, MC, V.
The Pullman City visitors' centre houses historic photos and Pullman-related items, such as a buffet table from the Pullman mansion, ornamental decor from the old Hotel Florence and the 'Perfect Town' award given to Pullman. Brochures for a self-guided walking tour are available, though there are also monthly guided tours in summer.

Eat, Drink, Shop

Restaurants	**144**
Bars	**176**
Shops & Services	**190**

Features

The best Restaurants	144
Loop lunchin'	147
Made in Chicago	150
Sweet things	155
Up all night	157
Meat beat manifesto	158
The brunch bunch	166
Going native	172
The best Bars	176
The golden gander	185
Smoke alarm	189
The best Shops	190
Where to shop	192
Designs for life	198
Farmers' markets	205
Golden oldies	210

Stone Lotus Lounge. *See p266.*

Restaurants

Eat your way around the world without leaving the Windy City.

Ever since the World's Columbian Exposition of 1893, at which America got its first taste of shredded wheat and Aunt Jemima pancakes, the Windy City has been making culinary history. These days, though, Chicago gets more attention for its high-end restaurants, such as **Charlie Trotter's**, and for its experimental eateries, among them **Alinea** and **Schwa**, than for its snack shacks. If you've got money to burn, the fine dining here is second to none.

That said, there are innumerable cheaper establishments here, notably the ethnic eateries in every corner of the city. Chicago is home to more Mexicans than any US city except LA, and the range of Mexican food is terrific. Head to Maxwell Street Market for dollar tamales, or to Pilsen taquerias such as **Nuevo León** for bargain mole. Heading upscale, the seasonal menus served by Rick Bayless at his **Frontera Grill** highlight various regions of Mexico.

After you've gone south of the border, take your tastebuds on a trip to India and Pakistan up on the city's far North Side, along W Devon Avenue. Amid the sari shops and electronics outlets sit revered curry houses such as **Hema's Kitchen** and kebab havens including **Chopal Kebab & Steak**. Across in Uptown, near where W Argyle Street meets N Broadway Street, Little Saigon holds a host of Vietnamese restaurants; you can't go wrong with the banh mi at **Ba Le** or the pho at **Pho Xe Tang**. Chinatown is also worth a look: fiery Sichuan food doesn't get better than at **Lao Sze Chuan**. And Thai spots have seen a surge in popularity of late, thanks in part to a local foodie who took it upon himself to translate the Thai-language menus at the likes of **Sticky Rice** and **TAC Quick Thai**. Anglo eaters can now order the same authentic dishes that once were only available to Thai-speakers; ask for the 'secret menu'.

You'll find a noticeable increase in the use of organic and local products at many mid-level restaurants around town. Chefs at trend-setting spots such as **North Pond**, **Blackbird**, **Lula Café**, **Naha**, **HotChocolate** and **Scylla** are dedicated to sourcing everything from free-range chicken to baby beets from local farms, and have been the driving force behind the city's popular Green City Market (*see p205* **Farmers' markets**). And while meat and potatoes will never go out of style here, old-school favourites such as the **Chicago Chop House** are now supplemented by the somewhat over-the-top presentations at **Primehouse David Burke** and the grass-fed beef at chef Shawn McClain's **Custom House**.

INFORMATION

Competition for tables at some smart and/or hip restaurants can be tough; if in doubt, always call ahead and book your spot. Chicago is generally a casual city, but gents should wear jackets at posh spots such as **Everest**. Prices given below are for an average main course.

The best Restaurants

For a blow-out breakfast
Breakfast Club (*p169*), Crêpe & Coffee Palace (*p158*), Ina's (*p165*), M Henry (*p162*) or West Egg Café (*p166* The brunch bunch).

For a lovely lunch
Bittersweet Pastry Shop (*p159*), Eleven City Diner (*p146*), HotChocolate (*p171*), Spa Café (*p147* Loop lunchin') or Sweet Maple Café (*p168*)

For a dazzling dinner
Alinea (*p155*), Blackbird (*p165*) Charlie Trotter's (*p157*), DeLaCosta (*p153*) or Schwa (*p173*).

For city specialities
Al's Italian Beef (*p150*), Chicago Chop House (*p150*) or Pizzeria Due (*p152*).

For a room with a view
Everest (*p144*), Japonais (*p152*) or North Pond (*p159*).

The Loop

For lunch specialists in the Loop, *see p147* **Loop lunchin'**.

Everest

440 S LaSalle Street, at W Van Buren Street (1-312 663 8920/www.everestrestaurant.com). El: Blue, Brown, Orange, Pink or Purple to LaSalle; Red to Jackson. **Open** 5.30-9.30pm Tue-Thur; 5-10pm Fri, Sat. **Main courses** $35. **Credit** AmEx, Disc, MC, V. **Map** p325 H13 ❶ French

Eat, Drink, Shop

Monster matzo balls and mean milkshakes at the **Eleven City Diner**. *See p146.*

The view from the 40th floor of the Chicago Stock Exchange is enchanting enough that you could eat burgers and be happy. Happily, renowned chef Jean Joho has higher standards and insists on applying his Alsatian roots and classical French training to seasonal American ingredients. Look for dishes such as black cod encrusted in pumpernickel horseradish, and creamy chestnut soup with duck confit.

Nick's Fishmarket

1 Bank One Plaza (51 S Clark Street), at W Monroe Street (1-312 621 0200/www.nicksfishmarketchicago. com). El: Blue or Red to Monroe; Brown, Green, Orange, Pink or Purple to Adams. **Open** 11.30am-2pm, 5-10pm Mon-Thur; 11.30am-2pm, 5-11pm Fri; 5-11pm Sat. **Main courses** $28. **Credit** AmEx, DC, Disc, MC, V. **Map** p325 H12 ❷ Seafood
Peanut butter and jelly. Cagney and Lacey. Romance and… fish. At least that's the vibe at this upscale institution, where the only thing that gets in the way of a couple's canoodling is the single rose on the table. It's common to see pairs feeding each other forkfuls of crispy citrus-ginger salmon or deep-red slices of seared tuna. If PDA isn't your idea of appetising, head upstairs for some pub grub at Nick's Grill.

Patty Burger

72 E Adams Street, between S Wabash & S Michigan Avenues (1-312 987 0900). El: Blue or Red to Monroe; Brown, Green, Orange, Pink or Purple to Adams. **Open** 7am-9pm Mon-Fri; 10am-6pm Sat, Sun. **Main courses** $4. **Credit** AmEx, DC, Disc, MC, V. **Map** p325 J12 ❸ Classic American
This home-grown fast food hub serves the best quick burger in the Loop: hand-formed Black Angus patties on buttered and griddled brioche buns with

lettuce, tomato, onion and 'special sauce' (ketchupy mayo). The fries are dead ringers for McDonald's, so you could always skip them and save room for one of the to-die-for chocolate peanut butter shakes.

Rhapsody

Symphony Center, 65 E Adams Street, between S Wabash & S Michigan Avenues (1-312 786 9911/ www.rhapsodychicago.com). El: Blue or Red to Monroe; Brown, Green, Orange, Pink or Purple to Adams. **Open** *Mid June-mid Sept* 11.30am-2pm, 5-9pm Mon-Thur; 11.30am-2pm, 5-10pm Fri, Sat. *Mid Sept-mid June* 11.30am-2pm, 5-9pm Mon-Wed; 11.30am-2pm, 5-10.30pm Thur-Sat; 4.30-9pm Sun. **Main courses** $22. **Credit** AmEx, DC, Disc, MC, V. **Map** p325 J12 ❹ Contemporary American
Given its built-in clientele of music fans, Rhapsody could get away with sub-par food and rushed preshow (pre-cooked) meal deals. Luckily, it doesn't try. The seasonal menu includes enticing appetisers such as braised rabbit cannelloni (spiked with sage, oregano and blue cheese), followed by the likes of tamarind-glazed pork with caramelised quince, or pan-roasted striped bass with celery-root fondant.

Russian Tea Time

77 E Adams Street, between S Michigan & S Wabash Avenues (1-312 360 0000/www.russiantea time.com). El: Blue or Red to Monroe; Brown, Green, Orange, Pink or Purple to Adams. **Open** 11am-9pm

❶ Purple numbers given in this chapter correspond to the location of restaurants on the street maps. *See pp322-332.*

Custom House.

The South Loop

Chicago Firehouse

1401 S Michigan Avenue, at E 14th Street (1-312 786 1401/www.chicagofirehouse.com). El: Green, Orange or Red to Roosevelt. **Open** 11.30am-4pm, 5-10pm Mon-Fri; 5-10pm Sat; 4-9pm Sun. **Main courses** $25. **Credit** AmEx, DC, Disc, MC, V. **Map** p324 J15 ❼ Classic American

Some believe that dining in the beautiful surroundings of this 1904 former fire station is worth any price; others grumble that cedar-planked Dover sole with browned butter should never cost $39, no matter how flavourful it is. Thankfully, the rest of the menu is fairer on the wallet: the CF 104 Tower, tender prosciutto encasing three sprigs of asparagus and mascarpone, is a heavenly starter, while the hearty pot roast falls apart with the touch of a fork.

Custom House

500 S Dearborn Street, at W Congress Parkway (1-312 523 0200/www.customhouse.cc). El: Blue or Red to Jackson; Brown, Orange, Pink or Purple to Library. **Open** 7.30-10am, 11.30am-2pm, 5-10pm Mon-Fri; 7.30-10.30am, 5-10pm Sat; 7.30am-2pm, 5-9pm Sun. **Main courses** $24. **Credit** AmEx, DC, Disc, MC, V. **Map** p325 H13 ❽ Classic American

This sleek steakhouse comes courtesy of chef Shawn McClain, also of Green Zebra (*see p169*) and Spring (*see p173*). A delicious cured sturgeon starter goes Eastern Euro with apple matchsticks, juniper berries and pumpernickel toast, while perfectly braised baby lamb gets thick rounds of fennel sausage, al dente cannellini beans, roasted carrots and turnips. And, of course, there's steak: expertly prepared bone-in rib-eye, prime sirloin and skirt steak, served with seasonal sides such as orange and vanilla-laced salsify.

Eleven City Diner

1112 S Wabash Avenue, between E 11th & E 12th Streets (1-312 212 1112/www.elevencitydiner.com). El: Green or Orange to Roosevelt/Wabash; Red to Roosevelt/State. **Open** 7.30am-10pm Mon-Thur; 7.30am-midnight Fri; 9am-midnight Sat; 9am-9pm Sun. **Main courses** $10. **Credit** AmEx, Disc, MC, V. **Map** p324 J14 ❾ Classic American

Owner Brad Rubin scoured the country to research this Jewish deli/diner, with impressive results. His pastrami is tender, fatty and full of flavour; the milk shakes are thick; the matzo balls are enormous, fluffy things; and the roast chicken is as good as any grandmother's, Jewish or otherwise. Rubin holds his own as the host, giving this place enough character to become a fixture in its own right. **Photo** *p145*.

Manny's Coffee Shop & Deli

1141 S Jefferson Street, at W Roosevelt Road (1-312 939 2855/www.mannysdeli.com). Bus 12. **Open** 5am-4pm Mon-Sat. **Main courses** $7. **Credit** AmEx, Disc, MC, V. **Map** p324 G14 ❿ Classic American

Mon-Thur, Sun; 11am-midnight Fri, Sat. **Main courses** $20. **Credit** AmEx, Disc, MC, V. **Map** p325 J12 ❺ Eastern European

This institution proves excess is best. Slide into a cosy booth and start the assault with classic borscht, sour cream-slathered dumplings and caviar blini. After that, order creamy beef stroganoff or oniony, nutmeg-laced, ground-beef-stuffed cabbage rolls. Finish with hot farmer's cheese blintzes or Klara's apricot-and-plum strudel, a family recipe from the restaurant's matriarch. Skip the wine and plump for a flight of house-infused vodkas.

Vivere

71 W Monroe Street, between S Clark & S Dearborn Streets (1-312 332 7005/www.italianvillage-chicago. com). El: Blue or Red to Monroe; Brown, Green, Orange, Pink or Purple to Madison. **Open** 11.30am-2.30pm, 5-10pm Mon-Thur; 11.30am-2.30pm, 5-11pm Fri; 5-11pm Sat. **Main courses** $20. **Credit** AmEx, DC, Disc, MC, V. **Map** p325 H12 ❻ Italian

The best of the three restaurants found under one roof in the Italian Village, Vivere boasts a menu as contemporary as its decor; quite a feat when the dining room resembles an Italian baroque version of Alice's Wonderland. The wine list has won awards, while the regional menu is a balance of solid classics and interesting twists on house-made pastas, seafood stews and grilled game. Try the sage-scented, pheasant-filled agnolottini, or the butternut squash-ricotta ravioli in rosemary brown butter with toasted hazelnuts.

Eat, Drink, Shop

Loop lunchin'

Although a few highfalutin restaurants and low-down bars do hold the fort during the evenings, and many of the area's hotel restaurants offer pretty decent food, most of the best eating options in the Loop are lunchtime specialists. Here are six of the best spots at which to replenish your energy supplies after a trek around the city's hub...

At the top of the list, somewhat surprisingly, is Macy's, which has brought celeb chef Rick Bayless into the fold to run **Frontera Fresco** (111 N State Street, at W Washington Street, 1-312 781 4884; *pictured below*). Tortas, quesadillas, tamales, salad and soup are among the offerings at this terrific seventh-floor food counter, but fillings run against notions of fast-food spots. Smoked pork loin and apple-wood bacon top the torta Cubana; steak joins garlicky mushrooms and chipotle sauce for an earthy huarache. Lines can rival the weekend queues at Frontera (*see p151*).

The closest thing Chicago has to *Seinfeld*'s Soup Nazi, **Perry's** (174 N Franklin Avenue, at W Randolph Street, 1-312 372 7557, www.perrysdeli.com) is a lunchtime Loop institution. Random trivia questions are barked over a loudspeaker; the no-cellphones policy is fiercely enforced. Your wait will be rewarded with deli classics such as matzo ball soup, egg salad sandwiches, and hot and juicily marbled pastrami.

Just going on the name, **Spa Café** (112 W Monroe Street, at N Clark Street, 1-312 551 0000) sounds like some posh spot where the tanned and toned prance around with cucumbers over their eyes. It's not – they prance around sipping cucumber water (which is incredibly good, by the way). The rest of us

can make tasty, filling combos from dozens of moreish options such as cumin-carrot and peanut butter soup, and grilled quesadilla with chicken, brie, leeks, mango and cilantro, all for less than $8.

Carnivores who hate eating with vegetarians will find peace at the **Oasis Café** (17 S Wabash Avenue, at W Madison Avenue, 1-312 558 1058), a Middle Eastern find. Daily specials are usually less than $7, among them Moroccan chicken pastille and couscous packed with sweet potatoes, roasted eggplant and steamed spinach. Alternatively, go with houmous and falafel.

It's tough to find a great salad bar in the Loop that doesn't charge $20 for five chickpeas, eight spinach leaves and a drizzle of dressing. But the traders at the Chicago Board of Trade have the value-for-money thing figured out: **Cellars Market** (141 W Jackson Boulevard, at S LaSalle Street, 1-312 427 3444), CBOT's basement cafeteria, has a killer salad bar at which a one-pound container of salad costs a mere $6.99... regardless of how much salad you manage to cram into it.

All manner of old-school entertainers have swung by the ancient **Miller's Pub** (134 S Wabash Avenue, at W Adams Street, 1-312 263 4988) down the years: the array of photographs on the wall is a virtual who's who of Atlantic City favourites. It's busy at lunchtime with Loop workers treating themselves to baby-back ribs or burgers, but the place merits mention for one further reason: it serves the same menu at 1am as it does at 1pm, making it one of the latest-opening kitchens in the Loop.

The most quintessentially Chicagoan restaurant is neither a steakhouse nor a lab-like kitchen putting out cutting-edge cuisine: it's this 65-year-old cafeteria. Before you queue, decide what you want. You'll pass by plates of Jell-O and chicken salad, but the line will move too quickly for you to make a snap decision. Overwhelmed? Simply grab one of the inhumanely oversized corned beef or pastrami sandwiches, a potato pancake on the side and, for dessert, a packet of Tums.

Tamarind

614 S Wabash Avenue, between E Harrison & E Balbo Streets (1-312 379 0970). El: Red to Harrison. **Open** 7am-11pm Mon-Fri; 11am-11pm Sat, Sun. **Main courses** $13. **Credit** AmEx, Disc, MC, V. **Map** p325 H13 ⓫ Pan-Asian

This cute spot is part slick and part casual, with soothing bamboo-decked green walls and eager-to-please staff. Jump around the massive, multicultured menu and you'll find an array of great dishes, from Chinese soup dumplings to ponzu-drizzled sashimi and Vietnamese-style grilled lemongrass beef. The generous cuts of sushi are tasty (but pricey) and the signature duck soup is a standout, but the red curry is a bit gloopy and not nearly as spicy as the menu warns. No matter: dozens of other dishes do the trick.

Chinatown

Cuatro

2030 S Wabash Avenue, between E Cullerton & E 21st Streets (1-312 842 8856/www.cuatro-chicago. com). El: Red to Cermak-Chinatown. **Open** 5pm-midnight Mon; 5-10pm Tue; 5pm-2am Wed-Sat; 10am-3pm, 5-10pm Sun. **Main courses** $18. **Credit** AmEx, DC, Disc, MC, V. **Map** p324 H16 ⓬ Latin American

The eclectic diners that gather at this lounge-like venue near Chinatown may be too busy ogling each other to notice, but chef Bryan Garcia (of New York's La Rosa and Chicago's Adobo Grill) and chef de cuisine Chris Barron (of Opera) turn out damn good nuevo Latino fare. Standouts include a zesty seafood cocktail, crispy flautas stuffed with agave-roasted beef, tender beer-braised short rib, and Brazilian moqueca fish stew; in general, it's the creative compositions that elevate the dishes to star status.

Lao Sze Chuan

2172 S Archer Avenue, between W Wentworth & W Princeton Avenues (1-312 326 5040/www.lao szechuan.com). El: Red to Cermak-Chinatown. **Open** 11.30am-midnight daily. **Main courses** $10. **Credit** AmEx, DC, Disc, MC, V. **Map** p324 H16 ⓭ Chinese

The best spot in town for Sichuan cuisine, Lao Sze Chuan uses Sichuan pepper, dried chillies, garlic and ginger to create an array of addictive flavours. Top choices include the Chengdu dumplings, crispy Chinese aubergine with ground pork, dry chilli string beans, twice-cooked pork, ma po tofu, Sichuan prawns and 'chef's special' dry chilli chicken. Or just choose at random: you won't be disappointed.

Spring World

2109a S China Place, between W Wentworth Avenue & W Canal Street (1-312 326 9966). El: Red to Cermak-Chinatown. **Open** 10.30am-10pm Mon-Thur; 10.30am-10.30pm Fri-Sun. **Main courses** $10. **Credit** MC, V. **Map** p324 G16 ⓮ Chinese

Spring World's owners are from Yunan, which explains the touches of puckery vinegar flavours and spicy red chillies that characterise the food. Try the hand-shredded chicken with spicy sesame vinaigrette dotted with peanuts, garlic, sesame seeds and spring onion slivers, or the crispy whole tilapia topped with tangy garlic-ginger-chilli paste. Other favourites include spicy baby chicken with ginger and crispy spring onion cake, perfect for dipping in the chilli sesame oil on the table.

Three Happiness Restaurant

209 W Cermak Road, between S Wentworth & S Princeton Avenues (1-312 842 1964). El: Red to Cermak-Chinatown. **Main courses** $8. **Credit** AmEx, DC, Disc, MC, V. Chinese

This Chinatown gem is a world away from the giant Three Happiness on Wentworth. Regulars toss 'little' before the name to avoid confusion, pack the tables, ignore the far-from-spotless decor and skip the so-so appetisers in favour of black pepper beef with rice noodles (ordered 'crispy'), stir-fried Dungeness crab in chilli-seafood XO sauce (the delicious mess is best spooned over rice), crispy salt-and-pepper shrimp and Cantonese-style crispy-skin chicken.

Tamarind.

Made in Chicago

No food factory tour is ever as dazzling as Charlie's fictional spin around Willy Wonka's chocolate factory. Fortunately, though, none are as dangerous. Take the trio of Chicago institutions that offer curious foodies the chance to see how some of the region's favourite local foodstuffs (and, for that matter, drinkstuffs) are produced: you'll learn a little and get a few free tastes into the bargain, but there's virtually no chance of you blowing up like a purple beachball or drowning in a river of chocolate.

Tours of the delicious-smelling base of **Intelligentsia Coffee** (1850 W Fulton Street, between N Wolcott Avenue & N Wood Street) begin with a rundown of the company history and a 101 on coffee-growing, with visitors standing around the vast roasters and learning java terminology. If you're an information hog, squeeze towards the front: the roasting machine is loud. Tours are held on the first and third Saturdays of the month; your seven-buck admission also gets you unlimited fresh-brewed coffee on site, plus a half-pound bag of freshly roasted java to take home. Reservations are recommended; make yours on 1-312 521 7963 or at www.intelligentsiacoffee.com.

If you'd like dessert with your coffee, head north-west to the **Eli's Cheesecake** factory (6701 W Forest Preserve Avenue, at N Montrose Avenue). The complex machinery on show during the tours is interesting, but it's easy to feel guilty as you watch the staff slaving away over hot stoves. Still, the journey ends on a high, when guests can take their pick from a range of desserts; among them is crème caramel cheesecake, baked with caramel, butter shortbread and Southern Comfort. Tours are held daily at 1pm; admission is $3 and bookings aren't required, but all visitors must wear rubber-soled shoes with closed toes. Call 1-773 308 7000 or visit www.elicheesecake.com.

There are, of course, times when booze-fuelled cheesecake simply won't cut it. At those times, you may care to consider the tours of the **Goose Island Brew Pub** (*see p181*). At 3pm every Sunday, a brewmaster leads visitors to a drippy, dank basement and outlines the beer-making process. It's nothing beer hounds won't have heard before, but the tour ends with a tasting that's well worth the $5 charge. After talking a little about each brew, the brewmaster then passes around a pitcher. You don't get that at Wonkaville.

see p181

The Near North Side

River North

Al's Italian Beef

169 W Ontario Street, between N Wells Street & N LaSalle Boulevard (1-312 943 3222/www.alsbeef. com). El: Brown or Purple to Chicago; Red to Grand. **Open** 10am-midnight Mon-Thur; 10am-3am Fri, Sat; 11am-10pm Sun. **Main courses** $4. **Credit** AmEx, DC, Disc, MC, V. **Map** p326 H10 ⑮ Classic American

They say the Italian beef sandwich was invented in Chicago, and who's to argue? Once you've ordered, unwrap your 'beef' (you ordered peppers on it, right?), spread the paper like a tablecloth, grab your sandwich with both hands and hold it in front of you. To take a bite, lean towards the sandwich. *Never* move the sandwich towards you: doing so will spill juices all over your clothes. If you're simulta-neously working on a messy side of cheese fries, which you should be, you don't need the added risk.

Café Iberico

739 N LaSalle Street, between W Superior Street & W Chicago Avenue (1-312 573 1510/www.cafe iberico.com). El: Brown, Purple or Red to Chicago. **Open** 11am-11.30pm Mon-Thur; 11am-1.30am Fri; noon-1.30am Sat; noon-11pm Sun. **Tapas** $5. **Credit** DC, Disc, MC, V. **Map** p326 H10 ⑯ Spanish

The wait at this always-packed tapas joint can be long, but once inside, things go pretty quickly. Cheap plates of patatas bravas and croquetas de pollo arrive almost immediately; more complicated dishes, like a sumptuous chicken breast stuffed with spinach and cheese, take longer. But with a plate of Manchego and a pitcher of sangria to tide you over, you won't even notice the wait.

Chicago Chop House

60 W Ontario Street, between N Dearborn & N Clark Streets (1-312 787 7100/www.chicagochophouse.com). El: Red to Grand. **Open** 11.30am-11pm Mon-Thur, Sun; 11.30am-11.30pm Fri, Sat. **Main courses** $30. **Credit** AmEx, Disc, MC, V. **Map** p326 H10 ⑰ Classic American

Visiting businessmen head upstairs to this brown-stone-housed institution for white-tablecloth service, pricey wines and huge porterhouses fit for kings. A better bet is the subterranean piano bar, where the walls are covered with vintage photos and the high wooden tables are packed with loud storytellers and unapologetic carnivores. Go for the creamed spinach-topped baked clams, the New York strip (ask for it 'charred') and the fatty but tasty lamb chops.

Crofton on Wells

535 N Wells Street, at W Grand Avenue (1-312 755 1790/www.croftononwells.com). El: Brown or Purple to Merchandise Mart; Red to Grand. **Open** 11.30am-2pm, 5-10pm Mon-Fri; 5-10pm Sat. **Main courses** $30. **Credit** AmEx, Disc, MC, V. **Map** p324 H16 ⓳ Contemporary American

Hopefully, Suzy Crofton likes the clean, contemporary look of her restaurant: as owner, manager, sommelier and chef, she spends a lot of time there. Her seasonal American cooking includes the appetising likes of a sweet and succulent pork tenderloin topped with apple chutney and poblano cream. Other cult-worthy dishes include a salad of Maytag blue cheese and firm, fresh pears, and chicken roasted in a fiery ground chipotle and molasses peppercorn sauce.

Cyrano's Bistrot & Wine Bar

546 N Wells Street, between W Grand Avenue & W Ohio Street (1-312 467 0546/www.cyranosbistrot. com). El: Brown or Purple to Merchandise Mart; Red to Grand. **Open** 11.30am-2pm, 5-10pm Mon-Fri; 5-11pm Sat; 5-9pm Sun. **Main courses** $16. **Credit** AmEx, DC, Disc, MC, V. **Map** p326 G10 ⓲ French

Via the assortment of vintage movie posters, Cyrano de Bergerac's nose pokes its way into every corner of this charming bistro, just as the town of Bergerac influences the menu. Chef Didier Durand has built a loyal following for his south-western French fare, which includes the likes of crisp-skinned rotisserie duck with orange sauce. The bread pudding, made with kumquat preserves and Grand Marnier, is revered. There's music in the downstairs space several nights a week (Wed-Sat).

Frontera Grill

445 N Clark Street, between W Hubbard & W Illinois Streets (1-312 661 1434/www.fronterakitchens.com). El: Brown or Purple to Merchandise Mart; Red to Grand. **Open** 11.30am-2.30pm, 5.20-10pm Tue; 11.30am-2.30pm, 5-10pm Wed, Thur; 11.30am-2.30pm, 5-11pm Fri; 10.30am-2.30pm, 5-11pm Sat. **Main courses** $15. **Credit** AmEx, DC, Disc, MC, V. **Map** p326 H11 ⓴ Mexican

Over the past decade, Rick Bayless has expanded his empire via a packaged food line, several cookbooks and various turns on TV. Unlike other chefs with his level of celebrity, however, Bayless has kept close to the kitchen. Lucky us. Since opening its doors in 1987, Frontera has offered a vibrant slice of Mexico City, serving intensely flavoured, impeccably fresh Mexican food. Chow down on bright ceviches, earthy moles, wood-grilled steaks tucked into house-made tortillas, smoky masa boats loaded with roasted chillies, and insanely good Margaritas.

Gino's East

633 N Wells Street, at W Ontario Street (1-312 943 1124/www.ginoseast.com). El: Brown or Purple to Chicago. **Open** *Summer* 11am-11pm Mon-Sat; noon-11pm Sun. *Winter* 11am-9pm Mon-Thur; 11am-11pm Fri, Sat; noon-9pm Sun. **Main courses** $20. **Credit** AmEx, DC, Disc, MC, V. **Map** p326 H10 ㉑ Pizza

Though this institution for Chicago-style pizza is no longer at its original Superior Street location, the famous graffiti-covered wooden walls were transported here when they moved. The famous deep-dish has a cornmeal crust devoid of the usual butter glaze, so it's not as greasy (but also not as flavourful) as that dished up by its competitors. Instead, the

Upper-crust: **Quartino** serves up some of Chicago's best thin-crust pizzas. *See p152.*

punch comes from the tangy and ripe sauce. Try the half-spinach, half-sausage concoction, letting it sit for a minute when it arrives (to avoid a runny mess).

Japonais

600 W Chicago Avenue, at N Larrabee Street (1-312 822 9600/www.japonaischicago.com). El: Brown or Purple to Chicago. **Open** 11.30am-11pm Mon-Thur; 5-11.30pm Fri, Sat; 5-10pm Sun. **Main courses** $25. **Credit** AmEx, DC, MC, V. **Map** p326 F10 ㉒ Japanese

Spend a million bucks building on an undeveloped stretch of the Chicago River and you too can have a restaurant capable of transporting Chicagoans to a distant land. The space is swanky, sexy and vibrant; the modern Japanese food served within it centres on superb-quality raw fish, presented simply as sashimi or whacked out into tasty rolls. Don't leave without having the Kobe carpaccio, the Tokyo drums, the crab nigiri, or Le Quack Japonais.

Le Lan

749 N Clark Street, between W Superior Street & W Chicago Avenue (1-312 280 9100/www.lelan restaurant.com). El: Red to Chicago. **Open** 5.30-10pm Mon-Wed; 5.30-11pm Thur-Sat. **Main courses** $26. **Credit** AmEx, DC, Disc, MC, V. **Map** p326 H10 ㉓ French/Vietnamese

Subtle French-Vietnamese fusion food served in a slightly Asian, minimalist room. Start with the tasty noodle salad, a crispy glass noodle-filled spring roll resting on wakame-garlic-dressed greens. Best-bet entrées include roast duck breast with seared foie gras in green cardamom jus, and perfectly grilled bass over nutty bulgar. The sheep's milk flan is a good place to end, but don't miss the Vietnamese coffee. Tuesday's $32 three-course deal is good value.

Nacional 27

325 W Huron Street, between N Franklin & N Orleans Streets (1-312 664 2727/www.nacional27. net). El: Brown or Purple to Chicago. **Open** 5.30-10pm Mon-Thur; 5.30pm-midnight Fri, Sat. **Main courses** $19. **Credit** AmEx, DC, Disc, MC, V. **Map** p326 G10 ㉔ Latin American

DJs spinning and customers dancing in the dining room may not be to everyone's taste, but the food at Nacional 27 is a treat. Chef Randy Zweiban takes his inspiration from Latin America and comes up with luscious seasonal eats such as braised beef cheeks with potatoes and onion confit, honey-orange-glazed quail with white beans and house-smoked bacon, and a bubbling cazuela of chorizo, chickpeas, spinach and piquillo peppers. On Wine Down Wednesdays, a five-course tasting menu with wine pairings costs $44.

Naha

500 N Clark Street, at W Illinois Street (1-312 321 6242/www.naha-chicago.com). El: Red to Grand. **Open** 11.30am-9.30pm Mon-Thur; 5.30-10pm Fri, Sat. **Main courses** $30. **Credit** AmEx, DC, Disc, MC, V. **Map** p326 H11 ㉕ Contemporary American

Chef Carrie Nahabedian's upmarket and snazzy yet pomp-free restaurant marries great service to a seasonal menu that reads like a who's who in regional, sustainable foods. Past offerings include seared scallops with spring asparagus, English peas and celery root purée, soft-shell crabs with heirloom tomatoes and white corn grits, and brioche-crusted halibut with spring morels and a salad of pea shoots and green beans. An excellent option.

Pepper Canister

509 N Wells Street, between W Illinois Street & W Grand Avenue (1-312 467 3300). El: Brown or Purple to Merchandise Mart; Red to Grand. **Open** 11am-2am Mon-Fri; 5pm-3am Sat. **Main courses** $10. **Credit** AmEx, DC, Disc, MC, V. **Map** p326 G10 ㉖ Irish

Kick healthy eating fads in the teeth by indulging in the Irish-ish menu at this smarter-than-average pub (named, since you ask, after a church in Dublin). Forget the saucy chips, which are really just skimpy American fries, and go greasy with the Irish breakfast, complete with fat slabs of sweet fried ham and soft, meaty sausages, or the toastie special, a buttery, oniony, cheesy mess of a grilled sandwich.

Phil Stefani's 437 Rush

437 N Rush Street, between W Hubbard & W Illinois Streets (1-312 222 0101/www.stefani restaurants.com). El: Red to Grand. **Open** 11am-10pm Mon-Thur; 5-11pm Fri, Sat. **Main courses** $24. **Credit** AmEx, DC, Disc, MC, V. **Map** p326 J11 ㉗ Classic American

No run-down rooms, no grumpy service, no cigar puffing at the tables… In the world of steakhouses, Phil Stefani's slick, cosmopolitan version is as refreshing as shrimp cocktail (which, by the way, is decent, but the crispy roast quail perched on top of a fluffy polenta-and-Gorgonzola soufflé is a better way to start). If you're up for steak, expect expertly prepared porterhouses, with a well-seasoned crust hiding tender flesh. But if it's lighter fare you're after, dig into the roast red king salmon.

Pizzeria Due

619 N Wabash Avenue, between E Ohio & E Ontario Streets (1-312 943 2400). El: Red to Grand. **Open** 11am-1.30am Mon-Thur, Sun; 11am-2.30am Fri, Sat. **Main courses** $15. **Credit** AmEx, DC, Disc, MC, V. **Map** p326 H10 ㉘ Pizza

This crowd-pleasing sister to the 60-year-old Uno (29 E Ohio Street, at N State Street, 1-312 321 1000) features a cosy dining room and bar that reeks of old Chicago, complete with a black and white tiled floor, historical photos, and Ditka memorabilia. Knife-and-fork, deep-dish pizza is the raison d'être, with a rich, pastry-like crust that gets crisp from its time in a black iron pan. It's the vehicle for a massive amount of cheese and fillings, with tomato sauce ladled on top.

Quartino

626 N State Street, at E Ontario Street (1-312 698 5000/www.quartinochicago.com). El: Red to Grand. **Open** 11.30am-1am Mon-Sat; 4pm-midnight Sun. **Small plates** $5. **Credit** AmEx, DC, Disc, MC, V. **Map** p326 H10 ㉙ Italian

This cavernous dining room is decked out in rustic Italian style with subway tiles and mismatched chairs. Chef John Coletta keeps things authentic with house-made salami-like beef bresaola, spicy soppressata and duck prosciutto served with giardiniera and mostarda. The pizza is among the better thin-crust versions in town (go for the margherita), and small plates of grappa-cured salmon and braised pork-filled ravioli are impressive. **Photo** *p151.*

Zocalo

358 W Ontario Street, between N Orleans & N Kingsbury Streets (1-312 302 9977/www.zocalo chicago.com). El: Brown or Purple to Chicago. **Open** 11.30am-11pm Mon-Thur; 5pm-1am Fri, Sat; 5-10pm Sun. **Small plates** $8. **Credit** AmEx, DC, Disc, MC, V. **Map** p326 G10 ⑳ Mexican
The Castañedas of the Lalo's chain have set up in River North with this contemporary setting, offering plenty of creative cocktails, and a menu of smallplates such as chicken in mole negro; soft, shredded beef steamed in banana leaf; and shrimp, scallops and calamari served in an excellent guajillo-garlic sauce. Don't miss the trio of guac appetiser, and if you fancy a ceviche, try the camarones, fresh limedrenched shrimp that are perfect with a Margarita.

The Magnificent Mile & Streeterville

Avenues

108 E Superior Street, between N Rush Street & N Michigan Avenue (1-312 573 6754/http://chicago. peninsula.com). El: Red to Chicago. **Open** 5.30-10pm Tue-Thur; 5.30-10.30pm Fri; 5-10.30pm Sat. **Degustation** $70. **Credit** AmEx, DC, Disc, MC, V. **Map** p326 J10 ㉛ Contemporary American
Chef Graham Elliot Bowles dishes up some culinary treats at this eatery just off Michigan Avenue, but he's a bit more grounded and reliant on seasonal ingredients than the whimsical chef-wizards with whom he's often compared. Recent creations include a garlic-nettle risotto and kangaroo (yes, kangaroo) with flavours of eucalyptus, melon and lime. The formal dining room glows golden with a view of the Magnificent Mile below.

Copperblue

Lake Point Tower (Illinois Street entrance), 505 N Lake Shore Drive, at E Illinois Street (1-312 527 1200/www.copperbluechicago.com). El: Red to Grand. **Open** 5.30-10.30pm Tue-Thur; 5.30-11.30pm Fri-Sun. **Main courses** $26. **Credit** AmEx, Disc, MC, V. **Map** p326 K10 ㉜ Contemporary American
Chef-owners Michael Tsonton and Victor Newgren keep their restaurant low-key, despite a setting that screams 'big night out'. The menu divides first and second courses into 'Work', featuring 'humble and down to earth' dishes such as roast pork shoulder and grilled shrimp with blue crab salad, and 'Play', which includes 'whimsical and fun' plates of organic duck two ways and braised rabbit empanadas.

DeLaCosta

River East Arts Center, 465 E Illinois Street, between N Peshtigo Court & N Lake Shore Drive (1-312 464 1700/www.delacostachicago.com). El: Red to Grand. **Open** 11.30am-2.30pm, 5-10pm Mon-Wed; 11.30am-2.30pm, 5-11pm Thur, Fri; 5-11pm Sat; 5-10pm Sun. **Main courses** $28. **Credit** AmEx, DC, Disc, MC, V. **Map** p326 K11 ㉝ Latin American
Chef Adam Schop is doing a fantastic job at Douglas Rodriguez's nuevo Latino enterprise. Take in the surroundings (think Rio-style carnival) while starting with a killer muddled cocktail. The ceviches may be the signature dish, but try instead hot starters such as the watercress-topped duck confit flatbread and the brandade littered with tiny, tart-hot guindilla peppers and razor-thin garlic chips. For mains, don't miss the suckling pig with glistening, crackly skin, perfectly sweet plantains and lard-rich black-bean purée.

Eat, Drink, Shop

Copperblue.

Keeping it simple at **Lux Bar**.

Eppy's Deli
224 E Ontario Street, between N St Clair Street & N Fairbanks Court (1-312 943 7797). El: Red to Grand. **Open** 8am-8pm daily. **Main courses** $6. **Credit** AmEx, MC, V. **Map** p326 J11 ❸ Classic American

'Larry the Jew' is at the helm of this slick underground operation, which has all the chutzpah of a New York deli but none of the grit. Ordering your sandwich on the marbled rye is the best bet; whether you go with thinly sliced turkey or celery-flecked tuna salad, the goods are piled high. Sides such as tangy potato salad, not to mention an array of mustards, keep punters happy, but it's the gooey, heart-stopping, grilled Reuben that's the real selling point.

NoMI
800 N Michigan Avenue, between E Chicago Avenue & E Pearson Street (1-312 239 4030/www.nomi restaurant.com). El: Red to Chicago. **Open** 6.30am-2pm, 5.30pm-1am Mon-Fri; 7am-2pm, 5.30pm-1am Sat, Sun. **Main courses** $36. **Credit** AmEx, DC, Disc, MC, V. **Map** p326 J10 ❸ Eclectic

Christophe David took over NoMI's kitchen from Sandro Gamba in 2006, but he barely missed a beat. That said, the menu has changed: small cuts of top-quality sushi are now a highlight, and David injects Indian notes into dishes such as a peekytoe crab-and-avocado salad with curry mayo. The room is stunning, with a view of the Mag Mile that makes a cocktail in the lounge very appealing.

Primehouse David Burke
616 N Rush Street, at W Ontario Street (1-312 660 6000/www.davidburke.com). El: Red to Grand. **Open** 7-11am, 11.30am-3pm, 5-10.30pm Mon-Thur, Sun; 7-11am, 11.30am-3pm, 5-11.30pm Fri, Sat. **Main courses** $33. **Credit** AmEx, DC, Disc, MC, V. **Map** p326 J10 ❸ Classic American

Once ensconced in this luxe yet modern eaterie, start with the crab cake, with impeccable meat shaped like a maki roll and crusted in Japanese pretzels. All the meat comes from animals sired by Prime, Burke's Kentucky-based bull: the filet is unstoppably tender and rich, the strip less so. The desserts are creative (fill-your-own doughnuts, anyone?). Burke has managed to create something a little different here. But it's not so different that your parents won't like it.

Tru
676 N St Clair Street, at E Huron Street (1-312 202 0001/www.trurestaurant.com). El: Red to Chicago. **Open** 5.30-10pm Mon-Thur; 5.30-11pm Fri, Sat. **Prix fixe** $95. **Credit** AmEx, DC, Disc, MC, V. **Map** p326 J10 ❸ Eclectic

Locals in the habit of splurging are familiar with Rick Tramonto and Gale Gand's contemporary creations at special-occasion prices. But the secret to indulging without selling a kidney is the amuse-bouche collection, three courses of what TRU calls 'quartets' (four individual creations) available to those not too snobby to eat in the lounge. Twelve tastes for $45 is a steal, starting with cold bites such as fluke sashimi with radish salad, then trademark soups like blistered corn with white corn ice and finally sample-sizes of entrées including seared cumin-crusted squab with tart huckleberries.

The Gold Coast

Lux Bar
18 E Bellevue Place, at N Rush Street (1-312 642 3400/www.luxbar.com). El: Red to Clark/Division. **Open** 10.30am-midnight Mon-Thur; 8.30am-midnight Fri-Sun. **Main courses** $15. **Credit** AmEx, DC, Disc, MC, V. **Map** p326 J10 ❸ Classic American

The food and space at this Gibson's offshoot seem to be imported from a simpler era, with dishes such as luscious filet mignon 'sliders' and impeccably juicy fried chicken presented without fanfare. The straightforward approach can go awry (the turkey burgers are bland), but for the most part it's a gem.

Le Petit Paris
260 E Chestnut Street, between N DeWitt Place & N Lake Shore Drive (1-312 787 8260/www.lepetit paris.net). El: Red to Chicago. **Open** 5-10pm daily. **Main courses** $20. **Credit** AmEx, Disc, MC, V. **Map** p326 J9 ❸ French

There was nothing wrong with the old Le Petit Paris, but there was nothing extraordinary about it, either. However, with celebrated Chicago chef Michael Foley in the kitchen, things are really looking up. The dining room is still lavish and the menu is still full of French classics like mushroom-laden

Eat, Drink, Shop

beef bourguignonne and luscious veal 'Marengo'. However, Foley regularly sneaks in new dishes, such as artichoke fritters with a tart lemon mayonnaise.

Ritz-Carlton Dining Room

160 E Pearson Street, between N Michigan Avenue & N Mies van der Rohe Way (1-312 266 1000). El: Red to Chicago. **Open** 6-10pm Wed, Thur; 6-11pm Fri, Sat; 10.30am-3pm, 6-10pm Sun. **Degustation** $75. **Credit** AmEx, DC, Disc, MC, V. **Map** p326 J9 ⓴ Contemporary American

Former sous chef Mark Payne took over the reins of this revered restaurant in 2006. Put yourself in his hands with the vegetarian spring degustation that includes sunchoke (Jerusalem artichoke) soup with garlic purée, and a morel mushroom and spring onion tart. Your only regret will be eating it in the stately dining room rather than on a green lawn.

Spiaggia

980 N Michigan Avenue, between E Oak Street & E Walton Place (1-312 280 2750/www.levyrestaurants. com). El: Red to Clark/Division. **Open** 6-9.30pm

Mon-Thur; 5.30-10.30pm Fri, Sat; 6-9pm Sun. **Main courses** $37. **Credit** AmEx, DC, Disc, MC, V. **Map** p326 J9 ㉑ Italian

Chefs Tony Mantuano and Missy Robbins marry imported Italian foodstuffs with top-notch American ingredients and a deep understanding of cuisine from the north of the boot. Kobe tartare glows with truffle oil, langoustines melt in your mouth, wood-roasted sea bass gets punch from olives and orange essence, filet is boosted with a marrow crust, and pastas are made fresh daily. Toss in perfect service and you have a night that's well worth a week's salary. One of the city's best fine dining experiences.

Old Town & Lincoln Park

Old Town

Alinea

1723 N Halsted Street, between W North Avenue & W Willow Street (1-312 867 0110/www.alinea-restaurant.com). El: Red to North/Clybourn.

Sweet things

An array of cakes, pastries and other treats serve as temptations down at **Sarah's Pastries & Candies** (11 E Oak Street, at N State Street, Gold Coast, 1-312 664 6223, www.sarahscandies.com; *pictured*), but it's the chocolate that may prove toughest to resist. Sarah Levy and her team (which includes her mother) will blind you with enormous smiles before tempting you with Chocolate Delights, habit-forming clusters of caramelised almonds, roasted pistachios and crispy rice; crispy Royaltines, similar to the Delights but with cake wafers instead

of pistachios; and Chocolate Enchantments, molasses caramel lollipops coated in chocolate.

The great thing about Karen Gerod's **Swim Café** (1357 W Chicago Avenue, at N Ada Street, West Town, 1-312 492 8600, www.swimcafe.com) is that you can head there with the (relatively) honest intention of eating healthily from its menu of salads and sandwiches. If you're then distracted by the aroma of still-warm baked goods... who could blame you? Try the fluffy mini blueberry scones, the dense pumpkin muffins (baked with oats), or the delectable chocolate-mocha cookies. If you're still hungry, insanely rich chocolate-bread pudding serves as a terrific dessert.

Speaking of insanely rich, how about three bucks for a cupcake? The informatively named **Cupcakes** (613 W Briar Place, at N Broadway Street, Lakeview, 1-773 525 0817, http://chicagocupcakes.com) does pretty much what its name suggests. The colourful and organic little things are gone in a bite, but the quality is more important than the quantity: try the absolutely adorable raspberry-lemonade cupcake, which tastes surprisingly like a cool glass of the stuff.

Open 5.30-9.30pm Wed-Sun. **Degustation** $125. **Credit** AmEx, DC, Disc, MC, V. **Map** p327 F7 ⑫
Contemporary American

Chef Grant Achatz has entered year two of his tenure at the restaurant that *Gourmet* anointed number one in the USA. What's the fuss? Simply put, this is food like you've never seen before. Sit back and enjoy a show that plays with textures, temperatures and notions of 'normal' cuisine, while remaining grounded in season and flavour. Recent menu stunners have included squab with peppercorn custard, sorrel and strawberries; cocoa-coated watermelon with cubed Kobe beef; and a parfait of porcini purée, almond ice-cream and powdered ham. Flawless.

¡Salpicon!

1252 N Wells Street, between W Scott & W Goethe Streets (1-312 988 7811/www.salpicon.com). El: Red to Clark/Division. **Open** 5-10pm Mon-Thur; 5-11pm Fri, Sat; 11am-2.30pm, 5-10pm Sun. **Main courses** $20. **Credit** AmEx, DC, Disc, MC, V. **Map** p327 G8 ⑬ Mexican

This swanky Mexican spot is known for its drinks: the Margaritas are perfect, and the wine list has been recognised by *Wine Spectator*. However, Priscila Satkoff's food is excellent, especially the traditional salsas, quesos fundido and earthy moles with handmade tortillas. Authentic Mexican flavours, from blue marlin ceviche to lacy crepas filled with goat's milk caramel, are explained by the warm, friendly staff in the lively, art-splashed dining room.

Lincoln Park

Charlie Trotter's

816 W Armitage Avenue, between N Halsted & N Dayton Streets (1-773 248 6228/www.charlietrotters. com). El: Brown or Purple to Armitage. **Open** 6-11pm Tue-Thur; 5.30-11pm Fri, Sat. **Degustation** $125. **Credit** AmEx, DC, Disc, MC, V. **Map** p327 F6 ⑭ Contemporary American

Trotter remains one of the best chefs in the US: not only can he keep up with the younger talent, he actually trained many of them. There's no à la carte at his signature restaurant, so go full throttle with the impeccable, contemporary six-course tasting menu and tack on wine pairings. Trotter changes the menu every other week or so; salutations to the season might include hamachi sashimi with kalamata-olive sorbet, and roast monkfish served alongside black trumpet mushrooms and crispy hominy.

Chicago Pizza & Oven Grinder Co

2121 N Clark Street, between W Dickens & W Webster Avenues (1-773 248 2570/www.chicago pizzaandovengrinder.com). El: Brown or Purple to

Up all night

Launching a throwback restaurant is easy: simply purchase retro fixture reproductions and open the doors. Preventing a genuine, old-school diner from fading into a razed memory is tougher in a city where sushi is more popular than steak and eggs. But the owners of a few 24-hour diners in Chicago are fighting to hold on to their little piece of round-the-clock Americana, no matter how high or how tempting the offers for them to sell.

'Home Depot offered me a million dollars for this corner,' insists George Liakopoulos, standing at the 1939-vintage **White Palace Grill** (1159 S Canal Street, at W Roosevelt Road, South Loop, 1-312 939 7167). Liakopoulos declined, saying diners are in his blood: his father owned a handful, and he himself presided over Lincoln Avenue's Golden Apple through the 1980s and '90s.

Liakopoulos spent half a million bucks cleaning up the White Palace and Wicker Park's **Hollywood Grill** (1601 W North Avenue, at N Ashland Avenue, 1-773 395 1818) after buying them in 2000. The White Palace may now have shiny new vinyl booths and a laminated menu touting 'modern' dishes such as taco salad, but the cops, hard-hats and third-shift coffee drinkers don't seem to notice: they order 'the usual' just the same. The new menu gets more wear among the hipsters and yuppies over at Hollywood.

When Don Wageman opened **Don's Humburgers** (1837 S Western Avenue, at W 18th Place, 1-312 733 9351), his counter-only grill in 1955, he misspelled hamburger simply to turn heads. His old place is now run by Michael Schellerer and David Ambroz, but the grilled onion-topped, double humburger remains the best-seller, keeping Don's afloat despite the looming golden arches across the street.

At the **Diner Grill** (1635 W Irving Park Road, at N Marshfield Avenue, 1-773 248 2030), the dining car-like landmark Arnold DeMar's father opened in 1946, mini-jukeboxes line the counter and a TV sputters out *The Three Stooges*. As DeMar talks of passing the diner to his son, his wife Sheila yells, 'We wouldn't sell it for a million bucks. It's been there since I was a kid, for all of our kids, our neighbours, our neighbours' kids... It's our little part of Chicago'.

Armitage. **Open** 4-11pm Mon-Thur; 4pm-midnight Fri; 11.30am-midnight Sat; 11.30pm-11pm Sun. **Main courses** $11. **No credit cards**. **Map** p327 G6 ⑮ Pizza

Since 1972, this cheery underground institution has been luring Chicagoans with the promise of famous sandwiches and pizzas. The signature Pizza Pot Pies are more like bread bowls filled with pizza sauce and melted cheese. But the grinders, such as an Italian combination that piles on Genoa salami and smoked ham, are so mammoth, crispy and warm, and the salads topple with such insane quantities of artichoke hearts, olives and peppers, that you'll forgive them.

Crêpe & Coffee Palace
2433 N Clark Street, between W Fullerton Parkway & W Arlington Place (1-773 404 1300). El: Brown, Purple or Red to Fullerton. **Open** 10am-9pm Mon-Thur; 9am-10pm Fri, Sat; 9am-9pm Sun. **Main courses** $7. **Credit** AmEx, DC, Disc, MC, V. **Map** p328 G5 ⑯ Algerian

The name may scream 'brunch', but this lively spot is also excellent for lunch or dinner. Savoury crêpes start out vegetarian, with the option to add as much

Meat beat manifesto

Eat, Drink, Shop

As the gateway to the West, Chicago was the transport hub for the agricultural products of America's ranching states. Steak is prominent in the city even today, but the industry has moved on apace. Want to know how your beef made it from farm to place? Read on…

ANGUS
A breed developed by the Scots but now raised throughout the world, Angus cows produce meat that has more marbling (flecks of fat running through the meat) than other animals. This generally translates to tastier beef.

DRY-AGED AND/OR WET-AGED
When beef is held in a cooler at a meat market or restaurant for 18 to 30 days, it loses water. Known as dry-ageing, the process tenderises the meat and intensifies its flavour. Conversely, wet-aged steaks are vacuum-packed and then put in a cooler to tenderise for between seven and 28 days. However, since the meat isn't losing moisture, there isn't the same concentration of flavour you get from dry-ageing.

GRASS-FED
A grass-fed cow, which is to say a cow whose diet was at least 80 per cent grass, has about a third to a half of the saturated fat of a grain-fed cow, and higher levels of omega-3s and vitamin E. It's better for you, then, but it's also less juicy, so the meat should be cooked a bit less in order to keep it from drying out.

KOBE AND/OR WAGYU
Kobe is beef from a Wagyu cow, but only if it comes from Kobe, Japan. Kobe beef isn't exported from Japan, where it goes for around $100 a pound. Technically speaking,

what you're getting in the US is Kobe-style beef from American-raised Wagyu cows (or, more commonly, a crossbreed of Angus and Wagyu).

MEAT GRADES
The USDA slaps one of eight grades on to all meat products, but Prime, Choice and Select are the only grades you'd ever find in a steakhouse. Prime has the highest amount of marbling, Choice has moderate marbling and Select has some marbling. Beyond that, it's hamburger meat; further down the scale and you're talking hot-dog quality.

ORGANIC AND/OR NATURAL BEEF
There's no clear standard on what constitutes 'natural' beef, but the term 'organic' can only apply to animals raised on organic feed and which weren't given any antibiotics or hormones. As with most organic foods, it's debatable whether you can taste a difference.

meat (chicken, smoked salmon, snails) as you like. But the palace crêpe, bursting with arugula (rocket), goat's cheese and roasted garlic, is packed with so many rich flavours that you won't miss your pound of flesh. Organic cappuccinos, glasses of cucumber water and free bowls of soup make the deal as sweet as the mango-and-ginger crêpe buena.

Fixture

2706 N Ashland Avenue, between W Wrightwood Avenue & W Diversey Parkway (1-773 248 3331/ www.fixturechicago.com). Bus 9, 76. **Open** 5pm-midnight daily. **Small plates** $9. **Credit** DC, Disc, MC, V. **Map** p328 D4 ⑰ Eclectic
This easy-to-miss space is now a small-plates spot with cleverly named wine flights, a DJ in the front lounge and, in the shape of Sarah Nelson, a young, talented chef. The global menu features stunners such as roast suckling pig with habanero-barbecue sauce and pineapple marmalade, caramelised onion-topped buffalo sliders (buffalo hamburgers), and peppered elk carpaccio with goat's cheese and honey-drizzled mâche greens (lamb's lettuce).

Half Shell

676 W Diversey Parkway, between N Orchard & N Clark Streets (1-773 549 1773). El: Brown or Purple to Diversey. **Open** 11.30am-midnight Mon-Sat; noon-midnight Sun. **No credit cards. Map** p328 F4 ⑱ Fish & seafood
'We close when we feel like closing' and 'Nothin' but cash, no exceptions' are among the variety of perfect-for-the-setting quips you might overhear from the bartender-server on a visit to this 38-year-old seafood spot. Grab a table in the tiny, fairy light-strewn room and start with the chowderific Mulligan stew and crispy calamari. For more fried goodness, go for the 32-Pointer entrée, a crunchy pile of smelts, perch, frogs' legs, clam strips and fat shrimp.

Maza

2748 N Lincoln Avenue, between W Schubert Avenue & W Diversey Parkway (1-773 929 9600). El: Brown or Purple to Diversey. **Open** 5-11pm Mon-Thur, Sun; 5pm-midnight Fri, Sat. **Main courses** $12. **Credit** AmEx, MC, V. **Map** p328 E4 ⑲ Middle Eastern
The métier of this mellow place is flavour-packed Middle Eastern grub. Start with fuul medames: warm fava beans simmered in mouth-puckering herbs, lemon juice and olive oil. Next, try the whole red snapper grilled to crispy, salty, juicy perfection. The dining room here is warm and romantic. Don't leave until you've had the flaky, buttery, house-made baklava, baked on the premises nightly.

North Pond

2610 N Cannon Drive, between W Fullerton Parkway & W Diversey Parkway (1-773 477 5845/www.north pondrestaurant.com). Bus 76, 151, 156. **Open** 11.30am-2pm, 5.30-10pm Tue-Fri; 5.30-10pm Sat; 11am-2pm, 5.30-10.30pm Sun. **Main courses** $30. **Credit** AmEx, DC, Disc, MC, V. **Map** p328 G4 ㊿ Contemporary American

This rustic, prairie-style hideaway (on a small pond) offers views of an unobstructed city skyline. Chef Bruce Sherman puts as much thought into his organic, seasonal food as the local farmers who grow it; dishes might include grilled walleye pike with artichoke purée, fava beans and lemon cream for dinner, and gingersnap pancakes with spiced quince syrup, sunny-side-up egg and venison bratwurst for brunch. North Pond is a dreamily enjoyable restaurant, if pricey.

Riccardo Trattoria

2119 N Clark Street, between W Dickens & W Webster Avenues (1-773 549 0038). El: Brown, Purple or Red to Fullerton. **Open** 5-10pm Tue-Fri; 5-11pm Sat; 4-9pm Sun. **Main courses** $18. **Credit** AmEx, DC, Disc, MC, V. **Map** p328 G6 ⑤ Italian
Chef Riccardo Michi's family founded the Bice restaurant empire in Milan; he was the chef at its first stateside location (New York, '87) before heading to Chicago. Don't miss the bacon-topped roasted quail with crispy polenta cake; the orecchiette with wild-boar sausage, garlicky rapini and pecorino cheese; or the double-cut lamb chops. Become a regular, and the thickly accented Italian waiters might cap off your meal with ricotta cheesecake.

Wiener's Circle

2622 N Clark Street, between W Wrightwood Avenue & W Drummond Place (1-773 477 7444). El: Brown or Purple to Diversey. **Open** 11am-4am Mon-Thur, Sun; 11am-5am Fri, Sat. **Hot dogs** $3. **No credit cards. Map** p328 F4 ㊿ Classic American
Having had quite enough of drunk yuppies talking crap at them, the sassy hot dog girls behind the counter of this classic roadside shack have developed their own brand of smack-talking that's become synonymous with a late-night dog run here. Get a Chicago red hot with the traditional fixings (mustard, onion, neon-green relish, pickle spear, tomato, celery salt and sport peppers), plus thick-cut fries.

Lakeview & around

Lakeview & Wrigleyville

For gay-slanted restaurants in Boystown, *see p244.*

Bittersweet Pastry Shop

1114 W Belmont Avenue, between N Clifton & N Seminary Avenues (1-773 929 1100/www. bittersweetpastry.com). El: Brown, Purple or Red to Belmont. **Open** 7am-7pm Tue-Fri; 8am-7pm Sat; 11am-6pm Sun. **Main courses** $7. **Credit** MC, V. **Map** p329 E2 ㊾ Classic American
Stop by around midday for chef Judy Contino's pastries and desserts, and the chances are that you'll end up lunching in the charming bakery café. You can't go wrong with any of the handful of daily menu options, such as carrot jalapeño soup, spinach salad with blue cheese and lemon vinaigrette, and

roasted aubergine and goat's cheese sandwiches. It's excellent light fare before you dive into that picture-perfect meringue tart.

Café 28

1800 W Irving Park Road, at N Ravenswood Avenue (1-773 528 2883/www.cafe28.org). El: Brown to Irving Park. **Open** 5.30-9pm Mon; 11am-2.30pm, 5.30-10pm Tue-Thur; 11am-2.30pm, 5.30-10.30pm Fri; 9am-2pm, 5.30-10.30pm Sat; 9am-2pm, 5.30-9pm Sun. **Main courses** $16. **Credit** AmEx, DC, Disc, MC, V. **Map** p330 C0 ❷ Cuban
Cuban food goes upmarket at this pleasant, contemporary spot. Standards are dressed up with fancy touches such as saffron cream, garlic polenta and sun-dried tomato pesto. It's competently executed, but with less oomph than the dramatic menu suggests. Ropa vieja, flanked by crunchy, sugary plantains, is juicy and tender, although somewhat pricey. An eclectic crowd and excellent Mojitos help compensate.

HB

3404 N Halsted Street, between W Roscoe Street & W Newport Avenue (1-773 661 0299). El: Brown, Purple or Red to Belmont. **Open** 5-10pm Tue-Fri; 9am-3pm, 5-11pm Sat; 9am-3pm, 5-10pm Sun. **Main courses** $16. **Credit** AmEx, Disc, MC, V. **Map** p329 F2 ❸ Eclectic
Now that the *Food Network* hype surrounding the Hearty Boys has died down, it's possible to grab a table in this funky-cosy BYOB. Good thing, too: the dishes turned out by chef Joncarl Lachman are seasonal and fresh. Try lamb steak over warm, curry-citrus chickpea salad, or roasted bass with bitter greens flecked with raisins and roasted tomatoes.

Laschet's Inn

2119 W Irving Park Road, between N Hoyne & N Hamilton Avenues (1-773 478 7915/www.laschets inn.com). El: Brown to Irving Park. **Open** 2-10.30pm Mon-Fri; noon-10.30pm Sat; noon-10pm Sun. **Main courses** $13. **Credit** AmEx, DC, Disc, MC, V. **Map** p330 B0 ❺ German
At first sight, you might think this is simply a charming German pub. It is, and has been since 1971, but it's also now a prime spot for rouladen: thin beef rolled with bacon, onions and pickles. The comfort-food staple is served with tasty brown gravy, braised cabbage and fluffy spaetzle dumplings; recommended alternatives include hackepeter (rich steak tartare on rye with capers and onions) and lox rouladen (herbed cream cheese and smoked salmon rolls).

Mrs Murphy & Sons

3905 N Lincoln Avenue, between W Byron Street & W Larchmont Avenue (1-773 248 3905/www.irishbistro. com). El: Brown to Irving Park. **Open** 5.30-10pm Tue-Thur; 5.30-11pm Fri; 11am-2.30pm, 5.30-11pm Sat; 11am-2.30pm, 5-10pm Sun. **Main courses** $16. **Credit** AmEx, Disc, MC, V. **Map** p330 ❼ Irish
Soda bread followed by black and white pudding? Not so much. This Irish bistro serves food you might find in modern Dublin, which means that Guinness isn't just on the epic beer list but also in a rich onion

and white cheddar soup. Bangers and mash arrives as savoury lamb sausage and fingerling potatoes that have been roasted with Morbier cheese and apples, all served on a fragrant cedar plank.

Salt & Pepper Diner

3537 N Clark Street, between Cornelia Avenue & Eddy Street (1-773 883 9800). El: Red to Addison. **Open** 7am-10pm Mon-Thur; 7am-midnight Fri, Sat; 7am-4pm Sun. **Main courses** $6. **No credit cards.** **Map** p329 E1 ❺ Classic American
There's more chrome and grease than in a motorcycle repair shop, but that's how you know a diner is worth its spit. The decor's no retro throwback: the original Lincoln Avenue location has been around since 1965. Top choices from the standard diner menu include gooey, juicy cheeseburgers; hot, crispy fries; thin omelettes overstuffed with sautéed vegetables; and tall, thick milkshakes.

Sola

3868 N Lincoln Avenue, at W Byron Street (1-773 327 3868/www.sola-restaurant.com). El: Brown to Irving Park. **Open** 5.30-10pm Mon-Wed; 11.30am-2pm, 5.30-10pm Thur; 11.30am-2pm, 5.30-11pm Fri; 10am-2pm, 5.30-11pm Sat; 10am-2pm, 5.30-10pm Sun. **Main courses** $19. **Credit** AmEx, DC, Disc, MC, V. **Map** p330 C0 ❺ Eclectic
Carol Wallack's Hawaiian-influenced food is a tropical relief from blustery Chicago winters, but it's in the summer that the pavement patio and refreshing flavours on the seafood-heavy menu can be put to best use. Cool down with poke (a Hawaiian-style ceviche that changes daily); a trio of tuna tartares flanked by cucumber salsa; or halibut with papaya, mango, cucumber and ginger-braised peaches.

Sticky Rice

4018 N Western Avenue, between W Irving Park Road & W Cuyler Avenue (1-773 588 0133/www. stickyricethai.com). Bus 49, X49, 80, X80. **Open** 11.30am-11pm Mon-Thur; 11.30am-midnight Fri, Sat; noon-10pm Sun. **Main courses** $5. **Credit** AmEx, Disc, MC, V. **Map** p330 A0 ❻ Thai
Kritsana Moungkeow keeps her customers' interest with new tangy concoctions every couple of weeks. Favourites include house-made spicy fermented pork sausage, probably Chicago's best gang hung lay (pork in sweet, garlicky, ginger-laden curry), and khua kae, a stir-fry of chicken, baby corn, aubergine, shredded lime leaves and roasted rice powder with a gingery citrus tang. Translations of the Thai-language menu are available, as is a vegetarian list.

TAC Quick Thai

3930 N Sheridan Road, between W Dakin Street & W Irving Park Road (1-773 327 5253). El: Red to Sheridan. **Open** 11am-10pm Mon, Wed-Sat; 11am-9.30pm Sun. **Main courses** $8. **Credit** AmEx, MC, V. Thai
The once-tiny Thai joint at the top of many locals' favourites list has more than doubled in size. Luckily, the kitchen isn't having trouble keeping up with the crowds that flood the simple, minimalist room. The

Small is beautiful at **Wakamono**, which offers a Japanese take on tapas.

old standouts are still found on the translated Thai-language menu, among them never-fail flavour explosions such as tart and smoky pork-and-rice sausage, ground chicken with crispy basil and pre-served eggs, and the best, richest, earthiest beef noo-dle dish in town, the brisket-packed boat noodles.

Wakamono
3317 N Broadway Street, between W Aldine Avenue & W Buckingham Place (1-773 296 6800). El: Brown, Purple or Red to Belmont. **Open** *4-11.30pm daily.* **Small plates** $5. **Credit** AmEx, MC, V. **Map** p329 F2 ⑤⑪ Japanese
It's shocking that such a cool-conscious place uses the word 'japas' (Japanese tapas). But as it turns out, the joke is on the traditionalists: small plates of dishes such as fresh tofu sprinkled with chilli oil and peanuts, and prosciutto topped with ponzu sauce, crunchy toasted shallots and charred asparagus are a brilliant, unexpected combination. The sushi is impeccable, too, and the staff smile as they serve it.

Roscoe Village

Hot Doug's
3324 N California Avenue, at W Roscoe Street (1-773 279 9550/www.hotdougs.com). Bus 52, 152. **Open** *10.30am-4pm Mon-Sat.* **Hot dogs** $3. **No credit cards.** Classic American
Doug Sohn's homage to encased meat is packed with suits, students and blue-collar lunch-breakers, who stand together in longer-than-ever queues and put up with limited hours to feast on classic Chicago dogs and brats served with an untouchable flair for

flavour. There are veggie dogs for vegetarians, bagel dogs for kids, speciality dogs (cranberry and cognac chicken sausage) for high-brow types, and the famous fries cooked in duck fat (Fri and Sat only).

Kaze
2032 W Roscoe Street, between N Seeley & N Hoyne Avenues (1-773 327 4860/www.kazesushi.com). El: Brown to Paulina. **Open** *5-11pm daily.* **Main courses** $15. **Credit** AmEx, DC, Disc, MC, V. **Map** p330 B2 ⑥② Japanese
Gifted with the hands of a warrior, chef Macku slays fish instead of dragons at his sophisticated Japanese storefront. The food is a form of fusion that dresses up nigiri with seasonal, cooked toppings. Dishes include creations such as white-fish tempura wrapped in shrimp and drizzled with parsley butter, and pan-fried minced pheasant breast smothered in creamy brie and white miso sauce. Tuesday nights are a steal: four courses with wine pairings for $45.

Turquoise Café
2147 W Roscoe Street, between N Hamilton Avenue & N Leavitt Street (1-773 549 3523/www.turquoise dining.com). El: Brown to Paulina. **Open** *11am-11pm Mon-Thur; 11am-midnight Fri, Sat; 9am-10pm Sun.* **Main courses** $16. **Credit** AmEx, DC, Disc, MC, V. **Map** p330 B2 ⑥③ Turkish
Highlights at this stylish Turkish eaterie include the manti (Turkish ravioli stuffed with bits of lamb in a creamy yoghurt and chilli oil sauce), whole slabs of juicy, salt-crusted sea bass, and some of the best houmous around. Savvy regulars skip the fill-ing entrées and instead fuel up on starters and sides such as lightly fried zucchini pancakes with chilled

yoghurt dip, heavenly scalloped potatoes bubbling in heavy cream, and char-grilled calamares with tons of fresh lemon.

Victory's Banner
2100 W Roscoe Street, at N Hoyne Avenue (1-773 665 0227/www.victorysbanner.com). El: Brown to Addison. **Open** 8am-3pm Mon, Wed-Sun. **Main courses** $7.50. **Credit** AmEx, Disc, MC, V. **Map** p330 B2 🅖🅔 Vegetarian

There's an interesting distraction during the long wait for a table at this sunny vegetarian spot, as a TV shows Indian guru Sri Chinmoy lifting heavy things: a crew of firemen, a helicopter, a plane. Impressive stuff, it must be said, but we're bigger believers in the two-inch-thick French toast slathered in peach butter and maple syrup, or the pesto-laden free-range scrambled eggs in the so-called satisfaction promise, which comes with crispy potatoes and crusty bread.

Volo
2008 W Roscoe Street, between N Damen & N Seeley Avenues (1-773 348 4600/www.volo restaurant.com). El: Brown to Addison. **Open** 5-11pm Mon-Thur; 5pm-midnight Fri, Sat. **Small plates** $10. **Credit** AmEx, Disc, MC, V. **Map** p330 B2 🅖🅔 Eclectic

Owner Jon Young of Kitsch'n on Roscoe has teamed up with chef Stephen Dunne, formerly at mk, to open this small-plates wine bar. Dunne's best dishes are the rich ones: intense confit of duck leg with sweet garlic purée, seared diver scallops topped with over-easy quail eggs and caviar, and buttery stewed escarole and white beans. The cracker-crust pizza is crisp and just salty enough, with toppings such as goat's cheese and sun-dried tomatoes.

Andersonville, Edgewater & Uptown

Ba Le
5018 N Broadway Street, between W Argyle Street & W Winnemac Avenue (1-773 561 4424). El: Red to Argyle. **Open** 8am-8pm daily. **Sandwiches** $3. **No credit cards**. Vietnamese

When the French controlled Vietnam, baguettes crossed cultures, with the banh mi sandwich turning out to be one of the most appealing results of this culinary fertilisation. They're plentiful in this area, but Ba Le creates most of the bread used by its rival restaurants. Sample the barbecue pork and the Ba Le special, which piles house-made pâté, brawn and sliced pork on to a crusty baguette along with tangy carrot and daikon slivers, cilantro (coriander) and jalapeño. Save room for a shrimp spring roll.

Hopleaf
5148 N Clark Street, between W Winona Street & W Foster Avenue (1-773 334 9851/www.hopleaf.com). El: Red to Berwyn. **Open** 5-11pm Mon-Thur, Sun; 5pm-midnight Fri, Sat. **Main courses** $16. **Credit** AmEx, DC, Disc, MC, V. Belgian

When it's cold, you'll find locals bellied up to the bar at Hopleaf with Belgian brews in hand. However, food is also a forte: fleeting flavours such as a salad of roasted beet and quick-pickled brussels sprouts dotted with pear-orange chutney, beer-mustard dressing and pickled egg, or a late-autumn medley of braised cabbage, baked apples and pears that goes perfectly with an assortment of four smoky pork sausages.

Marigold
4832 N Broadway Street, between W Lawrence Avenue & W Gunnison Street (1-773 293 4653/ www.marigoldrestaurant.com). El: Red to Lawrence. **Open** 5.30-10pm Tue-Thur, Sun; 5.30-11pm Fri, Sat. **Main courses** $16. **Credit** AmEx, Disc, MC, V. Indian

Owner Sandeep Malhotra and chef Monica Riley (formerly of Meritage, Hopleaf and Treat) have combined wits to create this modern, upmarket Indian eaterie. The jewel-toned room is date-worthy, the wine list is pairing-friendly, and contemporary dishes such as garam masala-dusted scallops, duck leg confit with blistered green beans, and seared peppercorn-crusted thick yoghurt with orange-coriander dressed greens are worth the extra dough.

M Henry
5707 N Clark Street, between W Hollywood & W Edgewater Avenues (1-773 561 1600). El: Red to Bryn Mawr. **Open** 7am-2.30pm Tue-Fri; 8am-3pm Sat, Sun. **Main courses** $8. **Credit** AmEx, MC, V. Classic American

The owners of this adorable, sunny café are committed to organics and offer meat-free options, but they're OK with cheese, butter and sugar now and then. Try the thick, dense blueberry pancakes and a breakfast sandwich of eggs, Swiss cheese, applewood-smoked bacon and green peppers. If that's too good and gooey, there's always the Vegan Epiphany, an organic tofu scramble that may live up to its name.

Pho Xe Tang
4953-55 N Broadway, at W Argyle Street (1-773 878 2253). El: Red to Argyle. **Open** 8.30am-10pm Mon-Sat; 8.30am-9pm Sun. **Main courses** $7. **Credit** Disc, MC, V. Vietnamese

Known simply as Tank to anglophones, this spot is the answer for indecisive diners wandering Argyle Street. Authentic dishes are done well, and staff are able to converse in English. Lotus root salad shows everything this cuisine can be: limey and minty, with shrimp flavour, crunchy peanuts and a subtle chilli kick. Creamy coconut-milk chicken curry gets oomph from sweet and new potatoes.

The Northwest Side

Noon O Kabab
4661 N Kedzie Avenue, between W Eastwood & W Leland Avenues (1-773 279 8899/www.noonokabab. com). El: Brown to Kedzie. **Open** 11am-10pm Mon-*

Thur; 11am-11pm Fri, Sat; 11am-9pm Sun.
Main courses $10. **Credit** AmEx, DC, Disc,
MC, V. Middle Eastern

There's something appealing about this casual room, brightened with colourful tile murals. Or perhaps it's just the food: the smoky baba ganoush, the cinnamon-and-tomato braised lamb shank, and the kebabs. Ah, the kebabs: marinated steak cubes, tender chicken breast hunks and oniony mince wrapped around skewers and charred outside but still juicy within, plopped down on the fluffiest of rice alongside char-grilled tomatoes and onions.

La Oaxaqueña

3382 N Milwaukee Avenue, between W Pulaski Road & W Keeler Avenue (1-773 545 8585). El: Blue to Irving Park. **Open** 10am-10.30pm Mon-Thur; 10am-11.30pm Fri-Sun. **Main courses** $9. **Credit** AmEx, DC, Disc, MC, V. Mexican

Food from Mexico's Oaxaca region is hard to find in Chicago. Happily, this place excels at cooking it. The Huatulco torta is the stuff of dreams: a huge sandwich that layers house-made chorizo, caramelised onions, a slather of pinto beans and fresh avocado atop amazing cesina (thin beef that's marinated for two days in lemon, salt and oregano and then grilled). Other enticing options include the roast Cornish hen smothered in Oaxacan mole.

The Far North Side

Hema's Kitchen

6406 N Oakley Avenue, between W Devon & W Arthur Avenues (1-773 338 1627). Bus 49B, 155. **Open** 11am-10pm daily. **Main courses** $9. **Credit** AmEx, Disc, MC, V. Indian

After rounds of chicken masala, lamb vindaloo, mattar paneer (peas and cheese) and chickpea curry at Hema Potla's eaterie, you certainly won't be lost in a sea of sameness. Start with flaky vegetable samosas, then order all of the above for the table; don't forget the fluffy rice, dense parathas and cooling mango lassis. Potla has opened a second spot in Lincoln Park, where the food is just as impressive.

San Soo Gap San

5247 N Western Avenue, at W Berwyn Avenue (1-773 334 1589). Bus 11, 49, 92. **Open** 24hrs daily. **Main courses** $15. **Credit** AmEx, Disc, MC, V. Korean

Charcoal-fuelled, DIY Korean barbecues take centre stage here. The wang kalbi and dai ji kalbi are marinated (not saturated) in their respective sauces, leaving the flavour of the high-quality meat to shine. Use lettuce leaves, spring onions and peanutty sauce to make mini wraps with the meat. Alternatively, get stuck into hae moul pajun (egg pancake packed with shrimp and calamares).

Udupi Palace

2543 W Devon Avenue, at N Maplewood Avenue (1-773 338 2152/www.udupipalace.com). Bus 49B, 155. **Open** 11.30am-10pm daily. **Main courses** $8. **Credit** AmEx, DC, Disc, MC, V. Indian

This South Indian spot is renowned for its dosais, which come in nearly a dozen varieties. Lentils abound (the menu is all vegetarian); other good bets include the vegetable pullav (a cardamom, clove and cinnamon-laced rice dish with fresh carrots and green beans), flaky samosas with a touch of sweetness from the occasional raisin, spicy chickpea masala, and the 'Madras-style' okra curry by which regulars swear.

Avec. *See p165.*

Eat, Drink, Shop

Time Out
Travel Guides

USA

Time Out Boston

Time Out California

Time Out Chicago

Time Out Las Vegas

Time Out Los Angeles

Time Out Miami

Time Out New York

Time Out San Francisco

Time Out Washington, DC

**Available at all good bookshops
and at timeout.com/shop**

Time Out
Guides

The Near West Side

The West Loop & Greektown

Avec

*615 W Randolph Street, between N Jefferson &
N Desplaines Streets (1-312 377 2002/www.avec
restaurant.com). El: Green or Pink to Clinton.* **Open**
3.30pm-midnight Mon-Thur; 3.30pm-1am Fri, Sat;
3.30-10pm Sun. **Small plates** $10. **Credit** AmEx,
DC, Disc, MC, V. **Map** p325 F12 ⑥⑥ Mediterranean

A tiny space that looks like a sauna, Avec has communal seating, doesn't take reservations and is loud as hell. But it still works. The small plates make it easy to try a bit of this and that: rustic Mediterranean mainstays such as chorizo-stuffed dates and salty brandade are unbeatable; the cod starter dotted with caper berries and topped with crisp speck is another winner. **Photo** *p163*.

Blackbird

*619 W Randolph Street, between N Jefferson & N
Desplaines Streets (1-312 715 0708/www.blackbird
restaurant.com). El: Green or Pink to Clinton.* **Open**
11.30am-2pm, 5.30-10.30pm Mon-Thur; 11.30am-2pm,
5.30-11.30pm Fri, Sat. **Main courses** $28. **Credit**
AmEx, DC, Disc, MC, V. **Map** p325 F12 ⑥⑦
Contemporary American

This revered dining room manages to keep the focus on food while still holding its status as the place to see and be seen at. Chef Paul Kahan uses local produce and meats to create contemporary takes on classic seasonal flavours. Expect dishes such as roast breast of guinea hen with Georgia peaches, cauliflower, roasted young shallots and white-corn panisse in summer; and crispy rainbow trout with house-made smoked bacon, rapini, maitake mushrooms, butternut squash and candied pecans in winter.

Butter

*130 S Green Street, between W Adams & W Monroe
Streets (1-312 666 9813/www.butterchicago.com).
Bus 8, 156.* **Open** 5.30-10pm Mon-Wed, Thur;
5.30-11pm Thur-Sat. **Main courses** $28.
Credit AmEx, DC, Disc, MC, V. **Map** p330 F12 ⑥⑧
Contemporary American

This airy and stylish spot was named after chef Ryan Poli's favourite ingredient. Just don't tell the toned and tanned patrons who take their liquid diet in the plush upstairs lounge on weekends. If you come to eat, start with lobster tails from the raw bar and the deconstructed tuna niçoise salad. For the main event, stick with pastas: wild mushroom risotto, say, or linguine dotted with peas and mint.

Carnival

*702 W Fulton Street, at N Union Avenue (1-312
850 5005/www.carnivalechicago.com). Bus 8, 65.*
Open 11.30am-2.30pm, 5-10.30pm Mon-Thur;
11.30am-2pm, 5-11.30pm Fri, Sat; 5-10pm Sun.
Main courses $20. **Credit** AmEx, DC, Disc, MC, V.
Map p330 F11 ⑥⑨ Latin American

When an eatery this size (there are 400 seats) is this busy, it must be doing something right. Jerry Kleiner's colourful design is impressive, though it's not quite as pleasing as the Mojitos and Margaritas. On the pan-Latin menu, you'll find variations on traditional fare: oxtail pupusas, white-fish tacos and roasted ancho-barbecue salmon. The juicy ropa vieja is top notch, but it's the crowd here that entertains the most.

De Cero

*814 W Randolph Street, between N Green &
N Halsted Streets (1-312 455 8114/www.decero
traqueria.com). El: Green or Pink to Clinton.* **Open**
11am-2pm, 5-10pm Mon-Thur; 11.30am-2pm, 5-11pm
Fri; 5-11pm Sat. **Main courses** $13. **Credit** AmEx,
DC, Disc, MC, V. **Map** p330 F11 ⑦⓪ Mexican

The swank set pull on their skinny jeans and stilettos and head to this modern taqueria for the boisterous scene, the hibiscus Margaritas and the contemporary dishes such as ahi tuna tacos topped with mango salsa. The fresh corn tamales shine with straight-off-the-cob flavour that perfectly complements a traditional lime 'rita.

Follia

*953 W Fulton Avenue, between N Sangamon & N
Morgan Streets (1-312 243 2888/www.folliachicago.
com). El: Blue to UIC-Halsted.* **Open** 5-11pm
Mon-Thur, Sun; 5pm-midnight Fri, Sat. **Main
courses** $15. **Credit** AmEx, DC, Disc, MC, V.
Map p330 E11 ⑦① Italian

Bruno Abate has decorated his high-style Italian restaurant with a wall of simulated grass and mannequins dressed in flashy couture, but the diverse crowd here comes for the food, not the fashions. The paper-thin pizzas from a wood-burning oven are particularly recommended (try the napoletana, topped with oregano and anchovies), as are the pastas.

Ina's

*1235 W Randolph Street, between N Racine
Avenue & N Elizabeth Street (1-312 226 8227/
www.breakfastqueen.com). Bus 20.* **Open** 7-9pm
Mon-Fri; 8am-9pm Sat; 8am-2pm Sun. **Main
courses** $8. **Credit** AmEx, DC, Disc, MC, V.
Map p330 E12 ⑦② Classic American

Judging from the long weekend queues, people seem willing to wait for their scrapple (a crispy, slightly spicy polenta-like dish flanked by eggs and chorizo) and so-called heavenly hots (sour cream pancakes with fruit compote) on the breakfast menu at this peach. The same comfort-food theme can be found at dinner, when Ina cooks her famous fried chicken and, on weekends, a 'Friday night in Brooklyn' special of matzo ball soup and brisket.

Meiji

*623 W Randolph Street, between N Jefferson &
N Desplaines Streets (1-312 887 9999/www.meiji
restaurant.com). El: Green or Pink to Clinton.*
Open 11.30am-2.30pm, 5-11.30pm Mon-Thur;
11.30am-2.30pm, 5pm-12.30am Fri; 5pm-12.30am
Sat. **Main courses** $18. **Credit** AmEx, Disc, MC, V.
Map p330 F11 ⑦③ Japanese

Eat, Drink, Shop

The brunch bunch

Nothing says 'weekend' in Chicago quite like brunch. The city is dotted with diners, cafés and restaurants offering a special menu during the day on weekends, but it takes a keen nose to sniff out the leaders of the pack.

Finding a half-decent breakfast in the Loop on weekends can be tricky. Happily, help is at hand to the west. **Ina's** (*see p165*) dishes up fabulous breakfasts every day of the week, but **Wishbone** (*see p167; pictured*) comes into its own on weekends. On the Near North Side, head for the **West Egg Café** (620 N Franklin Court, at E Ontario Street, 1-312 280 8366), which does astonishing things with eggs, or **Heaven on Seven** (600 N Michigan Avenue, entrance at E Ohio & N Rush Streets, 1-312 280 7774, www.heavenonseven.com), which serves amazing Cajun-styled brunches.

You can find a fancy French dress in almost any store on Halsted Street and Webster Avenue in Lincoln Park. When it comes to fancy French toast, **Toast** (746 W Webster Avenue, at N Burling Street, 1-773 935 5600) has enjoyed a monopoly for years, but **Gracie's** (1119 W Webster Avenue, between N Seminary & N Clifton Avenues, 1-773 528 1788, http://graciesonwebster.net) aims to change that. Chef Wade Fortin has upped the ante with his Death by Chocolate French toast, which tops chocolate brioche with a white chocolate-banana crème anglaise.

In Lakeview, the original **Orange** (3231 N Clark Street, at W Belmont Avenue, 1-773

549 4400) invented 'frushi' (fruit sushi). Rather than squeezing in with the others, take a short walk south to **Erwin** (2925 N Halsted Street, at W Oakdale Avenue, 1-773 528 7200, www.erwincafe.com), where the brunch menu sticks to American classics. Alternatively, try Ted's Hangover Helper at the **Harmony Grill** (3159 N Southport Avenue, at W Belmont Avenue, 1-773 525 2528). We don't know who Ted is, but from the looks of his fried salami, pesto scrambled eggs and potato-topped sandwich, he must be dangerously close to liver failure.

In Andersonville, **M Henry** (*see p162*) gets plaudits for its healthy, organic takes on sweet and savoury eats. However, sometimes even its blueberry pancakes aren't worth the wait. If it's full, walk down Clark to French bistro **La Tache** (1475 W Balmoral Avenue, at N Clark Street, 1-773 334 7168, www.latache chicago.com), where the Sunday-only brunch menu includes skirt steak and eggs, and a croque madame oozing with white cheddar and topped with two fried eggs.

Over in Wicker Park, there's always a crowd sipping coffee and munching French toast at the **Bongo Room** (*see p170*). If it's too busy, wander up to **Francesca's Forno** (*see p171*), where Italian-tinged dishes such as pancetta-arugula BLT flanked by pecorino and truffle oil-laced fries should soak up some of the previous night's damage. As, for that matter, should the very decent Bloody Marys.

The emphasis at this swanky spot is on sushi, which generally pleases novices and traditionalists. Over-the-top rolls bursting with cream cheese and tempura crunch are balanced by ultra-fresh, razor-thin sashimi cuts of fatty tuna and fluke (a flat fish), as well as rarer cuts like fatty yellowtail and shirauo (ice fish). However, Meiji also dabbles in other Japanese dishes, among them egg-custard soup, tofu wrapped in dried nori with dashi broth, and tonkatsu (crispy, panko-encrusted pork loin).

9 Muses

315 S Halsted Street, between W Jackson Boulevard & W Van Buren Street (1-312 902 9922). El: Blue to UIC-Halsted. **Open** 11am-2am Mon-Fri, Sun; 11am-3am Sat. **Main courses** $7. **Credit** AmEx, DC, Disc, MC, V. **Map** p330 F13 ⑳ Greek
Do the young Greeks who pack this trendy, clubby restaurant know something you don't? Yes, and they probably want to keep this place to themselves. Still, it's hard to stay away when you're in the mood for Greek munchies such as florina peppers (two roasted red peppers stuffed with creamy feta), loukanika (a pork-lamb sausage), 'toasts' (panini, basically) and huge gyro platters, all washed down with Mythos beer. If you can stop yourself talking by shovelling in food, nobody will know you don't belong.

One Sixtyblue

1400 W Randolph Street, between N Ada Street & N Ogden Avenue (1-312 850 0303/www.onesixtyblue. com). El: Green or Pink to Ashland. **Open** 5.30-10pm Mon-Thur; 5.30-11pm Fri, Sat. **Main courses** $25. **Credit** AmEx, DC, MC, V. **Map** p330 D11 ⑳
Contemporary American
The perfect venue for a special night out, partly because of the gorgeous space, but mostly thanks to Martial Noguier, the city's most underrated chef. His contemporary French food incorporates seasonal American produce, and hits all the right buttons: sweet, sour, salty, bitter and savoury. The vast menu ranges from free-range veal and big, fat delmonico steaks to light bites such as baby coho salmon wrapped in wild rice blinis.

Santorini

800 W Adams Street, at S Halsted Street (1-312 829 8820). El: Blue to UIC-Halsted. **Open** 11am-midnight Mon-Thur, Sun; 11am-1am Fri, Sat. **Main courses** $17. **Credit** AmEx, DC, Disc, MC, V. **Map** p330 F12 ⑳ Greek
The Kantos family imports organic olive oil and oregano from the family farm in Sparta to use at Santorini. The whole, grilled red snapper needs nothing more than a squeeze of lemon to show off its subtle flavour. You may jump a little every time somebody screams 'opa!' and a ball of flaming saganaki cheese erupts at a nearby table. But if your nerves can handle it, your taste buds will thank you.

Sushi Wabi

842 W Randolph Street, between N Green & N Peoria Streets (1-312 563 1224/www.sushiwabi.com). El: Green or Pink to Clinton. **Open** 11.30am-2pm, 5-11pm

Mon, Tue, Sun; 11.30am-2pm, 5pm-midnight Wed-Fri; 5pm-midnight Sat. **Nigiri** $3. **Credit** AmEx, DC, Disc, MC, V. **Map** p330 F11 ⑳ Japanese
The sushi is so incredibly fresh here that it's hard to be snide about the scene (aloof, black-clad servers dishing out pre-party snacks to clubgoers over a soundtrack spun by a Sade remix-loving DJ). Flash-cooked, citrus-tinged shrimp are placed on cool green-tea soba noodles; spicy, vinegar-tossed coleslaw is topped with tempura soft-shell crab that's drizzled with wasabi honey.

Venus Greek-Cypriot Cuisine

820 W Jackson Boulevard, between S Halsted & S Green Streets (1-312 714 1001/www.venuschicago. com). El: Blue to UIC-Halsted. **Open** 11am-11pm Mon-Thur; 11am-2am Fri; 4pm-3am Sat; noon-11pm Sun. **Main courses** $17. **Credit** AmEx, Disc, MC, V. **Map** p330 F12 ⑳ Greek
This sprawling spot is famed for its Cypriot cuisine. The owners have taken the traditional, rustic food and added some upmarket touches to the menu and the space. Try the halloumi cheese and the tender, six-hour slow-baked lamb (served in foil), or go for the pastitsio tsoukas, long noodles layered with ground beef and covered in a crispy béchamel topping. Everything is made to order; enjoy the wait while downing a bottle from the Greek wine list.

Wishbone

1001 W Washington Boulevard, at N Morgan Street (1-312 850 2663/www.wishbonechicago.com). Bus 8, 20. **Open** 7am-3pm Mon; 11am-3pm, 5-9pm Tue-Thur; 11am-3pm, 5-10pm Fri; 8am-3pm, 5-10pm Sat; 8am-3pm Sun. **Main courses** $10. **Credit** AmEx, DC, Disc, MC, V. **Map** p330 E12 ⑳ Classic American
Southern staples such as grits and biscuits can be hard to find here. But this West Loop eaterie is on a mission to bring 'mornin' hon' hospitality to the heartland. The brunch is often touted as the city's best; that's doubtful, but it's hard to fault the plate-size fruit pancakes and savoury corncakes (add hot sauce), the dense corn muffins and buttery biscuits, and the spicy andouille chicken sausage.

Little Italy & Heart of Chicago

Bruna's

2424 S Oakley Avenue, between W 24th Place & W 24th Street (1-773 254 5550). El: Blue (Cermak branch); Green or Pink to Western. **Open** 11am-10pm Mon-Thur; 11am-11pm Fri; 3-11pm Sat; 1-10pm Sun. **Main courses** $18. **Credit** AmEx, DC, Disc, MC, V. Italian
This old-school favourite opened way back in 1933, which explains the faded travel posters and weary saloon decor. But the kitchen is far from tired, going beyond typical pastas and parmigianas to specialise in rustic dishes from Siena, owner Luciano Silvestri's boyhood home. Tucked between the chicken vesuvio and the stuffed shells are a rich ravioli filled with porcini mushrooms, and a some-what spirited penne alla puttanesca.

Eat, Drink, Shop

Bravo Tapas & Lounge. *See p170.*

such as shaved ginger-topped aji (horse mackerel), meaty blue-fin and rich, grilled yellow-fin collar. The restaurant runs a BYOB policy.

RoSal's

1154 W Taylor Street, between S May Street & S Racine Avenue (1-312 243 2357/www.rosals.com). El: Blue to Racine. **Open** 4-9pm Mon-Thur; 4-10pm Fri, Sat. **Main courses** $18. **Credit** AmEx, DC, Disc, MC, V. **Map** p330 E14 ⑧ Italian

It's somehow still charming when the bubbly girl 'from da neighbourhood' explains how owners Roseanne and Salvatore (hence the name) came to open their Sicilian spot in Little Italy. Cuteness aside, though, the dependable old-school eats are among the best on the Taylor Street strip. Start off with the lightly charred but tender grilled calamares; follow it up with a pasta course of big, fat garlicky shrimp tossed with shells and broccoli, before getting stuck into the veal saltimbocca with a side of spinach.

Sweet Maple Café

1339 W Taylor Street, between S Ada & S Loomis Streets (1-312 243 8908). El: Blue or Pink to Polk. **Open** 7am-2pm daily. **Main courses** $5. **Credit** AmEx, MC, V. **Map** p330 D14 ⑧ Classic American

Most weekends, you'll find a crowd spilling on to this breakfast spot's sidewalk, watching servers carry plates laden with sweet-milk biscuits and bone-in ham. Those who stick it out will be rewarded with house-made muffins, or pancakes with sweet pockets of banana. At lunch, don't miss the Southern-inspired dishes such as fried catfish.

Pilsen

Mundial–Cocina Mestiza

1640 W 18th Street, between S Ashland Avenue & S Paulina Street (1-312 491 9908). El: Blue or Pink to 18th. **Open** 10am-10pm daily. **Main courses** $12. **Credit** AmEx, DC, Disc, MC, V. Mexican

This eclectic, upbeat spot has plenty of pedigree in the kitchen, concocting dishes from a menu that's part Mexican and part Mediterranean. The room is simple and casual, but the food goes beyond the surroundings. Try the mojarra empapelada (tilapia stuffed with chorizo, red onion, epazote leaves and jalapeño mayo, wrapped in foil and baked), or the cumin-coated quail with smoky camagua beans, roasted tomatillo and crisp watercress.

Nuevo León

1515 W 18th Street, between S Laflin Street & S Ashland Avenue (1-312 421 1517/www.nuevoleon restaurant.com). El: Blue or Pink to 18th. **Open** 7am-midnight daily. **Main courses** $10. **No credit cards.** Mexican

Since 1962, the Gutierrez family has been running this mecca for Mexican food, starting dinner in the bright, whimsically decorated space with an amuse-bouche. Don't fill up: there's much more to come, such as roast chicken pieces covered in a thick,

Haro

2436 S Oakley Avenue, between W 24th Place & W 25th Street (1-773 847 2400/www.harotapas. com). El: Blue (Cermak branch); Pink to Western. **Open** 5-11pm Tue-Thur; 5pm-1am Fri, Sat; 3-8pm Sun. **Main courses** $9. **Credit** AmEx, Disc, MC, V. Spanish

Pintxos, open-face sandwiches found in Basque bars, are the draw at Haro, though the selection changes daily. If you're lucky, you'll find the red pepper stuffed with spicy blood sausage, juicy lamb or the simple serrano-and-manchego combo. If not, fall back on tapas such as the huevos flamenco (a casserole of potatoes, chorizo and fried eggs) or baby eels (savoury and slick with olive oil).

Kohan

730 W Maxwell Street, between S Union Avenue & S Halsted Street (1-312 421 6254). El: Blue to UIC-Halsted. **Open** 11.30am-10pm Mon-Thur; 11.30am-11pm Fri; 5-11pm Sat; 4-9pm Sun. **Credit** AmEx, Disc, MC, V. Japanese

The service here is warm and welcoming enough to fool diners into believing this casual Japanese spot is an old favourite. Half the menu is dedicated to teppan (Benihana-style open grill) cooking; the teriyaki-glazed shrimp, steak and vegetables are tasty enough, but the sushi is more impressive. Stick to the specials board for supremely fresh catches

intense mole, and tacos de chorizo, house-made chorizo scrambled into an egg and wrapped in one of the famous tortillas. BYOB.

Wicker Park & around

Ukrainian Village & West Town

A Tavola

2148 W Chicago Avenue, between N Hoyne Avenue & N Leavitt Street (1-773 276 7567/www.atavola chicago.com). El: Blue to Chicago. **Open** 5.30-10pm Mon-Thur; 5.30-10.30pm Fri, Sat. **Main courses** $20. **Credit** AmEx, DC, Disc, MC, V. **Map** p331 B9 ⑥ Italian

This tiny dining room is tight on tables and menu items; there are about a dozen of each. However, what A Tavola lacks in size is made up for by its innate charm. The food is simple Italian fare: a duo of meaty mushrooms is dressed only with balsamic and thyme, and the roast chicken gets by on its golden, crisp skin. There's a fine line between simple and bland (the house-made tagliatelle bolognese teeters toward the latter), but it usually keeps its balance.

Bob San

1805 W Division Street, between N Wood & N Honore Streets (1-773 235 8888/www.bob-san.com). El: Blue to Division. **Open** 4.30-11.30pm Mon-Thur, Sun; 4.30pm-12.30am Fri, Sat. **Nigiri** $2.50. **Credit** AmEx, DC, MC, V. **Map** p331 C8 ⑥ Japanese

When the fish is this good, most customers can happily coexist with the Bucktown babes in pointy heels eating sashimi and sipping pinot grigio. Bob San's menu balances Japanese classics and fun rolls. The quality of the premium fatty tuna or yellowtail is great, and the creamy scallop nigiri and spicy white tuna roll are unforgettable.

Breakfast Club

1381 W Hubbard Street, between N Loomis & N Ada Streets (1-312 666 2372/www.chicagobreakfast club.com). El: Green or Pink to Ashland. **Open** 6am-3pm Mon-Fri; 7am-3pm Sat, Sun. **Main courses** $8. **No credit cards.** Classic American

The mother of all breakfast haunts holds strong in the middle of an industrial-ish yet residential 'hood. It's like granny's cosy kitchen, but with the morning news flowing via a stream of chatty city employees, laptop-wielding businessmen and convivial construction workers. All and sundry fuel up on wholegrain pancakes, football-size omelettes and biscuits with sausage-packed gravy.

Dodo

935 N Damen Avenue, at W Walton Street (1-773 772 3636). Bus 50, 66. **Open** 7am-3pm Mon-Fri; 8am-2pm Sat, Sun. **Main courses** $7. **No credit cards.** **Map** p331 B9 ⑥ Classic American

The omelettes at Kim Dalton's breakfast-and-lunch spot are fluffy and flecked with fresh parsley, while ground beef sandwiches are indulgent and the daily-changing, straightforward soups are comforting

and homely. However, Dalton's greatest feat is her Japanese pancake, a savoury, vegetable-stuffed flapjack that actually makes cabbage for breakfast sound like an appealing prospect.

Fan Si Pan

1618 W Chicago Avenue, between N Ashland & N Marshfield Avenues (1-312 738 1405). Bus 9, 66. **Open** 8am-9pm daily. **Main courses** $5. **Credit** AmEx, MC, V. **Map** p331 C9 ⑥ Vietnamese

Susan Furst gives Vietnamese staples a makeover at this insanely cute set-up. The spring rolls are super-sized and stuffed with sweet-and-salty hoi sin-marinated 'five star beef', while banh mi get contemporary fillings such as lime-tinged chicken and mango. Furst's house-made sauces add plenty to the dishes. The best bet, though, is the classic ham-and-pâté banh mi, a heavenly contrast of creamy and crunchy, salty and spicy. Most punters take away their food.

Flo

1434 W Chicago Avenue, between N Noble & N Bishop Streets (1-312 243 0477). El: Blue to Chicago. **Open** 8.30am-10pm Tue-Thur; 8.30am-11pm Fri, Sat; 9am-2.30pm Sun. **Main courses** $13. **Credit** AmEx, DC, Disc, MC, V. **Map** p331 D9 ⑥ Eclectic

Renee and Rodney Carswell's funky, casual room is an all-day draw for those after an interesting meal at a fair price. Brunch and breakfast menu standouts include such New Mexico-influenced tongue-scorchers as green chilli enchiladas and huevos rancheros, perfect when balanced with fresh fruit smoothies and strong coffee. At dinner, local and often organic produce appears in salads and sides for a list of comforting classics that could encompass fish tacos or chorizo meatloaf.

Green Zebra

1460 W Chicago Avenue, between N Bishop Street & N Greenview Avenue (1-312 243 7100/www.green zebrachicago.com). El: Blue to Chicago. **Open** 5.30-10pm Mon-Thur; 5-11pm Fri, Sat; 5.30-9pm Sun. **Main courses** $11. **Credit** AmEx, DC, Disc, MC, V. **Map** p331 D9 ⑥ Contemporary America

Shawn McClain's house of Zen is the only upmarket restaurant Chicago's meat-free (but seafood-happy) diners can truly call their own, so it's no surprise that the moss-coloured, Asian-tinged room gets packed. The menu is an exercise in subtlety from which diners should choose two to three small plates. Past standouts include white gazpacho with pears, white anchovies and grilled peppers, and roast halibut with toasted corn bread and heirloom tomato water.

May Street Market

1132 W Grand Avenue, at N May Street (1-312 421 5547/www.maystreetmarket.com). El: Blue to Grand. **Open** 10am-10pm Mon-Thur; 10am-11pm Fri, Sat. **Main courses** $19. **Credit** AmEx, Disc, MC, V. Contemporary American

Three reasons to check out this comfy-but-posh spot: chef-owner Alex Cheswick's (Tru, Le Français) comforting yet contemporary menu; the keenly priced, interesting wine list; and the inviting, amber-tinted room. Highlights of the former include a Maytag blue cheesecake with roasted apricots, arugula (rocket) and apricot ice; blue fin crab cakes with kohl-rabi and arugula salad; and free-form lasagne with braised fennel, forest mushrooms, asparagus and lentils.

Rudy's Taste

1024 N Ashland Avenue, between W Augusta Boulevard and W Cortez Street (1-773 252 3666). El: Blue to Division. **Open** 10am-10pm Mon, Tue, Thur-Sun. **Main courses** $12. **Credit** MC, V. **Map** p331 C9 ⑥ Latin American

This family operation is decorated with bright textile tablecloths and fresh flowers to comfortable, tropical effect. However, the food is still the draw, with Rudy Figueroa's native Guatemalan fare stealing the show. The plantain leaf-wrapped tamale is butter-smooth, studded with roasted pork chunks, roasted bell-pepper sauce, olives and capers.

West Town Tavern

1329 W Chicago Avenue, at N Throop Street (1-312 666 6175/www.westtowntavern.com). El: Blue to Chicago. **Open** 5-10pm Mon-Sat. **Main courses** $18. **Credit** AmEx, MC, V. **Map** p331 D10 ⑥ Contemporary American

Would that every neighbourhood had a cosy spot like this, serving unfussy food and fun wines, and enticing jeans and suits to mingle *sans* attitude. The popular antipasto plate, skillet-roasted mussels and 'campfire s'mores' are the pillars of the regular menu, but seasonal specials keep things interesting. Look for the likes of maple-roasted pork loin with risotto, grilled salmon with fennel and potato gratin.

Wicker Park & Bucktown

Bongo Room

1470 N Milwaukee Avenue, between W Evergreen Avenue & W Honore Street (1-773 489 0690/www. bongoroom.com). El: Blue to Damen. **Open** 7am-2.30pm Mon-Fri; 9am-2.30pm Sat, Sun. **Main courses** $10. **Credit** AmEx, Disc, MC, V. **Map** p331 C8 ⑨ Classic American

Hungover rock stars, early-rising soccer moms and everyone in between flock to this bright, cheery spot for fancy morning cocktails and a bite or two. Amid the menu's run-of-the-mill numbers are some dishes worth the often long wait. The black bean and sweet potato burrito is satisfying, especially smothered in tomatillo salsa. The chocolate tower French toast is a luxurious pile of chocolate bread smothered in what is essentially melted banana crème brûlée.

Le Bouchon

1958 N Damen Avenue, between W Homer Street & W Armitage Avenue (1-773 862 6600/www.le bouchonofchicago.com). El: Blue to Western. **Open** 5.30-11pm Mon-Thur; 5pm-midnight Fri, Sat. **Main courses** $16. **Credit** AmEx, DC, Disc, MC, V. **Map** p331 B6 ⑨ French

Yes, it's crowded. Yes, it's smaller than most studio apartments. Yes, you'll have to wait at the tiny bar, even with a reservation. But this is the closest thing

Chicago has to a Paris bistro. Regulars have their favourites: the flaky, caramelly onion tart; the robust onion soup with gruyère; the butter-topped steak flanked by perfect frites; and the hard-to-find seared veal kidneys with mustard sauce. Only snootier waiters could make your experience more French.

Bravo Tapas & Lounge

2047 W Division Street, between N Damen & N Hoyne Avenues (1-773 278 2727/www.bravotapas. com). El: Blue to Division. **Open** 11am-3pm, 5-10pm Mon-Wed; 11am-3pm, 5-11pm Thur; 11am-3pm, 5pm-midnight Fri; 5pm-midnight Sat; 5-10pm Sun. **Tapas** $9. **Credit** AmEx, Disc, MC, V. **Map** p331 B8 ㉒ Spanish

This three-level tapas spot is just the place at which to sip sangria and people-watch. Head upstairs for a lofty lounge feel, downstairs for a clubby vibe, or the patio if the weather's nice. Whatever the choice, start with a Mojito. Tapas, such as tender grilled calamares, or chorizo-studded dates wrapped in bacon, are among the best bets. Brunch and lunch have been added recently, but loud Spanish music and sparkly-topped patrons might not translate well into daylight. **Photo** *p168*.

Café Absinthe

1954 W North Avenue, between N Winchester & N Damen Avenues (1-773 278 4488). El: Blue to Damen. **Open** 5.30-10pm Mon-Thur, Sun; 5.30-11pm Fri, Sat. **Main courses** $24. **Credit** AmEx, DC, Disc, MC, V. **Map** p331 B7 ㉝ Contemporary American

A decade ago, it was considered daring to venture down the alley here. Now the neighbourhood is gentrified, it's harder to get a table at weekends. What hasn't changed is the cuisine: simple, seasonal ingredients brought together without fuss. Duck breast is moist inside, crisp outside and comes with tasty duck confit ravioli on caramelised onions, wilted arugula (rocket) and Asian mushrooms.

Café Matou

1846 N Milwaukee Avenue, between W Leavitt & W Moffat Streets (1-773 384 8911/http://cafematou. com). El: Blue to Western. **Open** 5-10pm Tue-Thur; 5-11pm Fri, Sat; 5-9pm Sun. **Main courses** $20. **Credit** AmEx, DC, Disc, MC, V. **Map** p331 B6 ㉞ French

It takes skill to pull off a dish like les deux poissons conserves au fenouil marine. Chef Charlie Socher does it with a perfect fennel relish that brings out the best in the house-cured salmon and the marinated white anchovies. Not everything at this charming venue is as intricate; the ever-changing menu of rich flavours might include venison 'scallops' in a syrah sauce, pork loin breaded with pecans, and linguine with ramps. In other words, food that's simple, hearty and delicious enough to get the job done.

Coast

2045 N Damen Avenue, between W McLean & W Dickens Avenues (1-773 235 5775/http://coastsushi bar.com). El: Blue to Western. **Open** 4pm-midnight Mon-Sat; 4-10pm Sun. **Nigiri** $2.50. **Credit** AmEx, Disc, MC, V. **Map** p331 B6 ㉟ Japanese

Bullish decor and brilliant patatas bravas at **Del Toro**.

This BYOB spot knows how to exploit sushi's sex appeal while maintaining the vibe of a low-key local favourite. Slippery morsels of tuna, yellowtail and salmon are served in a dark, sultry dining room full of minimalist furniture. The focus is top-quality raw fish, but liberties are taken, with success. Ceviche maki pairs lime-marinated scallop with mango, cilantro (coriander) and jalapeño; salmon gets stuffed in a spring roll, fried and served with green curry dipping sauce for non-traditional yet delicious results.

Il Covo

2152 N Damen Avenue, between W Shakespeare & W Webster Avenues (1-773 862 5555/www.ilcovo chicago.com). El: Blueto Western. **Open** 5-10pm Mon-Thur, Sun; 5-11pm Fri, Sat. **Main courses** $20. **Credit** AmEx, DC, Disc, MC, V. **Map** p331 B6 ⬤ Italian

An Italian joint with an Australian chef could make for global disaster, but Luka Lukic has shown plenty of promise. Hits include the herbal deep-fried zucchini flowers, perfectly prepared pastas (try the spaghetti with Morton Bay bugs, which are sweet, buttery crustaceans from Australia), and the deliciously crispy pizzas topped with prosciutto. Definitely one to watch.

Del Toro

1520 N Damen Avenue, between W Le Moyne Street & W Pierce Avenue (1-773 252 1500). El: Blue to Damen. **Open** 5-10.30pm Mon-Thur; 5-11pm Fri, Sat; 10am-3pm Sun. **Small plates** $7. **Credit** AmEx, MC, V. **Map** p331 B7 ⬤ Spanish

Come to this Spanish small-plates spot (where blood-red fabrics and bullish details echo the name) for late-night bites coupled with a glass or two of sparkling cava. Or try brunch, where Andrew Zimmerman takes liberties with Spanish tradition for awesome results: a flaky croissant is stuffed with serrano ham, Mahón cheese and scrambled eggs and served with spicy patatas bravas. The roasted strawberry crêpes and the blackcurrant mimosa are sweet highlights.

Francesca's Forno

1576 N Milwaukee Avenue, at W North Avenue (1-773 770 0184/www.miafrancesca.com). El: Blue to Damen. **Open** 11.30am-10.30pm Mon-Thur; 11.30am-11pm Fri; 10am-11.30pm Sat; 10am-10.30pm Sun. **Small plates** $8. **Credit** AmEx, Disc, MC, V. **Map** p331 B7 ⬤ Italian

The hip and hungry pack this branch of Francesca's to eat small plates of simple Italian fare for dinner, but brunch is the better bet. The BLT contains pancetta, arugula and a lemon mayo, plus a handful of Pecorino and truffle oil-laced fries. Thin pizza crust is the base for smoked salmon, soft-scrambled eggs, crème fraîche and red onion slivers. The 'panettone' French toast is topped with sweet mascarpone cream, fresh berries and balsamic vinegar.

Honey 1 BBQ

2241 N Western Avenue, between W Lyndale Street & W Belden Avenue (1-773 227 5130). El: Blue to Western. **Open** 11am-11pm Tue-Thur; 11am-midnight Fri, Sat; 1-9pm Sun. **Main courses** $9. **No credit cards. Map** p331 A5 ⬤ Classic American

The father and son behind this rib house employ real wood (rather than gas) to impart smoky flavour on slow-cooked slabs. The new place has a handful of tables and chairs in the simple dining area, and is already doing double the usual business, which means patrons no longer have to call ahead two hours to request ribs; the turnover means the Adams family are smokin' around the clock.

HotChocolate

1747 N Damen Avenue, between W Willow Street & W St Paul Avenue (1-773 489 1747). El: Blue to Damen. **Open** 11.30am-2pm, 5.30-10pm Tue, Wed; 11.30am-2pm, 5.30-11pm Thur; 11.30am-2pm, 5.30pm-midnight Fri; 10am-2pm, 5.30pm-midnight Sat; 10am-2pm, 5-10pm Sun. **Main courses** $14. **Credit** AmEx, MC, V. **Map** p331 B7 ⬤ Contemporary American

Don't let the name fool you: chef-owner Mindy Segal's talent extends beyond desserts. Settle into the loungey, comfy, chocolate-toned dining room and start with seasonal savoury dishes such as

Eat, Drink, Shop

lemon-scented sole with heirloom tomatoes and fennel salad, or Carr Valley's Krema Kasa cheese rolled into flatbread with lamb sausage. Leave room for the warm chocolate soufflé tart with salted caramel ice-cream, one of the most decadent dishes in town.

Irazu
1865 N Milwaukee Avenue, at N Oakley Avenue (1-773 252 5687). El: Blue to Western. **Open** 11am-9pm Mon-Sat. **Main courses** $8. **No credit cards.** **Map** p331 A6 ⓑ Central American
Never tried Costa Rican food? Here's your safe entry. It's simple, authentic, cheap, casual and friendly. Start with hearts of palm salad – huge, tangy stalks on a bed of shredded cabbage that's been tossed in a lime vinaigrette with radishes, cilantro (coriander), cucumber, pickled beets and ripe avocado. Another standout is the pepito sandwich, a toasted, gooey combo of juicy rib-eye steak, caramelised onions and mild cheese on French bread. Bring malbec to match.

Mas
1670 W Division Street, at N Paulina Street (1-773 276 8700). El: Blue to Division. **Open** 5.30-10pm Mon-Thur, Sun; 5.30-11pm Fri, Sat. **Main courses** $22. **Credit** AmEx, MC, V. **Map** p331 C8 ⓑ Latin American
John Manion's nuevo Latino joint puts out addictive food, such as a flaky empanada oozing with goat's cheese, mushrooms and walnuts or tilapia and shrimp

ceviche in a tequila-spiked citrus-coconut-milk blend. Vegetarians will love the roasted acorn squash filled with wild mushrooms and boniato (a sweet potato). A tropical cocktail list is the perfect excuse to linger amid the hot pre-club weekend crowd.

Milk & Honey
1920 W Division Street, between W Wolcott & W Winchester Avenues (1-773 395 9434/www. milkandhoneycafe.com). El: Blue to Division. **Open** 7am-4pm Mon-Fri; 8am-5pm Sat; 8am-4pm Sun. **Main courses** $7. **Credit** AmEx, Disc, MC, V. **Map** p331 C8 ⓑ Classic American
This sunny, friendly sandwich-and-coffee joint helps kick-start the day with baked goods and speciality coffees, but it's the sandwiches that score highly for lunch. Top choices? The goat's cheese panini laced with white truffle oil, and the BLT made with extra-thick bacon. The weekend crowd can be a bitch, so be prepared to fight your way to the front.

Piece
1927 W North Avenue, between N Wolcott & N Winchester Avenues (1-773 772 4422). El: Blue to Damen. **Open** 11.30am-2am Mon-Fri; 11am-3am Sat; Sun. **Main courses** $13.50. **Credit** AmEx, DC, Disc, MC, V. **Map** p331 C7 ⓑ Pizza
If it looks like a bar, smells like a bar and sounds like a bar, then… do the maths. Two things keep Piece on track: great house brews and expertly

Going native

Lasagne? No problem. Sushi? Easy. If you want a Laotian salad or a Somalian suqar, then there are fewer options, but options there nonetheless are...

The decor of the **Latin Sandwich Café** (4009 N Elston Avenue, at W Irving Park Road, Irving Park, 1-773 478 0175, www.latinsandwichcafe.com) doesn't exactly scream Chile. However, owner Orietta Lippians maintains that the Chilean dishes on the menu are available nowhere else in Illinois. Don't miss the Chilean sandwiches, which operate on the principle that everything's better with avocado.

Restaurateur Nguyen and his wife Hoa opened **Café Nhu-Hoa** (1020 W Argyle Street, between N Sheridan Road & N Kenmore Avenue, Uptown, 1-773 878 0618) in 1987, a lifetime in restaurant years. However, it's still going strong, serving a menu of dishes from Vietnam and (the USP) their native Laos. Order the sticky rice and mash up each handful into a small pad. Then order the papaya salad, the beef jerky, the galangal-and-lemongrass-spiked sausage, and the larb beef salad (lettuce, beef and

chewy organ meat). Use the rice pad to scoop everything into your mouth. Marvellous.

A quick glance at the menu of **Mount Everest** (630 Church Street, Evanston, 1-847 491 1069, www.mteverestrestaurant.com) might lead you to think you're in north India. However, owner Ramakamt Kharel is from Nepal, and this is the only restaurant in the city with Nepalese dishes on the menu. Manager Sunny Sharma asserts that 'compared to Indian food, Nepalese food is less spicy and less oily, with no dairy products'. Try the chicken momo or jhane ko daal, a comforting lentil dish.

Somalian food borrows from India (spices), Italy (spaghetti) and Ethiopia (injera), so a visit to **Banadir** (6221 N Clark Street, at W Thorne Avenue, North Side, 1-773 443 2778) takes in three continents. Garaad Samatar and Amina Garad, the attentive hosts, opened the restaurant in 2003, since when it's become as much Somali community centre as eaterie. Still, the food is terrific: the injera, served with breakfast, is a perfect wrap for beef suqar, a rich stew that's also available for dinner.

Hachi's Kitchen. *See p174.*

Scylla's seafood-stocked menu is constantly changing. Step into the two-storey, A-frame restaurant to sample from the latest line-up, which in the past has included the likes of chilled yellow tomato and vanilla bean soup with poached shrimp; crispy soft shell crab with bing cherries, olives, caper berries and English peas; and anise-scented baba with blackberry-muscatel sauce and cantaloupe sorbet.

Spring

2039 W North Avenue, between W Damen &
W Hoyne Avenues (1-773 395 7100/www.spring
restaurant.net). El: Blue to Damen. **Open** 5.30-
10pm Tue-Thur; 5.30-10.30 Fri, Sat; 5.30-9pm Sun.
Main courses $25. **Credit** AmEx, DC, Disc, MC, V.
Map p331 B7 **107** Contemporary American
There's flair in chef Shawn McClain's cooking, the way he uses Asian elements and local ingredients to create dishes that are both subtle and opulent. The upmarket Zen decor is snooze-inducing, but you'll want to be awake when popping plump Kumomoto oysters in your mouth, or marvelling over paper-thin potato 'ravioli' hiding scallops, or scraping up all the truffle-mascarpone risotto under the seared snapper. Several vegetarian choices are offered nightly.

Humboldt Park & Logan Square

Bonsoiree

2728 W Armitage Avenue, at N Fairfield Avenue
(1-773 486 7511). El: Blue to California. **Open**
11am-9.30pm Tue-Fri; 9am-3pm Sat, Sun. **Main**
courses $11. **Credit** AmEx, Disc, MC, V. Eclectic
Try to ignore the fact you're eating in a tiny takeaway, as the service and food equal that of much fancier establishments. Rack of lamb comes with a demi-glace so delicious it's drinkable; rich Spanish tortillas are layered with Manchego; and Grand Marnier is put to good use in the sugary French toast.

Fat Willy's Rib Shack

2416 W Schubert Avenue, between N Western & N
Artesian Avenues (1-773 782 1800/www.fatwillys
ribshack.com). Bus 49, X49, 76. **Open** 11.30am-
10pm Mon-Thur, Sun; 11.30am-11pm Fri, Sat.
Main courses $9. **Credit** MC, V. Classic American
Instead of the South Side tradition of 'cue cash 'n' carry, here there's an actual dining room, a comfy no-frills spot with a beer and wine list and a house cocktail called the Hogarita (a cranberry and citrus Margarita). For starters, go for the smoky, greasy rib tips and the ever-so rich mac and cheese. Move on to a slab of baby backs and the beef brisket sandwich with caramelised onions and horseradish.

Feed

2803 W Chicago Avenue, at N California Avenue
(1-773 489 4600). Bus 52, 66. **Open** 11am-10pm
Mon-Fri; 3-10pm Sat, Sun. **Main courses** $7.
No credit cards. Classic American
There's a fine line between kitsch and authenticity, and this homely chicken shack sits on it. Despite the crowds of gay Moby lookalikes, Starter-jacket-clad

cooked pizzas. Choose your pizza style – red, white or New Haven-style 'plain' (red sauce, no mozzarella) – then start piling on goat's cheese, spinach, meatballs, anchovies and, if you're really going New Haven-style, clams or mashed potatoes. Accompany it with a pitcher of crisp Golden Arm, and you'll never disparagingly say 'pizza and beer joint' again.

Schwa

1466 N Ashland Avenue, between W Julian &
W Le Moyne Streets (1-773 252 1466/www.schwa
restaurant.com). El: Blue to Division. **Open** 5.30-
10.30pm Tue-Sat. **Main courses** $22. **Credit** MC, V.
Map p331 C7 **105** Contemporary American
Michael Carlson was recently named one of *Food &*
Wine's best new chefs, so you're looking at a month's wait for a table here. The draw is the cosy vibe (BYOB fine dining?) and the wow-factor Carlson and sous chef Nathan Klingbail deliver by turning seasonal creations into works of avant-garde art. There's now a tasting menu format: a three-course and a seven. Expect eats such as date purée topped with turmeric ice-cream, a deconstructed panzanella salad, and a lobster and gooseberries combo.

Scylla

1952 N Damen Avenue, between W Homer Street &
W Armitage Avenue (1-773 227 2995/www.scylla
restaurant.com). El: Blue to Western. **Open** 5.30-
10pm Tue-Thur; 5.30-11pm Fri, Sat; 5.30-9pm Sun.
Main courses $23. **Credit** AmEx, DC, Disc, MC, V.
Map p331 B6 **106** Contemporary American

Eat, Drink, Shop

Café Trinidad. *See p175.*

teenagers and yuppie moms, Feed still feels the way you'd imagine a rural Kentucky chicken shack to be. And that's good. It means juicy rotisserie chickens flanked by pitta, salsa, sides including sweet corn pudding and finales such as apple pie.

Fonda del Mar

3749 W Fullerton Avenue, between N Ridgeway & N Hamlin Avenues (1-773 489 3748). El: Blue to Logan Square. **Open** *5-10pm Mon-Thur; 5-11pm Fri; 11.30am-2pm, 5-11pm Sat; 11.30am-2pm Sun.* **Main courses** $12.50. **Credit** DC, Disc, MC, V. Mexican
Raul Arreola's menu is a nod to Mexican fish houses known as marisquerías. Firm white fish chunks get tossed with jalapeño, cilantro (coriander) and lime juice for lively ceviche; whole red snapper is topped with a dark-green veracruzana sauce; and fish tacos are flanked by a bowl of smoky squid and octopus-laden guajillo broth. But Arreola's greatest achievement is from the land: borrego en mole negro (four petite lamb chops paired with a rich mole).

Hachi's Kitchen

2521 N California Avenue, between W Altgeld Street & W Logan Boulevard (1-773 276 8080). El: Blue to California. **Open** *4.30-11pm Mon-Thur; 4.30pm-midnight Fri, Sat; 3.30-10pm Sun.* **Nigiri** $2.50. **Credit** AmEx, MC, V. Japanese
Jim Bee's followers now have a new sushi venue in which to sample his creations. Hachi is Japanese for bee; doubly fitting, as Bee's place has been buzzing since it opened. The decor is sleek, the saké and wine lists are packed with ideal sushi partners, and the innovative starters and maki steal the show from the thick, glossy cuts of expected fish varieties. Try the crunchy-creamy tuna masako. **Photo** *p173.*

Lula Café

2537 N Kedzie Boulevard, between W Albany Avenue & W Linden Place (1-773 489 9554/www.lulacafe.com). El: Blue to Logan Square. **Open** *9am-10pm Mon, Wed, Thur; 9am-11pm Sat; 9am-6pm Sun; 11.30am-2pm Sun.* **Main courses** $13. **Credit** AmEx, MC, V. Contemporary American
This low-key, local-art-filled room is one of the best seasonal American restaurants in town. Certain classics (like the much-loved roast chicken) are kept on the menu, while specials are constantly rotated. Examples include grilled artichokes with peppery mizuna greens and prosciutto ribbons; lobster and ramps with ricotta gnocchi; and wild nettle risotto with white asparagus, golden beets, blood orange and black walnuts. It's first come, first served.

Maiz

1041 N California Avenue, between W Cortez & W Thomas Streets (1-773 276 3149). Bus 53, 66, 70. **Open** *5-10pm Tue-Sun.* **Main courses** $7. **No credit cards.** Mexican
Carlos Reyna's restaurant offers every type of corn creation under the sun. The banana leaf-steamed tamale is delicious, with a feather-light exterior of smooth masa hiding tender shredded chicken boosted with green chillies. The empanadas are the lightest and flakiest in town. Sopes (lightly griddled, dense corn patties) can be topped with everything from pastor (roasted pork) to huitlacoche (mushroom-like corn fungus) to spinach.

Ñ

2977 N Elston Avenue, at W Rockwell Street (1-773 866 9898). Bus 9, 73. **Open** *6pm-2am Tue-Fri; 6pm-3am Sat.* **Main courses** $12. **Credit** MC, V. Latin American

Eat, Drink, Shop

The clubby, dimly lit sister to Tango Sur, Ñ is a lot like escaping to Buenos Aires but without the inflation. An unconsciously chic gang of international exiles sip Mojitos and flirt to Latin house at either the front bar or at tables for two. The best picadas (starters) are the simple, garlicky aubergine and the mixto plate of empanadas and beef milanesa with bright and tangy chimichurri sauce. More substantial fare includes tender short ribs.

The South Side

Blu 47

4655 S King Drive, at E 47th Street (1-773 536 6000/www.blu47restaurant.com). El: Green or Red to 47th. **Open** 11am-3pm, 5-10.30pm Tue-Sat; 10am-3pm, 5-10.30pm Sun. **Main courses** $18. **Credit** AmEx, DC, Disc, MC, V. Classic American
This upmarket eatery is hidden on the second floor of a nondescript commercial complex, but the eclectic menu (soul food transcended) makes it worth finding. Start with spicy conch fritters or crab cakes, then go for the chipotle ribs or steak roulade au poivre. Chef David Blackmon's signature bayou catfish is a tasty dish of two crispy fillets stuffed with Cajun spiced crab meat on a bed of grilled vegetables. Reservations are vital, especially for jazz night (Thur).

Café Trinidad

557 E 75th Street, between S Rhodes & S St Lawrence Avenues (1-773 846 8081). El: Red to 79th. **Open** 11am-3pm Tue-Thur; 11am-9pm Fri, Sat; 2-7pm Sun. **Main courses** $9. **Credit** AmEx, DC, Disc, MC, V. Caribbean
The Caribbean rhythms bouncing out of the speakers are as happy as the family running this gem: three generations, with Grandma in the kitchen, the daughter taking orders and the little ones clearing tables. Try the roti wrap, a giant, paper-thin, crêpe-like bread that's filled with curried potato, chickpeas and fantastic jerk chicken. **Photo** *p174.*

Harold's Chicken Shack #24

407 E 75th Street, at S Vernon Avenue & S King Drive (1-773 488 9533). El: Red to 79th. **Open** 11am-3am Mon-Thur; 11am-5am Fri, Sat; 1pm-3am Sun. **Main courses** $5. **No credit cards.** Classic American
For years, outposts of this 'chicken king' takeaway empire have multiplied like rabbits, making it nearly impossible to go five blocks without bumping into one. This dive will beat. Order the four- or six-wing plate, ask for it 'fried hard' (extra crispy) with pepper (lemon-pepper if you want zing) and get both mild and hot sauce on the side for dipping.

Lagniappe

1525 W 79th Street, at S Justine Street (1-773 994 6375). Bus 9. **Open** 11am-8pm Tue-Thur, 11am-10pm Fri, Sat. **Main courses** $8. **Credit** AmEx, DC, Disc, MC, V. Classic American
This amazin' Cajun spot used to offer takeaway-only, but now the owner has added tables and chairs. Smoky, thick gumbo has a spicy roux base, white

rice, baby shrimp and chunks of andouille sausage. Jambalaya is rich with tomato and bright with herbs; dirty rice is authentic and earthy from spleen; and the shrimp po' boy is unforgettable.

La Petite Folie

1504 E 55th Street (in the Hyde Park Shopping Center), at S Lake Park Avenue (1-773 493 1394/ www.lapetitefolie.com). Metra 55th-56th-57th Street. **Open** 11.30am-late Tue-Fri; 5pm-late Sat, Sun. **Main courses** AmEx, DC, Disc, MC, V. **Map** p332 Y17 ❿ French
Classic French in Hyde Park? Yep. A mid-life career change prompted chef Mary Mastricola to open this almost-hidden, slightly upmarket spot five years ago. Both the wine list (French, tasty stuff) and the menu (stalwarts including venison pâté, trout almondine and Alsatian choucroute garni) are well priced. Older theatre-goers pack the room at the start of the evening to gobble up the early $30 three-course prix fixe (5-6.30pm).

Soul Vegetarian East

205 E 75th Street, at S Indiana Avenue (1-773 224 0104/www.soulvegetarian.com). El: Red to 79th. **Open** 7am-10pm Mon-Thur; 7am-11pm Fri; 8am-11pm Sat; 8am-9pm Sun. **Main courses** $7. **Credit** AmEx, DC, Disc, MC, V. Vegetarian
In a family atmosphere for vegans looking to escape boring lentil hell, this neighbourhood stalwart's 'BBQ Twist' sandwich (made from wheat gluten) is as close to real barbecue pulled pork as vegetarians will get. And somehow the fried cauliflower tastes like chicken. If you've the time, sit for the full Sunday dinner: salad with tangy house dressing, fake chicken pot-pie, collard greens, corn and potatoes.

Uncle John's

337 E 69th Street, at S Prairie Avenue (1-773 892 1233). El: Red to 69th. **Open** noon-11pm Mon-Thur, noon-1am Fri, Sat. **Main courses** $9. **No credit cards.** Classic American
Arkansas native Mack Sevier produces some of the best barbecued food in town. Go for the rib tips and hot-links combo. The rib tips are smoky, extremely juicy, meatier than elsewhere and crisp around the edges. The hot links contain searing bits of red chilli and have a smoky, porky, sage-packed flavour: like a spicy breakfast sausage. Takeaway only.

Yassa

716 E 79th Street, between S Evans & S Langley Avenues (1-773 488 5599). El: Red to 79th. **Open** 11am-11.30pm daily. **Main courses** $10. **Credit** AmEx, Disc, MC, V. African
Yassa's Senegalese chef uses slow methods of cooking mingled with the wild flavour of West African spices to make Old World, yet innovative, dishes. These might include mafe, a thick stew of lamb with ground peanuts and habanero peppers, or succulent chicken yassa (grilled chicken marinated in mustard powder, vinegar and lemon juice). Accompanying the giant portions of meat, poultry and fish is wonderfully fluffy jollof rice.

Bars

Diverse dives and stirring cocktails.

Dr Samuel Johnson, who wrote one of the most famous dictionaries of the English language, is quoted as saying that 'there is no greater gift that mankind has bestowed upon itself than the corner tavern inn'. Richard M Daley, whose father spent most of his life mangling said language, begs to differ.

In the early 1900s, a hard-working printer, meatpacker or pharmacist could pick from as many as 7,600 taverns for his happy hour cocktail. No longer. When Da Mare took office in 1989, there were more than 3,000 taverns in operation. But thanks to revoked licences and a law Daley reinstated that allows residents to vote their neighbourhoods dry, the number has been cut by almost two-thirds in less than two decades.

Nevertheless, the surviving taverns, liquor store bars, old-man bars and dives are as gritty as they've ever been, holding on to their position as anything-goes, everyone's-welcome watering holes. For a dive-minus-danger feel, try downtown bike messenger hangout **Cal's Liquors**. For a dose of divey blues with a side of crudely painted porn, head to the **Old Town Ale House**. And the leading twang-tavern remains **Carol's Pub**, where the $1.50 Busch bottles do wonders to encourage a bit of two-steppin'.

Seemingly worlds away, the posh and polished cocktail crowd has its pick of the litter when it comes to swank sipping spots, with hotel bars such as **J Bar**, **Whiskey Blue**,

Base, **Aria** and **Le Bar** leading the pack. But while visitors can surely pay to play at any of the upscale enclaves, you can't buy cool. For that, you'll have to head to hipster hangs where Blue State ideas mingle with indie rock and DIY fashion. The **Rainbo Club**, **Danny's Tavern** and the **Inner Town Pub** remain the hipster hotspots, but you could pretty much take your pick of bars in the Wicker Park and Ukrainian Village neighbourhoods and run into the beercan-toting, neckerchief-wearing crowd.

Whatever style of bar you favour, you'll find that most holler 'last call' a little before 2am (3am on Saturdays). Luckily, the presence of a handful of 4am bars – the metal-punk **Exit**, last-ditch pick-up spot **Estelle's**, everyman's favourite sardine can the **Continental** – mean that your bender can go on for a little while longer. Find a 24-hour diner to kill a couple of those in-between hours, and you can start all over again come 7am.

The Loop

Aria
Fairmont Hotel, 200 N Columbus Drive, at E Lake Street (1-312 444 9494/www.ariachicago.com). El: Brown, Green, Orange, Pink or Purple to State; Red to Lake. **Open** 11.30am-midnight Mon-Thur, Sun; 11.30am-1am Fri, Sat. **Credit** AmEx, DC, Disc, MC, V. **Map** p325 J11 ❶

A surprising number of locals hang out at this hotel bar (for the hotel, *see p55*), mostly attracted by its hip-but-not-trying-too-hard atmosphere. There are plenty of comfortable places to sit: the bar stools, the tiny tables in the middle of the room and the leather booths are all appealing options. During the holidays, try the pumpkin nog, a secret holiday elixir (served by request only) designed to help numb the pain of family get-togethers.

Base
Hard Rock Hotel, 230 N Michigan Avenue, at E Lake Street (1-312 345 1000/www.hardrockhotelchicago. com). El: Brown, Green, Orange, Pink or Purple to State; Red to Lake. **Open** 11am-2am Mon-Thur, Sun; 11am-3am Fri, Sat. **Credit** AmEx, DC, Disc, MC, V. **Map** p325 J11 ❷

The best Bars

For rising up
J Bar. *See p179.*

For diving down
Cal's Liquors. *See p177.*

For nouveau Wicker Park
Rodan. *See p188.*

For scotch on the rock ('n' roll)
Delilah's. *See p181.*

For making yourself at home
Danny's Tavern. *See p187.*

Eat, Drink, Shop

Cal's Liquors, just as beautifully basic on the inside.

Lounging on low-slung leather chairs and couches among a crowd of young post-workers, sipping a Bellini to the musical accompaniment of Dogs Die in Hot Cars, it's easy to forget you're in a hotel lobby (*see p57*). Until, that is, a tourist mom in a hot pink T-shirt barrels through pushing a huge stroller. As the night wears on, the drinkers get hipper, the beats get louder and the tourists get some sleep.

Cal's Liquors

400 S Wells Street, at W Van Buren Street (1-312 922 6392/www.drinkatcalsbar.com). El: Blue, Brown, Orange, Pink or Purple to LaSalle. **Open** 7am-7pm Mon-Thur; 7am-2am Fri, Sat. **Credit** AmEx, Disc, MC, V. **Map** p325 G13 ❸
Cal himself slings insults and Old Style in this fabulously grubby Loop dive, where a handful of stools are warmed by bike messengers, construction workers and the occasional gritty punk there to check out bands with names such as Urinal Mints and Rabid Rabbit banging out music from a corner of the room.

Monk's Pub

205 W Lake Street, between N Wells & N Franklin Streets (1-312 357 6665). El: Blue, Brown, Green, Orange, Pink or Purple to Clark; Red to Lake. **Open** 9am-2am Mon-Fri. **Credit** AmEx, DC, Disc, MC, V. **Map** p325 G11 ❹
For more than 30 years, this tavern has cornered the Loop market for medieval-themed dive-bar drinking. Beyond the heavy doors, you'll find an after-work crowd of suits and occasional skirts downing beer and adding to the piles of peanut shells.

17 West

17 W Adams Street, between S State & S Dearborn Streets (1-312 427 3170/www.17westchicago.com). El: Blue or Red to Monroe; Brown, Green, Orange, Pink or Purple to Adams. **Open** 10.45am-9pm Mon-Wed; 10.45am-4pm Thur-Sat. **Credit** AmEx, MC, V. **Map** p325 H12 ❺
The old Berghoff bar has been cleaned up, complete with a name change and a new, frilly Martini list. Now that the old wall that separated the eating and

drinking areas has been taken down, the room is a little airier. However, the century-old German pub was always all about its gorgeous, room-length wooden bar, full of a mix of tourists, after-work suits and afternoon drinkers.

Whiskey Blue

172 W Adams Street, between S LaSalle & S Wells Streets (1-312 782 4933/www.starwoodhotels.com/whotels). El: Blue or Red to Jackson; Brown, Orange, Pink or Purple to Quincy. **Open** 4pm-2am daily. **Credit** AmEx, DC, Disc, MC, V. **Map** p325 H12 ❻
Just as out-of-town scenesters are drawn to stay at the W City Center, so its bar lures its fair share of local hipsters, scattered across its lounge-worthy leather chairs. Models moonlight as waitresses, serving sexed-up singles looking to clink Cosmos as the evening draws in. The well-stocked bar lives up to its name; try a Manhattan if you're feeling nostalgic.

The South Loop & Chinatown

The South Loop

Grace O'Malley's

1416 S Michigan Avenue, between E 14th & E 16th Streets (1-312 588 1800/www.graceomalleychicago.com). El: Green, Orange or Red to Roosevelt. **Open** 11.30am-2am Mon-Sat; 9.30am-2am Sun. **Credit** AmEx, DC, Disc, MC, V. **Map** p324 J15 ❼
Once you've spent an evening in this quasi-Celtic enterprise, perched up at the beautiful and shiny wooden bar, you may be moved to consider staying in the South Loop forever just to make it your local hangout. Be prepared to drool when the guy next to you orders a burger on one of the soft pretzel buns.

Weather Mark Tavern

1503 S Michigan Avenue, between E 14th & E 16th Streets (1-312 588 0230/www.weathermarktavern.com). El: Green, Orange or Red to Roosevelt. **Open** 11.30am-2am Mon-Fri; 10.30am-3am Sat; 10.30am-2am Sun. **Credit** Disc, MC, V. **Map** p324 J15 ❽

Wine at **Swirl** (*left*), or champagne cocktails at **J Bar**? Your call. *See p179.*

If you thought the days of sailor bars were over, think again: this cheery, nautically themed hangout, complete with full-size sails dividing the long room into canoodling areas, has brought it back, albeit with a South Loop twist (think sun-kissed yuppie boaters rather than pirates). No boat of your own? Refreshing cocktails, among them the lemongrass-spiked Almost Stormy, help sail you away.

Chinatown

Bertucci's Corner

300 W 24th Street, at S Princeton Avenue (1-312 225 2848). El: Red to Cermak-Chinatown. **Open** 11am-10pm Mon-Thur; 11am-11pm Fri; 4-11pm Sat; 3-9pm Sun. **Credit** AmEx, Disc, MC, V.
Bertucci's is primarily a restaurant, but it's always grand to stop in for a Peroni at the bar and rub elbows with the old Italian locals who remember Chinatown before it was Chinatown. The joint's been around since '33; the regulars from those days are long gone, but they're immortalised in a dusty photo hanging behind the bar, and with mugs hanging from the ceiling. Hungry? Hearty pastas or sausage and peppers will do the job.

The Near North Side

River North

Billy Goat Tavern

Lower level, 430 N Michigan Avenue, at E Hubbard Street (1-312 222 1525/www.billygoattavern.com).

El: Red to Grand. **Open** 6am-2am Mon-Fri; 10am-3am Sat; 11am-2am Sun. **No credit cards.** **Map** p326 J11 ❾
A stream of tourists is drawn here by two claims to fame: the curse laid on the Cubs by the bar's then-owner Bill Sianis when he was turned away from a game (*see p50*), and the 'cheezborger' skit on *Saturday Night Live* that it inspired. Still, the Billy Goat remains a fine bar: grimy, charm-chocked and frequented by the kind of cursing newsmen who've been coming here since the days of Mike Royko.

Bin 36

339 N Dearborn Street, at W Kinzie Street (1-312 755 9463/www.bin36.com). El: Brown or Purple to Merchandise Mart; Red to Grand. **Open** 5-10pm Mon-Thur; 5-11pm Fri, Sat; 5-9pm Sun. **Credit** AmEx, DC, Disc, MC, V. **Map** p325 H11 ❿
Post-work, loosened-tie types love to spend happy hour at this River North wine bar that side-saddles the House of Blues. Who can blame them? The wine flights are affordable and interesting, the cheese selection is one of the best in town, and the black-board of 'tavern shared plates' offers just enough sustenance to soak up another round.

Celtic Crossings

751 N Clark Street, between W Superior Street & W Chicago Avenue (1-312 337 1005). El: Brown or Purple to Chicago. **Open** 2pm-2am Mon-Fri, Sun; 2pm-3am Sat. **Credit** AmEx, DC, Disc, MC, V. **Map** p326 H10 ⓫
It usually takes nothing but a four-leaf-clover cut out of construction paper to make a bar 'Irish', but this tchotchke-filled River North pub is a little different:

certified by the James Joyce Society, it's actually full of Real Live Irish People. Throw down that Guinness with confidence: this is the real thing, or as close as you'll find to it in this part of town.

Clark Street Ale House

742 N Clark Street, between W Superior Street & W Chicago Avenue (1-312 642 9253). El: Red to Chicago. **Open** 4pm-4am Mon-Fri; 4pm-5am Sat; 5pm-4am Sun. **Credit** AmEx, DC, Disc, MC, V. **Map** p326 H10 ⑫

A handful of people come to this dim, homely pub and hang out without ever ordering a drink, choosing instead to sit atop wooden stools and chat up the bartender. But resistance may prove trickier once you've spied the two dozen beers on tap, most of them domestic gems such as the Great Lakes Brewing Company's Eliot Ness.

Fado

100 W Grand Avenue, at N Clark Street (1-312 836 0066/www.fadoirishpub.com). El: Red to Grand. **Open** 11.30am-2am Mon-Fri; 9am-2.30am Sat, Sun. **Credit** AmEx, DC, Disc, MC, V. **Map** p326 H10 ⑬

Yes, it's a chain, but don't let that deter you. All three floors of this dark, wood-filled and slightly over-stylised Irish pub are packed with young professionals getting sloshed as they loosen their ties and tongues. After trying the Black Velveteen, a smooth and sweet blend of Guinness and cider, you may be inclined to join them.

J Bar

James Hotel, 616 N Rush Street, at E Ontario Street (1-312 660 7200). El: Red to Grand. **Open** 6pm-2am Tue-Fri; 8pm-3am Sat. **Credit** AmEx, Disc, MC, V. **Map** p326 J10 ⑭

These two slick rooms in the James Hotel (*see p63*) are awash with shiny mirrored tiles and video art, a perfectly slick backdrop for the richest and prettiest people in Chicago to sup on Martinis garnished with olive and blue cheese lollipops. It's usually so packed that you might even have to stay overnight in order to snag a seat. **Photo** *p178*.

Le Bar

Sofitel, 20 E Chestnut Street, at N Wabash Avenue (1-312 324 4000). El: Red to Chicago. **Open** 3pm-1am Mon-Wed, Sun; 3pm-2am Thur-Sat. **Credit** AmEx, DC, Disc, MC, V. **Map** p326 H9 ⑮

This sensual sipping spot inside the Sofitel draws a good crowd of locals along with the resident out-of-towners. Plush leather stools, a cool-to-the-touch chrome bar and well-made (and incredibly expensive) cocktails lend it a cosmopolitan vibe, but it's the bad techno that gives it that authentically European edge.

Motel Bar

600 W Chicago Avenue, at N Larrabee Street (1-312 822 2900). El: Brown or Purple to Chicago. **Open** 4pm-2am Mon-Fri; 6pm-3am Sat; 6pm-2am Sun. **Credit** AmEx, MC, V. **Map** p326 F10 ⑯

The boys behind Division Street restaurant Mas (*see p172*) are also the ones to thank for this low-lit, earth-toned lounge. It's nothing like any motel you'll have checked into recently, but you'll dig the throwback classic cocktails, the 'room service' comfort food, the unpretentious staff and the eclectic jukebox.

Redhead

16 W Ontario Street, between N State & N Dearborn Streets (1-312 640 1000/www.theredheadpianobar. com). El: Red to Grand. **Open** 7pm-4am Mon-Fri, Sun; 7pm-5am Sat. **Credit** AmEx, DC, Disc, MC, V. **Map** p326 H10 ⑰

The piano-bar fiend who likes his joints a little more Grace than Will will probably find that this long-standing, upmarket basement spot hits all the right notes. But even though the guys here aren't gay, they are at least well dressed: bouncers inspect outfits as well as IDs, and flip-flops and T-shirts won't get through the door.

Rossi's

412 N State Street, between W Kinzie & W Hubbard Streets (1-312 644 5775). El: Red to Grand. **Open** 7am-2am Mon-Fri, Sun; 7am-3am Sat. **No credit cards. Map** p326 H11 ⑱

Like a secret chamber of debauchery, the red door to this State Street bar reveals no sign of what's inside. Turns out it's a dark, cabin-like and oddly characterful space with a mixed crowd of lewd yuppies and bitter locals. Pissed off? Up to no good? You'll fit in just fine.

Swirl

111 W Hubbard Street, between N Clark & N LaSalle Streets (1-312 828 9000). El: Brown or Purple to Merchandise Mart; Red to Grand. **Open** 5pm-2am Tue-Fri; 7pm-3am Sat. **Credit** AmEx, Disc, MC, V. **Map** p326 H11 ⑲

With so many wine bars opening around town, it's good to know that there's a bona-fide wine lounge to which one can escape. With toothsome pizzas, jazz acts playing on weekends and decor straight out of a West Elm catalogue, it's easy to forget that wine is the focus at Swirl. But there are plenty of gems to be found on the 50-bottle list. **Photo** *p178*.

The Magnificent Mile & Streeterville

Lucky Strike Lanes

322 E Illinois Street, between N Fairbanks & N McClurg Courts (1-312 245 8331). El: Red to Grand. **Open** 11am-2am Mon-Fri, Sun; 11am-3am Sat. **Credit** AmEx, DC, Disc, MC, V. **Map** p326 J11 ⑳

The original LA outpost of Lucky Strike is a fave on *Entourage*. Chicago's branch is more local and less celeb-studded, but you can still feel (and act) like one of the beautiful people as you down drinks and munch on better-than-you'd-expect grub in the wine bar. Alternatively, make it more casual by playing pool or bowling while you quaff a cold one.

Eat, Drink, Shop

This dim and cavernous basement bar holds a secret underground community of sexy, friendly people and cheap drinks ($2 sangria on Tuesdays, $3 chocolate Martinis on Wednesdays, half-price drinks on Thursdays), both of which you'll want to get to know better. You might do well to investigate the food menu before things get out of hand.

Red Lion Pub

2446 N Lincoln Avenue, between W Fullerton Avenue & W Altgeld Street (1-773 728 8933). El: Brown, Purple or Red to Fullerton. **Open** noon-1.30am daily. **Credit** AmEx, MC, V.
Map p328 F5 ㉜

Imported scotches aren't the only spirits served at this imitation Brit-pub: listen up and you could tune in to the occasional ghost story. If you ask nicely, silver-tongued owner Colin Cordwell may take a break from carefully eyeing DePaul students' IDs to brag about all the spooked former employees of his supposedly haunted haunt. The food menu, inevitably, includes fish and chips.

Rose's Lounge

2656 N Lincoln Avenue, between W Wrightwood Avenue & W Diversey Parkway (1-773 327 4000). El: Brown or Purple to Diversey. **Open** 4pm-2am Mon-Fri, Sun; 4pm-3am Sat. **No credit cards.**
Map p328 E4 ㉝

Rose, the cute Eastern European owner-bartender, hasn't changed a thing since the '70s at her divey taproom. A shingled awning hangs over the back of the bar, wood panelling lines the walls and plenty of eclectic grandma knick-knacks mingle with the bottles of liquor. With a buck buying you either seven plays on the jukebox or a mug of Old Style, even the prices are old-fashioned.

Shoes Pub

1134 W Armitage Avenue, between N Seminary and N Clifton Avenues (1-773 871 4640). El: Brown or Purple to Armitage. **Open** 3pm-2am Mon-Fri; 11am-2am Sat, Sun. **No credit cards.**
Map p328 E6 ㉞

This hole-in-the-wall favourite is worlds apart from its neighbourhood competition: no-nonsense bartender Karen has more sass than all of Armitage's boutique salesgirls combined. Al (a fixture who 'kinda' works there) asserts that it's 'the joint where you take your funny, drunk uncle'. The darts competition is fierce; in addition to a Hank-Willie-Johnny jukebox, it's BYOCD.

Lakeview & around

Lakeview & Wrigleyville

For gay and lesbian bars in Boystown, *see p246.*

Cubby Bear

1059 W Addison Street, at N Clark Street (1-773 327 1662/www.cubbybear.com). El: Red to Addison. **Open** *Cubs home games* 10am-2am Mon-Sat; 11am-1am Sun. *Other times* 4pm-2am Mon-Fri; 11am-3am Sat; 11am-2am Sun. **Credit** AmEx, Disc, MC, V.
Map p329 E1 ㉟

Rock 'n' roll all night at Lincoln Park local **Delilah's**. *See p181.*

Cubs fans pack the sticky floor of this Wrigleyville hangout before and during the game, but it's after the home team has lost (or, less frequently, won) that the joint really gets busy. Murphy's Bleachers (3655 N Sheffield Avenue, at W Waveland Avenue, no phone) also draws Cubs fans in their hundreds, but this is the next best thing to being at the game.

Gingerman Tavern

3740 N Clark Street, between W Waveland Avenue & W Grace Street (1-773 549 2050). El: Red to Addison. **Open** 3pm-2am Mon-Fri; noon-3am Sat; noon-2am Sun. **No credit cards. Map** p329 E1 ㊱
The two coin-op pool tables suck, but the Gingerman is still a great place for a game of pool. The talent varies widely, from journeyman players who run the table to apprentice drinkers who struggle to hold a cue. A fine range of beers helps make this the best local bar for the meathead-avoider.

Hungry Brain

2319 W Belmont Avenue, between N Oakley & N Western Avenues (1-773 935 2118). El: Brown to Paulina. **Open** 8pm-2am Tue-Fri, Sun; 8pm-3am Sat. **No credit cards.**
This converted theatre has kept its artsy charm with thrift-store finds galore. Art-school dropouts flank the Ms Pac-Man/Galaga game and the great juke-box, while friendly bartenders serve cheap beers with a smile. An old piano, couches and a coffee table sit on the small stage, which gets occasional use for one-night shows.

L & L Tavern

3207 N Clark Street, between W Belmont & W Aldine Avenues (1-773 528 1303). El: Brown, Purple or Red to Belmont. **Open** 2pm-2am Mon-Thur; noon-2am Fri, Sun; noon-3am Sat. **No credit cards. Map** p329 F2 ㊲
The Clark and Belmont 'hood has a unique mix of runaway trannnies, wasted Cubs fans and local renters who love a bargain. This no-frills Lakeview tavern keeps the madness at bay with friendly bartenders, who've been known to buy rounds during afternoon *Jeopardy*. Other alcoholic highlights include a $2 beer of the month and two dozen Irish whiskeys.

Resi's Bierstube

2034 W Irving Park Road, between N Seeley & N Hoyne Avenues (1-773 472 1749). El: Brown to Irving Park. **Open** 2pm-2am Mon-Fri; 2pm-3am Sat; 3pm-midnight Sun. **Credit** MC, V. **Map** p330 B0 ㊳
This longstanding North Side favourite comes into its own in warmer weather, when you should supplement some of the great Deutsch food with a glass or two of the Franziskaner *weissbier*. The beer garden could use some better seating to replace the weathered benches, but the massive trees and German beer lanterns give it a cosy vibe.

Sheffield's

3258 N Sheffield Avenue, between W Belmont Avenue & W School Street (1-773 281 4989/http://sheffieldschicago.com). El: Brown, Purple or Red to

Belmont. **Open** 3pm-2am Mon-Fri; noon-3am Sat; noon-2am Sun. **Credit** AmEx, DC, Disc, MC, V. **Map** p329 E2 ㊴
In winter, all three rooms of this casual bar are packed. During the summer, the huge beer garden turns into a laid-back college reunion on weekend nights, with baseball-capped dudes and spaghetti-strapped chicks flanking the outdoor bar for $2 'Bad Beers of the Month' (Old Milwaukee and Stroh's, say). Food is cooked over a charcoal grill.

Spot 6

3343 N Clark Street, at W Buckingham Place (1-773 388 0185). El: Red to Addison. **Open** 5pm-2am Mon-Fri, Sun; 5pm-3am Sun. **Credit** MC, V. **Map** p329 E2 ㊵
It's tricky to peg this place. At times it feels like a neighbourhood bar, yet with a loungey vibe. Factor in the pool table and cheap drinks, and you have an ambitious hole in the wall. Bands play at weekends, so maybe it's really a music venue. Whatever the case may be, there's something for more or less everyone.

Sylvie's Lounge

1902 W Irving Park Road, at N Wolcott Avenue (1-773 871 6239). El: Brown to Irving Park. **Open** 4pm-2am Mon-Fri; 4pm-3am Sat; 7pm-2am Sun. **No credit cards. Map** p330 C0 ㊶
Long known as a host of highly competitive darts tournaments, this family-run, two-room bar now fancies itself as a rock venue for young acts getting their feet wet. Old Town School of Folk Music students favour the open-mic nights; on other evenings, the cheap cover indicates that things are below pro-level. The mostly bottled beers are no bargain, but this is still a good spot to check out local up-and-comers.

Twisted Spoke

3369 N Clark Street, at W Roscoe Street (1-773 525 5300/www.twistedspoke.com). El: Brown, Purple or Red to Belmont. **Open** 11am-2am Mon-Fri; 9am-3am Sat; 9am-2am Sun. **Credit** AmEx, MC, V. **Map** p329 E2 ㊷
This motorcycle-themed mainstay is a biker bar for kinder, gentler, weekend warriors and their admirers. Beer is the drink of choice, but a nice whiskey list offers an alternative. Don't miss Saturday's midnight Smut & Eggs, when vintage porn plays on the tube as the kitchen rolls out the brunch menu.

Roscoe Village

Four Moon Tavern

1847 W Roscoe Street, between N Wolcott & Ravenswood Avenues (1-773 929 6666). El: Brown to Paulina. **Open** 5pm-2am Mon-Fri; 10am-3am Sat; 10am-2am Sun. **Credit** AmEx, DC, Disc, MC, V. **Map** p330 C2 ㊸
A wood-panelled ceiling, a pool table, Texas longhorn skulls, assorted beer memorabilia and a jukebox stocked with jazz, standards and even bluegrass all combine to make this a nice spot in which to relax

over a well-made cocktail or a regionally brewed beer. Staff and patrons dabble in theatre, so keep an eye out for local play postings.

Johnny's
3425 N Lincoln Avenue, at W Roscoe Street (1-773 248 3000). El: Brown to Paulina. **Open** 9am-2am daily. **No credit cards**. **Map** p330 C1 ㊹
To get into this old-timey watering hole, Johnny himself has to buzz you in. Once you're inside, it's nostalgia central: a '60s jukebox, retro beer posters, old newspapers lying in the corner and even Christmas decorations from way back when. Better still, if the longtime proprietor enjoys talking to you, he'll keep the beer flowing past closing time.

Andersonville, Edgewater & Uptown

Carol's Pub
4659 N Clark Street, between W Wilson & W Leland Avenues (1-773 334 2402). El: Red to Wilson. **Open** 9am-2am Mon, Tue; 11am-4am Wed-Fri, Sun; 11am-5am Sat. **No credit cards**.
A honky-tonk in Sheridan Park with $1.50 Busch bottles, country and western karaoke on Thursdays, and music from the house band Diamondback on weekends. A pool table out back, a greasy grill and a Hank-filled jukebox round out the grit fest.

Moody's Pub
5910 N Broadway Street, between W Rosedale & W Thorndale Avenues (1-773 275 2696/www.moodys pub.com). El: Red to Thorndale. **Open** 11.30am-1am Mon-Sat; noon-1am Sun. **No credit cards**.
The beer garden at Moody's has the reputation of being one of the best in Chicago, which is why it's often rammed with ass-to-elbow crowds. The beer-and-burger haven is actually more enjoyable in winter, when you can snag a table by the fireplace and get cosy with your date. Bring a flashlight to read the menu: the place is so dark that you could carry on an affair with your spouse sat across the room.

Simon's Tavern
5210 N Clark Street, between W Foster & W Farragut Avenues (1-773 878 0894). El: Red to Berwyn. **Open** 11am-2am Mon-Fri, Sun; 11am-3am Sat. **No credit cards**.
If you're lucky, you can snag a couch out back by the fireplace at Simon's, where you can take in the cool vintage bar (built in the '30s to resemble a bar on the *SS Normandie*), sip some seasonal grog and check out the friendly neighbourhood crowd.

Lincoln Square & Ravenswood

Glunz Bavarian Haus
4128 N Lincoln Avenue, at W Warner Avenue (1-773 472 0965/www.glunzbavarianhaus.com). El: Brown to Irving Park. **Open** noon-2am Tue-Sun. **Credit** AmEx, DC, Disc, MC, V.

Deutschland takes a lot of pride in its beer. So before you get schnitzel-faced at this friendly German restaurant, sample some of the dozen or so ales and lagers on tap. If you don't know your *weizen* from your *dunkel*, the waitresses are happy to make recommendations; as, for that matter, are the German-American families sitting nearby.

Northwest Side

Fifth Province Pub
4626 N Knox Avenue, between W Wilson & W Leland Avenues (1-773 282 7035/www.irishamhc. com/5thprovince). El: Blue to Montrose. **Open** 4pm-12.30am Fri, Sat. **Credit** MC, V.
An Irish American Heritage Center wouldn't be an Irish American heritage centre without an on-site pub, would it? Supplementing a library and museum, this weekends-only hangout serves Guinness, hearty pub food and live music. If everyone were as beer-minded as the Irish, cultural institutions would be flooded with the thirsty and eager-to-learn.

Martini Club
4933 N Milwaukee Avenue, at W Gale Street (1-773 202 9444). El: Blue to Jefferson Park. **Open** 2pm-2am Mon-Fri; 2pm-3am Sat; 4pm-2am Sun. **Credit** AmEx, MC, V.
Polish Pride abounds at this swank, low-lit cocktail lounge: artful black-and-white photos of Krakow's Wawel area adorn the walls, sugar-sweet Euro pop trickles from the loudspeakers and everyone seems to be drinking vodka. The booths are comfortable, the crowd is friendly and everything on the Martini list is irresistible.

Montrose Saloon
2933 W Montrose Avenue, at N Richmond Street (1-773 463 7663). Bus 78. **Open** 2pm-2am Mon-Thur; noon-2am Fri, Sun; noon-3am Sat. **No credit cards**.
This ideal neighbourhood dive is somehow still overlooked. The wood panelling is balanced out by exposed brick, a fantastic tin ceiling and stained-glass lamps hanging over the bar, while the giant outdoor patio is one of the area's best-kept secrets: toss horseshoes, play the bean-bag game, or just drink and smoke. Don't mind the condo-dwellers across the street complaining about the noise: they'll either move soon or come down to join you.

The Near West Side

The West Loop & Greektown

Cobra Lounge
235 N Ashland Avenue, at W Walnut Street (1-312 226 6300/www.cobralounge.com). El: Green or Pink to Ashland. **Open** 11am-2am Mon-Fri; 5pm-3am Sat; 8pm-2am Sun. **Credit** MC, V. **Map** p330 D11 ㊺
This industrial-outskirts spot opened in 2006 and quickly became the best meet-up spot in the city for the ink-and-metal crowd. Ageing punks and young

The golden gander

It started, as most small businesses tend to start, with a big idea and a small amount of money. In 1986, fortysomething company man John Hall was waiting for a delayed plane when he stumbled on a magazine article about microbrewed beer. Call it inspiration or call it a mid-life crisis, but Hall decided there and then that Chicago needed such a brewery, and that he was just the man to start it. Despite the fact that he had precisely no experience of the brewing industry, Hall quit his job and set up shop close to the then-scruffy intersection of North and Clybourn Avenues. Two years later, the **Goose Island Brew Pub** opened its doors.

Fast-forward a couple of decades, and Goose Island has grown from an on-a-whim business start-up to one of the 30 largest breweries in the country, despite never distributing its beer beyond the Midwest. Hall's original pub (*see p181*) has grown from humble beginnings into a buzzing scene, with staff supplementing the ever-changing list of beers with food and even guided tours (*see p150*). In recent years, it's been joined by a sibling up near Wrigley Field (3535 N Clark Street, at W Addison Street, 1-773 832 9040), which has a sporting twist. All the while, the company has increased its profile by sponsoring and supporting a whole host of local events, from beer festivals to bike rides.

The selling point, though, remains the award-winning beer, most of it now brewed out of the company's plant in West Town under the supervision of brewmaster Greg Hall (John's son). Honker's Ale remains the best-seller, a deeply moreish and surprisingly creamy-tasting pale ale that's widely available throughout the city; other brewpub perennials include a pungent IPA and the richly flavoured Nut Brown Ale. Some beers are seasonal: Christmas Ale emerges each year in the run-up to the holidays, while summer sees the less charismatic 312 wheat beer soar in popularity. Others are brewed in what amount to limited editions, such as the glorious Pere Jacques (reminiscent of Belgian brew Orval). And still others come and go in the blink of an eye: check www.gooseisland.com to see what's on tap during the week you're here.

While Goose Island remains very much a Chicago company (it has even used the slogan 'Drink Local'), it's about to get a lot more visible. The firm signed a distribution deal with Anheuser-Busch in 2006, vastly increasing its reach across the Midwest and the rest of the US. Some local beer hounds were up in arms about the marriage, but the brewery remains proud of its independence. 'It's the same beer from the same brewery,' insists Greg Hall, 'only now it's on a different truck.' It still tastes good to us.

Eat, Drink, Shop

hipsters mix beneath a high ceiling and walls done out in reds and blacks, all to a soundtrack that emanates from one of the best jukeboxes in town. There's a separate plush room for dining, but the grub alone isn't worth a special trip.

Fulton Lounge

955 W Fulton Street, at N Morgan Street (1-312 942 9500/www.fultonlounge.com). Bus 65. **Open** 5pm-2am Mon-Fri; 5pm-3am Sat. **Credit** AmEx, Disc, MC, V. **Map** p330 E11 ⑯
Saturday nights at this Fulton district hot spot are packed. You may have to queue to get in, and then wait once at the bar; it's a good thing the expertly made cocktails are worth it. Opt for a weekday when there's space to take in the charming bookshelves, the exposed brick walls and diverse crowd. Then, perhaps, you'll be able to see what the fuss is about.

Wicker Park & around

Ukrainian Village & West Town

Club Foot

1824 W Augusta Street, between N Wood & N Honore Streets (1-773 489 0379). El: Blue to Division. **Open** 8pm-2am Mon-Fri, Sun; 8pm-3am Sat. **No credit cards. Map** p331 C9 ⑰
Fans of VH1's *I Love the '80s* will be in heaven at Club Foot, surrounded by walls plastered with vintage concert tees and glass cases jam-packed with every collectible toy from the decade that taste forgot. During the week, there's room to take it all in, but weekends get crammed with locals rocking white belts as they shoot pool to a DJed mix of punk, indie rock and occasionally polka (well, this is Ukrainian Village).

Inner Town Pub

1935 W Thomas Street, at N Winchester Avenue (1-773 235 9795). El: Blue to Division. **Open** 3pm-2am Mon-Fri, Sun; 3pm-3am Sat. **No credit cards. Map** p331 B9 ⑱
Crammed with more clutter than your eccentric aunt's house, this former speakeasy serves cheap booze (all shots are $3) and warm salted nuts in true dive-bar fashion. Indie-rockers on their way to the Empty Bottle (*see p256*) take advantage of the free pool, while a smattering of toothless old-timers keep it gritty with war stories and phlegmy coughs.

Matchbox

770 N Milwaukee Avenue, between W Carpenter Street & W Ogden Avenue (1-312 666 9292). El: Blue to Chicago. **Open** 4pm-2am Mon-Fri, Sun; 4pm-3am Sat. **Credit** AmEx, DC, Disc, MC, V.
If the thought of being crammed inside this tiny boxcar of a bar makes you a little bit nervous, just relax. In nice weather, the patio practically doubles the capacity of the place, and is the perfect spot in which to throw back one of the top-shelf Margaritas. Even if the patio's not open for business, the house-made infused vodkas and perfect Gimlets more than make up for the tight squeeze.

Cobra Lounge. *See p184.*

Rainbo Club

*1150 N Damen Avenue, between W Haddon Avenue
& W Division Street (1-773 489 5999). El: Blue to
Division.* **Open** 4pm-2am Mon-Fri, Sun; 4pm-3am
Sat. **No credit cards. Map** p331 B7 ⑨
The bittersweet reality of great little dives is that
they often lose their charm when they get overrun
by masses of clingers-on. Somehow, this spot has
managed to remain an underground favourite. The
local artists and musicians who frequent it hold on
to terra firma with cheap drink in hand, awaiting a
turn in the photo booth while nodding to everything
from Aesop Rock to Black Sabbath.

Wicker Park & Bucktown

Celebrity

*1856 W North Avenue, between N Honore Street
& N Wolcott Avenue (1-773 365 0091/www.celeb
chicago.com). El: Blue to Damen.* **Open** 7pm-2am
Tue-Fri; 7pm-3am Sat. **Credit** AmEx, MC, V.
Map p331 C6 ⑩
Wicker Park gets its bling on with yet another one
of these not-quite-a-bar-but-not-quite-a-club joints.
The crowd's as diverse as the drinks, which range
from cans of Old Style to bottles of Cristal. If you're
not into DJs and graffiti art, forget it. But then you're
probably in the wrong 'hood anyway.

Charleston

*2076 N Hoyne Avenue, at W Charleston Street
(1-773 489 4757). El: Blue (O'Hare branch) to
Western.* **Open** 3pm-2am Mon-Fri; noon-2am Sat,
Sun. **No credit cards. Map** p331 B6 ⑪
Will the hipsters, yuppies, freaks, dirty old men and
bluegrass bands that pack this tchotchke-ridden corner taproom, easily one of Bucktown's neighbourhood favourites, lose any of their charm now that
the place is officially smoke-free? Not really; they'll
just smell better.

Danny's Tavern

*1951 W Dickens Avenue, between N Damen & N
Winchester Avenues (1-773 489 6457). El: Blue to
Damen.* **Open** 7pm-2am Mon-Fri, Sun; 7pm-3am Sat.
No credit cards. Map p331 C6 ⑫
The floors of this converted house in Bucktown
shake so much from the weight of hot-footed trendsetters that you'd think the place is seconds from
caving in. Most of the dancing is done to a mix of
hip hop, electro and rock on the weekends, plus a
insanely popular first-Wednesday funk party called
Sheer Magic, but there are plenty of nooks and crannies in which to sit back, relax and people-watch.

Estelle's

*2013 W North Avenue, at N Milwaukee Avenue
(1-773 782 0450). El: Blue to Damen.* **Open** 7pm-
4am Mon-Fri, Sun; 7pm-5am Sat. **No credit cards.**
Map p331 B7 ⑬
Can't take the occasionally hipper-than-thou crowd
at the Rainbo Club (*see above*)? This low-key sanctuary should do the trick. No one's trying to out-cool

anyone here, though later on, they're definitely trying to pick each other up. Still, feel free to strike up
a conversation with a stranger over late-night bar
eats, served until 3am.

Exit

*1315 W North Avenue, between N Ada & N
Throop Streets (1-773 395 2700/www.exitchicago.
com). El: Red to North/Clybourn.* **Open** 9pm-
4am Mon-Fri, Sun; 9pm-5am Sat. **Credit** AmEx,
Disc, MC, V.
Thursday is fetish night and Monday offers punk
rock, but this haunt for the black-clad is rolling with
freaks virtually every evening of the week. As with
any pop-culture clique, Exit tends to have an insid-
ers-only feel, but brave souls looking for their
Ministry and PBR fix have to start somewhere.
There's a $5 cover on weekends.

Lemmings

*1850 N Damen Avenue, between W Moffat &
W Cortland Streets (1-773 862 1688). El: Blue
to Damen.* **Open** 4pm-2am Mon-Fri; noon-3am
Sat; noon-2am Sun. **Credit** AmEx, DC, MC, V.
Map p331 B6 ⑭
Don't take the name literally: there's a nice crowd
here, but the joint isn't packed with followers, so you
can usually find a seat from which to soak up the
comforting vibe. Those who drink here generally
want to try to keep things low-key, but they're running out of competition on the Ms Pac-Man machine.
An excellent, mellow option.

Leopard Lounge

*1645 W Cortland Street, between N Marshfield
Avenue & N Paulina Street (1-773 862 7877/www.
leopardlounge.com). Bus 9, 73.* **Open** 6pm-2am
Tue-Fri; 6pm-3am Sat. **Credit** AmEx, Disc, MC, V.
Map p331 C6 ⑮
The animal prints, the pin-up girls, the Neil Diamond
impersonators… you won't have seen this much
kitsch since the B-52s broke up (they did break up,
right?). But true lounges are rare in this part of town,
and besides, the Leopard gets extra points for being
big enough that you can usually snag a seat and
quiet enough that you can usually eavesdrop on an
adjacent conversation.

Map Room

*1949 N Hoyne Avenue, between W Homer Street &
W Armitage Avenue (1-773 252 7636). El: Blue
(O'Hare branch) to Western.* **Open** 6.30am-2am Mon-
Fri; 7.30am-3am Sat; 11am-2am Sun. **Credit** AmEx,
Disc, MC, V. **Map** p331 B6 ⑯
There's barely room for another beer on the killer
list at the Map Room, nor is there space for any more
Bucktown locals around the pool table. Tuesday is
International Night, which means food from a dif-
ferent ethnic spot around town each week. Plates are
free with an order of two drinks.

Marshall McGearty Tobacco Lounge

*1553 N Milwaukee Avenue, between W Honore
Street & N Damen Avenue (1-773 772 8410/
www.mmsmokes.com). El: Blue to Damen.*

Open 11am-midnight Mon-Thur, Sun; 11am-2am Fri, Sat. **Credit** AmEx, Disc, MC, V. **Map** p331 B7 **57**

This 2006 opening, owned by tobacco behemoth RJ Reynolds, aims to circumvent the city's smoking ban (*see p189* **Smoke Alarm**) by trading as a tobacco retailer, hawking hand-rolled cigarettes alongside drinks both alcoholic and caffeinated. Part café and part bar, it offers a retro vibe in which to plug in your laptop, scrawl some emo poetry or engage in a bout of Battleship.

Nick's Beergarden

1516 N Milwaukee Avenue, between W Honore Street & N Damen Avenue (1-773 252 1155/ www.nicksbeergarden.com). El: Blue to Damen. **Open** 4pm-4am Mon-Fri, Sun; 4pm-5am Sat. **Credit** AmEx, MC, V. **Map** p331 C7 **58**

The rumble of the train drowns out your conversation in the beer garden every five minutes, but that's a small price to pay for a laid-back afternoon. Servers are attentive, and the crowd outside is pretty relaxed: the only shit-talking will be going on around the Golden Tee machine or at the pool table. Until, that is, when the rest of the neighbourhood's bars close at 2am, when the line outside can get unruly.

Phyllis' Musical Inn

1800 W Division Street, at N Wood Street (1-773 486 9862). El: Blue to Division. **Open** 3pm-2am Mon-Fri; 3pm-3am Sat; 1pm-2am Sun. **No credit cards.** **Map** p331 C8 **59**

One of Wicker Park's first live music spots continues to book local acts that play original material as opposed to dreary covers. They're not always great, but the garden patio is: a scrappy mix of chairs and tables, a basketball hoop and groups of friends gassing over cheap drinks makes for a potentially classic summer night.

Pontiac Café

1531 N Damen Avenue, between W Wicker Park & W Pierce Avenues (1-773 252 7767). El: Blue to Damen. **Open** 3pm-2am Mon-Fri, Sun; 11.30am-3am Sat. **No credit cards.** **Map** p331 B7 **60**

It's impossible to be in the Wicker Park triangle and not hear the din from this converted gas station's patio. Aside from the insanely popular Friday-night live-band karaoke, DJs and bands fill the air with music, as an anything-goes crowd gawks at custom bicycles, shiny motorcycles and other passers-by.

Quencher's Saloon

2401 N Western Avenue, at W Fullerton Avenue (1-773 276 9730/www.quenchers.com). El: Blue to California. **Open** 11am-2am Mon-Fri, Sun; 11am-3am Sat. **No credit cards.** **Map** p331 A5 **61**

This 25-year-old beer bar on the Bucktown/Logan Square border has one of the most diverse crowds in the area. The well-heeled eye each other on weekends just as local beer nerds meet to taste the 200 choices during the week, while drunk punks wander in whenever. The various tribes peacefully co-exist in the spacious rooms, all in the name of beer.

Rodan

1530 N Milwaukee Avenue, between N Damen Avenue and W Honore Street (1-773 276 7036/ http://rodan.ws). El: Blue to Damen. **Open** 9pm-2am Mon-Fri; 10pm-3am Sat. **Credit** AmEx, Disc, MC, V. **Map** p331 C7 **62**

Compact but handsomely designed in modern blues and wood, Rodan fulfills the fantasy of the hipster who's moved on from squalid nights sucking PBRs in no-name dives. The menu includes reliably filling Asian and South American dishes and Japanese white ales. DJs spin wildly eclectic sets to their own tastes, and the big video screen and weekly live avant-jazz make it a multimedia mecca.

Zakopane

1734 W Division Street, between N Hermitage Avenue & N Wood Street (1-773 486 1559). El: Blue to Division. **Open** 7am-2am Mon-Fri; 7am-3am Sat; 11am-2am Sun. **No credit cards.** **Map** p331 C8 **63**

If you're lucky, you'll stumble into Zakopane on a night when the Anna Kournikova lookalike bartender is working, pouring vodka drinks with a heavy hand. But any night will do at this wood-panelled, Polish-owned watering hole. The old drunks are quick to challenge you at pool, and the young Poles are obsessed with the jukebox that spits out Polish versions of early '90s American chart-toppers.

Humboldt Park & Logan Square

Continental

2801 W Chicago Avenue, at N California Avenue (1-773 292 1200). Bus 52, 66. **Open** 5pm-4am Mon-Fri; 9am-5am Sat; 9am-4pm Sun. **Credit** AmEx, Disc, MC, V.

In its past life as Hiawatha, the only thing you'd pick up here was a six-pack of cheap beer to lug next door for a chicken dinner at Feed. Lately, though, the century-old dive has been transformed into a slick little enclave in which the late-night crowd can scope each other out and suck down the last liquor of the night to the sound of the DJ's all-rock repertoire.

Weegee's Lounge

3659 W Armitage Avenue, at N Lawndale Avenue (1-773 384 0707). Bus 53, 73, 82. **Open** 5pm-2am daily. **Credit** AmEx, Disc, MC, V.

Ten years from now, when this strip of Armitage is populated with coffee shops and vintage clothing stores, this old-school, soul record-playing, classic cocktail-mixing bar will be overrun with hipsters vying for their turn in the photo booth. Start hanging out here now so you can say that you knew it in the good old days.

The South Side

Cove Lounge

1750 E 55th Street, between S Hyde Park Boulevard and S Everett Avenue (1-773 684 1013). Metra 55th-56th-57th Street. **Open** 10am-2am daily. **No credit cards.** **Map** p332 Z17 **64**

The payoff from the nautical theme hinted at in the name of this blue-collar hangout is decidedly small: aside from a light fixture made from a ship's wheel and a few anchor-shaped coat hooks, it's really just a standard shot-and-a-beer dive. The crowd is comprised primarily of townies, with overflow from the crowd at the nearby Woodlawn Tap (*see below*).

Schaller's Pump

3714 S Halsted Street, between W 37th & W 38th Streets (1-773 376 6332). El: Red to Sox-35th. **Open** 11am-2am Mon-Fri; 4pm-3am Sat; 3-9pm Sun. **No credit cards.**

There's no better place in which to cheer on your team than this blue-collar institution close to US Cellular Field. Arrive at least a half-hour before game time if you're planning on eating (longer if you're actually planning on going to the game rather

than just watching it in the bar), and you definitely should: just-like-Mom-made classics include crispy pork tenderloin smothered in perfect pan gravy and greaseless fried chicken. Doting servers, cheap beer and a living room atmosphere all help.

Woodlawn Tap

1172 E 55th Street, between S University & S Woodlawn Avenues (1-773 643 5516). Metra 55th-56th-57th Street. **Open** 10.30am-2am Mon-Fri; 11am-3am Sat; 11am-2am Sun. **No credit cards.** **Map** p332 X17 ⑥⑤

Just off of the U of C campus, Jimmy's (as it's affectionately called by those in the know, after original owner Jimmy Wilson) is the favoured spot for the scholars to rub elbows with undergrads and working-class neighbourhood regulars. Cheap burgers are washed down with even cheaper beer.

Smoke alarm

In the wake of high-profile bans in the state of California and in the city of New York, not to mention numerous less well publicised ordinances across the country, Chicago has become the latest in an increasingly long list of American places aiming to stamp out cigarettes in indoor public places. When the Chicago Clean Indoor Air Ordinance went into effect on 16 January 2006, smoking was banned in all local sports stadiums, concert venues and restaurants. And then, in July 2008, all bars and taverns will be forced to comply with the ban. Well, almost all of them...

When they drafted the new law, the City Council allowed a get-out clause for establishments that install a sophisticated

air filtration system. In early 2007, no clear-cut plans had been laid out for the approval (or otherwise) of these systems, but the loophole turns the ban from a health issue into a financial one. Upmarket bars with the dough to shell out for a ventilation system will be exempt from the law, while the little neighbourhood taverns that Mayor Daley seems to dislike will have to abide by it, and will surely suffer as a result. Also exempt will be the **Marshall McGearty**

Tobacco Lounge (*pictured; see p187*), which has thus far ducked the law because more than 65 per cent of its sales are of tobacco or tobacco-related accessories.

The muscle behind classic Chicago spots in tony neighbourhoods – Gibson's in the Gold Coast, for example – have already dropped a million dollars on air filtration systems to ensure that their cigarette- and cigar-puffing clientele will still be planted firmly in their regular seats even after 2008. The bars and taverns that can afford systems get to keep their smoking customers, but many believe that they're also likely to see increases in business as smokers scour the city for places to puff. The rich, in other words, get richer, while everyone else gets left out in the cold.

Shops & Services

It's not just Michigan Avenue that's magnificent for shoppers.

Not long ago, Chicago's shopping scene ranked a long way behind New York and Los Angeles, and was built on Marshall Field's, Carson Pirie Scott and not a lot else. That's no longer the case. For one thing, Marshall Field's and Carson Pirie Scott have both gone, the former bought by Macy's and the latter shut down in early 2007. But in the meantime, a bevy of boutiques has brought international style back to the City of Big Shoulders, supplementing an already impressive roster of local retail talent.

TAX & DUTY

Local sales tax of 9% will be added to all purchases at the counter. If you're taking goods out of the country, you'll be liable for tax and duty on goods worth more than a certain sum (£145 for travellers returning to the UK).

General

Malls

Century Shopping Center

2828 N Clark Street, at W Diversey Parkway, Lakeview (1-773 929 8100). El: Brown or Purple to Diversey. **Open** 10.30am-9pm Mon-Fri; 10.30am-6pm Sat; noon-6pm Sun. **Map** p328 F4.
A small mall highlighted by a cinema and a Bally's Total Fitness (1-773 929 6900, www.ballys.com), plus Aveda (1-773 883 1560, www.aveda.com), Express for Men (1-773 665 2192, www.express fashion.com) and Victoria's Secret (1-773 549 7405, www.victoriassecret.com).

Chicago Place

700 N Michigan Avenue, at E Superior Street, Magnificent Mile (1-312 642 4811/www.chicago-place.com). El: Red to Chicago. **Open** 8am-7pm daily. **Map** p326 J10.
Saks Fifth Avenue (*see p193*) is the main attraction at this chichi mall, but you can also pick up hand-made papier mâché items and frames at Kashmir Handicrafts (1-312 751 8825) or remote-controlled gadgets at Peace Expo (1-312 642 0968).

900 N Michigan

900 N Michigan Avenue, at E Walton Street, Magnificent Mile (1-312 915 3916/www.shop900. com). El: Red to Chicago. **Open** 10am-7pm Mon-Sat; noon-6pm Sun. **Map** p326 J9.
The six-floor 900 N Michigan mall offers the city's only full-scale Bloomingdale's (*see p192*), alongside

Gucci (1-312 664 5504, www.gucci.com) and J.Crew (1-312 751 2739, www.jcrew.com), a Garber Furs store (1-312 642 6600) and a Truefitt & Hill boutique (1-312 337 2525, www.truefittandhill.com).

Northbrook Court

2171 Northbrook Court, off Route 41 (via I-94), Northbrook (1-847 498 1770/www.northbrookcourt. com). **Open** 10am-9pm Mon-Sat; 11am-6pm Sun.
As malls go, this one's more pleasing than most, with branches of the Apple Store (1-847 205 2020, www.apple.com) and Aveda (1-847 509 9354, www. aveda.com), Louis Vuitton (1-847 714 1004, www. louisvuitton.com) and Abercrombie & Fitch (1-847 562 4032, www.abercrombie.com).

Oakbrook Center

Off I-88 (Cermax Road exit), Oak Brook (1-630 573 0700/www.oakbrookcenter.com). **Open** 10am-9pm Mon-Sat; 11am-6pm Sun.
Neiman Marcus (1-630 572 1500, www.neiman marcus.com) is the poshest of the department stores at this outdoor mall. Elsewhere, run-of-the-mill stores such as Gap (1-630 573 5145, www.gap.com) and Guess? (1-630 954 2838, www.guess.com), are supplemented by the more exotic likes of the Discovery Channel Store (1-630 928 0706, http://shopping.discoverychannel.com), Urban Outfitters (1-630 586 9611, www.urbanoutfitters.com) and even Tiffany & Co (1-630 574 7900, www.tiffany.com).

Westfield North Bridge

520 N Michigan Avenue, at E Grand Avenue, Magnificent Mile (1-312 327 2300/www.westfield. com). El: Red to Grand. **Open** Mid Apr-Dec 10am-

The best Shops

For readers
Myopic Books. See p194.

For resters
Asha Gold Coast. See p210.

For rascals
Uncle Fun. See p214.

For roamers
Flight 001. See p207.

For racers
Londo Mondo. See p214.

A bookworm's bonanza: the **Seminary Cooperative Bookstore**. *See p193.*

8pm Mon-Sat; 11am-6pm Sun. *Jan-Mid Apr* 10am-7pm Mon-Sat; noon-6pm Sun. **Map** p326 J10.

Nordstrom (*see p192*) is the flagship at this 100-store development on the Magnificent Mile, but Hugo Boss (1-312 660 0056, www.hugoboss.com), Oilily (1-312 822 9616, www.oilily-world.com) and an entire floor of kid-friendly stores, among them a vast Lego Store (1-312 494 0760, http://shop.lego.com), also appeal to the largely non-native shoppers.

Water Tower Place

835 N Michigan Avenue, at E Chestnut Street, Magnificent Mile (1-312 440 3166/www.shopwater tower.com). El: Red to Chicago. **Open** 10am-9pm Mon-Fri; 10am-8pm Sat; noon-6pm Sun. **Map** p326 J9.

Now that Lord & Taylor has closed, Macy's (*see p192*) dominates, with support from clothes shops such as Banana Republic (1-312 642 7667, www. bananarepublic.com), French Connection (1-312 932 9460, www.frenchconnection.com) and Abercrombie & Fitch (1-312 787 8825, www.abercrombie.com).

Woodfield Shopping Center

Off Route 53 S (Woodfield Road exit), via I-90, Schaumburg (1-847 330 1537/www.shop woodfield.com). **Open** 10am-9pm Mon-Sat; 11am-6pm Sun.

Five department stores, including a Sears (1-847 330 2356, www.sears.com) and a Nordstrom (1-847 605 2121, www.nordstrom.com), are joined by Crate & Barrel (1-847 619 4200, www.crateandbarrel.com), inspiring apothecary CO Bigelow (1-847 517 7167, www.bigelowchemist.com) and a Mac-packed Apple Store (1-847 240 6280, www.apple.com). This was once the largest mall in the country.

Outlet malls

Chicago Premium Outlets

1650 Premium Outlets Boulevard, off I-88 (exit at Aurora, Farnsworth Avenue North), Aurora (1-630 585 2200/www.premiumoutlets.com/chicago). **Open** 10am-9pm Mon-Sat; 10am-6pm Sun.

Drive about an hour outside the city limits to shop at 100-odd outlet stores, from posh brands such as Salvatore Ferragamo (1-630 236 9720, www.ferra gamo.com) and hipster favourites like Diesel (1-630 236 5514, www.diesel.com) to everyday chains including Gap (1-630 499 5068, www.gap.com).

Gurnee Mills

6170 W Grand Avenue, off I-94/I-294 (exit at Route 132, W Grand Avenue), Gurnee (1-847 263 7500/ www.gurneemills.com). **Open** 10am-9pm Mon-Fri; 10am-9.30pm Sat; 11am-7pm Sun.

A JC Penney Outlet (1-847 855 0470, www.jc penney.com) and TJ Maxx (1-847 855 0146, www.tj maxx.com) draw bargain-hunters; an Abercrombie & Fitch Outlet (1-847 855 2819, www.abercrombie. com) and a Disney Outlet (1-847 856 8239, www.dis ney.com) are among the 100-plus stores that keep them at this somewhat unpleasant spot.

Department stores

Barneys New York

25 E Oak Street, at N Rush Street, Gold Coast (1-312 587 1700/www.barneys.com). El: Red to Clark/Division. **Open** 10am-7pm Mon-Sat; noon-6pm Sun. **Credit** AmEx, MC, V. **Map** p326 H9.

Where to shop

THE LOOP

There's not much notable retail activity in the Loop, but bargain-hunters should hightail it to State Street, where a number of department stores and clothing shops offer jaw-dropping steals.

THE NEAR NORTH SIDE: THE MAGNIFICENT MILE & THE GOLD COAST

Between the Chicago River and Water Tower Place, Michigan Avenue – aka the Magnificent Mile – is a consumerist paradise, packed with enormous department stores and multi-level flagships for countless big-ticket brands. As you might expect, it's packed on weekends.

The nearby Gold Coast isn't named after the colour of the credit cards wielded by shoppers, but it might as well be. The boutiques on Oak Street sell the poshest clothes that (someone else's) money can buy.

OLD TOWN & LINCOLN PARK

In the village-like streets of these two smartening neighbourhoods, independent clothing boutiques happily coexist next to outposts of national niche brands. Fertile shopping drags include Clark Street.

LAKEVIEW & AROUND

The chains that have encroached upon Lincoln Park haven't all made it up to Lakeview, which is still dominated by independent stores. Clark Street contains its fair share of stores, especially north of Belmont.

WICKER PARK & AROUND

These two rapidly gentrifying (some would say gentrified) 'hoods are awash with arty stores selling cool clothing, high-design home decor and funky accessories, plus a handful of great bookstores and music shops. Much of the action is around the three-way junction of Damen, North and Milwaukee Avenues.

THE SOUTH SIDE: HYDE PARK

The streets surrounding the University of Chicago are dotted with bookstores and record shops, all offering excellent value.

Barneys has transferred its New York City sophistication lock, stock and barrel to Chicago, and packed the attitude for good measure. Professionals and socialites head here for top designer and private-label apparel: clothing, jewellery, bags, shoes and accessories. Up in Lincoln Park, the two-storey Co-Op is a hipper, more youthful version of Barneys proper, albeit only slightly less expensive than its namesake.

Other locations: Barneys New York Co-Op, 2209-2211 N Halsted Street, at W Webster Avenue, Lincoln Park (1-773 248 0426).

Bloomingdale's

900 N Michigan Shops, 900 N Michigan Avenue, at E Walton Street, Magnificent Mile (1-312 440 4460/www.bloomingdales.com). El: Red to Chicago. **Open** 10am-8pm Mon-Sat; 11am-7pm Sun. **Credit** AmEx, MC, V. **Map** p329 J9.

On a Mag Mile awash with tradition, Bloomies is about having fun. A must for the younger shopper, its six levels are packed with fashions for the free-spirited; in particular, don't miss the shoe department. For the home and furniture store, *see p212*.

Macy's

111 N State Street, at E Randolph Street, the Loop (1-312 781 1000/www.macys.com). El: Blue to Washington; Brown, Green, Orange, Pink or Purple to Randolph; Red to Lake. **Open** 10am-8pm Mon-Sat; 11am-6pm Sun. **Credit** AmEx, DC, Disc, MC, V. **Map** p325 H12.

Chicagoans decried the loss of the Marshall Field's name, but the nine levels of this landmark department store remain impressively stocked with clothes, furniture, iPods (sold from vending machines) and everything in between. Sample the famous Frango mints, lunch in the Walnut Room or at the impressive, seventh-floor food counter, gaze at the Tiffany-domed atrium and check the stores-within-a-store, including shirtmaker Thomas Pink and bath-and-body import Lush.

Neiman Marcus

737 N Michigan Avenue, at E Chicago Avenue, Magnificent Mile (1-312 642 5900/www.neiman marcus.com). El: Red to Chicago. **Open** 10am-7pm Mon-Sat; noon-6pm Sun. **Credit** AmEx, Disc, MC, V. **Map** p326 J10.

Neiman Marcus woos shoppers with a refreshingly airy interior, haute fashions (from classic establishment names such as Chanel to up-and-comers), luxurious accessories and tempting baked goods. Price is generally no object for shoppers, resulting in a pricing structure that's led wags to nickname it 'Needless Markup'.

Nordstrom

520 N Michigan Avenue, at E Grand Avenue, Magnificent Mile (1-312 464 1515/www.nordstrom. com). El: Red to Grand. **Open** 10am-8pm Mon-Sat; 11am-6pm Sun. **Credit** AmEx, DC, Disc, MC, V. **Map** p326 J10.

Nordstrom is known for its wide range of fashions, particularly in footwear, and its attentive customer service. Check in your bags with the store concierge if you're power shopping. The in-store café is perfect for winding down at lunch, but you'll need to get there by 12.30pm to snag a booth.

Saks Fifth Avenue

Chicago Place, 700 N Michigan Avenue, at E Superior Street, Magnificent Mile (1-312 944 6500/ www.saks.com). El: Red to Chicago. **Open** 10am-7pm Mon-Sat; noon-6pm Sun. **Credit** AmEx, DC, Disc, MC, V. **Map** p326 J10.

Favoured by Chicago's upper crust since 1929, five years after it opened in New York, Saks Fifth Avenue favours traditional fashions over wild trends. Expect a wide range of high-quality apparel for women and children, supplemented with stylish accessories. Dash across the street to the classy menswear store (No.717).

Sears

2 N State Street, at W Washington Street, the Loop (1-312 373 6040/www.sears.com). El: Blue to Washington; Brown, Green, Orange, Pink or Purple to Randolph; Red to Lake. **Open** 9.45am-8pm Mon-Sat; noon-7pm Sun. **Credit** AmEx, Disc, MC, V. **Map** p325 H12.

Sears is still trying hard to update its image, particularly when it comes to fashions for men, women and children. It's all very affordable, if hardly exciting. Still, it's the only place downtown where one can shop for a washing machine and kitchen curtains. **Other locations**: throughout the city.

Specialist

Books & magazines

General

Barnes & Noble

1130 N State Street, at W Cedar Street, Gold Coast (1-312 280 8155/www.barnesandnoble.com). El: Red to Clark/Division. **Open** 9am-10pm Mon-Sat; 10am-10pm Sun. **Credit** AmEx, DC, Disc, MC, V. **Map** p326 H9.

In a gratifying break from the norm, the on-the-ball staffers at this wood-panelled store make a genuine effort to find the book you're looking for. The magazine section is large and varied. **Other locations**: 1441 W Webster Avenue, at N Clybourn Avenue, Lincoln Park (1-773 871 3610); 659 W Diversey Parkway, at N Clark Street, Lakeview (1-773 871 9004).

Borders Books & Music

830 N Michigan Avenue, at E Pearson Street, Magnificent Mile (1-312 573 0564/www.borders. com). El: Red to Chicago. **Open** 9am-11pm Mon-Thur; 8am-11pm Fri, Sat; 9am-9pm Sun. **Credit** AmEx, DC, Disc, MC, V. **Map** p326 J9.

The Mag Mile's megalithic, four-storey Borders has laid-back staff that are willing to help… if, that is, you can find any among the huge crowds. Head downstairs to peruse the excellent children's book section or visit the second-level café to sample a cup of coffee and the latest magazines. **Other locations**: 150 N State Street, at W Randolph Street, the Loop (1-312 606 0750); 2817 N Clark Street, at W Diversey Parkway, Lakeview (1-773 935 3909).

Seminary Cooperative Bookstore

5757 S University Avenue, at E 58th Street, Hyde Park (1-773 752 4381/www.semcoop.com). Metra: 59th Street. **Open** 8.30am-9pm Mon-Fri; 10am-6pm Sat; noon-6pm Sun. **Credit** AmEx, Disc, MC, V. **Map** p332 X12.

Right in the hub of Hyde Park's 'bookstore row', the Seminary Coop is revered by local academics. There are obscure texts galore, leaving even the most intrepid bookworm happy. The 57th Street location offers tomes of a more general nature. **Photo** *p191.* **Other locations**: Newberry Library Bookstore, 60 W Walton Street, at N Dearborn Street, Gold Coast (1-312 255 3520); 1301 E 57th Street, at S Kimball Avenue, Hyde Park (1-773 684 1300).

Unabridged Bookstore

3251 N Broadway Street, at W Belmont Avenue, Lakeview (1-773 883 9119/www.unabridgedbooks. com). El: Brown, Purple or Red to Belmont. **Open** 10am-9pm Mon-Fri; 10am-7pm Sat, Sun. **Credit** AmEx, Disc, MC, V. **Map** p329 F2.

This indie bookstore largely reflects the make-up of the neighbourhood in which it sits: it's particularly strong on gay and lesbian literature. Amble downstairs to check out the sizeable children's and travel sections, and look out for the sale stock.

Specialist

Abraham Lincoln Book Shop

357 W Chicago Avenue, at N Orleans Street, River North (1-312 944 3085/www.alincolnbookshop.com). El: Brown or Purple to Chicago. **Open** 9am-5pm Mon-Wed, Fri; 9am-7pm Thur; 10am-4pm Sat. **Credit** MC, V. **Map** p326 G10.

History buffs shouldn't miss this 60-year-old dealer in Lincolnabilia and Civil War lore, which sells a sizeable variety of books, autographs and prints. The store was the founding site of the Civil War Round Table, a discussion group that keeps alive stories of the blue and the grey.

Children in Paradise Bookstore

909 N Rush Street, at E Delaware Street, Gold Coast (1-312 951 5437/www.childreninparadise.com). El: Red to Chicago. **Open** 10am-7pm Mon-Fri; 10am-8pm Sat; noon-5pm Sun. **Credit** AmEx, MC, V. **Map** p326 H9.

Literature for littl'uns is the focus at this Gold Coast bookstore. Sit in on one of its story hours and watch young ones squirm in their Prada-clad mothers' laps.

Eat, Drink, Shop

Computer cravings? Take a bite at the big **Apple Store**. *See p195.*

Prairie Avenue Bookshop

418 S Wabash Avenue, at E Van Buren Street, the Loop (1-312 922 8311/www.pabook.com). El: Blue or Red to Jackson; Brown, Orange, Pink or Purple to Library. **Open** 10am-6pm Mon-Fri; 10am-4pm Sat. **Credit** AmEx, Disc, MC, V. **Map** p325 H13.

One of the Midwest's most impressive architectural bookstores stocks 15,000 titles on architecture, interiors, city planning and graphic design. Get cosy in the sit-around furniture by Frank Lloyd Wright, Mies van der Rohe and Le Corbusier.

Quimby's Bookstore

1854 W North Avenue, at N Milwaukee Avenue, Wicker Park (1-773 342 0910/www.quimbys.com). El: Blue to Damen. **Open** noon-10pm Mon-Fri; 11am-10pm Sat; noon-6pm Sun. **Credit** AmEx, Disc, MC, V. **Map** p331 B7.

Find the newest in small press, underground and self-published magazines at this Wicker Park staple, or check out the decent comic and book selections.

Savvy Traveller

310 S Michigan Avenue, at E Jackson Boulevard, the Loop (1-312 913 9800/www.thesavvytraveller. com). El: Blue or Red to Jackson; Brown, Green, Orange, Pink or Purple to Adams. **Open** 10am-7.30pm Mon-Sat; noon-5pm Sun. **Credit** Disc, MC, V. **Map** p325 J13.

The fine local interest section, the phenomenal range of tomes and maps for adventures to all corners of the globe, the wide selection of globes and the various items of luggage and travel gear combine to make this everything a travel store should be.

Women & Children First

5233 N Clark Street, at W Foster Avenue, Andersonville (1-773 769 9299/www.womenand childrenfirst.com). El: Red to Berwyn. **Open** 11am-7pm Mon, Tue; 11am-9pm Wed-Fri; 10am-7pm Sat; 11am-6pm Sun. **Credit** AmEx, Disc, MC, V.

This welcoming, queer-friendly spot is as much a community meeting place as it is a bookstore. Frequent readings, for women and kids alike, draw established authors and up-and-coming activists.

Used & antiquarian

After-Words New & Used Books

23 E Illinois Street, at N State Street, River North (1-312 464 1110). El: Red to Grand. **Open** 10.30am-10pm Mon-Thur; 10.30am-11pm Fri; 10am-11pm Sat; noon-7pm Sun. **Credit** AmEx, MC, V. **Map** p326 H11.

New, used and out-of-print volumes. Customers can access the internet using store computers, and are even able to order customised stationery.

Myopic Books

1564 N Milwaukee Avenue, at N Damen Avenue, Wicker Park (1-773 862 4882/www.myopicbook store.com). El: Blue to Damen. **Open** 11am-11pm Mon-Sat; 11am-10pm Sun. **Credit** MC, V. **Map** p331 C7.

Staffers at this three-storey shop are serious about the no-cellphones policy, which makes for an enjoyably quiet environment. Everything from foreign fiction to cookbooks is represented. Prices are fair, and you can even get a cheap coffee as you browse.

Powell's

1501 E 57th Street, at S Harper Avenue, Hyde Park (1-773 955 7780/www.powellchicago.com). Metra: 55th-56th-57th Street. **Open** 9am-11pm daily. **Credit** MC, V. **Map** p332 Y17.

Powell's processes hundreds of remainders a day. The South Side stores have strong academic sections, while the North Side branch has a large art and photography selection and also features a rare book room.

Other locations: 828 S Wabash Avenue, at W 8th Street, South Loop (1-312 341 0748); 2850 N Lincoln Avenue, at W Wolfram Street, Lakeview (1-773 248 1444).

Electronics & photography

The Magnificent Mile is home to the **Apple Store** (No.679, at E Erie Street, 1-312 981 4104, www.apple.com, **photo** *p194*), **Tweeter** (No.900, at E Delaware Place, 1-312 664 3100, www.twtr.com), and a major **Nokia** store (No.543, at E Grand Avenue, 1-312 670 2607, www.nokiausa.com). There's also a large **CompUSA** nearby (101 E Chicago Avenue, at N Rush Street, 1-312 787 6776, www. compusa.com), plus a branch of **Bang & Olufsen** (15 E Oak Street, at N State Street, 1-312 787 6006, www.bang-olufsen.com).

Central Camera
230 S Wabash Avenue, at E Jackson Boulevard, the Loop (1-312 427 5580/www.central-camera.com). El: Blue or Red to Jackson; Brown, Green, Orange, Pink or Purple to Adams. **Open** 8.30am-5.30pm Mon-Fri; 8.30am-5pm Sat. **Credit** AmEx, DC, Disc, MC, V. **Map** p325 H12.
The knowledgeable service here hasn't changed much during its century in business, but the stock certainly has: these days, it's packed with digital imaging equipment, as well as more old-fashioned gear. The repair service is a valued extra.

Saturday Audio Exchange
1021 W Belmont Avenue, at W Kenmore Avenue, Lakeview (1-773 935 4434/www.saturdayaudio.com). El: Brown, Purple or Red to Belmont. **Open** 5.30-9pm Thur; 10.30am-5.30pm Sat; noon-4pm Sun. **Credit** AmEx, Disc, MC, V. **Map** p329 E2.
Thanks to great prices and smart, unpushy staff, this local fave thrives despite its limited opening hours. Brands include Denon, Musical Fidelity and Grado; stock is a mix of new and used equipment. The on-site repair facility is another bonus.

Fashion

Children
There's a **Gap Kids** in Water Tower Place (*see p191*; 1-312 944 3053, www.gap.com), while cheery Dutch import **Oilily** has a shop in Westfield North Bridge (*see p190*; 1-312 527 5747, www.oilily-world.com). **Carter's** (1565 N Halsted Street, at W North Avenue, Old Town, 1-312 482 8603, www.carters.com) sells very inexpensive sleepwear and playwear.

Grow
1943 W Division Street, at N Damen Avenue, Wicker Park (1-773 489 0009/www.grow-kids.com). El: Blue to Damen. **Open** 10am-6pm Tue-Fri; 10am-7pm Sat. **Credit** AmEx, Disc, MC, V. **Map** p331 B8.

This cute-as-can-be Wicker Park store sells hand-picked nursery furniture and organic kids' attire with modern aesthetics.

LMNOP
2570 N Lincoln Avenue, at W Wrightwood Avenue, Lincoln Park (1-773 975 4055/www.carters.com). El: Brown, Purple or Red to Fullerton. **Open** 10am-6pm Mon-Fri; 10am-5pm Sat; 11am-4pm Sun. **Credit** AmEx, MC, V. **Map** p328 E4.
More design-oriented and less cutesy than many of its kiddie counterparts, this shop stocks small labels, many of them European. There's a play area, too.

Madison & Friends
940 N Rush Street, at E Oak Street, Gold Coast (1-312 642 6403/www.madisonandfriends.com). El: Red to Clark/Division. **Open** 10am-6pm Mon-Wed; 10am-6.30pm Thur, Sat; 11am-5pm Sun. **Credit** AmEx, MC, V. **Map** p326 H9.
The owners of this boutique strive hard to put some hipness (and designer cachet) into kids' clothes. Sizes range from newborns to teens.

Psychobaby
1630 N Damen Avenue, at W North Avenue, Wicker Park (1-773 772 2815/www.psychobabyonline.com). El: Blue to Damen. **Open** 10am-6pm Mon-Wed, Fri, Sat; 10am-8pm Thur; 11am-5pm Sun. **Credit** AmEx, Disc, MC, V. **Map** p331 B7.
Tots and toddlers get outfitted in funky fashions at this Wicker Park operation, where the clothes are a real antidote to traditional frilly togs. Educational toys, shoes and books round out the selection.

Designer
A stroll down fashionable E Oak Street between State Street and Michigan Avenue turns up big names, among them **Hermès** (No.110, 1-312 787 8175, www.hermes.com), **Jil Sander** (No.48, 1-312 335 0006, www.jilsander.com), **Kate Spade** (No.101, 1-312 654 8853, www.katespade.com), **Prada** (No.30, 1-312 951 1113, www.prada.com), **Ultimo** (No.114, 1-312 787 1171, www.ultimo.com) and **Yves Saint Laurent** (No.51, 1-312 751 8995, www.ysl.com). The north end of N Michigan Avenue, between Superior and Oak Streets, yields the world's largest **Ralph Lauren** (No.750, 1-312 280 1655, www.polo.com), plus **Giorgio Armani** (No.800, 1-312 751 2244, www.armani.com), **Gucci** (in the 900 N Michigan Shops, 1-312 664 5504, www.gucci.com), **J Mendel** (No.919, 1-312 981 1725, www.jmendel.com) and **Chanel** (No.935, 1-312 787 5500, www.chanel.com).

Active Endeavors
853 W Armitage Avenue, at N Fremont Avenue, Lincoln Park (1-773 281 8100/www.activeendeavors. com). El: Brown or Purple to Armitage. **Open** 10am-7pm Mon-Fri; 10am-6pm Sat; noon-6pm Sun. **Credit** AmEx, Disc, MC, V. **Map** p328 F6.

Though this men's and women's retailer sounds like a store for sporting goods, it's actually a chic boutique filled with all the sort of labels you see on Hollywood starlets. You'll find names such as Paul & Joe, Ulla Johnson and Rag & Bone alongside other buzzworthy brands.

Blake

212 W Chicago Avenue, at N Wells Street, River North (1-312 202 0047). El: Brown or Purple to Chicago. **Open** 10.30am-7pm Mon-Fri; 10.30am-6.30pm Sat. **Credit** AmEx, DC, Disc, MC, V. **Map** p326 G10.

You'll need to be buzzed in to browse the pricey frocks from Dries Van Noten, Marni and others, but the selection is worth the initial awkwardness. That said, the easily intimidated should head elsewhere, as the staff's attitude can be somewhat chilly.

Eskell

953 W Webster Avenue, at N Sheffield Avenue, Lincoln Park (1-773 477 9390/www.eskell.com). El: Brown, Purple or Red to Fullerton. **Open** 11am-7pm Tue-Sat; noon-6pm Sun. **Credit** AmEx, Disc, MC, V. **Map** p328 E5.

Young arty types depend on Eskell to find tiny designer labels, many from New York's hippest enclaves. The house line displays beautiful use of pattern and texture in its dresses and separates.

Etre

1361 N Wells Street, at W Burton Place, Old Town (1-312 266 8101/www.etrechicago.com). El: Brown or Purple to Sedgwick. **Open** 11am-7pm Mon-Fri; 11am-6pm Sat; noon-5pm Sun. **Credit** AmEx, Disc, MC, V. **Map** p327 H8.

Hard-to-come-by lines from Europe mingle with the latest from designers such as Anna Sui and Rebecca Taylor. A girl can dress smartly from head to toe choosing from the shop's bags, heels and jewellery.

Hejfina

1529 N Milwaukee Avenue, at W North Avenue, Wicker Park (1-773 772 0002/www.hejfina.com). El: Blue to Damen. **Open** noon-6pm Mon, Sun; 11am-7pm Tue-Sat. **Credit** AmEx, DC, MC, V. **Map** p331 C7.

Cool and sleek, this lifestyle boutique offers fashions for men and women; many are from international designers and most are exclusive to the store. If you've read about it in *Nylon*, you'll find it here first.

Helen Yi

1645 N Damen Avenue, at W North Avenue, Bucktown (1-773 252 3838). El: Blue to Damen. **Open** 11am-7pm Mon-Sat; noon-5pm Sun. **Credit** AmEx, MC, V. **Map** p331 B7.

Make sure your credit card is in good shape when you visit this spacious women's boutique. After you've seen the lovely clothes from Chloe, Evie Kilcline and Plein Sud, you'll struggle not to splurge.

Ikram

873 N Rush Street, at E Chicago Avenue, Gold Coast (1-312 587 1000/www.ikram.com). El: Red to Chicago. **Open** 10am-6pm Mon-Sat. **Credit** AmEx, DC, Disc, MC, V. **Map** p326 J10.

Ikram Goldman learned the rag trade at Ultimo before opening her boutique. The *Sex and the City* girls would revel in the global scope of the high-end fashions, flirty footwear and unique jewellery.

Jake

3740 N Southport Avenue, at W Grace Street, Wrigleyville (1-773 929 5253/www.shopjake.com). El: Brown to Southport. **Open** 11am-7pm Mon-Fri; 10am-6pm Sat; noon-5pm Sun. **Credit** AmEx, MC, V. **Map** p329 D1.

The best-dressed men and women in Chicago have Jake at the top of their must-shop list. The owners attend fashion shows in Paris and New York to find graceful, modern lines from the likes of 3.1 Phillip

Hejfina.

Designs for life

Chicago's nickname may be the City of Big Shoulders, but it's increasingly becoming a city of nipped waistlines and sleek silhouettes. The city doesn't yet have an international reputation for fashion, but that's changing: Mayor Daley formed the city's first Fashion Advisory Council in 2006, the same year that saw the launch of Fashion Focus Chicago, a yearly festival of runway shows and shopping events. Here are a few designers worth watching...

If you're after classic menswear, remember the name **Kent Nielsen**. The former computer professional's eye for clean lines translates to well-tailored suits, and his shirts are perfectly crisp (from Jake; see p197). For a look that's a bit less conservative, step into Bynum & Bang's Victorian-inspired boutique (2143 W Division Street, at N Hoyne Avenue, Wicker Park, 1-773 384 4546, http://bynum andbang.com) to see **Tom Bynum**'s tapered blazers and flattering trousers, an outfit you can complete with a silk **Lee Allison** tie (pictured; from Apartment No.9; see p200). Allison's 'four-in-hands', as he calls them, have cheeky prints and a 'remove before sex' message hidden in the tipping.

For women, buzzed-about duo **Vatit Itthi** create breathtakingly elegant gowns out of sumptuous silks and unexpected colour combinations. Available from Helen Yi (see p197), the clothing isn't cheap, but it's the most gorgeous souvenir you could find. For a seductive cocktail-party look, turn to **Orlando Espinoza**'s curve-conscious silk dresses and jersey separates (from Jake), sexy without being obvious.

On the more casual side, look out for **Double Stitch**, a funky line of crocheted dresses designed and modelled by identical twins (from Macy's; see p192). **Lara Miller** works with sustainable fibres such as bamboo, and her fantastic, geometrically based knit garments can be flipped around and worn in different ways (from P.45, see p199). **Michelle Tan** (see p199), another daywear designer, fuses futuristic shapes with traditional Asian cuts.

Chicago also has its share of accessory designers. **Diego Rocha** uses Italian leather in his line of chic, sophisticated handbags (from Macy's), while **Vanessa Penna** reworks vintage Japanese obis into versatile silk scarves (from Jake). And for a look at the very newest names on the scene, head to **Habit** (1951 W Division Street, at N Damen Avenue, Wicker Park 1-773 342 0093, www.habitchicago.com), where owner Lindsay Boland stocks her own Superficial line along with one-off pieces by recent Art Institute grads. If you want to see the future of Chicago design, make this your first stop.

Lim and Cloak. Considering the scary price tags, service is friendlier than you might expect. **Other locations**: 939 N Rush Street, at W Oak Street, Gold Coast (1-312 664 5553).

Kaveri
1211 W Webster Avenue, at N Racine Avenue, Lincoln Park (1-773 296 2141). El: Brown, Purple or Red to Fullerton. **Open** 11am-7pm Mon-Fri; 10am-6pm Sat; noon-5pm Sun. **Credit** AmEx, Disc, MC, V. **Map** p328 E5.
Professional women hit this laid-back store to browse trendy yet dressy selections from Edun, Ulla Johnson and Trovata. Look for luxurious accessories, such as Gryson bags (designed by a Marc Jacobs alum).

Michelle Tan
1872 N Damen Avenue, at W Cortland Street, Bucktown (1-773 252 1888). El: Blue to Damen. **Open** 11am-7pm Mon-Sat; noon-5pm Sun. **Credit** MC, V. **Map** p331 B6.
Local womenswear designer Tan specialises in unconventional cuts, unfinished hems and minimalist colours. She also sells complementary pieces by other rising designers.

Nicole Miller
1419 N Wells Street, at W Schiller Street, Old Town (1-312 664 3532/www.nicolemiller.com). El: Red to Chicago. **Open** 10am-6pm Mon, Thur-Sat; 10am-7pm Tue, Wed; noon-5pm Sun. **Credit** AmEx, Disc, MC, V. **Map** p326 H9.
Alluring yet tasteful designs for the active, contemporary woman, plus a good choice of silk ties for the man in her life.

Ouest
1063 W Madison Avenue, at S Aberdeen Street, Greektown (1-312 421 2799/www.shopouest.com). Bus 20. **Open** noon-6pm Mon; 11am-7pm Tue-Fri; 10am-6pm Sat; noon-5pm Sun. **Credit** AmEx, Disc, MC, V. **Map** p330 E12.
This posh women's boutique stocks designer lines from France, including Stella Forrest, Vanessa Bruno, Barbara Bui and Sonia by Sonia Rykiel. The look is contemporary but classic, and rather *cher*.

P.45
1643 N Damen Avenue, at W North Avenue, Wicker Park (1-773 862 4523/www.p45.com). El: Blue to Damen. **Open** 11am-7pm Mon-Sat; noon-5pm Sun. **Credit** AmEx, Disc, MC, V. **Map** p331 B7.
This super-hip shop, which features a wonderful sweeping interior created by famed local designer Suhail, is a piece of SoHo in Chicago. The young proprietresses of the industrial-chic space buy exclusive designs from local and New York up-and-comers, which they sell on at hefty prices.

Robin Richman
2108 N Damen Avenue, at W Webster Avenue, Bucktown (1-773 278 6150). El: Blue (O'Hare branch) to Western. **Open** 11am-6pm Mon-Sat; noon-5pm Sun. **Credit** AmEx, Disc, MC, V. **Map** p331 B5.

A Bucktown staple for hip men's and women's clothing. Antique-looking items (handsome bags, semi-precious jewellery and the like) make the atmosphere both rustic and ravishing.

Roslyn
2035 N Damen Avenue, between W McLean & W Dickens Avenues, Bucktown (1-773 489 1311). El: Blue to Damen. **Open** 11am-7pm Tue-Sat; noon-6pm Sun. **Credit** AmEx, Disc, MC, V. **Map** p331 B6.
At Roslyn, the racks of women's clothes are organised by label, each of which is accompanied by a biography. You'll appreciate the nuance: most of the pricey pieces are by rising (read: just-out-of-school) designers. Though the focus is on versatile women's separates, a 'Boyfriend Rack' supplies men with two-in-one Nicholas K jackets and Filson bags.

Scoop
1702 N Milwaukee Avenue, at W Wabansia Avenue, Wicker Park (1-773 227 9930/www.scoopnyc.com). El: Blue to Damen. **Open** 11am-7pm Mon-Sat; noon-6pm Sun. **Credit** AmEx, Disc, MC, V. **Map** p331 B7.
There's something for the whole fashionable family here, including Jimmy Choo slingbacks, Earnest Sewn denim for kids and John Varvatos sweaters for men. Prices aren't cheap, but there's often a good selection of items on sale.

Tangerine
1719 N Damen Avenue, at W North Avenue, Bucktown (1-773 772 0505). El: Blue to Damen. **Open** 11am-7pm Mon-Sat; noon-5pm Sun. **Credit** AmEx, MC, V. **Map** p331 B7.
Tangerine and P.45 (*see above*) were retail pioneers on the block; both still cater to hipsters with good cash flow. There are plenty of takers for the chic accessories, French footwear and feminine designs from Helen Wang, Nanette Lepore and Trina Turk.

Discount
See also p191 **Outlet malls**.

Beta Boutique
2016 W Concord Place, between N Damen & N Milwaukee Avenues, Bucktown (1-773 276 0905/ www.betaboutique.com). El: Blue to Damen. **Open** 11am-7pm Thur-Sat; noon-5pm Sun. **Credit** AmEx, Disc, MC, V. **Map** p331 B7.
Frugal fans of fashion will find plenty to love in this shop. Prices on hundreds of contemporary designer pieces are whittled down by 40-90%.

General
Many of the country's familiar chains are down on Michigan Avenue, among them cheap-chic staple **H&M** (No.840, at E Chicago Avenue, 1-312 640 0060, www.hm.com), posh and preppy **Banana Republic** (No.835, at E Chicago Avenue, 1-312 642 7667, www.bananarepublic. com) and **Gap** (No.555, at W Grand Avenue,

1-312 494 8580, www.gap.com). Water Tower Place is home to **French Connection** (1-312 932 9460, www.frenchconnection.com) and **Mango** (1-312 397 9800, www.mango.com). Cheap and cheery **Old Navy** has a store in the Loop (35 N State Street, at W Washington Street, 1-312 551 0522, www.oldnavy.com).

The Gold Coast is home to high-concept, high-priced chains **Anthropologie** (1120 N State Street, at E Elm Street, 1-312 255 1848, www.anthropologie.com) and **Diesel** (923 N Rush Street, a E Walton Street, 1-312 255 0157, www.diesel.com). Wicker Park, meanwhile, contains branches of **Urban Outfitters** stores (1521 N Milwaukee Avenue, at N Damen Avenue, 1-773 772 8550, www.urbanoutfitters. com) and **American Apparel** (1563 N Milwaukee Avenue, at N Damen Avenue, 1-773 235 6778, www.americanapparel.net).

Alcala's Western Wear

1733 W Chicago Avenue, at N Ashland Avenue, West Town (1-312 226 0152/www.alcalas.com). Bus 66. **Open** 9.30am-8pm Mon, Thur, Fri; 9.30am-7pm Tue, Wed, Sat; 9.30am-5pm Sun. **Credit** AmEx, DC, Disc, MC, V. **Map** p331 C9.
Wanna rodeo? Slip on the stetson to wallow in this shop's selections of jeans, hats and cowboy boots (some 10,000 pairs). Menswear predominates, with a smattering of shirts and jackets for cowgirls.

Apartment No.9

1804 N Damen Avenue, at W Churchill Street, Bucktown (1-773 395 2999). El: Blue to Damen. **Open** 11am-7pm Mon-Fri; 11am-6pm Sat; noon-5pm Sun. **Credit** AmEx, Disc, MC, V. **Map** p331 B7.
It's virtually impossible to look bad after shopping here, so stylish and timeless are the offerings. Staff specialise in helping men who need fashion guidance. The back room generally has great discounts on clothes by the likes of Rogan and Paul Smith.

Belmont Army

1318 N Milwaukee Avenue, at N Paulina Street, Wicker Park (1-773 384 8448/www.belmontarmy. com). El: Blue to Division. **Open** 11am-7pm Mon-Sat; noon-5pm Sun. **Credit** AmEx, Disc, MC, V. **Map** p331 C8.
March your way into this bright and tidy army and navy surplus store. You can dress like a soldier if you like, but most shoppers prefer to choose from the selections of cool trainers and youthful streetwear.

Krista K Boutique

3458 N Southport Avenue, at W Roscoe Street, Wrigleyville (1-773 248 1967/www.kristak.com). El: Brown to Southport. **Open** 11am-7pm Mon-Fri; 10am-6pm Sat; noon-5pm Sun. **Credit** AmEx, DC, Disc, MC, V. **Map** p329 D2.
Neighbourhood gals rely heavily on Krista K for its all-occasion sensibilities. There's a little bit of everything here: jeans, dresses, suits and even a maternity line. The apparel is stylish but never OTT.

Penelope's

1913 W Division Street, at N Damen Avenue, Wicker Park (1-773 395 2351/www.penelopeschicago.com). El: Blue to Division. **Open** 11am-7pm Mon-Sat; noon-6pm Sun. **Credit** AmEx, MC, V. **Map** p331 B8.
Recovering indie rockers swarm this adorable store, where guys and girls get their fill of slightly mod clothes, shoes and accessories. It's one of the only stores in the city to stock French cult label APC and the work of Brooklyn designers Lewis Cho.

TK Men

1909 W North Avenue, at N Wolcott Avenue, Wicker Park (1-773 342 9800/www.tkmen.com). El: Blue to Damen. **Open** noon-6pm Mon, Sun; 11am-8pm Tue-Sat. **Credit** AmEx, Disc, MC, V. **Map** p331 C7.
A former Hollywood stylist operates this men's shop, which lures shopping-phobic males with treats such as beer and video games. The casual clothes tend to be trendy, but there's also plenty of weekend garb for professional guys who want to unwind.

Tula

3738 N Southport Avenue, between W Grace Street & W Waveland Avenue, Wrigleyville (1-773 549 2876). El: Brown to Southport. **Open** 11am-7pm Mon-Fri; 10am-6pm Sat; noon-5pm Sun. **Credit** MC, V. **Map** p329 D1.
Ageless dressing with a European bent is the theme at this women's shop, which highlights casual clothing by mostly continental designers. It's grown-up without being old-lady; women of all ages should find something that works.

Vive la Femme

2048 N Damen Avenue, at W Armitage Avenue, Bucktown (1-773 772 7429/www.vivelafemme.com). El: Blue to Damen. **Open** 11am-7pm Mon-Fri; 10am-6pm Sat; 11am-5pm Sun. **Credit** AmEx, Disc, MC, V. **Map** p331 B6.
Plus-sized women don't deserve frumpy frocks, which is why this big-girl boutique is a must-visit if you're a size 12 (UK size 14) or larger. The styles here complement curves rather than hide them; size-two twiglets often envy the designs.

Vintage

Beatnix

3400 N Halsted Street, at W Roscoe Street, Wrigleyville (1-773 281 6933). El: Brown, Purple or Red to Belmont. **Open** 11am-11pm Mon-Thur; 11am-midnight Fri, Sat; noon-10pm Sun. **Credit** MC, V. **Map** p329 F2.
This colourful bazaar has outfits and accessories, both new and used, to keep club kids, drag queens and muscle boys looking their best. Past the 'pimp shoes' at the back sits a great collection of wigs.

Hollywood Mirror

812 N Belmont Avenue, at N Halsted Street, Lakeview (1-773 404 2044/www.hollywoodmirror. com). El: Brown, Purple or Red to Belmont. **Open** 11am-9.30pm Mon-Thur; 11am-10pm Fri, Sat; 11am-7pm Sun. **Credit** AmEx, Disc, MC, V. **Map** p329 F2.

Hollywood Mirror. *See p200*.

This retro shop has a huge selection of weathered jeans, bowling shirts and jackets, plus old-school furniture on the lower level and a wide array of nostalgic items upstairs. **Photo** *p201*.

LuLu's at the Belle Kay

3862 N Lincoln Avenue, at W Grace Street, Lakeview (1-773 404 5858). El: Brown to Addison. **Open** 11am-6pm Tue-Fri; 11am-5pm Sat; noon-5pm Sun. **Credit** AmEx, MC, V.

An elegant fainting couch completes the salon setting for LuLu's neatly arranged vintage handbags, furs, clothing and jewellery.

Silver Moon

1755 W North Avenue, at N Wood Street, Wicker Park (1-773 235 5797/www.silvermoonvintage.com). El: Blue to Damen. **Open** noon-8pm Tue-Sat; noon-5pm Sun. **Credit** MC, V. **Map** p331 C7.

Aerosmith's fashion stylist has amassed an exquisite collection of men's and women's clothes from the 1890s onwards, all in immaculate condition.

Yellow Jacket

2959 N Lincoln Avenue, at W Wellington Avenue, Lincoln Park (1-773 248 1996/www.yellowjacket vintageclothing.com). El: Brown or Purple to Diversey. **Open** noon-7pm Mon-Sat; noon-5pm Sun. **Credit** MC, V. **Map** p329 D3.

This bright and colourful store offers well-organised T-shirts and trousers, along with a selection of retro suits and seasonal merchandise.

Fashion accessories

Cleaning & repairs

Brooks Shoe Service

55 E Washington Boulevard, at N Michigan Avenue, the Loop (1-312 372 2504/www.brooksshoeservice. com). El: Brown, Green, Orange, Pink or Purple to Madison; Blue or Red to Monroe. **Open** *June-Aug* 8am-5.30pm Mon-Fri. *Sept-May* 8am-5.30pm Mon-Fri; 10am-3pm Sat. **Credit** AmEx, Disc, MC, V. **Map** p325 J12.

The third generation of the Morelli family is still here, repairing footwear for socialites, retailers and everyday Joes. They're also experts at restoring vintage shoes and bags. A delivery service is available.

Gibson Couture Cleaners

3447 N Southport Avenue, at W Roscoe Street, Wrigleyville (1-773 248 0937). El: Brown to Southport. **Open** 7am-7pm Mon-Fri; 7am-4pm Sat. **Credit** AmEx, Disc, MC, V. **Map** p329 D2.

The cognoscenti entrust their formals to this specialist in garment care. The tab will be steeper than at your corner cleaner, but you'll have peace of mind.

Jewellery

For salt-of-the-earth shopping, hit **Jeweler's Row**, a strip of jewellery stores on S Wabash Avenue between Washington and Jackson in the Loop. In particular, try the **Jeweler's Center** (5 S Wabash Street, at E Washington Street, 1-312 853 2057, www.jewelerscenter. com), home to 150 jewellers. On a rather grander note, **Tiffany & Co** has a shop on the Magnificent Mile (No.730, at E Superior Street, 1-312 944 7500, www.tiffany.com).

Fleur

3149 W Logan Boulevard, at N Milwaukee Avenue, Logan Square (1-773 395 2770/www.fleurchicago. com). El: Blue to Logan Square. **Open** 10am-7pm Tue-Sat; 10am-4pm Sun. **Credit** AmEx, MC, V.

Escape from the roar of traffic by stepping into this plant-filled wonderworld. Once you've sniffed all the flowers you can stand, browse the selections of stationery and jewellery. **Photo** *p203*.

K Amato Designs

1229 W Diversey Avenue, at N Magnolia Avenue, Lakeview (1-312 882 1366/www.k-amato.com). El: Blue to Diversey. **Open** by appointment. **Credit** AmEx, Disc, MC, V. **Map** p328 E4.

This local jewellery designer's huge work space doubles as a by-appointment boutique. The line ($30-$100) includes strands of beads, delicate chokers and golden chains with adornments, as well as dangling earrings and matching bracelets.

Left Bank

1155 W Webster Avenue, at N Racine Avenue, Lincoln Park (1-773 929 7422/www.leftbankjewelry. com). El: Brown, Purple or Red to Fullerton. **Open** noon-7pm Tue-Thur; noon-5pm Fri; 11am-5pm Sat; noon-4pm Sun. **Credit** Disc, MC, V. **Map** p328 E5.

The owner specialises in jewellery made in France, as well as unique gift items with that Parisian *je ne sais quoi*. This romantic boutique also features dazzling, bejewelled bridal tiaras and custom veils.

Silver Room

1442 N Milwaukee Avenue, at N Wood Street, Wicker Park (1-773 278 7130/www.thesilverroom. com). El: Blue to Damen. **Open** 11am-8pm Mon; 11am-8pm Tue-Sat; 11am-6pm Sun. **Credit** AmEx, Disc, MC, V. **Map** p331 C8.

The in-house DJ says it all, really: this is one style-conscious shop. Specialising in semi-precious jewellery, it also sells hats and super-fly sunglasses.

Leather goods & luggage

For travel-oriented shop **Flight 001**, *see p207*.

Hats Plus

4706 W Irving Park Road, at N Milwaukee Avenue, Irving Park (1-773 286 5577/www.hats-plus.com). El: Blue to Irving Park. **Open** 10am-6pm Mon-Wed, Fri, Sat; 10am-8pm Thur; 11am-5pm Sun. **Credit** AmEx, Disc, MC, V.

It's a hike from downtown, but men who take their headgear seriously will want to venture north for the city's largest choice in felt, fur, wool, straw and more. There's a small millinery department for women.

Fleur. *See p202.*

Shebang

1616 N Damen Avenue, at W North Avenue, Wicker Park (1-773 486 3800/www.shopshebang.com). El: Blue to Damen. **Open** 11am-7pm Mon-Sat; 11am-5pm Sun. **Credit** AmEx, MC, V. **Map** p331 B7.
Shebang's good-quality handbags and rare jewellery designs draw everyone from indie rockers to smart-dressed office workers after a chic accessory.

Spare Parts

2947 N Broadway Street, at W Wellington Avenue, Lakeview (1-773 525 4242/www.sparepartschicago. com). El: Brown or Purple to Wellington. **Open** 11am-8pm Mon-Sat; noon-5pm Sun. **Credit** AmEx, MC, V. **Map** p329 F3.
More or less any accessory can be found at this Boystown fave. The belts, handbags, wallets and sunglasses are versatile, lending themselves to just about any area of the fashion spectrum. Jewellery comes from Patricia Locke, bags from Paris Focus.

Lingerie

There are **Victoria's Secret** stores (www. victoriassecret.com) in Water Tower Place (*see p191*) and Century Shopping Center (*see p190*).

G Boutique

2131 N Damen Avenue, at W Charleston Street, Wicker Park (1-773 235 1234/www.boutiqueg.com). El: Blue to Damen. **Open** 11am-7pm Mon-Sat; noon-5pm Sun. **Credit** AmEx, MC, V. **Map** p331 B6.
One look at the bright pink facade of this skivvies boutique and you know what's in store: frills, lace, and sauciness. Cosabella thongs share space with sumptuous French underthings; if you're feeling naughty, pick up a vibrating rubber duckie.

Isabella Fine Lingerie

1101 W Webster Avenue, at N Seminary Avenue, Lincoln Park (1-773 281 2352/www.shopisabella. com). El: Brown, Purple or Red to Fullerton. **Open** 11am-7pm Tue-Fri; 11am-6pm Sat; noon-5pm Sun. **Credit** AmEx, MC, V. **Map** p328 E5.
A cocoon of whisper-soft silk, this glamorous boutique features designs by Cosabella, Le Mystère, On Gossamer and Parah. Kick back on the lounge room sofa among the pyjamas, swimwear and cosy robes.

Raizy

1944 N Damen Avenue, at W Armitage Avenue, Bucktown (1-773 227 2221/www.shopraizy.com). El: Blue (O'Hare branch) to Western. **Open** 11am-7pm Mon-Sat; 11am-5pm Sun. **Credit** AmEx, MC, V. **Map** p331 B6.
A girly girl's paradise, this confection of a shop stocks frilly French lingerie, hard-to-find cosmetic lines and bath products for pampering.

Shoes

Nordstrom and **Bloomingdale's** (for both, *see p192*) are famed for their selections of women's shoes.

Eat, Drink, Shop

City Soles/Niche

2001 W North Avenue, at N Damen Avenue,
Wicker Park (1-773 489 2001/www.citysoles.com).
El: Blue to Damen. **Open** 11am-8pm Mon-Wed, Sat;
11am-9pm Thur, Fri; 11am-6pm Sun. **Credit** AmEx,
Disc, MC, V.
Step into this emporium for beautifully crafted
designer heels and cool loafers for guys.
Other locations: 3432 N Southport Avenue, at
W Roscoe Street, Wrigleyville (1-773 665 4233).

Hanig's

660 N Michigan Avenue, at E Erie Street, Gold
Coast (1-312 642 5330/www.hanigs.com). El: Red
to Chicago. **Open** 9am-8pm Mon-Fri; 9am-7pm Sat;
11am-6pm Sun. **Credit** AmEx, DC, Disc, MC, V.
Map p326 J10.
Looking for comfort as well as style? The two don't
have to be mutually exclusive, as demonstrated by
Hanig's shoes and boots for men and women. You'll
find European and Canadian brands among the
ample selection of kicks.

Josephine

1405 N Wells Street, at W North Avenue, Old
Town (1-312 274 0359/www.josephineonline.com).
El: Red to Clark/Division. **Open** 11am-6pm Mon-Sat.
Credit AmEx, Disc, MC, V. **Map** p327 H7.
Breathtakingly beautiful women's heels – only in the
most fabulous styles – fill this glamorous, chande-
lier-adorned shoe salon. Prices begin at around $350,
but the free peeks are worth your time.

Lori's Designer Shoes

824 W Armitage Avenue, at N Dayton Street,
Lincoln Park (1-773 281 5655/www.lorisdesigner
shoes.com). El: Brown or Purple to Armitage.
Open 11am-7pm Mon-Thur; 11am-6pm Fri; 10am-
6pm Sat; noon-5pm Sun. **Credit** AmEx, Disc, MC, V.
Map p328 F6.
A fave with shoe-crazed women, Lori's has one of
the city's largest ranges of American and European
designer shoes, all at between 10% and 30% less
than department store prices. Great bags, too.

St Alfred

1531 N Milwaukee Avenue, at N Damen Avenue,
Wicker Park (1-773 486 7159). El: Blue to Damen.
Open noon-8pm Mon-Sat; 11am-6pm Sun.
Credit AmEx, MC, V. **Map** p331 C7.
Hip-hoppers and hipsters clamour over the selection
of limited-edition sneakers, some of which are dis-
tributed exclusively at this smallish store.

Food & drink

Alcohol

House of Glunz

1206 N Wells Street, at W Division Street, Gold
Coast (1-312 642 3000/www.houseofglunz.com).
El: Red to Clark/Division. **Open** 9am-8pm Mon-Fri;
10am-7pm Sat; 2-5pm Sun. **Credit** AmEx, MC, V.
Map p327 H8.

The city's oldest wine shop harbours some of the
world's oldest wines: several vintages date back as
far as the early 1800s.

Kafka Wine Co

3325 N Halsted Street, at W Buckingham Place,
Lakeview (1-773 975 9463/www.kafkawine.com).
El: Brown, Purple or Red to Belmont. **Open** noon-
10pm Mon-Sat; noon-7pm Sun. **Credit** AmEx, Disc,
MC, V. **Map** p329 F2.
Need proof that it's not necessary to spend a fortune
to pick up a good vino? More than 90% of the 250-
plus wines here cost less than $15. The knowledge-
able staff are only too happy to help novices choose
a bottle.

Sam's Wine & Spirits

1720 N Marcey Street, at W Willow Street, Old
Town (1-312 664 4394/www.samswine.com).
El: Red to North/Clybourn. **Open** 8am-9pm Mon-
Sat; 11am-6pm Sun. **Credit** AmEx, DC, Disc, MC, V.
Sam's stocks Chicago's largest selection of import-
ed wines alongside assorted other alcohols, includ-
ing many rare brands and bottles.

Bakeries

See also p155 **Sweet things**.

Bittersweet

1114 W Belmont Avenue, at N Racine Avenue,
Lakeview (1-773 929 1100/www.bittersweetpastry.
com). El: Brown, Purple or Red to Belmont.
Open 7am-7pm Tue-Fri; 8am-7pm Sat; 8am-6pm
Sun. **Credit** MC, V. **Map** p329 E2.
Pastry chef Judy Contino's café/bakery is a charming spot in which to linger over a salad, quiche or
other bistro fare. The scones, cakes, croissants, tarts
and cookies practically fly out of the store.

Lutz Continental Pastry Shop

2458 W Montrose Avenue, at N Western Avenue,
Lincoln Square (1-773 478 7785/www.lutzcafe.com).
El: Brown to Montrose. **Open** 7am-7pm Mon-Thur,
Sun; 7am-8pm Fri, Sat. **Credit** MC, V.
This sophisticated 54-year-old pâtisserie is famous
for its German delicacies, among them Black Forest
gâteau. If you feel like something stronger, there are
also a number of rum- and liqueur-soaked cakes.

Swedish Bakery

5348 N Clark Street, at W Summerdale Avenue,
Andersonville (1-773 561 8919). El: Red to Berwyn.
Open 6.30am-6.30pm Mon-Fri; 6.30am-5pm Sat.
Credit AmEx, DC, Disc, MC, V.
You'll have to fight through a throng to get to the
tantalising array of cookies, breads and pastries at
this 70-year-old classic, which is why there's always
free coffee on tap while you're waiting.

Sweet Thang

1921 W North Avenue, at N Damen Avenue,
Wicker Park (1-773 772 4166). El: Blue to Damen.
Open 7am-8pm Mon-Thur; 7am-9pm Fri, Sat; 8am-
8pm Sun. **Credit** AmEx, Disc, MC, V. **Map** p331 B7.

Farmers' markets

THE LOOP
Over the last few years, a pair of farmers' markets have set up in the Loop on Tuesdays: **Federal Plaza** (W Adams & S Dearborn Streets) hosts a market every week from mid May to late October, with the **Prudential Building Plaza** (E Lake Street & N Beaubien Court) competing for a piece of the action from early June. Thursdays from mid May to late September are also busy, with farmers' markets at **Daley Plaza** (W Washington & N Dearborn Streets) and the park at **311 S Wacker Drive** (at W Jackson Boulevard). And on Saturdays from mid June to mid October, farmers hawk their wares at **Printers Row** (S Dearborn & W Polk Streets). All markets run from 7am to 2pm.

THE NEAR NORTH SIDE
There's a biggish farmers' market held every Saturday (June to October) around the junction of **W Division & N Dearborn Streets** in the Gold Coast neighbourhood, kicking off at 7am and running until 2pm. If you're not here on a weekend, content yourself with the

market held every Tuesday from 10am until 6pm right by the **Museum of Contemporary Art** in Streeterville (June to October).

OLD TOWN & LINCOLN PARK
Perhaps the city's most prestigious farmers' market, the **Green City Market** (www.chicago greencitymarket.org) takes place every Wednesday and Saturday (7am-1.30pm, mid May to late October) in Lincoln Park itself, north of N LaSalle Street along the path between N Clark Street and N Stockton Drive. In November and December, it moves indoors to the **Peggy Notebaert Museum**, running every Wednesday and Saturday from 9am to 1pm. Saturday also sees a market at the junction of **W Armitage & N Orchard Avenues** (7am-2pm, June to October).

LAKEVIEW & AROUND
The neighbourhoods north of Lincoln Park are dotted with farmers' markets between early June and the end of November. There are markets every Tuesday in **Lincoln Square** (at N Lincoln & N Western Avenues), every Saturday in **Lakeview** (N Halsted Street & W Grace Street) and **Edgewater** (W Thorndale Avenue & Broadway), and every Sunday in **Roscoe Village** (W Belmont & N Wolcott Avenues). All run from roughly 7am to 2pm.

WICKER PARK & AROUND
There's a weekly farmers' market in **Wicker Park** itself (W Schiller Street & N Damen Avenue), held every Sunday from 7am to 2pm. Four hours later, another market gets under way over in **Logan Square** (W Logan Boulevard & N Milwaukee Avenue), ending around 4pm. Both are open between June and October.

Owner Bernard Runo's French training shines through in his buttery croissants, pastries and quiches. Kick back and sip an Italian coffee.

Coffee & tea

Argo Tea Café
958 W Armitage Avenue, at N Sheffield Avenue, Lincoln Park (1-312 873 4123/www.argotea.com). El: Brown or Purple to Armitage. **Open** 6am-11pm Mon-Fri; 7am-10pm Sat, Sun. **Credit** MC, V. **Map** p328 E6.

High ceilings lend a European feel to this purveyor of black, green, oolong, white and herbal teas, served hot (Carolina honey) or iced (sparkling passion fruit). The shop also offers tasty coffee and baked goods, plus free wireless access.
Other locations: 16 W Randolph Street, at N State Street, the Loop (1-312 553 1551); 819 N Rush Street, at W Chicago Avenue, River North (1-312 951 5302).

Intelligentsia
53 E Randolph Street, at N Michigan Avenue, the Loop (1-312 920 9332/www.intelligentsiacoffee.com). El: Blue to Washington; Brown, Green, Orange, Pink

City of Chicago Store. *See p207.*

or Purple to Randolph; Red to Lake. **Open** 6am-8pm Mon-Thur; 6am-10pm Fri; 7am-10pm Sat; 7am-7pm Sun. **Credit** AmEx, Disc, MC, V. **Map** p325 J12.

Barristas at Intelligentsia compete for (and often win) awards for artistry in cappuccino creation. A variety of house-blend beans is for sale by the pound, as are sundry coffee-making essentials. **Other locations:** 53 W Jackson Boulevard, at S State Street, the Loop (1-312 253 0594).

Julius Meinl

3601 N Southport Avenue, at W Addison Street, Wrigleyville (1-773 868 1857/www.meinl.com). El: Brown to Southport. **Open** 6am-10pm Mon-Thur; 6am-midnight Fri; 7am-midnight Sat; 7am-10pm Sun. **Credit** AmEx, Disc, MC, V. **Map** p329 D1.

Austrian Julius Meinl started roasting coffee beans in 1862. Modelled after his famed Viennese coffeehouses, this inviting spot certainly looks (and feels) the part. Order apple strudel to accompany your coffee or hot chocolate, served on a silver tray.

General supermarkets

Jewel Food Stores, a workhouse of a supermarket, has numerous locations, including a 24-hour Gold Coast store (1210 N Clark Street, at W Division Street, 1-312 944 6950). Local favourite **Dominick's**, another general supermarket, also has many branches around

town, including a 24-hour store in West Town (1340 S Canal Street, at W Maxwell Street, 1-312 850 3915, www.dominicks.com).

On a more exotic level, the city contains several branches of **Whole Foods Market**, the wildly popular (and often wildly expensive) organic supermarket chain: in River North (50 W Huron Street, at N Dearborn Street, 1-312 932 9600), Lincoln Park (1000 W North Avenue, at N Sheffield Avenue, 1-312 587 0648) and Lakeview (3300 N Ashland Avenue, at W Henderson Street, 1-773 244 4200). All are open 8am-10pm daily. Cheery health food chain **Trader Joe's** also has three Chicago locations: in River North (44 E Ontario Street, at N Wabash Avenue, 1-312 951 6369), Lincoln Park (1840 N Clybourn Avenue, at W Willow Street, 1-312 274 9733) and Lakeview (3745 N Lincoln Avenue, at W Waveland Avenue, 1-773 248 4920). Each opens 9am-10pm daily.

Fox & Obel

401 E Illinois Street, at N Fairbanks Court, Streeterville (1-312 410 7301/www.fox-obel.com). El: Red to Grand. **Open** 7am-9pm daily. **Credit** AmEx, Disc, MC, V. **Map** p326 J11.

Just what Chicago needs: a gourmet food emporium (cheeses, just-baked goods, fresh fish, etc) with an in-store café. Moochers fill up on free samples.

Provenance Food & Wine

2528 N California Avenue, at W Logan Boulevard, Logan Square (1-773 384 0699/www.provenance foodandwine.com). El: Blue to California. **Open** noon-9pm Tue-Sat; noon-7pm Sun. **Credit** AmEx, Disc, MC, V.

Everything you need for a perfect picnic in the park can be found inside this friendly gourmet shop. Sample wine from boutique vintners, then pick up some wonderfully stinky cheese and Red Hen bread.

Treasure Island

75 W Elm Street, at N Clark Street, Gold Coast (1-312 440 1144/www.treasureislandfoods.com). El: Red to Clark/Division. **Open** 7am-10pm Mon-Fri; 7am-9pm Sat, Sun. **Credit** Disc, MC, V. **Map** p327 H8.

Billed as a European supermarket, Treasure Island sells exotic foodstuffs and dainties next to laundry detergents and potato chips. It's useful for those hard-to-find cooking ingredients. **Other locations:** throughout the city.

Specialists

See also p205 **Farmers' markets**.

Aji Ichiban

2117-A S China Place, Chinatown Square, Chinatown (1-312 328 9998). El: Red to Cermak-Chinatown. **Open** 10am-8pm Mon-Thur, Sun; 10am-9pm Fri, Sat. **Credit** MC, V.

Feeling adventurous? Head here for obscure Japanese gummy candies, seaweed-hugged crackers and, inexplicably, a knitting shop in the back.

L'Appetito

30 E Huron Street, at N State Street, River North (1-312 787 9881/www.lappetito.com). El: Red to Grand. **Open** 7.30am-6.30pm Mon-Fri; 9am-6.30pm Sat. **Credit** AmEx, MC, V. **Map** p326 H10.
A great Italian grocery store with imported meats, cheeses and pastas, plus the best submarine sandwiches in the city.
Other locations: John Hancock Center, 875 N Michigan Avenue, at E Chestnut Street, Magnificent Mile (1-312 337 0691).

Delicatessen Meyer

4750 N Lincoln Avenue, at N Western Avenue, Lincoln Square (1-773 561 3377/www.delicatessen meyer.com). El: Brown to Western. **Open** 9am-7pm Mon-Sat; 10am-5pm Sun. **Credit** AmEx, Disc, MC, V.
German expats flock here for a taste of the old country. Family-owned and operated since 1953, this European deli features imported meats, cheeses, coffees and wines, plus candies and fresh breads.

Garrett Popcorn Shop

670 N Michigan Avenue, at E Erie Street, Magnificent Mile (1-312 944 2630/www.garrett popcorn.com). El: Red to Grand. **Open** 9am-9pm Mon-Thur; 9am-10pm Fri, Sat; 9am-8pm Sun. **Credit** AmEx, MC, V. **Map** p326 J10.
At almost any time of the day, customers craving Garrett's caramel corn form a line outside its small storefronts, lured by the sugary aroma that wafts down the block.
Other locations: 2 W Jackson Boulevard, at N State Street, the Loop (1-312 360 1108); 26 E Randolph Street, at N State Street, the Loop (1-312 630 0127).

Mitsuwa Marketplace

100 E Algonquin Road, Arlington Heights (1-847 956 6699/www.mitsuwa.com). **Open** 9am-8pm daily. **Credit** AmEx, Disc, MC, V.
This Japanese megamart is worth the 30-minute drive. Slurp udon in the food court, browse sashimi-ready fish, peruse imported beauty goods and stuff yourself silly with all the snacks you can handle.

Stanley's Fruits & Vegetables

1558 N Elston Avenue, at W North Avenue, Old Town (1-773 276 8050). El: Red to North/Clybourn. **Open** *Apr-Sept* 6am-10pm Mon-Sat; 7am-9pm Sun. *Oct-Mar* 7am-9pm Mon-Sat; 7am-8pm Sun. **Credit** AmEx, MC, V.
Home chefs are devoted to the high-quality and jaw-droppingly inexpensive organic produce at this Old Town staple.

Vosges Haut-Chocolat

Westfield North Bridge, 520 N Michigan Avenue, at E Grand Avenue, Magnificent Mile (1-312 644 9450/www.vosgeschocolate.com). El: Red to Grand. **Open** 10am-8pm Mon-Sat; 11am-6pm Sun. **Credit** AmEx, Disc, MC, V. **Map** p326 H10.

Two childhood friends run this gourmet *chocolatier*, which specialises in truffles but also turns out chocs accented with rare spices and flowers. The Aztec hot chocolate contains cinnamon and chipotle powder.
Other locations: Peninsula, 108 E Superior Street, at N Rush Street, Magnificent Mile (1-312 337 2888).

Gifts & souvenirs

Chicago's museums conveniently offer some of the best souvenirs. Fun, funky *objets d'art* are available at the **Chicago Architecture Foundation** shop (*see p80*), while the **MCA** (*see p100*) store features plenty of unusual items, and the **Art Institute** (*see p78*) sells gifts and art books. The store at **Symphony Center** (*see p253*) has a range of high-culture souvenirs.

Art Effect

934 W Armitage Avenue, at N Bissell Street (1-773 929 3600/www.arteffectchicago.com). El: Brown or Purple to Armitage. **Open** 10am-7pm Mon-Thur; 11am-6pm Fri; 10am-6pm Sat; 11am-5pm Sun. **Credit** AmEx, MC, V. **Map** p328 E6.
This fun, airy shop has loads of nifty gift items: tiny calculators, antique brooches and household accessories of French provenance, plus cool, casual clothing (for women and kids), and wonderful jewellery.

City of Chicago Store

163 E Pearson Street, at N Michigan Avenue, Magnificent Mile (1-312 742 8811/www.chicago store.com). El: Red to Chicago. **Open** 9am-5pm Mon-Sat; 10am-5pm Sun. **Credit** AmEx, MC, V. **Map** p326 J9.
Out-of-service street signs and parking meters are among the cast-offs sold at this unique gift shop. Conventional souvenirs include ceramics, books, posters, T-shirts and CDs. **Photo** *p206*.

Flight 001

1133 N State Street, at W Division Street, Gold Coast (1-312 944 1001/www.flight001.com). El: Red to Clark/Division. **Open** 10am-8pm Mon-Sat; noon-6pm Sun. **Credit** AmEx, DC, Disc, MC, V. **Map** p327 H8.
Designed to mimic the interior of a 747, this mod travel shop offers an excellent selection of traditional and fashionable luggage, plus travel gift ideas.

Gallery 37 Store

66 E Randolph Street, at N Wabash Avenue, the Loop (1-312 744 7274/www.gallery37.org). El: Blue to Washington; Brown, Green, Orange, Pink or Purple to Randolph; Red to Lake. **Open** 10am-6pm Mon-Fri; 11am-4pm Sat. **Credit** Disc, MC, V. **Map** p325 H12.
One-of-a-kind paintings, sculptures, ceramics and other art objects created by apprentice artists. All proceeds go to not-for-profit organisations.

Paper Boy

1351 W Belmont Avenue, at N Southport Avenue, Lakeview (1-773 388 8811). El: Brown to Southport. **Open** noon-7pm Mon-Fri; 11am-7pm Sat; 11am-5pm Sun. **Credit** AmEx, MC, V. **Map** p329 D3.

Eat, Drink, Shop

The best selection of cards in town is supplemented by a great range of stationery, wedding invites and other funky impulse items. It's owned by the same man behind nearby collectibles shop Uncle Fun (*see p214*).

Paper Doll

2048 W Division Street, at N Damen Avenue, Wicker Park (1-773 227 6950/www.paperdollchicago.com). El: Blue to Damen. **Open** 11am-7pm Tue-Fri; 11am-6pm Sat; 11am-5pm Sun. **Credit** Disc, MC, V. **Map** p331 B8.

House pug Maude welcomes you to this treasure trove of fantastic and funky items you don't really need but still simply *have* to have. It'll be difficult to tear yourself away from the cool letterpress stationery, journals and quirky nicknacks.

Poster Plus

200 S Michigan Avenue, at E Adams Street, the Loop (1-800 659 1905/www.posterplus.com). El: Blue or Red to Jackson; Brown, Green, Orange, Pink or Purple to Adams. **Open** 10am-6pm Mon-Wed; 10am-8pm Thur; 10am-7pm Fri, Sat; 10:30am-6pm Sun. **Credit** AmEx, Disc, MC, V. **Map** p325 J12.

Poster art is the main draw at this three-storey emporium, but the first floor offers some interesting souvenirs (notebooks, umbrellas, magnets). Don't miss the reproductions of vintage Chicago posters and postcards.

RR#1

814 N Ashland Avenue, at W Chicago Avenue, West Town (1-312 421 9079/www.rr1chicago.com). Bus 9, 66. **Open** 11am-7pm Mon-Sat; noon-5pm Sun. **Credit** AmEx, Disc, MC, V. **Map** p331 C9.

Set in a 1930s apothecary, this dimly lit but brilliantly stocked store has something for everyone. Along with a selection of hard-to-find natural bodycare lines, it also carries fun doodads and postcards with an international bent.

Tatine

1742 W Division Street, at N Wood Street, Wicker Park (1-773 342 1890/www.tatinecandles.com). El: Blue to Division. **Open** 11am-7pm Tue-Fri; 11am-6pm Sat; noon-5pm Sun. **Credit** AmEx, MC, V. **Map** p331 C8.

Hand-poured in small batches, the soy candles here come in wonderful scents such as tomato leaf, new-mown hay and even saké. **Photo** *p209*.

Health & beauty

Complementary medicine

Cortiva Institute

18 N Wabash Avenue, at E Madison Street, the Loop (1-312 753 7990/www.cortiva.com). El: Brown, Green, Orange, Pink or Purple to Madison; Blue or Red to Monroe. **Open** 9am-7pm Mon-Fri; 9am-6pm Sat; 9am-5pm Sun. **Credit** AmEx, Disc, MC, V. **Map** p325 J12.

Massage-therapy students offer low-priced massages in this spa-like environment. A small retail area in the lobby sells healing massage oils, neck supports and other homeopathic remedies.

Ruby Room

1743-1745 W Division Street, at N Wood Street, Wicker Park (1-773 235 2323/www.rubyroom.com). El: Blue to Damen. **Open** 10am-7pm Mon-Fri; 9am-7pm Sat; 10am-6pm Sun. **Credit** AmEx, MC, V. **Map** p331 C8.

This enormous yet cosy 'healing sanctuary' has guides to help visitors select crystals, traditional Chinese medicine herbs and flower essences. The vibe is slightly new-agey, but the luxurious environment and fees are far from earthy.

Cosmetics & skincare

Benefit

852 W Armitage Avenue, at N Halsted Street, Lincoln Park (1-773 880 9192/www.benefit cosmetics.com). El: Brown or Purple to Armitage. **Open** 11am-7pm Mon-Wed; 10am-8pm Thur; 10am-7pm Fri, Sat; noon-6pm Sun. **Credit** AmEx, MC, V. **Map** p328 F6.

Drop in for a brow wax at this cheekily retro beauty spot. Its cosmetics counter majors in smart solutions for common problems such as redness, puffy eyes and fine lines.

Bravco Beauty Centre

43 E Oak Street, at N State Street, Gold Coast (1-312 943 4305/www.bravcobeautycentre.com). El: Red to Chicago. **Open** 9am-6.30pm Mon-Sat; 11am-5pm Sun. **No credit cards. Map** p326 H9.

A phenomenal variety of high-end salon brands in hair and skin care products are available at Bravco Beauty Centre, many offered at discounted prices. A second-storey addition offers a savvy selection of cosmetics and accessories.

CO Bigelow Apothecary

Water Tower Place, 835 N Michigan Avenue, at Chicago Avenue, Magnificent Mile (1-312 642 0551/www.bigelowchemist.com). El: Red to Chicago. **Open** 10am-9pm Mon-Fri; 10am-8pm Sat; noon-6pm Sun. **Credit** AmEx, Disc, MC, V. **Map** p326 J9.

A more modern sister store to New York's first pharmacy, this is a veritable repository of hard-to-find personal care items from around the world. The house lines of tonics and lotions are based on decades-old formulations.

Endo-Exo Apothecary

2034 N Halsted Street, at W Armitage Avenue, Lincoln Park (1-773 525 0500/www.endoexo.com). El: Brown or Purple to Armitage. **Open** 11am-7pm Mon-Thur; 11am-7pm Fri; 10am-6pm Sat; 11am-5pm Sun. **Credit** AmEx, Disc, MC, V. **Map** p328 F6.

Grab new skincare products and cosmetics (look for the Sundari and Poole lines), get your make-up done by a pro, and check out the vintage compacts at Endo-Exo.

Tatine. See p208.

Hairdressers

Ajés the Salon
648 W Randolph Street, at N Desplaines Street, West Loop (1-312 454 1133). Bus 14, 20, 56. **Open** 9am-6pm Wed-Fri; 6am-1pm Sat. **Credit** AmEx, Disc, MC, V. **Map** p330 F12.
Sisters flock to Ajés for braids, locks, weaves, colourings, cuts and styling. The full-service salon also offers manicures and pedicures.

Art + Science
1971 N Halsted Street, at W Armitage Avenue, Lincoln Park (1-312 787 4247/www.artandscience salon.com). El: Brown or Purple to Armitage. **Open** 10am-9pm Tue-Thur; 10am-8pm Fri; 9am-6pm Sat. **Credit** Disc, MC, V. **Map** p328 F6.
Trendsetters are loathe to give up the secrets to their hip haircuts, but this place is almost always the source. The glass-fronted location is something of a see-and-be-seen place.
Other locations: 1554 N Milwaukee Avenue, at N Damen Avenue, Wicker Park (1-773 227 4247).

Big Hair
2012 W Roscoe Street, at N Damen Avenue, Roscoe Village (1-773 348 0440). El: Brown to Paulina. **Open** 10am-6pm Mon-Fri; 10am-4pm Sat; noon-3pm Sun. **No credit cards. Map** p330 B2.
Twenty bucks will buy you an of-the-moment 'do from this punky, retro salon. The catch? You may have to queue, as appointments aren't offered.

Strange Beauty Show
1261 N Paulina Avenue, at N Milwaukee Avenue, Wicker Park (1-773 252 9522/www.strange beautyshow.com). El: Blue to Division. **Open** 11am-10pm Tue-Sat; noon-6pm Sun. **Credit** MC, V. **Map** p331 C8.
This attitude-free salon-cum-gallery is a cheery, rock 'n' roll kind of place at which to get a quick snip ($25-$45) while supping on a house cocktail.

State Street Barbers
1151 W Webster Avenue, at N Racine Street, Lincoln Park (1-773 477 7721). El: Brown or Purple to Armitage. **Open** 8am-9pm Mon-Thur; 10am-7pm Fri; 8am-5pm Sat; 9am-5pm Sun. **Credit** MC, V. **Map** p328 E5.
An inviting, old-fashioned barbershop that offers haircuts and hot lather shaves, as well as shoe shines and repairs. Ask about the first-visit discount.
Other locations: 1547 N Wells Street, at W North Avenue, Old Town (1-312 787 7722).

Opticians

In the Loop, **Macy's** (*see p192*) and **Sears** (*see p193*) have optical counters.

D/Vision Optical
1756 W Division Street, at N Wood Street, Wicker Park (1-773 489 4848/www.dvoptical.com). El: Blue to Division. **Open** noon-8pm Mon-Thur; noon-6pm Fri, Sun; 10am-6pm Sat. **Credit** AmEx, Disc, MC, V. **Map** p331 C8.
Top-of-the-line designer collections, many of them European, fill this hip specs and sunglasses shop.

Eye Want
1543 N Milwaukee Avenue, at N Damen Avenue, Wicker Park (1-773 782 1744/www.eyewanteyewear. com). El: Blue to Damen. **Open** noon-7pm Mon-Fri; noon-5pm Sat. **Credit** AmEx, Disc, MC, V. **Map** p331 B7.

Dusty Groove America, a happy hunting ground for vinyl junkies. *See p213.*

See p213.

Love the thrill of the dig? Take a tour of this massive three-floor warehouse, which is filled to the rafters with beautiful and unusual furniture. Highlights include fireplace mantels, claw-foot bathtubs and bathroom fixtures.

Urban Remains

410 N Paulina Street, at W Kinzie Street, West Town (1-312 523 4660/www.urbanremains chicago.com). El: Green or Pink to Ashland. **Open** 11am-7pm daily. **Credit** MC, V. **Map** p330 C11.

Housed in a former turn-of-the-century bottling company, this unconventional shop stocks architectural artefacts and antiques. You might find Victorian-era doorknobs, sconces from the Chicago Board of Trade, and the owner's series of old-timey photographs – a steal at just $25.

White Attic

5408 N Clark Street, at Bryn Mawr Avenue, Andersonville (1-773 907 9800/www.thewhite attic.com). El: Red to Bryn Mawr. **Open** noon-7pm Wed-Fri; 10am-6pm Sat; noon-5pm Sun. **Credit** AmEx, Disc, MC, V.

White Attic's owners hunt for vintage pieces of furniture and then lovingly restore them, right down to the little details. The original *objets d'art* reflect the charming but not precious vibe.

Garden stores & florists

Green

1718 N Wells Street, at W St Paul Avenue, Old Town (1-312 266 2806). El: Brown or Purple to Sedgwick. **Open** 9am-7pm Mon-Sat; 11am-6pm Sun. **Credit** MC, V. **Map** p327 H7.

This Old Town oasis sells an enormous variety of orchids, tropical plants and other flowering fronds, but is also a source of antique Chinese porcelains and ethnographic art from Africa, Asia and South America.

A New Leaf Studio & Garden

1645 N Wells Street, at W North Avenue, Old Town (1-312 642 1576/www.anewleafchicago.com). El: Brown or Purple to Sedgwick. **Open** 9am-8pm Mon-Fri; 9am-7pm Sat; 9am-6pm Sun. **Credit** AmEx, Disc, MC, V. **Map** p327 H7.

Originally a plant store, this popular florist also sells antiques, pottery, candles and home accessories from around the world.
Other locations: 1818 N Wells Street, at W Menomenee Street, Old Town (1-312 642 8553).

Sprout Home

745 N Damen Avenue, at W Chicago Avenue, West Town (1-312 226 5950/www.sprouthome.com). Bus 50, 66. **Open** 10am-8pm Mon-Fri; 10am-7pm Sat, Sun. **Credit** AmEx, Disc, MC, V. **Map** p331 B10.

You'll find clever modern design pieces for the homeat Sprout, including mod-print plates and stick-on decals for walls. During the warmer months, an outside garden is filled with beautiful plants and trees.

Homewares

Bloomingdale's Home & Furniture Store

600 N Wabash Avenue, at E Erie Street, River North (1-312 324 7500/www.bloomingdales.com). El: Red to Grand. **Open** 10am-8pm Mon-Sat; 11am-7pm Sun. **Credit** AmEx, MC, V. **Map** p326 H10.

Situated in the former Medinah Temple building, this fabulous store has four levels of homewares, furniture, rugs and bedding, plus all kinds of luxury items. Call ahead for details of the cooking demos.

Haus

5405 N Clark Street, at W Balmoral Avenue, Andersonville (1-773 769 4000/www.hauschicago. com). El: Red to Berwyn. **Open** 11am-7pm Tue-Thur; 11am-8pm Fri, Sat; noon-5pm Sun. **Credit** AmEx, Disc, MC, V.

This locally focused boutique has a well-curated collection of ceramics and pottery, including work by West Loop glass artists F2 and sustainable-wood tables by Berwyn woodworker Nevin Peters.

ID

3337 N Halsted Street, at W Roscoe Street, Wrigleyville (1-773 755 4343/www.idchicago.com). El: Brown, Purple or Red to Belmont. **Open** 11am-7pm Tue-Thur; 11am-6pm Fri; 10am-5pm Sat; noon-5pm Sun. **Credit** AmEx, Disc, MC, V. **Map** p329 F2.

This über-minimalist home accessories store features expertly selected gadgets, exquisite Swedish furniture, bath products, stylish eyewear and a small range of unusual wooden clutch bags.

Lille

1923 W North Avenue, at N Damen Avenue, Wicker Park (1-773 342 0563/www.lilleashop.com). El: Blue to Damen. **Open** 11am-6pm Mon-Sat; noon-5pm Sun. **Credit** AmEx, Disc, MC, V. **Map** p331 B7.

Lille's gallery-like setting makes you feel as if you're buying a work of art. Find high-tech gadgets for the home, as well as tasteful decorative accessories.

Willow Home & Body

908 N Damen Avenue, at W Iowa Street, West Town (1-773 772 0140/www.shopwillow.com). Bus 50, 66. **Open** 11am-6pm Tue, Sat; 11am-7pm Wed-Fri; noon-4pm Sun. **Credit** MC, V. **Map** p331 B9.

Nature inspires the independently designed tableware, pillows and knick-knacks at this charmingly cosy spot. You can pop by for excellent brow waxes and thorough facials in the small room out back.

Music

General

The pick of the chains in town is the **Virgin Megastore** (540 N Michigan Avenue, at E Grand Avenue, Magnificent Mile, 1-312 645 9300, www.virgin.com).

Dr Wax

1121 W Berwyn Avenue, at N Winthrop Avenue, Edgewater (1-773 784 3333/www.drwax.com). El: Red to Berwyn. **Open** 11.30am-7pm daily. **Credit** AmEx, Disc, MC, V.

A selection of rap, jazz, soul and imports on CD and vinyl, both new and used. Staff are friendly. **Other locations:** 5225 S Harper Avenue, at E 52nd Street, Hyde Park (1-773 493 8696).

Evil Clown

4314 N Lincoln Avenue, at W Montrose Avenue, Lincoln Square (1-773 509 0708/www.evilclowncd. com). El: Brown to Western. **Open** noon-9pm Mon-Sat; noon-7pm Sun. **Credit** AmEx, MC, V.

Listen on headphones before you buy at this tidy little indie rock shop. It stocks CDs only, both new and second-hand.

Hyde Park Records

1377 E 53rd Street, at S Kenwood Avenue, Hyde Park (1-773 288 6588/www.hydeparkrecords.net). Metra: 55th-56th-57th Street. **Open** 11am-8pm daily. **Credit** MC, V. **Map** p332 Y16.

A few blocks north of the University of Chicago campus, this terrific retailer stocks healthy selections of soul, hip hop and jazz on vinyl and CD, plus ample selections of indie rock and hundreds of (mostly 20th-century) classical discs.

Rock Records

175 W Washington Street, at N Wells Street, the Loop (1-312 346 3489). El: Blue, Brown, Green, Orange, Pink or Purple to Washington. **Open** 9am-6.30pm Mon-Fri; 10am-4pm Sat. **Credit** AmEx, Disc, MC, V. **Map** p325 H12.

The name is something of a misnomer, as this unassuming store also stocks healthy selections of rap and Top 40 stock. It lacks the cred of other shops, but it's good in a pinch.

Specialist & used

Dusty Groove America

1120 N Ashland Avenue, at W Division Street, Wicker Park (1-773 342 5800/www.dustygroove. com). Bus 9, 70. **Open** 10am-8pm daily. **Credit** AmEx, Disc, MC, V.

Hip hoppers, house partiers and other savvy sorts buy their vinyl at this well-organised shop, which hawks an array of obscure and imported dance-related discs. **Photo** *p212.*

Gramaphone Records

2843 N Clark Street, at W Diversey Parkway, Lakeview (1-773 472 3683/www.gramaphone records.com). El: Brown or Purple to Diversey. **Open** 11am-9pm Mon-Fri; 10.30am-8.30pm Sat; noon-7pm Sun. **Credit** AmEx, Disc, MC, V. **Map** p328 F4.

DJs shop at this store for vinyl, mix tapes and some CDs. Those who aren't au fait with the scene might feel a little out of their depth.

Jazz Record Mart

25 E Illinois Street, at N Wabash Avenue, River North (1-312-222-1467/www.jazzmart.com). El: Red to Grand. **Open** 10am-8pm Mon-Sat; noon-7pm Sun. **Credit** AmEx, Disc, MC, V. **Map** p326 H11.

One of the best music collections in the city. The music is often divided by regions (there's a whole bin just for Chicago blues), and the new and used CDs are supplemented by large selections of albums (some still sealed), R&B singles and even 78s.

K-Starke

1109 N Western Avenue, at W Division Street,
Wicker Park (1-773 772 4880). El: Blue to Division.
Open 11am-8pm Mon-Sat; noon-7pm Sun. **Credit**
MC, V. **Map** p331 A9.
Specialising in rare vinyl and hard-to-find 45s, this
off-the-beaten-path shop draws DJs with its selections of obscure house, jazz, soul, reggae, Italo disco
and punk wax. If it's underground, it may well be
available here.

Reckless Records

1532 N Milwaukee Avenue, at N Damen Avenue,
Wicker Park (1-773 235 3727/www.reckless.com).
El: Blue to Damen. **Open** 10am-10pm Mon-Sat;
10am-8pm Sun. **Credit** AmEx, Disc, MC, V.
Map p331 B9.
Perhaps the best used-CD all-rounder in the city, the
Wicker Park branch of Reckless has decent selec-
tions of CDs in more or less all genres.
Other locations: 3161 N Broadway Street, at W
Belmont Avenue, Lakeview (1-773 404 5080).

Record Dugout

6055 W 63rd Street, at S McVicker Street, South
Side (1-773 586 1206). El: Red to 63rd. **Open** noon-
7pm daily. **No credit cards**.
Vinyl geeks sift through breathtakingly large piles
of used records (no CDs!) at this South Side hangout,
hunting for hyper-rare rock, pop, soul and R&B singles. A must-visit.

Sport & fitness

The Magnificent Mile is made a little less
magnificent by the presence of **Niketown**
(669 N Michigan Avenue, at E Huron Street,
1-312 642 6363, www.nike.com).

Londo Mondo

1100 N Dearborn Street, at W Division Street, Gold
Coast (1-312 751 2794/www.londomondo.com). El:
Red to Clark/Division. **Open** 10am-7pm Mon-Fri;
10am-7pm Sat; 11am-6pm Sun. **Credit** AmEx, Disc,
MC, V. **Map** p327 H8.
This longstanding resource for athletic women has
oodles of swimsuits, flip-flops, in-line skates and a
small selection of jeans and tees.

Lululemon Athletica

2104 N Halsted Street, at W Armitage Avenue,
Lincoln Park (1-773 883 8860/www.lululemon.com).
El: Brown or Purple to Armitage. **Open** 10am-6pm
Mon-Wed; 10am-7pm Thur-Sat; 11am-6pm Sun.
Credit AmEx, MC, V. **Map** p328 F6.
Super-stylish yoga gear, from mats to clothing,
draws a crowd that insists on looking alluring while
doing asanas.

Sportmart

620 N LaSalle Street, at W Ontario Street, River
North (1-312 337 6151/www.sportsauthority.com).
El: Red to Grand. **Open** 9am-9.30pm Mon-Fri; 9am-
9pm Sat; 10am-7pm Sun. **Credit** AmEx, Disc, MC, V.
Map p326 H10.

This eight-storey flagship store has entire floors
given over to virtually every athletic pursuit. Watch
out for the busloads of tourists who create a frenzy
over the pro sports memorabilia.
Other locations: 3134 N Clark Street, at W Belmont
Avenue, Lakeview (1-773 871 8501).

Viking Ski Shop

3422 W Fullerton Avenue, at N Kimball Avenue,
Logan Square (1-773 276 0732/www.vikingski.com).
El: Blue to Logan Square. **Open** May-Sept call for
details. Oct-Apr 11am-9pm Mon, Tue, Thur; 11am-
6pm Wed, Fri; 10am-5pm Sat; 11am-5pm Sun.
Credit AmEx, Disc, MC, V.
Arguably *the* destination for skiers in the Midwest,
Viking has more than 30 years of experience fitting
the entire family with ski equipment and general
cold-weather gear.

Windward Sports

3317 N Clark Street, at W Belmont Avenue,
Lakeview (1-773 472 6868/www.windwardsports.
com). El: Brown, Purple or Red to Belmont. **Open**
11am-6pm Mon; 11am-8pm Wed, Thur; 11am-7pm
Fri; 11am-5pm Sat, Sun. **Map** p329 F3. **Credit**
AmEx, Disc, MC, V. **Map** p329 F2.
All manner of snowboarding, skateboarding, kite-
boarding, wakeboarding and windsurfing gear is
offered at this Lakeview store, which is also a safe
bet for swimwear, sunglasses and sandals. Rentals
are also available.

Toys & games

For the **Lego Store**, *see p191*.

Quake

4628 N Lincoln Avenue, at W Eastwood Avenue,
Uptown (1-773 878 4288). El: Red to Lawrence.
Open 1-6pm Mon, Wed-Fri; noon-6pm Sat; noon-5pm
Sun. **Credit** MC, V.
The place to find that elusive Mystery Date game or
that *Nightmare Before Christmas* figurine, along
with retro lunchboxes, *Star Wars* swag and board
games from the '60s and '70s.

Rotofugi

1953 W Chicago Avenue, at N Damen Avenue,
West Town (1-312 491 9501/www.rotofugi.com).
Bus 50, 66. **Open** noon-8pm Tue-Sat; noon-5pm Sun.
Credit AmEx, Disc, MC, V. **Map** p331 B10.
Grown-up kids rush to this Japanese-inspired toy
shop to pick up limited-edition vinyl dolls, plush
toys and poseable figures. There's almost always a
cool art exhibition on show.

Uncle Fun

1338 W Belmont Avenue, at N Southport Avenue,
Lakeview (1-773 477 8223/www.unclefunchicago.
com). El: Brown, Purple or Red to Belmont. **Open**
noon-7pm Tue-Fri; 11am-7pm Sat; 11am-5pm Sun.
Credit AmEx, MC, V. **Map** p329 D2.
Kids young and old will love digging through draw-
ers jammed full of plastic squirt cameras, fake barf
and the like, all at quite reasonable prices.

Arts & Entertainment

Festivals & Events	216
Art Galleries	221
Children	225
Comedy	230
Dance	233
Film	236
Gay & Lesbian	240
Music	250
Nightclubs	263
Sports & Fitness	271
Theatre	278

Features

The best Festivals	216
Hug a hoodie	218
The best Galleries	221
The best Kids' stuff	225
The real Kid Rock	229
The best Comedy	230
Bronze mettle	232
The best Dance venues	233
Fringe benefits	235
The best Screens	237
The best Gay spots	240
Read all about it	244
Ride him, cowboy	249
The best Classics	250
The best Rock & pop	253
Artists in residence	258
The best Blues & jazz	259
The best Clubs	263
Club culture	265
Baby, let's play house	268
The best Sports	271
Spare change	273
Life cycle	274
The best Theatres	278
What's in a name?	282

Navy Pier. *See p225*.

Festivals & Events

Let off some steam in the city with a shindig for all seasons.

As the temperatures dip below zero, Chicagoans gather for winter festivities both ancient and modern. But when the warm weather blows in from the lake, the city springs into life in a blaze of festivals, block parties and other open-air shenanigans. It's as if Chicago has suffered through the hibernation of the often harsh winters purely to spend the summer outdoors.

In particular, Grant Park gets inundated with day-trippers, queueing up to take in a packed programme of festivals focused on music, movies and even food. The lakefront is regularly filled with funseekers taking in headline-grabbers such as the **Chicago Air & Water Show**. The trick with these high-profile events is to plan ahead, arrive early (especially in summer) and get used to the fact that the only place to eat will be immediately adjacent to a fly-covered garbage can.

Fun and games abound at the city's many neighbourhood festivals, street fairs and block parties (*see p218* **Hug a hoodie**), which have a more relaxed pace than their downtown counterparts. Many are tied to the city's ethnic communities, all of which proclaim their heritage with at least one event a year.

INFORMATION & TICKETS

For advance information on these and other events around the city, contact the **Mayor's Office of Special Events** (1-312 744 3315, www.cityofchicago.org/specialevents) or the **Chicago Office of Tourism** (1-312 744 2400, www.cityofchicago.org/tourism), which publishes a quarterly guide to seasonal events. *Time Out Chicago* offers weekly listings of festivals and events in its Around Town section, and also publishes an annual guide to summer events that's available as both a pull-out guide in the magazine and online at www.timeout.com/chicago. The Friday editions of the *Chicago Tribune* and the *Chicago Sun-Times* do their bit with regular pull-out event guides. All events in this section are free and family-friendly unless stated.

Spring

For **Around the Coyote**, *see p219*.

Spring & Easter Flower Show

Garfield Park Conservatory *300 N Central Park Boulevard, at W Lake Street, West Side (1-312 746 5100/www.garfield-conservatory.org). El: Green to Conservatory-Central Park Drive.* **Date** Feb-May.
Lincoln Park Conservatory *2391 N Stockton Drive, at W Fullerton Parkway, Lincoln Park (1-312 742 7736/www.chicagoparkdistrict.com). El: Brown, Purple or Red to Fullerton.* **Date** Feb-May. **Map** p328 G5.

Lincoln Park Conservatory and the Garfield Park Conservatory display a collage of the first blooms to defy the icy hold of winter, with refreshments, children's activities and music. The opening reception is held at Garfield Park.

St Patrick's Day

Downtown *Columbus Drive, from E Balbo Drive to E Monroe Street, the Loop (1-312 744 2400/www.cityofchicago.org). El: Blue or Red to Jackson; Brown, Green, Orange, Pink or Purple to Adams.* **Date** Sat nr 17 Mar. **Map** p325 H11-H13.
South Side *around S Western Avenue, at 103rd Street, South Side (1-773 393 8687/www.southside irishparade.org). Bus 49, 103.* **Date** Sun nr 17 Mar.

During election years, the candidates all magically become Irish for the duration of St Patrick's Day, which is celebrated with serious abandon by locals and suburbanites regardless of whether or not they have any connection to the Emerald Isle. Downtown, the Chicago River is dyed green at 10.45am on the nearest Saturday to the day itself (it's best viewed from the upper level of the Michigan Avenue Bridge, at Wacker Drive), before a parade works its way through the Loop. The celebrations are rather more authentic on the South Side, with a rougher, tougher parade down S Western Avenue from 103rd to 115th. Bring a spare liver.

Great Chicago Places & Spaces

Around the city (1-312 744 3370/www.cityofchicago. org). **Date** 3 days, late May.

A weekend-long event devoted to Chicago's famous architecture. The Chicago Architecture Foundation (www.architecture.org) oversees tours by bus, train,

The best Festivals

For aerial acrobatics
Chicago Air & Water Show. *See p219.*

For a four-hour workout
Chicago Marathon. *See p219.*

For a sweet-toothed treat
Garfield Park Chocolate Show. *See p220.*

Don't rain on their parade: **Chicago Carifete**. See p219.

trolley and foot. Dozens of tours cover everything from CTA rail stations to the City Hall rooftop garden, district-cooling plants to skyscrapers. Most tours are free, but require registration at the CAF's ArchiCenter (see p80), from 7.30am each day.

Summer

For Chicago's celebrated neighbourhood festivals, held sporadically throughout the summer, see p218 **Hug a hoodie**.

Andersonville Midsommarfest

N Clark Street, between W Foster Avenue & W Berwyn Street, North Side (1-773 665 4682/ www.starevents.com). El: Purple or Red to Berwyn. **Date** wknd, June.
Andersonville is famous as the home of Chicago's formerly prominent Swedish community, a history that's celebrated each summer with this traditional-ish free outdoor event around Clark Street. Some 50,000 locals descend to watch maypole dancers, munch street food and generally make merry.

Printers' Row Book Fair

S Dearborn Street, between W Congress Parkway & W Polk Street, South Loop (1-312 222 3986/ www.printersrowbookfair.org). El: Blue to LaSalle; Red to Harrison. **Date** wknd, June. **Map** p324 H13.
Once the wellspring of the city's publishing prosperity, Printers' Row rekindles its heritage once a year with this weekend-long festival in the South Loop. More than 150 booksellers show up to sell books new and used, with authors on hand to give readings and sign copies of their works.

Taste of Chicago

Grant Park, the Loop (1-312 744 2400/www.tasteof chicago.us). El: Brown, Green, Orange, Pink or Purple to Adams; Red to Monroe. **Date** 10 days, late June-early July. **Map** pp324-325 J11-J14.
Only about 1% of Chicago's 5,000 restaurants are represented at this ten-day festival in Grant Park, but the event nonetheless draws an astonishing three million visitors. Entry is free; instead, you pay for tickets which you can then exchange for grub. Large crowds at weekends and evenings mean finding a seat is tricky. There's also music and a range of family-friendly activities.

Independence Day Fireworks

Grant Park, the Loop (1-312 744 2400/www.cityof chicago.org). El: Brown, Green, Orange, Pink or Purple to Adams; Red to Monroe. **Date** 3 July. **Map** pp324-325 J11-J14.
On the day before Independence Day, huge crowds descend on Downtown to sway to live bands, before turning their eyes to the sky to watch a spectacular fireworks display at around 9.30pm. The display is best viewed from Grant Park (where the Taste of Chicago event will be in full swing) or along the

---

▶ Festivals and events dedicated to a single art form are featured in the relevant chapter: **art** (*p222*), **comedy** (*p230*), **dance** (*p234*), **film** (*p238*), **music** (*p252* & *p254*) and **clubbing** (*p267*).
▶ For **gay & lesbian events**, see *p243*.

Arts & Entertainment

Hug a hoodie

Fun as they often are, Chicago's blockbuster summer festivals are often packed with more visitors than locals. For a real window into city life, venture off the tourist track into the city's residential neighbourhoods, which take it in turns to celebrate summer with their own block parties. Streets are blocked off for the weekend, and vendors provide meals of the deep-fried or between-a-bun variety while musicians of varying talent provide entertainment. Entry prices can be steep, but many neighbourhoods turn over the cash to charity or re-invest it in the community. A schedule can be obtained from the Mayor's Office of Special Events (*see p216*); it's also

worth looking out for the free festivals guide published by *Time Out Chicago* magazine each summer.

Many block parties tend to reflect the neighbourhoods in which they're set. Wicker Park's **Summerfest** (late July) features an array of indie-rock, buzz-bin bands spread over two days, while **Summer on Southport** (late July) welcomes the young families that make up much of modern-day Lakeview's population, and the Near West Side's **West Fest** (mid August) is altogether artier. Others are rather more basic (a couple of bands, a couple of kegs, a couple of cops) but no less enjoyable for their lack of flash.

A few events offer great food: Greektown's **Taste of Greece** (late August; *pictured*), for example. And though Taylor Street is usually considered Chicago's Little Italy, but Heart of Italy, a more off-the-beaten-path locale to the south-west, takes centre stage every June with **Festa Pasta Vino**, aka the Heart of Italy Food & Wine Festival (www.festapastavino. com). In past years, the free celebration of Italian food and culture has included plenty of tastings and cooking demos, and even a working replica of Rome's Trevi fountain.

Chicago reputedly boasts a larger Polish population than any city on earth except Warsaw. Accordingly, the **Taste of Polonia** (www.copernicusfdn.org), held each year in Jefferson Park on the first weekend in September, is a serious party. Along with more pierogis than you could possibly carbo-load, there's entertainment from the likes of hip hop act Funky Polak and even, if you are lucky, a few Polish Elvis impersonators.

lakefront. There are further festivities (and even more fireworks) on Independence Day itself over at Navy Pier (*see p101*).

Dearborn Garden Walk

N Dearborn, N State, N Astor and N LaSalle Streets & N Sandburg Terrace, between W Goethe Street and W North Avenue, Gold Coast (1-312 632 1241/ www.dearborngardenwalk.com). El: Red to Clark/ Division. **Date** Sun, mid July. **Map** p327 G8-H8.
America's oldest garden walk (it's been running since the 1950s) works its way around the luxurious homes and gardens of the Gold Coast, taking in around 20 private gardens. Garden items and refreshments are sold en route, and there's also music. The tickets, which usually cost around $30, include a copy of a coffee-table book entitled *The Gardens of Chicago's Gold Coast*.

Venetian Night

Lake Michigan, from the Adler Planetarium to Monroe Harbor, the Loop (1-312 744 2400/www. cityofchicago.org). El: Brown, Green, Orange, Pink or Purple to Adams; Red to Harrison or Jackson. **Date** Sat, late July. **Map** pp324-325 K12-K14.
Boat owners celebrate by adorning their crafts with lights and parading them along the waterfront. A brilliant fireworks display concludes the evening.

Bud Billiken Day Parade & Picnic

From 39th Street, at S King Drive, to Washington Park, at E 51st Street, Hyde Park (1-312 744 2400/ www.budbillikenparade.com). El: Green to 51st or Indiana. **Date** 2nd Sat in Aug. **Map** p332 X16.
This African American parade, the largest of its kind in the nation, has been held since 1929, when *Chicago Defender* founder Robert Abbott decided to

stage an event to celebrate South Side family values. The event begins on 39th Street and King Drive, and proceeds south to Washington Park, rounding off with a big barbecue. The patron, Bud Billiken, is associated with an ancient mythical Chinese guardian angel of children.

Chicago Air & Water Show
North Avenue Beach, at North Avenue & from W Oak Street to W Diversey Parkway (1-312 744 3370/ www.cityofchicago.org). Bus 151. **Date** wknd, Aug. **Map** pp326-328 G4-H9.
If you didn't know this free event was due to take place in early August, the sonic booms that bounce off the Gold Coast high-rises as planes soar past them make it impossible to avoid. Some two million people head to the lakefront each year to watch the spectacular aerobatic and aquatic stunt performers.

Chicago Carifete
Around Hyde Park, centred on E 59th Street (1-773 509 4942/www.chicagocarifete.com). Metra: 59th Street. **Date** Sat, late Aug. **Map** p332 Y18.
This free celebration of Caribbean culture includes a masquerade procession through the streets of Hyde Park. Costumed bands with steel drummers keep the parade in stride; stalls offer Caribbean cuisine and other cultural wares. **Photo** *p217.*

Around the Coyote Festival
Around Wicker Park & Bucktown (1-773 342 6777/ www.aroundthecoyote.org). El: Blue to Damen. **Date** wknd, early Sept. **Map** p331.
The Coyote in question is the Northwest Tower in Wicker Park; this free festival, now approaching its 20th anniversary, contains a variety of events within a stone's throw of it. ATC began as an artists' open house, with local painters and sculptors welcoming the public to their studios. Now it takes in readings, screenings and a other performances. There's also a smaller winter edition in February.

Autumn

German-American Festival
4700 N Lincoln Avenue, at W Lawrence Avenue, Lincoln Square (1-630 653 3018). El: Brown to Western. **Date** wknd, Sept.
Kind of a diet Oktoberfest, this German-American Festival is similar to its Bavarian counterpart, with the notable exception of the stewed masses. The festival coincides with the Von Steuben Day Parade down Lincoln Avenue on the Saturday.

Redmoon Spectacle
Location varies (1-312 850 8440/www.redmoon.org). **Date** 1wk, Oct.
Each year, this not-for-profit theatre company stages an impressive outdoor spectacle, taking in puppetry, music and dazzling special effects. In recent years, Redmoon has staged a Hallow's Eve parade in Logan Square, and set a lake on fire in Chinatown's Ping Tom Park. What will they think of next?

Columbus Day Parade
Columbus Drive, from E Balbo Drive to E Monroe Street, the Loop (1-312 744 2400/www.cityofchicago. org). El: Blue or Red to Jackson; Brown, Green, Orange, Pink or Purple to Adams. **Date** 2nd Mon in Oct. **Map** p325 H11-H13.
Chicago's Italian-American community celebrates the so-called discovery of America with a massive parade through the Loop on this national holiday.

LaSalle Bank Chicago Marathon
Start/finish: Grant Park, on S Columbus Drive, near Buckingham Fountain, the Loop (1-312 904 9800/ www.chicagomarathon.com). El: Blue or Red to Monroe; Brown, Green, Orange, Pink or Purple to Adams. **Date** Sun, late Oct. **Map** p325 J13.
The city all but shuts down as nearly 40,000 sweaty athletes race along a 26.2-mile (42.1-kilometre) course that's among the fastest in the world. Starting from Grant Park, runners head up via Lincoln Park to Wrigleyville, then turning on their heels before coming back down through Old Town, out into the West Loop, south through Pilsen and across via Chinatown into Grant Park and the finish line.

Chicago Humanities Festival
Around Chicago (1-312 661 1028/www.chfestival. org). **Date** 2wks, late Oct/early Nov.
Get up close and personal with big (and small) names in literature, film and artfor a programme of lectures, readings and panel discussions that fall under a usually timely theme (in 2006, it was Peace & War: Facing Human Conflict).

Chicago Air & Water Show.

Arts & Entertainment

Hallowe'en

Around Chicago (www.cityofchicago.org/ specialevents). **Date** around 31 Oct.

Dust off your broomstick and try on your bedsheets. Every October, the city of Chicago organises three weeks of Hallowe'en celebrations, fronted by the suitably scary Mayor Daley.

Day of the Dead

Mexican Fine Arts Center Museum, 1852 W 19th Street, at S Damen Avenue, Pilsen (1-312 738 1503/ www.mfacmchicago.org). El: Blue to 18th Street or Hoyne. **Date** 1 day, early Nov.

This celebration honours the gone-but-not-forgotten with exhibits at the Mexican Fine Arts Center Museum (*see p124*) in the heart of the Midwest's largest Mexican community. Alongside the displays of macabre but curiously joyous art and other accoutrements, a procession kicks off at the St Precopious School (1625 S Allport Street, at W 16th Street, Pilsen) and ends up at the museum.

Winter

In addition to the events below, the City of Chicago stages a variety of events in January and February for its **Winter Delights** series.

Christmas Around the World

Museum of Science & Industry, 5700 S Lake Shore Drive, at E 57th Street, Hyde Park (1-773 684 1414/ www.msichicago.org). Metra: 55th-56th-57th Street. **Date** mid Nov-early Jan. **Map** p332 Z17.

For the last 60-plus years, the Museum of Science & Industry has staged a simultaneous exhibition on and celebration of the ways in which the festive season is observed all over the globe. In addtion to Christmas, there are events based around Diwali, Hanukkah, Kwanzaa and Chinese New Year, with regular theatre, dance and music shows to jolly along the proceedings.

Zoolights

Lincoln Park Zoo, 2200 N Cannon Drive, at W Webster Avenue, Lincoln Park (1-312 742 2000/ www.lpzoo.com). El: Brown, Purple or Red to Fullerton. **Date** late Nov-early Jan. **Map** p328 H5.

The zoo stays open late through the holidays, and the atmosphere is dazzling. Evening visitors are guided along the winding pathways by a sprawling display of illuminated designs, many of them shaped like animals. If the lights leave you dazed, the hot cider and chainsaw-wielding ice sculptors are sure to wake you up.

Christkindlmarket

Daley Plaza, W Washington Boulevard & N Dearborn Street, the Loop (1-312 644 2662/www.christkindl market.com). El: Blue to Washington; Brown, Green, Orange, Pink or Purple to Randolph; Red to Lake. **Date** late Nov-late Dec. **Map** p325 H12.

The German-American Chamber of Commerce converts Daley Plaza into a German-style market, with German food and arts on tap.

McDonald's Thanksgiving Parade

State Street, from Congress Parkway to Randolph Street, the Loop (1-312 781 5681/www.chicago festivals.org). El: Blue or Red to Jackson, Monroe or Washington; Brown, Green, Orange, Pink or Purple to Adams, Madison or Randolph. **Date** Thanksgiving Day. **Map** pp325 H11-H13.

Chicago's holiday season truly gets under way with this big parade along 'that great street' in the Loop, starring everything from a giant inflatable Elmo to lawnchair-toting dads clad in massive underwear. Events start at 8.30am and conclude by 11am.

Holiday Tree Lighting Ceremony

Daley Plaza, W Washington Boulevard & N Dearborn Street, the Loop (1-312 744 2400/www. cityofchicago.org). El: Blue to Washington; Brown, Green, Orange, Pink or Purple to Randolph; Red to Lake. **Date** late Nov. **Map** p325 H12.

A giant 80-foot (25-metre) tree constructed from smaller evergreens is illuminated at Daley Plaza the night after Thanksgiving, usually around 4pm. Four giant toy sentries tower over onlookers and an enormous toy train roams around the plaza's corner.

Pre-Kwanzaa Celebration

South Shore Cultural Center, 7059 S Shore Drive, at E 71st Street, South Side (1-773 256 0149/ www.chicagoparkdistrict.com). Metra: South Shore. **Date** mid Dec.

Kwanzaa, an East African word meaning 'first fruits of the harvest', is a time for celebration in Africa. The South Shore Cultural Center marks the event with music, dance and Afro-centric lectures

Chinatown New Year Parade

Along S Wentworth Avenue, Chinatown (1-312 326 5320/www.chicagochinatown.org). El: Red to Cermak-Chinatown. **Date** 1st Sun after Chinese New Year (early Feb). **Map** p324 H16.

Chicago celebrates Chinese New Year with an array of festivities, all held in Chinatown. The calendar generally includes parades, banquets, concerts, dance performances and a fanfare of fircrackers.

Chicago Auto Show

McCormick Place, 2301 S Lake Shore Drive, South Side (1-312 791 7000/www.chicagoautoshow.com). Bus 2, 3, X3, 4, 6, 10, 14, 21, 26, 28. **Date** 10 days, early Feb.

A chance for petrolheads to check out what's new in motoring. Close to 1,000 different vehicles are on display at this annual showcase, along with accessories, collectables and car-themed exhibits.

Garfield Park Chocolate Show

Garfield Park Conservatory, 300 N Central Park Avenue, at W Lake Street, West Side (1-312 746 5100/www.garfieldconservatory.org). El: Green to Conservatory-Central Park Drive. **Date** 2nd wknd in Feb.

Start your Valentine's Day celebrations early with a sugar high. Thousands of samples of chocolate are distributed, with storytelling and craft stalls adding to the messy merriment.

Art Galleries

The art of the matter.

Roy Boyd Gallery. *See p222*.

Chicago's art scene is known for its youthful edge. The School of the Art Institute of Chicago helps attract many fresh-faced youngsters to the city, who make their mark by opening experimental galleries and artist-run spaces. The scene is, or can be, a little low-key: opening hours vary (always call ahead), and some spaces admit visitors by appointment only. Don't be surprised if someone offers you a Pabst Blue Ribbon while you're browsing.

The best Galleries

For young up-and-comers
Rhona Hoffman. *See p223*.

For old-school artists
Corbett vs Dempsey. *See p224*.

For ancient artefacts and historical finds
Douglas Dawson. *See p224*.

That said, the gallery circuit in Chicago isn't all about its up-and-comers: many galleries and collectors, among them **Donald Young** and **Richard Gray** (for both, *see p223*), carry significant clout in the art world. Touring galleries of such stature is a bit like a trip to a free museum. Just try not to be intimidated by the pristine walls and the snarling assistant behind the front desk.

INFORMATION

Chicago's largest gallery hub is the intersection of Superior and Franklin Streets in **River North**, while the **West Loop** warehouse district is home to a number of interesting and innovative galleries. However, while **Wicker Park** and **Bucktown** were an artists' boom town a decade ago, many of its galleries have been forced out by rising rents.

Pick up a copy of *Time Out Chicago* or the *Chicago Reader* for weekly listings of all galleries, alternative and mainstream. *Chicago Gallery News* (www.chicagogallerynews.com), a free quarterly available at many galleries, covers the scene and maps out the city's various art districts.

The Near North Side

River North

In 1976, about a dozen pioneering galleries settled in River North, surpassing the number on Michigan Avenue and the museum-centric neighbourhood of Hyde Park. Dealing in everything from mid-century to contemporary American art, the scene gathered pace until a

▶ Chicago's art museums and non-commercial galleries are listed in the Sightseeing sections of this guide: the **Art Institute of Chicago** (*p78*), the **Arts Club of Chicago** (*p101*), the **Loyola University Museum of Art** (*p98*), the **Mary & Leigh Block Museum of Art** (*p117*), the **National Museum of Mexican Art** (*p125*), the **Museum of Contemporary Art** (*p101*), the **National Vietnam Veterans' Art Museum** (*p92*), the **Renaissance Society** (*p139*), the **Smart Museum of Art** (*p142*) and the **Ukrainian Institute of Modern Art** (*p129*).

Festivals Art

Art Chicago & Artropolis

Merchandise Mart, N Wells Street, at W Kinzie Street, River North (1-312 527 4141/ www.artchicago.com). El: Brown or Purple to Merchandise Mart. **Date** Apr. **Map** p326 G11.
More than 100 dealers bring their wares to Art Chicago each year for a long weekend of schmoozing; 20,000 members of the public show up to join in. Since 2006, when dealer Thomas Blackman sold up, it's been held in the Merchandise Mart; an expansion in the programme for 2007 added numerous other events across the city under the banner of Artropolis. Admission includes entry to the concurrent International Antiques Fair.

Bridge Art Fair

Location varies (1-312 421 2227/ www.bridgeartfair.com). **Date** Apr.
The Bridge Art Fair started out as the NOVA (Network of Visual Art) Young Art Fair, a hip and cheap alternative to Art Chicago, but has grown into a major event. Many works no longer fall into the 'affordable' price bracket, but time spent browsing still offers a glimpse of the art world's rising stars.

Version

Locations in Bridgeport, Wicker Park, Bucktown & the Loop (1-773 837 0145/ http://versionfest.com). **Date** Apr-May.
The city's political artists and provocateurs convene at this festival of anti-corporate exhibitions and events. Join a protest, see an exhibition or sit back and eat organic wieners.

57th Street Art Fair

Hyde Park, at 57th Street & Kimbark Avenue, Hyde Park (1-773 493 3247/www.57thstreet artfair.org). Metra 55th-56th-57th Street.
Date June. **Map** p332 Y17.
The Midwest's oldest juried art fair showcases a slightly hokey range of visual arts from more than 250 artists for the benefit of 100,000-plus attendees.

Select Media Festival

Locations in Bridgeport, Wicker Park, Bucktown & the Loop (1-773 837 0145/ http://selectmediafestival.org). **Date** Oct.
New media exhibits, film and video screenings, performances and raging parties are all crammed into this annual festival.

---

fire in April 1989 incinerated dozens of the local galleries. The cause of the fire was never discovered, but it led some galleries to flee the area for a fresh start in the West Loop.

River North still has the greatest concentration of art dealers in Chicago, but edgy art and hip venues are conspicuous by their absence these days. Many of the area's established galleries market their work to the traditional tastes of the type of customer who also comes to peruse the pricey furniture shops just south of Franklin Street as part of a joint art-and-matching-couch shopping trip. Most galleries in the area open between 10am and 6pm from Tuesday to Friday, and roughly 11.30am to5pm on Saturdays, though it's best to call ahead before making a special trip.

A handful of galleries focus on artists who live and work in Chicago, and grace the pages of Alan Artner's notoriously temperamental art column in the *Chicago Tribune*. The **Roy Boyd Gallery** (739 N Wells Street, at W Chicago Avenue, 1-312 642 1606, www.royboydgallery.com; **photo** *p221*) shows abstract, highly textured work from a corral of gallery artists: painters, fiber-artists and Imagists. The works of beloved local artist Ed Paschke often hang on the walls of the **Maya Polsky Gallery** (215 W Superior Street, at N Wells Street, 1-312 440 0055, www.mayapolskygallery.com), while the **Carl Hammer Gallery** (740 N Wells Street, at W Chicago Avenue, 1-312 266 8512, www. hammergallery.com; **photo** *p223*) mounts outrageous exhibitions that often come with a quasi-naive aesthetic: Henry Darger's epic and disturbing drawings of grade-schoolers have featured here in the past.

Arty fare of a more international flavour fills the rooms of the **311 W Superior Street** building. In the rear, former Milwaukee Museum director **Russell Bowman** (Suite 115, 1-312 751 9500, www.bowmanart.com) hangs mid-century to contemporary works from Warhol to Kara Walker, along with the occasional Pollock painting. One of the two galleries operated by **Stephen Daiter** (Suites 404 & 408, 1-312 787 3350, www.stephendaiter gallery.com) is dedicated to contemporary work, and contains mostly documentary-style photography. At the front of the building, **Printworks** (Suite 105, 1-312 664 9407, www.printworkschicago.com) has a whimsical collection of prints, including art by artist/ novelist Audrey Niffenegger and political provocateur Leon Golub.

Across the street, **Judy Saslow** (300 W Superior Street, at N Franklin Street, 1-312 943 0530, www.jsaslowgallery.com) puts on large exhibitions by outside artists, while **Catherine Edelman** (300 W Superior Street, at N Franklin Street, 1-312 266 2350, www.edelmangallery.com) hangs a rather haphazard mix of contemporary photography. Directly east, **Zg** (300 W Superior Street, at N Franklin Street, 1-312 654 9900,www.zggallery.com) keeps things lively with vibrant paintings and installations by young, up-and-coming artists.

Two galleries slightly off the beaten path boast huge spaces and fill them with big-scale art. To the north-east, **Alan Koppel** (210 W Chicago Avenue, at N Wells Street, 1-312 640 0730, www.alankoppel.com) shows modern and contemporary artists, from Man Ray to Jeff Koons. And at the south-western tip of the district sits **Zolla Lieberman** (325 W Huron Street, at N Orleans Street, 1-312 944 1990, www.zollaliebermangallery.com), which still shows work by artists it represented back when it became the first gallery to set up shop in the then-industrial neightbourhood back in 1976. Among them are horse sculptor Deborah Butterfield and conceptualist Buzz Spector.

The Magnificent Mile & Streeterville

Many of the galleries on Michigan Avenue sell little more than posters and knick-knacks. The two main exceptions are both found in the towering **John Hancock Center** (875 N Michigan Avenue, at E Delaware Place; *see p98*. **Richard Gray** (Suite 2503, 1-312 642 8877, www.richardgraygallery.com), better known for his New York outfit than his original gallery in Chicago, has had a hand in the careers of David Hockney, Jennifer Bartlett and Jaume Plensa, the creator of the fantastic Millennium Park fountain. **Valerie Carberry** (Suite 2510, 1-312 397 9991, www.valeriecarberry.com), meanwhile, is *the* place in Chicago for post-war American art.

Old Town & Lincoln Park

Before a Starbucks could be found on every corner, the North Side was a desolate area, where the cheap housing attracted working artists. Today, older galleries are sprawled throughout the North Side, but prices generally prevent new spaces from moving in. One leftover from the mid-century is Lincoln Park's **Contemporary Art Workshop** (542 W Grant Place, at N Cleveland Avenue, 1-773 472 4004, www.contemporaryartworkshop.org), a

not-for-profit space founded in 1949 by Leon Golub, John Kearney and others. Working artists fill the studios upstairs, above an exhibition space that's been the springboard for many a contemporary artist.

The Near West Side

The West Loop & River West

Galleries began to trickle into the West Loop in the mid 1990s and the scene has hardly slowed down since, with converted warehouse spaces changing hands constantly. In recent years, though, the district seems to have settled a little, and with it has come gentrification: an influx of pricey eateries, deafening dance clubs and trendy apartments has turned this former meatpacking district into one of Chicago's hippest 'hoods. Galleries here are generally open 11am-6pm from Tuesday to Saturday.

Rhona Hoffman (118 N Peoria Street, at W Randolph Street, 1-312 455 1990, www.rhoffmangallery.com) was one of the first galleries to move to the area. Hoffman was once married to neighbouring gallerist **Donald Young** (933 W Washington Boulevard, at N Sangamon Street, 1-312 455 0100, www.donaldyoung.com). While Hoffman offers an eclectic selection (digital art followed by an exhibitition of ancient Indian pieces), Donald Young has

Shock tactics at **Carl Hammer**. *See p222.*

Bronzeville Children's Museum

Evergreen Plaza, 9600 Western Avenue, at 96th Street, Evergreen Park (1-708 636 9504/www. bronzvillechildrensmuseum.com). Bus 49, 49A. **Open** 10am-4pm Tue-Sat. **Admission** $3; $2 children. **No credit cards.**

The only African American children's museum in the country, this noble enterprise way down on the South Side is chock full of interactive exhibits about local and national black history.

Chicago Children's Museum

700 E Grand Avenue, at Navy Pier, Streeterville (1-312 527 1000/www.chichildrensmuseum.org). El: Red to Grand. **Open** 10am-5pm Mon-Wed, Fri, Sun; 10am-8pm Thur, Sat. **Admission** $8; $7 over-65s; free under-1s; free to families 5-8pm Thur, and under-15s on 1st Mon of mth. **Credit** AmEx, Disc, MC, V. **Map** p326 K10.

Kids will have a blast here, but they might also learn something at the 15 permanent exhibits and the one or two touring shows usually on display. Aspiring archaeologists can dig for dino bones in a replica excavation pit, while cooped-up urban kids can get a dose of green space in the indoor Big Backyard, which combines technology and art to create a fantastical Chicago neighbourhood backyard that changes with the seasons. The museum's satellite operation is an unusual one: Kids on the Fly, a free interactive exhibition on the departures level of Terminal 2 at O'Hare International Airport.

Kohl Children's Museum

2100 Patriot Boulevard, Glenview (1-847 832 6600/www.kohlchildrensmuseum.org). Metra: North Glenview. **Open** *June-Aug* 9.30am-5pm Mon-Sat; noon-5pm Sun. *Sept-May* 9.30am-noon Mon; 9.30am-5pm Tue-Sat; noon-5pm Sun. **Admission** $6.50; $5.50 over-55s; free under-1s. **Credit** AmEx, Disc, MC, V.

This new state-of-the art, eco-friendly museum is well worth the trip to the Glen, a newly developed community on the site of the former Glenview Naval Air Station. Catering to kids aged eight and under, the Kohl has 36,000sq ft (3,350sq m) of indoor exhibition space, including a pint-sized grocery store and

a water play area where budding seafarers can design their own boats and control movement with water and air jets (clothes dryers are available, free of charge). Habitat Park, the museum's two acres of outdoor exhibition space, provides year-round access to the outdoors in a fenced-off site with a landscaped garden, a sculpture trail and interactive tools to encourage kids to connect with the environment. In other words, get good and dirty for the ride back.

Wonder Works

6445 W. North Avenue, at Elmwood Avenue, Oak Park (1-708 383 4815/www.wonder-works.org). Bus 72. **Open** 10am-5pm Wed-Sat; noon-5pm Sun. **Admission** $5; free under-1s. **No credit cards.**

Oak Park's Wonder Works is a small museum that really feels more like a big playroom, with five main exhibits encouraging learning through creative play. There's something for kids of all ages: at Lights, Camera, Action!, young 'uns can dress up and act on stage, while North Avenue Art Works is an art studio where creative types can work with paint, crayons and other crafty tools.

Parks & gardens

Over in **Millennium Park** (*see p75*), kids get a kick out of kicking off their shoes and frolicking in the water around the two 50-foot (15-metre), glass-brick towers that face one another at Crown Fountain. The faces of 1,000 Chicagoans flash continually across screens on the towers; periodically, one will purse their lips and water will spout out, making it seem like the person is spitting on the crowd below.

The highlight of a visit to **Lincoln Park** (*see p109*) for many kids is a wander around the Lincoln Park Zoo. The Children's Zoo offers an up-close-and-personal view of animals and throws in a crash course on conservation, while the Farm-in-the-Zoo is a working replica of a Midwestern farm, complete with red barns housing cows, sheep and horses. Best of all, admission is free.

Navy Pier. *See p225.*

Not far from Lincoln Park sits **Oz Park**, famous for its silver statue of the Tin Man from *The Wizard of Oz* (the story's author, L Frank Baum, lived in Chicago). Sports facilities include basketball, volleyball and tennis courts, and a softball field . There's a Dorothy's Play lot for the little ones, and – of course – a yellow brick road.

If the rug rats still have some leftover energy you'd like them to expend, head to the 185-acre **Garfield Park** about four miles west of the Loop, where you'll find a playground, baseball diamonds, soccer fields, basketball and tennis courts, a pool, a lagoon, a bike path and a couple of sandpits. The conservatory (1-312 746 5100, www.garfield-conservatory.org), one of the US's largest, is a delightful spot when it's gloomy outside.

Sundae best at **Margie's Candies**.

Eat, drink, shop

Restaurants

Chicago is teeming with child-friendly cafés and restaurants. Here are a few favourites.

Big Bowl
60 E Ohio Street, at N Wabash Avenue, River North (1-312 951 1888/www.bigbowl.com). El: Red to Grand. **Open** 11.30am-10pm Mon-Thur, Sun; 11.30am-11pm Fri, Sat. **Main courses** $8-$18. **Credit** AmEx, Disc, MC, V. **Map** p326 H10.
Looking to expand Junior's culinary repertoire beyond McNuggets? Try this Chinese-Thai restaurant, where the kids' menu lists steamed dumplings, satays and stir-frys, and is printed with games that go beyond the usual mazes and wordsearches.
Other locations: 6 E Cedar Street, at N State Street, Gold Coast (1-312 640 8888).

Cereality Cereal Bar & Café
100 S Wacker Drive, at W Monroe Street, the Loop (1-312 506 0010/www.cereality.com). El: Brown, Orange, Pink or Purple to Quincy. **Open** 6am-6pm Mon-Fri; 8am-4pm Sat. **Main courses** $3-$6. **Credit** AmEx, MC, V. **Map** p325 G12.
This outpost of the national chain serves dozens of name-brand hot and cold cereals in various ways: in snack bars, as smoothies, in parfaits, as trail mixes and, of course, in bowls with milk. All are made by 'cereologists', who work in their pyjamas. At the toppings bar, you can spruce up your Corn Flakes with nuts, fruits or candies.

Ed Debevic's
640 N Wells Street, at W Erie Street, River North (1-312 664 1707/www.eddebevics.com). El: Red to Chicago. **Open** 11am-9pm Mon-Thur; 11am-11pm Fri; 9am-11pm Sat; 9am-9pm Sun. **Main courses** $6-$14. **Credit** AmEx, Disc, DC, MC, V. **Map** p326 H10.
The gum-snapping staff are part of the attraction at the Chicago branch of this ersatz 1950s diner chain, serving a side order of insults and wisecracks along with the burgers. The staff have been known to jump up on the counters and boogie along to the piped-in music.

Foodlife
Water Tower Place, 835 N Michigan Avenue, at E Pearson Street, Magnificent Mile (1-312 335 3663/ www.foodlifechicago.com). El: Red to Chicago. **Open** 10.30am-9pm Mon-Sat; 11am-9pm Sun. **Main courses** $8-$15. **Credit** AmEx, Disc, MC, V. **Map** p326 J9.
You'll find something to please everyone from your vegetarian sister to your burger-loving teen at this funky food court on the mezzanine level of the Water Tower Place mall. The range of food at the 13 kiosks takes in Asian stir-frys, pizzas and barbecue, a far cry from standard fast-food options.

Margie's Candies
1960 N Western Avenue, at W Armitage Avenue, Bucktown (1-773 384 1035/www.margiescandies. com). El: Blue to Western. **Open** 9am-midnight daily. **Main courses** $4-$8. **Credit** AmEx, Disc, MC, V. **Map** p331 A6.
In the neighbourhood since 1921, this soda fountain is revered as much for its desserts as it is for its ancient, charming wait staff. There's a menu of ho-hum salads and sandwiches, but the crowds come for the ice-cream, served in a seemingly endless array of sundae combinations. Margie's also makes its own boxed chocolates and candies, so you can keep the kids' sugar highs going even after you leave.

Shops

For toy shops, *see p214*; for children's clothing shops, *see p195*.

Arts & entertainment

In addition to the venues detailed below, the glammed-up **Navy Pier** (*see p101*) offers plenty for the young 'uns, including an IMAX cinema (*see p239*), a futuristic McDonald's with a laser-light show, a 150-foot (46-metre) Ferris wheel and, in winter, an ice rink.

Dave & Buster's

1030 N Clark Street, at W Oak Street, Gold Coast (1-312 943 5151/www.daveandbusters.com). El: Red to Clark/Division. **Open** 11.30am-midnight Mon-Wed, Sun; 11.30am-1am Thur-Sat. **Admission** $5 after 10pm Fri, Sat. **Credit** AmEx, DC, Disc, MC, V. **Map** p326 H9.

Though the focus here is on arcade games, Dave & Buster's offers everything from shuffleboard to high-tech virtual reality kits. Frazzled adults can take the edge off with a cocktail.

Different Strummer

4544 N Lincoln Avenue, at W Wilson Avenue, Lincoln Square (1-773 751 3398/www.oldtown school.org). El: Brown to Western. **Open** 10am-9pm Mon-Thur; 10am-5pm Fri-Sun. **Credit** AmEx, Disc, MC, V.

Part of the Old Town School of Folk Music (*see p259*), the Different Strummer store offers plenty for the budding muso: CDs, videos and toy instruments, as well as real ones made especially for younger players. Check out the school's concert schedule for kids' performances.

Other locations: 909 W Armitage Avenue, at N Fremont Street, Lincoln Park (1-773 751 3410).

Down in the Basement

Blue Chicago (South), 536 N Clark Street, at W Grand Avenue, River North (1-312 661 1003/www.bluechicago.com). El: Red to Grand. **Admission** $5; under-12s free. **Open** 8pm-midnight Sat. **Credit** AmEx, MC, V. **Map** p326 H10.

Little ones get glum, too, but the Gloria Shannon Blues Band feels their pain every Saturday evening at this all-ages blues show in the Blue Chicago Store (for the sister clubs, *see p260*). No alcohol is served.

WhirlyBall

1880 W Fullerton Avenue, at N Wolcott Avenue, Wicker Park (1-773 486 7777/www.whirlyball.com). Bus 50, 74. **Open** 10am-2am Mon-Fri; noon-3am Sat; noon-2am Sun. Over-21s only after 5pm; minors in large parties allowed with restricted access. **Admission** *Walk-ins* $10/person per 30mins. *Pre-bookings* $180/hr Mon-Thur; $200/hr Sat, Sun. **Credit** AmEx, Disc, MC, V. **Map** p331 C5.

Two teams spin around a 4,000sq ft (370sq m) court, attempting to scoop up a ball and whip it at a backboard. Think polo in bumper cars. Kids must be aged 12 or over, and be at least 54in (137cm) tall.

Theatre

Several professional theatre companies around the city are dedicated solely to kids. The **Chicago Shakespeare Theatre** offers the Bard to babes with its Family Series; productions have included *MacHomer*, with Homer Simpson as the tragic King Macbeth.

Chicago Children's Theatre

1464 N Milwaukee Avenue, at W Evergreen Street, Wicker Park (1-773 227 0180/www.chicagochildrens theatre.org). El: Blue to Damen. **Tickets** $7.50-$35. **Credit** AmEx, Disc, MC, V. **Map** p331 C8.

This multi-million-dollar venture launched in 2006 with the aim of bringing high-end children's productions to young theatregoers. The company doesn't yet have a home of its own, instead staging shows at theatres throughout the city.

Chicago Playworks for Families & Young Audiences

DePaul's Merle Reskin Theatre, 60 E Balbo Drive, at S Wabash Avenue, South Loop (box office 1-312 922 1999/http://theatreschool.depaul.edu). El: Red to Harrison. **Tickets** $8. **Credit** Disc, MC, V. **Map** p325 H13.

Founded as the Goodman Children's Theater in 1925 and now run by the Theater School at DePaul University, Chicago Playworks is one of the country's oldest continuously running children's companies. The playhouse presents three productions each season, supplemented by post-show discussions, backstage tours and ice-cream socials.

Emerald City Theatre

Apollo Theater, 2540 N Lincoln Avenue, at W Wrightwood Avenue, Lincoln Park (1-773 935 6100/www.emeraldcitytheatre.com). El: Brown, Purple or Red to Fullerton. **Tickets** $13; $10 children. **Credit** AmEx, Disc, MC, DC, V. **Map** p328 E4.

Jolly kids' fare, such as a modern musical version of *The Nutcracker* and a theatrical take on *The Jungle Book*, is offered by this fine establishment in its digs at the Apollo Theater in Lincoln Park.

Directory

Babysitting & childcare

American Childcare Services

1-312 644 7300/www.americanchildcare.com. **Credit** AmEx, Disc, MC, V.

A large staff of sitters provides childcare services to hotel guests. Expect to pay $18.50 per hour, with a four-hour minimum and a $20 agency fee. Clients should book at least 24 hours in advance; note that there is also a 24-hour cancellation policy. Group childcare is available for conventioneers.

North Shore Nannies

1-847 864 2424/www.northshorenannies.com. **Credit** *Agency fee* AmEx, MC, V. *Nanny* cash/cheque only.

This agency offers a nanny service at hotels for $12 per hour (with a four-hour minimum) plus parking charges. For other non-hotel sitting services, it's $10 per hour (again, with a four-hour minimum) or $120 for overnight service, plus $5 per night for each additional child. With all sitting services, an additional agency fee of $18 applies for up to six hours, $30 for seven to 12 hours and $40 for 12 to 24 hours. Book ahead, especially for weekends.

The real Kid Rock

It's a typical Saturday at FitzGerald's (*see p256*), the legendary roots roadhouse just west of Chicago. As music blares from the speakers, the fans dance around the room, bobbing their heads in rhythm to the music. When the lead singer tells the audience to let loose, everyone screams; a few even rush the stage. But there's one notable difference about these groupies: most of them aren't yet out of nappies.

Welcome to a day in the life of **Ralph Covert**, a Chicago rocker who, performing under the name Ralph's World (Covert plays solo and with a rotating group of musicians), has become the reigning king of a new brand of kiddie pop. Mom and dad dig his music as much as their kids, but then these moms and dads were weaned on rock, and want their youngsters to listen to music with the same aesthetic values. Covert has stepped into the breach, borrowing from disco, blues, pop and even punk in his kid-friendly tunes.

Covert made a name for himself in the early 1990s as the lead singer of the Bad Examples, a pop-rock band that briefly enjoyed mainstream success in the US. After he himself became a parent, Covert agreed to teach a music class for kids at Chicago's popular Old Town School of Folk Music, but on his own terms, bringing along his daughter Fiona and not playing, in his words, any 'painful crap'. He quickly gained a reputation as the 'edgy' teacher, playing his class songs by the likes of the Who before eventually coming up with original material to chase away his own boredom and woo his young audiences.

Covert began recording his kids' music in the summer of 2000 to huge acclaim: his sixth album, 2005's *Green Gorilla, Monster And Me*, was even nominated for a Grammy as Best Musical Album for Children. Although Covert now has a national following, he still plays plenty of concerts around Chicago, many of which sell out months in advance (for details of upcoming shows, check www.ralphsworld.com). Parents and kids happily sing along together to 'The Coffee Song'

('M-O-M-M-Y needs C-O-F-F-E-E / D-A-D-D-Y needs C-O-F-F-E-E / I want a latte, a cappuccino / And tonight I think I'll have a little vino'), but his biggest hit at live shows is 'Barnyard Blues', a song that could hook the crowd at any blues club. Kids have fun shouting animal sounds back at Covert, while parents get a kick out of the improvised yet familiar riffs, including one that sounds suspiciously like the opening jam from 'Purple Haze'.

The key to Covert's success is his realisation that the formula for pleasing kids and adults isn't much different from the one he used when writing for the Bad Examples (who still occasionally play together). 'Ninety per cent of it is the same,' he says. 'A Bad Examples song might be about longing for love, while a Ralph's World one might be about longing for a pet. Both songs have to be musically rich with strong lyrics. Kids can't connect with yearning for a great love, but they can connect with wanting an elephant for a pet. It's all about communicating with your audience.'

Comedy

Whose line is it anyway?

In Chicago, comedy means improv. The vast majority of the city's comedy venues specialise in extemporised performance, and have done so since the form was essentially invented in the city in the late 1950s. Giants of the genre such as Chris Farley, Elaine May, Mike Nichols, John and James Belushi, Bill Murray, Shelley Long and George Wendt all honed their comic craft in the city, as did recent *Saturday Night Live* and *MADtv* stars including Amy Poehler and Stephnie Weir. Pioneering venue **Second City** has since been joined by a number of competitors, all putting their own different spin on the form.

Stand-up comics occasionally get to take a turn in the spotlight. **Zanies** hosts nationally known stand-ups nightly, while a handful of weekly shows showcase local talent, among them the **Lincoln Lodge** and **The Elevated** (Wednesdays at 8.30pm, Cherry Red, 2833 N Sheffield Avenue, Lakeview, www.theelevated. com). But if you're looking for laughs, you really need to make it up as you go along.

INFORMATION AND TICKETS

Pick up a copy of *Time Out Chicago*, which offers listings for almost every venue in town. Tickets can be bought directly from the box offices. A number of improv troupes don't perform in a set location; check listings for details of their movements.

Venues

Annoyance Productions

Annoyance Theatre, 4840 N Broadway Street, at W Gunnison Street, Uptown (1-773 561 4665/www. annoyanceproductions.com). El: Red to Lawrence. **Shows** 8pm Mon, Tue; 8pm & 10.30pm Thur; 8pm, 10.30pm & midnight Fri, Sat. **Tickets** $2-$15. **Credit** MC, V.

The ever-irreverent Annoyance sits alone on a particular echelon of respectability in Chicago's comedy scene, mostly because they love to curse and offend. However, their shows are rather better than that description might indicate: behind the obvious in-your-face bombast lies some of the city's best improv and sketch comedy writing. Mick Napier, one of the founders of the company, is held to be something of a comedy guru. As such, the shows he directs are often the most reliable, although Susan Messing's *Messing With a Friend* is also a favourite. The company's Uptown theatre, which opened in summer 2006, is a beautiful space. **Photo** *p231*.

ComedySportz of Chicago

777 N Green Street, at W Chicago Avenue, West Town (1-312 327 2000/www.comedysportzchicago. com). El: Blue to Chicago. **Shows** 8pm Thur; 8pm & 10pm Fri; 6pm, 8pm & 10pm Sat. **Tickets** $17. **Credit** AmEx, Disc, MC, V.

ComedySportz is the Starbucks of its field, though it's no surprise that Chicago hosts one of its stronger franchises. The schtick is simple: two teams battle each other at improv games, complete with a scoreboard. The performers are generally talented, but the place is aimed more at providing harmless fun for the masses than extending the boundaries of the

Festivals
Comedy

Staged over a week in late April each year, the **Chicago Improv Festival** (www.chicagoimprovfestival.org) manages to attract improvisers from all over the world, while also showcasing the best local talent. The schedule was pared back a little in 2007; many shows are held at the Athenaeum Theatre (*see p283*).

January's **Chicago Sketch Festival** (www.chicagosketchfest.com) draws a similar mix of local and national talent to what has become the largest sketch comedy festival in the country. Almost 100 shows are held during the ten-day event, staged at the Theatre Building (*see p284*) on the second weekend in January.

The best Comedy

For future Saturday Night Livers
iO Chicago. See *p231*.

For eventual MADtv stars
Second City. See *p232*.

For current Starbucks baristas
Playground. See *p232*.

Clockwise from top: Peter Renaud, Jennifer Estlin and Josh Walker at the **Annoyance**. *See p230.*

art. After its historic theatre was demolished to make way for condominiums, the company was somewhat nomadic for a while, but plans to return to Lakeview in spring 2007.

iO Chicago

3541 N Clark Street, at W Addison Street, Wrigleyville (1-773 880 0199/www.iochicago.net). El: Red to Addison. **Shows** times vary, daily. **Tickets** free-$14. **Credit** Disc, MC, V. **Map** p329 E1.

The most respected Chicago venue for hardcore improv (alumni here have included the likes of Andy Richter, Mike Myers and founder Charna Halpern), iO Chicago takes as its house speciality a long-form style called the Harold. Created by Del Close, it features improvising teams creating fluid acts that loosely revolve around a single audience suggestion. However, it's just one of numerous shows at this two-space venue that's busy every night with a young, party-hearty crowd; indeed, after Second City, it's the most famous comedy venue in town. Oh, and the name? It was formerly called the ImprovOlympic, but the International Olympic Committee felt violated.

Jokes & Notes

4641 S King Drive, at E 46th Place, Bronzeville (1-773 373 3390/www.jokesandnotes.com). El: Green to 47th Street. **Shows** 7.30pm Wed, Thur; 8pm & 10.30pm Fri, Sat; 8pm Sun. **Tickets** $10-$20. **Credit** MC, V.

See p232 **Bronze mettle**.

Lincoln Lodge

4008 N Lincoln Avenue, at W Irving Park Avenue, Lincoln Square (1-773 296 4029/www.thelincoln lodge.com). El: Brown to Irving Park. **Shows** 9pm Thur, Fri. **Tickets** $8 (1-drink min). **No credit cards.** **Map** p330 B0.

Perhaps *the* place to see locally grown stand-up comedy, the Lincoln Lodge has cultivated a cult following. Shows routinely sell out (reservations can be made in advance, but are only guaranteed until 8.45pm), and comedians are encouraged to perform their edgiest material. The hosts play up the lodge feel, often donning fedoras and showcasing oddball variety acts. There's no stand-up show like this in town; though performers vary week to week, you're guaranteed a few good sets at each show.

Playground

3209 N Halsted Street, at W Belmont Avenue,
Lakeview (1-773 871 3793/www.the-playground.
com). El: Brown, Purple or Red to Belmont. **Shows**
times vary, nightly. **Tickets** free-$10. **Credit** Disc,
MC, V. **Map** p329 F3.

This improv specialist features plenty of nascent
troupes and even hosts something called the
Incubator, where lonely improvisers pay a small fee
to meet each other. Purely in terms of entertainment,
it's a little hit and miss. That said, in a typical night,
four troupes will each perform 30-minute long-form
acts, one of which is bound to be funny. There are
usually two shows a night, with three on Fridays
and Saturdays (and one on Mondays). A weekly
highlight, on Saturdays at 10.30pm, is gameshow
spoof *Don't Spit the Water* (www.dontspitthe
water.com), in which an array of comedians try to
get audience members to laugh so hard that... well,
you can guess the rest. Sit a couple of rows back.

Bronze mettle

In the 1940s, Bronzeville was the centre
of Chicago's black culture, a hotbed of
jazz musicians, writers and others of an
artistic bent. Six decades later, **Jokes &
Notes** (*see p231*) is helping to return the
neighbourhood to the primacy of its glory
days. The venue opened in January 2006
with an impressive set-up in its South
Side premises: an expansive stage,
murals of classic comedians and flat-
screen video monitors.

'Jokes & Notes offers a different flavour
of comedy from North Side clubs,' believes
owner Mary Lindsey, known to many on the
local scene through her now-defunct South
Loop venue All Jokes Aside. 'All people
are welcome, though our focus is primarily
on showcasing minority talent. Performers
are given free rein to express themselves
and their stories however they want.'

From Friday to Sunday, the club pairs
local wannabes with nationally known
African American comedians, including a
number of *Def Comedy Jam* veterans.
The stand-up bookings were initially
so successful that some customers
overlooked Jokes & Notes' other
programming: Wednesday sees an
anything-goes open-mike night, while
Thursdays offer a variety show. 'It's
important to offer a mix of entertainment,
though – comedy, jazz, spoken word –
as a tribute to Bronzeville's past,' believes
Lindsey. 'The history of this area is deeply
rooted in all sorts of expression.'

Second City

1616 N Wells Street, at W North Avenue, Old Town
(1-312 337 3992/www.secondcity.com). El: Brown or
Purple to Sedgwick. **Shows** *Main stage* 8.30pm Mon-
Thur; 8pm & 11pm Fri, Sat; 7pm Sun. *ETC stage*
8pm Thur; 8pm & 11pm Fri, Sat; 7pm Sun. *Donny's*
Skybox times vary, Thur-Sun. **Tickets** $12-$24.
Donny's Skybox $3-$12. **Credit** AmEx, Disc, MC, V.
Map p327 G7.

The grandaddy of all comedy theatres, Second City
is the brand name for funny business in town.
Founded in 1959, it's a well-polished machine and a
top tourist attraction, but deservedly so. The city's
best comics perform here, waiting to be snatched
away by *Saturday Night Live* or *Mad TV*, but the
humour is still cutting-edge and the political digs at
conservatism suitably shameless. A different – and
often gutsier – revue plays in the ETC Theatre, with
Donny's Skybox given over to student performances.
Get there early on weekends, as most shows sell out.

Zanies

1548 N Wells Street, at W North Avenue, Old Town
(1-312 337 4027/www.zanies.com). El: Brown or
Purple to Sedgwick. **Shows** 8.30pm Tue-Thur, Sun;
8.30pm, 10.30pm Fri; 7pm, 9pm, 11.15pm Sat.
Tickets $22-$50 (2-drink min). **Credit** MC, V.
Map p327 G7.

Though the one major stand-up club in the city to
survive the post-1980s bust doesn't create much of
a buzz, it's a reliable place to see seasoned local
comics you've never heard of, as well as the odd
national act. The likes of Jackie Mason sometimes
show up to try out new material. A typical night
features an MC, an opening comic and a headliner.
Audiences tend to be loud and boorish.

Classes

While the likes of Bill Murray and Chris Farley
have graduated from the Chicago stage to the
national TV screen, a few souls have sat in the
audience thinking 'I can do that'. Most of them
can't, of course. But some venues offer courses
to help the wannabes improve at improv.
Classes start at around $200 for an eight-week
programme, though some of the theatres offer
unpaid internships in exchange for free classes.

Second City (*see above*) offers numerous
classes in its Old Town space, from beginners'
lessons to the Conservatory Level, which is
geared towards those who are serious about
taking to the stage one day. Those more
interested in long-form should try out **iO
Chicago** (*see p231*), which offers five tiers of
classes alongside performance-level lessons for
the students who get stage time in its theatre.
For *Whose Line is it Anyway?*-style laughs,
head to **ComedySportz of Chicago** (*see
p230*). **Annoyance Productions** (*see p230*),
meanwhile, teaches its brand of offbeat and
slightly offensive humour in its Uptown theatre.

Dance

The city's movers and shakers.

Hubbard Street Dance Chicago.

Chicago's dance scene is as broad and diverse as the city itself. Whether you're looking for experimental dance or traditional ballet, flamenco or bharata natyam, you'll find it here, particularly if you visit between September and May when the season is at its height.

INFORMATION AND TICKETS

Time Out Chicago and the *Chicago Reader* are your best bets for listings and reviews; the *Chicago Tribune* and the *Chicago Sun-Times* both list dance events and run reviews. The calendar at the excellent **www.seechicago dance.com** is searchable by date, company, venue and genre; the site also offers ticket discounts. For tickets, contact the theatre box offices, Ticketmaster (1-312 902 1400, www. ticketmaster.com) or TicketWeb (www.ticket web.com). If you're looking for classes or studio space, go to www.chicagoartistsresource.org.

Major companies

Hubbard Street Dance Chicago
1-312 850 9744/www.hubbardstreetdance.com.
Founded in 1977 by choreographer Lou Conte, Hubbard Street has built up a thoroughly deserved reputation as Chicago's premier dance company. Now under the artistic direction of Jim Vincent, the

company has phased out its identity as a jazz-based troupe and entered the realm of contemporary dance with an international flavour with a repertoire that takes in works by Naharin, Forsythe and Duato. The group is often on tour, but performs annually at the new Harris Theater for Music & Dance (*see p234*).

Joffrey Ballet of Chicago
1-312 739 0120/www.joffrey.com.
One of the major American ballet companies, Joffrey emigrated to Chicago from New York in 1995, and is now resident at the Auditorium Theatre (*see p234*). The eclectic repertoire is strong on American choreographers, reconstructions of historic Ballet Russe era works and full-length classics.

Luna Negra Dance Theater
1-312 337 6882/www.lunanegra.org.
Founded in 1999 by Cuban-born Eduardo Vilaro, still the artistic director, this vibrant company is now a major player on the Chicago dance scene. The group creates, performs and teaches contemporary dance by Latino choreographers. The repertory includes original works by Vilaro, as well as pieces by Ron DeJesus, Vicente Nebrada and Pedro Ruiz.

Muntu Dance Theatre of Chicago
1-773 602 1135/www.muntu.com.
This dynamic troupe is strongly connected to its South Side community, but also maintains ties with dancers and musicians in Africa, who visit for residencies and performances. Under the artistic direction of Amaniyea Payne, the company draws on traditional African and African American dance and music to create original works. In addition to performing annually at Navy Pier's Skyline Stage and other venues, the company is in the midst of a major project to build its own arts centre.

The best Venues

For grand old ballet
Auditorium Theatre. See p234.

For edgy new dance
Dance Center of Columbia College. See p234.

For major Chicago troupes
Harris Theater for Music & Dance. See p234.

Festivals Dance

The big event on the calendar each year is **Dance Chicago** (1-773 989 0698, www.dancechicago.com). Founded in 1995, the festival aims to highlight the quality and variety of local dance, and features local companies performing throughout November at the Athenaeum Theatre (*see p234*). Tickets are available from the Athenaeum box office.

During the summer, members of the public are invited to dig out their dancing shoes for **Chicago SummerDance** (1-312 742 4007, www.cityofchicago.org/summerdance), a free festival held in a number of city parks (on a rotating basis) that invites the public to trip the light fantastic through a variety of dance styles. One-hour lessons in everything from ballroom dancing to Irish step-dance are followed by two hours of hoofing, often to live bands.

River North Chicago

1-312 944 2888/www.rivernorthchicago.com.
Now more than a decade old, this hip and sexy touring troupe has created a trademark breezy style with a strong emphasis on accessibility; co-artistic director Sherry Zunker Dow has even described River North as 'the dance company for the MTV generation'. Most of the choreography comes from Chicago-based artists.

Major venues

Athenaeum Theatre

2936 N Southport Avenue, at W Oakdale Avenue, Lakeview (1-773 935 6860/www.athenaeumtheatre. com). El: Brown or Purple to Wellington. **Box office** 3-7pm Tue-Fri. **Tickets** $15-$30. **Credit** AmEx, Disc, MC, V. **Map** p329 D3.
Built in 1911 as a recreation centre for the German community that once populated the neighbourhood, the 900-seat Athenaeum Theatre has old-fashioned red velvet seats and a gilded ceiling with allegorical paintings, but the rest of the building recalls one of its past lives as a girls' high school. The main stage is used for the annual Dance Chicago in November (*see p234* **Festivals**).

Auditorium Theatre

50 E Congress Parkway, at S Wabash Avenue, the Loop (1-312 922 2110/www.auditorium theatre.org). El: Blue or Red to Jackson; Brown, Orange, Pink or Purple to Library. **Box office** noon-6pm Mon-Fri. **Tickets** $25-$130. **Credit** AmEx, Disc, MC, V. **Map** p325 J13.

This gorgeous theatrical palace, built by famed architects Louis Sullivan and Dankmar Adler, is an internationally recognised landmark, boasting perfect acoustics. Home to the Joffrey Ballet (*see p233*), it hosts an international dance series that includes world-class companies such as Alvin Ailey and the Kirov Ballet. Depending on your cashflow and connections, you could find yourself sitting pretty in the orchestra or communing with the gods near the golden ceiling.

Dance Center of Columbia College

1306 S Michigan Avenue, at W 13th Street, South Loop (1-312 344 8300/www.dancecenter.org). El: Green, Orange or Red to Roosevelt. **Box office** 9am-5pm Mon-Fri. **Tickets** $18-$26. **Credit** AmEx, Disc, MC, V. **Map** p324 H15.
The only dance-dedicated theatre in Chicago is managed by the dance department of Columbia College, the city's most progressive centre for dance education. The programming reflects this, with appearances by touring and national artists mixed in with performances by prominent local choreographers, faculty programmes and student choreographic workshop nights. The level of the touring work is high: in 2006, the modern 272-seat centre hosted the Richard Alston Dance Company, Quasar Dance Company from Brazil and Bebe Miller, among others. Student and faculty shows are usually free, and the quality often surpasses that of independently produced performances elsewhere in the city.

Harris Theater for Music & Dance

205 E Randolph Street, between N Stetson Avenue & N Columbus Drive, the Loop (1-312 334 7777/ www.harristheaterchicago.org). El: Brown, Green, Orange, Pink or Purple to Randolph; Red to Lake. **Box office** noon-6pm daily. **Tickets** $20-$90. **Credit** AmEx, MC, V. **Map** p325 J12.
Completed in late 2003 as part of the Millennium Park complex, this ultra-modern 1,500-seater is a not-for-profit venture providing an outlet for local music and dance groups. The venue is mostly underground: if you arrive at the street entrance with orchestra-level tickets in hand, you'll need to navigate several levels of concrete floors and hard stairs, so wear comfortable shoes. The interior is pared-down and white, with Dan Flavin-esque neon lighting. Inside the vast theatre itself, sightlines are excellent. Chicago's major dance companies perform here, among them Hubbard Street, Giordano Jazz Dance Chicago, the Luna Negra Dance Theater, River North and the Muntu Dance Theatre.

Links Hall

3435 N Sheffield Avenue, at N Clark Street, Wrigleyville (1-773 281 0824/www.linkshall.org). El: Red to Addison. **Box office** 9am-5pm Mon-Fri. **Tickets** $10-$15. **No credit cards. Map** p329 E2.
Founded in 1979 by a small group of choreographers, this intimate studio/theatre is still going strong, with multidisciplinary programming that takes in a healthy portion of experimental dance by local and international artists.

Museum of Contemporary Art

*220 E Chicago Avenue, at Mies van der Rohe Way,
Streeterville (1-312 280 2660/www.mcachicago.org).
El: Red to Chicago.* **Box office** 10am-8pm Tue;
10am-5pm Wed-Sun. **Tickets** $20-$24. **Credit**
AmEx, DC, Disc, MC, V. **Map** p326 J10.

The MCA's elegant, modern theatre is set up perfectly for viewing dance: the 300-odd seats are arranged on a deep slope, starting at the same level as the stage and rising to look down on it. The programming is excellent, too: the MCA is one of the city's most important theatres for touring contemporary dance companies. Attending performances here is a good way to stay in touch with what's hot on the international and national dance scenes.

Ruth Page Center for the Arts

*1016 N Dearborn Avenue, at W Oak Street,
Gold Coast (1-312 337 6543/www.ruthpage.org).
El: Red to Clark/Division.* **Box office** 9am-9pm
daily. **Tickets** $7-$25. **Credit** MC, V. **Map**
p326 H9.

Heiress, dancer and notable American choreographer Ruth Page established this home for dance smack in the middle of the swanky Gold Coast. In addition to studios and a dance library, the 90-year-old building houses a handsome 200-seat theatre, which is rented out to many small- or medium-sized dance companies and independent choreographers. You can expect to see ballet, modern dance and jazz styles.

Fringe benefits

In addition to its big-ticket venues and organisations, Chicago has hundreds of smaller troupes that together make up a healthy fringe scene. Some aspire to the aesthetic of the more established companies, while others represent cultural diversity and/or artistic experimentation. All perform off the beaten path in smaller theatres; a few stage shows in unconventional locations such as art galleries or swimming pools.

Breakbone DanceCo

1-773 841 2663/www.breakbone.com.
Post-feminist, punk-rock slam dancing with a strong video component. Your teenage kid will enjoy it.

Chicago Moving Company

*1-773 880 5402/www.chicagomoving
company.org.*
CMC hosts an annual alternative dance festival every autumn at its North Side venue, the Hamlin Park Field House (3035 N Hoyne Avenue, at W Berry Avenue).

Ensemble Español

1-773 442 5930/www.neiu.edu/~eespanol.
Led by Dame Libby Komaiko, this troupe has been preserving and promoting high-calibre Spanish dance for almost 30 years.

Hedwig Dances

1-773 871 0872/www.hedwigdances.com.
A modern dance company resident at the Chicago Cultural Center (*see p80*).

Lucky Plush Productions

1-773 862 9484/www.luckyplush.com.
Original, lush choreography with compelling imagery by artistic director Julia Rhoads and interdisciplinary collaborators.

Lucky Plush Productions.

Natya Dance Theatre

1-312 212 1240/www.natya.com.
Classical Indian *bharata natyam* in a contemporary context.

The Seldoms

1-312 328 0303/www.theseldoms.org.
Intellectually stimulating dance-theatre by a small collective of choreographers and performance artists.

Thodos Dance Chicago

*1-312 266 6255/www.thodosdance
chicago.org.*
Thodos showcases the talents of choreographer Melissa Thodos, but is also devoted to developing the talents of its members through an annual New Dances programme.

Film

On the screen and behind the scene, Chicago's a hot ticket.

Brew & View at the Vic Theatre. *See p237.*

Chicago has been a big movie town for as long as film has existed as a commercial medium. It was the centre of film production throughout much of the silent era, when it boasted more theatres per capita than any other city. The dominant studio of the era, the Essanay Film Manufacturing Company, churned out 14,000 titles, including star vehicles for Charlie Chaplin, Gloria Swanson and Wallace Beery. But Chaplin's defection to Hollywood in 1916 both presaged and contributed to the company's collapse the following year.

However, even as the major production companies moved to Los Angeles, where the climate permitted year-round production of Westerns, Chicago continued to control the distribution side of the business. And as technology liberated film-makers from the sound stage, the city came back into favour as a location, a renaissance that began with James Stewart's 1948 true-crime drama *Call Northside 777*. Chicagoans tend to fetishise *The Blues Brothers* and *Ferris Bueller's Day Off* as iconic representations of their city's spirit, though connoisseurs favour 1993's *Mad Dog and Glory* and the 1969 docu-drama *Medium Cool*.

Regrettably, two of Chicago's most historic neighbourhood cinemas, the Biograph (where John Dillinger was shot by the FBI) and the

3 Penny, recently went dark after a run of service that stretched back to the nickelodeon era. (The Biograph has since reopened as a theatre; *see p282*.) However, the city does still offer a variety of idiosyncratic alternatives to the multiplex experience. The **Music Box** is a gorgeously preserved mini movie palace, where screenings of arthouse, foreign and cult films are often preceded by a Wurlitzer organ recital. The **Davis Theater** has been screening movies in Lincoln Square since 1918. And for hardcore film buffs, no trip to the city is complete without a pilgrimage to Hyde Park to catch a flick presented by **Doc Films** at the **University of Chicago Doc Films** (*see p237*), where the eclectic programming is all over the cinematic map.

INFORMATION AND TICKETS

Weekly film listings are available in *Time Out Chicago* and at www.timeout.com/chicago/nowplaying, as well as in the *Chicago Tribune*, the *Chicago Sun-Times*, *RedEye* and the *Chicago Reader*. To buy tickets in advance, either visit the theatre in person, call the numbers listed below or log on to the theatre's website. Parents should note that many Chicago movie theatres won't admit children under six years old after 6pm.

Cinemas

Mainstream & first-run

The cinemas listed below are the city's better first-run houses, though there are multiplexes galore dotted around the Chicagoland region. The **Century 12** in Evanston is favoured by purists (the sound quality is excellent) and drivers (there's free parking across the street).

AMC Loews 600 N Michigan *600 N Michigan Avenue, entrance at N Rush Street & E Ohio Street, Magnificent Mile (1-312 255 9340/www.amc theatres.com). El: Red to Chicago.* **Tickets** $9.50; $7.50 before 6pm Mon-Thur, before 4pm Fri-Sun; $5 before noon Sat, Sun; $6.50-$8.50 discounts. **Credit** AmEx, Disc, MC, V. **Map** p326 J10.

AMC River East 21 *322 E Illinois Street, at N Columbus Drive, Streeterville (1-847 765 7262/ www.amctheatres.com). El: Red to Grand.* **Tickets** $9.50; $7.50 before 6pm Mon-Thur, before 4pm Fri-Sun; $5 before noon Fri-Sun; $6.50-$8.50 discounts. **Credit** AmEx, Disc, MC, V. **Map** p326 J11.

Century 12 Evanston & CinéArts 6 *1715 Maple Avenue, at Church Street, Evanston (1-847 492 0123/www.cinemark.com). El: Purple to Davis.* **Tickets** $9.25-$9.75; $6.25 before 6pm Mon-Fri, before 2pm Sat, Sun; $5.75-$7.75 discounts. **Credit** MC, V.

Davis Theater *4614 N Lincoln Avenue, at W Montrose Avenue, Lincoln Square (1-773 784 0893/www.davistheater.com). El: Brown to Montrose.* **Tickets** $8; $5.50 before 6pm; $5.50 discounts. **No credit cards.**

Kerasotes Webster Place 11 *1471 W Webster Avenue, at N Clybourn Avenue, Lincoln Park (1-800 326 3264/www.kerasotes.com). El: Brown, Purple or Red to Fullerton.* **Tickets** $9.25-$9.75; $6.50 before 6pm Mon-Thur, before 4pm Fri-Sun; $5 before noon Fri-Sun; $6.50-$8.50 discounts. **Credit** AmEx, Disc, MC, V. **Map** p328 D5.

Village Theatre *1548 N Clark Street, at W North Avenue, Old Town (1-312 642 2403/www.village theatres.com). El: Brown or Purple to Sedgwick.* **Tickets** $7; $5 before 6pm; $5 discounts. **Credit** MC, V. **Map** p327 H7.

Indie & revival

In addition to the movie theatres listed below, there are also regular screenings at venues as varied as the Skokie Public Library and **Delilah's** bar in Lincoln Park (*see p181*).

Block Cinema

Mary & Leigh Block Museum of Art, Northwestern University, 1967 S Campus Drive, Evanston (1-847 491 2448/www.blockmuseum.northwestern.edu). El: Purple to Davis. **Tickets** $6; $4 discounts. **No credit cards.**

This campus series screens an interesting mix of classic and contemporary films from around the world in a small but state-of-the-art facility. In summer, weather permitting, the series moves outdoors.

Brew & View at the Vic Theatre

3145 N Sheffield Avenue, at W Belmont Avenue, Lakeview (1-773 929 6713/www.brewview.com). El: Brown, Purple or Red to Belmont. **Tickets** $5. **No credit cards. Map** p329 E3.

Movie-going becomes a social pursuit at the Brew & View. When the Vic isn't hosting concerts (*see p254*), it screens newish movies and older flicks for all of five bucks, and serves cheap beer by the pitcher. If the mood takes you, follow the drunken crowd and start yelling retorts at the screen. The best seats are on the balcony. **Photo** *p236.*

Chicago Filmmakers

5243 N Clark Street, at W Berwyn Avenue, Andersonville (1-773 293 1447/www.chicagofilm makers.org). El: Purple or Red to Berwyn. **Tickets** $8; $7 discounts. **Credit** MC, V.

This Andersonville set-up, one of two operations run by the not-for-profit Chicago Filmmakers enterprise, screens a selection of experimental films a few times a month, with occasional screenings at other venues such as the Cinema Borealis in Wicker Park. The group also stages all sorts of classes and workshops, and provides more general behind-the-scenes support for local moviemakers.

Doc Films, University of Chicago

Max Palevsky Cinema, Ida Noyes Hall, 1212 E 59th Street, at S Woodlawn Avenue, Hyde Park (1-773 702 8575/www.docfilms.uchicago.edu). Metra: 55th-56th-57th Street. **Tickets** $5. **No credit cards. Map** p332 Y18.

The 'Doc' is short for 'documentary', reflecting this film society's origins as the International House Documentary Film Group; founded in 1940, but with its origins eight years earlier, it's purportedly the longest-running student film society in the country. These days, the programme is wider: the range of titles, screened every night of the academic year at the 490-seat Max Palevsky Cinema, is a shrewdly selected mix of arthouse, cult and classic work, balanced by more popular fare.

Facets Multimedia

1517 W Fullerton Avenue, at N Ashland Avenue, Lincoln Park (1-773 281 4114/www.facets.org). El: Brown, Purple or Red to Fullerton. **Tickets** $9. **Credit** AmEx, Disc, MC, V. **Map** p328 D5.

The best Screens

For gracious Art Deco ambience
Music Box. *See p239.*

For film geek subculture
Doc Films. *See p237.*

For no-budget experimentalism
Chicago Filmmakers. *See p237.*

Arts & Entertainment

Festivals Film

As befits a city with such a long and lustrous cinematic history, Chicago abounds with film festivals of all stripes. We've detailed the biggest and best below, in chronological order. However, there are many others throughout the year, including an array of screenings in summer and a programme of experimental short films screened as part of September's **Around the Coyote** festival in Wicker Park (*see p218*). Check *Time Out Chicago* each week for details.

European Union Film Festival

Gene Siskel Film Center; details p239 (1-312 846 2600/www.siskelfilmcenter.org). **Date** Mar.
This expertly vetted showcase of new European works runs for a good portion of March each year at the Siskel Center.

Chicago Asian American Showcase

Gene Siskel Film Center; details p239 (1-312 846 2600/www.faaim.org. **Date** Apr.
This two-week event offers an eclectic selection of features, docs and experimental films by or about Asian-Americans.

Chicago Latino Film Festival

Various venues (1-312 431 1330/www. latinoculturalcenter.org). **Date** Apr-May.
Established in 1984, the two-week CLFF is the best of the city's ethnic film festivals. Screenings are staged at Facets (*see p237*), the Siskel Center (*see p239*) and Landmark's Century Centre Cinema (*see p239*).

Onion City Experimental Film & Video Festival

Various venues (1-773 293 1447/ www.chicagofilmmakers.org). **Date** June.
Sponsored by Chicago Filmmakers (*see p237*), this two-day event is more cerebral than its psychotronic cousin, the Chicago Underground Film Festival (*see right*).

Chicago Outdoor Film Festival

Grant Park, the Loop (1-312 742 7638/ www.cityofchicago.org/specialevents). **Date** July-Aug.
This perennially popular series offers screenings every Tuesday for two months each summer. If you don't want to be stuck behind a pole or a crowd of around 5,000 people, arrive hours ahead of time, drop a blanket on the ground and get picnicking.

Black Harvest International Festival of Film & Video

Gene Siskel Film Center; details p239 (1-312 846 2600/www.siskelfilmcenter.org). **Date** Aug.
Chicago's annual two-week showcase for films that celebrate black culture.

Chicago Underground Film Festival

Music Box; details p239 (www.cuff.org). **Date** Aug.
Transgression, subversion and partying are the order of the day. Leave the kids at home.

Chicago International Film Festival

Various venues (1-312 683 0121/ www.chicagofilmfestival.org). **Date** Oct.
The oldest competitive film festival in North America programmes around 100 features and documentaries — a compromise between the dauntingly huge Toronto International Film Festival and the hyper-exclusive New York Film Festival. Most screenings are held at the AMC River East 21 (*see p237*), Landmark's Century Centre Cinema (*see p239*) and the Thorne Auditorium at the NWU campus in Streeterville (375 E Chicago Avenue).

Chicago International Children's Film Festival

Facets Multimedia; details p237 (1-773 281 9075/www.cicff.org). **Date** Oct.
This ten-day event is the largest children's film festival in North America.

Festival for Cinema of the Deaf

1-847 332 2464/www.cimi.ws. **Date** Oct.
Two-day event shows captioned Hollywood films and works made for deaf audiences.

Reeling: the Chicago Gay & Lesbian International Film Festival

Various venues (1-773 293 1447/ www.reelingfilmfestival.org. **Date** Nov.
Held at theatres around town, this ten-day event is the second-oldest US gay festival.

New French Cinema

Facets Multimedia; details p237 (1-773 281 9075/www.facets.org **Date** Dec.
Chicago's most high-minded arthouse presents this carefully curated ten-day round-up of new Gallic movie-making.

This no-nonsense, not-for-profit Lincoln Park venue is a cinephile's wildest fantasy. That's because it is committed to screening rare and forgotten films that simply aren't seen elsewhere, with a strong bias towards film history, non-fiction pieces and experimental films. The larger theatre usually screens classic and (often esoteric) contemporary works, while the smaller theatre is primarily dedicated to documentaries and even more obscure productions. Many of the 40,000-plus titles housed in this nationally esteemed video library are all but impossible to find elsewhere.

Film Row Cinema

Columbia College, 1104 S Wabash Avenue, at W 11th Street, South Loop (1-312 344 8829/ www.colum.edu). El: Green, Orange or Red to Roosevelt. **Tickets** free. **No credit cards.** **Map** p324 H14.

The weekly screenings programme at Columbia's swell new downtown facility is aimed at bringing the richness of world cinema to the public.

Gene Siskel Film Center

164 N State Street, at W Randolph Street, the Loop (showtimes 1-312 846 2800/office 1-312 846 2600/www.artic.edu/webspaces/siskelfilmcenter). El: Brown, Green, Orange, Pink or Purple to State; Red to Lake. **Tickets** $9; $7 discounts. **Credit** AmEx, MC, V. **Map** p325 H12.

Named for the former *Tribune* critic who found national fame when TV producers paired him with *Sun-Times* film writer Roger Ebert. Though Siskel died in 1999, his spirit lives on in this modern, refined complex, associated with the Art Institute of Chicago (*see p221*). The two state-of-the-art theatres feature experimental American work, new foreign movies, classic revivals, themed retrospectives and other festivals.

Landmark's Century Centre Cinema

2828 N Clark Street, at W Diversey Parkway, Lakeview (1-773 509 4949/www.landmarktheatres. com). El: Brown, Purple or Red to Belmont. **Tickets** $9.50; $7 before 6pm Mon-Fri, 1st show Sat, Sun; $7-$7.50 discounts. **Credit** AmEx, MC, V. **Map** p328 F4.

Though it's tucked away in a yuppie mall, this seven-screen cinema concentrates on films at the artier end of the spectrum, and does a great job of screening them. Upon purchasing your ticket, ask the disillusioned but very funny and friendly punk-rock staff their opinion of the movie you're about to see. The theatre is one of the hosts of the Chicago International Film Festival (*see p238* **Festivals**).

LaSalle Bank Cinema

4901 W Irving Park Road, at N Lamon Avenue, Irving Park (1-312 904 9442). Bus 54, 54A, 80. **Tickets** $5; $3 discounts. **No credit cards.**

Classic, vintage and forgotten films, including some silent movies, are given new life in the back of this old bank building on Saturday nights at 8pm.The tickets are cheap, the retrospectives are complete and scholarly and the overall experience is terrific.

Gene Siskel Film Center.

Music Box

3733 N Southport Avenue, at W Waveland Avenue, Wrigleyville (1-773 871 6604/www.musicboxtheatre. com). El: Brown to Southport. **Tickets** $9.25; $8.25 1st show Mon-Thur; $7.25 before noon Sat, Sun. **No credit cards.** **Map** p329 D1.

The darling of Chicago movie houses. Two intimate theatres screen first-run arthouse and foreign films, supplemented by matinée and midnight screenings of everything from Marx Brothers classics to cheesy 1970s 3-D porn. But the vintage organ (sometimes employed to accompany silent films) and Moorish meets Tinseltown decor are even more memorable. For cinematic heaven, sneak a cheeseburger into the main theatre for a morning matinée of a black-and-white classic and look up at the projected moving clouds and mechanical stars on the ceiling.

Navy Pier IMAX Theatre

600 E Grand Avenue, at Lake Michigan, Streeterville (1-312 595 5629/www.imax.com/chicago). El: Red to Grand. **Tickets** $10.50; $8.50-$9.50 discounts. **Credit** AmEx, MC, V. **Map** p326 K10.

When it comes to cinema, bigger does not always equal better. Still, this IMAX set-up persists in its programme of large-format movies, some of which can be spectacular. Alongside the obligatory nature films and high-budget animations, the cinema also screens occasional 35mm blockbusters. Down south, the Omnimax Cinema at the Museum of Science & Industry (*see p139*) offers a similar eyeful.

Gay & Lesbian

The Midwest's 'mo mecca.

To make up for its miles of empty prairie and its location in one of the so-called 'fly-over' states, Chicago has always been boastful of its achievements: the tallest building, the deepest-dished pizza, the oldest ballpark and so on. Gay Chicago is no different. The state of Illinois led the US in repealing its anti-sodomy laws, while Chicago was among the first cities in the world to designate a district as officially gay and lesbian (note the rainbow-striped phallic columns on Halsted Street). The mayor proudly supports same-sex marriages (note the word 'marriage', not 'civil union'), and the Chicago Gay & Lesbian Hall of Fame (www.glhalloffame.org) is the only municipally funded organisation of its kind in the US.

In truth, queer Chicago doesn't really stand comparison to its coastal counterparts, but let's do it anyway. The nightlife is a little more cutting-edge and fashion-conscious in LA or San Francisco. However, at 1.30am, bartenders in those two cities are shouting last call, while they're just getting warmed up over here. The Big Apple is glitzier, but the Windy City is more affordable. Indeed, the only real difference is that here, you won't see Amanda Lepore in the corner of the discos being ogled by glamorous twinks.

The city is queer central for Midwesterners (Boystown is home to many red state refugees), which makes the diversity astonishing. Gays and lesbians aren't marginalised in Chicago: the 400,000 queer folk in the city are made up of homos and homemakers, doctors and dykes, actors and activists, twinks, leather folk, bears, circuit queens, lipstick lesbians and just about every other group and sub-group you can pack into one city. Something for everyone? You bet.

HOMO HABITATS

Boystown is the city's main gaybourhood; indeed, the name is sanctioned by Mayor Daley. The area is officially bordered by Addison Street to the north, Broadway Street to the east, Belmont Avenue to the south and Halsted Street to the west, but it really includes anywhere within a stone's throw where gays are currently dwelling. Broadway is best for shopping and dining, while Halsted Street is the nightlife hub.

Andersonville, an old Swedish enclave to the north, is Chicago's other key gay area. The queer scene has its origins in the 1990s, when lesbians discovered its historic charms while searching for cheaper rents. The boys soon followed; today, it's a self-satisfied mishmash of trendy restaurants, gay hangouts and furniture stores, all centred along Clark Street. The folk here are less showy than in Boystown, and double strollers (and doubled rent prices) are appearing with increasing regularity.

While Boystown and Andersonville are the city's two identifiably gay areas, gay life thrives all over town. **Wicker Park** is a mecca for alterna-queers who eschew gay-identified bars in favour of metrosexual hipster hangouts, while the 40-plus crowd has taken up in **River North**. And just about everyone, gay or straight, is in search of the ever-elusive next big neighbourhood. Look for a mix of people in **West Town**, the **Ukrainian Village**, **Logan Square** and **Lincoln Square**.

In general, Chicago is very accessible for gay visitors. Most queer attractions are within easy reach of downtown; indeed, in Boystown and Andersonville, they're all within easy reach of each other. You may want to break out the button-up shirt for one or two fancier digs along casual-conservative Halsted Street, but T-shirt and jeans are the norm just about everywhere. While your time in the gay 'hoods is likely to be hassle-free, muggings sometimes occur. Take as much care as you would in any big city.

This might be the Midwest, but cruising is common in Chicago. Popular haunts include Lincoln Park (the park itself, not the yuppie 'hood); you can also score pretty much anywhere from Montrose Harbor all the way up to the Hollywood Beach (also an excellent gay beach by day). If a car flashes its lights at you or a furtive glance is cast your way, you're in business. But the Chicago police are no fools:

Arts & Entertainment

Big Chicks. *See p245.*

Joie de Vine: the perfect tonic for oenophiles of all orientations. *See p245.*

we suggest you either head somewhere else with your new-found mate or, at the very least, that you use some discretion. Alternatively, head to www.gay.com and enter the fetish room of your choice, or just dig into pure sleaze at www.craigslist.org. Always play safe: HIV infection is just as prevalent here as elsewhere.

LESBIAN LIFE

The easiest way for girls to come out of the closet is to walk into the **Closet** on Broadway (*see p246*), or to take the Red line to Berwyn and head into **Girltown**, aka Andersonville. **Star Gaze** (*see p246*) shines brightest, boasting the city-est babes and a bodacious patio, though classy dykes should try lesbian wine bar **Joie de Vine** (*see p245*).

In general, though, you'll fare better at the city's weekly and monthly events. Chances, a alternative dance party at **Subterranean** (2011 W North Avenue, at N Damen Avenue, Wicker Park, 1-773 278 6600, www.subt.net), draws a pretty even male/female mix, while Women Wanna Play, on the fourth Thursday of the month at **Crew Bar & Grill** (*see p246*), and Dirty Girl Thursdays, weekly at the **Lakeview Broadcasting Company** (3542 N Halsted Street, at W Addison Street, Lakeview, 1-773 857 2444, www.lbcchicago.com), are both tilted at girls alone. The regular girlie parties

hosted by ChixMix at **Circuit** (*see p248*) are worth a look, as are Slut-n-Strut at **Déjà Vu** (2624 N Lincoln Avenue, at W Wrightwood Avenue, Lincoln Park, 1-773 871 0205, www. dejavuchicago.com) and the dyke night at **Spy Bar** (*see p266*). Always call ahead or check local listings before you make the trip.

INFORMATION & MEDIA

Time Out Chicago includes plenty of gay events listings each week. In addition, the vestibule of any eaterie or meeterie in Andersonville and Boystown will have high-rise stacks of the free gay papers. The *Chicago Free Press* and bastard sister the *Windy City Times* (twin sufferers of an acrimonious media divorce) both delve into local and national issues while also including all-important nightlife information. *Identity* covers the politics of race and culture; *Nightspots*, with its compact map and addresses of manjoints, fits snugly into a back pocket.

As shiny as a waxed chest, *Boi* contains listings, fluff pieces and the occasional article on amphetamines or abs. *Gay Chicago* has full listings of happenings and have-to-dos; if you want to be escorted, there are ads aplenty in the back pages. *Pink* magazine is the glossiest of them all, supplementing generally well-written articles with a business directory for the queer community (hence its original title, *Pink Pages*).

Chicago's only all-music radio show for the gay community airs on WLUW 88.7 FM every Tuesday from 6pm to 8pm. Hosts Erik and Ali of Think Pink Productions keep their queer ears to the ground and spin the best in alternative sounds. Online, the city has become something of a hotbed of queer podcasting: check out the wildly popular Feast of Fools (www.feastof fools.net), PNSexplosion (www.pnsexplosion. com) and the Daily Purge (www.thedailypurge. net), among others.

Eat, Drink, Shop

Restaurants & cafés

Andersonville

Francesca's Bryn Mawr

1039 W Bryn Mawr Avenue, at N Sheridan Road (1-773 506 9261). El: Red to Bryn Mawr. **Open** 11.30am-2pm, 5-9pm Mon; 11.30am-2pm, 5-10pm Tue-Thur; 11.30am-2pm, 5-11pm Fri; 5-11pm Sat; 5-9pm Sun. **Main courses** $15-$30. **Credit** AmEx, Disc, MC, V.

There are a dozen or so versions of this hip Italian hangout throughout the city and suburbs, but only this one is nicknamed Mancesca's. You can't swing a fettuccini noodle without hitting half a dozen tables of same-sex couples chowing down excellent pasta, or (less frequently) large parties of guppies ordering tons of vino and checking out both the daily specials and the handsome waitstaff. **Other locations**: throughout the city.

Hamburger Mary's

5400 N Clark Street, at W Balmoral Avenue (1-773 784 6969). El: Red to Bryn Mawr. **Open** 11am-11pm Mon-Thur; 11am-midnight Fri; 10am-midnight Sat; 10am-11pm Sun. **Main courses** $8-$11. **Credit** AmEx, Disc, MC, V.

Chicago gets its very own version of the ubiquitous queer hamburger chain. The burgers come in every combination of ingredients imaginable (Buffy the Hamburger Slayer, anyone?), and are out of this

world. Wash them down with a constant flow of beer, before your bill arrives in a high heel. Upstairs, Mary's Attic (open Wed-Sat only) couples tasty late-night fare with themed nights such as Paper Doll, a drag show hosted by local persona Vanity Fair. Expect crowds on weekends.

Jin Ju

5203 N Clark Street, at W Foster Avenue (1-773 334 6377). El: Red to Berwyn. **Open** 5-9.30pm Tue, Wed; 5-10.30pm Thur; 5-11.30pm Fri, Sat. **Main courses** $8-$15. **Credit** AmEx, Disc, MC, V.

Brick walls and a subdued sexiness draw a mixed crowd, who nibble on fiery spare ribs (you must) and sip Sojutinis, a potable crafted with a Korean grain liquor that's made from sweet potatoes (again, you must). Finish with the ginger ice-cream: it's so good that you'll want to lick someone else's spoon.

M Henry

5707 N Clark Street, at W Hollywood Street (1-773 561 1600). El: Red to Bryn Mawr. **Open** 7am-2.30pm Tue-Fri; 8am-3pm Sat, Sun. **Main courses** $8-$15. **Credit** AmEx, MC, V.

Come the weekend, you can't get in the door here. However, you'll still want to try, simply to taste the most scrumptious blueberry and walnut pancakes this side of the Mississippi. The wait can be long, but it's a friendly queue full of attractive possibilities.

Tomboy

5402 N Clark Street, at W Balmoral Avenue (1-773 907 0636/www.tomboyrestaurant.com). El: Red to Bryn Mawr. **Open** 5-10pm Mon-Thur; 5-11pm Fri, Sat. **Main courses** $15-$25. **Credit** AmEx, Disc, DC, MC, V.

Previously BYOB (bring your own butch, as well as own wine and worldly-wise proclivities), this tasty lesbian-run bistro in Andersonville now has a fully licensed bar. Reasonably priced, Tomboy is also handsomely appointed and appropriately low-lit for under-the-table napkin snatching.

Tweet

5020 N Sheridan Road, at W Argyle Avenue (1-773 728 5576/www.tweet.biz). El: Red to Argyle. **Open** 9am-3pm Mon, Wed-Sun. **Brunch** $7-$12. **No credit cards**.

Festivals Gay & lesbian

Gays, straights and everything in between jam Boystown during the fourth weekend in June for the city's annual **Pride** celebrations (1-773 348 8243, www.chicagopridecalendar.org). The events calendar takes in talks, film screenings, discussions and performances, all culminating in Sunday's Pride Parade.

Six weeks later, the largest street festival in the Midwest rolls into Boystown, along

Halsted Street between Belmont Avenue and Addison Street. **Northalsted Market Days** (1-773 883 0500, www.northalsted.com), staged over the first weekend in August, is basically a two-day outdoor gay bar with bands, DJs, street vendors and shirtless studs galore. Don't miss it.

For **Reeling: the Chicago Gay & Lesbian International Film Festival**, see p238.

Having put a lid on its evening operations, Michelle Fire's Uptown restaurant is now free to concentrate on its daytime service. Tweet serves giant helpings of breakfast favourites, with a wonderful coffee cake *amuse-bouche* to start. Most of the food is made with organically grown and locally produced ingredients.

Boystown

Ann Sather

929 W Belmont Avenue, at N Sheffield Avenue (1-773 348 2378/www.annsather.com). El: Brown, Purple or Red to Belmont. **Open** 7am-3pm Mon, Tue; 7am-9pm Wed-Sun. **Main courses** $9-$12. **Credit** AmEx, MC, V. **Map** p329 E2.

Known for its sticky buns (oh, *please*), this hospitable, gay-run Swedish enclave has been around for half a century. The place is cheap, cosy and, despite its Nordic roots, emphatically all-American in its cuisine. Ann Sather's owner, Tom Tunney, was elected as the city's first openly gay alderman in 2003. **Other locations**: 3411 N Broadway Street, at W Roscoe Street, Boystown (1-773 305 0024); 3416 N Southport Avenue, at W Roscoe Street, Lakeview (1-773 404 4475); 5207 N Clark Street, at W Foster Avenue, Andersonville (1-773 271 6677).

Caribou Coffee

3300 N Broadway Street, at W Aldine Avenue (1-773 477 3695/www.cariboucoffee. com). El: Brown, Purple or Red to Belmont. **Open** 5.30am-10pm daily. **Credit** AmEx, Disc, MC, V. **Map** p329 F2.

This coffee house has multiple locations; this branch – aka Cruisabou – is in the heart of Boystown. Come here to chat with your mates, but look elsewhere if you're looking to… well, look elsewhere – there's a quieter location on Halsted Street.
Other locations: throughout the city.

HB Café

3404 N Halsted Street, at W Newport Avenue (1-773 661 0299). El: Red to Addison. **Open** 5-10pm Tue-Thur; 5-10.30pm Fri; 9am-2pm, 5-10.30pm Sat; 9am-2pm, 5-10pm Sun. **Main courses** $15-$25. **Credit** AmEx, Disc, MC, V. **Map** p329 F1.

There's almost nothing but tables for two in this cramped Boystown hangout, ensuring almost every guest has one thing on his mind. Just make sure you get the seat facing the window, so your partner has his eyes on you and not on the boys on Halsted. Dig into new American dishes such as brown sugar-crusted salmon, courtesy of owners (and Food Network stars) Dan Smith and Steve McDonagh.

Read all about it

In June 1987, the **Henry Gerber/Pearl M Hart Library** hosted a book sale from its small basement premises on the edge of Boystown. Visitors to the gay and lesbian collective could find in its small library essays and literature about the AIDS crisis, old flyers that circulated during the heyday of gay liberation, lesbian pulp novels with worn-down spines and physique magazines featuring oiled-up young men. It wasn't much of a collection, but it was enough to attract the attention of a young woman named Karen Sendziak, who stopped to check out the sale.

It rained that afternoon. As volunteers began to bundle up the books and take them inside, Sendziak found herself joining in their rescue efforts. That fall, she attended her first volunteer meeting. Fast-forward two decades, and Sendziak is the president of the board of directors and curator of the archives, now based up in Edgewater. The library celebrated its 25th anniversary in 2006, an impressive feat considering that the project nearly folded in 1987 following the deaths of Gregory Sprague, the library's founder, and Joe Gregg, its longtime librarian.

Sprague's vision for a gay and lesbian archive began in the early 1980s. He knew of the ONE Institute (now the ONE National Gay

& Lesbian Archives) in Los Angeles and the Lesbian Herstory Archives in New York, both founded in the '70s, but he worried that Chicago's contribution was being ignored. 'Gay history, as it was being written, was bicoastal,' says Sendziak. 'It completely ignored the Midwest.' Sprague named his fledgling organisation after two local gay-rights pioneers: Henry Gerber, who founded the Society for Human Rights (the US's first gay rights organisation) in 1924, and Pearl Hart, a pioneering lesbian attorney who practised in the city until her death in 1975.

Over the years, the library has weathered its share of trouble, not least among them the kind of financial difficulties inevitable for an organisation that depends on community donations. Still, it has steadily built its membership through innovative events programming, which takes in film screenings, exhibitions, readings and even GLBT academic salons, where students discuss their theses with the community. (For details of the library's contact information and opening hours, *see p305*.) When praised for her role in its survival, Sendziak defers credit to the library's founder. 'It was Gregory Sprague,' she says. 'One person, one vision. He was annoyed – that was it.'

Intelligentsia

3123 N Broadway Street, at W Barry Street (1-773 348 8058/www.intelligentsiacoffee.com). El: Brown, Purple or Red to Belmont. **Open** 6am-10pm Mon-Thur, Sun; 6am-11pm Fri; 7am-11pm Sat. **Credit** AmEx, Disc, MC, V. **Map** p329 F3.

Putty-toned walls, soothing tunes, scattered-pattern seating, Adirondack chairs out front in summer… yep, it's Boystown's very own independent coffeehouse, popular with the anti-Starbucks crowd. For tours of the factory, *see p150* **Made in Chicago**. **Other locations**: 53 W Jackson Boulevard, at S Dearborn Street, the Loop (1-312 253 0594); 53 E Randolph Street, at S Wabash Avenue, the Loop (1-312 920 9332).

Kit Kat Lounge & Supper Club

3700 N Halsted Street, at W Waveland Avenue (1-773 525 1111/www.kitkatchicago.com). El: Red to Addison. **Open** 5.30pm-2am Tue-Sun. **Main courses** $13-$26. **Credit** AmEx, DC, Disc, MC, V. **Map** p329 F1.

One look at the pretty garnishes beyond the lip of the bar (cherries, chunks of watermelon, umbrella-spiked pineapples) and you just know it's fruity 'n' juicy in here. Funkadelic drag queens make appearances and lip-synch, but it's the extensive Martini menu that really rocks.

Melrose

3233 N Broadway Street, at W Melrose Street (1-773 327 2060). El: Brown, Purple or Red to Belmont. **Open** 24hrs daily. **Main courses** $6-$14. **Credit** MC, V. **Map** p329 F2.

It's 4am, you're in mid-hangover, and there's a frightening plate of greasy food staring you in the face. It really doesn't get much better than this. Besides, the Melrose is your last chance to decide if that bar pick-up sitting across from you is really worth taking home.

Nookies Tree

3334 N Halsted Street, at W Buckingham Place (1-773 248 9888). El: Brown, Purple or Red to Belmont. **Open** 7am-midnight Mon-Thur, Sun; 24hrs Fri, Sat. **Main courses** $5-$12. **No credit cards**. **Map** p329 F2.

March in here for munchies, brunchies and grilled American cheese sandwiches. It's an inevitable, even obligatory destination, right on the Boystown strip; everybody goes there, night and day, and so should you. There are two other branches, but this one's got the gaydar. **Other locations**: Nookies, 1746 N Wells Street, at W St Paul Avenue, Old Town (1-312 337 2454); Nookies Too, 2114 N Halsted Street, at W Dickens Avenue, Lincoln Park (1-773 327 1400).

X/O

3441 N Halsted Street, at W Newport Avenue (1-773 348 9696/www.xochicago.com). El: Red to Addison. **Open** 5.30-11pm Mon-Wed; 5.30pm-2am Thur, Fri; 5.30pm-3am Sat; 11am-3pm, 5.30-11pm Sun. **Main courses** $9-$23. **Credit** AmEx, Disc, DC, MC, V. **Map** p329 F2.

Stop wasting your time at Sidetrack (*see p247*) and Roscoe's (*see p247*): if you can't pick up someone beautiful at this clubby, small-plates nightspot, you're just not trying. Choose from tons of tiny tasting items, such as pan-fried Chesapeake Bay softshell crabs or beautiful grilled octopus salad. It's unlikely, however, that your trick will go down as well as X/O's chocolate orgasm dessert.

Elsewhere

Speakeasy Supper Club

1401 W Devon Avenue, at N Glenwood Avenue, Rogers Park (1-773 338 0600/www.speakeasysupperclub.com). El: Red to Granville. **Open** 5-10pm Mon-Thur, Sun; 5-11pm Fri, Sat. **Main courses** $19-$23. **Credit** AmEx, DC, Disc, MC, V.

This upscale lez-owned joint in Rogers Park is the sexiest spot uptown. The new American menu is full of half-portions perfect for sharing, and the gorgeous lesbians enjoying cigarettes at the bar make secondhand smoke taste appealing. You can enjoy cabaret performances while you dine, thanks in part to co-owner and out artist Michael Feinstein.

Bars

Andersonville

Big Chicks

5024 N Sheridan Road, at W Argyle Avenue (1-773 728 5511/www.bigchicks.com). El: Red to Argyle. **Open** 4pm-2am Mon-Fri; 3pm-3am Sat; 11am-2am Sun. **No credit cards**.

This charming speakeasy-style saloon is more akin to an East Village hangout than it is to a Chicago joint. Owner Michelle Fire gives away free shots at midnight and rolls out an all-you-can-eat Sunday buffet. The clientele is a mixed bag of scruffy neighbourhood locals, relaxed twentysomethings and lesbians on the loose. Everyone gets along, especially on the tiny, packed dancefloor. **Photo** *p241*.

Chicago Eagle

5015 N Clark Street, at W Winnemac Avenue (1-773 728 0050). El: Red to Argyle. **Open** 8pm-4am Mon-Fri, Sun; 8pm-5am Sat. **No credit cards**.

Clomping through the trailer of a semi truck gets you into this cruisy, bruisy leather bar. Upstairs, you can sit and get your boots spit-shined; downstairs in the Pit, there's a chain-link fence pen for impounding naughty 'prisoners'. There's almost always a DJ.

Joie de Vine

1744 W Balmoral Avenue, at N Ravenswood Avenue (1-773 989 6846). Bus 22. **Open** 5pm-midnight Mon-Thur; 5pm-2am Fri; 5pm-3am Sat; 2pm-midnight Sun. **Credit** AmEx, Disc, MC, V.

Starry-eyed romantics will quickly fall in love with this lesbian wine bar, where flickering candles and soft house music are combined with an encyclopedia of international wines and some light bites. Most nights, it's just a regular bar, where oenophiles of all orientations pull up a stool and swill pinot. But on weekends, it looks more like a casting call for *The L Word*, with plenty of stylish lezzies gossiping, holding hands and leaving lipstick marks all over the glassware. **Photo** *p242*.

Star Gaze

5419 N Clark Street, at W Foster Avenue (1-773 561 7363). El: Red to Berwyn. **Open** 6pm-2am Wed-Fri; 6pm-3am Sat; noon-2am Sun. **Credit** AmEx, Disc, MC, V.

This laid-back lesbian hangout is a reminder that Andersonville used to be a gaybourhood firmly dominated by dykes. You can take salsa lessons on Friday night or party with trannies every other Thursday – and, yes, the pool tables are almost always in use.

Boystown

Cell Block

3702 N Halsted Street, at W Waveland Avenue (1-773 665 8064/www.cellblock-chicago.com). El: Red to Addison. **Open** 4pm-2am Mon-Fri; 2pm-3am Sat; 2pm-2am Sun. **Credit** AmEx, DC, Disc, MC, V. **Map** p329 F1.

Ever wanted to go to jail? Come on in. It's seedy and cagey, with a leather dress code enforced by burly, nipple-clamped sergeants patrolling entry into the backroom (aka the Holding Cell). The third Wednesday of every month is No Hair Night, with free buzzing for all.

Closet

3325 N Broadway Street, at W Buckingham Place (1-773 477 8533). El: Brown, Purple or Red to Belmont. **Open** 2pm-4am Mon-Fri; noon-5am Sat; noon-4am Sun. **No credit cards.** **Map** p329 F2.

This little lesbian bar is a safe stone's throw away from the hustle and muscle of Halsted Street. It's the perfect place to have a beer with the ladies while watching the straight folk push their strollers down Broadway. Things really get rolling after 2am on weekends, when boys and girls mix as easily as a vanilla-chocolate swirl ice-cream.

Cocktail

3359 N Halsted Street, at W Roscoe Street (1-773 477 1420). El: Brown, Purple or Red to Belmont. **Open** 4pm-2am Mon-Fri, Sun; 4pm-3am Sat. **Credit** AmEx, Disc, MC, V. **Map** p329 F2.

The perfect corner bar for sissies who love sissies, Cocktail has huge windows that make Halsted a two-way street to cruise and be cruised. Go-go boys groove at Spank, the Tuesday- and Thursday-night randy rendezvous. The perfect place to meet and greet in the early evening, and the in-house jukebox rocks.

Crew Bar & Grill

4804 N Broadway Street, at W Lawrence Avenue (1-773 784 2739/www.worldsgreatestbar.com). El: Red to Lawrence. **Open** 11.30am-2am Mon-Fri; 11am-2am Sat, Sun. **Credit** MC, V. **Map** p329 F2.

Barely two years young, this sports bar has broken away from the Boystown pack with a novel Uptown location, a crowd that's welcoming to both men and women, and plenty-of-fun monthly parties such as

Minibar. *See p247.*

Frat Boy Fridays, Women Wanna Play and God Save the Queens. A perfect place to watch the Cubs lose in the company of both gays and lesbians. The mini-burgers on the appetisers menu are irresistible.

Minibar

3341 N Halsted Street, at W Buckingham Place (1-773 883 1800/www.minibarchicago.com). El: Red to Addison. **Open** 7pm-2am Mon-Fri; 5pm-3am Sat; 5pm-2am Sun. **Credit** AmEx, Disc, MC, V. **Map** p329 F2.

Hold your Martini glass and your nose up in the air at this tiny new jet-set lounge for the pretentious and beautiful. Music is kept to a low roar, which enables conversation (and potential hook-ups). Indulge Sundays feature a rotating line-up of DJs. Don't forget to check out the wine bar and tasting lounge next door. **Photo** *p246*.

Roscoe's

3356 N Halsted Street, at W Roscoe Street (1-773 281 3355/www.roscoes.com). El: Red to Addison. **Open** noon-2am Mon-Fri; noon-3am Sat; 11am-2am Sun. **Admission** $5 after 10pm Sat. **Credit** Disc, MC, V. **Map** p329 F2.

This horny Gen-Y romper room has everything a queer kid could ask for, including drinks specials, loads of cute boys and plenty of entertainment courtesy of Chicago's 'finest' drag queens. It's a lovely tavern, with loads of exposed brick, a cosy outdoor patio, and plenty of nooks and crannies for making out in. Expect queues on weekends.

Sidetrack

3349 N Halsted Street, at W Buckingham Place (1-773 477 9189/www.sidetrackchicago.com). El: Red to Addison. **Open** 3pm-2am Mon-Fri, Sun; 3pm-3am Sat. **Credit** AmEx, DC, Disc, MC, V. **Map** p329 F2.

This juggernaut of a bar is famous not just in Boystown but across the country. Stare at videos or stare at men in any number of rooms, including the cavernous glass bar or the sparkling roof deck. There's a comedy night on Thursday. Girls are welcome, but will find themselves in the minority.

Elsewhere

Jackhammer

6406 N Clark Street, at W Devon Avenue, Rogers Park (1-773 743 5772). Bus 22. **Open** 4pm-4am Mon-Thur; 4pm-5am Fri; 2pm-5am Sat; 2pm-4am Sun. **Credit** AmEx, Disc, MC, V.

This place draws a delightful mix of guys in jeans and T-shirts or military fetish gear, plus street-tuff trannies, adventurous clubgoers and leather folk. The main room is dominated by a dancefloor; once a month, it hosts Flesh Hungry Dog Show, a queer rock cabaret. While a new upstairs lounge hints that the place might go mainstream, the downstairs Hole bar is strictly for the adventurous, and the rotation of gay porn on the monitors will always keep it sleazy. The isolated location means the lovely outdoor patio remains open after midnight in summer.

Manhandler Saloon

1948 N Halsted Street, at W Armitage Avenue, Old Town (1-773 871 3339). El: Brown or Purple to Armitage. **Open** noon-4am Mon-Fri, Sun; noon-5am Sat. **No credit cards. Map** p328 F6.

If someone cryogenically froze 1970s gay life and defrosted it in the 21st century, they'd end up with this place. Located among aromatherapy shops and yuppie bistros, this dimly lit watering hole is the kind of place where old men stare at you too long. Still, it's nice to come here to imagine those heady days of gay lib when moustaches and short shorts ruled, and safer sex was still light years away.

Shops & services

Andersonville

His Stuff

5314 N Clark Street, at W Foster Avenue (1-773 989 9111). El: Red to Berwyn. **Open** 11am-9pm Tue-Fri; 11am-7pm Sat; noon-6pm Sun. **Credit** AmEx, Disc, MC, V.

Only two years old but more natty than bratty, this Andersonville haberdasher's is undeniably stylish.

Women & Children First

5233 N Clark Street, at W Foster Avenue (1-773 769 9299/www.womenandchildrenfirst.com). El: Red to Berwyn. **Open** 11am-7pm Mon, Tue; 11am-9pm Wed-Fri; 10am-7pm Sat; 11am-6pm Sun. **Credit** AmEx, Disc, MC, V.

A cheery and inclusive must-visit both for feminist and child-oriented literature, this well-stocked bookstore specialises in lesbian and gay titles, music, videos and magazines.

Boystown

For the **Unabridged Bookstore**, which contains a sizeable selection of gay and lesbian literature, *see p193*.

Batteries Not Included

3420 N Halsted Street, at W Roscoe Street (1-773 935 9900/www.toysafterdark.com). El: Brown, Purple or Red to Belmont. **Open** 11am-midnight daily. **Credit** AmEx, MC, V. **Map** p329 F2.

Half of the profits of this gadget and goo shop go to charity. The owner's so nice, he'll even let you test out the lubes before you purchase. Here, the customer always comes first.

Beatnix

3400 N Halsted Street, at W Roscoe Street (1-773 281 6933). El: Red to Addison. **Open** noon-10pm Mon-Thur, Sun; 11am-midnight Fri, Sat. **Credit** MC, V. **Map** p329 F2.

This vast vintage store in the middle of Boystown is a favourite clothes closet for club kids, drag queens, bull dykes and muscle boys. It offers a sexy selection of tuxes (the queers must cater, you know) and a cute vortex in the corner devoted to wigs.

Gay Mart

3457 N Halsted Street, at W Cornelia Avenue (1-773 929 4272). El: Red to Addison. **Open** 11am-7pm Mon-Thur, Sun; 11am-8pm Fri, Sat. **Credit** Disc, MC, V. **Map** p329 F2.

The gaudy and goofy rooms here are overflowing with gay-themed cards, novelties, jewellery and stuff adorned with rainbows and schlongs. Shop 'til you drop your inhibitions and then cross over to Hydrate *(see p249)* for a drink.

Universal Gear

3153 N Broadway Street, at W Belmont Avenue (1-773 296 1090/www.universalgear.com). El: Brown, Purple or Red to Belmont. **Open** 10am-9pm Mon-Thur; 10am-10pm Fri, Sat; 11am-8pm Sun. **Credit** AmEx, Disc, MC, V. **Map** p329 F3.

Pretty boys do the folding in this menswear-only shop, which hawks threads from the likes of Jocko, Energie and DKNY, as well as more underwear than you could sniff in a lifetime.

Arts & Entertainment

Bathhouses & boothstores

Andersonville

Man's Country

5015 N Clark Street, at W Argyle Street (1-773 878 2069). El: Red to Argyle. **Open** 24hrs daily. **Admission** $10 lifetime member. **No credit cards.**

This Andersonville bathhouse, which bills itself as 'more fun than a barrel of hunkies', contains three floors of nakedness, with singles, doubles and fantasy rooms. Plunge into the huge whirlpool or the steam room and say hello to the thirtysomethings.

Boystown

Ram

3511 N Halsted Street, at W Cornelia Avenue (1-773 525 9528). El: Red to Addison. **Open** 24hrs daily. **Admission** prices vary. **Credit** Disc, MC, V. **Map** p329 F2.

Porn and playthings are sold up front at this heavy-duty hangout. Pay for entry to the rear room, then wander the narrow, labyrinthine hallways.

Steamworks

3246 N Halsted Street, at W Belmont Avenue (1-773 929 6080/www.steamworksonline.com). El: Brown, Purple or Red to Belmont. **Open** 24hrs daily. **Admission** $6 membership; $14 lockers; $20-$50 room rentals. **Credit** AmEx, MC, V. **Map** p329 F2.

There are 70 private rooms at this sani-tastic tiled romphouse, plus a gym, a sauna and hot hunks galore, pitching their towel tents all over the place.

Thursday is the night to visit. Like a challenge? Butt up against the atti-dudes on the weekends.

Elsewhere

Bijou Theater

1349 N Wells Street, at W Evergreen Avenue, Old Town (1-312 943 5397/www.bijouworld.com). El: Brown or Purple to Sedgwick; Red to Clark/Division. **Open** 24hrs daily. **No credit cards.** **Map** p327 H8.

Owned and operated by porn producer Steven Toushin since 1970, this pioneering establishment screens dirty movies in a Victorian townhouse. It sounds slightly quaint, until the hardcore flicks and exotic dancers unreel and undress.

Nightclubs

The venues below are specifically gay-oriented, but many other clubs are also big with queers. Among them are **Berlin** *(see p269)* and, on Mondays, the **Boom Boom Room** *(see p268* **Baby, let's play house)**. Queues are long at weekends, Sundays are a local favourite, and on Tuesdays everybody stays in and rents a DVD.

Boystown

Charlie's

3726 N Broadway Street, at W Waveland Avenue (1-773 871 8887). El: Red to Addison. **Open** 3pm-4am Mon-Fri, Sun; 3pm-5am Sat. **Admission** free-$20. **Credit** AmEx, MC, V. **Map** p329 F1.

If you don't know how to dance country-style, Charlie's offers lessons several nights a week. But it's not homos doin' the hoedown that pack this queer country club: it's the circuit queens and the style-conscious who join the queues around 2am, when the crowds ditch their cowboys hats in exchange for some high-energy fun.

Circuit

3641 N Halsted Street, at W Addison Street (1-773 325 2233/www.circuitclub.com). El: Red to Addison. **Open** 9pm-4am Thur, Fri, Sun; 9pm-5am Sat. **Admission** $5-$15. **Credit** AmEx, Disc, MC, V. **Map** p329 F1.

This venerable club has had its fair share of woes, including a dispute with local condo dwellers that gave it a bruising a few years back, but it still knows how to churn out a late-night dance party. Latin men dish and dance together on Thursdays and Sundays, while hip hop homos and lady-lovin' ladies each get a monthly party of their own.

Hydrate

3458 N Halsted Street, at W Belmont Avenue (1-773 975 9244/www.hydratechicago.com). El: Brown, Purple or Red to Belmont. **Open** 8pm-4am Mon-Fri, Sun; 8pm-5am Sat. **Admission** $3-$10 Thur-Sun. **Credit** MC, V. **Map** p329 F2.

Ride him, cowboy

After audiences saw Jake Gyllenhaal bending down beside a mountain stream wearing nothing but a pair of cowboy boots in *Brokeback Mountain*, Chicagoan gay men started wearing their jeans a little tighter. However, the local gay country and western scene has long been impressive. Gear up over at **Alcala's Western Wear** (*see p200*) before two-stepping on to the circuit...

Most gay Chicagoans go to **Charlie's** (*see p248*) for the after-hours dance parties. But it's also the biggest gay western venue in the city, with resident rancher Michael B and DJ Micha spinning country tunes most nights. Free two-step and line-dancing lessons are offered on Mondays and Wednesdays, and a couple of drag-hosted events punctuate the week. Party boys come here to fondle in the wee hours, but the pair of glittering cowboy boots hanging above the dancefloor reminds them that at Charlie's, country rules.

Elsewhere, **Touché** (6412 N Clark Street, at W Devon Avenue, Uptown, 1-773 465 7400, www.touchechicago.com) caters mostly to a leather crowd, but stages regular cowboy themed events. Every other month, the Rodeo Riders (www.rodeoriderschicago.org) host a night at the venue; the Illinois Gay Rodeo Association (www.ilgra.com) also stage regular meetings here in advance of their annual rodeo each August.

On the South Side, **Chesterfield's** (1800 W Pershing Road, at S Wood Street, 1-773 247 4403, www.clubchesterfields.com) draws seas of pretty boys, neighbourhood regulars and gangsta queers, but also attracts plenty of dudes wearing cowboy hats. If you're into early 20th-century SoCal Mexican rancher chic, head here.

If you've got two left feet, try the **Chi-town Squares** (www.iagsdc.org/chi-townsquares), the city's gay square-dancing club. The group hosts classes for beginners every Monday at the Ebenezer Church Community Center (1650 W Foster Avenue, at N Ashland Avenue, Andersonville), with lessons for more experienced dancers later in the week. Various social events and dances are staged throughout the year: check out the website more details.

Hydrate manages to lure some of the city's best DJs for its wildly busy after-hours scene, but there's plenty going on here every night, including Martinis and manicures on Tuesdays and monthly lube wrestling.

Spin
800 W Belmont Avenue, at N Halsted Street (1-773 327 7711/www.spin-nightclub.com). El: Brown, Purple or Red to Belmont. **Open** 4pm-2am Mon, Tue, Thur, Fri; 8pm-2am Wed; 2pm-3am Sat; 2pm-2am Sun. **Admission** free-$5. **Credit** MC, V. **Map** p309 F2.
Up front, it's a video bar; out back, there's darkness and dancing. The crowd leans towards gay males and their straight female friends; leave your 'tude at the door. Friday's Shower Power sees contestants vie for prizes by getting drenched as seductively as possible.

Theatre & piano bars

For **Jackhammer**, which hosts queer-oriented indie-rock night Flesh Hungry Dog Show on the third Friday of each month, *see p247*. For the **Bailiwick Repertory** theatre, *see p279*.

Baton Lounge
436 N Clark Street, at W Illinois Street, River North (1-312 644 5269/www.thebatonshowlounge.com). El: Brown or Purple to Merchandise Mart; Red to Grand. **Shows** 8.30pm, 10.30pm, 12.30am Wed-Sun. **Admission** $10-$14. **Credit** DC, Disc, MC, V. **Map** p326 H10.

Chicago's prime drag venue allows only pre-ops to perform; these quasi-queens are so strut-alicious that straight men, as well as gay men's moms, have been known to swoon. Clap your mitts for Mimi Marks, the Marilyn Monroe-esque belle of the circuit ball, and don't miss October's Miss Continental Pageant.

Gentry
440 N State Street, at W Illinois Street, River North (1-312 836 0933/www.gentryofchicago.com). El: Red to Grand. **Open** 4pm-2am Mon-Fri, Sun; 4pm-3am Sat. **Admission** free. **Credit** AmEx, DC, Disc, MC, V. **Map** p326 H10.
Deep-throated songbirds croon cabaret-style at this smooth and easy piano bar, from Hairspray to Harry Connick Jr and back again. The branch in Boystown bursts with twentysomethings; downtown, the crowd tips toward the mid-century.
Other locations: 3320 N Halsted Street, at W Buckingham Place, Boystown (1-773 348 1053).

Homolatte
No Exit Café, 6970 N Glenwood Avenue, at W Morse Avenue, Uptown (1-773 743 3355). El: Red to Loyola. **Open** 7pm-1am Fri-Sun. **Admission** $22. **No credit cards**.
With performances by, for and about word-hungry queers, this weekly showcase of gay, lesbian and transgendered musicians and writers is hosted by Scott Free, the kinda angry, very talented, one-time falsetto soprano for the Lavender Light Gospel Choir.

Arts & Entertainment

Music

From classic rock to classics that rock.

Classical & Opera

Classical music has a strong presence in Chicago, led by the **Chicago Symphony Orchestra** and the **Lyric Opera of Chicago**. The city's two major ensembles are both tied to sizeable venues: the Lyric to the Civic Opera House, and the CSO to Symphony Center and, in summer, the outdoor Ravinia Festival. Touring orchestras and soloists pass through town often, filling out a calendar that's usually busy. Some events are seasonal, such as the springtime series staged in the Harris Theater by the **Chicago Opera Theater**, and the summer seasons at **Ravinia** and **Millennium Park**. Others run year-round, chiefly the excellent and eclectic programme of free concerts at the Chicago Cultural Center's **Preston Bradley Hall**.

The city boasts a number of smaller ensembles, which play around town with varying degrees of regularity. Among them are the **Chicago Chamber Musicians** (1-312 819 5800, www.chicagochambermusic.org), who play a six-concert season at Gottlieb Hall and a lunchtime concert on the first Monday of the month at Preston-Bradley Hall; the **Callisto Ensemble** (1-312 566 9318, www.callisto ensemble.com), also found regularly at Gottlieb Hall; **Music of the Baroque** (1-312 551 1414, www.baroque.org), at the Harris Theater; and the forward-thinking **Chicago Sinfonietta** (1-312 236 3681, www.chicagosinfonietta.org), which performs at Symphony Center and, as of 2006, at the Adler Planetarium (*see p89*). Contemporary music has a strong following, thanks to the **International Contemporary Ensemble** (1-312 494 2655, www.iceorg.org), **Fulcrum Point** (1-773 935 1768, www.fulcrum point.org), **Contempo** (http://contempo. uchicago.edu), the **MAVerick Ensemble** (1-312 771 4916, www.maverickensemble.com), and the CSO's **MusicNOW** group.

INFORMATION AND TICKETS

The weekly *Time Out Chicago* magazine carries comprehensive music listings; the free *Chicago Reader* weekly and the *Chicago Tribune* also have information on upcoming shows. Tickets for the CSO, Lyric Opera and the Ravinia Festival are available through their respective box offices, as well as through **Ticketmaster** (1-312 902 1500, www.ticketmaster.com), but you'll need to book ahead: many concerts are part of subscription series and sell out well ahead of time. Tickets aren't always sold in advance for smaller chamber concerts.

Venues

In addition to the venues listed below, it's worth investigating the **Harris Theater for Music & Dance** (*see p234*), a modern underground venue that's home to the splendid, cutting-edge **Chicago Opera Theater** (1-312 704 8414, www.chicagooperatheater.org). For outdoor concerts in **Grant Park**, **Millennium Park** and **Ravinia**, *see p252* **Festivals**.

Civic Opera House

20 N Wacker Drive, at E Madison Street, the Loop (1-312 332 2244/www.lyricopera.org). El: Brown, Green, Orange or Purple to Washington. **Box office** *noon-6pm Mon-Sat. Mid Sept-Mar also Sun on performance days.* **Tickets** *$40-$170.* **Credit** AmEx, DC, Disc, MC, V. **Map** p325 G12.

As soon as you clap eyes on the lobby's opulent, almost garish art deco design, you'll realise that subtlety isn't the order of the day at the Civic Opera House, built in 1929 by utilities magnate Samuel Insull (*see p19*). The Lyric Opera of Chicago has made its home here since 1954, and now presents eight productions here each season. It's regularly ranked as one of the top opera companies in the country, boasting a talented stable of singers alongside an excellent orchestra (under the musical direction of former BBCSO chief conductor Sir Andrew Davis). It's also one of the most traditional, in terms of the choice of repertoire and the ways in which it's staged: if you like your opera stars dressed in tights, this is the place for you. But if the Lyric rarely breaks new

The best Classics

For 50 violinists in tuxes
Symphony Center. *See p253.*

For ten singers in frilly outfits
Civic Opera House. *See p250.*

For a string quartet in suits
Mandel Hall. *See p251.*

Stars of the Lyric Opera sing for their supper at the **Civic Opera House**. *See p250.*

ground, the numbers speak for themselves: on average, the company plays to 95% capacity, no mean feat in a room that holds 3,500.

Around Christmas, look out for the Do-it-Yourself Messiah, a Chicago tradition in which have-a-go locals join a local orchestra of amateurs in a rousing rendition of Handel's classic. Admission is free, but you'll need to book your ticket in advance.

Ganz Hall at Roosevelt University

430 S Michigan Avenue, at E Van Buren Street, the Loop (1-312 341 3780/www.roosevelt.edu). El: Blue or Red to Jackson; Brown, Orange, Pink or Purple to Library. **Box office** none. **Admission** usually free. **No credit cards. Map** p325 J13.

Formerly a hotel banqueting hall and a masonic lodge, this impressive space now stages recitals by student and faculty members at Roosevelt's Chicago College of Performing Arts, alongside regular concerts by visiting soloists and ensembles. The acoustic lends virtually every instrument a rich resonance.

Lyon & Healy Hall

168 N Ogden Avenue, at W Randolph Street, West Loop (1-800 595 4849/www.lyonhealy.com/hall). El: Green or Pink to Ashland. **Box office** from 6.45pm on performance nights. **Tickets** $30. **Credit** AmEx, Disc, MC, V. **Map** p330 D11.

This recent addition to the local music scene, a 200-capacity hall housed in (and run by) the Lyon & Healy harp factory, is highlighted by its unusual design: the stage is backed by a huge window, offering concertgoers breathtaking views of downtown. The music's pretty good, too: L&H's own recitals series includes some impressive names, while many local musicians also rent out the space for their own independent concerts.

Mandel Hall at the University of Chicago

1131 E 57th Street, at S University Avenue, Hyde Park (1-773 702 8069/http://music.uchicago.edu). Metra 55th-56th-57th Street. **Box office** times vary. **Tickets** $5-$35. **No credit cards. Map** p332 X17.

The distinguished, century-old Mandel Hall plays host to internationally recognised string quartets, opera singers (in recital) and early music groups. Many of today's classical stars, among them violinist Hilary Hahn, made their Chicago debuts here. The University of Chicago also stages occasional concerts in the lovely Rockefeller Memorial Chapel, nearby on its Hyde Park campus.

Merit School of Music, Gottlieb Concert Hall

38 S Peoria Street, between W Monroe & W Madison Streets, West Loop (1-312 786 9428/www.meritmusic.org). El: Blue to UIC-Halsted. **Box office** times vary. **Tickets** free-$20. **Credit** varies. **Map** p330 F12.

This cosy 372-seat hall opened in 2005 at a local music college and has been embraced by the city's chamber ensembles: the Callisto Ensemble, the Orion Ensemble and the Chicago Chamber Musicians have all played here. The near-Downtown location is a boon both to musicians and concertgoers.

PianoForte Chicago

410 S Michigan Avenue, between E Van Buren Street & E Congress Parkway (1-312 291 0000/www.pianofortechicago.com). El: Blue or Red to Jackson; Brown, Orange, Pink or Purple to Library. **Open** 10am-5pm daily. **Tickets** $10-$20. **Credit** MC, V. **Map** p325 J13.

Located in Solon S Beman's Fine Arts Building (*see p32*), the PianoForte Foundation exists to promote and sell the small but revered range of Fazioli pianos. To those ends, it stages a bijou range of concerts in its showroom; regular Saturday-afternoon piano recitals are supplemented by the Fazioli Salon Series every Friday lunchtime, for which all tickets are free.

Preston Bradley Hall

Chicago Cultural Center, 78 E Washington Boulevard, at N Michigan Avenue, the Loop (1-312 744 6630/www.cityofchicago.org/culturalaffairs). El: Blue to Washington; Brown, Green, Orange, Pink or Purple to Randolph; Red to Lake. **Open** 8am-7pm Mon-Thur; 8am-6pm Fri; 9am-6pm Sat; 10am-6pm Sun. **Tickets** free. **No credit cards.** **Map** p325 J12.

The original site of Chicago's public library hosts regular concerts under the world's largest (and, for that matter, most expensive) Tiffany dome. Any number of classical music events are staged here, with musicians from the nearby Chicago Symphony often among the artists. You're guaranteed to find classical performances at 12.15pm every Monday (as part of the hall's LunchBreak series) and Wednesday (in the Dame Myra Hess Memorial Concert Series), and at 3pm on Sundays.

Festivals Classical & opera

Grant Park Music Festival at the Jay Pritzker Pavilion

Millennium Park, the Loop (www.millennium park.org). El: Blue or Red to Washington; Brown, Green, Orange, Pink or Purple to Randolph. **Date** June-Aug. **Tickets** free. **No credit cards. Map** p325 J12.

Imbued with his trademark architectural drama, Frank Gehry's striking outdoor concert hall in Millennium Park did a mighty job at counteracting Chicago's downtown griminess when it opened in 2004. The Grant Park Orchestra plays free concerts here in summer, and there are also regular world music and jazz events. The pavilion has room for 11,000 listeners, 4,000 on permanent seating and the rest camped out on the lawn, and the acoustic set-up is astonishing: the trellis that loops over the lawn carries a sound system that's concert hall quality.

Ravinia Festival

Ravinia Park, Green Bay Road, Highland Park (1-847 266 5100/www.ravinia.com). Metra: Ravinia Park. **Date** June-Aug. **Tickets** 25¢-$100. **Credit** AmEx, DC, Disc, MC, V.

The outdoor Ravinia Festival has kept the classical scene hopping in summer for decades. The biggest and most famous of the three stages is the Ravinia Pavilion, which presents concerts by the Chicago Symphony alongside occasional big-name galas, concert performances of popular operas and pop gigs. The 3,200 covered seats at the pavilion are supplemented by a huge expanse of picnic-friendly lawn. Elsewhere on site, the 850-seat Martin Theatre hosts concerts by chamber groups, and the smaller Bennett-Gordon Hall features a variety of college-age performers. Ravinia's Steans Institute trains young musicians, and the concerts in which they feature are often the highlights of the season.

Ravinia Festival.

St Paul's Church

*2335 N Orchard Street, at W Fullerton Avenue,
Lincoln Park (1-773 348 3829/www.stpaulsucc
chicago.org). El: Brown, Purple or Red to Fullerton.*
Box office contact individual ensembles for tickets.
Tickets free-$20. **Credit** varies. **Map** p328 F5.
Rebuilt after the Chicago Fire, this vaguely Gothic
cathedral supplements its religious activities with
concerts. Music of the Baroque are among the ensembles that play here from time to time.

Symphony Center

*220 S Michigan Avenue, at E Adams Street, the
Loop (1-312 294 3000/www.cso.org). El: Blue or
Red to Jackson; Brown, Green, Orange, Pink or Purple
to Adams.* **Box office** 10am-6pm Mon-Sat; 11am-
4pm Sun. **Tickets** $10-$200. **Credit** AmEx, DC,
Disc, MC, V. **Map** p325 J12.
A multi-million-dollar renovation in 1997 turned the
Symphony Center into a veritable music mall. Its pri-
mary role, of course, is as the home of the Chicago
Symphony Orchestra, which performs in Orchestra
Hall every weekend from autumn to early summer.
Daniel Barenboim retired as the CSO's music director in June 2006, leaving an orchestra with a rich
sound and flexible expression. His post wasn't filled
immediately, but with eminent Dutchman Bernard
Haitink and ultra-precise Pierre Boulez serving as
regular guest conductors, the orchestra was left in
capable hands.

The hall's programme is supplemented by occasional visits from touring soloists, small ensembles
and orchestras; Saturday-morning family concerts;
sporadic pop and rock shows; and occasional concerts from the Civic Orchestra of Chicago (the CSO's
training orchestra for young musicians) and the
Chicago Youth Symphony Orchestra (www.cyso.
org). Also on site is a learning centre, a music-themed
restaurant (Rhapsody; *see p145*) and a shop selling
CDs and gifts. Next door is the Chicago chapter of
the National Academy of Recording Arts & Sciences.

Rock & Roots

The blues (*see pp260-261*) gets all the headlines,
and not without good reason. But Chicago's rock
scene is every bit as vital, and has been for a
while. The 1980s saw the emergence from the
city of such disparate styles as industrial metal
(courtesy of Ministry and the Wax Trax label),
and house (which takes its name from the
now-defunct Warehouse club), while the 1990s
spawned an insurgent country scene that
continues to thrive. Three of the country's best
independent labels – Touch & Go, Thrill Jockey
and Drag City – are based here; at the other end
of the spectrum, Kanye West and Common have
given local hip hop international currency. Is it
any wonder that Sufjan Stevens wrote an entire
album about Illinois? With so many Chicagoan
music stories, he'd need a box set to do it justice.

INFORMATION AND TICKETS

For comprehensive reviews and listings of the
latest concerts and events, check the weekly
Time Out Chicago magazine, also online at
www.timeout.com/chicago. The *Chicago
Reader* also carries listings and previews.

In giant venues such as the **Allstate Arena**
and the **United Center**, shows keep regular
hours, starting around 7.30pm and wrapping
up by 10.30pm. The smaller clubs, up to **Metro**
or even **House of Blues** size, keep later
hours: gigs start about 9pm and finish between
midnight and 1am, with everything running
an hour later on Fridays and Saturdays. Shows
not designated 'all-ages' are only open to those
over the age of 21. Always carry a photo ID.

Tickets for many club shows are available
only at the door. However, tickets for bigger
bands are sold in advance, either through the
venue or via an agency such as **Ticketmaster**
(1-312 902 1500, www.ticketmaster.com).

Venues

Major arenas & stadiums

Several major sporting venues host occasional
gigs. **Soldier Field** (1-312 559 1212; *see p272*),
home of the Chicago Bears, welcomes the likes
of the Rolling Stones when it's not too cold,
while the **United Center** (1-312 455 4500; *see
p272*) stages shows by big-name acts when it's
not hosting the Bulls or the Blackhawks. On the
South Side, the Chicago Fire's **Toyota Park**
(1-708 598 6666; *see p272*) also presents big
gigs. And multi-band summer extravaganzas
such as Ozzfest often roll into the **First
Midwest Bank Amphitheatre** out in Tinley
Park (1-708 614 1616, www.livenation.com).

The **Charter One Pavilion at Northerly
Island**, formerly as Meigs Field (1-312 540
2000, www.northerlyislandpavilion.com),
hosts a handful of open-air concerts, as does
the Skyline Stage at **Navy Pier** (www.navy
pier.com). The **Jay Pritzker Pavilion** in
Millennium Park (*see p252* **Festivals**) and

The best Rock & pop

For arena rock
AllState Arena. *See p254.*

For indie rock
Empty Bottle. *See p256.*

For roots rock
FitzGerald's. *See p256.*

Festivals Rock, roots, blues & jazz

In addition to the festivals listed below, you can often catch bands playing at the various neighbourhood festivals and block parties around the city each summer. *Time Out Chicago* carries weekly listings, but look out in particular for the block party at the **Hideout** (*see p257*) over a weekend in September, which features a ton of terrific local alt-rock acts. Tickets (around $15 a day) benefit local charities, and usually sell out in advance. There's also lots of music staged as part of the **Taste of Chicago** festival (*see p217*).

Chicago Gospel Festival
Millennium Park, the Loop (www.millennium park.org). El: Blue or Red to Monroe; Brown, Green, Orange, Pink or Purple to Randolph. **Date** wknd, early June. **Map** p325 J13.
The big-name performers at this three-day free event perform at the Pritzker Pavilion, but there are also two other stages, one of which is devoted to young performers.

Chicago Blues Festival
Grant Park, the Loop (www.cityofchicago.org/ specialevents). El: Blue or Red to Jackson; Brown, Green, Orange, Pink or Purple to Adams. **Date** 4 days, early June. **Map** pp324-325 J11-J14.

Held over four days in early June, the Chicago Blues Festival is the biggest of all the city's free music festivals, attracting more than half a million visitors each year. The biggest names play at the Petrillo Music Shell (2006 saw turns from Bettye LaVette and Bobby 'Blue' Bland), but there are also five other stages on hand to showcase smaller local acts.

Intonation
Union Park, 1501 W Randolph Street, at N Ogden Avenue, West Town (www.intonation musicfest.com). **Date** wknd, late June. **Map** p330 D11.
Started in 2005 by Pitchfork but curated the following year by *Vice* magazine, this two-day festival spotlights buzz-bin bands (the Streets, Bloc Party) and failsafe veterans (Robert Pollard, the Boredoms). Tickets usually cost around $20 per day or $35 for the weekend.

Chicago Country Music Festival
Grant Park, the Loop (www.cityofchicago.org/ specialevents). El: Blue or Red to Jackson; Brown, Green, Orange, Pink or Purple to Adams. **Date** wknd, early July. **Map** pp324-325 J11-J14.

---

the **Petrillo Music Shell** in Grant Park (www.cityofchicago.org) stage free shows in summer, and the **Ravinia Festival** (*see p252* **Festivals**) supplements its classical line-ups with occasional pop shows.

Allstate Arena
6920 Mannheim Road, Rosemont (1-847 635 6601/ www.allstatearena.com). El: Blue to Rosemont, then Pace bus 223 or 250. **Box office** 11am-7pm Mon-Fri; noon-5pm Sat. **Tickets** $20-$100. **Credit** AmEx, Disc, MC, V.
The venue known to many longtime locals as the Rosemont Horizon attracts mainstream star power, from Queen to Justin Timberlake, as well as Latin, country and world music acts.

UIC Pavilion
1150 W Harrison Street, at S Racine Avenue (1-312 413 5700/www.vcsa.uic.edu). El: Blue to Racine. **Box office** noon-6pm Mon-Fri; noon-4pm Sat. **Tickets** $25-$75. **Credit** Disc, MC, V. **Map** p330 E13.
Big stars occasionally play the UIC Pavilion, usually home to the university's sports teams. However, you're more likely to find multi-band bills and festivals, such as local heroes Fall Out Boy playing with half a dozen other popular emo bands.

Rock & roots venues

In addition to the clubs and theatres listed below, a number of other venues stage shows. The **Chicago Theatre** (175 N State Street, at W Lake Street, the Loop, 1- 312 462 6363, www. thechicagotheatre.com) has welcomed everyone from Dolly Parton to the White Stripes of late; the **Auditorium Theatre** (50 E Congress Parkway, at S Wabash Avenue, 1-312 922 2110, http://auditoriumtheatre.org) also presents big-ticket acts; and the more casual **Vic Theatre** (*see p237*) welcomes alt-rock bands when it's not showing movies. **Darkroom** and **Sonotheque** (for both, *see p270*) host shows by hot local acts when they're not majoring in DJ culture, while **Cal's Liquors** (*see p177*) stages free shows on Fridays and Saturdays by noisy local acts. There are also great free gigs at the Chicago Cultural Center's **Preston Bradley Hall** (*see p252*).

Abbey Pub
3420 W Grace Avenue, at N Elston Avenue, Avondale (1-773 478 4408/www.abbeypub.com). El: Blue to Addison. **Tickets** free-$25. **Credit** AmEx, DC, Disc, MC, V.

This weekend-long event at the Petrillo Music Shell isn't as high-profile as Grant Park's other music festival, but it does offer big-name acts: in 2006, Jo Dee Messina and Glen Campbell headlined (not together). Admission is free.

Pitchfork Music Festival

Union Park, 1501 W Randolph Street, at N Ogden Avenue, West Town (www.pitchfork media.com). Date wknd, late July. Map p330 D11.
The locally based but globally known online zine stage a two-day festival each year out in Union Park. Expect to see the likes of Will Oldham and Yo La Tengo on the bill alongside a few wild cards (in 2006, Os Mutantes). Tickets are around $20 a day.

Lollapalooza

Grant Park, the Loop (www.lollapalooza.com). El: Blue or Red to Jackson; Brown, Green, Orange, Pink or Purple to Adams. Date wknd, early Aug. Map pp324-325 J11-J14.
Starting life as an alt-rock travelling show in the grunge-era '90s, Lollapalooza has made Chicago its home in the last few years. Big names in music – Red Hot Chilli Peppers, Kanye West and Ryan Adams in 2006 –

play a variety of stages over three days. A pass for the entire festival costs a not insubstantial $150.

Chicago Jazz Festival

Grant Park, the Loop (www.cityofchicago.org/specialevents). El: Blue or Red to Jackson; Brown, Green, Orange, Pink or Purple to Adams. Date 4 days, early Sept. Map pp324-325 J11-J14.
Held over the Labor Day weekend, this four-day festival welcomes many big names to Grant Park. In 2006, the opening show at Symphony Center (with Joshua Redman and Kurt Elling) was followed by three days of free shows from the likes of Joe Lovano, Lee Konitz and the Rebirth Brass Band. With the exception of the Symphony Center show, tickets are free.

Chicago World Music Festival

Various venues (www.cityofchicago.org/specialevents). Date 1 wk, mid Sept.
This week-long wing-ding allows Chicagoans to travel the globe without leaving the city, via a sprawling bill of more than 60 artists from virtually every continent. Events are held everywhere from Millennium Park to branches of Borders: check online for details.

There are two sides – literally – to this Northwest Side spot. On one is a small Irish pub that hosts energetic folk and traditional performances most nights. On the other is one of the city's premier venues for independent hip hop, where you can catch anyone from local act MC Diverse to conscious hip hop artists such as Little Brother. Indie rock acts such as Spoon and Cat Power also stop by regularly.

Aragon Ballroom

1106 W Lawrence Avenue, at N Winthrop Avenue, Uptown (1-773 561 9500/www.aragon.com). El: Red to Lawrence. Tickets $30-$50. Credit AmEx, MC, V.
This beautiful, ornate and capacious space opened as a ballroom in 1926. These days, though, it serves as one of the biggest music venues within the city limits. The 4,500-capacity room hosts groups such as Black Eyed Peas, Slayer and Death Cab for Cutie.

Beat Kitchen

2100 W Belmont Avenue, at N Hoyne Avenue, Lakeview (1-773 281 4444/www.beatkitchen.com). Bus 50, 77. Tickets $7-$20. Credit AmEx, MC, V.
This tidy, welcoming little corner bar in the north of the city has hosted innumerable debut shows, many of them in the punk and alt-rock varieties.

However, it also stages sporadic gigs from more well-known and sometimes rootsy acts such as Festus, Missouri's Bottle Rockets.

California Clipper

1002 N California Avenue, at W Augusta Boulevard, Humboldt Park (1-773 384 2547/www.california clipper.com). Bus 52, 66, 70. Tickets free. No credit cards.
This fun, folksy bar, one of the bigger rockabilly hangouts in the city, welcomes some of Chicago's finer weekly country-swing performers, such as local favourite Susie Gomez. The booths are comfy, while the back room is low-key but spacious.

Congress Theater

2135 N Milwaukee Avenue, between W Maplewood Avenue & W Rockwell Street, Humboldt Park (1-773 486 6672/www.congresschicago.com). El: Blue to Western. Tickets $20-$50. Credit Disc, MC, V.
This sizeable, slightly oddball venue hosts a diverse range of shows, featuring everyone from mainstream alt-rockers such as the Killers and Modest Mouse to nationally known Latino groups and even occasional hip hop and dancehall acts. The calibre of the bookings has improved of late.

Empty Bottle.

Double Door

1572 N Milwaukee Avenue, at N Damen Avenue,
Wicker Park (1-773 489 3160/www.doubledoor.com).
El: Blue to Damen. **Tickets** $5-$20. **Credit** AmEx,
Disc, MC, V. **Map** p331 B7.
Located in the very heart of the nightlife action in
Wicker Park, the Double Door is essentially the lit-
tle brother to the Metro (*see p257*), which books its
acts. Many older local bands play here, among them
longtime popular duo Local H, alongside occasion-
al turns from touring groups (everyone from the
Lemonheads to Scritti Politti).

Elbo Room

2871 N Lincoln Avenue, at W George Street,
Lakeview (1-773 549 5549/www.elboroomchicago.
com). El: Brown or Purple to Diversey. **Tickets**
$5-$10. **Credit** AmEx, Disc, MC, V. **Map** p329 D3.
The music may be played in the basement, but don't
mistake the Elbo Room for a dive. With a rotating
roster of local, usually undiscovered rock bands, and
comfortable, eye-level sightlines, there might not be
a better place to find out that your neighbour's rock
band doesn't actually suck.

Empty Bottle

1035 N Western Avenue, at W Cortez Street,
Wicker Park (1-773 276 3600/www.emptybottle.
com). Bus 49, 70. **Tickets** $7-$12. **Credit** AmEx,
Disc, MC, V. **Map** p331 A8.
Don't be fooled by its unassuming storefront: this is
Chicago's premier indie rock club, hosting cutting-
edge bands from home and abroad. The annual
Adventures in Modern Music festival, co-sponsored
by British magazine *The Wire*, is internationally
renowned. If you need to get away from the noise
for a while, the club has a comfortable front room,
complete with a pool table and friendly cat, Radley,
curled up on the couch. A great venue.

Fireside Bowl

2648 W Fullerton Avenue, between N Talman &
N Washtenaw Avenues (1-773 486 2700/www.
firesidebowl.com). El: Blue to California. **Tickets**
$5-$10. **Credit** AmEx, Disc, MC, V.
This bowling alley was the city's premier all-ages
punk venue for years. It shut down for a while, but
it recently reopened to host the occasional over-21s
show – usually local bands, usually punk and usually on Sundays. Sadly, you can't bowl during the
shows, otherwise this club really would be our
favourite in the city.

FitzGerald's

6615 W Roosevelt Road, at East Avenue, Berwyn
(1-708 788 2118/www.fitzgeraldsnightclub.com).
El: Blue to Oak Park. **Tickets** $5-$15. **Credit**
Disc, MC, V.
Perhaps Chicago's premier roots music showcase,
this homey haunt out in Berwyn features an array
of zydeco, country, rockabilly and blues acts alongside occasional big band jazz. All-acoustic country
bands perform in a side bar.

Heartland Café

7000 N Glenwood Avenue, at W Lunt Avenue,
Rogers Park (1-773 465 8005/www.heartlandcafe.
com). El: Red to Morse. **Tickets** free-$5. **Credit**
Disc, MC, V.
This Rogers Park restaurant offers acoustic entertainment of a country/folk bent. Local regulars the
Long Gone Lonesome Boys are typical of the kind
of thing you can expect, though the venue also features a weekly open-mic poetry and music night, as
well as a Saturday radio show broadcast on WLUW
88.7 FM. Adjacent to the venue (and sharing the
same fantastic kitchen), the Red Line Tap (1-773 338
9862) books small-time but usually endearing rock,
folk, country and punk bands.

going for it. The majority of bands featured on the smaller Back Porch stage are blues acts, playing in a well-lit setting meant to look like a juke joint but actually resembling a modern art museum.

Lakeshore Theater
3175 N Broadway Street, between W Briar Place & W Belmont Avenue, Lakeview (1-773 472 3492/ www.lakeshoretheater.com). El: Brown, Purple or Red to Belmont. **Tickets** $10-$15. **Credit** Disc, MC, V. **Map** p329 F2.
Better known as a theatre venue, this North Side spot has recently started featuring all-ages music shows booked by the Empty Bottle crew (*see p256*). It's an intimate venue with comfy bucket seats and excellent sightlines, ideal for acoustic sets.

Logan Square Auditorium
2539 N Kedzie Boulevard, at W Albany Avenue, Logan Square (1-773 252 6179/www.logansquare auditorium.com). El: Blue to Logan Square. **Tickets** $8-$20. **No credit cards.**
This all-ages, 750-capacity Logan Square spot resembles nothing so much as a high-school gym – it's no wonder local radio station WLUW hosts its annual indie rock prom here. The acoustics leave much to be desired, but some of the gigs (many of which are booked by the team at the Empty Bottle; *see p256*) really are can't-miss, starring everyone from the Fall to the Eagles of Death Metal.

Martyrs'
3855 N Lincoln Avenue, at W Berenice Avenue, Lakeview (1-773 404 9494/www.martyrslive.com). El: Brown to Irving Park. **Tickets** $6-$30. **Credit** Disc, MC, V.
This rather plain, mid-sized space has hosted big names such as Wilco, Los Lobos and Bernie Worrell in the past, but in recent years has exposed Chicago to a welter of jazz-fusion, world music and jam acts. On the first Thursday of the month, it stages the Big C Jamboree, Chicago's only all-rockabilly showcase and open mic night.

Metro
3730 N Clark Street, between W Waveland & W Racine Avenues, Wrigleyville (1-773 549 0203/ www.metrochicago.com). El: Red to Addison. **Tickets** $5-$20. **Credit** AmEx, Disc, MC, V. **Map** p329 E1.
One of the city's older and more famous clubs hosts a variety of mid-sized national touring acts of all genres, from rock to electronica. It's also known for hosting larger showcases of local bands: the annual Chicago Rocks fest, for example, at which you can catch a slew of the city's top hip hop artists all on one night. Downstairs, you'll often find excellent DJs at the Smartbar (*see p269*).

Morseland
1218 W Morse Avenue, between N Lakewood Avenue & N Sheridan Road, Rogers Park (1-773 764 8900/www.morseland.com). El: Red to Morse. **Tickets** free-$10. **Credit** AmEx, Disc, MC, V.

Hideout
1354 W Wabansia Avenue, between Elston Avenue & Throop Street, Wicker Park (1-773 227 4433/ www.hideoutchicago.com). Bus 72. **Tickets** $5-$12. **No credit cards.**
Appropriately named (it's tucked away in an industrial corridor), the Hideout serves as both an unpretentious, friendly local bar and a don't-miss roots venue. Some of the city's best alt-country acts got their start in the backroom, which also plays host to rock groups, readings and other non-music events. Its block party (*see p254* **Festivals**) is always a blast. Rugged string band Devil in a Woodpile play in the front bar every Tuesday for free.

HotHouse
31 E Balbo Drive, between S State Street & S Wabash Avenue, the Loop (1-312 362 9707/www.hothouse. net). El: Red to Harrison. **Tickets** $5-$15. **Credit** AmEx, MC, V. **Map** p325 H13.
This not-for-profit venue hosts the city's most adventurous musical programme in a gorgeous, art-crammed space. The crowd here is among the most diverse in the city, with college kids mingling with urban bohos. Bookings lurch from global world music imports to homegrown avant-jazzers.

House of Blues
329 N Dearborn Street, at W Kinzie Street, River North (1-312 923 2000/www.hob.com). El: Red to Grand. **Tickets** $10-$40. **Credit** AmEx, Disc, MC, V. **Map** p326 H11.
Presenting some of the best national and international touring acts through one of the city's finest sound systems, the Chicago edition of this chain is especially beautiful (check out the lush bathrooms). Purists scorn the place, but any venue that runs the gamut from Common to Frankie Knuckles to T-Model Ford in a single week must have something

Artists in residence

Touring acts come and go, but some things on Chicago's music scene stay the same. A handful of bands play week-in, week-out residencies, welcoming a mix of hardcore regulars and curious visitors. All are well worthy of your time and attention, and all are free, but don't forget to show some love when the tip jar comes around.

Devil in a Woodpile's weekly gig at the Hideout (*see p257*; Tuesdays at 9.30pm, free) is like an old-fashioned hootenanny, only hipper. The group performs in the bar instead of on a stage, and singer Rick Sherry doesn't even use a mic – he just hollers like a street vendor. Sherry, guitarist Joel Paterson and double bassist Tom Ray stomp and strut through an assortment of jug-band blues tunes, a genre that most can't pull off without being overtly cute.

As one of Chicago jazz's most overlooked musical treasures, it makes sense that free-jazz keyboardist **Jim Baker** would find a creative home in a dive bar (Hotti Biscotti; *see p262*). Along with drummer Steve Hunt, bassist-guitarist Brian Sandstrom and Liquid Soul saxophonist Mars Williams, Baker has created what is an endangered species in Chicago jazz: a jam session that matters (Tuesdays at 8pm, free). The music ranges from quiet, icy reveries to squealing cackles of delight, with surprise

guests virtually guaranteed for the second set. It's all done by 10.30pm; if you leave a little early, you'll have time to careen down to the South Side and catch **Von Freeman**'s more straight-ahead weekly session at his own New Apartment Lounge (*see p262*; Tuesdays at 9pm, free).

The **Hoyle Brothers** began their happy-hour residency at the Empty Bottle (*see p256*; Fridays at 5.30pm, free) in 2002, and its earthy, no-frills authentic country always attracts a full house. There's nothing ostentatious about the Brothers (who aren't related) as they play off the stage, cracking jokes as they artfully flow through crowd-pleasing Merle Haggard covers and some excellent originals. And since there's no cover charge, says singer Jacque Judy, 'We're the best dang band in your price range.'

Devil in a Woodpile.

Thanks to a recent makeover, this Rogers Park club has become the single best destination on the Far North Side for hip hop, dub and jazz. Whether you're watching a live jazz band or a bona fide turntablist, the cushy environment aids enjoyment.

Mutiny

2428 N Western Avenue, between W Fullerton Avenue & W Montana Street, Logan Square (1-773 486 7774/http://themutiny.bravepages.com). Bus 49, 74. **Tickets** free. **No credit cards**.

The dive to end all dives is tucked away close to the expressway. The backroom stage has a chipping ceiling, but the beer's cheap and it's a fun place to see that friend-of-a-friend's band play. Getting booked is relatively easy, so lots of local groups often play their first gigs here.

Nite Cap Lounge

5007 W Irving Park Road, at N Lavergne Avenue, Northwest Side (1-773 282 8654/www.nitecaplive.com). El: Blue to Irving Park. **Tickets** $5-$8. **No credit cards**.

This out-of-the-way venue used to host heavy metal shows, but has moved on to presenting hardcore and garage bands. The bar in the music room is circular and located smack-dab in the middle of the action.

Note

1565 N Milwaukee Avenue, at N Damen Avenue (1-773 489 0011/www.thenotechicago.com). El: Blue to Damen. **Tickets** $5-$10. **Credit** AmEx, MC, V. **Map** p331 B7.

Formerly known as the Blue Note, this straightforward Wicker Park bar is right in the centre of the madness. While the local rock acts it books are sometimes so-so, the hip hop nights are excellent: be sure to stop by late on a Saturday (it's open until 5am) to hear some of the city's better hip hop DJs.

Old Town School of Folk Music

4544 N Lincoln Avenue, between W Sunnyside & W Wilson Avenues, Ravenswood (1-773 728 6000/ www.oldtownschool.org). El: Brown to Western. **Tickets** $15-$30. **Credit** AmEx, MC, V.

There are occasional shows at the Old Town School's Old Town location (909 W Armitage Avenue, at N Fremont Street). However, the bigger concerts staged by this loveable local institution, featuring folk, blues, country and world music acts, are held up in the more capacious Ravenswood space. Don't miss the annual Old Town Folk & Roots Festival in July. It's still a school, too, by the way: call for details of the many and varied music classes.

Park West

322 W Armitage Avenue, at N Clark Street, Lincoln Park (1-773 929 1322/www.parkwestchicago.com). El: Brown or Purple to Armitage. **Tickets** $15-$20. **Credit** MC, V. **Map** p328 G6.

This smarter-than-average, relatively intimate venue in Lincoln Park books a roster of interesting acts, anyone from Sean Lennon to Sharon Jones & the Dap Kings. Note that it's a 10-15-minute walk from Armitage station; if you can't be bothered taking it, the 11 or 22 buses will drop you far closer.

Riviera Theatre

4746 N Racine Avenue, at N Broadway Street, Uptown (1-773 275 6800/www.rivieratheatre. com). El: Red to Lawrence. **Tickets** $20-$45. **No credit cards.**

The Riv is generally considered to be the sister rock club to the Aragon (*see p255*), a few blocks away. With a capacity of around 2,500, the jazz-age theatre isn't quite as big as its neighbour, but the acoustics are much better. Those afraid of heights should probably give the steep balcony seating a miss.

Schubas Tavern

3159 N Southport Avenue, at W Belmont Avenue, Lakeview (1-773 525 2508/www.schubas.com). El: Brown, Purple or Red to Belmont. **Tickets** $5-$15. **Credit** AmEx, MC, V. **Map** p309 D3.

Much like the Empty Bottle (*see p256*), this small club books some of the best indie touring acts around, as well as staging folk and country shows, and month-long residencies from local groups with a national profile. You can hang out in the front bar area without paying cover for the shows; if you're under 21, go straight to the back room, which stages plenty of all-ages and over-18 shows. The Harmony Grill serves up a mean brunch at weekends.

Subterranean

2011 W North Avenue, at N Damen Avenue, Wicker Park (1-773 278 6600/www.subt.net). El: Blue to Damen. **Tickets** $5-$15. **Credit** AmEx, DC, Disc, MC, V. **Map** p331 B7.

Set right in the heart of Wicker Park, this upstairs club rarely disappoints. The bookings, which lean towards indie, are usually excellent; local acts are supplement by occasional touring bands. There's a lofty balcony high above the stage if you don't want to rub shoulders with the crowd.

Uncommon Ground

1214 W Grace Street, at N Clark Street, Wrigleyville (1-773 929 3680/www.uncommonground.com). El: Red to Addison. **Tickets** $15 min purchase in dining room. **Credit** Disc, MC, V. **Map** p329 E1.

One of Chicago's most beloved coffeehouses hosts the city's best weekly open mic night alongside shows from local and touring folk artists. Thanks to a much-ballyhooed set by the then-unknown Jeff Buckley in 1994, the cosy shop even has an annual tribute to the late singer-songwriter in November that draws an international audience.

Wild Hare

3530 N Clark Street, between W Cornelia Avenue & W Eddy Street, Wrigleyville (1-773 327 4273/ www.wildharereggae.com). El: Red to Addison. **Tickets** $5-$12. **No credit cards.** **Map** p329 E2.

One of the few places left to see authentic Caribbean music in the city, the Wild Hare boasts live reggae and dub music seven nights a week. Come on a Monday and you might also catch some local hip hop.

Wise Fools Pub

2270 N Lincoln Avenue, between W Belden & W Webster Avenue, Lincoln Park (1-773 929 1300/ www.wisefoolspub.com). El: Brown, Purple or Red to Fullerton. **Tickets** $5-$10. **Credit** AmEx, MC, V. **Map** p328 F5.

One of the first North Side blues venues was reborn a few years ago, and now serves primarily as a showcase for local jam and cover bands such as Mr Blotto.

Blues & Jazz

Without Chicago, the blues wouldn't have been the same. And without the blues, Chicago would be a different town. From the 1910s to the 1950s, African Americans from the south flocked to the city in what became known as

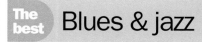

The best Blues & jazz

For blues belters
Blue Chicago. *See p260.*

For brass blowers
Green Mill. *See p262.*

For star power
Buddy Guy's Legends. *See p260.*

the Great Migration. A handful plugged in their guitars and invented the Chicago blues, an electrified, energetic take on traditional Delta sounds. The reverberations bounced around the world and came back again, influencing the likes of the Rolling Stones and Eric Clapton. Many clubs in Chicago these days cater to tourists, but you can still find musicians playing with the passion of their predecessors. For more on the blues in Chicago, see pp45-48.

The jazz scene here is vibrant, too, with international touring acts supplementing a local scene that takes in such disparate names as Von Williams and Ken Vandermark. The **Association for the Advancement of Creative Musicians** (http://aacmchicago.org), which stages shows at the **Velvet Lounge**, is a powerhouse of African American jazz.

INFORMATION AND TICKETS

The weekly *Time Out Chicago* magazine carries comprehensive listings and previews. Few club shows here start before 9pm, and many kick off nearer 10pm. At many jazz venues, the band will play two sets, wrapping up at 1am or later. A few clubs sell tickets or accept reservations in advance, especially for bigger-name acts (Buddy Guy at Buddy Guy's Legends, for example). If in doubt, call ahead or check online.

Venues

Blues & R&B

Blues fans should also check the line-ups at the **Chicago Cultural Center** (*see p252*), the **HotHouse** (*see p257*), the **Old Town School of Folk Music** (*see p259*) and the **Red Line Tap** (*see p256* Heartwood Café), all of which often features blues acts on their rosters. In addition, the 4,200-capacity, 45-year-old **Arie Crown Theatre** (2301 S Lake Shore Drive, 1-312 791 6190, www.ariecrown.com) regularly hosts shows by middle-of-the-road blues and R&B acts.

B.L.U.E.S.

2519 N Halsted Street, between W Altgeld Street & W Lill Avenue (1-773 528 1012/www.chicagobluesbar.com). El: Brown, Purple or Red to Fullerton. **Tickets** $5-$8. **Credit** AmEx, DC, Disc, MC, V. **Map** p328 F5.
The 'other' popular Lincoln Park blues club, more traditional and down-home compared to Kingston Mines' fluorescent sports-bar atmosphere. Popular acts include local stalwarts such as Li'l Ed and Jimmy Johnson. If you've never done blues karaoke, be sure to stop by on Sunday afternoons and belt your heart out.

Blue Chicago

Blue Chicago North *736 N Clark Street, at W Superior Street, River North (1-312 642 6261). El: Brown, Purple or Red to Chicago.*
Blue Chicago South *536 N Clark Street, at Grand Avenue (1-312 661 0010). El: Brown or Purple to Merchandise Mart; Red to Grand.* **Both** *www.bluechicago.com.* **Tickets** $5-$8. **Credit** AmEx, MC, V. **Map** p326 H10.
These two related nightclubs are so similar in style that they're virtually interchangeable. Both focus primarily on local female blues vocalists like Shirley Johnson and Big Time Sarah, and draw a crowd thick with tourists.

Buddy Guy's Legends

754 S Wabash Avenue, at E 8th Street, South Loop (1-312 427 0333/www.buddyguys.com). El: Red to Harrison. **Tickets** $10-$15. **Credit** AmEx, DC, Disc, MC, V. **Map** p325 H13.
If you want to see Guy perform at his own club, stop by in January when he takes over the schedules. If you show up the other eleven months of the year, you may well see him sitting at the bar, overseeing the whole operation: he's more than just a name on the sign outside. There are acoustic blues sets on Fridays and Saturdays at 5.30pm. And if you like Louisiana cuisine, the kitchen has just what you need.

Kingston Mines

2548 N Halsted Street, at W Wrightwood Avenue, Lincoln Park (1-773 477 4646/www.kingstonmines.com). El: Brown, Purple or Red to Fullerton. **Tickets** $12-$15. **Credit** AmEx, DC, Disc, MC, V. **Map** p328 F4.
This polite Lincoln Park club has an unusual set-up – two different bands in two different rooms on two different stages, with MC Frank Pellegrino keeping things moving at all times. Expect to find local bands that lean in a rock direction while playing standards such as (*I'm Your*) *Hoochie Coochie Man*, though the club occasionally hooks out-of-town acts as well.

Lee's Unleaded Blues

7401 S South Chicago Avenue, at E 74th Street (1-773 493 3477). Bus 30, 71, 75. **Tickets** free. **No credit cards.**
Since the demise of the original Checkerboard, Lee's has inherited the title of the South Side's leading blues bar, and with good reason. Open only since 1980, it books a variety of local acts, with the very excellent Johnny Drummer & the Starlighters in residency every Saturday night. There's never a cover.

New Checkerboard Lounge

5201 S Harper Court, at 52nd Street, Hyde Park (1-773 684 1472). Metra 55th-56th-57th Street. **Tickets** free-$5. **No credit cards. Map** p332 Y16.
Forced out of its old Bronzeville digs after building difficulties, this legendary old blues club has found a new and rather swankier home in a Hyde Park strip mall. The booking policy remains the same as ever, with popular blues performers such as Vance Kelly appearing regularly. **Photo** *p261.*

Blues in the night, at the **New Checkerboard Lounge**. *See p260*.

Rosa's Lounge

3420 W Armitage Avenue, at N Kimball Avenue, West Side (1-773 342 0452/www.rosaslounge.com). El: Blue to Belmont. **Tickets** $5-$12. **Credit** AmEx, Disc, MC, V.

Located in a working-class West Side neighbourhood, this family-run spot is owned by fine local drummer Tony Mangiullo and his mother, after whom the place is named. The schedule mixes local musicians (including a weekly jam hosted by Tony) and underground out-of-town acts with growing reputations. A full crowd makes Rosa's seem cosy rather than congested, a sign of a good venue.

Smoke Daddy

1804 W Division Street, at N Wood Street, Wicker Park (1-773 772 6656/www.thesmokedaddy.com). El: Blue to Division. **Admission** free. **Credit** AmEx, Disc, MC, V. **Map** p331 C8.

This barbecue joint hosts live music seven nights a week, alternating between blues and jazz with occasional intrusions from country and rockabilly acts. The food's good, too.

Jazz & experimental music

The **Jazz Showcase**, Chicago's leading jazz venue for decades, was forced to close in 2006 when the lease on its River North property expired. It hopes to reopen in 2007; check www.jazzshowcase.com for details.

The **Auditorium Theatre** (*see p254*), the **Chicago Cultural Center** (*see p252*) and the **HotHouse** (*see p257*) also host jazz shows. On Mondays, **Myopic Books** in Wicker Park (*see p194*) puts on performances of low-key jazz and electronica; Sundays see experimental musicians play over at the **Hungry Brain** (*see p183*).

Andy's

11 E Hubbard Street, between N State Street & N Wabash Avenue, River North (1-312 642 6805/www.andysjazzclub.com). El: Red to Grand. **Tickets** $5-$10. **Credit** AmEx, MC, V. **Map** p326 H11.

This mainstream jazz haven runs regular, low-key residencies with some of Chicago's most respected scene elders, Von Freeman and Mike Smith among them. It's a comfortable, intimate space; on top of the music, an evening here is improved by one of the very decent steaks.

Davenport's

1383 N Milwaukee Avenue, at W Wolcott Avenue, Wicker Park (1-773 278 1830/www.davenportspiano bar.com). El: Blue to Division. **Tickets** $10-$30. **Credit** AmEx, Disc, MC, V. **Map** p331 B7.

On the edge of Wicker Park's vibrant nightlife quarter, Davenport's specialises in old-fashioned cabaret reinterpreted by younger, hipper performers. The venue itself is colourful and modern, a far cry from

Green Mill.

what you might expect given the line-ups. There's often more than one show on any given night; call ahead to check start and finish times.

Green Dolphin Street
2200 N Ashland Avenue, at W Webster Avenue, Lincoln Park (1-773 395 0066/www.jazzitup.com). Bus 9, 73. **Tickets** free-$20. **Credit** AmEx, DC, MC, V. **Map** p328 D5.
This capacious spot close by the river is as much restaurant as jazz club, but the food's decent enough that no one's grumbling. The jazz tends toward the light side, though there are also regular Latin sessions and, on Mondays, the quasi-legendary Boom Boom Room (*see p268* **Baby, let's play house**).

Green Mill
4802 N Broadway, at W Lawrence Avenue, Uptown (1-773 878 5552/www.greenmilljazz.com). El: Red to Lawrence. **Tickets** free-$10. **Credit** MC, V.
Al Capone and other gangsters used to hang here in the 1920s, but these days it's all about the music. Owner Dave Jemilo, who returned the club to its original lustre in the 1980s, books smart bebop and free jazz with a discriminating ear. Local favourites Kurt Elling and Patricia Barber both maintain residencies throughout the year (Elling's here every Wednesday, if he's not on tour). Come early, as it's usually understandably busy.

Hotti Biscotti
3545 W Fullerton Avenue, at N Drake Avenue, Logan Square (1-773 772 9970). El: Blue to Belmont. **Tickets** free. **No credit cards.**

This dive bar in Logan Square may not be as well-funded as its competition, but its idiosyncratic weekly acts – like free jazz synth wizard Jim Baker on Tuesdays – are well worthy of the diversion.

Katerina's
1920 W Irving Park Road, between N Wolcott & N Damen Avenues, Lakeview (1-773 348 7592/ www.katerinas.com). El: Brown to Irving Park. **Tickets** free-$10. **Credit** AmEx, MC, V.
Den mother Katerina supports local jazz and world music like few others. Inside her cosy venue you can catch gypsy violinist Alfonso Ponticelli, jazz chanteuse T Monique, sporadic world music gigs and even local jam bands.

New Apartment Lounge
504 E 75th Street, at S Eberhart Avenue, South Side (1-773 483 7728). El: Red to 79th. **Tickets** free. **No credit cards.**
This unashamedly kitschy bar and jazz venue is worth the schlep down to the South Side. It's owned by local saxophonist Von Williams, who leads a popular late-night jam session on Tuesdays that attracts talent from colleges and training grounds all over Illinois.

Pops For Champagne
601 N State Street, at E Ohio Street, River North (1-773 472 1000/www.popsforchampagne.com). El: Red to Grand. **Tickets** free-$15. **Credit** AmEx, DC, Disc, MC, V. **Map** p326 H10.
Having relocated from its Lakeview premises at the tail end of 2006, Pops hopes to continue its tradition of showing high-quality mainstream jazz in a very swanky setting. Even if you're not a champagne type, it's still worth a look, thanks to residencies from a number of the city's finest straight-ahead pianists and vocalists.

6ODUM
2116 W Chicago Avenue, between N Hoyne Avenue & N Leavitt Street, Ukrainian Village (no phone/ www.lampo.org). Bus 50, 66. **Tickets** check listings for details. **No credit cards. Map** p331 B9.
Shows at 6Odum (pronounced 'odum') are infrequent, but it remains one of the best places in which to see experimental music – not just in Chicago, but in the entire US. Artists from all over the globe show up here and make everything from provocative tape experiments to saxophone skronking. Check the website for updates.

Velvet Lounge
67 E Cermak Road, between E Michigan & E Wabash Avenues, Chinatown (1-312 791 9050/ www.velvetlounge.net). El: Red to Cermak-Chinatown. **Tickets** free-$20. **No credit cards.**
The address is different (the original location was a few blocks east), but the booking policy remains the same at this pioneering, treasurable venue. Run by veteran saxophonist Fred Anderson, the club concentrates on free jazz, with high-calibre guests such as Paul Motian and Henry Grimes joining the locals.

Nightclubs

Home is where the house is.

While New York and LA might boast more star sightings on the street than in the sky, America's third city has a layered approach to clubbing. You can go out every night of the week in Chicago without hearing the same DJ twice, spending as little or as much cash as you want. There's glitz if you want it, but there's also plenty of grit. Indeed, much of the city's best nightlife is slightly underground.

At the swanky end of the spectrum are clubs in River North such as **RiNo** and the **Stone Lotus Lounge**, which go all out for exclusivity. The strangulating dress codes of yore have loosened of late, thanks to designer jean culture and the realisation that a room full of identically dressed people doesn't make for a great social mix. However, the dreaded velvet rope is still in use. The best way past it is to RSVP a promoter online or show up a bit earlier than party time. For more on how best to enjoy clubbing in Chicago, *see p265* **Club culture**.

Bear in mind that many of the city's new hot spots need only stay jammed for six months in order to be worthwhile investments for their owners, after which they can be left to rot. Knowing whether the party people have moved on can be tricky, but a number of promoters, among them Surreal and Exact, have loyal followings of sociable people that move from place to place in River North. Bump into that crowd and you could easily trick yourself into believing you've landed in South Beach.

Further down the ladder from the River North hangouts sit a clutch of venues that put their emphasis on the music. Chief among them is **Smartbar**, spruced up in 2006 with a redesign of its previously penitential looks and the addition of a world-class sound system to

RiNo. *See p266.*

match the cutting-edge DJ programming. Elsewhere, check out **Sonotheque**: with its high design and boutique bookings, it has fast established itself as a hub for the broken beat, IDM, mod, electro and dark wave scenes, but can also turn down and dirty from time to time.

In recent years, Chicago has taken its history as the birthplace of house more seriously. Stars of the '90s house resurgence, such as Derrick Carter and Cajmere, play regularly, but gigs from old-timers like Farley Jackmaster Funk are also frequent. The **Boom Boom Room** (*see p268* **Play house**) is probably the longest running house night in America and attracts a wide spectrum of clubbers.

On the other end of the spectrum, indie rock clubs are increasingly reliant on DJ-oriented nights, and a number of bars host DJs. **Danny's Tavern** (*see p187*) offers everything from downbeat electronica to a long-running soul gig, while **Delilah's** (*see p181*) cranks up the punk and country. It's also worth remembering that Chicago is an immigrant destination with ethnic

The best | Clubs

For hip hop chic
Boutique. *See p267.*

For real Chicago house
Ohm. *See p270.*

For a hint of everything
Sonotheque. *See p270.*

Arts & Entertainment

enclaves producing scenes of their own. Whether it be Puerto Rican reggaeton joints or the Eastern European family of clubbers, there are several parallel nightlife universes that beg exploring if you ever get bored.

INFORMATION AND TICKETS

The weekly *Time Out Chicago* magazine carries the most comprehensive listings, previews and features on the local clubs scene. It's also worth checking record stores such as **Reckless** (*see p214*), **Gramaphone** (*see p213*), **Borderline** (3333 N Broadway Street, at W Buckingham Place, Lakeview, 1-773 975 9533, www.border linemusic.com) and **Kstarke** (1109 N Western Avenue, at W Thomas Street, West Town, 1-773 772 4880) for flyers. Many DJ events are listed online at **www.deephousepage.com**, while the forums at **http://purefuture.com** often contain flyers plugging underground gigs.

Aside from **Smartbar** and **Crobar**, and any **Pure Future** promotions, venues don't generally sell tickets in advance. However, at some clubs, you can call or email ahead to get on a list offering cheaper admission. Although the city's public transport system does run into the night, not all lines are open 24 hours, and those that are don't always offer a frequent service. Always carry a cab number. For more on getting around town, *see pp300-302*.

Clubs

The Loop

Hard Drive

Hyatt Regency, 151 E Wacker Drive, at N Michigan Avenue (1-312 239 4544/www.harddrivechicago. com). El: Brown, Green, Orange, Pink or Purple to State; Red to Lake. **Open** 10pm-4am Fri, Sat. **Admission** $10-$20. **Credit** AmEx, Disc, MC, V. **Map** p325 J11.
Big and bad, Hard Drive is the converted atrium of a large hotel (*see p58*), making for a pleasant spaciousness but little intimacy and questionable acoustics. It's heavy on gimmickry: video remixes play to energetic trance and electro dance tracks, smoke machines cranking all the while. Attention-seekers head to a dance floor encircled by a moat.

Wet

209 W Lake Street, at N Wells Street (1-312 223 9232/www.wetchicago.com). El: Blue, Brown, Green, Orange, Pink or Purple to Clark; Red to Lake. **Open** 9pm-4am Mon, Wed-Fri, Sun; 9pm-5am Sat. **Admission** free-$20. **Credit** AmEx, MC, V. **Map** p325 G11.
A downtown rowhouse club, Wet has a marine-themed decor (it's wet as in water, so get your mind out of the gutter) and attracts a diverse clientele that

wants a little bit of Vegas/Miami decadence in its nightlife. An industry night on Sunday attracts poly-sexual, go-for-broke party people with hip electro and house sounds.

The Near North Side

River North

Buzz

308 W Erie Street, at N Franklin Street (1-312 475 9800/www.buzztheclub.com). El: Brown or Purple to Merchandise Mart. **Open** 10pm-4am Mon, Tue, Thur, Fri; 5pm-4am Wed; 10pm-5am Sat; 7pm-2am Sun. **Admission** $10-$15. **Credit** AmEx, MC, V. **Map** p326 G10.
This River North club with a loft look is an ace destination for Latin beats, salsa rhythms and hip hop cuts. It's also quite the picture of diversity. Casual and classy Latinos pack the floor for a popular Wednesday salsa night, but weekends draw all kinds of folk for house and hip hop.

Cabaret Cocktail Boutique

15 W Hubbard Street, between N State & N Dearborn Streets (1-312 245 3100/www.cabaret chicago.com). El: Red to Grand. **Open** 9pm-2am Wed-Fri; 9pm-3am Sat. **Admission** $10-$20. **Credit** AmEx, Disc, MC, V. **Map** p326 H11.
Glitzy, gaudy and Vegas-inspired, River North's Cabaret Cocktail Boutique is more of a magnet for tourists and suburban adventurers than for serious clubbers. Still, with Moulin Rouge-style dancing girls and a different DJ every night, it's an experience worth… well, experiencing, even if it's about as subtle as a velvet punch.

Enclave

220 W Chicago Avenue, between N Wells & N Franklin Streets (1-312 654 0234/www.enclave chicago.com). El: Brown or Purple to Chicago. **Open** 10pm-2am Thur; 9pm-2am Fri; 9pm-3am Sat. **Admission** free-$20. **Credit** AmEx, Disc, MC, V. **Map** p326 G10.
The handsome, open and woody loft look of this spacious River North club balances out the sexed-up, usually hip hop-fuelled parties that happen from Thursday through the weekend. Big name radio DJs, platform dancers and MCs keep it lively. Promoter Tony Macey has a loyal following that comes out for DJ Flipside's grindworthy DJ sets. When it closes, traffic heads to nearby RiNo (*see p266*).

Moda

25 W Hubbard Street, at N Dearborn Street (1-312 670 2200/www.clubmodachicago.com). El: Red to Grand. **Open** 10pm-4am Wed-Fri; 10pm-5am Sat. **Admission** $5-$20. **Credit** AmEx, MC, V. **Map** p326 H11.
The servers and bartenders wear designer threads at this couture-themed club, which often hosts sexy fashion shows for beautiful wannabes who don't mind paying a pile for their drinks. The DJs spin

Club culture

Five tips to improve your time spent on the Chicago clubs scene...

Go online and get on the RSVP list. You can RSVP for upcoming events through almost every promoter and club in town, entitling you to free or reduced admission. All you need to do is let the promoter know in advance how many of you will be turning up. Note that the list is often thrown out of the window after 11pm, so be sure to know what time you need to be on the scene.

Know the dress code. No, we don't like them either. But it's a good idea to know the code. 'No gym shoes, no baggy jeans and no sports attire' is an almost universal rule these days, at least in River North, and T-shirts don't always work either. Guys should also bear in mind that they're a lot more likely to get in if there are women in their party.

Consider bottle service. The downside of bottle service – which, for the uninitiated, entails paying a large sum of money for a table reservation and a bottle of liquor at a club – is that it means forking out as much as $200 for the privilege of sitting down with your friends. The upside is that, if done right, it can make things a lot easier and perhaps

even cheaper: anyone signing up for bottle service gets to skip both the queues and the cover charge, and is all but guaranteed good service all night. Some clubs allow four people per bottle (which generally cost $150-$200), but others permit six, making it even more worthwhile.

Hit industry nights. Weekends are crazy-busy in Chicago, and sometimes crazy-expensive to boot. A better bet are industry nights, catering to city denizens who work at restaurants, bars and clubs, or in music or fashion. The lines are usually non-existent and the crowds a bit more tight-knit... and often hipper, more streetwise and more music-focused.

Be safe. Since the high-profile catastrophe of 2003, when 21 patrons died at the over-crowded E2 venue during a panic brought on by the use of pepper spray, clubs have come under increased scrutiny from the authorities for capacity violations. Always be vigilant: look for the exits on arrival and leave immediately if the venue seems over capacity. Blatant drug use is rare in clubs these days: many people seem to score and use elsewhere.

Join the ladies (and men) who lounge at **Sonotheque**. *See p270.*

up-to-the-minute remixes and catchy European house, while barely-clad dancers pump up the vibe. The vodka and champagne bar affords a perch from which to view the 25-and-up crowd striking a pose.

Ontourage

157 W Ontario Street, at N Wells Street (1-312 573 1470/www.ontouragechicago.com). El: Brown or Purple to Merchandise Mart. **Open** 9pm-2am Thur, Fri; 9pm-3am Sat. **Admission** $10-$20. **Credit** AmEx, MC, V. **Map** p326 H10.

Finally settling down into a solid identity having changed hands on innumerable occasions down the years, Ontourage caters to a big-night-out crowd from the 'burbs with money to burn. The futuristic, bi-level club, bathed in pink and blue light, has two dance floors. Music is mainly house and hip hop.

RiNo

343 W Erie Street, at N Orleans Avenue (1-312 587 3433/www.rinolounge.com). El: Brown or Purple to Merchandise Mart. **Open** midnight-4am Wed; 10pm-4am Thur, Fri; 10pm-5am Sat. **Admission** $10-$20. **Credit** AmEx, MC, V. **Map** p326 G10.

If location is everything, then Ri(ver)No(rth) makes sure you know where it's at. Inside, it feels like a wealthy socialite's loft party for pretty people. The casually trendy ladies seem to love dancing on the furniture, which makes sense when you consider that they're usually already drunk when they arrive at 1am. On Sundays, things get extra naughty with schoolgirl uniform-clad bartenders. **Photo** *p263.*

Sound-Bar

226 N Ontario Street, at W Franklin Street (1-312 787 4480/www.sound-bar.com). El: Brown or Purple to Chicago. **Open** 9pm-4am Fri; 9pm-5am Sat. **Admission** $10-20. **Credit** AmEx, Disc, Cash, MC, DC, V. **Map** p326 G10.

After opening in 2003, the sleek, modern Sound-Bar quickly became a prime venue in which to hear big-name DJs spinning techno and house. In 2006, it turned to more Miami-style beats, but some of its biggest nights have been bhangra blowouts. Each room on its two levels, including the VIP-only round bar, features a DJ.

Spy Bar

646 N Franklin Street, at W Erie Street (1-312 587 8779/www.spybarchicago.com). El: Brown or Purple to Chicago. **Open** midnight-4am Wed; 10pm-4am Thur, Fri, Sun; 10pm-5am Sat. **Admission** $5-$20. **Credit** AmEx, MC, Disc, V. **Map** p326 G10.

Once a week, the sexy, underground Spy Bar brings in headline-grabbing DJ talent that spins techno, progressive and house courtesy of dance promoter Purefuture. On the whole, it's moderate on attitude and high on intimacy.

Stone Lotus Lounge

873 N Orleans Street, between W Chestnut & W Locust Streets (1-312 440 9680/www.stonelotus lounge.com). El: Red to Chicago. **Open** 9pm-2am Tue-Fri; 9pm-3am Sat. **Admission** $10-$20. **Credit** AmEx, Disc, MC, V. **Map** p326 G9.

Serene but sexy design, gourmet dining and spa services all figure at this much-hyped addition to the River North scene. But aside from the opportunity to nibble in the carpeted basement lounge, it's basically business as usual for the posing and boogeying clubbers that jam its boutique confines.

Vision/Excalibur

640 N Dearborn Street, at W Ohio Street (1-312 266 1944/www.excaliburchicago.com). El: Red to Grand. **Open** 7pm-4am Mon-Fri, Sun; 7pm-5am Sat. **Admission** free Mon-Wed, Sun. $10-$20 Thur-Sat. **Credit** AmEx, Disc, DC, MC, V. **Map** p326 H10.

Yuppies, suburbanites and a slightly older tourist crowd flock to this four-clubs-in-one mega-venue, which boasts a jaw-breaking, bass-pumping sound system. It's both pricey and cheesy, but money talks: name DJs play at Vision regularly, and promoters PureFuture host one of the city's hottest club nights on Saturdays. The adjacent, castle-like Excalibur is a right royal tourist magnet.

Y Bar

224 W Ontario Street, at N Franklin Street (1-312 274 1880/www.ychicago.com). El: Red to Grand. **Open** 9pm-2am Thur, Fri; 9pm-3am Sat. **Admission** $20. **Credit** AmEx, Disc, MC, V. **Map** p326 G10.
The upmarket sibling to the nearby Sound-Bar plays up the bottle service angle with luxury seating and model-like bartenders. But with the aid of a booming sound system that pumps out house and hip hop, the designer-clad clientele raises the roof.

The Gold Coast

Bar Chicago

9 W Division Street, at N State Street (1-312 654 1120/www.barchicago.com). El: Red to Clark/Division. **Open** 9pm-4am Thur; 8:30pm-4am Fri; 8:30pm-5am Sat. **Admission** $6-$10. **Credit** AmEx, MC, V. **Map** p327 H8.
Right on Division, and dontcha just know it: the DJ will never play anything you haven't heard a zillion times. Gung-ho staff encourage outrageous behaviour: a typical night will find half a dozen gals shaking it on the bar. There's no style or sophistication, but that's the way (uh-huh, uh-huh) they like it.

Level

1045 N Rush Street, at W Cedar Street (1-312 397 1045/www.levelchicago.com). El: Red to Clark/Division. **Open** 8pm-4am Tue, Thur, Fri, Sun; 8pm-5am Sat. **Admission** $5-$20. **Credit** AmEx, Disc, MC, V. **Map** p326 H9.
Simply for its second-level window on the Rush Street circus of seduction, Level is worth the price of admission. This being the Gold Coast, bottle service is big and there's often a celeb or two at a table amid the big spenders. Seasoned DJs deliver trance, house and hip hop to Martini-fuelled partygoers.

Old Town & Lincoln Park

Old Town

Boutique

809 W Evergreen Avenue, at N Halsted Street (1-312 751 8700/www.theboutiquelifestyle.com). El: Red to North/Clybourn. **Open** 10pm-4am Fri, Sun; 10pm-5am Sat. **Admission** $5-$20. **Credit** AmEx, MC, V. **Map** p327 F8.
Chicago hip hop's reputation for tailored chic with street cred is realised in this three-tiered lounge. Hip-hop manager John Monopoly is a partner in the venture, and you can't turn around without bumping into an aspiring actress/model/whatever. The likes of Diddy and Kanye West (plus entourages) can be seen on occasion, but the veneer of elitism is mostly a ruse: the members-only policy has never taken hold.

Crobar

1543 N Kingsbury Street, at W Weed Street (1-312 266 1900/www.crobarnightclub.com). El: Red to North/Clybourn. **Open** 10pm-4am Wed, Fri; 10pm-5am Sat. **Admission** $10-$20. **Credit** AmEx, Disc, MC, V.
The original member of a now-international franchise got a makeover in 2003, highlighted by a glass-enclosed VIP area and a more open dance floor. The young and rich returned in droves and have pretty much stayed in residence. Hang in the mezzanine and watch the fashion show unfold. The midweek Latin night has added reggaeton to the menu.

Zentra

923 W Weed Street, at N Sheffield Avenue (1-312 787 0400/www.zentranightclub.com). El: Red to North/Clybourn. **Open** 10pm-4am Thur, Fri, Sun; 10pm-5am Sat. **Admission** $7-$20. **Credit** AmEx, DC, Disc, MC, V.
Zentra's eastern decor has faded slightly: you won't be finding any hookahs around here. Instead, its Jack night on Fridays has become the raging home of Chicago house's big names from Roy Davis Jr to Derrick Carter, with some Detroit techno now and then. In the lounges and basement are less experienced spinners and hip hop residents.

Lincoln Park

Bacchus

2242 N Lincoln Avenue, at W Belden Avenue (1-773 477 5238). El: Brown, Purple or Red to Fullerton. **Open** 7pm-2am Wed-Fri; 7pm-3am Sat. **Admission** free-$5. **Credit** AmEx, MC, V. **Map** p328 F5.
Bacchus introduced sports bar-dominated Lincoln Park to the lounge a while back. The club is pretty reserved, with loungers of the twentysomething, khaki-clad, Kate Spade bag-toting variety. Jager bombs flow freely, and DJs spin familiar tunes.

Liar's Club

1665 W Fullerton Street, at N Ashland Avenue (1-773 665 1110). El: Brown, Purple or Red to Fullerton. **Open** 8pm-4am Mon-Fri, Sun; 8pm-3am Sat. **Admission** free-$5. **Credit** AmEx, DC, Disc, MC, V. **Map** p328 D5.

Festivals Clubs

The city has become home to a number of dance music festivals in recent years. While the house-oriented Move event failed to attract an audience in 2006, the city-sponsored **Chicago SummerDance** festival (*see p234* **Festivals**) features a weekly outdoor electronic night that has proved massively popular.

Also in 2006, Purefuture launched **PureNation** (www.purenationlive.com), a Labor Day weekend shindig at the Charter One Pavilion on Northerly Island (the old Meigs Field) that starred Tiesto, Deep Dish and others. Keep an eye out for it in future years.

Baby, let's play house

Essentially invented at the Warehouse club in the late 1970s and early '80s, Chicago house laid the foundation for much of the dance and electronic music of the past 20 years. Given its origins, then, it's strange that it has often had to fight hard to get noticed in the city. The original 1980s sound of the Trax Records era has made a comeback in hipster and DJ circles in recent years, but one club never stopped believing in four-to-the-floor beats, soulful vocals and good vibes, or in the urban egalitarian aspect of the music.

Held on Mondays at Green Dolphin Street (*see p262*), the **Boom Boom Room** has been running for almost 15 years. Charging only a moderate cover ($10, free before midnight with an RSVP), boasting a relaxed dress code and starting late in the evening (10pm), it's long attracted the city's seriously studied house heads. However, it also draws an ultra-diverse crowd that's willing to sacrifice any productivity on its Tuesdays. Originally a gay night, it has come to attract a broader range of clubbers: made-up kids and businessmen, gays and straights, the deep-pocketed and the cash-strapped, the fit and the not-so-fit.

DJ Lego, the club's longtime resident, has moved on to pastures new in recent years, with Chicago heavy Mark Grant taking his place as the main room DJ. While he spins, the green room out back is headed up by Just Joey and Uncle Milty. However, guest DJs are also fairly common, whether up-and-coming Chicagoans or international stars. The only constant is the music: all house, all the time, right through until 5am. The result is one of Chicago's truly legendary club nights.

This unpretentious hangout for the low-maintenance rock 'n' roll crowd has an impressive collection of Kiss memorabilia. It hosts mashup, grime and drum 'n' bass nights, but mostly pumps out classic rock and punk on the small slanted dance floor.

MaxBar

2247 N Lincoln Avenue, between W Belden & W Webster Avenues (1-773 549 5884/www.maxbar chicago.com). El: Brown, Purple or Red to Fullerton. **Open** 9pm-4am Wed-Fri; 9pm-5am Sat. **Admission** free-$5. **Credit** AmEx, Disc, MC, V. **Map** p328 F5.
The folks that own Crobar (*see p267*) made over this space in 2006 to give Lincoln Parkers an upmarket option just steps from all the pubs and sports bars. It's a bit schizophrenic, playing the fancy saloon up front but turning fully modern and clubby in the rear. There's an overlooking VIP area, a compact and crowded dance floor, and platforms for vogueing. It draws a post-collegiate, young professional crowd still getting its sea legs for nightlife.

Neo

2350 N Clark Street, at W Fullerton Avenue (1-773 528 2622/www.neo-chicago.com). El: Brown, Purple or Red to Fullerton. **Open** 10pm-4am Mon-Fri, Sun; 10pm-5am Sat. **Admission** free-$5. **No credit cards. Map** p328 G5.
Somehow, the unrepentantly goth Neo has survived since 1979 in the rarefied yuppied air of Lincoln Park. Down an alley from the pricey condos of Clark Street, you'll find a dark cave with bargain-basement drinks, sparse decor and unpretentious staff. The crowd could be extras from a Nine Inch Nails video, and DJs spin plenty of classic industrial along with punk, electronica and New Wave. Creative attire is encouraged but in no way required.

Lakeview & around

For information on gay nightclubs in Boystown, *see p248*.

Berlin

954 W Belmont Avenue, at N Sheffield Avenue (1-773 348 4975/www.berlinchicago.com). El: Brown, Purple or Red to Belmont. **Open** 8pm-4am Mon; 5pm-4am Tue-Fri; 5pm-5am Sat; 8pm-4am Sun. **Admission** free-$7. **No credit cards. Map** p329 E2.
Anything goes at this libidinous free-for-all, which draws a healthy mix of gays and straights. The music ranges from industrial and '80s to new club sounds. Ralphi Rosario spins disco on the last Wednesday of the month.

Cherry Red

2833 N Sheffield Avenue, at W Diversey Parkway (1-773 477 3661/www.cherryredchicago.com). El: Brown or Purple to Diversey. **Open** 9pm-2am Tue-Fri; 9pm-3am Sat. **Admission** free-$5. **Credit** AmEx, MC, V. **Map** p328 E4.
Your average 21- to 30-year-old, hip, urban, typical Lincoln Park clubbers flock like moths to this super lounge's red glow, which boasts a more laid-back

vibe than its bigger rivals. Two DJs a night spin a mix of hip hop, trance and house, but don't be too surprised if you hear the hottest dance hit *du jour* several times a night.

Smartbar

3730 N Clark Street, between W Waveland & W Racine Avenues (1-773 549 0203/www.smartbar chicago.com). El: Red to Addison. **Open** 10pm-4am Wed-Fri, Sun; 10pm-5am Sat. **Admission** $5-$15. **Credit** AmEx, V. **Map** p329 E1.
A makeover in 2006 slicked up this Wrigleyville joint (twinned with the Metro; *see p257*) and brought back a vibrant young crowd. Best of all, it added a world-class Funktion One sound system, one of less than half-a-dozen in the US. Cutting-edge DJs from Europe, Detroit and Chicago form the bulk of the house, techno and electro bookings, but local mashup and indie jocks rule on bargain weeknights.

The Near West Side

The West Loop

Chromium

817 W Lake Street, at N Halsted Street (1-312 666 7230/www.chromiumniteclub.com). El: Green or Pink to Ashland. **Open** 9pm-2am Fri; 9pm-3am Sat. **Admission** $10-$20. **Credit** AmEx, MC, V. **Map** p326/p330 F11.
A streetwise, chrome-fronted venue out in the West Loop's Warehouse District, Chromium draws a healthy crowd of weekend warriors with a taste for Latin beats and New York DJs. Saturday is the night to go, when salsa and merengue pump through the sound system.

Funky Buddha Lounge

728 W Grand Avenue, at N Halsted Street (1-312 666 1695/www.funkybuddha.com). El: Blue to Grand. **Open** 9pm-2am Mon-Fri, Sun; 9pm-3am Sat. **Admission** $5-30. **Credit** AmEx, MC, V. **Map** p326 F10.
These two cosy but well-ventilated rooms bulge with hip hop, frequent live PAs and cameos from R&B and rap stars, all of which combine to keep the lines long. Earlier in the week, local mashup jocks and visitors from Berlin and New York drop in for guest turns. Staged every Tuesday, Outdanced! is the city's hippest gay night.

Rednofive

440 N Halsted Street, at W Hubbard Street (1-312 733 6699/www.rednofive.com). El: Blue to Grand. **Open** 10pm-4am Thur, Fri; 10pm-5am Sat. **Admission** $10-$20. **Credit** AmEx, DC, Disc, MC, V. **Map** p326/p330 F11.
Outside, this bi-level club strings up the velvet rope to block the rabble; behind the bouncers, it goes for an old world elegance, chiefly by offering more celeb-friendly booths upstairs. Hip hop and house get spiked by live percussion and usually provoke go-for-broke dancing.

Arts & Entertainment

Reserve Ultra Lounge

858 W Lake Street, at N Peoria Street (1-312 455 1111/www.reserve-chicago.com). El: Green or Pink to Clinton. **Open** 9pm-2am Tue-Fri; 10pm-3am Sat. **Admission** free-$20. **Credit** AmEx, Disc, MC, V. **Map** p330 F11.

Reserve has gone for the celeb-magnet, bottle-service combo. Unusually, though, it's stayed hot long after opening, which means that genuine stars can sometimes be spotted here. The cosy first level works well for schmoozing; upstairs is for posing and taking a turn on the dance floor. The bartenders and servers are eye-catching, but the doormen can be shockingly inept at keeping things under control.

Transit

1491 W Lake Street, at N Ogden Avenue (1-312 491 8600/www.transit-usa.com). El: Green or Pink to Ashland. **Open** 10am-4pm Fri; 10pm-5am Sat. **Admission** $10-$20. **Credit** AmEx, MC, V. **Map** p330 D11.

This converted industrial space has been translated into the biggest of the many clubs on Lake. It boasts a clean futuristic look and a powerful sound system. A young set (straight out of UIC) packs the place, posing, downing vodka-Red Bulls and listening to hip hop, house and, on the mezzanine, R&B.

Victor Hotel

311 N Sangamon Street, between W Wayman Street & W Fulton Market (1-312 773 6900/www.victor hotelchicago.com). Bus 8. **Open** 8pm-2am Wed-Fri; 8pm-3am Sat. **Admission** free-$10. **Credit** AmEx, Disc, MC, V. **Map** p330 F11.

Even the most dedicated party person some day outgrows sweaty clubs. This is where they head when the day rolls around. Fashionistas and professionals eat sushi and suck down high-end cocktails in an open space, while DJ Miki plays house and loungier stuff in the company of pals from NY's Cielo.

Wicker Park & around

Ukrainian Village

Darkroom

2210 W Chicago Avenue, at N Leavitt Street (1-773 276 1411/www.darkroombar.com). Bus 50, 66. **Open** 9pm-2am Mon-Fri, Sun; 9pm-3am Sat. **Admission** free-$8. **Credit** AmEx, Disc, MC, V. **Map** p331 D9.

This unpretentious Ukrainian Village night spot has gradually upgraded its sound and stage features, enabling it to turn from rock bar to DJ den. Reggae, hip hop and house now predominate, but rock, indie and electro nights are still frequent. Somehow, it's never become overly hip, which might be because it needs a headcount of 100 before it starts to fizz.

Sonotheque

1444 W Chicago Avenue, at N Ashland Street (1-312 226 7600). Bus 66. **Open** 9pm-2am Mon-Fri, Sun; 9pm-3am Sat. **Admission** free-$10. **Credit** AmEx, Disc, MC, V. **Map** p331 D9.

There's no sign outside this lounge club for serious music lovers, but you'll find exceptional programming within. Black-clad hipsters queue outside the matte-silver building for popular monthly get-downs such as Dark Wave Disco, and underground stars including Diplo or Four Tet unleash beats for a tight-knit crowd of creative types. **Photo** *p266.*

Wicker Park & Bucktown

Debonair Social Club

1575 N Milwaukee Avenue, at W North Avenue (1-773 227 7990/www.debonairsocialclub.com). El: Blue to Damen. **Open** 6pm-2am Mon-Fri; 6pm-3am Sat; noon-6pm Sun. **Admission** free. **Credit** AmEx, MC, V. **Map** p331 B7.

Having opened in late 2006, Debonair combines star-quality bookings (Tommie Sunshine, Steve Aoki) with dark and modern design. Video art screens on an upstairs wall. Downstairs comes with an illicit red-light-district vibe, as DJs play electro, rock and club hits to frisky hipsters making out on the dance floor. It's usually jammed with young folks sporting magazine-ready looks.

Four (IV)

1551 W Division Street, at N Ashland Avenue (1-773 235 9100/www.fourchicago.com). El: Blue to Division. **Open** 9pm-4am Tue-Fri; 9pm-5am Sat. **Admission** free-$20. **Credit** AmEx, Disc, MC, V. **Map** p331 D8.

An unspectacular interior redesign of this nightclub (formerly Big Wig) resulted in an uninviting cold chrome look and a lack of room in which to dance. But the DJ bookings are respectable, with homegrown house and hip hop hustlers playing the crow's nest every week. Open late, too.

Ohm

1958 W North Avenue, at N Damen Avenue (1-773 278 4646/http://ohmnightlife.com). El: Blue to Damen. **Open** 9pm-4am Wed-Fri; 9pm-5am Sat. **Admission** $10-$20. **Credit** AmEx, Disc, MC, V. **Map** p331 B7.

This dancer's club hit Wicker Park in November 2006, playing up its handsome classic looks and formidable sound system. The Chicago-centric DJ programming concentrates on house, but leaves room for classic hip-hop as well as techno and electro in a separate room dubbed the Bridge. The biggest attraction might be space: with more than 6,000 square feet (560 square metres) of dance floor, there's room to freak out properly.

Tini Martini

2169 N Milwaukee Avenue, at W Rockwell Avenue (1-773 269 2900/www.tinimartini.com). El: Blue to Western. **Open** 9pm-2am Mon-Fri, Sun; 9pm-3am Sat. **Admission** free-$10. **Credit** AmEx, MC, V. **Map** p331 A6.

Tini Martini doubled in size relatively recently, which means that the bar can host two different dance parties next to each other on the same night. Techno, house and hip hop events are frequent.

Sports & Fitness

Shoot some hoops, cheer on the Cubs or go jump in the lake.

You can blame it on the so-called 'Second City' complex, which sees locals take great glory in triumphing over big-town rivals. You can pin it on the long-established blue-collar culture, or perhaps on the waves of European and Latin American immigration. But whatever the reason, Chicago lives and dies by the fortunes of its sporting teams. The town has more major-league teams within its city limits than any other in the US, and the local pride is palpable. When the White Sox won baseball's World Series in 2005, an incredible 1.75 million fans jammed the Loop for the ticker-tape celebration. Conversely, when the Bears of the NFL were bumbling their way through the late 1990s, winters here were even bleaker than usual.

While watching sports is popular, whether from the bleachers, the sofa or the barstool, participating in them comes a close second. The Chicago winter isn't built for outdoor activity, unless you're into skating, but in summer you can hardly move for the hordes of cyclists and joggers, Frisbee-chuckers and softball teams. Those of more leisurely inclinations may prefer to cast their fishing lines into Lake Michigan, rack up at a local pool hall, or strike out at one of Chicago's many bowling alleys.

For information on upcoming games and opportunities for participation, see the Sports section in the weekly *Time Out Chicago*.

Spectator sports

Baseball

Despite the **Chicago Cubs**' dismal play in recent years, cosy old Wrigley Field remains perpetually popular. It's unsurprising: the stadium is far easier on the eye than the team was under manager Dusty Baker, fired in 2006 after a dismal season. Most of the team's 81 home games are played during the day; tickets are pricey and hard to come by, but every sports fan should take in at least one game here.

It's a very different story on the South Side. The **Chicago White Sox** play in a rather less appealing stadium than their North Side

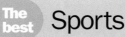

The best Sports

For shooting
Chris's Billiards. *See p276.*

For getting your skates on
McCormick Tribune Ice Rink. *See p277.*

For escaping the traffic
Lakefront Trail. *See p275.*

rivals, a concrete shell that sits in a bleak and featureless corner of the city. However, the team has played very well in recent years, constantly challenging for honours in the tough AL Central division and even winning the World Series in 2005. Sell-outs are relatively rare, at least during the week, but it's far tougher than it once was to get a great seat. The smart fans head here for home games on Mondays, when the majority of seats are half-price.

For more on the lengthy catalogue of misery that constitutes the history of baseball in Chicago, *see pp49-52.*

Chicago Cubs *Wrigley Field, 1060 W Addison Street, at N Clark Street, Wrigleyville (1-773 404 2827/www.cubs.com). El: Red to Addison.* **Season** Mar-Oct. **Tickets** $14-$65. **Credit** AmEx, DC, Disc, MC, V. **Map** p329 E1.

Chicago White Sox *US Cellular Field, 333 W 35th Street, at S Shields Avenue, Bridgeport (1-312 674 1000/http://chicago.whitesox.com). El: Red to Sox-35th.* **Season** Mar-Oct. **Tickets** $16-$59. **Credit** AmEx, DC, Disc, MC, V.

Basketball

The **Chicago Bulls** dominated the NBA in the 1990s, but when Michael Jordan quit in 1997, the team fell apart. Between 1999 and 2001, the team won just one of every five of its games; put off by the team's terrible play and by ill feeling resulting from the 1999 lockout, the previously loyal fans decided to stay away. Under former Phoenix coach Scott Skiles, the Bulls have improved in recent years, with a nucleus of young players supplemented by veteran center Ben Wallace. Tickets are getting increasingly hard to come by: try to book yours in advance if at all possible.

Chicago Bulls *United Center Arena, 1901 W Madison Street, at N Damen Avenue, West Loop (1-312 462 2849/www.nba.com/bulls). El: Blue to Medical Center.* **Season** Nov-Apr. **Tickets** $10-$125. **Credit** AmEx, DC, Disc, MC, V. **Map** p330 C12.

Football

The **Chicago Bears** enjoyed their glory years in the mid 1980s under the guidance of Mike 'Da Coach' Ditka, an irascible loudmouth who led the team to a Super Bowl triumph in 1986. After a spell in the doldrums during the 1990s and early 2000s, the team has come back to life in recent years by winning ugly, cruising to success in 2006 behind a substandard offense but an awesome defense. With a relatively young nucleus of players in place, the Bears appear primed for a dominant run.

Soldier Field, the team's home, remains a Chicago institution – but only just. Built in the early 1920s as a monument to America's war dead, the stadium was subjected to extensive and frankly brutal renovations at the turn of the 21st century, making the facility much more modern and comfortable but draining away much of its brusque charm in the process. The major overhaul resulted in the stadium getting taken off the National Register of Historic Places.

Chicago Bears *Soldier Field, 425 E McFetridge Place, at S Lake Shore Drive, Museum Campus (1-847 615 2327/www.chicagobears.com). El: Green, Orange or Red to Roosevelt.* **Season** Aug-Jan. **Tickets** $60-$340. **Credit** AmEx, DC, Disc, MC, V. **Map** p324 J15.

Hockey

In 2004, ESPN ranked the 121 major-league sporting franchises in the US across a number of categories. The **Chicago Blackhawks** came in 121st, and haven't improved much since. 'Dollar' Bill Wirtz remains one of the most despised team owners in American sports, both for his frugality in putting together a team and for his quixotic policy of not allowing the team's home games to be broadcast on local TV. On the ice, the team qualified for the playoffs just once between 1997 and 2006, almost impossible to do given the generous post-season structure of the NHL. The Hawks showed a few signs of life in the 2006-07 season, but the United Center is only ever sold out when local rivals Detroit and St Louis come to town.

Chicago Blackhawks *United Center, 1901 W Madison Street, at N Damen Avenue, West Loop (1-312 943 4295/www.chicagoblackhawks.com). El: Blue to Medical Center.* **Season** Oct-Apr. **Tickets** $10-$250. **Credit** AmEx, Disc, MC, V. **Map** p330 C12.

Soccer

For whatever reason, soccer will never be more than a marginal sport in the US. However, the **Chicago Fire** have found themselves a tidy little market in Chicago, drawing crowds of more than 10,000 to the 16 games the team plays each year at shiny new Toyota Park.

Chicago Fire *Toyota Park, 7000 S Harlem Avenue, Bridgeview (1-888 657 3473/ http://chicago.fire.mlsnet.com). El: Orange to Midway, then shuttle bus.* **Season** Apr-Nov. **Tickets** $20-$45. **Credit** AmEx, Disc, MC, V.

Active sports & fitness

Sure, Chicago has four seasons like everywhere else. But forget spring, summer, autumn and winter for a moment. There are really only two different times of year here: when it's warm enough to leave the house and when it isn't.

Spare change

The 2005 arrival in Chicago of Hollywood's Lucky Strike Lanes marked yet another step in the hipsterisation of bowling. The Streeterville alley is shooting unashamedly for an upmarket clientele, but if the thought of sipping shiraz between frames makes you want to hurl, don't fret. The city has lanes to fit every vibe, so lace up your rented shoes and see if you can still break a hundred. For listings details, *see p275.*

The aforementioned **Lucky Strike Lanes** is 36,000 square feet (3,350 square metres) of low-lit, throwback cool. There's a wine bar, fancy foods (ancho-citrus chicken skewers, say), a dress code and a 21-and-over policy that comes into effect every night at 9pm. Best of all, it brings in new bowling shoes about once a month, good news for those of us who never trusted that bowling-alley disinfectant spray.

Lucky Strike Lanes might have landed here with a splash, but it didn't invent the upmarket bowling concept. In the House of Blues hotel, **10pin** started calling itself a 'bowling lounge' when it opened its 24 lanes in 2004. Like Lucky Strike, 10pin sports ritzy eats and top-shelf booze, plus a club-quality sound system and a ton of flat-panel video screens, the perfect distraction for those in your party who find the actual bowling a touch dull. Although the shoes might not always be brand new, you can upgrade to 'cool' kicks (slick-bottomed wing tips) for an extra buck.

Unlike cooler-than-thou lounges downtown, **Timber Lanes** up on Irving Park Road keeps the whippersnappers at bay with a lack of bells and whistles. We're not just

talking about smoke machines and dancing lights: the alley's eight lanes don't even have automatic scoring, so you'll have to learn how to count up the pins yourself. There's a similarly old-school set-up at **Southport Lanes** (*pictured*), where the pins are reset by hand at the end of each frame. It's one of only ten hand-set alleys in the US.

While most bowling alleys reserve a couple of weekend hours for the black-lit and Led Zep-soundtracked Rock 'n' Bowl conceit, the **Diversey River Bowl** turns the lights down low at the drop of a hat. Every night except Mondays, the fog machines kick in, the 'intelligent', sound-activated lights flare up and a DJ busts out the classic rock.

All bowling alleys have bars, but the Chicago locations of the **Seven Ten Lounge** give over more space to eating and drinking than to bowling: each branch is equipped with eight lanes, two rooms of four apiece in both locations. The tavern-cum-alleys split the difference between bowling's old and new schools: they're not as self-consciously hip as the dance club-style joints, but they're more sophisticated than the snack bar and league-night places.

While Chicago's weather is notorious, recent years have seen a succession of relatively mild winters, and the sight of people jogging by the water in February is not as unusual or odd as it once was. But summer is when the city really goes berserk. The **Lakefront Trail** (*see p275*) gets packed out with skaters, cyclists and runners during warmer weather, all competing for the best views over the city. A ride or a

jog along this stretch is one of the finest sightseeing bargains in town.

Before you get out and about, pick up the invaluable monthly *Windy City Sports* magazine (1-312 421 1551, www.windycity sports.com), which offers information on just about every amateur sport in the Chicago area. The magazine is available free in sporting goods stores, bookshops and health clubs.

Basketball

The **Chicago Park District** (1-312 742 7529, www.chicagoparkdistrict.com) maintains more than 1,000 baseketball courts in the city. Many are in fine nick, while others are in disrepair. Regardless of condition, though almost all of them are packed on sunny summer's afternoons.

Hoops the Gym

1001 W Washington Boulevard, at N Morgan Street, Greektown (1-312 850 4667). El: Green or Pink to Clinton. **Open** 24hrs daily, on reservation. **Rates** $110/hr. **Credit** MC, V. **Map** p330 E12.

If you're willing to pay to play, Hoops is where Jordan wannabes congregate to see who's got game (along with MJ himself, who prepared for his 2001 comeback here). The seemingly sizeable fee becomes reasonable when split between a big group.

Boating

Although it helps, you don't have to be Donald Trump to enjoy Lake Michigan up close and personal. Several groups offer sailing lessons, among them the **Chicago Sailing Club** (Belmont Harbour, 1-773 871 7245, www.chicagosailingclub.com).

Life cycle

Founded in 2000, the **Working Bikes Cooperative** (*see p275*) has two main aims: reducing unnecessary waste in Chicago, and providing help for developing countries. The two ambitions don't initially seem to have much in common, but one is entirely dependent on the other. First, the WBC salvages discarded and unwanted bikes from around Chicagoland, which are then scrubbed up by a gang of volunteers and shipped abroad. Roughly 5,000 cycles a year are delivered to countries such as Ghana and Zambia, a ground-level relief effort that helps needy locals rejuvenate their communities.

This noble and worthy enterprise is funded through a small storefront on Western Avenue, from which the WBC sells roughly 2,500 revivified bikes a year to Chicagoans and a handful of adventurous visitors. The cycles range from sit-up-and-beg, three-speed Schwinn Suburbans to speedy racers, all nursed carefully back to life by local volunteers. You won't be getting anything flash for your money, but the price is right: only a handful of bikes cost more than $100, and most sell for less ($50-$75 is standard). And remember, it's all in a terrific cause.

If you're a moderately experienced city rider, and especially if you're here outside winter, cycling is a terrific way to travel around Chicago, whether you plan to tour the city's sights or simply trundle up and

down the Lakefront Trail a few times. Other companies in the city offer bike rentals, but the rate charged per couple of days is roughly what it costs to buy a bike outright from the WBC. One nice option worth considering is to buy a WBC bike when you arrive, then give it back to the co-op as a donation when you're ready to leave town. Everyone wins.

Bowling

For more, *see p273* **Spare change**.

Diversey River Bowl *2211 W Diversey Parkway, at N Logan Boulevard, Bucktown (1-773 227 5800/ www.drbowl.com). El: Blue to Western.* **Open** *June-Aug* noon-2am Mon-Fri, Sun; 9am-3am Sat. *Sept-May* noon-2am Mon-Fri, Sun; noon-3am Sat. **Rates** *Per lane* $10-$32/hr. *Shoes* $3. **Credit** AmEx, Disc, MC, V.

Lucky Strike Lanes *322 E Illinois Street, at N Columbus Drive, Streeterville (1-312 245 8331/ www.bowlluckystrike.com). El: Red to Grand.* **Open** 11am-2am Mon-Fri, Sun; 11am-3am Sat. *Per game* $4.95-$6.95. *Per lane* $45-$65/hr. *Shoes* $3.95. **Credit** AmEx, Disc, MC, V. **Map** p326 J10.

Seven-Ten Lounge *2747 N Lincoln Avenue, at W Diversey Parkway, Lakeview (1-773 472 1601/www. theluckystrike.com). El: Brown or Purple to Diversey.* **Open** 5pm-midnight Mon-Wed; 5pm-2am Thur, Fri; noon-3am Sat; noon-midnight Sun. **Rates** *Per lane* $20/hr. *Shoes* $2. **Credit** AmEx, DC, Disc, MC, V. **Map** p328 E4.

Southport Lanes *3325 N Southport Avenue, at W Henderson Street, Lakeview (1-773 472 6600/www. theluckystrike.com). El: Brown to Southport.* **Open** noon-2am Mon-Fri; 10.30am-3am Sat; 11.30am-1am Sun. **Rates** *Per lane* $20/hr. *Shoes* $2. **Credit** AmEx, DC, Disc, MC, V. **Map** p329 D2.

10pin *330 N State Street, at the Chicago River, River North (1-312 644 0300/www.10pinchicago. com). El: Red to Grand.* **Open** 11am-1am Mon-Thur, Sun; 11am-2am Fri; 11am-3am Sat. **Rates** *Per game* $4.95-$6.95. *Per lane* $70/hr. *Shoes* $3.95-$4.95. **Credit** AmEx, DC, Disc, MC, V. **Map** p325 H11.

Timber Lanes *1851 W Irving Park Road, between N Ravenswood & N Wolcott Avenues, North Side (1-773 549 9770/www.timberlaneschgo.com). El: Brown to Irving Park.* **Open** 11am-6.30pm, 10pm-2am Mon, Tue; 11am-4pm, 9.30pm-2am Wed; 11am-5pm, 11pm-2am Thur; 11am-4pm, 10pm-2am Fri; 3-5.45pm, 9pm-3am Sat; 4pm-2am Sun. **Rates** *Per game* $2-$2.50. *Per lane* $20/hr. *Shoes* $2. **Credit** MC, V. **Map** p330 C0.

Cycling

Cycling in Chicago is a contact sport, or can be. Wear a helmet, be vigilant against erratic driving, use lights at night, and be sure always to secure your bike with a U-lock. However, if you're used to riding in big cities, riding around Chicago should be straightforward, perhaps even fun. The roads are wide, straight and (crucially) flat, and drivers generally pay attention to cyclists and to the increasingly impressive network of bike lanes.

Dedicated bike lanes and trails are springing up around the city all the time. In 2006, Mayor Daley announced ambitious plans to increase the network to a total of 500 miles as part of his Bike 2015 strategy (www.bike2015plan.org). However, the best route in town is one of the oldest: the 18-mile **Lakefront Trail**, which

runs between Kathy Osterman Beach near Andersonville and 71st Street on the South Side. Whether you choose to do all or part of the trail, it's an easy and often beautiful ride, especially if you steer clear of the busy summer weekends. Finding the path is as easy as riding a bike: head for the lake (east of wherever you are, unless you're swimming in it), and look for the yellow lines. For more on the trail, *see p111* **Taken for a ride**.

For more on riding in Chicago, contact the **Chicago Bicycle Federation** (1-312 427 3325, www.biketraffic.org), which publishes the excellent *Chicagoland Bike Map* of local bike trails ($6.95 non-members). There's more useful information at http://chicagobikes.org.

Bike rentals are available from **On the Route**, a Lakeview specialist store; **Bike Chicago**, a tourist-tilted operation with branches on Navy Pier, at the North Avenue Beach and at Foster Beach; and **Bobby's Bike Hike** (*see p72*), which offers the best rental rates of all. For more on the **Working Bikes Cooperative**, a charitable organisation that sells serviceable bikes at knockdown prices, *see p274* **Life cycle**.

Bike Chicago *Millennium Park, the Loop (1-888 245 3929/www.bikechicago.com). El: Blue or Red to Washington; Brown, Green, Orange, Pink or Purple to Randolph.* **Open** *Summer* 6.30am-8pm Mon-Fri; 8am-8pm Sat, Sun. *Spring, Fall* 6.30am-7pm Mon-Fri; 9am-7pm Sat, Sun. *Winter* 6.30am-6.30pm Mon-Fri. **Rates** $8-$15/hr; $29-$59/day. **Credit** AmEx, Disc, MC, V. **Map** p326 K10.

On the Route *3146 N Lincoln Avenue, at N Ashland Avenue, Lakeview (1-773 477 5066/ www.ontheroute.com). El: Brown to Southport.* **Open** 11am-8pm Mon-Fri; 11am-5pm Sat, Sun. **Rates** $35-$50day; $125-$195/week. **Credit** AmEx, Disc, MC, V. **Map** p329 D3.

Working Bikes Cooperative *1125 S Western Avenue, at Roosevelt Road, West Side (1-312 421 5048/http://workingbikes.org). Bus 12.* **Open** noon-5pm Wed, Sat, Sun. **No credit cards**. **Map** p309 D3.

Fishing

The easiest fish to catch in Lake Michigan are alewives, which float to the shore in summer. Dead. A whiff of defunct alewife, and you'll know to leave 'em be. Thankfully, most of the alewives have now been eaten by the Pacific salmon that in turn spawned a huge charter fishing industry. The lake also boasts many other live fish: perch are the most sought-after catch among pier anglers, while the smelt fishing season is a sight to behold.

You'll need a licence to fish legally in Illinois; they're available to over-16s at bait stores (check the *Yellow Pages*), sporting goods stores, currency exchanges or the City Clerk's office.

Arts & Entertainment

The **Illinois Department of Natural Resources** (1-312 814 2070/http://dnr.state.il.us) offers guides on where to fish. For starters, try Chicago's parks (details from the **Chicago Park District** on 1-312 742 7529); the **Forest Preserve District of Cook County** (1-800 870 3666, www.fpdcc.com); and, of course, **Lake Michigan**. You can cast off the shore at **Belmont Harbor** (3200 North, 1-312 742 7673), **Diversey Harbor** (2800 North, 1-312 742 7762), **Monroe Harbor** (100 South, 1-312 742 7643) or **Burnham Harbor** (1600 South, 1-312 742 7009).

Fitness clubs

Many hotels have a fitness facility on site or offer an 'in' at a nearby club. However, if yours doesn't, there are plenty of options. Among the more popular clubs are **Bally Total Fitness** (25 E Washington Street, at N State Street, the Loop, 1-312 372 7755, www.ballyfitness.com), a chain with numerous local branches, and the **Lakeshore Athletic Clubs** (there's one at 441 N Wabash Avenue, River North, 1-312 644 4880, www.lsac.com), of which there are four scattered around the city. There's even a branch of UK favourite **Holmes Place** (355 E Grand Avenue, Streeterville, 1-312 467 1111, www.holmesplaceus.com). Daily membership is available at all, costing around $15-$20 a day.

Golf

The Chicago Park District runs a half-dozen courses around the city, details of which can be found at www.cpdgolf.com.

Cog Hill Golf & Country Club

12294 Archer Avenue, Lemont (1-866 264 4455/ www.coghillgolf.com). Metra Lemont. **Open** *Summer* 6am-9pm daily. *Winter* 6am-5pm daily. **Rates** $36-$138. **Credit** Disc, MC, V.
A series of four 18-hole courses. The most expensive is Dubsdread, home to the Western Open each July, but the other three offer a decent challenge. Call for details of afternoon and twilight rates.

Jackson Park

S Hayes Drive, at E 63rd Street, South Side (1-312 245 0909/www.cpdgolf.com). Metra: 63rd Street. **Open** sunrise-sunset daily. **Rates** *Non-residents* $22.50-$25.50. **Credit** MC, V. **Map** p331 Z18.
The Chicago Park District's (and city's) only 18-holer should challenge even low handicappers. Club rental is available.

Sydney R Marovitz Course

3600 N Recreation Drive, in Lincoln Park (1-312 742 7930). El: Red to Addison. **Open** sunrise-sunset daily. **Rates** *Non-residents* $19.75-$22.75. **Credit** MC, V. **Map** p329 G1.

This nine-hole Lincoln Park course enjoys a fantastic setting. The course is good, too, but you'll need to book ahead (allow up to 14 days in advance).

In-line skating

Chicago drivers tend not to notice skaters until one slams against the hood of their car. However, there's safety in numbers at the **Road Rave**, a summer skate similar to the Friday Night Skate events held in other cities around the world. The skate leaves from Daley Plaza, at the corner of Dearborn and Washington Streets in the Loop, at 7.30pm on the first Friday of the month from May to October, and is suitable for skaters of all grades. Experienced street skaters can also join a longer Road Rave event on the third Friday of the month (May to September). Off the road, the **Lakefront Trail** (*see p275*) is a pleasant way to while away an afternoon. Skates can be hired from **Londo Mondo** and **Windward Sports** (for both, *see p214*), and from **Bike Chicago** (*see p275*).

Pool

In many Chicago bars, the unspoken pool-table rule is that the winner keeps the table. However, you can rent a table by the hour at **Chris's Billiards** (*see below*), one of the town's better pool halls, or at the **Gingerman** (*see p183*), a fine Wrigleyville bar.

Chris's Billiards

4637 N Milwaukee Avenue, at W Lawrence Avenue, Jefferson Park (1-773 286 4714). El: Blue to Jefferson Park. **Open** 9.30am-2am daily. **Rates** $6.25-$7.50/hr. **Credit** AmEx, Disc, MC, V.
Pool, billiards and snooker, with tournaments for the true hustler and lessons for the true hack. Some sequences for *The Color of Money* were filmed at this North Side joint.

Running

The **Chicago Area Runners Association** (1-312 666 9836, www.cararuns.org) has information on upcoming races and ideal running routes, though you might be fine simply jogging along the **Lakefront Trail** (*see p275*). For the **Chicago Marathon,** *see p219*).

Skating & sledding

Wintertime visitors can sled courtesy of the Chicago Park District (1-312 747 7529, www.chicagoparkdistrict.com), which operates a number of toboggan runs with wooden chutes. City-run rinks, such as those in **Millennium Park** (*see p277*) and at **Daley Bicentennial Plaza**, are generally open from

late November to mid March. From December until early January, there's also a (quite expensive) ice rink on **Navy Pier**.

McCormick Tribune Ice Rink at Millennium Park

McCormick Tribune Plaza, Millennium Park, 55 N Michigan Avenue, at E Randolph Street (1-312 742 5222/http://millenniumpark.net/ice/icerink.html). El: Blue to Washington; Brown, Green, Orange, Pink or Purple to Randolph; Red to Lake. **Open** *late Nov-mid Mar* 10am-10pm Mon, Fri, Sun; 10am-8pm Tue-Thur, Sat. **Admission** free. *Skate hire* $5. **Map** p325 J12.
This 16,000sq ft outdoor skating rink is totally free, but there's a catch: skate hire costs $7.

Soccer

Given Chicago's large Latin American population, it's no surprise that the beautiful game is popular in the city. Some of the liveliest action happens just off the lake at Montrose Avenue. For details of local games, contact the **Illinois Soccer Association** (1-773 283 2800, www.illinoissoccer.org) or the **National Soccer League of Chicago** (1-773 237 1270, www.nslchicago.org).

Swimming

In summer, thick-skinned aquanauts swim from Navy Pier north towards the Oak Street Beach. Buoys protect swimmers from boats, at least theoretically. The season officially runs from Memorial Day to Labor Day, but some beaches are sporadically closed because of high levels of water toxicity.

The Chicago Park District (1-312 747 7529, www.chicagoparkdistrict.com) operates numerous indoor swimming pools that are both free and, on the whole, well maintained. Among the best is **Welles Park**, a full-size pool in a great Lincoln Square building (2333 W Sunnyside Avenue, at N Western Avenue, 1-312 742 7511).

Tennis

With more than 600 courts around Chicago, it's easier to find a net than a partner. Fees vary wildly. If you prefer to play indoors, there are courts at a few health clubs in the city, such as the Lincoln Park branch of the **Lakeshore Athletic Club** (*see p276*). The most central public court is situated along the lakefront; for details of others, call the Chicago Park District (1-312 742 7529, www.chicago parkdistrict.com).

Daley Bicentennial Plaza

337 E Randolph Street, at N Columbus Drive, the Loop (1-312 742 7648). El: Blue to Washington; Brown, Green, Orange, Pink or Purple to Randolph; Red to Lake. **Open** 7am-10pm Mon-Fri; 9am-5pm Sat, Sun. **Rates** $5-$7/hr. **Credit** Disc, MC, V. **Map** p325 J12.
Rally beneath the skyscrapers on the city's most stunningly located tennis court.

Volleyball

Along the lake, there are pick-up games galore. Try **Foster Beach** (at Foster Avenue), **Montrose Beach** (at Montrose Avenue), and the **North Avenue Beach** (at North Avenue), the Centre Court of Chicago beach volley. *See also p102* **Beachy keen**.

Theatre

From Shakespeare to showtunes.

If you walk through the lobby of an average mid-sized Chicago theatre, you'll probably spot a few familiar faces amid the black and white photos of plays gone by. Step back and look at the whole wall, though, and you'll realise that the handful of famous names are just a few tiles in a larger mosaic. Surrounding them are countless scrappy punks who, since the late 1960s, have been toiling to change Chicago from a hot-dog-and-baseball town to a thriving hub of American theatre.

The city's theatrical alumni include blazing mavericks (David Mamet, John Malkovich), comfort-food TV stars (Laurie Metcalf, David Schwimmer) and acting titans (Brian Dennehy, Joan Allen). Most of them will gladly use their reputations to promote the city, but they'll also concede that Chicago theatre's real lifeblood is its storefront scene, a booming collection of itinerant young troupes, non-professional but sturdy companies and well-weathered producing groups. There's something for just about everybody.

INFORMATION AND TICKETS
The weekly *Time Out Chicago* magazine carries comprehensive theatre listings, plus reviews of major shows. Other resources include the free *Chicago Reader* weekly, the *Chicago Tribune*'s 'Friday' section (which carries most theatre ads), and the generally accurate monthly listings magazine published by the **League of Chicago Theatres** (LCT; www.chicagoplays.com), freely available in many hotels.

Many Chicago theatres, especially the small ones, stage performances only from Thursday to Sunday. On Fridays and Saturdays, late-night shows typically begin around 11pm. It's generally best to buy tickets direct from theatre

box offices in order to avoid surcharges; however, most resident companies and touring shows also sell seats via the ubiquitous Ticketmaster (1-312 902 1400, www.ticketmaster.com), with smaller companies preferring Ticketweb (www.ticketweb.com). Prices are all over the map, from $10-$20 at fringe venues to $60 or more at venues such as the Goodman.

Many shows sell half-price tickets for the same day's performance from the LCT's three **Hot Tix** booths: in the Loop (78 E Randolph Street, at N Michigan Avenue), at the Water Works (163 E Pearson Street, at N Michigan Avenue) and in Skokie (at the North Shore Center for the Performing Arts, 9501 N Skokie Boulevard). All are open from 10am to 6pm Tuesday to Saturday, and from 11am to 4pm on Sunday. Each morning, a list of shows for which cheap seats are available is posted at www.hottix.org. Some theatres list their shows several days in advance, which allows you to buy (for example) half-price tickets for Saturday's show on a Thursday.

Major companies

There are so many theatres in Chicago that what follows is a necessarily selective list. Check *Time Out Chicago* for reviews of the latest shows when you're in town.

Note that the box office hours listed in this section apply when there is no performance at the specified theatre. On days when there is a scheduled show, hours are generally extended until showtime and occasionally beyond.

American Theater Company
1909 W Byron Street, at N Lincoln Avenue, Irving Park (1-773 929 1031/www.atcweb.org). El: Blue to Irving Park. **Box office** *During shows* 10am-6pm Tue, Wed; 10am-8pm Thur, Fri; 3-8pm Sat; 1-3pm Sun. *Other times* 10am-6pm Tue-Fri. **Tickets** $10-$35. **Credit** AmEx, MC, V. **Map** p330 C0.
This professional troupe has steadily built its reputation by producing classic (and occasionally new) plays about the American experience. The scale of the productions tends to be practical and tasteful, while the acting is characterised by hearty, often blue-collar energy.

Artistic Home
1420 W Irving Park Road, at N Southport Avenue, Lakeview (information 1-773 404 1100/tickets via Ovation Tix 1-866 811 4111/

The best Theatres

For the hits
Broadway in Chicago. See p281.

For the misses
A Red Orchid Theatre. See p278.

For the maybes
Steppenwolf Theater Company. See p278.

www.theartistichome.org). El: Brown to Irving Park.
Box office *Ovation Tix* 24hrs daily. **Tickets** $20-
$22; $17-$19 discounts. **Credit** *Ovation Tix* AmEx,
Disc, MC, V.
Devoted to forgotten and/or underloved American
classics, this Equity theatre seats a whopping 28 people. But if you're interested in rediscovering works
by masters and seeing them interpreted by leading
kitchen-sink actors, you'll be scrambling for a seat.

Bailiwick Repertory

*1229 W Belmont Avenue, at N Racine Avenue,
Lakeview (1-773 883 1090/www.bailiwick.org).
El: Brown, Purple or Red to Belmont.* **Box office**
10am-6pm Mon-Wed; 10am-8pm Thur-Sat; noon-6pm
Sun. **Tickets** $20-$42. **Credit** AmEx, Disc, MC, V.
Map p329 E3.
The Bailiwick company is largely devoted to the
politics of gay identity (and, sometimes, the
unabashed thrills of gay sex), and the quality of its
shows is mixed. However, the group also hosts
smaller companies in its large main theatre and two
studio spaces, and produces quality musicals, often
family-oriented. Just be wary of the stage debuts of
screen actors billed as 'power tops'.

Black Ensemble Theater

*4520 N Beacon Street, at W Sunnyside Avenue,
Uptown (1-773 769 4451/www.blackensemble
theater.org). El: Red to Wilson.* **Box office** 10am-
5pm Mon-Fri; 11am-3pm Sat. **Tickets** $40; $35
discounts. **Credit** AmEx, Disc, MC, V.
BET founder Jackie Taylor traffics in the almost
destructive but ultimately redemptive lives of black
musical legends. Her biographical revue-tributes
are by no means literary masterpieces, but the roof-
raising performances of songs originally recorded
by the likes of Etta James and Jackie Wilson make
up for any deficiencies in the script.

Chicago Shakespeare Theater

*800 E Grand Avenue, at Navy Pier, Streeterville
(1-312 595 5600/www.chicagoshakes.com).
El: Red to Grand.* **Box office** 10am-5pm Mon;
10am-7.30pm Tue-Fri; 10am-8pm Sat; noon-5pm
Sun. **Tickets** $40-$67. **Credit** AmEx, Disc, MC, V.
Map p326 K10.
In less than 20 years, this unpretentious Bardic
troupe moved from the back of a Lincoln Park pub
to a mouthwatering, multi-million-dollar facility in
Navy Pier with a main stage modelled on the Swan
Theatre in Stratford-upon-Avon. Shakespeare's
plays usually get streamlined, populist treatments;
trimmings include dynamic international programming and, in the studio space, matchbox-sized
reimaginings of Sondheim musicals. Use the intermission to take in the spectacular lakefront views.

Court Theatre

*5535 S Ellis Avenue, at E 55th Street, Hyde Park
(1-773 753 4472/www.courttheatre.org). Metra:
55th-56th-57th Street.* **Box office** noon-5pm daily.
Tickets $36-$54; 10%-25% discounts. **Credit**
AmEx, Disc, MC, V. **Map** p332 X17.

Strawdog Theatre Company. *See p282.*

The Court has stood its ground for five decades on
the University of Chicago campus, mounting classics
from Sophocles to Stoppard. However, in the last few
years, groovy deconstructions of vintage musicals
and a heightened interest in African American writers have thickened the mix.

Goodman Theatre

*170 N Dearborn Street, at W Randolph Street, the
Loop (1-312 443 3800/www.goodmantheatre.org).
El: Blue, Brown, Green, Orange, Pink or Purple to
Clark; Red to Lake.* **Box office** 10am-5pm Mon-Sat;
noon-5pm Sun. **Tickets** *Albert Theatre* $20-$68.
Owen Theatre $20-$68. **Credit** AmEx, Disc, MC, V.
Map p325 H12.
A standard-bearer among the nation's regional the-
atres and the downtown grande dame of Chicago's
professional scene, the Goodman is anchored by

Tony-winning director Robert Falls, whose hallmark productions of American classics (*Death of a Salesman, Long Day's Journey Into Night*) are indicative of the theatre's mainly deluxe but traditional fare. A commitment to ethnically diverse programming (check the trailblazing Latino festival every other August) sets it apart from its contemporaries, and there's also a great production of *A Christmas Carol* every year.

Lookingglass Theatre Company

Water Tower Water Works, 821 N Michigan Avenue, at E Pearson Street, Magnificent Mile (1-312 337 0665/www.lookingglasstheatre.org). El: Red to Chicago. **Box office** 10am-showtime Tue-Fri; noon-showtime Sat, Sun. **Tickets** $20-$58. **Credit** Disc, MC, V. **Map** p326 J9.

The most recognisable face in the lobby belongs to old *Friend* David Schwimmer, but the roster of productions staged by this spectacle troupe are sitcom-free. Taking its name from the hallucinatory world of Lewis Carroll, the playful 20-year-old company put itself on the map by mounting *cirque*-influenced, highly physical renditions of myths and classic literary works. Notable among the tribe is visual auteur Mary Zimmerman, whose pool-set *Metamorphoses* won her a Tony award. The company has recently added a small studio to its digs in the Water Tower's pumping station.

Neo-Futurists

Neo-Futurarium, 5153 N Ashland Avenue, between W Foster Street & W Farragut Avenue, Andersonville (1-773 275 5255/www.neofuturists.org). El: Red to Berwyn. **Tickets** $8-$13. **No credit cards**.

Too Much Light Makes the Baby Go Blind, Chicago's longest-running play, stars a game, if somewhat scrappy, ensemble of writer-performers attempting to perform 30 mini-plays in 60 minutes. The resulting late-night hour is, in equal parts, block party and populist performance art. To ensure you get seats, you need to show up no later than 10.45pm, as no bookings are taken. Tickets cost $7 plus whatever number shows up when you roll a dice: turn up a '1' and you pay $8, but if you roll a '6', your ticket costs $13. If the show sells out, the troupe treat the entire audience to pizza.

Next Theatre

927 Noyes Street, at Ridge Avenue, Evanston (1-847 475 1875 ext 2/www.nexttheatre.org). El: Purple to Noyes. **Box office** noon-6pm Tue-Sat; from 2hrs prior to showtime Mon, Sun. **Tickets** $20-$40; $10-$36 discounts. **Credit** AmEx, Disc, MC, V.

New York theatre regulars who tend to frequent the less commercially corrupted, more esoteric spaces off-Broadway will feel at home in this small venue at the Noyes Cultural Arts Center. Favouring the likes of Caryl Churchill and Suzan Lori-Parks, the artistically progressive and technically accomplished Next Theatre company is well worth the trip to Evanston for anyone seeking a non-passive theatre experience.

Profiles Theatre

4147 N Broadway Street, at W Gordon Terrace, Lakeview (1-773 549 1815/www.profilestheatre.org). El: Red to Sheridan. **Box office** 1pm-showtime daily. **Tickets** $20-$25. **Credit** AmEx, Disc, MC, V.

Much of what goes on in this dingy hovel is not for the tender-hearted. The plays can be brutal (Neil LaBute and Adam Rapp are regularly on the bill), and the audience's close proximity to the actors might generate discomfort. But the umpteen acting awards racked up by the ballsy troupe are no accident. When paired with quality material, the players create harrowing and memorable theatre.

A Red Orchid Theatre

1531 N Wells Street, at W North Avenue, Old Town (1-312 943 8722/www.aredorchidtheatre.org). El: Brown or Purple to Sedgwick. **Box office** noon-5pm Mon-Fri. **Tickets** $14-$20. **No credit cards**. **Map** p327 G7.

Few Chicago spaces are more intimate than A Red Orchid's, and few artistic ensembles are more willing to test theatrical limits. Whether they're experimenting with the more bizarre works of Pinter and Ionesco or trying out bold new work, you'll be struck by the gutsy performances, the crafty designs and the gritty essence of the city's storefront scene.

Redmoon Theater

1438 W Kinzie Street, at N Ashland Avenue, West Loop (1-312 850 8440/www.redmoon.org). El: Green or Pink to Ashland. **Box office** 9am-5pm Mon-Fri. **Tickets** free-$35. **Credit** AmEx, MC, V. **Map** p330 D11.

Redmoon performances are sporadic; you'll have to chase them all over the city limits to catch them. But if you can hunt them down, you'll be treated to the kind of large outdoor spectacle that has made the renegade puppet troupe a Chicago institution. Performing in parks and other public venues, as well as at their warehouse on Kinzie, Redmoon presents pageants with often large, age-diverse casts and European-influenced visual flourishes. Many of the opulent trimmings are made from recycled junk.

Steppenwolf Theatre Company

1650 N Halsted Street, at W North Avenue, Lincoln Park (1-312 335 1650/www.steppenwolf.org). El: Red to North/Clybourn. **Box office** 11am-5pm Mon-Sat; 1-5pm Sun. **Tickets** *Main theatre* $50-$65. *Garage* $20-$30. **Credit** AmEx, Disc, MC, V. **Map** p327 F7.

Accruing an international mythology in less than three decades, Steppenwolf is perhaps the most famous acting ensemble in the US (paging Gary Sinise, Johns Malkovich and Mahoney, Laurie Metcalf, Martha Plimpton). The sweaty group of twentysomething upstarts has graduated to fancy digs on Halsted Street since its founding. But the lineup of new and classic plays, and the dynamic Traffic series of one-off performances and lectures from arts-and-letters giants, staged in no fewer than three performance venues (upstairs and downstairs spaces, plus a funkier garage that often features storefront troupes), can still get the blood pumping.

Arts & Entertainment

Strawdog Theatre Company

3829 N Broadway Street, at W Grace Street, Lakeview (1-773 528 9696/www.strawdog.org). El: *Red to Sheridan.* **Box office** from 1hr before show. **Tickets** $15-$20. **Credit** Disc, MC, V. **Map** p329 F1.

Retaining its storefront sensibility even 20 years into its existence, the Strawdog gang still resides above a Mexican restaurant in Lakeview. Known for large-cast plays that show off a sizeable acting ensemble, the troupe tends to put twists on traditional fare, from Shakespeare to Chekhov. A newly renovated bar next door serves as a fine venue for late-night music and post-show shenanigans. **Photo** *p279.*

TimeLine Theatre Company

615 W Wellington Avenue, at N Broadway Street, Lakeview (1-773 281 8463/www.timelinetheatre. com). El: *Brown or Purple to Wellington.* **Box office** 10am-4pm Tue-Fri. **Tickets** $25; $15 discounts. **Credit** MC, V. **Map** p329 F3.

One of the storefront scene's Little Theatres That Could, this modest company (housed in a church) snags outstanding acting and design talent. The company's simple but evocative mission is to present stories inspired by history, which allows for a pro-gramme that ranges from *Copenhagen* to *Fiorello!.*

Victory Gardens Theater

2433 N Lincoln Avenue, at W Fullerton Avenue, Lincoln Park (1-773 871 3000/www.victorygardens. org). El: *Brown, Purple or Red to Fullerton.* **Open** Box office noon-8pm Tue-Sat; noon-4pm Sun. **Tickets** $26-$45. **Credit** AmEx, Disc, MC, V. **Map** p328 F5.

Victory Gardens is Chicago's highest-profile gener-ator of new plays. With an ensemble of 12 resident playwrights, among them Oscar-nominated screen-writer John Logan, the theatre's commitment to new work earned it 2001's regional theatre Tony. It recently moved into one of the city's most coveted venues, the sumptuous Biograph in Lincoln Park (where John Dillinger was gunned down).

Itinerant companies

Barrel of Monkeys

Information 1-773 281 0638/tickets 1-312 409 1954/www.barrelofmonkeys.org.

The Neo-Futurarium (*see p281*) hosts the squatters of this scrappy Monday-night performance troupe. The collective of excellent adult comedians perform *That's Weird, Grandma,* an ever-changing pro-gramme of short works written by local schoolkids. Even if most theatres weren't dark on Mondays, this quirky night out would still be a sparkling choice.

House Theatre of Chicago

Information 1-773 769 3832/tickets 1-773 251 2195/ www.thehousetheatre.com.

Making their mark by rakishly riffing on all things pop cultural (from *The Wizard of Oz* to samurai films via John Ford), the young ruffians of the House

What's in a name?

The origins behind the names of many theatre companies in Chicago are either plainly obvious or non-existent. The Black Ensemble Theatre and the Chicago Shakespeare Theater both do exactly what they say on the tin, while the name of the Timeline Theatre Company is a nod to its historical bent. Other company names, though, give theatregoers head-scratching pause for thought.

It sounds dainty, but **A Red Orchid Theatre** (*see p281*) takes its name from *Naked Lunch* by anything-but-dainty Beat writer William Burroughs. When one of his characters shoots up heroin, Burroughs describes the bit of blood that's sucked into the vial as looking like a red orchid. 'It's a little nihilistic, it's a little edgy, it's a little on the fringe,' says artistic director Guy Van Swearingen.

The **Remy Bumppo Theatre Company** (www.remybumppo.org) may be known as the city's foremost producer of plays proper and British, but the origins of its name suggests it's not so stuffy. Founding member (and current artistic director) James Bohnen owned a black labrador called Bumppo, named after the character Natty Bumppo in James Fenimore Cooper's *Leatherstocking Tales,* while fellow founder Carol Loewenstern had a cat called Remy, after the cognac Rémy Martin. '[The founders] were serious about producing plays,' says director of communications Stephanie Kulke, 'but they didn't put a lot of serious thought into naming their company.'

The name of **Theo Ubique** (1-773 743 3355, www.theoubique.org), a cabaret and musical company based in Rogers Park, was all Greek to us until we investigated. It turns out that it is Greek, at least in part: Theo translates as God; Ubique ('oo-bee-kway'), meanwhile, comes from Latin, and means 'encompassing all things'. Founding member Fred Anzevino turned to spirituality in the late 1990s, and wanted a name that echoes the Holy Theatre. However, atheists needn't worry. The work doesn't demand supplication to a deity: it's about the ritual and spiritual dimension of drama.

Theatre have, in less than five years, become one of Chicago's dominant storefront troupes. Their plays, pastiches of vaudeville, circus antics and traditional storytelling, have made them a favourite among both young theatregoers and older luvvies who like feeling youthful. They can usually be found raising hell at the Viaduct Theatre (discreetly located under an actual viaduct at 3111 N Western Avenue, at W Barry Avenue).

Porchlight Music Theatre

1-773 325 9884/www.porchlighttheatre.com.
Traditional musicals are hard to find in Chicago's city limits; they're mostly relegated to the huge Equity houses in the 'burbs. Yet Porchlight's steady stream of scaled-back but earnest chestnuts has found the company a loyal following. Their unofficial digs are in the Theatre Building Chicago (*see p284*).

Teatro Vista

1-312 494 5767/www.teatrovista.org.
Teatro Vista ('Theatre with a view') regularly premieres new plays and translations by Latino dramatists, from inside America's borders and out. In addition to the fine work it produces on its own, the company often gangs up with other local groups for hybrid co-productions. **Photo** *p284.*

Other venues

Athenaeum Theatre

2936 N Southport Avenue, at W Oakdale Avenue, Lakeview (information 1-773 935 6860/tickets from Ticketmaster 1-312 902 1500/www.athenaeum theatre.com). El: Brown or Purple to Wellington.
Box office *Theatre* 3-7pm Tue-Fri. *Ticketmaster* 24hrs daily. **Tickets** $10-$35. **Credit** *Ticketmaster* AmEx, Disc, MC, V. **Map** p329 D3.
This antiquated, cathedral-like building was once an annex to a mammoth neighbouring church. Now it has several studio theatres and a large proscenium main stage; between them they play landlord to shows of all shapes and sizes, including dance and performance art. Prices vary, but most of the performances cost less than $20.

Briar Street Theatre

3133 N Halsted Street, at W Belmont Avenue, Lakeview (1-773 348 4000/www.blueman.com). El: Brown, Purple or Red to Belmont. **Box office** 9am-10pm Mon-Sat; noon-7pm Sun. **Tickets** $49-$59. **Credit** AmEx, Disc, MC, V. **Map** p329 F3.
This bigger-than-it-looks theatre might appear rather prosaic from the outside, but most nights it's packed to the hilt with crowds who thrill to the colourful techno antics of Blue Man Group, which has occupied the space for years (and shows no signs of vacating soon).

Broadway in Chicago

Cadillac Palace Theatre *151 W Randolph Street, at N LaSalle Street, the Loop. El: Blue, Brown, Green, Orange, Pink or Purple to Clark; Red to Lake.* **Map** p325 H12.

Drury Lane Theatre Water Tower Place
175 E Chestnut Street, at N Michigan Avenue, Magnificent Mile. El: Red to Chicago. **Map** p326 J9.
Ford Center for the Performing Arts, Oriental Theatre *24 W Randolph Street, between N State & N Dearborn Streets. El: Blue, Brown, Green, Orange, Pink or Purple to Clark; Red to Lake.* **Map** p325 H12.
LaSalle Bank Theatre *18 W Monroe Street, between S State and S Dearborn Streets, the Loop. El: Blue or Red to Monroe; Brown, Green, Orange, Pink or Purple to Madison.* **Map** p325 H12.
All venues *Information 1-312 977 1700/tickets via Ticketmaster 1-312 902 1400/www.broadwayin chicago.com.* **Box office** *Theatres* hrs vary, but usually 10am-6pm Mon; 10am-showtime Tue-Sat; 11am-4pm Sun. *Ticketmaster* 24hrs daily. **Tickets** $15-$85. **Credit** AmEx, Disc, MC, V.
Three of the Loop's glorious old theatres have received a second lease of life courtesy of Broadway in Chicago, which uses them as a roadhouse for big-ticket touring shows. Gorgeous and resplendent, the 1926 Cadillac Palace retains the opulence of Golden-era vaudeville palaces, and now stages large-scale productions such as *The Lion King* and *Mamma Mia!*. The spectacularly renovated LaSalle Bank Theatre, formerly the Shubert Theatre, is the cosiest of the trio, and mixes touring shows with pre-Broadway try-outs of productions such as *Spamalot*. If you're reading this before the year 2030, there's a good chance that the rococo Oriental Theatre will be housing the colossally successful Broadway musical *Wicked*, which looks like it has the potential to outlast the Daley administration. Joining the Loop theatres is the Drury Lane Theatre at Water Tower Place, which was taken over by Broadway in Chicago in 2006.

Chopin Theatre

1543 W Division Street, at N Ashland Avenue, Wicker Park (1-773 278 1500/www.chopintheatre. com). El: Blue to Division. **Box office** 10am-8pm daily. **Tickets** $5-$40. **Credit** varies by show. **Map** p331 C8.
The home base for some of the city's most dynamic storefront troupes, Wicker Park's Chopin is a resolutely funky venue that consistently draws young audiences. In addition to a rotating door for visiting European companies, many of them Polish, the Chopin is a regular host to innovative companies such as Uma Productions, a resourceful troupe whose scenic designs place audiences inside the set; Collaboraction, which produces the annual short-fest-cum-rave Sketchbook; and Signal Ensemble and the BackStage Theatre Company, both of which create small-scale productions of classic plays.

Royal George Theatre

1641 N Halsted Street, at W North Avenue, Old Town (1-312 988 9000/www.theroyalgeorge theatre.com). El: Red to North/Clybourn. **Box office** 10am-6pm Mon; 10am-8pm Tue-Sat; noon-5pm Sun. **Tickets** $25-$50. **Credit** AmEx, MC, V. **Map** p327 F7.

Across the street from Steppenwolf sits this commercial venue that at any given time hosts two or three long-running hits at once, including the sweet Catholic-school satire *Late Nite Catechism*. The musicals that play here are generally small-scale revues rather than Broadway fare, but they often stay on their feet for years at a time.

Theatre Building Chicago

1225 W Belmont Avenue, at N Southport Avenue, Lakeview (1-773 327 5252/http://theatrebuilding chicago.org). El: Brown, Purple or Red to Belmont. **Box office** noon-6pm Wed; noon-showtime Thur-Sun. **Tickets** $10-$32. **Credit** AmEx, Disc, MC, V. **Map** p329 D3.

Since the 1970s, this three-stage rental house has been the incubator for countless storefront companies. Some feature the city's top-shelf Equity actors, while others are produced on a guv'ment cheese budget; in other words, the reviewers are your friends. The resident company regularly produces workshops and new musicals.

Theatre on the Lake

2400 N Lake Shore Drive, at W Fullerton Avenue, Lincoln Park (1-312 742 7529/www.chicagopark district.com). Bus 151. **Box office** mid June-mid Aug. **Tickets** $15-$20. **Credit** MC, V. **Map** p328 H5.

Offering a selection of the season's best storefront plays, the Theatre on the Lake is a decades-old summer tradition for Chicago families. The partially open-air space on Lake Michigan changes the feel of many of the plays from their original venues; the drafty acoustics and the sea-salt air can feel like a day at the docks. But, miraculously, more troupes overcome it than not, and the variety of the plays is a terrific sampler of the local scene.

Victory Gardens Theater Greenhouse

2257 N Lincoln Avenue, at W Webster Avenue, Lincoln Park (1-773 871 3000/www.victorygardens. org). El: Brown, Purple or Red to Fullerton. **Box office** noon-8pm Tue-Sat; 10am-4pm Sun. **Tickets** $20-$35. **Credit** AmEx, Disc, MC, V. **Map** p328 F5.

Once home to the Tony-winning Victory Gardens company (*see p282*), this facility now simply serves as a rental house with four theatres of varying sizes. Among the many dependable companies that call it home are the Eclipse Theatre, which devotes each of its seasons to a single American playwright; Shattered Globe, a long-standing, award-winning producer of mostly middle-class dramas; Remy Bumppo, a dapper and intelligent company that produces high-minded literary classics; About Face, a popular, classy producer of gay and gender-themed plays; MPAACT, which produces new and non-traditional African American works; and two Irish-slanted troupes, Seanachai and the Irish Repertory. On any given night, the lobby is usually bustling with diverse audiences.

Theatre with a view: Latino life is explored on stage at **Teatro Vista**. *See p283.*

Trips Out
of Town

Day Trips 286

Features
The best Trips 286
Kidding around 298

Maps
Day Trips 287
Milwaukee 293

Milwaukee Art Museum. *See p293.*

Day Trips

Head out of the Windy City for a breath of fresh air.

Chicagoans take great pride in their city, but there's also plenty to explore in the surrounding Midwestern states. Whether you're interested in presidential history of Honest Abe or a day's apple-picking, there are numerous options just an hour or two from the city.

Simple geography makes Chicago an ideal centre for touring the Midwest. Drive east from downtown Chicago and within half an hour you're in Indiana; in little more than an hour you're in Michigan. Wisconsin is only an hour's drive north (Milwaukee is a mere 90 minutes away), and you can get as far as the Mississippi River and neighbouring Iowa in less than three hours. Even St Louis, Missouri, can be reached by road in about five hours. Indeed, it's estimated that around 20 per cent of the nation's population lie within a reasonably comfortable one-day drive of the Windy City.

Lake Michigan, shared by Illinois, Indiana, Michigan and Wisconsin, is a great source of recreation. Sometimes wild and raging, often benevolently calm, the great inland sea provides beaches and yacht harbours, fishing and boating. It's also ideal for simply watching and dreaming, as it changes colour with weather and season from sombre gun-metal grey to bright and lively aquamarine blue.

TRANSPORT

We've included information on how to reach all the listed destinations from Chicago; for most you'll need a car. Long-distance bus services from Greyhound (see p300) are patchy and train services to many communities are non-existent, although Amtrak (see p300) does provide services to several of the places listed in this chapter. But mostly, you're best off hiring a car (see p302) and hitting the open road.

The best Day trips

For big-city culture
Milwaukee. See p293.

For small-town ambience
New Buffalo. See p291.

For beach-bum mellowness
Indiana Dunes. See p291.

Illinois

Small-town charm

Galena

Welcome to presidential country: Grant, Lincoln and Reagan all took root here. Driving the backroads east of Galena over the rolling terrain of one of the few hilly regions in prairie-flat Illinois, you may encounter a bright red stagecoach pulled by a pair of brown Belgian draught horses. An authentic reproduction of a 19th-century Concord stagecoach, it's one of many living history experiences that await in Galena, the quintessential time-warp town.

Established in the 1820s, Galena grew into a lead-mining boomtown at a time when Chicago was a tiny military outpost on the swampy lake shore. Today, the quaint little town (population 3,400) is rather calmer, but does offer a tourist-friendly motherlode of arts and crafts, antiques shops, winery tours, stylish bistros and about 40 B&Bs. More than 85 per cent of its buildings appear on the National Register of Historic Places; many now house shops and galleries.

Housed in an 1858 Italianate mansion, the **Galena/Jo Daviess County Historical Society & Museum** (211 S Bench Street, 1-815 777 9129, www.galenahistorymuseum. org, free-$4.50) takes visitors back to the time when Galena was the richest port north of St Louis, attracting more than 350 steamboats a year. It offers an audio-visual presentation and a peek into the original shaft of one of the lead mines to which Galena owes its existence.

You can soak up more history at the **Ulysses S Grant Home State Historic Site** (500 Bouthillier Street, 1-815 777 3310, www.granthome.com, closed Mon & Tue, $3), a reminder of the day (18 August 1865) when, with a jubilant procession, speeches and fireworks, proud citizens welcomed home their returning Civil War hero. Before going to war, Grant had worked at a Galena store owned by his father and run by his kid brothers. Upon his return, Grant was presented with a handsome, two-storey furnished brick mansion on Bouthillier Street, purchased for $2,500 by a group of wealthy Republicans a few months prior to his homecoming. Following his death, his children bequeathed the mansion to the city of Galena in 1904, which later turned it over to the state of Illinois. The house has since been restored to the way it appeared in drawings published in an 1868 edition of Frank Leslie's *Illustrated Newspaper*, with the addition of assorted Grantabilia.

Take time to wander away from touristy Main Street to discover the 'Artists' Row' section of Spring Street, dotted with a wide variety of one-of-a-kind shops, galleries and B&Bs. A few minutes from Main Street, you'll also find a chunk of Ireland. Opened in 2003, the **Irish Cottage & Frank**

O'Dowd's Irish Pub (9853 US Route 20 W, 1-815 776 0707, www.theirishcottageboutique hotel.com) nestle on a 20-acre site, a 75-room inn and Irish-themed pub and restaurant created by two first cousins from Ireland.

Galena is tucked away in Illinois's north-west corner, where Iowa, Wisconsin and Illinois converge near the Mississippi. A ten-minute drive takes you to spectacular views from the highest point in what otherwise is a monotonously flat state.

Getting there: Galena is 165 miles north-west of Chicago. By car, take I-90 (Northwest Tollway) to Rockford, then take US 20.

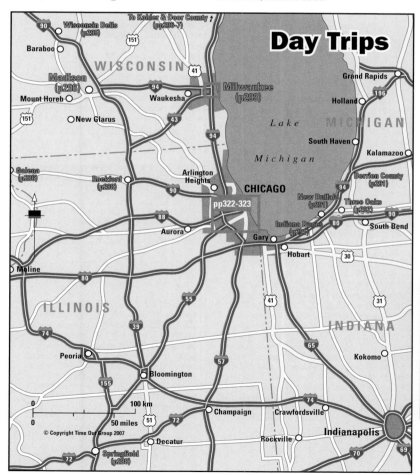

Land of Lincoln

Springfield

Abraham Lincoln died more than 140 years ago. However, the presence of the 16th president remains all-pervasive in his former home town. Many places where Honest Abe lived and worked have been so carefully restored that it's easy to believe he's only just left the building. A tall hat hangs on a peg in the hall of his former home, as though he'd only that moment slipped out to tend the garden or play with the kids.

Lincoln purchased the only home he ever owned for $1,200 and lived there for 17 years. Located in a leafy neighbourhood, it's operated by the National Park Service as the **Lincoln's Home National Historic Site** (S 8th Street, 1-217 492 4241, www.nps.gov/liho, free), with guided tours by park rangers. It was in the parlour that the gangly lawyer, who found chairs uncomfortable and frequently stretched out on the floor, was asked to run for president.

Opened in 2004, the **Abraham Lincoln Presidential Library & Museum** (112 N 6th Street, 1-217 782 5764, www.alplm.org, closed Sun, $3.50-$7.50) has become the city's flagship attraction. The family-friendly museum supplements its exhibits life with two short theatrical presentations; the holdings in the library are also very impressive.

The **Old State Capitol** (1 Old State Capitol Plaza, 1-217 785 7961, closed Mon, $2) is a fine example of Greek revival architecture. Built in 1837, it's been painstakingly restored and beautifully maintained, reflecting its important place in town history. Lincoln made his 'house divided' speech on slavery here in 1858; a scant seven years later, the body of the slain president lay in state in the same building. Tours are offered all year round.

Across from the Old State Capitol are the **Lincoln-Herndon Law Offices** (Adams Street, between 5th & 6th Streets, 1-217 785 7960, closed Mon, $1-$2), where Lincoln practised law. Cases were tried in the federal court below; Lincoln would sometimes lie on the office floor and observe courtroom proceedings through a peephole in the floorboards. Another must-see is the **Lincoln Depot** (10th & Monroe Streets, 1-217 544 8695), from where he delivered his famous farewell address – which some say ranks with the Gettysburg Address – on 11 February 1861 before departing for Washington, DC to assume the presidency. Inside the restored depot sit waiting rooms, a ticket seller's cage and an audio-visual re-creation of Lincoln's 12-day journey to his inauguration.

Springfield's most moving site is surely **Lincoln's Tomb** (1500 Monument Avenue, 1-217 782 2717, free). Each Tuesday evening at 7pm between June and August, a retreat ceremony is held in front of the tomb, with a drill, musket firing and the haunting sound of the Retreat and Taps played by a bugler. Captured in an inscription are the words spoken by Secretary of War Edwin M Stanton at Lincoln's death: 'Now he belongs to the ages.'

Although Lincoln is Springfield's most famous citizen, another of its native sons had an international reputation. Vachel Lindsay (1879-1931) was one of America's best-known poets during the early decades of the 20th century, and the **Vachel Lindsay Home** (603 S 5th Street, 1-217 524 0901, hours vary, $2) has been restored as a State Historic Site.

Architecture buffs should head for the **Dana-Thomas House** (301 E Lawrence Avenue, 1-217 782 6776, www.dana-thomas.org, closed Mon & Tue, $1-$3), one of the most well-preserved and complete of Frank Lloyd Wright's early Prairie School houses. The **Museum of Funeral Customs** (1440 Monument Avenue, 1-217 544 3480, www.funeralmuseum.org, closed Mon, $2-$4) is also worth a look, at least for the macabre of mind.

Getting there: Springfield is 200 miles south-west of Chicago. Take I-55 from Chicago to Springfield, exit 98-B (Clearlake).

The Rockford files

Rockford

If you think that Chicago has an inferiority complex, look at what Rockford has had to overcome. Some 20 years ago, it was a gritty industrial city with high unemployment. Since then, Illinois' second-largest city has enjoyed a renaissance. The turnaround isn't quite complete, but Rockford has become a surprisingly zesty getaway destination.

The highlight of a visit to Rockford is indubitably the **Anderson Japanese Gardens** (318 Spring Creek Road, Rockford, 1-815 229 9390, www.andersongardens.org, closed Nov-Apr, free-$6) a tranquil traditional Japanese garden containing 16th-century sukiya-style architecture. Paths wind around ponds containing Japanese koi, Chinese grass carp, crayfish and turtles, and past stone pagodas, four soothing waterfalls and a tea house, guesthouse and gazebo.

Another of Rockford's gems is more than 75 years old, returned to its former glory through an $18.5 million restoration. The **Coronado Theatre** (314 N Main Street, 1-815 968 5222, www.coronadotheatre.org) is a grand, lavish beauty: part Spanish castle, part Italian villa, wildly opulent and superbly decadent.

Springfield. *See p288.*

Rockford's **Erlander Home Museum**, a little piece of Scandinavia in Illinois.

Trips Out of Town

With a painted skyline of Moorish castles and a ceiling filled with twinkling star-lights, the effect is designed to resemble a Spanish courtyard on a summer's evening. Among acts who've graced its stage are Bob Hope, the Marx Brothers, Louis Armstrong and Liberace.

Grouped together in Riverfront Museum Park are a trio of excellent, newer museums: the **Discovery Center Museum** (711 N Main Street, Rockford, 1-815 963 6769, www.discoverycentermuseum.org, free-$5), a hands-on children's museum with a planetarium and a science park; **Rockford Art Museum** (711 N Main Street, Rockford, 1-815 968 2787, www.rockfordartmuseum.org, free-$5), downstate Illinois's largest art museum; and the splendid **Burpee Museum of Natural History** (737 N Main Street, Rockford, 1-815 965 3433, www.burpee.org, $3-$5), focusing on dinosaurs and Native American history.

Rockford's Swedish heritage dates back to a period in the 19th century when every sixth person in Sweden left for America. Many settled here, creating one of the largest Swedish settlements in the Midwest and establishing Rockford's pre-eminence in furniture making through their skilled craftsmanship. Many one-of-a-kind pieces made by Swedish craftsmen can be seen in a guided tour of the Victorian brick mansion owned by furniture magnate John Erlander, now run as the **Erlander Home Museum** (404 S 3rd Street, Rockford, 1-815 963 5559, www.swedishhistorical.org, closed Mon & Sat, $2-$5).

The stretch of the Rock River between Rockford and **Dixon** is picturesque to a fault. Along one especially pretty two-mile stretch, just south of Castle Rock State Park, the road is canopied by leafy branches dappled with sunlight. Though scenic Route 2 travels alongside much of the river's course along its west bank, the river twists and turns so much that you find yourself crossing it. Follow the river south to learn the story of the 'Plow that won the West'. At Dixon is the family home of Ronald Reagan, who moved here at age nine with his parents. The **Ronald Reagan Boyhood Home** (816 S Hennepin Avenue, Dixon, 1-815 288 3404, www.ronaldreaganhome.com, closed Nov-Mar and Mon-Fri in Feb, free-$3) is now a museum chronicling the formative years of the 40th president.

Getting there: Rockford is about 85 miles north-west of Chicago. Take the I-90 (Northwest Tollway) to Rockford. Follow US 2 along the Rock River between Rockford and Dixon.

Indiana

Indiana Dunes & vicinity

Just as Easterners cherish a trip to 'the shore', thousands of Chicagoans grow up looking forward to visiting 'the dunes'. Located along Indiana's north-western corner, this beach playground offers swimming, bodysurfing and the exhilaration of a romp down steep, sandy slopes after a leg-wearying climb to the summit. On a clear day, the Chicago skyline is visible from the shore, shimmering on the horizon.

The sloping white expanses of the dunes encompass the **Indiana Dunes State Park** (1600 North 25 E, Chesterton, 1-219 926 1952, www.state.in.us/dnr), Chicago's closest beach getaway and just an hour's drive from the city. Relax along the park's three miles of Lake Michigan-hugging shoreline, or explore more than 15,000 acres of dunes, bogs, marshes and prairie grounds in the surrounding **Indiana Dunes National Lakeshore** (Highway 12 & County Line Road, Chesterton, 1-219 926 7561, www.nps.gov/indu, free). The federal nature reserve spans 15 miles of shoreline and offers canoeing, hiking and other outdoor activities.

If you're up for a little more exertion than lying around on the beach, take a hike along the Mt Baldy Trail (Highway 12, Michigan City). It's less than a mile long, but hiking a sand dune isn't easy and you'll definitely feel it the next day. But the payoff is well worth it, particularly at sunset: a spectacular view of the Chicago skyline from an entirely new vantage point. Less adventurous types can take a flatter path around the 126-foot (38-metre) 'mountain' of sand, but be sure to snag a map at the **Dorothy Buell Memorial Visitor's Center** (Indiana Highway 49 & Munson Road, Chesterton, 1-219 926 7561). The centre boasts several interactive exhibits about the surrounding terrain, as well as a pleasant bookstore.

A trip to the dunes isn't complete without a stop at one of the area's clutch of riverboat casinos, the king of which is **Hammond's Horseshoe Casino** (777 Casino Center Drive, Hammond, 1-866 711 7463, www.horseshoe.com). It's the closest casino to the city: you can't miss its massive sign from the Chicago Skyway.

Getting there: By car, take the Chicago Skyway and I-80/90 and I-94 to Highway 49. By train, the Chicago South Shore & South Bend Railroad follows the curve of the Lake Michigan shoreline into Indiana and makes several stops in Lake and Porter Counties. Trains leave from Randolph Street station in the Loop.

Michigan

Just an hour and a half's drive from the city, Michigan's Harbor Country is a pretty amalgam of shabby-chic shops, bucolic B&Bs, tree-shaded paths, white-sand beaches and heavenly hamburgers. Here are three ways in which you could experience it.

New Buffalo & vicinity

Red Arrow Highway, which runs through the heart of Harbor Country, connects dozens of tiny beach towns that come to life during Michigan's balmy summer. The largest and most central destination is **New Buffalo** (population 2,200), located roughly an hour from the Loop. It's a sweet little place, well worth a wander.

After grabbing some fresh Michigan blueberries at **Jackson's Fruit Market** (2 E Buffalo Street, New Buffalo, 1-269 469 4029) stroll down Whittaker Street towards the centre of town. Lined with a few chic clothing shops, Whittaker is home to the **Stray Dog Bar & Grill** (245 N Whittaker Street, New Buffalo, 1-269 469 2727, www.eatatthedog.com), packed in summer with locals vying for a spot on its rooftop deck. Continue down the block to enjoy a day at the New Buffalo Beach, which offers casual surfing and an outpost of the popular Oink's ice-cream chain. After working up an appetite in the outdoors, head to **Redamak's** (616 E Buffalo Street, New Buffalo, 1-269 469 4522), where the tasty, no-frills burgers and fries have been satisfying locals since 1975.

About 20 miles up the road at **Warren Dunes State Park** (12032 Red Arrow Highway, Sawyer, 1-269 426 4013), giant piles of sand, some nearly 250 feet (75 metres) high, make a perfect perch from which to take in the lake. The surrounding woods provide more than six miles of trails, making it a great place for spotting wood ducks, opossum, foxes and all sorts of woodland creatures.

Getting there: New Buffalo is approximately 60 mile east of Chicago. Take I-90 east to the La Porte exit IN-39 (La Porte Road).

Berrien County wineries

The tri-county southwest region of Michigan has been designated an American Viticultural Area by the name of 'Lake Michigan Shore'. Tucked into the rolling hills and fertile valleys of Berrien County, little more than an hour's drive from the Loop, nearly a dozen wineries take advantage of the micro-climate, producing a range of wines that are sold locally and nationally. Visitors are generally welcome.

Among the best of the bunch is **Tabor Hill Winery** (185 Mount Tabor Road, Buchanan, 1-800 283 3363, www.taborhill.com, tours Apr-Nov, tastings year-round, free), which attracts couples in search of fine dining and romantic sunsets. Windows look out over the vineyards; on the horizon sit the dark, brooding humps of the dune ridges along Lake Michigan.

Rick Moersch was a winemaker at Tabor Hill for 14 years before he opened the **Round Barn Winery & Distillery** (10981 Hills Road, Baroda, 1-800 716 9463, www.heart ofthevineyard.com, free), in 1992. Tastings of more than two dozen wines are conducted in a 125-year-old barn, but the winery's most distinctive building is the eponymous round Amish barn. Discovered in northern Indiana, it was dismantled, transported 90 miles to this site and rebuilt by Amish craftsmen. A crescent-shaped copper bar features matching wall sconces decorated with alchemy symbols from the Middle Ages.

Family-owned and family-oriented **Lemon Creek Fruit Farm & Winery** (533 East Lemon Creek Road, Berrien Springs, 1-269 471 1321, www.lemoncreekwinery.com, closed Mon & Tue, free) is a vast working farm with a fruit stand, pick-your-own orchards, tractor rides for kids and abundant wildlife, including deer, foxes, hawks and owls, plus waterfowl that settle on a five-acre pond. The vineyards produce white wines ranging from dry chardonnay to sweet Vidal Blanc, reds that include an award-winning cabernet sauvignon, grape and raspberry sparkling wines, and three non-alcoholic sparkling juices. Just down the road is the **Domaine Berrien Cellars & Winery** (398 E Lemon Creek Road, Berrien Springs, 1-269 473 9463, www. domaineberrien.com), a popular picnic venue. The winery was opened in 2001 by Wally Maurer, who himself pours during the week.

The best of the bunch is **St Julian Winery** (716 S Kalamazoo Street, Paw Paw, 1-269 657 5568, www.stjulian.com, free), established in 1921 and Michigan's oldest winery by far. Located in Paw Paw, St Julian also has a tasting room at downtown Union Pier (9145 Union Pier Road, Union Pier, 1-269 469 3150), with a selection of fairly priced favourites.

Getting there: At the heart of the Lake Michigan Shore viticultural region is St Joseph, approximately 95 miles north-east of Chicago. Take I-94 east to the Stevensville exit. The winery exits are posted along I-94. Amtrak runs a service from Chicago to St Joseph.

Three Oaks

Modest in comparison to its neighbouring beach towns, Three Oaks (population 1,900) is a cultured gem amid the cluster of tourist destinations along the lake. A second home for many Chicagoans, the town provides the city comforts – fine dining, arts and entertainment – on a small-town scale.

Every summer, hundreds of visitors descend on the city for the annual Sound of Silents Film Festival at the restored, turn-of-the-century **Vickers Theatre** (6 N Elm Street, Three Oaks, 1-269 756 3522, www.vickerstheatre.com). The Vickers sponsors live music in the town's Dewey Cannon Park during the summer, and screens indie and art-house films all year round. Down the street is the **Acorn Theater** (107 Generations Drive, Three Oaks, 1-269 756 3879, www.acorntheater.com), a beautifully updated performance space located in the town's historic featherbone factory.

Three Oaks is also known for its visual arts and antiques. The **Aron Packer Gallery** (6 Linden Street, Three Oaks, 1-773 458 3150, closed Mon-Fri, free), a satellite to Packer's gallery in River North, specialises in 3D art and anonymous folk-art objects. Collectors of Heywood-Wakefield furnishings have long been commuting to **Springdale** (19 S Elm Street, Three Oaks, 1-269 756 9896, www.springdale furnishings.com, appointment only Tue & Thur); **Ipso Facto** (1 W Ash Street, Three Oaks, 1-269 756 3404, closed Mon-Fri) concentrates on accessories, artefacts and vintage-modern and antique finds. Also worth a look is **Rubbish** (13 N Elm Street, Three Oaks, 1-269 756 9242), which offers quirky, unique jewellery and second-hand clothing.

A handful of popular dining establishments are worth the quick drive from the lakeshore. **Froehlich's** (26 N Elm Street, Three Oaks, 1-269 756 6002, www.shopfroehlichs.com), pronounced 'fray-licks', oozes small-town charm. Nibble on delicious breads, sandwiches, cheeses, home-canned jams and other delights at this gourmet deli and bakery. Housed in a 100-year-old storefront, **Viola** (102 N Elm Street, Three Oaks, 1-269 756 9420) opened in April 2005, and now serves breakfast, lunch and afternoon tea. If you're staying for dinner, plan to linger at the upscale **Mesa Luna** (13 S Elm Street, Three Oaks, 1-269 756 7519), which already feels like an institution even though it's only been around since 2004. Local ingredients are worked into the creative American menu; the wine list includes bottles from Michigan.

Getting there: Three Oaks is approximately 80 miles east of Chicago. Take I-94 east to the US-12 E exit 4A to Three Oaks/Niles.

Wisconsin

Milwaukee

Milwaukee is as traditional as the oompah bands that it trots out periodically to celebrate its German heritage, and as contemporary as the experimental theatre that flourishes in the revitalised downtown historic districts. It has big-city assets: museums, galleries, orchestra, opera and ballet companies, lively nightlife, plenty of parkland and major league sports. Yet it's also quiet enough to please families, and compact enough to reward the day-tripper: the 90-minute commute from Chicago is well worth the effort, whether for an afternoon of art or a Friday night fish-fry.

While Milwaukee's German roots have ensured its reputation as a mecca for beer (Pabst, Schlitz, Blatz and, most famously, Miller were all started in Milwaukee by German families), it's recently become known for its stunning architecture. Chief among the recent additions to the town is undoubtedly the $100-million expansion of the **Milwaukee Art Museum** (700 N Art Museum Drive, 1-414 224 3200, www.mam.org, free-$8), designed by world-renowned architect Santiago Calatrava and completed in 2001. The extension was inspired by the museum's lakefront location: check out the cabled pedestrian bridge with a mast suggested by the form of a sailboat, the curving single-storey galleria reminiscent of a wave, and, most strikingly, the moving steel louvres, which pay homage to the wings of a bird. It's a credit to the museum's 20,000 works, including a significant number by Milwaukee native Georgia O'Keeffe, that the art itself is not overshadowed.

Trips Out of Town

In addition to its growing architectural reputation, Milwaukee's beer legacy remains. Although Miller is Milwaukee's only surviving megabrewery, it's complemented by several microbreweries that have started up over the past decade. At the same time, swathes of the admittedly small downtown area have been redeveloped to pleasing effect, most notably the Historic Third Ward, and new businesses are springing up around the city.

Much of the town's prosperity is mirrored in new downtown development, especially on the RiverWalk along the Milwaukee River, which the city hopes will bring in more visitors. A prime example of the city's revitalisation and flourishing performing arts scene is the 4,100-seat **Milwaukee Theatre** (Wisconsin Center District, 400 W Wisconsin Avenue, 1-414 908 6000), a $32 million makeover of the historic Milwaukee Auditorium, which opened in November 2003. The theatre features an elegant domed rotunda lobby and reception area, and hosts a range of Broadway shows as part of its programme of entertainments.

Culturally, Milwaukee's on the up. Aside from festivals, the biggest of which is late June's **Summerfest** (1-800 273 3378, www.summerfest.com), the **Milwaukee Symphony Orchestra** draw the crowds, and a number of theatre groups push drama further up the town's agenda. Incidentally, make sure you don't get the **Marcus Center for the Performing Arts** (929 N Water Street, 1-414 273 7121), downtown's main entertainment venue, confused with **Art's Performing Center** (144 E Juneau Avenue, 1-414 271 8288), a creatively named strip joint nearby.

Families love the **Milwaukee Public Museum** (800 W Wells Street, 1-414 278 2702, www.mpm.edu, free-$11), a three-floor natural history museum that holds some six million exhibits, but there are other attractions nearby; not for nothing is the area known informally as Museum Center. **Discovery World** (815 N James Lovell Street, 1-414 765 9966, www.discoveryworld.org, closed Mon, free-$15.95) is full of interactive exhibits; the **Humphrey IMAX Dome Theater** (800 W Wells Street, 1-414 319 4629, www.mpm.edu, $8) boasts a six-storey high screen and a 12,000-watt sound system.

The town's real must-see is the **Milwaukee County Zoo** (10001 W Bluemound Road, 1-414 771 3040, www.milwaukeezoo.org, prices vary). With 3,000 animals spread across 200 acres, it's one of the nation's largest and best zoos. Elsewhere, **Betty Brinn Children's Museum** (929 E Wisconsin Avenue, 1-414 390 5437, www.bbcmkids.org, closed Mon from Sept to May, $1-$5) is an interactive place

Milwaukee Art Museum. *See p293.*

designed for under-10s, while **America's Black Holocaust Museum** (2233 N 4th Street, 1-414 264 2500, www.blackholocaust museum.org, closed Mon & Sun, $5) is the only museum of its type in the US.

Down by the charming RiverWalk is the **Milwaukee County Historical Society Library & Museum** (910 N Old World 3rd Street, 1-414 273 8288, www.milwaukee countyhistsoc.org, $2), another interesting museum set in a lovely old building. One of Milwaukee's newest and most fascinating museums, the **William F Eisner Museum of Advertising & Design** (208 N Water Street, 1-414 847 3290, www.eisnermuseum.org, closed Mon & Tue, free-$5) provides colourful, interactive exhibits on how advertising impacts on our culture. For a more bizarre experience, take a trip out to the **International Clown Hall of Fame** (Suite 526, Tommy Thompson Youth Center, Wisconsin State Fair Park, 640 S 84th Street, West Allis, 1-414 319 0848, www.theclownmuseum.org, closed Sat & Sun, $3-$5). Fans of comically gargantuan shoes will find much to admire.

For a chance to soak up Brew City's history along with some suds, head to the **Miller Brewing Co** (4251 W State Street, 1-800 944 5483, www.millerbrewing.com, free), open for free (albeit self-aggrandising) tours. Learn how Frederic Miller started at a tiny Plank Street property, a replica of which sits outside the main plant; how the brewery churns out six gezillion bottles of Miller Lite a minute; and how Miller has five of the top ten selling beers in the US. Gratis beers are a fitting end to the brisk tour.

Shoppers and diners will be charmed by the Historic Third Ward, where boho boutiques, gastropubs and posh eateries line the refurbed blocks. In the heart of the district is the **Milwaukee Public Market** (400 N Water Street, 1-414 336 1111, www.milwaukeepublic market.org, closed Mon), refurbished in autumn 2005 in an effort to preserve the neighborhood's history as a public marketplace. In it you'll find dozens of vendors selling gourmet and organic produce, seafood from around the world, baked goods, flowers and, of course, pounds and pounds of cheese. But the proof, as they say, is in the pudding: it doesn't come much better than the frozen custard from **Leon's Frozen Custard Drive-In** (3131 S 27th Street, 1-414 383 1784), which reputedly acted as the inspiration for Arnold's Drive-In on *Happy Days*.

Getting there: By car, Milwaukee is approximately 90 miles north of Chicago on I-94. Milwaukee is a 90-minute train ride from Chicago's Union Station; services are frequent.

Water world

The Wisconsin Dells

Dispensing Hoopla with a capital 'H', the Wisconsin Dells remains one of the Midwest's great kid-pleasers. Adventure parks and video arcades, helicopter rides and go-kart races, mini-golf and hot-dogs… The Dells is the place to head when the kids whine about wanting something to do.

The Dells is forever reinventing itself, adding new attractions every season. None, though, has had as much impact as the indoor waterparks that have popped up all over town; indeed, the place now touts itself as the 'Waterpark Capital of the World'. Among the biggest and best are the elegant **Kalahari Resort & Convention Center** (1305 Kalahari Drive, 1-877 253 5466, www.kalahariresort.com); the golfer-friendly **Wilderness Hotel & Golf Resort** (511 E Adams Street, 1-800 867 9453, www.wilderness resort.com); and the enormous **Mt Olympus Water & Theme Park** (1701 Wisconsin Dells Parkway, 1-608 254 2490, www.mtolympus themepark.com), which expanded in 2006 by adding six new outdoor theme-park rides in addition to its 37 waterslides, two floating rivers, water basketball and shallow play-water areas. These wet and wild destinations have helped to transform the Dells from a strictly seasonal resort into a year-round tourist hub.

Despite its brash, noisy front, the Dells somehow remains the scenic destination it was back when 19th-century photographer Henry Hamilton Bennett first set out to capture the landscape. The towering sandstone cliffs and cool, fern-filled gullies remain unspoiled, and a tour of the upper and lower rivers by boat or aboard an amphibious 'duck', a World War II landing craft, are enjoyable outings (**Wisconsin Ducks**, 1-608 254 8751, www. wisconsinducktours.com, closed Dec-Mar, $9-$19.60). To see the Dells as Bennett saw them, visit the **HH Bennett Studio & History Center** (215 Broadway, 1-608 253 3523, www.hhbennett.wisconsinhistory.org, closed Mon-Fri from Nov to Apr, $5).

A number of shows keep kids on their toes. The **Famous Tommy Bartlett Thrill Show** (560 Wisconsin Dells Parkway, 1-608 254 2525, www.tommybartlett.com, closed Labor Day-Memorial Day, $11-$18) has been entertaining visitors for a while; magician **Rick Wilcox** (1666 Wisconsin Dells Parkway, 1-608 254 5511, www.rickwilcox.com, times & prices vary) is also a popular figure here.

Getting there: Wisconsin Dells is 188 miles north-west of Chicago. Take I-90 from Chicago to Dells exits 92, 89, 87, 85 (the best exit for downtown is 87).

Little town on the prairie

Madison

Every Saturday, almost 20,000 locals and tourists flock to the square around Wisconsin's neo-classical Capitol building. Although the building dates from 1917 and boasts a quite singular granite dome, it's neither history nor architecture that attracts the crowds. This is the **Dane County Farmers' Market** (www.madfarmmkt.org), awash with the thick aroma of freshly brewed coffee, the sweet scent of basil and the distinctive tang of hand-made cheeses. When you're ready for a break (or a snack), rest on the lawn or on the Capitol steps where there's often a concert going on.

This weekly ritual perfectly illustrates why Madison is so highly regarded by those who live here and those who visit. Built on an isthmus bordered by Lake Monona and Lake Mendota, it's a beautiful town with nature in its favour. Five lakes, 13 public beaches, 50 miles of bike paths and more than 200 parks draw the crowds in summer, when outdoor recreation focuses on biking, hiking, fishing and canoeing. But Madison has a full calendar of events and activities year-round. Winter sees the locals ice-skating, ice-fishing, skiing and sledding; and then there's even Polar Jam, a new winter festival scheduled for a weekend in January.

Culturally, Madison punches well above its weight, with a resident orchestra, a theatre and a full performing arts schedule at the University of Wisconsin at Madison. It keeps improving, too: the **Overture Center for the Arts** (201 State Street, 1-608 258 4177, www.overturecenter.com), added in 2004, focuses on local artists in a multitude of disciplines and styles. Special events include the Wisconsin Chamber Orchestra's outdoor concert series, Concerts on the Square, and the Art Fair on the Square, more approachable than Chicago's art festivals.

Downtown's 'Museum Mile' includes the **Madison Children's Museum** (100 State Street, 1-608 256 6445, www.madisonchildrensmuseum.org, free-$4); the **Madison Museum of Contemporary Art** (211 State Street, 1-608 257 0158, www.mmoca.org, closed Mon, free); the **University of Wisconsin-Madison's Chazen Museum of Art** (800 University Avenue, 1-608 263 2246, www.chazen.wisc.edu, closed Mon, free); the **Wisconsin Historical Museum** (30 N Carroll Street, 1-608 264 6565, www.wisconsinhistory.org/museum, closed Mon, $3-$4); and the **Wisconsin Veterans' Museum** (30 W Mifflin Street, 1-608 267 1799, http://museum.dva.state.wi.us, closed Sun, free).

The **Monona Terrace Community & Convention Center** (1 John Nolen Drive, 1-608 261 4000, www.mononaterrace.com, free), located on the shores of Lake Monona, was conceived by Frank Lloyd Wright more than 60 years ago, but wasn't completed until 1997 after decades of architectural and civic controversy. This world-class, five-level facility hosts conventions, meetings and special events; tours are offered daily (1pm, $3).

Elsewhere, clusters of boutiques, speciality shops and restaurants on King, Monroe and Williamson Streets capture the eclectic character of the city . The antiquarian bookstores around State Street draw collectors from Chicago and beyond in search of rare first editions.

Getting there: Madison is 145 miles north-west of Chicago. Take I-90 to Beltline Highway (US 12/18); follow signs to downtown (look for the Capitol dome symbol).

Soak it all in

Kohler

While Chicago has a bevy of day spas, Kohler, aka 'Destination Relaxation', offers a real escape. This small village, roughly two and a half hours north of Chicago, is home to the Midwest's premier spa and golf resort.

Synonymous with the famous plumbing manufacturing company founded there in 1873, the village of Kohler was developed as a planned community to service the factory's employees, who were showered with benefits. Its feel is anything but industrial, although many of the town's 2,000 residents work directly with the company.

At the town's centre is the **American Club** (Highland Drive, 1-800 344 2838, www.destinationkohler.com, $250-$1,060 per night), originally built to offer Kohler workers a place to rest their heads and now Wisconsin's most luxurious hotel. The club was opened in 1918 by then Kohler president Walter J Kohler, Sr, whose philosophy that 'a worker deserves not only wages, but roses as well' is evident in the fine craftsmanship of the traditionally restored, Tudor-style building. Its rooms and suites are spacious, and have the most exquisite bathrooms this side of the Mississippi.

The village's finest treasure is the **Kohler Waters Spa** (501 Highland Drive, 1-920 457 7777, www.destinationkohler.com/spa), accessible via an underground walkway from the American Club. Expanded by more than 50 per cent in 2000, the spa now offers an enormous 24,000 square feet (2,200 square metres) of relaxation space, the bulk of which is quietly tucked beneath the American Club's Carriage House annexe. Rooms can be booked here for in-room spa services.

Though standard massages, facials and finishing treatments are offered throughout the spa's 21 treatment rooms, experiencing the Kohler Waters Spa to the fullest means signing up for a bathing experience. The Aroma Sök invites you to relax in an infinity bath overflowing with effervescent, aromatic bubbles while chromatherapy adds to the mood. Other treatments are more invigorating than relaxing: the refreshing Highland Fling, for example, involves lying under a warm Vichy shower while buckets of warm water are thrown over you. There are even Golfer's Massages to aid die-hard indulgers in Kohler's two world-renowned golf courses: Blackwolf Run and Whistling Straits, which has hosted the PGA Championship and the Palmer Cup.

Lingering at the Waters Spa is a Kohler rite of passage. Guests of the American Club, and the more affordable Inn on Woodland Lake, have access to the spa's multiple whirlpools, plunge pools, saunas, steam rooms, lounge areas, fitness room and luxurious showers for the bargain price of $25 a day, which is waived when you indulge in any of the treatments. The general public is welcome to use the same amenities for an additional $10.

Getting there: By car, Kohler is approximately 145 miles from Chicago. Take I-94 to Milwaukee, then I-43 to Kohler.

Back to nature

Door County

Those who say the Midwest is landlocked have clearly never ventured to Door County, the long, elegant peninsula home to a serenely isolated cluster of communities anchored along Lake Michigan's westernmost dip into Wisconsin. Engulfing about a dozen towns and numerous

A trip to **Madison**? Sounds like a Capitol idea. *See p296.*

tiny villages on either side of the peninsula, and many surrounding islands, this 300-mile curved stretch of shoreline is popular in summer for sailing, fishing, hiking, canoeing and other water-based activities, but also serves as a peaceful winter getaway.

Door County's mainland peninsula has two sides – literally. The west side faces mild **Green Bay**, where winding roads connect tourist towns such as **Egg Harbor**, **Fish Creek** and **Ephraim**. The county's first inhabitants developed the sweeping **Sturgeon Bay** on the Lake Michigan (east) side of the land, the peninsula's county seat and only real city. With a population of 865, it's a typically friendly Midwestern town, but its spectacular surroundings stand in stark contrast to the cow-towns and corn country that surrounds Chicago.

Travel north a few miles along the peninsula for a real escape. Just south of the town of **Jacksonport**, you'll find **Cave Point and Whitefish Dunes State Park** (3275 Clarks Lake Road, Sturgeon Bay, 1-920 823 2400). Kick off your shoes, climb down the rocks and walk along the water until you can't go any farther.

Then find your way up to the rugged trail that winds along the lakefront. Climb over (and under) downed trees along the path en route to the state park, where an open beach and the highest dunes in Wisconsin await.

For those in search of island life with all the amenities, **Washington Island** (www.washingtonislandchamber.com), Door County's largest, offers an easy respite from the main peninsula's hustle and bustle. After arriving in Detroit Harbor, recreation awaits: Washington Island plays host to arts and gallery scenes, as well as a handful of museums, shopping districts and a first-rate golf course, the **Deer Run Golf Course & Resort** (1885 Michigan Road, 1-920 847 2017, seasonal hours). Take it all in from **Mountain Park**. Or if you're visiting during summer , stick around for Friday-night entertainment at the **Red Barn Park** and **Gislason Beach** (Rangeline Road at Detroit Harbor, 1-920 847 3064, free), where musicians perform country, jazz and more.

Getting there: By car, Door County is around 250 miles north of Chicago. Take I-94 to Milwaukee, then I-43 to Green Bay.

Kidding around

Some kids take immediately to Chicago, excited by the energy of the streets and the plethora of fabulous attractions. But if yours are a little less impressed with the big city, there are plenty of quieter spots in which they'll find plenty to keep them happy. Milwaukee is packed with child-friendly museums; in summer, the beaches of Indiana are a real treat for young 'uns. And here are three more day-trip destinations, all an easy car ride from Chicago.

Just across the Wisconsin state line lies a Wonka-esque fantasy for kids in the form of a 30-minute electric-train tour of the **Jelly Belly** warehouse (Pleasant Prairie, WI, 1-866 868 7522, www.jellybelly.com, 90 miles from Chicago). The tour stops along the way in front of jumbo video monitors for short films on company history and how the candy is made. Enormous jelly beans loom overhead when passing though 'Candy Alley', where jelly-bean mosaic portraits of US Presidents are on show. The ride ends at a sample bar, where everyone can get hopped up on free sweets just in time for the ride home. The free tours are offered daily from 9am to 4pm, and no reservations are needed.

The Amish and Mennonite community in Nappanee, Indiana has built a thriving tourism industry, drawing international visitors who want a taste of the area's famous shoofly pie and distinct culture. Families visiting the farmstead in the spring can tour the grounds of **Amish Acres** (1-574 773 4188, www.amishacres.com, 120 miles from Chicago) in a covered wagon, sample freshly tapped maple syrup and bond with barnyard animals. Overnight lodging packages at the Inn at Amish Acres are available, and your kids will be psyched to know that, contrary to traditional Amish custom, all the guestrooms are outfitted with cable television.

Over by Utica, IL, **Starved Rock State Park** (1-815 667 4211, http://dnr.state.il.us, 90 miles from Chicago) is best known to Chicagoans as a warm-weather hiking and camping spot where you can get an up-close look at massive rock formations thought to be more than 400 million years old. But in the early spring, the winter thaw combines with frequent rains to create spectacular waterfalls throughout the canyons. If there's late-season snow, rental skis are available for cross-country use through March. Starved Rock Lodge (1-800 868 7625, www.starvedrocklodge.com) is inside the park and has a kid-friendly indoor-pool complex.

Directory

Getting Around   300
Resources A-Z   303
Further Reference   311
Index   313
Advertisers' Index   320

Features

Travel advice   303
Climate   309
Passport update   310

Directory

Getting Around

By air

Chicago is served by two major airports.

O'Hare International

1-773 686 2200/www.flychicago.com.
O'Hare (ORD) is one of the largest and busiest airports in the world, and thus a little daunting. All domestic flights and international departures by domestic airlines use Terminals 1, 2 and 3. Non-US international airlines use Terminal 5, with two exceptions: Lufthansa and Iberia Airlines, which arrive at Terminal 5 but depart from Terminals 1 and 3 respectively. The terminals are linked by an airport train system.

The CTA provides a 24-hour El service on its Blue line between O'Hare and downtown Chicago. The journey takes around 45 minutes, but allow 10-15 minutes to travel between the station and the check-in desks or baggage carousels. Follow signs marked 'Trains to the city'. If you're still confused, pick up an airport map from one of the information stands. Like all CTA fares (*see below*), the journey costs $2.

The next cheapest option for getting into town is by **shuttle bus**. Continental Airport Express (1-888 284 3826, www.airportexpress.com), which has a booth in the baggage reclaim area, charges $25 single or $46 return for the journey downtown.

There's a **taxi** rank outside the baggage reclaim area of each terminal. The fare to downtown should come to about $35-$40 plus tip, though traffic on I-90 can extend the half-hour travel time, and the fare, at busy times, will be saved by using the Shared Ride scheme: up to four passengers can share a cab from O'Hare to downtown (as far north as Fullerton Avenue and as far south as McCormick Place) for $15 per person. During quiet spells it can take an inordinate amount of time to assemble a shared ride.

Midway International

1-773 686 2200/www.flychicago.com.
Considerably smaller than O'Hare, Midway (MDW) is used mostly by lower-cost airlines. However, it's also closer to the Loop, and rather easier to negotiate than sprawling O'Hare.

Travelling to and from town on the El is easy: simply take the Orange line, which runs to the Loop. The journey time is around 35 minutes, and the fare is the standard $2.

As with O'Hare, Continental Airport Express (1-888 284 3826, www.airportexpress.com) operate a **shuttle bus** into the city. The firm has a booth in the baggage reclaim; tickets cost $20 for a single or $36 for a round-trip ticket.

The **taxi** ride to downtown Chicago from Midway should cost around $25-$30 plus tip and take 20-25 minutes. The Shared Ride scheme allows for a flat fee of $10 per person.

By bus

Greyhound bus services (1-800 231 2222, www.greyhound.com) arrive at the main bus station (630 W Harrison Street, at S Desplaines Street, West Loop, 1-312 408 5800).

By rail

Amtrak trains (1-800 872 7245, www.amtrak.com) pull into Union Station, across the river from the Sears Tower (225 S Canal Street, between W Jackson & W Adams Streets, the Loop).

Transport in Chicagoland is overseen by the **Regional Transportation Authority (RTA)**. The service is split between the **Chicago Transit Authority (CTA)**, which runs buses and the elevated/subway train system (aka the 'El') in the city; the **Metra** rail network, which links city to suburbs; and **Pace**, a suburban bus system. For a map of the El network, *see p335*.

CTA *567 W Lake Street, IL 60661 (1-888 968 7282/1-312 664 7200/ www.transitchicago.com).* **Open** *By phone* 7am-8pm Mon-Fri.

Metra *547 W Jackson Boulevard, IL 60661 (1-312 322 6777/www.metrarail.com).* **Open** *By phone* 8am-5pm Mon-Fri.
Pace *550 W Algonquin Road, Arlington Heights, IL 60005 (1-847 364 7223/www.pacebus.com).* **Open** *By phone* 8am-5pm Mon-Fri.
RTA *Suite 250, 175 W Jackson Boulevard, IL 60604 (1-312 836 7000/www.rtachicago.com).* **Open** *By phone* 4.45am-1am daily.

CTA fares & tickets

The CTA operates a simple fare structure across the network, but prices vary depending on how you pay.

Short-term visitors might be best off with a **Visitor Pass**, which allows unlimited travel across the El and bus network for a flat fee. A one-day pass costs $5, with a two-day pass at $9, a three-day ticket at $12 and a five-day pass retailing at $18. Tickets are valid for 24 hours (or 48, 72 or 120 hours) from the first time the card is used, and are available from O'Hare (Blue line), Midway (Orange) and Chicago (Red) El stations, Union Station, the Chicago Cultural Center (*see p310*), the Water Works Visitor Center (*see p310*) and other locations. See www.transit chicago.com for a full list. The **CTA Full Fare Pass** is very similar ($5 for one day, $20 for seven days and $75 for 30 days), but is sold less widely.

Visitors planning to travel less often should consider a **Transit Card**, which bills travellers on a per-journey basis. The customer decides how much value to add to the card, available from vending machines at all El stations; when the money runs out (or runs low), you can recharge the card at any machine. Fares, automatically deducted when passengers pass the card through the reader on entering each bus or station, are $1.75 on buses and $2 on the El. If you make another journey within two hours of starting the first, you'll be charged a 'transfer' rate of 25¢; a further transfer is free.

The **Chicago Card** and **Chicago Card Plus** are electronic passes valid on El trains and on CTA and Pace buses. (Visitors from the UK may recognise the technology as similar to that of London's Oyster card.) When money runs low, it's topped up through a debit system tied to the user's credit or debit card. Fares across the network cost $1.75, a saving of 25¢ on each El journey; the transfer system is identical to the Transit Card. For each $20 added to the card, the customer receives a $2 bonus. The disadvantages, for short-term visitors, is that the card costs $5, and you can only apply for it in person at limited locations (see online for a list).

If you don't have a ticket, you can pay **cash** on buses, but the $2 fare doesn't entitle you to any transfers.

CTA trains

The CTA's elevated/subway train system, or the 'El', consists of eight colour-coded lines. It's generally fast and reliable, if a little creaky.

Most lines run every five to 15 minutes between around 4.30-5am and 12.30-1.30am. The main exceptions are the Red and Blue lines, which run around the clock (every 15-20 minutes in the dead of night), and the Purple line, which runs south of Howard only in rush hours (roughly 6-10am and 3-7pm). Care should be taken late at night. Destinations are shown on the platforms and on the front and side of trains.

Several El stations share the same name. There are stations called Chicago on the Red line

(at Chicago Avenue and State Street), on the Purple and Brown lines (at Chicago Avenue and Franklin Street in River North) and on the Blue line (at Chicago Avenue and Milwaukee Avenue on the West Side). For clarity, our listings include the line on which each station sits.

There are plenty of El stations in the Loop: in the area bounded by Wells Street, W Wacker Drive, Michigan Avenue and Van Buren Street, 48 blocks square, there are no fewer than 16 stops. We've listed the nearest one or two to each venue, but if you're travelling within the Loop, it'll be often be quicker to walk.

CTA buses

CTA bus stops are marked by white and blue signs listing the names and numbers of the routes they serve followed by the destination. Most routes run every ten to 15 minutes from dawn until at least 10.30pm daily. Night buses, known as 'Night Owls', run every half-hour on some routes.

Most routes stick to one north-south or east-west street, unless forced off it by one-way road system. Below are some of the more popular and/or useful routes:

8: Halsted
North- and southbound, the 8 runs along Halsted Street between Waveland Avenue in Lakeview and 79th Street on the South Side.

20: Madison
Westbound, the 20 runs on Madison Street from Michigan Avenue to Austin Boulevard in Oak Park. Eastbound, it turns on to Washington Boulevard at Halsted Street and then terminates at Washington and Michigan. In rush hours, its route is extended to the Illinois Center.

22: Clark
Southbound, the 22 runs on Clark Street between the far North Side and Polk Street in the Loop. The northbound route runs up Dearborn Street from Polk Street to Washington Square, where it joins Clark Street.

29: State
The 29 runs up State Street from the far South Side to Illinois Street just north of the Chicago River, where it turns east and heads to Navy Pier. The return journey follows the same route, but leaves Navy Pier along Grand Avenue until State.

36: Broadway
Southbound, the 36 runs from the far North Side down Broadway to Diversey Parkway, then heads south on Clark Street before joining State Street at Division and continuing south to Polk Street in the Loop. The northbound service begins at Polk, heading up Dearborn Street as far as Illinois Street where it joins State. At Division, it joins Clark, and at Diversey, it joins Broadway and continues to the far North Side.

66: Chicago
Runs east along Chicago Avenue between the far West Side and Fairbanks Court in Streeterville, then heads south on Fairbanks to Illinois Street and then east to Navy Pier. The westbound route is identical but for the fact it leaves Navy Pier along Grand Avenue instead of Illinois.

72: North
Runs along North Avenue between Lincoln Park and the far West Side. Service is extended during summer months to include a stop at North Avenue beach.

151: Sheridan
Runs in a circuitous fashion around the Loop, taking in Union Station then heading along Jackson, turning north on State, east on Washington and north again on Michigan Avenue. It joins Lake Shore Drive at Oak Street, passing through Lincoln Park and picking up Sheridan Road at Diversey. After turning left on Sheridan, it continues heading north.

Metra rail

The Metra is a 11-line rail system that serves 243 stations in Illinois and parts of Indiana. The Metra's Chicago termini are **LaSalle Station** (414 S LaSalle Street, at E Congress Parkway, the Loop); **Millennium Station** (E Randolph Street, at N Michigan Avenue, the Loop); the **Ogilvie Transportation Center** (500 W Madison Street, at S Canal Street, West Loop); and **Union Station** (*see p300*). Metra offers a variety of fares, from

Directory

simple single-route fares to ten-route tickets (saving 15 per cent) and a $5 pass that allows unlimited weekend travel.

Pace buses

Pace buses serve Chicago's suburbs. **Single fare** prices vary by route: a regular fare costs $1.50, with local fares at $1.25 and premium fares (on four routes that serve the Loop) costing $3. Reduced-price fares are available for 7-12s; under-7s ride free. CTA Chicago Cards are valid on all Pace routes, and Transit Cards are accepted on the vast majority of services. Pace also offers a number of reduced rate passes; among them is the **10-ride ticket**, which offers 11 rides for the price of ten.

Taxis

Taxis are prevalent in most Chicago neighbourhoods covered in this guide, and can be hailed on the street. Further out, and on the South Side, you'd be better off booking a taxi; staff in bars and restaurants are usually happy to do this for you.

Meters start at $2.25, then increase by 20¢ for every one-ninth of a mile or 36 seconds of waiting time. The first extra passenger (aged 12-65) is charged $1, with additional passengers adding a further 50¢ to the fare. Journeys to or from either airport incur an additional $1 charge. There is no fee for baggage. Tipping is optional, but expected.

Registered taxis are usually safe and reliable. However, if you have a complaint, call the **Department of Consumer Services** on 1-312 744 4006 or on 311. Below are listed four reliable firms.

American United *1-773 248 7600.*
Checker *1-312 243 2537.*
Flash *1-773 561 4444/ www.flashcab.com.*
Yellow *1-312 829 4222/ www.yellowcabchicago.com.*

Driving

While not furious as in New York or as tedious as in LA, traffic in Chicago can be wearying, especially in the Loop (weekdays) and the Near North Side (in rush hours, and on weekend nights). The city's grid system makes it easy to negotiate. But if you're staying in the centre of town and not planning to travel far beyond it, there's no point hiring a car.

The **American Automobile Association (AAA)** offers maps, guides and other perks to members of affiliated organisations, such as the British AA. Reach them by phone on 1-866 968 7222 or online at www.aaa.com.

Parking

Parking in Chicago is hugely expensive. Street parking is limited and meter-controlled, and parking in a car park costs upwards of $15 per day, twice that at hotels. Be careful not to park in a towing area: you'll end up paying the cost of retrieving your car from the pound on top of the fine. If you are towed, call the **Chicago Police Department** on 311 or 1-312 746 6000.

Car hire

Though some firms will rent cars to over-21s, you'll usually need to be 25 or over to rent a car. Rental rates should include unlimited mileage but will exclude taxes of 16 per cent.

When you rent, you'll be offered liability insurance and a collision-damage waiver. If you're not covered by your home policy, take both. It's pricey, but not as pricey as the bill you'll face should the worst come to the worst. UK travellers should note that while rental deals struck with the UK offices of the major firms include insurance, it's often cheaper to rent the car from the US office and rely for insurance on the good-value, year-long policy available from www.insurance4carhire.com. All the major rental companies have outlets at O'Hare and, in most cases, at Midway.

Rental companies

Alamo *US: 1-800 462 5266/ www.alamo.com. UK: 0870 400 4562/www.alamo.co.uk.*
Avis *US: 1-800 331 1212/www.avis.com. UK: 0870 606 0100/ www.avis.co.uk.*
Budget *US: 1-800 527 0700/ www.budget.com. UK: 0844 581 2231/www.budget.co.uk.*
Dollar *US: 1-800 800 3665/ www.dollar.com. UK: 0808 234 7524/www.dollar.co.uk.*
Enterprise *US: 1-800 261 7331/ www.enterprise.com. UK: 0870 350 3000/www.enterprise.co.uk.*
Hertz *US: 1-800 654 3131/www.hertz.com. UK: 0870 844 8844/ www.hertz.co.uk.*
National *US: 1-800 227 7368. UK: 0870 400 4581. Both: www.nationalcar.com.*
Thrifty *US: 1-800 847 4389/ www.thrifty.com. UK: 0808 234 7642/www.thrifty.co.uk.*

Cycling

As major American cities go, Chicago is pretty bike-friendly, with plenty of wide roads and bike lanes. For more on cycling in the city and details of bike hire firms, *see p275.*

The **CTA** and **Metra** allow bikes on trains outside of rush hours. For CTA, that means any time apart from 7-9am and 4-6pm (Mon-Fri only); on Metra, that means all trains except those that arrive in Chicago before 9.30am, and those that depart before 3pm and after 7pm (both Mon-Fri only). Bikes can be transported on the front of all CTA buses.

Water transport

Between May and August, **Shoreline** (1-312 222 9328, www.shorelinesightseeing.com) operates water taxi services that link Navy Pier with the Shedd Aquarium and Sears Tower. For sightseeing tours by boat, *see pp72-73.*

Resources A-Z

Addresses

Addresses follow the standard US format. The room and/or suite number usually appears after the street address, followed on the next line by the city name and the zip code.

Age restrictions

Buying/drinking alcohol 21
Driving 16
Sex (hetero- & homosexual) 17
Smoking 18

Attitude & etiquette

While Chicago is a buzzing metropolis, it's also in the heart of the Midwest, and comes with all the relaxed good manners that characterise its location. Some high-end restaurants will insist on jacket or jacket and tie (call to check), while some clubs operate a dress code (no gym shoes, baggy jeans or sports gear). But mostly, casual clothes are fine.

Business

Chicago's central location, not to mention its natural and man-made travel links, has long made it attractive to

industry and commerce. It's still an economic powerhouse: the city is visited by millions of business travellers each year, many of whom come to one of the huge conventions.

Conventions

The majority of Chicago's conventions occur at the vast **McCormick Place**: 2.2 million square feet (205,000 square metres) of exhibition space, 170,000 square feet (16,000 square metres) of banqueting, ballroom and meeting room space, spread over 27 acres. It's so large that you'll need to factor journey time into your appointments. The facilities are modern, but there's nothing to do within several blocks of the centre.

Two other venues also stage conventions and exhibitions: the modern **Festival Hall** at Navy Pier, and the **Donald E Stephens Convention Center** out in Rosemont.

Donald E Stephens Convention Center *5555 N River Road (near O'Hare Airport), Rosemont (1-847 692 2220/www.rosemont.com).*
Festival Hall *Navy Pier, 600 E Grand Avenue, at Lake Michigan, Near North (1-312 595 5300/ www.navypier.com). El: Red to Grand.* **Map** p326 K10.

McCormick Place Convention Complex *2301 S Lake Shore Drive, at E 23rd Street, South Side (1-312 791 7000/www.mccormickplace.com). Metra: 23rd Street.*

Couriers & shippers

DHL *1-800 225 5345/www.dhl.com.* **Credit** AmEx, Disc, MC, V.
FedEx *1-800 463 3339/www.fedex. com/us.* **Credit** AmEx, Disc, MC, V.
UPS *1-800 742 5877/www.ups.com.* **Credit** AmEx, Disc, MC, V.

Office services

All of the companies listed below have branches around the city; check online for more.

Alphagraphics *208 S LaSalle Street, at W Adams Street, the Loop (1-312 368 4507/http://us042.alpha graphics.com). El: Brown, Orange, Pink or Purple to Quincy.* **Open** 8am-6pm Mon-Fri. **Credit** AmEx, Disc, MC, V. **Map** p325 H12.
FedEx Kinko's *700 S Wabash Avenue, at E Balbo Drive, South Loop (1-312 341 0975/http://fedex.kinkos. com) El: Red to Harrison.* **Open** 7am-10pm Mon-Fri; 10am-5pm Sat, Sun. **Credit** AmEx, DC, Disc, MC, V. **Map** pp325 H13.
Office Depot *6 S State Street, at W Madison Street (1-312 781 0570/ www.officedepot.com). El: Blue or Red to Monroe; Brown, Green, Orange, Pink or Purple to Madison.* **Open** 8am-8pm Mon-Wed; 7am-10pm Thur-Sat; 10am-5pm Sun. **Credit** AmEx, Disc, MC, V. **Map** p325 H12.

Useful organisations

For **libraries**, *see p305*.

Consulates

Foreign embassies are located in Washington, DC, but many countries also have a consulate in Chicago.

British Consulate General *Suite 1300, Wrigley Building, 400 N Michigan Avenue, at E Hubbard Street, Magnificent Mile (1-312 970 3800/www.britainusa.com/chicago). El: Red to Grand.* **Open** 8.30am-5pm Mon-Fri. **Map** p326 J11.
Canadian Consulate General *Suite 2400, Two Prudential Plaza, 180 N Stetson Avenue, the Loop (1-312 616 1860/www.chicago.gc.ca).*

Travel advice

For current information on travel to a specific country, including the latest news on health issues, safety and security, local laws and customs, contact your home country's government department of foreign affairs. Most have websites with useful advice for would-be travellers.

Australia
www.smartraveller.gov.au

Canada
www.voyage.gc.ca

New Zealand
www.safetravel.govt.nz

Republic of Ireland
http://foreignaffairs.gov.ie

United Kingdom
www.fco.gov.uk/travel

USA
http://travel.state.gov

El: Red to Lake; Brown, Green, Orange, Pink or Purple to State. **Open** 8.30am-12.30pm, 1-4.30pm Mon-Fri. **Map** p325 J11.
Ireland Consulate *Suite 911, Wrigley Building, 400 N Michigan Avenue, at E Hubbard Street, Magnificent Mile (1-312 337 1868/ www.irelandemb.org). El: Red to Grand.* **Open** 10am-noon Mon-Fri. **Map** p326 J11.

Consumer

For complaints about shops, restaurants, cabs and the like, contact the **City of Chicago Department of Consumer Services** on 1-312 744 4006 or 311, or see www.cityofchicago. org/consumerservices.

Customs

International travellers go through US Customs directly after Immigration. Give the official the filled-in white form you were given on the plane.

Foreign visitors can import the following goods duty free: 200 cigarettes or 50 cigars (not Cuban; over-18s) or 2kg of smoking tobacco; one litre of wine or spirits (over-21s); and up to $100 in gifts ($800 for returning Americans). You must declare and maybe forfeit plants or foodstuffs. Check **US Customs** online for details (www.cbp.gov/xp/cgov/travel). **UK Customs & Excise** allows returning travellers to bring in £145 worth of goods.

Disabled

While Chicago is reasonably accessible to disabled visitors (a lot of the buses are fitted with lifts, there are lifts on elevated CTA platforms and the sidewalks have ramps), it is always wise to call ahead to check accessibility.

The **Mayor's Office for People with Disabilities** (1-312 744 7050, TTY 1-312 744 4964, www.cityofchicago.org) is a good source of general information about all aspects of disabled access in the city.

You can also contact the **RTA** (1-312 836 7000, TTY 1-312 836 4949, www.rtachicago.com) or the **CTA** (1-888 968 7282, TTY 1-888 282 8891, www.transit chicago.com) for information on public travel, or **Special Services** on 1-800 606 1282 well in advance to arrange accessible transportation.

Drugs

You only have to walk into any bar to realise how strict the Chicago authorities are about drugs: if they're going to be that wary about serving beers to under-21s, then drugs must also be heavily policed. They are, too: foreigners caught in possession of anything illegal may be treated harshly.

Electricity

US electricity voltage is 110-120V 60-cycle AC. Except for dual-voltage, flat-pin plug shavers, foreign appliances will usually need an adaptor.

Emergencies

For helplines, *see p305.* For hospitals, *see below.* For local police stations, *see p307.*

Ambulance, fire or police *911.*
Illinois Poison Control *1-800 222 1222.*

Gay & lesbian

Center on Halsted

2855 N Lincoln Avenue, at W Diversey Parkway, Lakeview (1-773 472 6469/www.centeronhalsted.org). **Map** p328 E4.
The Center on Halsted is housed in a temporary space while construction of its new building is completed. When it's ready, it will house more than a dozen LGBT groups. For the centre's helplines, *see p305.*

Chicago Area Gay & Lesbian Chamber of Commerce

1210 W Rosedale Street, at N Broadway Street, Lakeview (1-773 303 0167/www.glchamber.org). Built to assist and promote gay-owned businesses in the city.

Gerber-Hart Library

1127 W Granville Avenue, at N Broadway, North Side (1-773 381 8030/www.gerberhart.org). El: Red to Granville. **Open** 6-9pm Wed, Thur; noon-4pm Fri-Sun. **Admission** free. *Membership* $40.
See p244 **Read all about it.**

Health

For opticians, *see p209.*
For pharmacies, *see p210.*

Accident & emergency

Foreign visitors should ensure they have full travel insurance: health treatment can be pricey. Call the emergency number on your insurance before seeking treatment; they'll direct you to a hospital that deals with your insurance company.

For general information, call **Advocate Health** (1-800 323 8622, www.advocatehealth. com), which can connect you to a number of hospitals. There are 24hr emergency rooms at the locations listed below.

Northwestern Memorial Hospital *250 E Huron Street, at N Fairbanks Court, Streeterville (1-312 926 2000/www.nmh.org). El: Red to Chicago.* **Map** p326 J10.
Rush University Medical Center *1653 W Congress Parkway, at S Ashland Avenue, West Loop (1-312 942 5000/www.rush.edu). El: Blue to Medical Center.* **Map** p330 D13.
Stroger Cook County Hospital *1900 W Polk Street, at S Wood Street, West Loop (1-312 864 6000/ www.ccbh.org). El: Blue to Medical Center.* **Map** p330 C14.
University of Chicago Hospital *5841 S Maryland Avenue, at E 58th Street, Hyde Park (1-773 702 1000/ www.uchospitals.edu). Metra: 59th Street.* **Map** p332 X17.

Contraception & abortion

Planned Parenthood

6th floor, 18 S Michigan Avenue, at E Madison Street, the Loop (1-312 592 6700/www.plannedparenthood. com). El: Blue or Red to Monroe; Brown, Green, Orange, Pink or Purple to Madison. **Open** 9am-5.45pm Mon; 9am-3.45pm Tue; 8am-3.45pm Wed, Fri; noon-5.45pm Thur; 9am-12.45pm Sat. **Map** p325 H13.

A non-profit organisation that can supply contraception, treat STDs and perform abortions. **Other locations**: around the city.

Dentists

For dental referrals, call 1-800 577 7322.

HIV & AIDS

Howard Brown Health Center

4025 N Sheridan Road, at W Irving Park Road, Lakeview (1-773 388 1600/www.howardbrown.org). El: Red to Sheridan. **Open** 9am-9pm Mon-Thur; 9am-5pm Fri; 9am-3pm Sat. Comprehensive health services for the gay community, including primary care, anonymous HIV testing, support groups and research, as well as supplies of free condoms.

Helplines

Alcoholics Anonymous *1-312 346 1475/www.chicagoaa.org.*
Illinois HIV/STD Hotline *1-800 243 2437/www.idph.state.il.us.*
LGBT Info Line *1-773 929 4357/ www.centeronhalsted.org.*
Narcotics Anonymous *1-708 848 4884/www.chicagona.org.*
Rape Crisis *1-888 293 2080/ www.rapevictimadvocates.org*

ID

If you're planning on drinking in Chicago, then carry photo ID that contains your date of birth (a driving licence or a passport, say): you'll be carded if staff think that there's even a 1,000-to-1 chance that you're under 21.

Immigration

Immigration regulations apply to all visitors to the US. During the flight, you will be issued with an immigration form to present to an official on the ground. You'll have your fingerprints and photograph taken as you pass through. If you have a non-US passport, expect close questioning. For more on passports, *see p310* **Passport update**; for visas, *see p310.*

Insurance

Non-nationals should arrange comprehensive baggage, trip-cancellation and medical insurance before they leave. US citizens should consider doing the same. Read the small print: consequences of security scares, including cancelled flights, may not be covered.

Internet

Travellers with laptops should find it easy to get a Wi-Fi hook-up. Aside from **Screenz** (*see below*), there are few internet cafés here, but all branches of the Chicago Public Library have terminals. The **Harold Washington Library Center** (*see below*) has 78 terminals on which anyone can sign up for a free one-hour session, and 18 terminals for 15-minute sessions.

Screenz *2717 N Clark Street, at W Diversey Parkway, Lincoln Park (1-773 348 9300/www.screenz.com). El: Brown or Purple to Diversey.* **Open** 8am-midnight Mon-Thur; 8am-1am Fri; 9am-1am Sat; 9am-midnight Sun. **Credit** AmEx, Disc, MC, V. **Map** p328 F4.

Left luggage

Neither O'Hare or Midway offer any luggage storage facilities. However, you can leave bags in lockers at Union Station (*see p300*).

Legal help

Your first call in any serious legal embroilment should be to your insurance company (depending on your policy) or your consulate (*see p303*). The Chicago Bar Association offer a lawyer referrals service; call 1-312 554 2000 for details.

Libraries

In addition to the **Harold Washington Library Center**, the Chicago Public Library has branches on the **Near North Side** (310 W Division Street, at N Wells Street, 1-312 744 0991), in **Lincoln Park** (1150 W Fullerton Avenue, at N Racine Avenue, 1-312 744 1926) and in **Lakeview** (644 W Belmont Avenue, at Broadway, 1-312 744 1139). All are open from 9am to 9pm Monday to Thursday and from 9am to 5pm on Friday and Saturday. See www.chipublib.org for a full list of locations.

Harold Washington Library Center

400 S State Street, at W Congress Parkway, the Loop (1-312 747 4999/ www.chipublib.org). El: Blue or Red to Jackson; Brown, Orange, Pink or Purple to Library. **Open** 9am-7pm Mon-Thur; 9am-5pm Fri, Sat; 1-5pm Sun. **Map** p325 H13.
The main branch of the Chicago Public Library is the second largest library in the world. It houses two million volumes, plus a theatre, the Chicago Blues Archives, a number of meeting rooms and a large number of free-access computer terminals.

Lost property

Airports

If you lose an item at either Chicago airport near the ticket counters or close to the gates, contact your airline. If you lose anything in other areas, call the numbers below.

Airport public areas *O'Hare 1-773 686 2385. Midway 1-773 838 3003.*
Airport transit system *O'Hare 1-773 601 1817.*
Food courts *O'Hare 1-773 686 6148.*
Parking facilities *Both airports 1-773 686 7532.*
Security checkpoints *O'Hare 1-773 894 8760. Midway 1-773 498 1308.*

Public transport

If you lost something on public transport, contact the relevant company (*see p300*).

Taxi

If you lose something in a cab, call the taxi company. You'll need the number of the cab if you're going to get anywhere.

Media

Home to the country's third-largest media market and with a newspaper heritage to rival that of New York, Chicago is taken seriously as one of the US media's big-hitters.

Daily newspapers

Chicago Tribune

www.chicagotribune.com.
Founded in 1847, the *Tribune* is the most powerful paper in Illinois. Its strengths include sports, foreign news, and the entertainment-led 'Friday' supplement. However, nationally, the *Trib* is still perhaps unfairly considered a second-tier paper, which helps explain the presence of a special Midwest edition of the *New York Times*.

In recent years, the *Tribune* has been publishing **RedEye**, a morning tabloid comprised of articles from that morning's paper and specially commissioned entertainment pieces. It's available for free at or near most El stations.

Chicago Sun-Times

www.suntimes.com.
The *Sun-Times* is the *Trib*'s tabloid competitor. Though it offers gritty reporting on city politics and good coverage of Chicago sports, arts coverage is weak (with the notable exception of recuperating movie hack Roger Ebert), and most news stories are squeezed into a few paragraphs. Like the *Tribune*, it sells for 50¢.

Daily Herald & Daily Southtown

www.dailyherald.com & www.dailysouthtown.com.
The *Daily Herald* and the *Daily Southtown* round out Chicago's dailies, but neither attempts to compete with the *Trib* or *Sun-Times*. The *Herald* publishes zoned suburban editions, while the *Southtown* concerns itself only with the southernmost area of the city.

Magazines

Time Out Chicago

www.timeout.com/chicago.
Obviously we're a little biased, but we think our sister magazine is the essential publication for locals and visitors wanting to know what's going on in Chicago. Retailing for $2.50, available every Wednesday at newsstands and bookshops around the city, *Time Out Chicago* covers every corner of the city's arts and entertainment scene, with substantial coverage of shopping, eating and drinking. The format is similar to the magazines in London and New York.

Chicago Reader

www.chicagoreader.com.
The *Reader* is the dominant free weekly, distributed each Thursday in bars, cultural venues and distribution boxes around town. Revamped in recent years, the paper no longer carries the gravitas with which it made its name, and its listings are a little spotty. But it does still carry some good writing, and includes Dan Savage's notorious 'Savage Love' sex advice column.

The Onion

www.theonion.com.
The Onion is certain to startle anyone who isn't already familiar with its immensely popular website. In addition to the satire for which it's best known, it provides fine coverage of music and movies, and (like the *Reader*) the 'Savage Love' column. It's available free every week in bars and convenience stores.

Other publications

The rest of the street-corner boxes are filled with a variety of weekly, fortnightly and monthly freesheets. A few are specific to the locale in which they're found, while others, such the **Windy City Times** (www.wctimes.com) and the **Chicago Free Press** (www.chicagofreepress.com), are targeted at the gay community. **CS** (www.modernluxury.com) is a vehicle for advertisers and society photographers, while **Newcity** (www.newcitychicago.com) and **UR Chicago** (www.urchicago.com) are a pair of scrappy entertainment rags. Paid-for monthlies include **Chicago** magazine (www.chicagomag.com), an upscale, surprisingly cultured read, and **Where Chicago** (www.wheremagazine.com), tilted at the tourist market.

Radio

The more interesting sounds on Chicago's dial generally emanate from college stations: Northwestern's **WNUR** (89.3 FM, www.wnur.org); Columbia College's **WCRX** (88.1 FM, www.colum.edu/crx); **WDCB** (90.9 FM, www.wdcb.org) from the College of DuPage; Loyola University's **WLUW** (88.7 FM, www.wluw.org); the University of Chicago's **WHPK** (88.5 FM, http://whpk.uchicago.edu); and St Xavier University's **WXAV** (88.3 FM, www.wxav.com). The pick of the pack is **WBEZ** (91.5 FM, www.wbez.org), the city's public radio station, but the network was due to undergo a number of major programming changes in 2007.

The major FM rock stations, namely **WXRT** (93.1 FM, www.wxrt.com), **WKQX** (101.1 FM, www.q101.com) and **WTMX** (101.9 FM), are generally pretty bland. Pop kids may enjoy **WKSC** (103.5 FM, www.kisschicago.com), while those after classic rock should head for **WLUP** (97.9 FM, www.wlup.com) and those with a yen for oldies are directed to **WZZN** (94.7 FM, www.947trueoldies.com). Talk station **WCKG** (105.9 FM, www.1059freefm.com) brings together such unlikely bedfellows as Penn Jillette, Bill O'Reilly and the Chicago Bulls.

News, sport and mindless chat dominate on the AM dial. Sports-wise, **WBBM** (780 AM, www.wbbm780.com) is the home of the Bears; *Tribune*-owned **WGN** (720 AM, http://wgnradio.com) broadcasts Cubs games; and **WSCR** (670 AM, www.670thescore.com) broadcasts the White Sox and the Blackhawks.

Television

Chicago is home to numerous TV stations. In addition to the local affiliates of the major networks – **CBS2** (aka WBBM, http://cbs2chicago.com), **NBC5** (aka WMAQ, www.nbc5.com), **ABC7** (aka WLS, http://abc local.go.com/wls) and **Fox Chicago** (channel 32, aka WFLD, www.myfoxchicago.com) – the biggest station is **WGN-9** (http://wgntv.trb.com), an CW affiliate.

Money

The US dollar ($) is divided into 100 cents (¢). Coins run from the copper penny (1¢) to the silver nickel (5¢), dime (10¢), quarter (25¢), less-common half-dollar (50¢) and very rare dollar. Green notes or 'bills' come in denominations of $1, $5, $10, $20, $50 and $100. Some bills have recently been redesigned, but old-style bills remain legal currency.

ATMs

There are ATMs throughout the city: in banks, stores and even bars. ATMs accept Visa, MasterCard and American Express, as well as other cards, but almost all charge a usage fee. If you don't remember your PIN, most banks will dispense cash to cardholders.

Banks & bureaux de change

Most banks are open from 9am to 5pm Monday to Friday. Photo ID is required to cash travellers' cheques. Many banks don't exchange foreign currency, so arrive with some US dollars. If you arrive after 6pm, change money at the airport. If you want to cash travellers' cheques at a shop, note that some require a minimum purchase.

Stores that bill themselves as 'currency exchanges' will not help you exchange your currency: they're basically cheque-cashing services and don't accept foreign currency. Instead, try an AmEx office.

American Express *605 N Michigan Avenue, at E Ohio Street, Magnificent Mile (1-312 943 7840). El: Red to Chicago.* **Open** 8.30am-6pm Mon-Fri; 9am-5pm Sat. **Map** p326 J10.
Other locations: 55 W Monroe Street, at N Dearborn Street, the Loop (1-312 541 5440).

Credit cards

Bring at least one major credit card: they are accepted – often required – at nearly all hotels, restaurants and shops. The cards most widely accepted in

the US are American Express, Diners Club, Discover, MasterCard and Visa.

Lost or stolen cards

American Express *Cards* 1-800 992 3404. *Travellers' cheques* 1-800 221 7282.
Diners Club 1-800 234 6377.
Discover 1-800 347 2683.
MasterCard 1-800 622 7747.
Visa *Cards* 1-800 847 2911. *Travellers' cheques* 1-800 227 6811.

Tax

In Chicago, sales tax on the vast majority of goods is 9 per cent, which is not included in the price marked. Central restaurants levy a 10.25 per cent sales tax; for hotel rooms and services, the rate rises to a nasty 15.4 per cent.

Police stations

You don't have to report non-emergency crimes in person: phone them in on **311** (or, from out of town, 1-312 746 6000). The details will be taken and any paperwork can be sent to you at home. The city's most central police station is at 1718 S State Street (1-312 745 4290); for others, see www.cityof chicago.org/police.

Postal services

Post office opening hours in Chicago are usually 8am to 5pm Monday to Friday, with many branches also open on Saturday mornings. The main office is open 24 hours daily.

Post offices are usually open from 9am to 5.30pm Monday to Friday, 9am to 2pm Saturday; the vast majority are closed on Sundays. Phone 1-800 275 8777 or see www.usps.com for information on your nearest branch. Stamps can be bought at any post office and also at some hotel receptions, vending machines and ATMs. Stamps for postcards within the US cost 23¢; for Europe, the charge is 70¢. For couriers and shippers, *see p303.*

Main Post Office *433 W Harrison Street, at S Canal Street, West Loop. El: Blue to Clinton.* **Open** 24hrs daily. **Map** p325 G13.
The Loop *211 S Clark Street, at W Adams Street. Blue or Red to Jackson; Brown, Orange, Pink or Purple to Quincy.* **Open** 7am-6pm Mon-Fri. **Map** p325 H12.
River North *540 N Dearborn Street, at W Grand Avenue. El: Red to Grand.* **Open** 7.30am-6.30pm Mon-Fri; 7.30am-3pm Sat; 9am-2pm Sun. **Map** p327 H10.
Streeterville *227 E Ontario Street, at N St Clair Street. El: Red to Grand.* **Open** 8am-6pm Mon-Fri. **Map** p326 J10.
Lincoln Park *2405 N Sheffield Avenue, at N Fullerton Avenue. El: Brown, Purple or Red to Fullerton.* **Open** 8am-7pm Mon-Fri; 8am-3pm Sat. **Map** p328 E5.
Lakeview *1343 W Irving Park Road, at N Southport Avenue. El: Red to Sheridan.* **Open** 7.30am-7pm Mon-Fri; 8am-3pm Sat.
Wicker Park *1635 W Division Street, at N Ashland Avenue. El: Blue to Division.* **Open** 8.30am-7pm Mon-Fri; 8am-3pm Sat. **Map** p331 C8.

Religion

Devout travellers are in luck in Chicago. There are places of worship for almost every denomination you can imagine (and a few you can't).

Baptist
Unity Fellowship Missionary Baptist Church *211 N Cicero Avenue, at W Maypole Avenue, West Side (1-773 287 0267). El: Green to Cicero.* **Services** 7.45am, 10.45am.

Buddhist
Buddhist Temple of Chicago *1151 W Leland Avenue, at N Racine Avenue, Uptown (1-773 334 4661/ www.budtempchi.org). El: Red to Lawrence.* **Services** 11am Sun. **Map** p326 G9.

Catholic
Holy Name Cathedral *735 N State Street, at E Superior Street, River North (1-312 787 8040/www. holynamecathedral.org). El: Red to Chicago.* **Services** 6am, 7am, 8am, 12.10pm, 5.15pm Mon-Fri; 8am, 12.10pm, 5.15pm, 7.30pm Sat; 7am, 8.15am, 9.30am, 11am, 12.30pm, 5.15pm Sun. **Map** p326 H10.
Old St Mary's Church *1500 S Michigan Avenue, at S State Street, the Loop (1-312 922 3444). El: Green, Orange or Red to Roosevelt.* **Services** 8.30am, 12.10pm Mon-Fri; noon, 5pm Sat; 8.30am, 11.30am Sun. **Map** p325 H13.

Directory

Eastern Orthodox

St George Orthodox Cathedral
*917 N Wood Street, at W Iowa
Street, West Town (1-312 666
5179). El: Blue to Division.* **Services**
9.30am Sun. **Map** p331 C9.

Episcopal

St James Cathedral *65 E Huron
Street, at N Wabash Avenue,
Magnificent Mile (1-312 787 7360/
www.saintjamescathedral.org). El:
Red to Chicago.* **Services** 5.30pm
Wed; 12.10pm Thur, Fri; 8am,
10.30am Sun. **Map** p326 H10.

Jewish

Chicago Loop Synagogue
*16 S Clark Street, at W Madison
Street, the Loop (1-312 346 7370/
www.chicagoloopsynagogue.org).
El: Blue or Red to Monroe.*
Services 8.05am, 1.05pm, 4.40-5pm
(time depends on sunset) Mon-Fri;
9am, 3.45-4.30pm, 4.45-5.30pm
(depends on sunset) Sat; 9.30am,
4.45-5.30pm (depends on sunset) Sun.
Map p325 H12.
**Chicago Sinai Congregation
(Reform)** *15 W Delaware Place, at
N State Street, Gold Coast (1-312
867 7000/www.chicagosinai.org). El:
Red to Chicago.* **Services** 6.15pm
Fri; 11am Sun. **Map** p326 H9.

Lutheran

**First St Paul's Evangelical
Lutheran Church** *1301 N LaSalle
Street, at W Goethe Street, Gold
Coast (1-312 642 7172/www.fspauls.
org). El: Red to Clark/Division.*
Services 7am Wed; 8.30am, 11am
Sun. **Map** p327 H8.

Methodist

**First United Methodist Church
at the Chicago Temple** *77 W
Washington Boulevard, at N Clark
Street, the Loop (1-312 236 4548/
ww.chicagotemple.org). El: Blue,
Brown, Green, Orange, Pink or
Purple to Clark; Red to Washington.*
Services 7.30am, 12.10pm Wed;
5pm Sat; 8.30am, 11am Sun.
Map p325 H12.

Muslim

Downtown Islamic Center
*218 S Wabash Avenue, at E Jackson
Boulevard, the Loop (1-312 939
9095/www.dic-chicago.org). El:
Brown, Green, Orange, Pink or
Purple) to Adams; Blue or Red to
Jackson.* **Open** 10.30am-5.30pm
Mon-Fri. **Map** p325 H12.

Presbyterian

Fourth Presbyterian Church *126
E Chestnut Street, at N Michigan
Avenue, Near North (1-312 787
4570/www.fourthchurch.org). El: Red
to Chicago.* **Services** 8am, 9.30am,
11am, 6.30pm Sun. **Map** p326 J9.

Follow the same precautions as
you would in any urban area.
● Don't draw attention to
yourself by unfolding a huge
map and looking lost.
● Don't leave your purse or
wallet in a place where it could
easily be pickpocketed.
● Do beware of hustlers: while
one is disturbing you from the
front, another could be half a
block away with your cash.
● Do leave valuables in a
hotel safe if at all possible.
● Don't carry too much cash
at any one time. If you have
multiple credit cards, leave one
or more at the hotel in case of
emergencies.
● Do avoid deserted areas late
at night. Potentially dangerous
areas include pockets of the
Near West Side, especially
around Little Italy, and parts
of the South Side.

Smoking

Smoking is outlawed in
Chicago's restaurants, and
will be banned in the majority
of bars from 2008. For more,
see p189 **Smoke alarm**.

Study

It's only a matter of time
before some marketing genius
in the mayor's office comes up
with a slogan like 'City of Big
Learners'. The prevalence of
educational establishments in
Chicago is of obvious benefit to
the city, both academically and
economically.

The most prestigious college
is the **University of Chicago**
in Hyde Park (1-773 702 1234,
www.uchicago.edu). Other
prominent institutions include
the **University of Illinois
at Chicago** (UIC) in the
West Loop (1-312 996 7000,
www.uic.edu); **Loyola
University Chicago** (1-773
274 3000, www.luc.edu) and
Northwestern University
(1-847 491 3741, 1-312 503

8649, www.northwestern.edu),
both split over big campuses
on the Far North Side and
smaller downtown set-ups;
and **DePaul University**
(1-312 362 8000, www.depaul.
edu), based in Lincoln Park.
And then there are numerous
specialist establishments,
such as the **School of the
Art Institute** and **Columbia
College Chicago**.

In general, US universities
are more flexible about part-
time study than their European
counterparts. Stipulations for
non-English-speaking students
might include passing the
TOEFL (Test of English as
a Foreign Language); most
students also have to give
proof of financial support.

Telephones

Dialling & codes

There are five area codes in
the Chicago metropolitan area.
312 covers downtown Chicago
(roughly as far north, west
and south as 1600 on the
street grid); 773 covers the
rest of the city; the northern
suburbs are 847; the southern
and western suburbs are
708; and the areas to the
far west are 630. Numbers
prefaced by 1-800, 1-888,
1-866, and 1-877 are toll-free
within the US. Numbers
prefaced with 1-900 are
charged at a premium rate.

Direct dial calls

If you're dialling outside your area
code, dial 1 + area code + phone
number; on payphones, an operator
or recording will tell you how much
money to add.

Collect calls

For collect or when using a phone
card, dial 0 + area code + phone
number and listen for the operator/
recorded instructions. If you're
completely befuddled, dial 0 and
plead your case with the operator.

International calls

Dial 011 followed by the country
code listed just over the page. If you
need operator assistance with
international calls, dial 00.

Australia 61
Germany 49
Japan 81
New Zealand 64
UK 44

Operator services

Operator assistance 0
Emergency (police, ambulance and fire) 911
Local and long-distance directory enquiries 411

Public phones

In general, payphones are hard to find. But if you do come across one, it'll accept nickels, dimes and quarters. Check for a dialling tone before you start adding change. Local calls usually cost 35¢, though some firms operate payphones that charge exorbitant prices. The rate also rises steeply as the distance between callers increases (an operator or recorded message will tell you how much to add).

Mobile phones

Chicago operates on the 1900 GSM frequency. Travellers from Europe with tri-band phones will be able to connect to one or more of the networks here with no problems, assuming their service provider at home has an arrangement with a local network; check before leaving. European travellers with dual-band phones will need to rent a handset upon arrival.

Check the price of calls before you go. Rates may be hefty and, unlike in the UK, you'll probably be charged for receiving as well as making calls. It might be cheaper to rent or buy a mobile phone while you're in town: contact **Cellhire** (www.cellhire.com), who can deliver to your hotel.

Time

Chicago operates under US Central Standard Time (CST), six hours behind Greenwich Mean Time (GMT) and one hour behind Eastern Standard Time (EST). The border between Eastern and Central Standard Times is just to the east: Michigan and much of Indiana are on EST. From the first Sunday in April until the last Sunday in October, Daylight Saving Time puts the clocks forward an hour.

Tipping

First rule of tipping: don't be a tightwad. Waiters, bellhops and the like are paid a menial wage and many depend on tips to get by. In general, tip cab drivers, wait staff, hairdressers and food delivery people 15-20 per cent of the total tab. Tip bellhops and baggage handlers $1-$2 a bag. And in bars, bank on tipping around a buck a drink, especially if you want to hang around for a while. If you look after the bartender, they'll look after you.

Toilets

Public toilets are few and far between in Chicago. Head instead to a shopping mall, hotel, department store, shop with a café attached (such as Borders) or fast food outlet. Bars and restaurants can be a little sniffy unless you buy something while you're there.

Tourist information

The **Chicago Office of Tourism** dispenses information about the city for visitors online at www.choose chicago.com, by phone on 1-877 244 2246 (within the US) and 1-312 201 8847 (outside the US), and through three visitor centres within easy reach of most hotels.

The **Chicago Cultural Center** is the most useful of the three, stocked with tons of information on the town's attractions along with details of the centre's own excellent programme of events. It's also the starting point for all city-run guided tours (see pp72-73). The visitor centre at the **Chicago Water Works**, a 19th-century pumping station, includes a tourist information booth; the **City of Chicago Store** (see p207), which sells souvenirs and collectibles; and **Hot Tix**, which sells half-price tickets for theatres in the Chicago area (see p278). The newest of the visitor centres is in **Millennium Park**, and offers a fairly standard array of tourist information and other goodies.

Climate

	Average high	Average low	Average rain
Jan	32°F (0°C)	18°F (-8°C)	2.2in (5.6cm)
Feb	38°F (3°C)	24°F (-4°C)	1.8in (4.6cm)
Mar	47°F (8°C)	32°F (0°C)	3in (7.6cm)
Apr	59°F (15°C)	42°F (6°C)	3.6in (9.3cm)
May	70°F (21°C)	51°F (11°C)	3.7in (9.4cm)
June	80°F (27°C)	61°F (16°C)	4.3in (10.9cm)
July	84°F (29°C)	66°F (19°C)	3.7in (9.4cm)
Aug	83°F (28°C)	65°F (18°C)	3.9in (9.8cm)
Sept	76°F (24°C)	57°F (14°C)	3.2in (8.1cm)
Oct	64°F (18°C)	46°F (8°C)	2.7in (6.9cm)
Nov	49°F (9°C)	35°F (2°C)	3.3in (8.4cm)
Dec	37°F (3°C)	24°F (-4°C)	2.6in (6.7cm)

Directory

Passport update

People of all ages (children included) who enter the US on the Visa Waiver Progam (VWP; *see p310*) are now required to carry their own machine-readable passport, or MRP. MRPs are recognisable by the double row of characters along the foot of the data page. All burgundy EU and EU-lookalike passports issued in the UK since 1991 (that is, all that are still valid) should be machine readable. Some of those issued outside the country may not be, however; in this case, holders should apply for a replacement even if the passport has not expired. Check at your local passport-issuing post office if in any doubt at all.

The US's requirement for passports to contain a 'biometric' chip applies only to those issued from 26 October 2006. All new and replacement UK passports should be compliant, following a gradual phase-in. The biometric chip contains a facial scan and biographical data.

Though it is being considered for 2008 (when ID cards may be introduced), there is no current requirement for UK passports to contain fingerprint or iris data. The application process remains as it was, except for new guidelines that ensure that the photograph you submit can be used to generate the facial scan in the chip.

Further information for UK citizens is available from www.passport.gov.uk. Nationals of other countries should check well in advance of their journey whether their current passport meets the requirements for the time of their trip, at http://travel.state.gov/visa and with the issuing authorities of their home country.

Chicago Cultural Center
77 E Randolph Street, at N Michigan Avenue, the Loop (1-312 201 8847/1-877 244 2246/www.choosechicago.com). El: Blue to Washington; Brown, Green, Orange, Pink or Purple to Randolph; Red to Lake. **Open** 10am-6pm Mon-Fri; 10am-5pm Sat; 11am-5pm Sun. **Map** p325 J12.
Chicago Water Works
163 E Pearson Street, at N Michigan Avenue, Magnificent Mile (1-312 201 8847/1-877 244 2246/www.choosechicago.com). El: Red to Chicago. **Open** 7.30am-7pm daily. **Map** p326 J9.
Millennium Park *201 E Randolph Street, in the Northwest Exelon Pavilion, the Loop (1-312 201 8847/1-877 244 2246/www.choosechicago.com). El: Blue or Red to Washington; Brown, Green, Orange, Pink or Purple to Randolph.* **Open** Apr-Sept 9am-7pm daily. Oct-Mar 10am-4pm daily. **Map** p325 J12.

Visas

Under the **Visa Waiver Scheme**, citizens of 27 countries, including the UK, Ireland, Australia and New Zealand, do not need a visa for stays of less than 90 days (for business or pleasure). Mexicans and Canadians don't usually need visas but must have legal proof of citizenship. All other travellers must have visas. Given current security fears, it's advisable to double-check requirements before you set out. For more, *see p303* **Travel advice**, *p305* **Immigration** and *above* **Passport update**; *see also below* **Work**.

Visa applications can be obtained from the nearest US embassy or consulate. It's wise to send in your application at least three weeks before you plan to travel. If you require a visa more urgently you should apply via the travel agent who is booking your ticket. UK citizens should call the Visa Information Line: 09042 450100 (£1.20/min) or check www.usembassy.org.uk.

When to go

Climate

For average temperatures, *see p309*, but also factor in that summer can be very humid, winter brings 40 inches of snow and, year-round, there's the wind. Prepare for anything.

Public holidays

New Year's Day (1 Jan); **Martin Luther King Jr Day** (3rd Mon in Jan); **President's Day** (3rd Mon in Feb); **Memorial Day** (last Mon in May); **Independence Day** (4 July); **Labor Day** (1st Mon in Sept); **Columbus Day** (2nd Mon in Oct); **Veterans' Day** (11 Nov); **Thanksgiving Day** (4th Thur in Nov); **Christmas Day** (25 Dec).

Women

When walking at night – especially alone, which isn't ideal – take plenty of care: avoid unlit, deserted streets, and be alert for people trailing you. When travelling on trains at night, always try to pick a busy carriage.

Working in the US

For foreigners to work legally in the US, a US company must sponsor your application for an **H-1 visa**, which enables you to work in the country for up to five years. For the H-1 visa to be approved, your prospective employer must convince the Immigration Department that there is no American citizen qualified to do the job as well as you. Students have a much easier time. UK students can contact the **British Universities North America Club** (BUNAC) for help in arranging a temporary job and the requisite visa (16 Bowling Green Lane, London, EC1R 0QH, 020 7251 3472, www.bunac.org/uk).

Further Reference

Fiction

Nelson Algren
The Neon Wilderness (1947)
This collection of short stories made
Algren's name when it emerged, and
set the scene for novels such as *The
Man with the Golden Arm* (1949).
Saul Bellow *The Adventures
of Augie March* (1953)
A coming-of-age tale of sorts,
and one of several Chicago novels
by Bellow; check out, too, the
magisterial *Humboldt's Gift* (1975).
Sandra Cisneros
Loose Woman (1994)
Poems by the author of the fine *A
House on Mango Street*.
Theodore Dreiser
Sister Carrie (1900)
Perhaps the first great Chicago novel,
a tale of the corruption of a young
woman in the big bad city.
James T Farrell
Studs Lonigan (1935)
Farrell's three Lonigan stories, tell
of the coming of age of an Irish-
American in Chicago in the early
20th century.
Sara Paretsky
Indemnity Only (1982)
The first outing for Paretsky's 'tec
creation VI Warshawski, now a
veteran of a dozen hard-boiled
whodunnits, most recently *Fire
Sale* (2005).
Upton Sinclair *The Jungle* (1906)
Sinclair's masterpiece, which caused
a major sensation on publication, is
set in the Chicago stockyards.
Scott Turow
The Laws of Our Fathers (1996)
One of many page-turners from the
Chicago lawyer turned author; others
include *Presumed Innocent* (1987)
and *Personal Injuries* (1999).
Richard Wright *Native Son* (1940)
A prescient tale of murder and racial
issues in Chicago.

Non-fiction

Jane Addams
20 Years at Hull-House (1910)
An autobiography of sorts from the
pioneering social reformer.
Eliot Asinof *Eight Men Out* (1963)
The story of how the Chicago White
Sox threw the 1919 World Series.
**Richard Cahan &
Michael Williams**
Richard Nickel's Chicago (2006)
This paean to Nickel, who fought
an often solitary battle to save the
city's architecture, is packed with
beautiful photography.

**Adam Cohen & Elizabeth
Taylor** *American Pharaoh* (2000)
It's lazily written, but this biography
of Mayor Daley has enough to keep
the reader interested.
Nadine Cohodas
Spinning Blues into Gold (2000)
The story of Chess Records has been
waiting to be told for years; Cohodas
has done a fine job telling it.
Robert Cromie
The Great Chicago Fire (1958)
How the city lost its innocence. And
most of its buildings, too.
Peter Golenbock
Wrigleyville (1996)
Golenbock's history of the Chicago
Cubs is a highly entertaining read.
**James R Grossman, Ann Durkin
Keating & Janice L Reiff (eds)**
The Encyclopaedia of Chicago (2004)
Incomplete, almost wilfully so in
places, but still a treasure trove of
history, conjecture and anecdote.
LeAlan Jones & Lloyd Newman
Our America (1997)
Subtitled 'Life and Death on
Chicago's South Side', *Our America*
tells of life in Chicago's ghettos
through the eyes of two teenagers.
Erik Larson
The Devil in the White City (2004)
A wonderfully imaginative jaunt
around the 1893 World's Columbian
Exposition in the company of
architect Daniel Burnham and serial
killer HH Holmes.
Richard Lindberg
To Serve and Collect (1991)
A splendidly titled survey of police
corruption in Chicago 1855-1960.
David Garrard Lowe
Lost Chicago (rev.2000)
A wonderful book detailing some
marvellous Chicago buildings that
didn't survive the wrecking ball.
Elizabeth McNulty
Chicago Then and Now (2000)
Containing some beautiful old
photographs, this book places the
emphasis firmly on the 'then'.
Donald L Miller
City of the Century (1996)
'The epic of Chicago', reads the
wonderfully appropriate subtitle for
this, the definitive history of the city.
Mike Royko
One More Time (1999)
A collection of articles by the grand
old man of Chicago journalism. Also
worth a look is his exhilarating
biography of the former mayor *Boss:
Richard J Daley of Chicago* (1971).
Eric Schlosser
Fast Food Nation (2001)
Schlosser's classic tract is a kind
of 21st-century update to Sinclair's
The Jungle, and includes a
fascinating section on Chicago's
meatpacking industry.

Richard Schneirov et al (eds)
*The Pullman Strike and the Crisis
of the 1890s* (1999)
One of the city's defining moments
gets the essay treatment in this
surprisingly engrossing book.
Alice Sinkevitch (ed) *AIA Guide
to Chicago* (2004)
'AIA' stands for the American
Institute of Architects, which, with
the Chicago Architecture Foundation,
is behind this excellent survey of the
city's notable buildings.
Bob Skilnik *The History of
Beer and Brewing in Chicago
1833-1978* (1999)
A somewhat slight but largely
engrossing history of beer in this
most boozy of cities.
Carl Smith *The Plan of Chicago:
Daniel Burnham and the Remaking
of the American City* (2006)
How Daniel Burnham went about
rebuilding Chicago.
**David Starkey & Richard
Guzman (eds)** *Smokestacks and
Skyscrapers* (1999)
Chicago Writing 101, with extracts
from works by over 70 Chicago
writers. Useful.
Studs Terkel
Division Street: America (1967)
One of many worthwhile books
from the country's premier social
historian, and a local legend: others
include *Coming of Age* (1995) and
Working (1974).
Bill Veeck with Ed Linn
Veeck As in Wreck (1962)
The autobiography of the legendary
one-legged baseball executive who
planted the ivy at Wrigley Field
before later buying the White Sox.
Lynne Warren et al (eds)
Art in Chicago 1945-1995 (1996)
A survey of more than 100 artists
who worked in Chicago during the
50 years following World War II.

Poetry & drama

Gwendolyn Brooks
Selected Poems (1963)
An excellent collection of poetry from
the first African-American winner of
the Pulitzer prize.
**Ben Hecht & Charles
MacArthur** *The Front Page* (1928)
A classic stage work co-authored by
Ben Hecht, a notable local hack.
David Mamet
Mamet Plays 1 (1994)
A selection of stage works, including
Sexual Perversity in Chicago (1977)
and *American Buffalo* (1976).
Carl Sandburg
Selected Poems (1996)
This collection includes the classic
Chicago Poems (1916).

Films

About Last Night…
dir. Edward Zwick (1986)
The singles scene on Division Street forms the basis for this lame 1980s flick based on David Mamet's play *Sexual Perversity in Chicago*.

Backdraft *dir. Ron Howard* (1991)
Fire in Chicago, albeit 120 years after the biggest fire of them all.

The Blues Brothers
dir. John Landis (1980)
Feeble sketch extended to breaking point, or riotously funny romp? Either way, Chicago should get a credit alongside Belushi and Aykroyd.

The Break-Up
dir. Peyton Reed (2006)
Vince Vaughn and Jennifer Aniston go through a tough patch.

Chicago *dir. Rob Marshall* (2002)
Massively popular adaptation of the roaring '20s musical.

The Color of Money
dir. John Hughes (1986)
Paul Newman and Tom Cruise shoot some stick on the North Side.

Eight Men Out
dir. John Sayles (1988)
Sayles' retelling of the Black Sox tale succeeds despite its treacle-thick sympathies for 'Shoeless' Joe.

Ferris Bueller's Day Off
dir. John Hughes (1986)
Matthew Broderick bunks off school to hit countless local landmarks. 'Bueller? Bueller…? *Bueller!*'

The Fugitive
dir. Andrew Davis (1993)
Harrison Ford on the run.

Go Fish *dir. Rose Troche* (1994)
A winning Chicago-set romantic comedy with a twist: it's set on the lesbian scene.

Hardball *dir. Brian Robbins* (2001)
Keanu Reeves stars as a bum who takes over a Little League team from the projects of Cabrini-Green.

Henry: Portrait of a Serial Killer *dir. John McNaughton* (1986)
If you see anyone on Lower Wacker Drive claiming their car has broken down, keep driving.

High Fidelity
dir. Stephen Frears (2000)
Needless but surprisingly successful translation of Nick Hornby's London-set novel to Chicago.

Hoop Dreams
dir. Steve James (1994)
Enthralling documentary following two young MJ wannabes in Chicago.

The Lake House
dir. Alejandro Agresti (2006)
Strained supernatural romance with an architectural undertone and some nice on-location shots.

My Best Friend's Wedding
dir. PJ Hogan (1997)
Julia Roberts and Cameron Diaz find love (well, kinda) in the Windy City.

Risky Business
dir. Paul Brickman (1983)
A ludicrous plot – Tom Cruise plays a teenager on the make, Rebecca de Mornay his hooker acquaintance – is saved by sharp scripting.

Running Scared
dir. Peter Hyams (1986)
Billy Crystal stars with Gregory Hines in this comic cop flick.

The Untouchables
dir. Brian de Palma (1987)
Competent, Costner-starring retelling of the Capone-Ness battles of the '20s.

Music

Big Black
Songs About Fucking (1987)
Grim and grubby, fierce and fearsome. Leader Steve Albini has gone on to engineer a staggering number of indie notables.

Chicago Transit Authority
Chicago Transit Authority (1969)
After a name change, they carved out a career as purveyors of hideous soft rock. But Chicago's debut is a peach.

Common *Be* (2006)
Lonnie Lynn, Jr's breakthrough album, co-produced by fellow local lad Kanye West.

Bobby Conn *Homeland* (2004)
Playful – or, perhaps, just plain silly – alt-pop.

Felix da Housecat
Kittenz and Thee Glitz (2001)
As a teenager, Felix Stallings, Jr was a protégé of the legendary DJ Pierre.

Robbie Fulks
Country Love Songs (1996)
As his live show illustrates, Fulks defies categorisation, but this first record is an alt.country landmark.

The Handsome Family
In the Air (2000)
The best record from spooky alt. country duo Brett and Rennie Sparks, since relocated to New Mexico.

Howlin' Wolf
The Genuine Article (1951)
The best of Chester Arthur Burnett.

Curtis Mayfield *Superfly* (1972)
A revelatory piece of movie scoring, and a Blaxploitation classic.

Liz Phair *Exile in Guyville* (1993)
A startling rethink of the Stones' *Exile On Main Street*.

Tortoise *Standards* (2001)
The most accessible album from the post-rock doyennes. The earlier *TNT* makes a fine companion piece.

Muddy Waters
The Anthology 1947-1972 (2001)
Two discs cover the essential cuts of the pioneering bluesman.

Kanye West
Late Registration (2005)
Dazzling 21st-century hip hop.

Waco Brothers
Freedom and Weep (2005)
The most recent album from the rabble-rousing troupe.

Wilco *Yankee Hotel Foxtrot* (2002)
The disc that saw Jeff Tweedy shed the alt.country tag. The cover shot features the Marina City towers.

Various *Chicago 2018…*
It's Gonna Change (2000)
A fine survey of the city's alternative scene at the turn of the century.

Various *For a Life of Sin:*
A Compilation of Insurgent Chicago Country (1994)
Starring the likes of Robbie Fulks and the Bottle Rockets, the first release on Bloodshot Records is still a thrill-a-minute set.

Various *The Sound of Chicago House* (2006)
Marshall Jefferson, Sterling Void and a raft of others appear on this 2-CD set, a decent summary of the scene that revolutionised dance in the '80s.

Various *The Chess Story 1947-1975* (1999)
15 CDs, 335 tracks, and more or less everything you ever wanted to know about Chess Records but were afraid to ask. Plenty of smaller compilations do a decent job for less money.

Websites

www.chicagobloggers.com
A loose agglomeration of local bloggers.

www.chicagoist.com
Pithy, searching and occasionally laugh-out-loud news and comment on what's happening in town.

www.chicagoparkdistrict.com
Details on where to find the city's 500-plus parks, along with information on their amenities.

www.chicagotribune.com
Most of the newspaper's content is posted on this site, which is regularly updated with up-to-the-minute news and sports.

www.choosechicago.com
Masses and masses of information for visitors to the city, including maps and details of guided tours.

www.encyclopedia.chicago history.org
The content of this vast book (*see p311*), put together by the Newberry Library and the Chicago Historical Society, is available online.

www.cityofchicago.org
The city's homepage badly needs an overhaul. However, if you've got the patience to wade through the poorly structured menus, you'll be rewarded with plenty of information.

www.timeout.com/chicago
Listings, previews, reviews, features and plenty more besides. Your one-stop guide to what's on in the city.

www.transitchicago.com
Everything you ever wanted to know about the Chicago Transit Authority, including downloadable system maps (in PDF format), details of fares and timetables for trains and buses.

Directory

Index

Note: page numbers in **bold** indicate section(s) giving key information on topic; *italics* indicate illustrations.

a

accommodation 54-70
 best, the 54
 by price: deluxe 55, 56, 62, 63, 65, 66, 67; expensive 57, 58, 59, 60, 61, 63, 64, 67, 68; moderate 60, 61, 64, 68, 69; budget 59, 61, 62, 64, 65, 69, 70
 chains 61
 hostels 69
 hotel spas 66
 in film sets 57
 see also p319 Accommodation index
Addams, Jane 15, 17
addresses 303
Adler Planetarium 87, **89**
age restrictions 303
air travel 300
airports 300
aldermen 19
Alfred Caldwell Lily Pool 109
Andersonville 113
 bars 184
 bars, gay 245
 bathhouses 248
 nightclubs, gay 248
 restaurants 162
 restaurants, gay 243
 shops, gay 247
Andersonville Midsommarfest 217
antiques 211
Aon Center 35, 39, 79
Aragon Ballroom 114, *114*
Archbishop's Residence 105
architecture 31-40
 skyline, history of 38
 skyline, photo guide to 36
 tallest buildings 38
Around the Coyote Festival 219

art festivals 222
Art Institute of Chicago 34, 72, *76*, **78-79**
Arts Club of Chicago 101
Astor Court 104
Astor Street 104-105, *105*
attitudes & etiquette 303
Athenaeum Theatre 234
Auditorium Building 32, *78*, **80**, **234**

b

babysitting 228
Bahá'i Temple House of Worship 118, *118*
bakeries 204
ballet *see* dance
banks 307
bars 176-189
 best, the 176
 gay & lesbian 245-247
 smoking 189
 with microbrewery 185
 see also p320 Bars index
baseball 49-52, 271
 timeline 50-52
basketball 272, 274
Baum, L Frank 110
beaches **102-103**, 111
'Bean', the *see* Cloud Gate
Bears *see* Chicago Bears
beef *see* steak
Beer Baron Row 130, *130*
Belmont Marina 111
Berrien County, MI 291-292
bike hire 111
Biograph Theatre 110
Black Panthers 23, 24
'Black Sox' scandal 49
Block 37 development **38**, 40, 82
Blues Heaven 94
blues, the 45-48
 best, the 259
 festivals 254-255
 museums *47*, 48, 94, 137, *137*
 venues 259-262
boating 274
bookshops 193-195
bowling **273**, *273*, 275

Boystown 113
 bars, gay 246
 bathhouses 248
 nightclubs, gay 248
 restaurants, gay 244
 shops, gay 247
BP Bridge 77
brewers 130
Bridgeport 135, **137**
Bronzeville 135-137
Bronzeville Children's Museum 226
Brookfield Zoo 134
brunch 166
Buckingham Fountain 77
Bucktown 126, **130**
 accommodation 70
 bars 187-188
 galleries 224
 nightclubs 270
 restaurants 170-173
Bud Billiken Day Parade & Picnic 218
Bulls *see* Chicago Bulls
Burnham, Daniel 18, 32, 33, 34
bus travel 300
business 303

c

Cabrini-Green 28
Calder, Alexander 85
Capone, Al 21, 22, 42
Carbide & Carbon Building *see* Hard Rock Hotel
Carson Pirie Scott Building 34, 82
Cermak, Anton 'Tony' 22, 41, **42**, *42*
Cermak/Zangara affair 42
Chagall, Marc 85
Charnley House 104
Chase Tower 39
Chess brothers 46, 47, 48
Chess Records 47, 48, 94
Chicago Air & Water Show 219, *219*
Chicago Architecture Foundation 72
Chicago Auto Show 220
Chicago Bears 272
Chicago Blues Museum 47, 48, 137, *137*

Chicago Board of Trade Building 34, 35, **83**
Chicago Board Options Exchange 83
Chicago Botanic Garden 118
Chicago Bulls 272
Chicago Carifete *217*, 219
Chicago Children's Museum 101, **226**
Chicago Cubs 49-52, 113, 271
Chicago Cultural Center 34, 79, **80**, *81*
Chicago Defender Building 136
'Chicago Eight', the 23
Chicago Fire 14, *15*
Chicago Greeters 72
Chicago History Museum 105, **108**
Chicago History Museum 72, **108**
Chicago Humanities Festival 219
Chicago Mercantile Exchange 86
Chicago nicknames 24
Chicago Plan, the 34
Chicago politics 41-44
Chicago Race Riots 20
Chicago River 85-86
Chicago School, the 32, 33, 34
Chicago Temple 35, **83**
Chicago Theater 34, 82, **254**
Chicago Transit Authority *see* CTA
Chicago Water Works 98
Chicago White Sox 49-52, 137, 271
childcare 228
children 225-229
 best, the 225
 fashion 195
Chinatown 92, **93-94**, *94*
 accommodation 59-60
 bars 178
 restaurants 149
 early notoriety 18, 19
Chinatown New Year Parade 220
Chinatown Square 93

Chinatown Summer Fair 93
Chinese New Year Parade 93, **220**
Chinese-American Museum of Chicago 92, 93, **94**
Christkindlmarket 220
Christmas Around the World 220
churches & cathedrals
  Bahá'í Temple House of Worship 118, *118*
  Fourth Presbyterian Church 98
  Holy Name Cathedral 35, 95
  Holy Trinty Orthodox Cathedral 129
  Lake Shore Drive Synagogue 104
  Moody Church 108
  Old St Patrick's Church 120, *121*
  St James Cathedral 95
  St Michael's Church 35, 107
  St Nicholas Ukrainian Catholic Cathedral 129
  St Stanislaus Kostka 128
  Saint Therese Chinese Catholic Mission 92
  Sts Volodymyr & Olha Church 129
cinemas 237-239
Citicorp Center 86
City Hall 83
Civic Opera House 19, 86, **250**
Clarke House Museum 91
classical music 250-253
  best, the 250
  festivals 252
cleaning & repairs 202
climate 309
Cloud Gate 77
club culture 265
clubbing *see* nightlife
coffee & tea 205
Columbia Yacht Club 111
Columbus Day Parade 219
comedy 230-232
  African American 232
  best, the 230
  classes 232
  festivals 230
complementary medicine 208
consulates 303
consumer services 304
Cosa Nostra gangs 42

cosmetics 208
Couch Mausoleum 109
Coughlin, John 19
County Building 83
Courthouse Place 96
Covert, Ralph 229, *229*
cowboys, gay 249
Crilly Court 107, *107*
Crilly, Daniel 107
Crown Fountain 77
Crudup, Arthur 'Big Boy' 46
CTA 29, 300-301
  creation of 19
Cubs *see* Chicago Cubs
customs 304
cycling 29, 274, 275, **302**

d
Daley Bicentennial Plaza 77, 83
Daley Center *see* Richard J Daley Center
Daley, Richard J 22, 23, 24, *41*, **43**, 44
Daley, Richard M 25, 27-29, **44**
dance 233-235
  best, the 233
  festivals 234
  fringe companies 235
Day of the Dead 220
Dearborn Garden Walk 218
Dearborn Station 34
department stores 191-193
DePaul University 110
Depression, the 22
Dillinger, John 110
disabled information 304
Disco Demolition Night 51
Division Street Russian & Turkish Bathhouse **127**, *127*, 128
Door County, WI 297-298
Douglas, Stephen 136
Dragon Boat Races 93
Drake Hotel 65, 98
driving 302
drugs 304
Du Sable, Jean-Baptiste Point 12, 13
Dubuffet, Jean 84
DuSable Museum of African American History 139, *139*

e
Eastland, the 21, *21*
economic growth 14

18th Amendment 20, 22
El, the 86, **301**
electricity 304
electronics 195
elevated train *see* the El
Eli's Cheesecake Festival 218
emergencies 304
Ernest Hemingway Birthplace & Museum 131, *131*, **134**
Evanston 116-117
Everleigh Club 19
experimental music 263

f
Fallen Firefighter & Paramedic Memorial Park 111
farmers' markets 205
Farnsworth House 38
fashion 195-202
  accessories 202-204
  children 195
  designer 195-199
  designers, pick of 198
  discount 199
  general 199-200
  vintage 200-202
fashion designers 198
Federal Center 37
Festa Pasta Vino 218
Festival of Life 23
festivals & events 216-220
  art 222
  best, the 216
  classical music & opera 252
  comedy 234
  dance 234
  film 238
  food 217, 220
  gay & lesbian 243
  nightlife 267
  rock, blues & jazz 254-255
Field Museum 87, **89-90**, *89*
film 236-239
  best, the 237
  festivals 238
  set in Chicago 311
Fine Arts Building 32, **80**
First Ward, the 18, 19
Fisher Building 33
fishing 275
fitness clubs 276
Flat Iron Building 130
florists 212

food & drink
  ethnic 172
  festivals 217, 220
  made in Chicago 150
  pastries 155
  shops 204-207
football (American) 272
Fort Dearborn 13
Fortune House 105
400 N Lakeshore Drive 40
Fourth Presbyterian Church 98
Frances Willard House 116
Francis J Dewes Mansion 110
Frank Lloyd Wright Home & Studio 131, 133, **134**
Fulton Market 119
further reading 311

g
Gale house 132
Galena, IL 286-288
galleries 221-224
  best, the 221
gangsters *see* organised crime
garden stores 212
Garfield Park 119, 227
Garfield Park Chocolate Show 220
gay & lesbian 240-249
  advice & information 304
  bars 245-247
  best, the 240
  cowboys 249
  festivals 243
  library 244
  restaurants 243-245
  shops 247
Gehry, Frank 40, 77
German-American Festival 219
gift shops 207
Gingerbread House 130
Glencoe 118
Glessner House Museum 91
Glessner, John Jacob 91
goat, curse of 50
Gold Coast 95, 98, **101-105**
  accommodation 65-69
  bars 180
  nightclubs 267
  restaurants 154-155
  shops 192
Goldberg, Bertrand 93

Goldblatt Bros building 129
golf 276
Goose Island Brewery 150, **185**
Graham, Bruce 39
Grant Park 77
Great Chicago Places & Spaces 216
Greektown 119, **120-122**
bars 184-185
restaurants 165-167
Green Mill 114
greeters *see* Chicago Greeters
Grosse Point Lighthouse 116
Gurnee 117
gyms *see* fitness clubs

hairdressers 209
Hallowe'en 220
Handy, WC 46
Harbour Country, MI 291-292
Hard Rock Hotel 36, 57, 79
Harold Washington Cultural Center 136
Harold Washington Library 48, 83, 306
Harper, William Rainey 17, 18
Harpo Studios 120
Harris Theater for Music & Dance 77, **234**
Harrison, Carter (Jr) 19, 20
Harrison, Carter (Sr) 18, 19
Haymarket Square riot 15
health & beauty 208-211
health 304-305
Hellenic Museum & Cultural Center 120
helplines 305
Hemingway, Ernest 131, 134
Henry Gerber/Pearl M Hart Library 244
Hideout Block Party 218
Hilliard Homes 93
Hills House 132, *132*
Historic Pullman Foundation Visitors Center 142
history 12-26
timeline 26
hockey *see* ice hockey

Holabird, William 33, 34, 36
Holiday Tree Lighting Ceremony 220
Holy Name Cathedral 35
Holy Name Cathedral 95
Holy Trinty Orthodox Cathedral 129
Home Insurance Building 33
homewares 212
hospitals 304
Hotel Burnham 34, 58, 82
house music 268
Hubbard, Gurdon 13
Humboldt Park 126
bars 188
restaurants 173-175
Hunt, Richard 84
Hyatt Center 86
Hyde Park 135, **137-142**

ice hockey 272
ice skating 276
ID 305
IIT *see* Illinois Institute of Technology
Illinois Beach State Park 118
Illinois Institute of Technology 135
Illinois Regional Library for the Blind & Physically Handicapped 123
immigration 14, 15, 41-43, 305
in-line skating 276
Independence Day Fireworks 217
Indiana Dunes, IN 291
Insull, Samuel 19
insurance 305
InterContinental Hotel 63, 98
International Museum of Surgical Science 105
International Style, the 36
internet 305

James R Thompson Center 83
Jane Addams Hull-House Museum 122
Jay Pritzker Pavilion 40, 77

jazz 259-262
best, the 259
festivals 254-255
historic venues 114
Jazz Age, the 114
Jenney, William LeBaron 32
jewellery 202
Joffrey Ballet of Chicago 233
John Hancock Center 35, 39, 72, **98**, *99*
Jolliet, Louis 12
Jones, Ronald 85

Kapoor, Anish 77, 85
Kathy Osterman Beach 111
Kemey, Edward 85
Kenna, Michael 'Hinky Dink' 19
King, Martin Luther 22
Kinzie, John 13
Kohl Children's Museum 226
Kohler, WI 296-297
Koolhaas, Rem 135
Kwanusila 111

Lake Shore Drive 111
Lake Shore Drive Apartments 37
Lake Shore Drive Synagogue 104
Lakefront Trail 72, **111**, *111*
Lakeshore East *39*, 40, 79
Lakeview 112-115
accommodation 70
bars 182-183
farmers' markets 205
nightclubs 269
restaurants 159-161
shops 192
LaSalle Bank Chicago Marathon 219
LaSalle Bank Theatre 82, **283**
LaSalle Street 83-85
Latin School of Chicago 105
Law, Frederick 18
Lawndale 119
Leather Archives & Museum 115
leather goods 202
left luggage 305
legal help 305
lesbian *see* gay & lesbian

Levee, the 19
libraries 305
Lillstreet Art Center 115
Lincoln Park (the park) *108*, 109-110
Lincoln Park *108*, **109-110**, 226
accommodation 69
bars 181-182
farmers' markets 205
galleries 223
nightclubs 267
restaurants 157-159
shops 192
Lincoln Park Conservatory 109
Lincoln Park Zoo 109
Lincoln Park Zoo 72, **109**
Lincoln Square 115
bars 184
restaurants 162-163
lingerie 203
Little Italy 119, **123**
restaurants 167-168
Lloyd Wright, Frank 34, 131, **132-133**, *133*
Logan Square
bars 188
restaurants 173-175
Long Grove Historic Village 118
Loop, the *36*, 72, 73, **75-86**
accommodation 55-58
bars 176-177
farmers' markets 205
nightclubs 264
restaurants 144-146
shops 192
lost property 305
Loyola University Museum of Art 98
luggage 202
lunchtime snacks 147
Lurie Gardens 77

machine politics 41-44
Madison, WI 296, *297*
Madlener House 105
Magnificent Mile 95, *96*, **97-101**
accommodation 62-65
bars 179-180
galleries 223
restaurants 153-154
shops 192
malls 190-191
Manhattan Building 33
Marina City *31*, 39, 96
Marquette Building 33

Marquette, Father
  Jacques 12
Mary & Leigh Block
  Museum of Art
  117, *117*
Masonic Temple 35
Maxwell Street 122
McCormick Place 87
McCormick Place Bird
  Sanctuary 111
McCormick Tribune
  Bridgehouse &
  Chicago River
  Museum 79, **80**, *82*
McCormick Tribune
  Campus Center 135
McCormick Tribune
  Freedom Museum 97,
  100, *100*
McCormick Tribune Ice
  Rink 77, **277**
McCormick, Cyrus 13, 15
McDonald's
  Thanksgiving
  Parade 220
meat industry 120
media 306
Meigs Field airport 25
Melrose, Lester 46
Merchandise Mart 36
Merchandise Mart 97
Metra rail 301
Metropolitan
  Correctional Center 83
Michigan Avenue 79-81
Michigan Avenue
  Bridge 77, 97
Midwest Buddhist
  Temple 107
Mies van der Rohe,
  Ludwig 36, 37, 38, 39
Millennium Park 25,
  25, 40, **75-77**,
  111, 226
  Welcome Center 77
Milwaukee, WI 293-295,
  294
Miró, Joan 84
Mitchell Museum of the
  American Indian 116
Mob, the *see* organised
  crime
Monadnock Building
  32, 82
money 306
Monroe Harbor 111
Montgomery Ward
  Building 35
Montrose Beach 103
Moody Church 108
Moore House 132, *133*
Moore, Henry 85
Motor Row 94
murals 124

museums & galleries
  *African American
    culture*: Bronzeville
    Children's Museum
    226; DuSable
    Museum of African
    American History
    139, *139*
  archaeology: Oriental
    Institute Museum
    139, 140, **141**
  architecture: Frank
    Lloyd Wright Home
    & Studio 131, 133,
    134
  art: Art Institute of
    Chicago 34, 72, *76*,
    78-79; Arts Club of
    Chicago 101;
    Lillstreet Art Center
    115; Loyola
    University Museum
    of Art 98; Mary &
    Leigh Block
    Museum of Art 117,
    117; Museum of
    Contemporary Art
    95, **101**, **235**;
    National Museum of
    Mexican Art 123,
    125; National
    Vietnam Veterans'
    Art Museum 92;
    Renaissance Society
    139; River East Art
    Center 101; Smart
    Museum of Art 139,
    142; Ukrainian
    Institute of Modern
    Art 129
  blues, the: Blues
    Heaven 94; Chicago
    Blues Museum *47*,
    48, 137, *137*
  broadcast media:
    Museum of
    Broadcast
    Communications 97
  Chicago River:
    McCormick Tribune
    Bridgehouse &
    Chicago River
    Museum 79, **80**, *82*
  Chicago's history:
    Chicago History
    Museum 105, **108**;
    Clarke House
    Museum 91;
    Glessner House
    Museum 91; Jane
    Addams Hull-House
    Museum 122;
    Wood-Maxey-Boyd
    House 135

  Chinese culture:
    Chinese-American
    Museum of Chicago
    92, 93, **94**
  civil liberties:
    McCormick Tribune
    Freedom Museum
    97, **100**, *100*
  for children:
    Bronzeville
    Children's Museum
    226; Chicago
    Children's Museum
    101, **226**; Kohl
    Children's Museum
    226; Wonder
    Works 226
  Greek culture: Hellenic
    Museum & Cultural
    Center 120
  Hemingway: Ernest
    Hemingway
    Birthplace &
    Museum 131,
    131, **134**
  holograms: Museum
    of Holography 120
  Jewish culture: Spertus
    Museum 81
  Mexican culture:
    National Museum
    of Mexican Art 123,
    125
  *Native American
    culture*: Mitchell
    Museum of the
    American Indian
    116
  *natural history
    & science*: Field
    Museum 87, **89-90**,
    89
  Polish culture: Polish
    Museum of America
    128, **129**
  science: Museum of
    Science & Industry
    139-141, *142*
  sex: Leather Archives
    & Museum 115
  sports: National Italian
    American Sports
    Hall of Fame
    122, 123
  stained glass: Smith
    Museum of Stained
    Glass Windows 101
  surgery: International
    Museum of Surgical
    Science 105
  Swedish culture:
    Swedish American
    Museum Center 113,
    113, **115**

  *Temperance
    movement*: Frances
    Willard House 116
  Ukrainian culture:
    Ukrainian Institute
    of Modern Art 129;
    Ukrainian National
    Museum 129
  *wildlife &
    environment*: Kohl
    Children's Museum
    226; Notebaert
    Nature Museum 110
Museum Campus 72,
  87-90
Museum of Broadcast
  Communications 97
Museum of
  Contemporary Art 95,
  101, **235**
Museum of Holography
  120
Museum of Science &
  Industry 139-141, *142*
music 250-262
  best, the 250, 259
  festivals 252, 254-255
  house 268
  kiddie rock
  made in Chicago 312
  shops 213
music shops 213

n

National Italian
  American Sports Hall
  of Fame *122*, 123
National Museum of
  Mexican Art 123, **125**
National Vietnam
  Veterans' Art Museum
  92
Navy Pier 95, 100, **101**,
  111, *226*
NBC 5 Streetside TV
  Studio 98
NBC Tower 100
Near North Side
  95-105
  accommodation 60-69
  bars 178-180
  farmers' markets 205
  galleries 221-223
  nightclubs 264-269
  restaurants 150-155
  shops 192
Near South Side 135
Near West Side
  119-125
  bars 184-185
  galleries 223-224
  nightclubs 269-270
  restaurants 165-167

neighbourhood
overview 73
Ness, Eliot 22
Untouchables tour 73
Nevelson, Louise 84
New Buffalo, MI 291
Newberry Library 103
nightlife 263-270
best, the 263
festivals 267
gay 248
inside tips 265
North Avenue Beach
102, 111
North Pier 100
North Shore 116-118
Northerly Island Park 89
Northwest Tower 130
Northwestern University
116
Northwestern University
Settlement House 128
Notebaert Nature
Museum 110
Noyes Cultural Arts
Center 116
NWU *see* Northwestern
University

O'Banion, Dion 22
O'Hare International 300
Oak Park 131-134
Oak Park Conservatory
134
Oak Street 103-104
Oak Street Beach
103, 111
off-licences 204
Ohio Street Beach
101, 111
Old Colony Building 33
Old St Patrick's Church
120, *121*
Old Town 106-108
accommodation 69
bars 180-181
farmers' markets 205
galleries 223
nightclubs 267
restaurants 155-157
shops 192
Old Town Triangle 107
Olive Park 101
On Leong Merchants
Association Building
92
One Financial Place 84
One Prudential Plaza 79
opera 250-253
best, the 250
festivals 252
opticians 209

organised crime 21, 42
Oriental Institute
Museum 139, 140, **141**
Oz Park 110, 227

Pace buses 302
Paderewski House 130
Palmer House Hilton
58, 82
Palmer, Potter 101, 102
Palmolive Building 36
Paris métro sign 79
Parker house 132
parks & gardens
for children 226
Chicago Botanic
Garden 118
Fallen Firefighter &
Paramedic Memorial
Park 111
Garfield Park 119, 227
Grant Park 77
Illinois Beach State
Park 118
Lincoln Park *108*,
109-110, 226
Lurie Gardens 77
Millennium Park
25, *25*, 40, **75-77**,
111, 226
Northerly Island
Park 89
Oak Park
Conservatory 134
Olive Park 101
Oz Park 110, 227
Ping Tom Memorial
Park 93
Shakespeare Garden
109
passports 310
pharmacies 210
photography 195
Picasso, Pablo 84
piercing 211
Pilsen 119, **123-125**
galleries 224
murals 124, *124*
restaurants 168-169
Ping Tom Memorial
Park 93
Pinkerton, Allan 13
Pleasant
Home/Historical
Society of Oak Park
& River Forest 134
Plensa, Jaume 77, 85
police stations 307
Polish Museum of
America 128, **129**
Polish Roman Catholic
Union of America 128

political machines *see*
machine politics
political scandal 44
Polonia Triangle 128
Pontiac Building 80
pool 276
postal services 307
Prairie Avenue Historic
District 91-93, *91*
Prairie Style 34
Pre-Kwanzaa
Celebration 220
Printers' Row 80
Printers' Row Book Fair
217
Prohibition 20, 21, 22
public art 84-85, *84*
public transport 300-302
Pullman District 17, **142**
Pullman, George 17, 91,
142

R&B 262
rail travel 300
railroad strike 15
railway industry 14, 17
Randolph Street 83
Ravenswood 115
bars 184
Redmoon Spectacle 219
Reliance Building 82
religion 307
Renaissance Society 139
resident musicians 258
restaurants 144-175
best, the 144
by cuisine: African
175; Algerian 158;
Belgian 162;
Caribbean 175;
Central American
172; Chinese 149;
classic American
145, 146, 150, 152,
154, 159, 160, 161,
162, 165, 167, 168,
169, 170, 171, 172,
173, 175;
contemporary
American 145, 151,
152, 153, 155, 157,
159, 165, 167, 169,
170, 171, 173, 174;
Cuban 160; Eastern
European 146;
eclectic 154, 159,
160, 162, 169, 173;
fish & seafood 145,
159; French 144,
151, 154, 170, 175;
French/Vietnamese
152; German 160;

Greek 167; Indian
162, 163; Irish 152,
160; Italian 146,
152, 155, 159, 165,
167, 168, 169, 171;
Japanese 152, 161,
165, 167, 168, 169,
170, 174; Korean
163; Latin American
149, 152, 153, 165,
170, 172, 174;
Mediterranean 165;
Mexican 151, 153,
157, 163, 165, 168,
174; Middle Eastern
159, 162; pan-Asian
149; pizza 151, 152,
157, 172; Spanish
150, 168, 170, 171;
Thai 160; Turkish
161; vegetarian
162, 175; Vietnamese
162, 169
ethnic 172
for brunch 166
for cakes & pastries
155
for children 227
for lunch 147
gay & lesbian 243-245
24-hour dining 157
see also p319
Restaurants index
Richard J Daley Center
35, 39, 83
River East Art Center
101
River North 95-97
accommodation 60-62
bars 178-179
galleries 221
nightclubs 264-267
restaurants 150-153
River North Gallery
District 95
River West 119-120
Riviera Theatre 114
Robie House 34, 133,
139, **142**
rock & roots 253-259
best, the 253
festivals 254-255
Rockefeller, John D 17
Rockford, IL 288, 290,
290
Rogers Park 28, 115
rollerblading *see* in-line
skating
Rookery 34, 84
Root, John Welborn
33, 34
Roscoe Village 113
restaurants 161-162
running 276

Russell House 104
Ryerson House 104

S

safety & security 308
Saint Therese Chinese
    Catholic Mission 92
sales tax 190
St James Cathedral 95
St Michael's Church
    35, 107
St Nicholas Ukrainian
    Catholic Cathedral 129
St Patrick's Day 216
St Stanislaus Kostka 128
St Valentine's Day
    Massacre 22, 110
Sts Volodymyr & Olha
    Church 129
Santa Fe Building 80
Santa Fe Center 34
Sears Tower 35, *40*,
    85, **86**
Second City 24
Shakespeare Garden
    109, 117
Shedd Aquarium 87, **90**,
    111
shipping industry 14, 21
shoes 203
shops & services
    190-214
    best areas 192
    best shops 190
    gay & lesbian 247
    historic 210
    sales tax 190
Sianis, Billy 50
sightseeing 72-142
    best, the 72
    for children 225-227
    orientation 72
    overview 73
    tours 72-73
Sinclair, Upton 137
Six Flags Great America
    & Hurricane Harbor
    117
sledding 276
Smart Museum of Art
    139, **142**
Smith Museum of
    Stained Glass
    Windows 101
smoking 308
Smurfit-Stone Building
    79
soccer 272, 277
Soldier Field 89, 272
South Loop 73, **87-93**
    accommodation 58-59
    bars 177-178
    restaurants 146-149

South Side 135-142
    bars 188-189
    restaurants 175
    shops 192
    souvenirs 207
spas 66, **210**
Spertus Museum 81
sports & fitness
    271-277
    active sports 272-277
    best, the 271
    spectator sports
    271-272
sports shops 214
Spring & Easter Flower
    Show 216
Springfield, IL 288, *289*
Starr, Ellen Gates 15, 17
State Street 81-83
steak, guide to 158
Stella, Frank 85
Streeterville 100-101
    accommodation 62-65
    bars 179-180
    galleries 22-3
    restaurants 153-154
study 308
Sullivan, Louis 32
supermarkets 206
Swedish American
    Museum Center
    113, *113*, **115**
swimming 277
Symphony Center
    80, **253**

T

Taste of Chicago 217
Taste of Polonia 218
tattoos 211
taxis 302
telephones 308
Tempel Farms 118
temperance movement
    20, 21
tennis 277, *277*
theatre 278-284
    best, the 278
    gay 249
    unusual names 282
Three Oaks, MI 292
31st Street Beach 111
Thomas House 132
Thompson Center *see*
    James R Thompson
    Center
Thompson, William
    20, 21, 22
Three Arts Club 104
311 S Wacker Drive 86
330 N Wabash 37
333 W Wacker Drive 40
time 309

tipping 309
toilets 309
Torrio, Johnny 21
Tortilleria Sabinas
    factory 124
tourist information 309
tours, guided 72-73
toy shops 214
Transportation Building
    80
travel advice 303
Tree Studios 96
Tribune Tower 34**97**
Trump International
    Tower & Hotel 40, 97
12th Street Beach 102
21st Amendment 22
24-hour dining 157UIC
    see University of
    Illinois at Chicago
2 Riverside Plaza 36

U

Ukrainian Institute of
    Modern Art 129
Ukrainian National
    Museum 129
Ukrainian Village 126,
    128-129
    bars 186-187
    nightclubs 270
    restaurants 169-170
Union Station 86
Union Stock Yards
    20, 26
Unity Temple 133, **134**
University of Chicago
    17, 18, 139
University of Illinois at
    Chicago 122
Uptown 114, 115
    bars 184
    jazz venues 114
    restaurants 162
Uptown Theatre 114
US Cellular Field 52, 137

V

Veeck, Bill 51
Venetian Night 218
Victory Monument 136,
    136
visas 310
volleyball 277

W

W Wacker Drive 85-86
walks, guided
    Chinatown 92-94
    collegiate Hyde Park
    140-141

Pilsen 124-125
    public art 84-85
Washington Square 103
Washington, Harold
    25, 43, 44
Water Tower 98
Water Tower Place 39
water transport 302
Waters, Muddy 47
Waveland Field House
    111
Weathermen, the 23
websites 312
Wentworth, 'Long'
    John 13
West Loop 73, **119-120**
    bars 184-185
    galleries 223
    nightclubs 269
    restaurants 165-167
West Town 126,
    128-129
    bars 186-187
    restaurants 169-170
when to go 310
'White City' 18, **34**
White Sox *see* Chicago
    White Sox
Wicker Park 126,
    130, *130*
    accommodation 70
    bars 186-188
    farmers' markets 205
    galleries 224
    nightclubs 270
    restaurants 170-173
    shops 192
Williams, Eugene 20
Wilmette 118
Windy City 24
Winfrey, Oprah 120
winter of 1978-79
    23, 24
Wisconsin Dells, WI 295
women 310
Wonder Works 131, 226
Wood-Maxey-Boyd
    House 135
Working Bikes
    Cooperative 274, *274*
working in the US
    310
World's Columbian
    Exhibition 18, *18*, 34
World's Fair, second 22
Wrigley Building *32*, 34,
    35, **98**
Wrigley family 50, 52,
    113
Wrigley Field *49*, 50, 72,
    113, **272**
Wrigley Square 77
Wrigleyville 113
    restaurants 159-161

y

Yerkes, Charles Tyson 19
Yippies 23

z

Zangara, Giuseppe 42
Zion 118
Zoolights 220

Accommodation

Allerton Crowne Plaza 63
Amalfi Hotel 60
Arlington International House 69
Chicago International Hostel 69
Chicago Marriott 63
City Suites 70
Comfort Inn & Suites Downtown 61
Conrad Chicago 63, *65*
Courtyard by Marriott 64
Crowne Plaza Silversmith 55
Days Inn Lincoln Park 69
Drake 65
Embassy Suites Chicago Downtown Lakefront 64
Essex Inn 59
Fairfield Inn & Suites 64
Fairmont Chicago 55
Four Seasons 65
Gold Coast Guest House 68
Hampton Inn & Suites 61
Hard Rock Hotel 57
HI-Chicago 69
Hilton Chicago 58
Hilton Garden Inn 61
Hilton Suites 67
Hotel Allegro 57
Hotel Blake 58
Hotel Burnham 58
Hotel Indigo 67, *68*
Hotel Monaco *56*, 58
House of Blues 60, *62*
House of Two Urns B&B 70
Howard Johnson Inn 61
Hyatt Regency 58
Hyatt Regency McCormick Place 60
InterContinental Chicago 63
International House of Chicago 69
James Chicago 63
Majestic 70

Millennium Knickerbocker 67
Ohio House 62
Omni Chicago 62
Palmer House Hilton 58, *59*
Park Hyatt Chicago 62
Peninsula Chicago 62, *66*
Raffaello 67
Ray's Bucktown B&B 70
Red Roof Inn 64
Renaissance Chicago Hotel 56
Ritz-Carlton Chicago 65
Seneca 68
Sheraton Chicago Hotel & Towers 63
Sofitel Chicago Water Tower 66
Sutton Place 67
Swissôtel 56
Talbott Hotel 67
W Chicago City Center *55*, 56
W Chicago Lakeshore 64
Westin 68
Wheeler Mansion 59, *60*
Whitehall Hotel 69
Wicker Park Inn 70
Willows 70
Windy City Urban Inn 69

Restaurants

A Tavola 169
Al's Italian Beef 150
Alinea 155
Avec *163*, 165
Avenues 153
Ba Le 162
Banadir 172
Bittersweet Pastry Shop 159
Blackbird 165
Blu 47 175
Bob San 169
Bongo Room 166, 170
Bonsoiree 173
Le Bouchon 170
Bravo Tapas & Lounge *168*, 170
Breakfast Club 169
Bruna's 167
Butter 165
Café 28 160
Café Absinthe 170
Café Iberico 150
Café Matou 170
Café Nhu-Hoa 172
Café Trinidad *174*, 175
Carnival 165
Cellars Market 147
Charlie Trotter's 157

Chicago Chop House 150
Chicago Firehouse 146
Chicago Pizza & Oven Grinder Co 157
Coast 170
Copperblue 153, *153*
Il Covo 171
Crêpe & Coffee Palace 158
Crofton on Wells 15
Cuatro 149
Cupcakes 155
Custom House 146, *146*
Cyrano's Bistrot & Wine Bar 151
De Cero 165
Del Toro 171, *171*
DeLaCosta 153
Diner Grill 157
Dodo 169
Don's Humburgers 157
Eleven City Diner *145*, 146
Eli's Cheesecake 150
Eppy's Deli 154
Erwin 166
Everest 144
Fan Si Pan 169
Fat Willy's Rib Shack 173
Feed 173
Fixture 159
Flo 169
Follia 165
Fonda del Mar 174
Francesca's Forno 166, 171
Frontera Fresco 147, *147*
Frontera Grill 151
Gino's East 151
Goose Island Brew Pub 150
Gracie's 166
Green Zebra 169
Hachi's Kitchen *173*, 174
Half Shell 159
Harmony Grill 166
Haro 168
Harold's Chicken Shack #24 175
HB 160
Heaven on Seven 166
Hema's Kitchen 163
Hollywood Grill 157
Honey 1 BBQ 171
Hopleaf 162
Hot Doug's 161
HotChocolate 171
Ina's 165, 166
Intelligentsia Coffee 150
Irazu 172
Japonais 152
Kaze 161
Kohan 168

Lagniappe 175
Lao Sze Chuan 149
Laschet's Inn 160
Latin Sandwich Café 172
Le Lan 152
Lula Café 174
Lux Bar 154, *154*
M Henry 162, 166
Maiz 174
Manny's Coffee Shop & Deli 146
Marigold 162
Mas 172
May Street Market 169
Maza 159
Meiji 165
Milk & Honey 172
Miller's Pub 147
Mount Everest 172
Mrs Murphy & Sons 160
Mundial–Cocina Mestiza 168
Ñ 174
Nacional 27 152
Naha 152
Nick's Fishmarket 145
9 Muses 167
NoMI 154
Noon O Kabab 162
North Pond 159
Nuevo León 168
Oasis Café 147
One Sixtyblue 167
Orange 166
La Oaxaqueña 163
Patty Burger 145
Pepper Canister 152
Perry's 147
La Petite Folie 175
Le Petit Paris 154
Phil Stefani's 437 Rush 152
Pho Xe Tang 162
Piece 172
Pizzeria Due 152
Primehouse David Burke 154
Quartino *151*, 152
Rhapsody 145
Riccardo Trattoria 159
Ritz-Carlton Dining Room 155
RoSal's 168
Rudy's Taste 170
Russian Tea Time 145
¡Salpicon! 157
Salt & Pepper Diner 160
San Soo Gap San 163
Santorini 167
Sarah's Pastries & Candies 155, *155*
Schwa 173
Scylla 173
Sola 160

Soul Vegetarian East
 175
Spa Café 147
Spiaggia 155
Spring 173
Spring World 149
Sticky Rice 160
Sushi Wabi 167
Sweet Maple Café 168
Swim Café 155
TAC Quick Thai 160
La Tache 166
Tamarind 149, *149*
Three Happiness
 Restaurant 149
Toast 166
Tru 154
Turquoise Café 161
Udupi Palace 163
Uncle John's 175
Venus Greek-Cypriot
 Cuisine 167
Victory's Banner 162
Vivere 146
Volo 162
Wakamono 161, *161*
West Egg Café 166
West Town Tavern 170
White Palace Grill 157
Wiener's Circle 159
Wishbone 166, *166*, 167

Yassa 175
Zocalo 153

Bars
Aria 176
Le Bar 179
Base 176
Bertucci's Corner 178
Billy Goat Tavern 178
Bin 36 178
Cal's Liquors 177, *177*
Carol's Pub 184
Celebrity 187
Celtic Crossings 178
Charleston 187
Clark Bar 181
Clark Street Ale House
 179
Club Foot 186
Cobra Lounge 184, *186*
Continental 188
Cove Lounge 188
Cru Café & Wine Bar
 180
Cubby Bear 182
Danny's Tavern 187
Delilah's 181, *182*
Elm Street Liquors 180
Estelle's 187
Exit 187
Fado 179

Fifth Province Pub 184
Four Moon Tavern 183
Fulton Lounge 186
Gingerman Tavern 183
Glunz Bavarian Haus
 184
Goose Island Brew Pub
 150, 181, 185, *185*
Grace O'Malley's 177
Hungry Brain 183
Inner Town Pub 186
J Bar *178*, 179
Jet Vodka Lounge 180
Johnny's 184
L & L Tavern 183
Leg Room 180
Lemmings 187
Leopard Lounge 187
Lucky Strike Lanes 179
Map Room 187
Marshall McGearty
 Tobacco Lounge
 187, 189, *189*
Martini Club 184
Matchbox 186
Matisse 181
Monk's Pub 177
Montrose Saloon 184
Moody's Pub 184
Motel Bar 179
Nick's Beergarden 188

Old Town Ale House
 181, *181*
Phyllis' Musical Inn 188
PJ Clarke's 180
Pontiac Café 188
Quencher's Saloon 188
Rainbo Club 187
Red Lion Pub 182
Redhead 179
Resi's Bierstube 183
Rodan 188
Rose's Lounge 182
Rossi's 179
Schaller's Pump 189
17 West 177
Sheffield's 183
Shoes Pub 182
Simon's Tavern 184
Spot 6 183
Swirl 179
Sylvie's Lounge 183
Taps Lounge 180
Twisted Spoke 183
Weather Mark Tavern
 177
Weed's Tavern 181
Weegee's Lounge 188
Whiskey Blue 177
Woodlawn Tap 189
Zakopane 188
Zebra Lounge 180

Advertisers' Index

Chicago Office of Tourism	IFC

In Context

Blue Man Group	10
Chicago Transit Authority	16
Chicago Architecture Foundation	30
Carbon Neutral Flights	30
Days Inn Lincoln Park North	52

Sightseeing

Chicago Loop Alliance	74
Chicago's North Shore	88
Days Inn Lincoln Park North	88
Shoreline Sightseeing	138
CityPass	138

Restaurants

Hard Rock Café	148
Italian Village	156

Shops & Services

G Boutique	196
Poster Plus	196

Theatre

Steppenwolf Theater	280
Time Out Chicago	280
Time Out Shortlist Guides	IBC

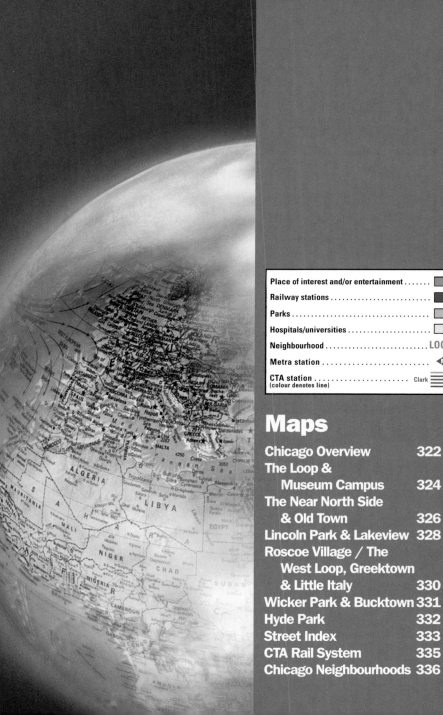

Place of interest and/or entertainment . . . .

Railway stations . . . .

Parks . . . .

Hospitals/universities . . . .

Neighbourhood . . . . **LOOP**

Metra station . . . . **Ⓜ**

CTA station . . . . Clark
(colour denotes line)

Maps

Chicago Overview   322
The Loop &
    Museum Campus   324
The Near North Side
    & Old Town   326
Lincoln Park & Lakeview 328
Roscoe Village / The
    West Loop, Greektown
    & Little Italy   330
Wicker Park & Bucktown 331
Hyde Park   332
Street Index   333
CTA Rail System   335
Chicago Neighbourhoods 336

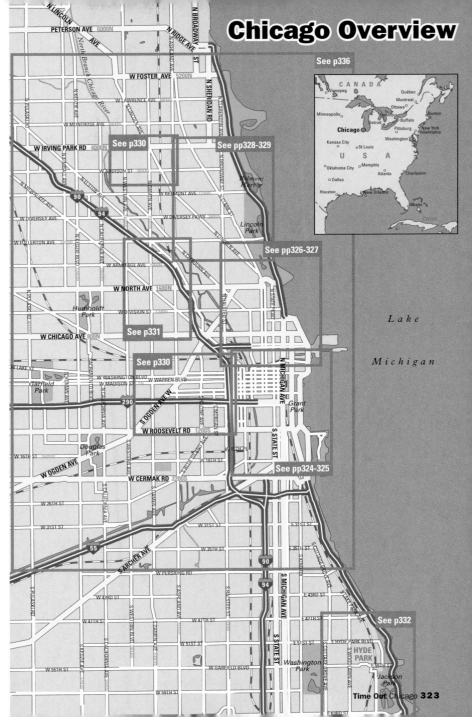

Chicago Overview

See p336

See p330

See pp328-329

See pp326-327

See p331

See p330

See pp324-325

See p332

Lake

Michigan

Belmont Harbor

Lincoln
Park

Grant
Park

HYDE
PARK

*Washington
Park*

*Jackson
Park*

Humboldt
Park

Garfield
Park

Douglas
Park

CANADA

Winnipeg
Québec
Ottawa
Montreal
Minneapolis
Toronto
Buffalo
Boston
Detroit
Pittsburg
New York
Chicago
Philadelphia
Kansas City
St Louis
Washington
Oklahoma City
Memphis
Dallas
Atlanta
Charleston
Houston
New Orleans
Miami

U S A

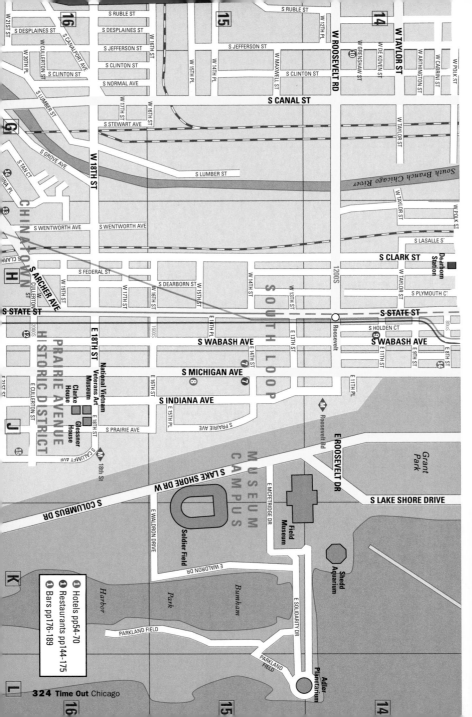

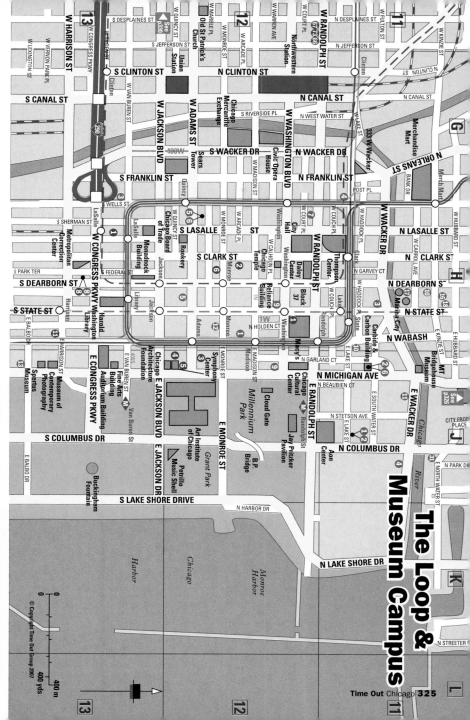

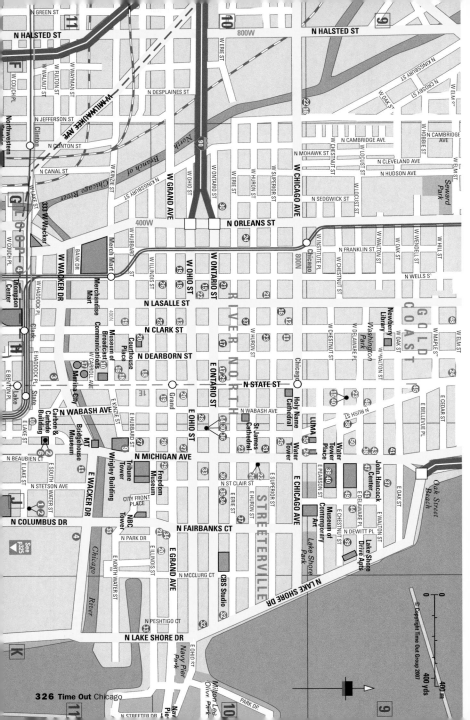

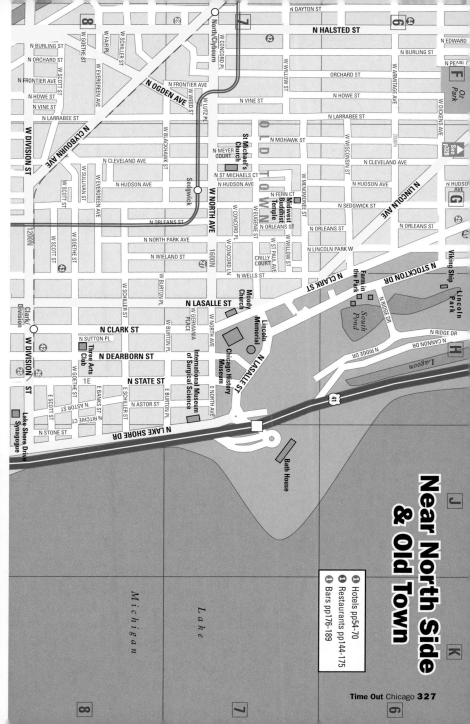

Near North Side & Old Town

- ❶ Hotels pp54-70
- ❶ Restaurants pp144-175
- ❶ Bars pp176-189

Lincoln Park & Lakeview

- **1** Hotels pp54-70
- **2** Restaurants pp144-175
- **3** Bars pp176-189

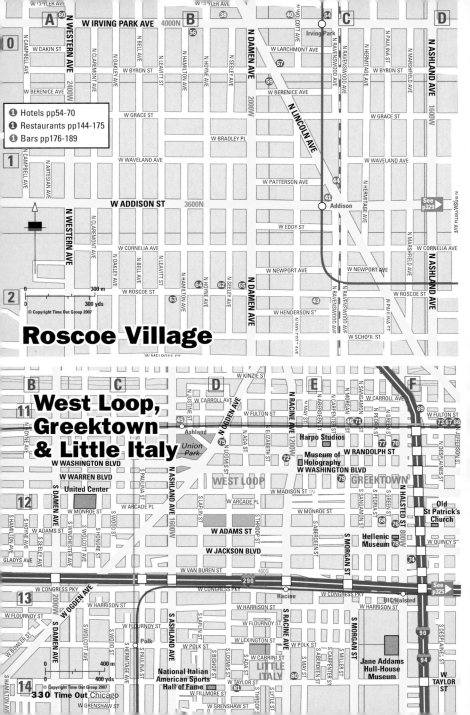

Wicker Park & Bucktown

W MEDILL AVE

W BELDEN AVE

W LYNDALE ST

Holstein Park

W PALMER ST

W WEBSTER AVE

W SHAKESPEARE AVE

W CHARLESTON ST

BUCKTOWN

W DICKENS AVE

W McLEAN AVE

W ARMITAGE AVE   2000N

W HOMER ST

W CORTLAND ST

W MOFFAT ST

W CHURCHILL ST

W WILLOW ST

W St PAUL AVE

W WABANSIA AVE

W CATON ST

W CONCORD PL

Flatiron Building

W NORTH AVE   1600N   W NORTH AVE

Padrewski House

Gingerbread House

W PIERCE AVE

W LE MOYNE ST

WICKER PARK

W SCHILLER ST

W EVERGREEN AVE

W POTOMAC AVE

W CRYSTAL ST

Division Street Russian & Turkish Bath House

W DIVISION ST   1200N   W DIVISION ST

Holy Trinity Orthodox Cathedral

St Volodymyr Ukranian Orthodox Cathedral

W AUGUSTA BLVD   W AUGUSTA BLVD

W WALTON ST

UKRAINIAN VILLAGE

W RICE ST

© Copyright Time Out Group 2007

W CHICAGO AVE   W CHICAGO AVE

0   400 m
0   400 yds

1 Hotels pp54-70
1 Restaurants pp144-175
1 Bars pp176-189

Time Out Chicago **331**

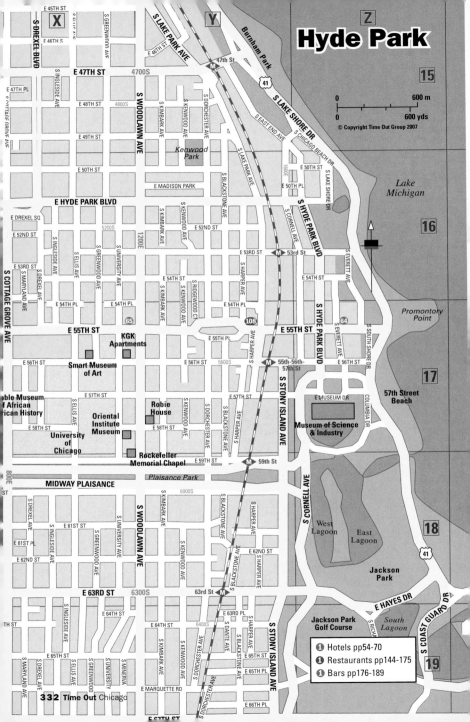

Hyde Park

Z

Y

X

S 45TH ST

S 46TH ST

E 47TH ST

4700S

S LAKE PARK AVE

Burnham Park

47th St

M

41

S LAKE SHORE DR

15

0   600 m
0   600 yds
© Copyright Time Out Group 2007

S DREXEL BLVD

S GREENWOOD AVE

E 48TH ST

4800S

S WOODLAWN AVE

S KIMBARK AVE

S KENWOOD AVE

S DORCHESTER AVE

E 49TH ST

Kenwood
Park

E 50TH ST

E MADISON PARK

S BLACKSTONE AVE

S LAKE PARK AVE

1600E

E 50TH ST

E 50TH PL

S EAST END AVE

S CHICAGO BEACH DR

S LAKE SHORE DR

Lake
Michigan

16

E HYDE PARK BLVD

E DREXEL SQ

E 52ND ST

5200S

1200E

S INGLESIDE AVE

S ELLIS AVE

S GREENWOOD AVE

S UNIVERSITY AVE

S KIMBARK AVE

S KENWOOD AVE

E 52ND ST

S RIDGEWOOD CT

S HARPER AVE

S CORNELL AVE

S HYDE PARK BLVD

S EVERETT AVE

E 53RD ST

M

53rd St

E 54TH ST

E 53RD ST

S MARYLAND AVE

S DREXEL AVE

E 54TH PL

E 54TH PL

65

E 54TH ST

E 54TH ST

108

E 55TH ST

E 55TH ST

64

Promontory
Point

S COTTAGE GROVE AVE

E 55TH ST

KGK
Apartments

Smart Museum
of Art

E 56TH ST

E 56TH ST

5600S

S HARPER AVE

55th-56th-
57th St

M

E 56TH ST

S EVERETT AVE

S SOUTH SHORE DR

17

57th Street
Beach

ble Museum
f African
rican History

E 57TH ST

Robie
House

Oriental
Institute
Museum

Rockefeller
Memorial Chapel

S ELLIS AVE

S KENWOOD AVE

E 58TH ST

S DORCHESTER AVE

S BLACKSTONE AVE

S HARPER AVE

E 57TH ST

S STONY ISLAND AVE

E MUSEUM DR

Museum of Science
& Industry

COLUMBIA DR

University
of
Chicago

E 59TH ST

M

59th St

MIDWAY PLAISANCE

800E

Plaisance Park

6000S

S DREXEL AVE

S INGLESIDE AVE

S GREENWOOD AVE

S UNIVERSITY AVE

S WOODLAWN AVE

S KIMBARK AVE

S KENWOOD AVE

S BLACKSTONE AVE

S HARPER AVE

S CORNELL AVE

West
Lagoon

East
Lagoon

18

41

E 61ST ST

E 61ST PL

E 62ND ST

E 62ND ST

Jackson
Park

E 63RD ST

6300S

63rd St

M

S STONY ISLAND AVE

E HAYES DR

E 63RD PL

E 63RD ST

6400S

E 64TH ST

TH ST

E 64TH ST

S INGLESIDE AVE

S KIMBARK AVE

S KENWOOD AVE

S DANTE AVE

S BLACKSTONE AVE

S HARPER AVE

Jackson Park
Golf Course

South
Lagoon

S RICH

S COAST GUARD DR

19

E 65TH ST

S MARYLAND AVE

S DREXEL AVE

S ELLIS AVE

S GREENWOOD AVE

S MINERVA

S UNIVERSITY

S DORCHESTER AVE

E MARQUETTE RD

S STONY ISLAND AVE

❶ Hotels pp54-70
❶ Restaurants pp144-175
❶ Bars pp176-189

332 Time Out Chicago